HINTS 'N' HELPS
HOUSEHOLD DICTIONARY

1990 Edition

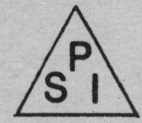

P.S.I. & Associates, Inc.
13322 S.W. 128th Street
Miami, Florida 33186

Acknowledgment is made with thanks for their courtesy in granting permission for the use of their materials to the New York City Fire Dept., Community Relations Div.

Copyright © 1974 by Ottenheimer Publishers, Inc.
All rights reserved.
Published under arrangements with Ottenheimer Publishers, Inc.
Printed in the U.S.A.

Cover 1989 P.S.I. Associates Inc.

A

Abrasives. Sanding is the most important stage in surface preparation—especially when clear finishing is wanted. All nail holes and cracks should be filled beforehand.

Coarse papers can be used for sanding—but always finish with a fine No. 0 glasspaper or its equivalent. Smoothness should be gauged by touch rather than sight. Always sand along the grain—sanding across the grain will leave scratches. On flat surfaces wrap the paper around a block and sand with a firm, even pressure. Keep the block level when sanding edges. If you sand at an angle this will round the edges.

When preparing the surface it is always best to sand by hand. An orbital sander saves time but leaves tiny circular scratches which have to be removed by hand. A disc sander cuts against the grain and leaves deep scratches.

After sanding, all dust should be removed with a rag dampened with turpentine before applying the finish.

The surface can be bleached after sanding to remove any unwanted color or to lighten dark timber for a clear finish. The bleach should be allowed to dry for about 48 hours. If the finish is applied too soon after the bleach, the surface may blister. Any raised grain should be sanded down with a No. 1 paper, then again with No. 0.

In using abrasive papers there is often a great temptation when smoothing a surface to hold the glasspaper or other abrasive paper in the fingers and rub it backwards and forwards as shown.

This should always be avoided, because it only results in the edges and corners being "dubbed" over to ruin the appearance.

This point is illustrated in the sketch where the edges and corner have lost their sharp, clean lines.

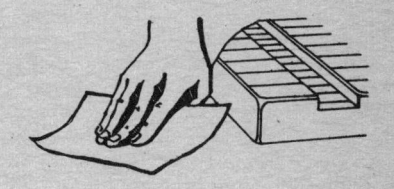

Always hold the abrasive paper on a flat rubbing block, preferably of cork or a wooden block faced with cork sheeting.

For irregular surfaces such as moldings, make a special block, shaping the edge to the reverse of the molding, and rub the work with this.

For the general run of work begin with medium 2-grade glasspaper and finish off with 00-grade if the work is to be enameled or finished with clear lacquer or any of the paint-on plastic products.

for Curved Moldings. You can improvise a very efficient sanding "block" for use along curved moldings or edges with an old pack of playing cards with a sheet of sandpaper wrapped around the edge of the deck. The edge can be pressed against the edge to be sanded, and pressure will force individual cards to slip in or out until the edge of the deck matches the contour of the molding. A tight grip will hold the

AC

deck of cards in this position so that it will serve as a firm backing for your sandpaper.

For the curves of chairbacks, Victorian carving, fluting, etc., steel wool takes the place of sandpaper. Powdered pumice and rottenstone are also fine abrasives.

for Inside Curves and Scroll Work. You can make the usually difficult job of sanding the edges of inside curves or cut-out scroll work much easier if you use a short piece of heavy dowel with the sandpaper wrapped around it. The diameter of the dowel of course depends on the radius of the curve being sanded.

for Irregular Surfaces. For easier sanding and less wear on your fingers, try using an old scrub brush with a strip of sandpaper folded over the bristles and secured with a strip of automobile inner tube rubber, as in the illustration. This is an especially efficient device when you are sanding uneven or irregular surfaces, since the bristles will follow and fit into all the depressions and crevices.

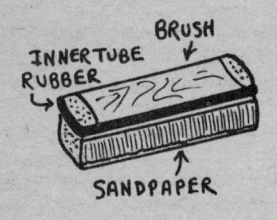

AC (Alternating Current), see ELECTRICITY, THEORY OF.

Acetate, see FIBERS, MAN-MADE.

Acid Stain, see STAIN REMOVAL.

Accordion Door, see CLOSET DOORS.

Acoustical Tile, see TILE, ACOUSTICAL.

Acrylic, see FIBERS, MAN-MADE.

Address Plaque. You can make a very attractive and novel rustic address plaque for your front yard by use of blowtorch. First outline your address numbers and, if you wish, your name, on some sheet asbestos. Then cut these out, and tack the numbers and letters in proper position on a board, which should be at least one-inch stock. Apply your blowtorch to the exposed wood around the figures, scraping away the charred wood and repeating the operation until your numbers and letters stand out in bold relief. Best to perform this work against some bricks, as illustrated, in the interest of fire prevention.

Adhesives.
for China Repair, see CHINA CARE.
Clear cements are desirable for repairing dishes, leather luggage, belts, shoes, book bindings, costume jewelry, models—most items where the repaired seam will show. Clear cements resist water and work equally well with rigid or flexible joints. One of the newer products even assures a bond that will survive a dishwasher. Clear cements can be used with leather, paper, wood, glass, china, ceramics and metals.

Contact cement provides an immediate bond (hence the name "contact"), requires no clamps and resists moisture, temperature extremes and fungus. Its uses include most laminating wall tiles, paneling, felt work and luggage repair. It works well with wood, cloth, leather, some rubbers and plastics, ceramics and metals other than copper. In use, however, it may be too weak for heavy loads, may discolor, and is flammable.

Crockery Cement. Here's an effective and easily-made cement you can mix for mending crockery. It takes quite a long time to dry, but it is well worth it, for it will stand up under heat and water. Just mix a little pure white lead with linseed oil, and use it very thick on the broken edges of your crockery. Let it set for at least a week.

Emergency.

1. Evaporated milk is a good emergency adhesive for a label, postage stamp, or snapshot.

2. When the adhesive on an envelope flap or a postage stamp fails to stick, try some nailpolish. It dries fast, and it sticks.

Epoxy glues are the strongest glues available. They will bond most materials including: wood, cloth, glass, leather, hard plastics, masonry, ceramics and metals. The resulting joints are strong: most work does not require clamps and epoxy joints resist moisture, heat and heavy loading. Epoxy glues are ideal for fastening fixtures to ceramic-tiled walls; repairing jewelry, dishes or masonry; or for bonds requiring high strength. Epoxies also do not work well with certain soft plastics or rubbers and in an unhardened state the glue may irritate the skin.

for Glass. A cement for attaching objects to glass can be made by melting together one part of resin and two parts of yellow wax.

Grout. Grout is Portland cement and water, with sometimes very fine sand added, used to fill in small cracks in concrete and masonry walls and frequently to bind ceramic tiles.

Homemade.

1. A good, harmless, odorless, and stainless glue can be made at home just be soaking plain cooking tapioca in water. The glue is especially good for the young child who likes to taste everything he uses.

2. One formula for a good household glue—add enough water to one cup of granulated laundry starch to produce a liquid of whipping cream consistency, then bring this to a boil, and allow to cool.

Mortar is Portland cement and sand, without the strength of concrete, used as adhesive to bind brick, concrete blocks, cinder blocks, and stone into walls and slabs.

Plastic Cement. Sometimes that special plastic cement that comes with plastic veneer has a way of becoming too thick and gummy for practical use. When this happens, close the bottle tight, soak it in warm water for a while, and it will regain its usable consistency.

Rubber-base. You can preserve a partially used portion of the adhesive for future use by pouring a layer of water over the remaining amount before closing the can.

Substitute. When something needs gluing, and you're out of the real thing, try substituting some colorless fingernail polish, which does the trick nicely for most gluing purposes.

Waterproof Cement. An excellent waterproof cement for any number of household repair jobs can be made with litharge and glycerin, mixed together into a smooth, thick paste.

White glues are the least expensive to use. They work well with wood, paper, cloth, leather, cardboard or cork. They set fast, provide a strong bond and are neither toxic nor flammable. Typical uses include: scrapbook pasteups, package sealing, wood-working (especially chair rungs and legs), upholstery-patching and patching wood veneers. White glues do not work well with metals, common rubbers, or many other nonporous materials such as plastics. Water, high humidity or heat may tend to weaken the bonds.

Adhesives, Use of. Read the manufacturer's instructions carefully.

If unsure of the materials being bonded, test a small area first.

Work where possible in a well-ventilated space away from open flames.

Make sure both surfaces to be joined are clean.

Test-align the parts before applying an adhesive.

No matter which type of glue is used, give it plenty of chance to dry.

If a less expensive glue will work for a job, use it. Don't overglue where you don't have to.

Applicators. You can make your own handy little glue applicator, which can be used over and over again. Slip a two-inch length of soft windshield wiper hose partly over an ordinary lead pencil. Then slit about one inch of the hose into strips 1/16-inch wide with some scissors.

Wooden tongue depressors, obtainable at almost any drugstore, make fine glue applicators and paint

ADHESIVES, USE OF

stirrers. And they're so reasonable in cost, you have no qualms about throwing them away when they have served their purpose.

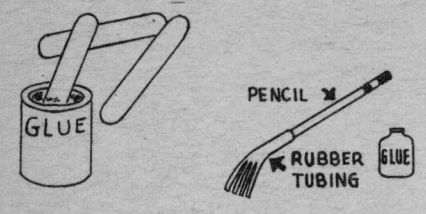

Bottle Stopper. When a bottle of glue is used often, it's a good idea to use a stub of candle as a stopper instead of a cap or cork. The candle will effectively seal the opening and will not stick.

Brush Holder. When you're doing some gluing, it's a familiar problem just what to do with your brush while it's not in use. Your glue brush won't pick up dirt or mess up your work-bench if you'll just solder a staple to the top of the can and rest the brush there.

Excess Removal. To loosen excess glue after a pasting job, rub the spots with cheesecloth dampened with alcohol.

Gluing Chairs, see CHAIR REPAIR.

Gluing Metal to Wood. To stick metal to wood, first soak the metal in acetone. When dry, use some household cement to attach it to the wood—being careful not to touch the cleaned area of the metal before cementing.

Gluing Small Items. When gluing chips of small pieces of china or furniture that cannot be clamped, hold the pieces in place while the glue is drying with a strip of cellophane tape.

Gluing Tip. If you are in the process of gluing two pieces of wood together and have no clamps on hand for holding them firmly together, apply your glue to both pieces, then rub the glue sides together until the glue begins to set. The pieces of wood will then hold just as well as if you had used clamps.

Gluing Wood, see WOOD CARE TIPS.

Mortar Repair. If some of the mortar joints in one of your outside brick walls are cracked or crumbling, chip out the broken mortar, blowing out all the crumbs with your vacuum cleaner. Then pack in a mixture of one part cement and three parts sand to the consistency of damp earth. Finish to match the old joints.

Softening. When vegetable glue has become dry and hard, it can be softened up to usable consistency again with some hot vinegar. Just add the vinegar drop by drop and keep stirring until the glue is soft. It's possible to use cold vinegar, too, but it sometimes takes several days to soak through and become effective.

Spreader. An ideal tool for the spreading of glue over large surfaces is an old hacksaw blade with its serrated edge. The teeth of this blade insure a good, even distribution of your glue.

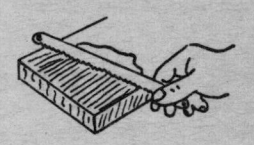

Storage.

1. A tube of household cement will be usable to the last drop if, after using it, you replace the cap carefully, put the tube in a small screw-top jar, and close it tightly.

ALUMINUM SHEETS

2. One of our pet annoyances is the necessity of using a wrench to loosen the cap of a glue jar or can. You can just throw the cap away, if you'd like to rid yourself of this trouble—and seal the container with some strips of cellulose tape, which can be removed very easily the next time you have to use the glue.

Adhesive Tape Remover. For cleaning the stains left on the skin by adhesive tape, fingernail polish remover does a first-rate job.

Air Conditioners, see COOLING.

Adhesive Tape Stain, see STAIN REMOVAL.

Adjustable Wrench, see TOOLS, HAND.

Air Mattress. Here is an easy way to deflate an air mattress used at a swimming pool. Disconnect the air plug and submerge the opposite end of the mattress in the water. The water will force all the air up to the plug. Slowly force more of the mattress under the water until it is completely submerged up to the plug. Be careful not to get the plug under water! In this way you don't have to roll, push, and squeeze the air out only to find when you are finished that the mattress still has some air in it.

Airplane Glue Stain, see STAIN REMOVAL.

Alabaster.
  Cleaning. Apply paste of spirits of turpentine and finely powdered pumice stone. Wash with soapy lather, rinse with clear water. Polish with dry cloth.
  Repair. Broken alabaster usually mends with household cement. After cleaning both edges, apply a thin coat of the cement, let dry, then apply a second coat to one edge and press together for several hours.

Alarms, see BURGLAR ALARMS.

Albumen Stain, see STAIN REMOVAL.

Alcohol Burner. Here's a handy little alcohol burner you can improvise from an empty India ink bottle, a cork, a short length of copper tubing, and a wick—a burner that will serve you well for small heating or melting jobs in your workshop. Punch a hole through your cork, and insert the tubing through this so that it projects about 1/2-inch on the top and the bottom. Then thread your wick through this, and with a little alcohol in your bottle, you're in business.

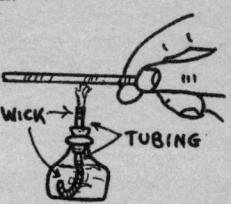

Alcohol Stain, see STAIN REMOVAL.

Alkyd Resin Paint, see PAINTS.

Alternating Current (AC), see ELECTRICITY, THEORY OF.

Aluminum foil makes an excellent cleanser. Use it on chrome and on golf clubs. Squeeze a handful into a ball, dampen and rub over the surface to be cleaned. Leaves it shiny and bright.

Aluminum Furniture, see FURNITURE CARE.

Aluminum Sheets.
  Cleaning. Mix ammonia, borax and water, and apply to the aluminum with a soft cloth. Another method is to wash with warm soapy water, then dry and polish with whiting.
  Cutting. When you have to cut an aluminum sheet or flashing, you can make an easy and neat job of this without any danger of producing a ragged edge, as is usually done with snips. Just use a straight-edge as your guide and score the metal with a linoleum knife or some other sharp tool. Then all you have to do is bend the metal back and forth until it breaks off on the line you have scored . . . quick, easy, and neat!

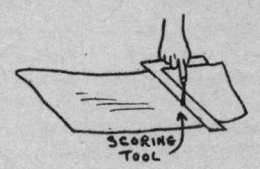

ALUMINUM WINDOW FRAMES

Deburring. When a number of aluminum sheets or articles have to be deburred on the edges after shearing, a hook scraper like the one shown in sketch (A) will do the work rapidly as it treats both sides of an edge in one operation.

The scraper is made by cutting a V notch in one end of a strip of steel and beveling the sides of the notch to form cutting and scraping edges.

The notched end is bent at a right-angle, and a grip is formed at the other end as shown in sketch (B).

The scraper is then hardened to retain its cutting edge.

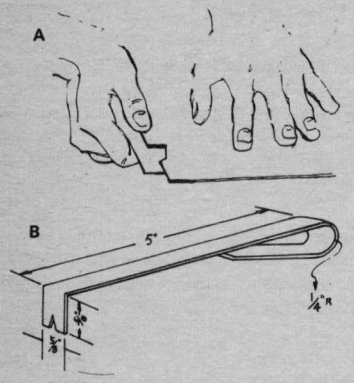

Repair. For large holes or tears in aluminum, if the edges are more than about 3/16-inch apart, cut a patch out of sheet aluminum, then clean this patch and the area around the hole with steel wool. Spread plastic aluminum or epoxy glue on the patch, and press down.

Aluminum Window Frames. Preserve a bright finish on aluminum window frames and doors with an annual coating of silicone, available in auto supply stores. Also, wiping silicone into the channels will make the windows slide easily in cold weather.

Aluminumware.

Cleaning. When aluminumware turns black, slowly stew some acid food (such as rhubarb, tomatoes, or the like) and watch the sparkle return to the aluminum. And, incidentally, the food itself won't be harmed.

Dent Repair. Dents in aluminumware can often be remedied by holding a block of wood over the concave side of the dent, then hammering out carefully with light taps and using a rubber mallet. Hammer from the edges of the dent to the center.

Hole Repair. Small holes in aluminumware cannot very well be repaired by soldering, but you can plug them very nicely with aluminum rivets. You should first round the hole by turning a tapered punch inside it, leaving the burr to be crushed against the rivet. Then, insert the rivet with the head inside the container and resting on a steel block, and finish your riveting.

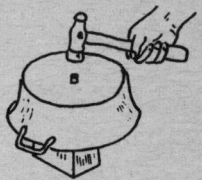

Stain Prevention. When cooking beans or rice, add a few drops of vinegar or lemon juice to the contents and this will prevent your aluminum pot from turning black, without changing the taste of your food.

Stain Removal, see STAIN REMOVAL.

Warp Prevention.

1. To avoid warping of an aluminum pan, don't overheat it. If a gas range is used, the tip of the flame should just touch the bottom of the vessel, never flare up around its sides. If an electric range is used, use high heat for only a few minutes, then switch to medium. Once the food is brought to cooking temperature, heat may be reduced to low.

2. Never let cold water run into a hot pan.

Amber requires regular attention. Rub with moistened whiting, then smear lightly with olive oil. Polish with flannel.

Ammonia Stain, see STAIN REMOVAL.

Amperage, see ELECTRICITY, THEORY OF.

Anchor. A very useable anchor for a light dinghy or other small boat can be fashioned from a discarded automobile spring. Fasten the spring leaf to the end of a length of pipe with an expansion bolt, and screw a stand pipe tee to the other end of the pipe to accommodate the rope. The car-spring arms will catch readily on the bottom and are strong enough to hold fast.

Andiron Cleaning. Add attractiveness to your woodburning fireplace by keeping those andirons in spick-and-span condition. Remove any deposits that collect on the andirons with some white gasoline (outdoors, of course), and follow this with a good washing with some non-gritty kitchen cleanser. Complete your cleaning job with some metal polish. Clean out any pitted areas with a vinegar-salt solution, then rinse quickly.

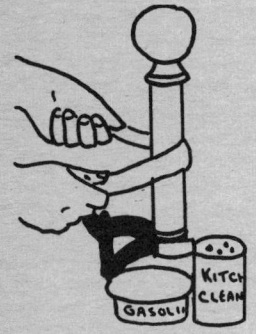

Anidex, see FIBERS, MAN-MADE.

Animal Care, see CAT CARE, DOG CARE.

Animal Stain, see STAIN REMOVAL.

Antique Furniture Finish, see FURNITURE REFINISHING.

Ants, see INSECTS.

Anvil. A very efficient and handy anvil for your workshop can be improvised by removing the handle from an old flatiron and turning the iron upside down. And, if you want to make it more permanent, you can bolt it down to your bench.

Apples, see FOODS.

Appliance Centers, Kitchen, see KITCHEN PLANNING.

Appliances.
Finding Cause of Trouble. You should keep in mind several rules when you are looking for the cause of appliance troubles. Be sure you don't rush the job. You should examine the appliance carefully before you try to pry it apart or cut through any of it. In most cases, the appliance has been designed so it can be opened for repairs, usually by removing screws or by taking off some snap-on panel. As a general rule, you'll find that the access opening is in a part of the appliance hidden from view—the bottom of a toaster, the back of a clock, or the side of a radio.

If you are prevented from taking off a covering by the presence of a shaft or some long part on the outer end of the appliance, you'll usually find a set screw or similar device holding the shaft. By removing this, you can take off the shaft and then the cover.

Some appliances, including large ones, have special parts sealed in a metal container so that you cannot replace it without cutting the container apart. Simply replace the entire sealed unit. Cutting into it will probably make it un-repairable anyway.
General Repair. It is almost always inadvisable to try to strip down and repair a large appliance like a refrigerator, an air-conditioner, or a television set. There are simply too many things that may be wrong, and repairs are extremely complicated. If you are an expert repairman, of course, go ahead. Usually, it's best to call in an expert.

Before you call in a pro, however, be sure you check the plug, the cord, and the convenience outlet. If the trouble lies here, fix the cord, the plug or the outlet. Incidentally, if any appliance won't work, the very first thing to check is to see that it is plugged in!

Large appliances are usually motor-driven. The kind of electric motor most often found in a home appliance is a universal type, one running on AC, and sometimes one running on DC. There are three things that can go wrong with electric motors: the motor will not start; the motor runs hot; the motor runs too slowly. Any of these difficulties may be caused by inadequate or defective power supply;

7

APPLIANCES

un-oiled or dirty parts; defects in the wiring of the motor; or a defective belt connection.

Check list. You can at least search out the probable trouble in a motorized appliance by using the following check list:

Check the power supply. Be sure the cord and socket are in working order. Make sure the cord is large enough to carry the proper current for the motor.

Check to see that the motor is properly oiled. If it is not, you may find a good oiling will check its running hot or slow. Pay attention to the oiling instructions that accompany the motor. Some are self-lubricating; never oil a part unless it is clearly marked OIL, or unless a lubricating chart accompanies the appliance. Follow directions if issued with the motor. You'll find the proper grade and type of oil named. If not, use light machine oil or an oil specifically made for electric motors.

Check the motor to see if it needs cleaning. If so, clean all grease and dirt out of the open windings with a clean, dry cloth or soft-bristled brush.

Check any belt adjustments and keep all oil or grease off the belt and pulley. Be sure the belt is tightly installed. Most belts are controlled by wing screws or slot bolts. Turn the screw or bolt until the belt is tight to the touch.

Noise Reduction. Here are some suggestions for reducing the noise created inside the home by various appliances and domestic equipment.

Some items such as refrigerators generate a certain amount of noise which, although not loud, can be extremely irritating.

Before buying any new equipment, make sure that you hear it in operation first.

Different makes of the same type of appliance have different noise levels, so listen to several carefully and remember that the sound you hear in a large shop may be greatly magnified in a small room.

It is not easy to cut down noise in a kitchen because of the large area of hard surfaces in the room.

Isolate refrigerators by placing on a pad of cork or rubber, and making sure they do not come in contact with the wall or cabinets at back or sides.

Some noise can be reduced, however, by lining the underside of the working top of cabinets with acoustic tiles. This will help to absorb sound from motor-driven electrical appliances such as mixing and beating machines.

Another place where you can use acoustic tiles is on the wall behind any motor-driven appliance, such as a washing machine, dishwasher or refrigerator.

Metal pedal bins will be a lot quieter if rubber gaskets are fitted round the lid. Line the inside of the bin, too, with a double thickness of paper to reduce noise. This precaution will also protect and keep the metal lining clean.

If a motorized extractor fan tends to be noisy, you should be able to improve matters by isolating it from the wall or window with strips of foam plastic.

Squeaking food mixers and beaters are an added irritation to the housewife, but they often hesitate to use oil to lubricate them in case it taints the food. The solution is to use a few drops of glycerine—it leaves no flavor.

Cups and plates that rattle inside a cupboard every time the door is opened can be dealt with by hanging the cups on plastic-covered hooks and standing the plates on one of the special plastic racks available as cupboard fittings.

Refrigerator Cleaning.

1. Don't use harsh, abrasive cleansers to scrub off messy smears and sticky fingerprints on the refrigerator. A good cleaning wax will do an efficient job, and will also leave a wax coating that will protect the surface and resist dirt.

2. A paste that often does a good job of perking up the appearance of an old refrigerator is a mixture of two tablespoons of paste silver polish, one teaspoon of liquid bleach and one teaspoon of liquid detergent.

Refrigerator Repair. Your refrigerator is a complex mechanism, and should be taken care of immediately if it begins to ail. You can handle some of the repairs and maintenance, but you should be able to tell what is wrong with the machine even if you have to call someone in to fix it.

If your refrigerator runs hot and emits a bad odor, the motor itself is defective. It is best not to do anything with it except to unplug it and call in a repairman.

If your refrigerator runs too much, you may have a dirty condenser, or the door may leak air, or you may have your refrigerator placed too near a wall or too close to a stove. A refrigerator with a condenser

APPLIANCE WATTAGE CHART

at the back should be at least 4 inches from a wall and 12 inches from a ceiling.

You should clean a refrigerator condenser at least once a year. It is located at the back or at the bottom of the box. Always disconnect the power before you touch it. Clean the box with a vacuum cleaner brush attachment or a long-handled brush. Instructions for cleaning the condenser come with the booklet of advice for keeping the refrigerator in running condition.

To check whether or not your refrigerator door leaks, place a thin piece of paper between the door and the frame and close the door. If you can pull the paper out without feeling a tug, the door gasket, or rubber lining, is loose and does not fit correctly. Unscrew the old gasket and replace it.

If your refrigerator needs too much defrosting, check for a leaky door, and then make sure you do not have the thermostat set too low. The temperature should be kept at about 40° or 45°. Below 35 degrees makes frost form too rapidly and causes faster defrosting demands.

Toaster Care. It is well to give the electric toaster a good cleaning every now and then. A fine paint brush proves very handy for this purpose, getting into the more inaccessible crevices. Never put the appliance into water, but clean it with a damp cloth. And always allow the toaster to cool thoroughly before attempting to clean it.

Waffle Iron Care. After using the waffle iron, wipe the grids lightly with a paper towel or soft cloth, and cool the iron with it lid up. Scub the grids with a fine wire brush, then brush with non-salted oil. Heat the iron for about ten minutes to recondition it, after which soak up the excess oil with a piece of bread placed between the grids.

The bright outside finish needs little care. If the batter runs out from a too-full grid onto the outside of the iron, leave it until it is set by the heat, then it will come off easily. Then clean with a damp cloth. Sometimes tiny brown spots appear on the outside, caused by particles of fat. These can be removed with a little fine scouring powder.

Appliance Wattage Chart. In order not to overload your electrical circuits, it is necessary to know exactly what wattage each appliance and fixture draws when it is in use.

Most small appliances can be handled by plugging them into regular convenience outlets. But it is a good idea to know the approximate amount of current each one draws. In the case of some appliances, like a refrigerator, the initial moment of switching on requires *several times* the normal wattage. That is the reason the lights sometimes dim when a refrigerator starts up. The same is true of an air conditioning unit.

The following is the average wattage of some ordinary household appliances:

APPLIANCE	WATTS
Fluorescent light	15-40
Table Lamp	50-100
Mixer	100
Radio	100
Built-in ventilating fan	100
Portable electric fan	100
Vacuum cleaner	125
Refrigerator	150
Floor lamps	150-300
Electric blanket	200
Television set	300
Automatic hand iron	1000
Portable heater	1000
Automatic rotisserie	1100
Waffle iron or sandwich grill	up to 1100
Coffeemaker	up to 1100
Electric sauce pan or skillet	1100
Deep-fat fryer	1350
Broiler-rotisserie	1320-1650
Electric roaster	1650
Iron	1650

There are some appliances which draw so much current that they should be placed on individual circuits and not be plugged into a regular circuit. Below is a typical list of these, and their average watt rate:

APPLIANCE	WATTS
Home freezer	350
Waste disposal	500
Automatic washer	700
Water pump	700
Fuel-fired heating plant	800
Built-in bathroom heater	1000-1500
Room air conditioner ¾-ton	1200
Dishwasher, waste-disposer	1500
Electric water heater	2000-4500
Built-in cook top	4000
Built-in oven	4000
240-volt electric clothes dryer	4500-9000
Electric range	8000-16000

(See also ELECTRIC CIRCUITS)

AQUARIUM CLEANING

Aquarium Cleaning. Unsightly deposits that often form at the water line of fish bowls and aquariums may be removed by rubbing with a cloth saturated in vinegar. Then rinse the bowl thoroughly before filling with fresh water.

Argyrol Stain, see STAIN REMOVAL.

Art Brush Holder. To prevent the bristles of a slender artist's brush from touching the bottom of a small-necked bottle when not in use, clip a bobby pin to the brush handle, and place it across the mouth of the bottle.

Artificial Flowers, see FLOWERS.

Asbestos Shingles, see ROOF SURFACES.

Ashtray, Stain on, see STAIN REMOVAL.

Asparagus, see FOODS.

Asphalt-Prepared Roll Roofing, see ROOF SURFACES.

Asphalt Shingle Roof, see ROOF SURFACES.

Asphalt Tile, see RESILIENT TILE FLOORS, TILE, ASPHALT.

Attic Fans, see COOLING.

Attic Finishing. An attic is usually a storage place for useless or outmoded possessions. Actually, the attic was put there for a specific purpose: to insulate the house below against excessive heat in the summer and excessive cold in the water. The air space provided by the sloping roof and the ceiling is a perfect insulation barrier.

However, most of us eventually want more use out of the attic area. And, with conditions in the rest of the house becoming more and more crowded, you turn toward the attic as a kind of final solution to one more living area.

It's not as expensive as you might think to change an attic into a room, especially if you do the work yourself. And the extra room will save you money in the long run. Think how much it would cost you to buy a new house just to get that extra room!

Remember one thing when planning that new room: the attic is an insulation chamber; be sure to keep some air pockets in your new plan.

Finishing off an attic differs from finishing off a basement in one very important consideration: in a basement all walls and ceiling are already extant; in an attic you'll have to put up your own walls and possible a ceiling.

First of all measure the floor area of the attic space you want to use. Then measure the height of the roof peak from the floor. With the measurement from roof peak to the point where floor and roof meet, you'll have all the measurements you need.

Draw this triangle on paper, marking the distances to scale. Hopefully the distance from peak to floor is about 10 feet or more, since you'll want your ceiling at least 7 feet above the floor, preferably 8 feet. Draw in a ceiling, at scale, about 7 feet from the floor. This will give you a good indication of the general profile of the room.

The walls are the next consideration. If each wall is at least 4 feet from floor to intersection with the roof slope, you should have enough room to put in desks, cabinets, dressers, and so on.

With this profile, you can get a pretty good idea of what your room will look like. The finished room will have a floor, ceiling, half-walls, and a slope from wall to ceiling on both sides of the room.

You can use the outside wall of the house—which probably already has a window—as the third side of your room. The fourth side will contain a door in a wall. You'll have to build the wall and put the door in it. Doors come in specified sizes—it's always a good idea to have a specific door size in mind when you're planning the room. You simply build the door and the frame around it so it will fit in when you're finished.

Framing. First of all you must rough in the studs. Using 2 by 4's, cut the wall studs about 2 inches shorter than the distance from the floor to the underside of the sloping roof sheathing. Then lay a strip of 2 by 4 along the floor exactly where you want your wall. Attach the studs at the proper 16-inch intervals along the plate, nailing with 10d nails from underneath. Then set the plate and studs upright, and attach the plate to the floor and the studs either directly to the rafters, or to a top plate secured to the rafters.

For the fourth wall, lay a 2 by 4 plate along the floor, cut out the section where the door will hang, and nail the plate to the floor. At 16-inch intervals, attach studs to the plate by toe-nailing in from opposite sides, and secure the studs at the top to the rafter running parallel to it. At the top of the door space, clearing the door where it will hang, nail a cross piece of 2 by 4 framing; then attach a cripple stud from the top of the frame to the roof rafter.

On the outside wall of the house, attach to the house studs at 8 feet from the floor a horizontal top plate for the ceiling. Work in from the wall and attach to each pair of rafters another horizontal ceiling joist all the way across the room.

Wiring. If you have any electrical wiring to do, do it yourself now, or have it done. It is a risky thing to do this yourself. You may run into insurance problems as well as the building codes.

Insulation. With the studs for the walls and the ceiling in place, and with the wiring all set, you are now ready to insulate. Using insulation batts, staple them across the rafters running all the way from the floor to the roof peak. Then attach insulation batts between the wall studs you have roughed in. Include batts between the ceiling rafters. A complete insulation job will leave three necessary air pockets around the room: above, and at the two sides of the walls. (See also INSULATION.)

Drywall. Simply measure the wall height carefully. Cut the drywall along the mark with a sharp utility knife, and break through by placing a 2 by 4 along the line of the break underneath and pressing down hard to snap it through. Place the drywall section against the studs and mark and cut out with a utility knife any holes for electric outlets and wall switches. Then attach the drywall with nails at intervals of 10 inches along each stud and floor and ceiling plates.

Tape the joints where the drywall sections meet and spackle. (See also DRYWALL.)

Molding. You'll notice the joint where the drywall meets the floor is probably a bad one. Attach a baseboard there, using regular baseboard molding. Attach the molding to the place where the ceiling and the wall meet, to cover any breaks. Use molding in the corners where necessary.

Attic Insulation, see INSULATION.

Attic, Unfinished. It is common practice these days for the builders of a house to leave the attic unfinished; but the necessary provisions are often arranged so that the attic can, at some later date, and at the convenience of the home owner, be made into one or more rooms. These "expansion attics," as they are sometimes called, offer a great many possibilities to the home mechanic who is willing to spend a little time, effort and money to add one or more attractive yet low cost rooms to his house. For example, as the family grows in size, an extra bedroom is a great convenience; or this same space can be used for a quiet study, private sitting room, playroom, or library. And finally, if the attic is large enough a complete and self-contained small apartment can be made out of it.

The finishing off of an attic bedroom or two can be accomplished by one man. However, if you are planning to raise a dormer, or add a bathroom or kitchen, you will need assistance. Before planning to raise a dormer, add a bathroom or kitchen, check your local building codes. You might require the services of an architect and other professionals for portions of these tasks.

Automatic Drill, see TOOLS, HAND.

Automatic Switch. Here's one way that the handyman can make his own automatic switch for turning on a light, radio, or other electrical device. It is fashioned from a spring-wound alarm clock and a pull-chain light socket, as in the illustration. Add an extension to the alarm-winding key on the back of the clock to take care of the string which is attached to the chain on the socket. Drill a hole crosswise through the extension to prevent the string from slipping on the shaft. Then screw a light bulb into the socket or a receptacle plug for whatever appliance you wish to be turned on or off.

Automobile.

Battery. Clean the terminals of the battery in the usual manner with baking soda and water, then after they are completely dry, paint them with rubber cement. The cement will prevent the formation of acid and, except for dust, keep the terminals clean.

AUTOMOBILE

Chrome Care.

1. A thin coat of regular automobile oil applied to the chrome on your car in the fall and periodically throughout the winter will cut down possible rust.

2. You can clean and shine up the chrome on automobile bumpers just by dipping a wad of aluminum foil into cold water, then rubbing away.

3. Remove water and stain spots from the chrome on your car with plain old lemon juice.

Emergency Equipment. Instead of discarding that old roller window shade, put it in the trunk of your car. When trouble comes on the road, unroll it and place it on the ground where you are working and your clothes will stay clean.

Fan Belt. If the fan belt in your car is squeaking annoyingly, a drop of either household glycerin or permanent anti-freeze will usually silence it.

Flares. It's a good idea to keep a couple of milk cartons in the trunk of your car. Then, if you are ever stuck on the road at night, each of these cartons will make a fine flare, burning almost fifteen minutes.

Fog Prevention. You can prevent the glass in your car's windshield from fogging or frosting if you will rub a cut onion over it, or the tobacco from a cigarette butt. Or, moist salt rubbed on the windshield, inside or out, will help keep it from frosting or icing.

Gasoline Stains. If a careless gasoline station attendant has let some gasoline run down the side of your car when filling your tank, this is sometimes very difficult to remove, especially after it has dried. Try using a tablespoon of kerosene to one cup water and this will usually remove the dried gasoline quickly.

Ice Traction.

1. During the winter, when there is danger of your car becoming stalled on icy roads, carry two pieces of corrugated-rubber doorway matting in the trunk of your car. Then, when traction becomes impossible on a slippery road, stretch out the mats in front of the rear wheels of your car. The mats will grip the road surface sufficiently to provide you the traction your car needs.

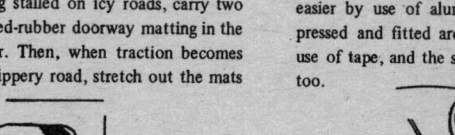

2. Composition roof shingles will get your car out of an icy rut as quickly as sand or ashes, and they certainly are much easier and cleaner to carry in your car trunk.

Identification. Trying to locate your car in a large parking lot or near a crowded recreation area is no laughing matter if you are in a hurry and your sense of direction is none too accurate. To help you find it again, tie a small flag or handkerchief to the radio aerial and push it up as far as it will go. This will help you spot your car, even at a distance.

Mud Traction. Here is one very practical use for some of those old, discarded automobile license plates. Link four or five of the old plates together with some wire or chain-repairing links, fold them into the luggage compartment of your car. Then, if ever you get stuck in the mud, you have your own ready-made mud track.

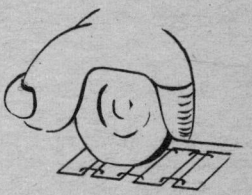

Oil Leak. If you suspect that your car has an oil leak, spread some newspapers on the garage floor under the front end and run the engine for a few minutes at a slow speed. Any oil leak will show on the paper.

Spray Painting. If you are going to spray-paint your car, you can make the job of masking your bumper guards, bumpers, headlamps, and other parts much easier by use of aluminum foil. This foil can be pressed and fitted around these parts without the use of tape, and the sheets can be used repeatedly, too.

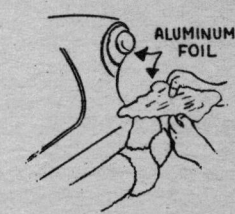

Tailpipe. If the tailpipe of your car persistently scrapes as you enter or leave a steep driveway, you can cut it without shortening it. Hacksaw a piece from the bottom of the pipe at a long angle. In this way, you will gain road clearance, yet the overhang keeps the bumper free of any possible exhaust stains.

Tar. Ordinary cooking oil or shortening may be used to remove tar from your car. Rub it on briskly with a clean cloth, let stand for a second or so, then rub off.

Touchup. Worn spots on the finish of your car can often be touched up with shoe polish. Rub in with a soft cloth, then cover with some auto wax.

Washing. A familiar annoyance, when shampooing the car, is a chamois that persists in wrinkling and rolling up as you rub. You can avoid this little headache if you'll just wrap your chamois around a cellulose sponge. The chamois will remain flat and smooth, and still retain enough flexibility to follow the contours of the car body. You can use the same sponge with which you washed the car.

White Wall Tires.

1. White sidewall automobile tires can be effectively cleaned with denatured alcohol to which a small amount of hydrogen peroxide has been added. Saturate a cloth with this solution, apply to the sidewalls, allow a minute or so to penetrate, repeat the application, then rub the dirt off with a clean, alcohol-dampened cloth.

2. Do not use steel wool or harsh scouring powder to remove curb markings on white-walled tires. They can scratch the surface. Instead, apply washing soda with a wet brush, then rinse.

Windshield Cleaner. Those spattered insects on the windshield and other parts of your car are easily removable with an application of a mixture consisting of two tablespoons of baking soda to one quart of water.

Windshield Defrosting. It's a good idea to keep a small jar or box of ordinary kitchen salt in your car throughout the cold winter months. Then, should you arrive at your parked car and find its windshield coated with ice, you can remove this by rubbing over it with some of your salt.

Windshield Steaming. An ordinary clean blackboard eraser is much handier than a bulky cloth for wiping steam from your car windows or windshield. When not in use, it fits nicely inside your glove compartment.

Windshield Wipers.

1. An ineffective windshield wiper on your car is often due to an accumulation of grease and dirt on the rubber blade. Clean it off now and then with a damp cellulose sponge sprinkled with dry baking soda.

2. If the windshield wipers on your car are not doing a proper job, try rubbing the blades with sandpaper to clean and smooth them.

Awl, see TOOLS, HAND.

Awnings.

Faded. Year after year you'll find that your awnings become dim and fade with age. If the awning is only one color, you can always dye it. You can even use house paint on the surface, if you add to it one-fourth the amount of turpentine. Apply the paint in a thin coat and brush it into the fibers.

Mildew Prevention. Awnings must be sprayed with anti-mildew compound each winter when you store them. You can apply the compound from an aerosol can. You can also water-proof an awning by painting it with a solution of 1 pound shaved paraffin in a gallon of turpentine or clean kerosene. Stretch the fabric when you paint it.

AWNING WINDOWS

Repairing. If you have a tear in your awning, you can repair it in several ways:

(1) You can sew a patch of the same material to the under side. (2) Buy a patching preparation and attach the material with that. (3) Try household cement or rubber cement.

In repairing the awning, lay it face down on a flat surface, cut the canvas and coat the patch and the awning separately with cement. Let this dry until it is strongly tacky, and then put the patch in position and hammer it into contact.

Awning Windows, see WINDOWS.

B

Bag Holder, see PAPER BAG HOLDER.

Baked Custard, see FOODS.

Ballast, see LIGHTING, FLUORESCENT.

Ball-Peen Hammer, see TOOLS, HAND.

Ballpoint Pens.
  1. Every now and then a ballpoint pen tip becomes clogged with excessive ink or fuzz. The quickest and easiest way to clean this point is to insert it in the filter portion of a cigarette. Just a few quick turns and it is ready for use. You don't even have to waste a fresh cigarette, as a butt works just as well.
  2. Have you ever had a ballpoint pen begin to skip and seemingly run out of fuel sooner than you think it should have? This is often due to the fact that the ink in the container has thickened or congealed. Try heating it by holding the point for a minute or so against a lighted electric light bulb, and this often has a way of giving one of these pens a new lease on life. Be careful not to overheat the pen, and thus soften its plastic case!

Bamboo Cleaning. Apply salt and water with a small brush. Rinse with clear water. Dry in open air, polish with soft duster.

Bamboo Furniture, see FURNITURE CARE.

Bananas, see FOODS.

Barbecue.
  Cleaning Tip. The next time you are planning a cook-out, if you take out a little time beforehand to coat the bottoms of your skillets and other cooking utensils with some liquid detergent, it will make the job of washing off their soot-blackened bottoms much easier and faster later on.

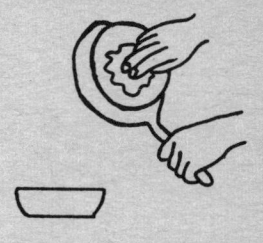

  Fire. An easy way to kindle a fire in your barbecue pit is to use a brick soaked in kerosene. Put the brick to soak a day or two in advance and use it in place of kindling wood. It will burn for a long time and keep the fire going, even if the fuel is damp.

  Grill. Here is an extremely simple, yet efficient, grill which can be set up in your backyard. It can be constructed of common bricks, cobblestones, or field stones. Before determining the exact size of the grill, buy your iron grillwork which is to be laid over the fire, and allow at least two inches at either end so that the grill can be firmly set into the side

BAR TOP

walls. First step is to excavate ten or twelve inches deep with the proper outside dimensions, then fill the bottom of the excavation with a layer of cinders and tamp them down to form a solid level base for the bottom of your pit. Your brick or stone should be firmly set in a concrete mortar. Then build your side walls up on this foundation high enough to allow room for building a fire comfortably, and the grillwork set in mortar over the pit.

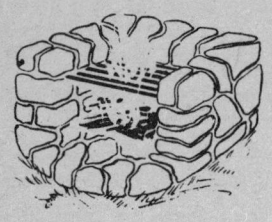

For a small family cookout, you can improvise a very efficient grill from a discarded iron Dutch oven or kitchen pot. Build your charcoal fire in this, then place a wire cake rack over it, and cook your steaks, hamburgers, or other meats on this rack. Then, for the sake of economy when you have finished your cooking, put the pot cover tightly on—and this will choke out the fire and enable you to use the charcoal again on some future cookout.

Outdoor Fireplaces. Outdoor fireplaces range from simple makeshift units to elaborate structures designed to harmonize with and enhance the appearance of the house and the landscape.

Plans for outdoor fireplaces are available from various sources. Magazines frequently feature articles on outdoor-fireplace design and construction.

If the fireplace is to be built with local labor and material, a relatively simple design, such as that shown is advisable.

Built-in features, such as ovens, cranes, grills, storage compartments, sinks, and benches, add to the appearance and convenience of fireplaces. Dealers in outdoor-fireplace equipment usually have catalogs listing types and sizes of accessory equipment.

Elaborately designed fireplaces that include many built-in features or that are an integral part of a building should be built by skilled labor.

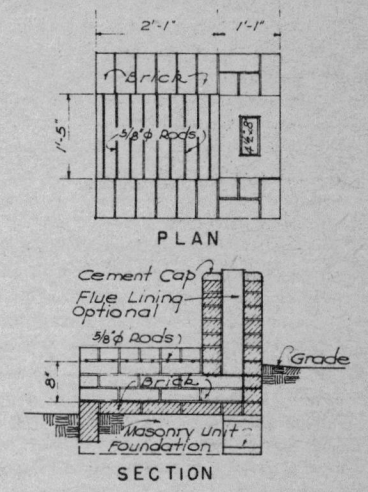

Bar Top. If you want to make an extra-attractive bar top, use some prefinished flooring, which is available in a number of patterns from pegged ranch to formal parquet. This makes the chore of finishing and polishing easy.

Baseboard, see MOLDINGS.

Basement Finishing.
1. **Measuring and Planning.** If you have decided that you are capable of finishing your basement, the first thing you should do is to make a planning chart, using graph paper. Measure the length, width and height that you would like your room to be when finished. Then, with the aid of your graph paper, allow each square to equal 6 inches or 12 inches, and mark out door openings, window areas and existing closet openings. If there are lolly columns, also indicate their locations.

Remember that plywood usually comes in 4 foot

BASEMENT FINISHING

and work it out carefully so that you do not have to cut the panels lengthwise. Always measure from the inside of the stud frame. For example, it will be easier to finish a 12 foot by 16 foot room than a 10 foot by 14 foot area.

Using your graph, it will be easy to figure out how much material you will need. Keep in mind that studs are 16 inches apart (it is usually suggested that you use double studs at all doorways). Many lumber yards will be happy to assist you in figuring your materials if you bring in a complete floor plan. Be sure to include overhead lights, wall plugs and switches. If girders and pipes for water and heating have to be covered, these should also be indicated.

2. Preparation of Masonry Walls. When masonry walls or concrete block are below ground level, they tend to be damp. Before you do anything else, check carefully for cracks. If you find them, repair them by chiseling out an inverted "V" and filling this with cement. Then see your lumber dealer for advice on the correct commercial compounds available as an initial sealer. Next use a vinyl plastic vapor barrier and insulator according to the manufacturer's directions.

Take your heating problems into consideration. Most basements do not have radiators. Can your existing system carry another radiator? If you have a hot air system, can you cut a register in the existing duct work? It is wise to check your local building codes and discuss any problem with a professional contractor. Many areas require the use of licensed help and the heating system tends to be a very complex job.

3. Framing. After you have properly sealed your walls, and arranged for heating, you are ready to start the framing for your covering. Build a frame of 2 x 3 lumber over the entire wall, as shown, using sixteenpenny nails. Nail shoe and plate to studs, then nail 1 x 2 furring strips to the back of the frame. This furs the frame away from the wall. Place your frame in correct position, and check with your level to make certain that it is plumb.

Next, nail the plate to the ceiling joists. Where ceiling joists run parallel to the frame, nail 2 x 4 catts 2 feet on centers. Use concrete nails to attach the shoe to the floor. This type of installation will not affect the waterproofing seal on your walls.

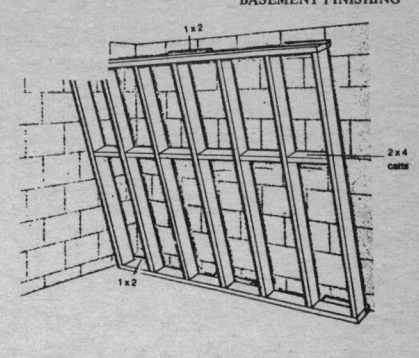

2 x 3 Frame

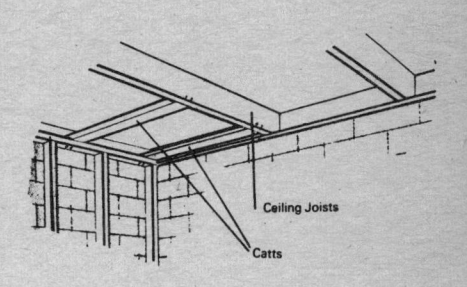

Ceiling Joists
Catts

4. Windows and Stairs. Most cellar windows are deep set. Simply continue the paneling into your windows. Your stairs can be enclosed, using relatively simple construction methods.

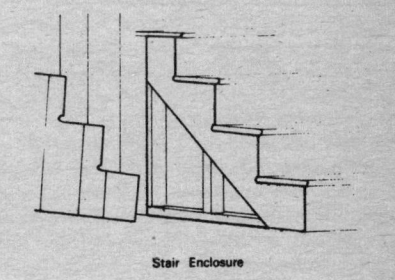

Stair Enclosure

17

BASEMENT FINISHING

5. Enclosing Columns and Beams. To hide lolly columns, build a simple strong box all around the column. A center beam enclosure is shown. Water and heating pipes are enclosed in the same way. Additional furring may be required around radiators or baseboard radiant heating.

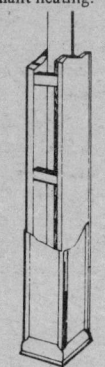

Enclosure for Lolly Column
showing finishing at base

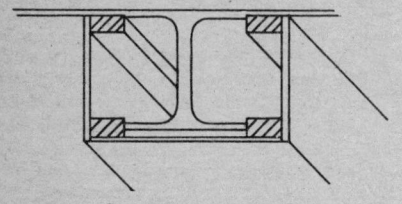

Center Beam Enclosure

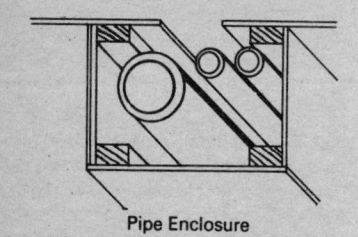

Pipe Enclosure

6. Electrical Installation. When your framing is complete, install your wall and ceiling outlets and switches. The switch and outlet boxes should finish flush with the face of your top covering. Ceiling lighting can be recessed between the joists.

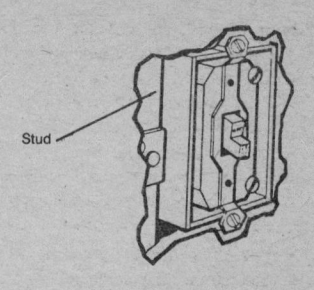

Stud

Switch Box

If you do not have a great deal of experience with electrical wiring, it is wise to hire a professional electrician to do this part of the job. As a matter of fact, many local codes require that you use only a licensed person for any electrical installation, so be sure to check before attempting to proceed on your own. (See also ELECTRIC SWITCHES, ELECTRIC WIRING.)

7. Wall and Ceiling Coverings. Today you have a wide variety of coverings available to finish your walls and ceilings. The least expensive, but most time-consuming to use is gypsum board because you will have to fill the seams and nail heads. The nail heads will have to be countersunk, filled with plaster and sanded down smooth and flush with the board. The seams will have to be filled with perforated tape and plaster. Use a 4-inch scraper for this job.

8. Ceilings. Before you do the walls, but after you have decided on the location of your ceiling lights, you may install your finished ceiling. If you are going to use gypsum board, paneling or plyboard, you will not need furring strips.

Ceiling tile is available in many convenient sizes; the most commonly used is 12 x 12 inches. These can be nailed, stapled or glued on with special adhesive, but the ceiling will have to be furred down from the joists first. The furring strips must be 12 inches centered and level. This may require shimming the strips. After the ceiling is furred, read the manufacturer's instructions carefully before installing the tile. (See TILE CEILING for general procedure.)

9. Walls. The most commonly used wall covering is plywood. It is now available in a variety of wood finishes, including surfwood, oak, chestnut, teak, rosewood, etc. The size ranges include 4 x 7 foot, 4 x 8 foot and 4 x 10 foot by 1/8-inch to 3/8-inch thick. The standard 1/4-inch is now preferred. For most basements, the 4 x 7 foot is sufficient.

Arrange the panels around the room in both daylight and artificial light. This enables you to get the proper sequence in the graining.

To install your paneling, start at a corner. If you have not been able to get your corners perfectly plumb, here is how your panels must be trimmed:

1. Measure 50" out from the corner and mark the wall with perfectly vertical (Plumb) line.

2. Hold the panel to fit against this line.

3. Mark the panel edge, parallel to the corner. If the walls are exceptionally rough, you might want to scribe. (See SCRIBING.)

4. Cut, plane, sand, or file carefully to fit the panel into the corner. It might not be necessary to scribe and fit to compensate for slight irregularities or for corners only slightly out of plumb . . especially if you are paneling both walls of an inside corner, or if you're planning to use inside corner molding. If in doubt, scribe. Butt edges against previously installed panels. Be sure to maintain a true plumb line, for good alignment at the next corner, doorway, etc. Cut off panel at edge going into the room corner, leaving an inch or more excess to permit scribing and/or accurate measuring to compensate for out-of-plumb corner. Keep panel edge exactly parallel with previously installed panel. (Slight irregularities will be concealed by corner molding.)

Paneling should be nailed to furring, studs, or sheathing with 1-inch brads or threepenny, 1-1/4-inch long finishing nails, every 6 inches along panel edges and every 12 inches along intermediate furring. Toe-nail (at an angle) at joints through bevels and grooves. Conceal nail heads with matching putty. Be careful not to dent or mark the panel face with hammer head. Use nailset.

10. Floors. Asphalt tile is the most usual covering for basement floors. Now that indoor-outdoor rug tiles are available, many people are using a combination of asphalt and rug. Check with your local dealer for his recommendation. (See RESILIENT TILE FLOORS.)

11. Trim. To finish off the areas around doors, windows, lolly columns, radiators, floor and ceiling, see your lumber dealer for the many varieties of ready-to-use trim now available.

Basements, Damp or Wet.

Causes. There can be many causes of wet or damp basements. The trouble can be minor, readily apparent, and easily corrected. Or, it can be a more serious condition, not readily detected from the surface and hard to correct. Test borings to determine the subsurface or ground water level should be taken during the wet season.

Following are some of the more common causes of wet or damp basements:

1. Condensation ("sweating") of atmospheric moisture on cool surfaces—walls, floor, cold-water pipes—in the basement. You will find damp spots on your basement wall exactly like those caused by seepage. But condensation does not come in through the wall, but rather from the moist air circulating inside the basement. It is extracted from the air in much the same way ice water in a pitcher forms sweat on the surface on a hot, moist summer day. Condensation will occur during hot, humid weather; but it can also occur during the winter months when warm air is pushed out by a clothes dryer or some other moisture-producing appliance. And you may easily confuse this kind of winter condensation with seepage.

To find out whether the dampness you have in your basement is caused by condensation or seepage, attach a pocket mirror to the wall of your basement in the middle of one of the damp areas. After leaving it overnight, examine it the following day. If the surface of the mirror is fogged over or covered with damp moisture, your problem is condensation. If the face of the mirror remains dry and the wall surface is damp, you can call it seepage.

2. No gutters and downspouts (or defective ones) to handle roof water from rain and snow. The free-falling water forms puddles or wet soil near or against the basement walls. Water leaks in or enters by capillarity.

3. The land is flat or slopes toward the house, permitting surface water (rain and melting snow) to drain down against the basement walls. Water leaks through cracks or other openings in the walls and causes wet spots on the walls or standing water on the floor.

4. Leaky plumbing or other sources of moisture increase the humidity of the basement air. Dense shrubbery and other plantings around the basement walls prevent good ventilation.

5. The subsurface or ground water level is close to the underside of the floor slab. Water rises through the slab by capillarity, producing dampness.

6. The subsurface or ground water level is higher than the basement floor. Water leaks in or enters by capillarity, causing standing water in the basement and, at times, dampness in the rooms above.

Chemical Demoisturizer. Calcium chloride is very effective for dispelling the dampness that occurs in many home basements. A good trick when using this is to pour it in a heap on top of a piece of window screening stretched across an enameled tray. Then, when the crystals of this salt have dissipated, pour off the liquid that has collected in the tray and reload the screen with some more calcium chloride.

Condensation. Condensation is a frequent cause of dampness in basements. It occurs when moisture in the basement air condenses on cool surfaces—walls, floor, cold-water pipes. It may be prevented or eliminated by preventing or removing excess moisture in the air.

Avoidable sources of moisture, such as leaky plumbing, should be eliminated. Exposed cold-water pipes should be insulated.

The basement should be well ventilated—sunlight and free movement of air can quickly dry out a basement. Trees and shrubbery around the basement should be pruned or thinned out to prevent heavy shading and to permit better air circulation.

Ventilation should be governed by weather conditions. In general, windows should be open night and day during fair weather and when it is cooler outside than inside the basement. During hot, humid weather or long rainy spells, windows should be closed because the outside air will probably contain more moisture than the basement air.

Laundering is the most common cause of excess humidity in basements. Washing clothes and drying them either on lines or in a mechanical dryer adds considerable moisture to the air. This excess moisture may be removed by use of a dehumidifier or an air conditioner.

Two types of dehumidifiers are available— chemical and mechanical refrigeration. Chemical types use silica-gel or other chemical to absorb moisture from the air. The chemicals must be replaced or dried out periodically. Mechanical-refrigeration types draw the air over a refrigerated coil (called a condenser), where the moisture condenses and drains off into a drain or a collection pan.

A window-installed air conditioner will cool the basement and remove moisture at the same time. Even better is a type of air conditioner designed to dehumidify as well as to cool. It will cool to a predetermined temperature and then automatically switch over to dehumidifying until the desired setting on a humidistat is reached.

Crack Repair. If there are leaks around the edges of your basement floor, chip out the cracked, soft and crumbly concrete with a cold chisel, blow out the residue with a vacuum cleaner, then fill the cracks with asphalt roofing cement or hot waterproofing pitch.

Flooding. A flooded basement can be a serious and expensive problem when the water interferes with the heating system or with drywall construction. If you have a basement below the water table in winter, you should know what to do as soon as flooding starts.

You should have a small electric pump ready for instant use. It works like a bilge pump in a boat and will push the water out quickly. The pump will give you temporary relief.

Improvement of Old Basements. Waterproofing the exterior surface of existing basement walls is usually more effective than interior treatment. Waterproofing methods would be the same as for new basements (see **Wall and Floor Construction**, below). If outside work is done, installation of a footing drain is recommended, if one is not already installed (see **Subsurface Drainage**, below).

Because of the labor or cost involved, or because of the presence of trees and shrubbery, it may not be practical to dig the trench required for outside waterproofing. In such case, draintile can be laid along the inside bottom of the footings. The tile should be embedded in coarse gravel and should lead to a drainage outlet. (If a drainage outlet cannot be provided, use of a sump pump and pit should be considered.) A drain installed inside the footings is not as effective as one installed outside, but it should eliminate water pressure.

A variety of commercial compounds are available for waterproofing or dampproofing both the exterior and the interior of existing basement walls. They vary in effectiveness. Manufacturers' directions should be followed in applying them.

Roof water properly disposed of will prevent the drainage of surface water into basements. (See GUTTERS AND DOWNSPOUTS.)

Subsurface Drainage. Deep, thorough drainage of the house site is important. In poorly drained soil or where the basement will be below the subsurface water level, draintile should be installed around the footings or at least on the sides where trouble may occur. This drain should be installed even though the walls and floor receive special waterproofing.

Good, 4-inch draintile should be used. It should be laid parallel with, and at the bottom of, the footings. The bottom of the tile must not be lower than the bottom of the footings. If the drain is below the footings, the footings may be undermined. The drain should slope very little—about ½ inch per 12 feet. Joints between sections of the tile should be open about the thickness of a knifeblade, and the top half should be covered with building felt or similar material to keep out dirt.

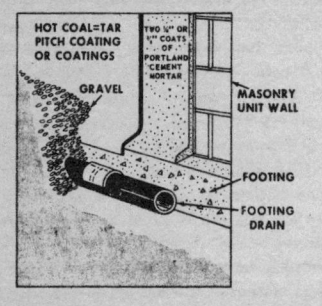

In normal, porous soil, the tile should be covered with 18 inches of screened gravel. In heavy, nonporous soil, the gravel should extend almost to the top of the excavation. In either kind of soil, fine gravel should be placed immediately over and around the tile to provide a good bedding and protection.

This footing drain and belt of gravel around the basement walls should drain off all seepage water and prevent the accumulation of water around the walls. This method is especially suitable on the upper side of a house located on a hillside, because a drainage outlet can usually be located within a short distance.

Under abnormal conditions, it may be necessary to drain deeper than the foundation. The draintile should be placed 4 to 5 feet away from the footings to prevent undermining them. Branch drains may be laid to take care of any springs that may appear when the excavation is completed.

Sump Pump, see SUMP PUMP.

Surface Drainage. Basements can become wet or damp when surface water drains down the walls. Drainage down the walls cannot be prevented, but should be minimized.

After a basement is built, the excavation around it is usually filled with loose dirt. To make this dirt less permeable to the passage of water, it should be free of pieces of masonry, mortar, and other waste material, and should be compacted as it is put into the excavation.

CAUTION: Do not backfill against concrete masonry basement walls until the first floor of the house is in place. Any movement of the walls may crack them.

If the ground is flat or slopes toward the house, build the ground up and grade it to a smooth, sharp slope that will drain away surface water. Extend the slope for at least 10 feet. Seed it with a good lawn grass, and rake and roll it. Sodding is a common practice and prevents the washing away of a newly graded area during heavy rains.

If possible, the basement windows should be entirely above the finished grade for maximum light and ventilation (at least 8 inches from the grade to the tops of the window sills). Windows or parts of windows that must be below grade should be protected by metal or masonry window wells. The bottom of a well should consist of gravel to permit good drainage.

Where a large area of land slopes toward the house, surface drainage should be intercepted and rerouted some distance from the house. Dig a shallow, half-round drainage ditch or depression designed to route the water around the house. Sod the ditch or plant grass in it. If a ditch is objectionable, draintile, with one or more catch basins at low spots, may be installed.

BASEMENTS, DAMP

Tar-Paper Barrier. Even though the roof gutters on a house may be in good shape, and the downspouts drain away from the house properly, the basement walls still may get damp after a good rain. The rain, which beats against the wall and runs down, may seep through the foundation before it can drain away. This can be overcome by digging a trench about 3 feet wide and 12 inches deep along the foundation on the damp side, the bottom of this trench sloping AWAY from the house. Clean the foundation and trowel on tar up to the ground level. Now take some 30-pound tar paper and lay it in the trench, turning up one edge about 6 inches and sticking it to the tarred wall. Fill the trench with dirt over the paper, and when rain running down the walls hits the tar-paper barrier, it will drain away from the wall.

Wall and Floor Construction. Construction required for the basement walls and floor depends largely upon soil drainage conditions. In well-drained soil, good, water-resistant construction may be adequate. In poorly drained soil or where the basement floor will be below the subsurface water level, watertight construction is required.

Cost and availability generally determine the material of which the walls will be built. Poured concrete and hollow-masonry units are most commonly used.

In well-drained soil, concrete that is properly mixed, placed, and cured should provide sufficient protection against moisture penetration. Hollow-masonry unit walls should receive two 1/4 or 3/8-inch coats of Portland cement mortar to help shed water down the walls and keep it out of joints. Application of the mortar, which is called parging, is discussed below.

The walls should have, or should be started on, substantial concrete footings. Properly designed footings prevent uneven settlement and possible cracking of the wall.

The floor should be an even concrete slab about 4 inches thick. A vapor barrier of polyethylene or 55-pound roll roofing should be placed under the slab. The floor should have a slight slope in one or two directions to aid in the removal of water that may enter the basement.

A floor drain can be installed to drain water, and will be useful for draining appliances or fixtures. The floor should slope toward a floor drain from all directions.

Depth of the basement floor below the finished grade will be established by house design. Deep basements are likely to be damper than shallow ones. Temperature, however, tends to be more uniform as the depth increases.

The basement should have enough windows for adequate light and ventilation. And as indicated in **Surface Drainage** (above), all windows should be above grade for maximum light and ventilation.

Waterproofing with Epoxy Resin. To get your basement ready for epoxy resin waterproofing, you must first remove all paint from the walls. If the paint is *rubber-* or *oil-based,* use caustic soda or a strong solution of trisodium phosphate in warm water. Remove *cold-water paint* and *calcimine* with muriatic (hydrochloride) acid and water. When you use this material, wear old clothes, heavy gloves, and goggles to protect your eyes. Mix the solution in a non-metal container, using a wooden paddle for stirring. Flush the walls afterward with clear water and dry thoroughly. You must clean *all* paint and impurities off the concrete wall, for epoxy resins will bond only to a clean, dry surface. *Cement paint* is the only kind you can leave on the wall before applying epoxy; cement paint contains enough cement to bond to the epoxy.

To apply epoxy resin, use a brush or trowel, depending on the consistency of the material used. The idea is to brush it on the walls, and trowel it on the floor. Since most of the pressure from the water comes up from underneath, be sure there is a solid layer of epoxy on the basement floor, possibly a thicker layer than on the walls. All epoxy continers have carefully worded instructions. Follow them exactly.

Watertight Construction. Poured concrete is recommended for watertight construction of the basement walls and floor, but hollow-masonry units are often used for the walls.

Choose one of these methods of waterproofing:
1. Close, compact, watertight construction of

the walls and floor themselves. This is called the integral method and is applicable only to poured-concrete construction.

2. Application of a bituminous membrane to the exterior surface of the walls and under the floor slab.

3. Application of two coats of Portland cement mortar to the exterior surface of the walls. This is called parging.

4. Application of polyethylene film, a vapor barrier material, to the exterior surface of the walls. Manufacturers' instructions should be followed in applying the material.

Integral Method. Good materials (cement, sand, and gravel) and first-class workmanship are essential for watertight concrete. Follow these general instructions in building the basement walls and floors.

Do the work in mild, dry weather. Fall is the best time, because the subsurface water level is usually low and temperatures are more favorable for making watertight concrete.

Use fresh Portland cement; clean, coarse sand; clean, sound gravel not over ¾ inch in diameter; and the smallest quantity of water that will give a smooth, workable mix. Do not use more than 6 gallons of water per sack of cement.

Mix the concrete thoroughly. Thorough mixing increases the strength and watertightness.

Pour the floor in one continuous operation and the walls in as nearly a continuous operation as possible. Leakage can occur at construction joints and at seams between pourings.

Work (vibrate or spade) the concrete in the forms only enough to eliminate honeycombing. Overworking it can cause a nonuniform mixture and reduce its strength and watertightness.

Properly protect and cure the concrete immediately after placing it. Freezing or rapid drying of the concrete by sun or wind can damage it and make it worthless.

Membrane. Overlapping layers of a prepared waterproofing felt or fabric are applied to the exterior surface of the walls and under the floor slab. The layers are coated and cemented together with hot coal-tar pitch.

The wall surface should be smooth, clean, and dry. Fill in holes and depressions with mortar. Knock off projections that could puncture the membrane. A coat of cement mortar may be applied over the membrane to protect the exterior surface against abrasions and puncture.

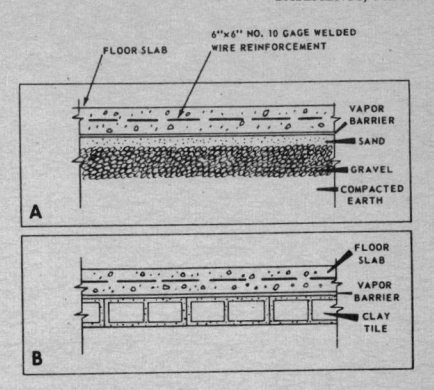

The floor membrane may be laid on a thin concrete subfloor or over hollow-tile or concrete units covered with a coat of mortar. The membrane should be turned up against the inside surface of the walls. After the floor slab has cured, the space between it and the walls is filled with hot coal-tar pitch.

If properly applied, the membrane is a very effective method of waterproofing. However, it is one of the more expensive methods, and, if leaks develop, they may be difficult to locate and costly to repair.

Parging. Two 1/4- or 3/8-inch coats of Portland cement mortar are applied to the exterior surface of the walls. The mortar should be mixed in the proportion of 1 part Portland cement to 2½ parts sand.

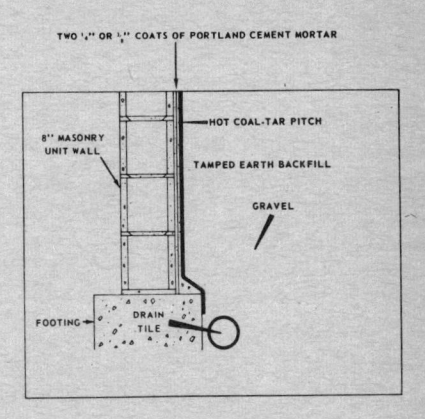

BATHROOM ACCESSORIES

The wall surface should be thoroughly cleaned to remove dirt and loose material. Just before the first mortar coat is applied, the wall should be moistened and given a brush coat of neat Portland cement grout. The second mortar coat should be applied before the first one sets firmly, and the first one should be lightly scratched with a stiff brush to obtain good bond between coats.

The surface of the second, or outside, coat should be steel-troweled to a smooth, impervious finish. Do not overwork the surface.

In very wet soils, the parged surfaces below grade may be given two coats of hot coal-tar pitch. The mortar must be dry when the coal-tar pitch is applied.

CAUTION: Any movement or other disturbance to the walls can crack the walls and mortar coating. Do not backfill dirt against the walls until the first floor of the house is in place.

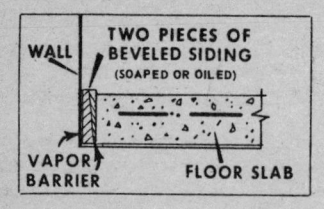

Under-the-floor Construction. In compact or clay-like soil, lay a 5-inch layer of compacted gravel. Follow with a 1-inch layer of tamped sand. Cover the sand with a vapor barrier such as polyethylene or 55-pound roll roofing. Pour the floor slab on the vapor barrier. Be careful not to break the material, because it will be ineffective at that point.

In very poorly drained soil, lay a 4-inch layer of clay tile or hollow-masonry units. Follow with the vapor barrier.

Roll roofing vapor barrier (but not polyethylene) should be turned up on the inside surface of the basement walls. A 1-inch space, formed as is shown above, should be left between the floor slab and walls. After the slab has cured, the two pieces of siding are removed and the space is filled with hot coal-tar pitch.

Bathroom Accessories.

Cabinet Rack. Here's an easily made, handy little rack for use in your bathroom cabinet, to hold toothpaste tubes, shaving cream, and other tubed preparations—thus eliminating the usual clutter of these small articles in your cabinet. Cut some slots of the proper size into a piece of aluminum (which is rustproof), bending the metal as shown, to allow room for the caps of the tubes. Fasten this to the bottom of the shelf, for suspending the various tubes.

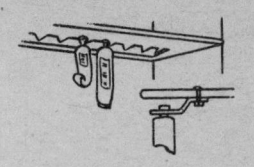

Clothes Hooks. Nonrusting hooks for hanging bathrobes and other clothing add convenience. Place the hooks from 5 feet 5 inches to 6 feet from the floor. They should be above eye level for safety.

Drying Lines and Racks. If clothes—especially those made of drip-dry and wash-and-wear fabrics—are to be dried in the bathroom, it is best to make special provision for the job, rather than depending on towel rods for hanging space.

Here are suggested ways to provide bathroom drying:

1. Place hooks in the walls at each end of the built-in tub for attaching clotheslines across the tub when needed.

2. Put a telescope rod with rubber suction cups over a recessed tub. This rod may be left in place permanently or stored after each use.

3. Mount a drying rack on which to hang hangers on the wall at one end or on the side of the tub. The rack will fold flat against the wall when not in use.

4. Install a clothesline reel with retractable plastic line over the bathtub. Line is hooked to opposite wall for use.

Grab Bars installed by the tub and shower are important safety features. A little time and money spent in buying and installing grab bars could prevent a costly and painful accident to a member of your family. Select sturdy metal bars. Make certain that they are firmly anchored.

An angled grab bar is shown in the shower-tub arrangement. Straight bars are available in various lengths and can be installed vertically, horizontally, or at an angle.

Paper Holders of china or metal can be recessed in the wall or fastened to the wall.

Place the paper holder so that its bar is about 30 inches from the floor, and if on a sidewall, about 6 to 8 inches beyond the front edge of the toilet.

Soap Holders for the tub and shower are usually recessed. Vitreous china and metal are commonly used materials. For tub use, place the soap holder at about the middle of the wall beside the tub and within easy reach from a sitting position in the tub.

In the shower stall, the soap holder is usually placed about shoulder height, and far enough forward so the shower spray does not reach it. Or, if you prefer, you can install a corner shelf in the shower stall for soaps, shampoos, and rinses.

Toothbrush and Tumbler Holder. These accessories are often combined, but can be bought separately. Those made of vitreous china are set into the tile wall. Metal holders may be recessed or wall mounted. Some of these accessories are stationary, others revolve and close flush with the wall. Revolving combination units hold soap, tumbler, and toothbrushes.

Towel Rod. Each family member needs rod space for a towel and washcloth. In addition, you will want some extra space for guest use. To hang a bath towel and washcloth folded once lengthwise re-quires 21 inches. If the washcloth is hung unfolded for quick drying, the washcloth and towel take up 28 inches of rod space.

Towel rods on the sides of the lavatory are a convenient height for small children. A towel pole provides for extra towels in a minimum of space.

Bathroom Fixtures.
Basin Drain Repair, see PLUMBING.
Bath Tub Drain, Clogged, see PLUMBING.
Care. Harsh gritty cleansers soon scratch the surface of a fixture regardless of the material of which it is made. To test the abrasiveness of a cleanser, put a small amount between two pieces of glass and rub them together. If the glass is scratched, the cleanser is too harsh to use on fixtures. Liquid detergents are recommended for fiberglass fixtures because of their somewhat softer finish.

Other precautions to observe in fixture care:

1. Do not use bathtubs or lavatories for washing venetian blinds or sharp-edged articles. If it is necessary to stand in the bathrub or to place a stepladder in it when washing walls and windows, cover the bottom of the tub with a rug or mat with a nonskid backing.

2. Do not drop bottles or other heavy objects in enameled fixtures. The surface can be chipped. Fiberglass fixtures are more resilient and not as subject to this type of damage.

3. Do not allow strong solutions including household and hair bleaches to stand in fixtures. Even acid resisting enamel will be damaged by continued contact with acid. Stains from iodine and burning cigarettes are the most difficult to remove from fiberglass fixtures. Take the precaution of rinsing the lavatory after using cosmetic lotions, hair tints, and medicines.

4. Do not allow faucets to drip constantly—the minerals in some water discolor and stain enameled surfaces.

5. Do not leave wet non-slip mats in tub. Some of them make permanent stains. Hang them to dry after each use before replacing in the tub.

Care During Installation. A careful workman protects bathroom fixtures from blows, scratches, falls, and other damage during delivery, room finishing, and installation. He sees that fixtures are well covered with suitable materials and that plaster, paints, and acids do not get on them.

The damaged surface of a porcelain fixture can-

BATHROOM FIXTURES

not be restored. Special repair materials of the same chemical composition as the basic material are available for fiberglass fixtures. When competently applied, the damaged areas can be restored to new condition.

Here are some tips on fixture care during finishing and installation:

1. Uncrate fixtures carefully. Leave protective wrappings on.

2. If fixtures are delivered uncovered, cover with several layers of strong wrapping paper held in place with tape; or cover with corrugated board, special coverings available from plumbing supply firms, or the special coatings that can be sprayed or brushed on.

3. Do not use newspaper or dyed paper next to enamel; they may leave permanent stains. Newspapers can be used for added protection if fixture is first covered with unprinted paper or plastic.

4. Avoil using paste made with flour to attach covering. Do not use sawdust as a protective filler. Flour paste and sawdust ferment when wet and produce an acid which etches the enamel.

5. Keep fixtures clear of tools, scrap lumber, wet paper or burlap, and other debris.

6. Remove carefully any plaster or cement on a fixture with water or a nongritty cleaning compound.

7. Soften paint drips with the recommended solvent and remove carefully.

Cleaning Tips.

1. That familiar ring around the bathtub will vanish if you'll rub it with paper toweling that has been moistened with kerosene. Then rinse off the lingering traces of kerosene aroma with soap and water.

2. To remove hair from your bathroom wash basin, dampen a small piece of toilet tissue and rub this over the bowl. The tissue will pick up the hair nicely and leave your bowl and drain clean.

Lavatories. Wall-hung lavatories are supported by special brackets or hangers. China or metal legs can be added to some designs. Be sure the legs can be adjusted to fit the desired height of your lavatory.

Whatever type of lavatory you choose, be sure to install it at a comfortable height for the adults of the family. A height of 33 to 36 inches from the floor suits most adults.

Lavatory cabinet combinations usually come in two heights—31 inches and 34 inches. If you war the counter surface on a lavatory cabinet to b higher, you can increase the height of the toe space

Materials. Bathroom fixtures are available at di ferent price levels. The price depends on th material of which the fixture is made, and the size color, and styling of the fixture.

Vitreous china is always used for toilets, and ma be used for lavatories. Porcelain enameled cast iro and pressed steel are used for tubs and lavatorie All white and colored china and porcelained enamel fixtures now on the market are acid resisting.

In recent years, good quality fiberglass fixture have become available. The gloss and color of th gel coat finish is similar in appearance to that c enameled or china fixtures and is resistant to ord nary household chemicals. Tub-shower units an shower stalls including the surrounding wall area ar of leakproof one-piece construction.

Porcelain enameled cast iron and steel tubs ar heavy. If remodeling, have joists checked by a experienced builder to make sure they will suppor the proposed installation. Fiberglass fixtures ar comparatively lightweight and therefore lend them selves to remodeling where the structure may no support the heavier fixtures.

Repair, see PLUMBING.

Shower Head, Dripping, see PLUMBING.

Showers. The most economical way to provide a shower is to add a shower head over the tub. If the shower fittings are installed at the time the bathroom is built, the pipes for the shower can be concealed in the wall. Shower fixtures with exposed pipes are available.

Shower heads are usually made of chrome-plated brass, and have swivel joints for directing the spray. Some models also have volume regulators, or both volume and spray regulators. A fitting that diverts the water from the tub faucets to the shower head is combined with the tub, but separate faucets or mixer valves for the shower can be used.

To insure head clearance for adults, the shower head should be installed at least 6 feet 2 inches from the floor. Tubs installed with shower heads can be enclosed with permanent rigid enclosures, or with shower curtains. Install the rod for the shower curtain at a height of 6 feet 6 inches.

For separate shower facilities, build a shower stall of masonry or tile, or buy a prefabricated enclosure. Prefabricated stalls come in porcelain enameled steel and fiberglass, and range in floor size from 30 by 30 inches to 36 by 36 inches to 34 by 48 inches. Height ranges from 74 to 80 inches. Prefabricated bases or receptors range in sizes from 32 by 32 inches to 32 by 48 inches.

Toilet Bowl Removal, see PLUMBING.
Toilet Float Ball Rapair, see PLUMBING.
Toilet Flushing Mechanism, see PLUMBING.
Toilet Intake Valve Repair, see PLUMBING.
Toilet, Non-Flushing, see PLUMBING.

Toilets are classified according to the water action used. The three types most commonly installed in homes are: Siphon jet, reverse trap, and washdown.

The *siphon jet* is the most expensive, and has the quietest action of any of the three types. The trapway, located at the rear of the bowl, and the water surface are extra large for maximum cleanliness. A deep water seal gives maximum protection from sewer gases.

The *reverse trap* has the same water action as the siphon jet, but a smaller trapway, less water surface, and not as deep a water seal.

The *washdown*, the least expensive of the three types, has the trapway at the front of the bowl. The flushing action is noisier, the water surface smaller, and the water seal not as deep as in the other two types.

One-piece toilets are neat in appearance and easily cleaned, but are more expensive than two-piece models. In two-piece toilets the tank is a separate unit attached to the bowl. Completely wall-hung toilets make it possible to clean the floor under and around the toilet.

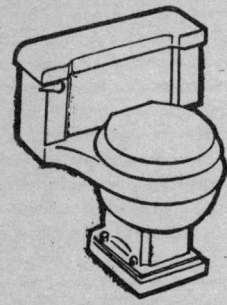

BATHROOM FIXTURES

WALL-HUNG.
Completely wall-hung toilets make it possible to clean the floor under and around the toilet.

TWO-PIECE WITH WALL-HUNG TANK.

Toilet Tank Sweating, see PLUMBING.
Toilet Trap, Clogged, see PLUMBING.

Tubs. Built-in tubs of cast iron and enameled steel must be partially supported by the studs to prevent their pulling away from the wall. A 2- by 4-inch support secured to the studs or special hangers are used. Fiberglass tubs and shower stalls have nailing flanges and are nailed directly to enclosing stud partitions.

Tubs for recess (fit flush between two walls) or for corner installation are 4, 4½, 5, or 5½ feet long. The 5-foot tub is the most used length. Tubs with widened rims are usually 32 or 33 inches wide; tubs with straight fronts, 30 or 31 inches wide.

ONE-PIECE.
One-piece toilets are neat in appearance and easily cleaned, but are more expensive than two-piece models.

27

BATHROOM FLOORS

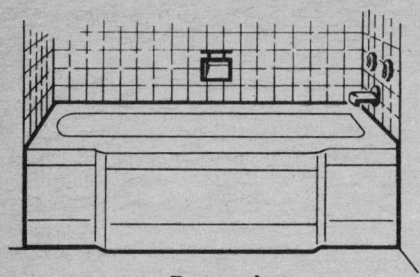

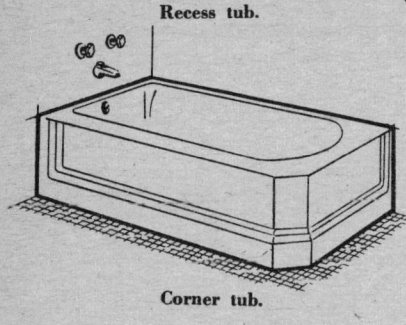

Recess tub.

Corner tub.

Square tubs are about 4 feet by 3½ or 4 feet, and are available for either recess or corner installation. Some styles have one built-in seat, others two. A square tub is heavier than a rectangular tub and may require additional framing for support.

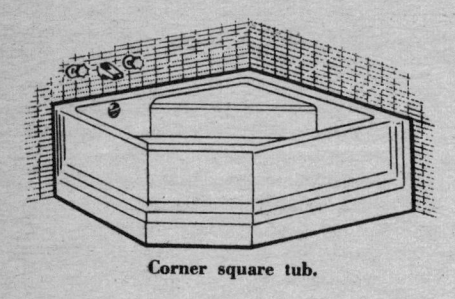

Corner square tub.

Receptor tubs are approximately 36 to 38 inches long, 39 to 42 inches wide, and 12 inches high. They are most suitable for shower installations, but, because of lower height, are also convenient for bathing children and others who need assistance.

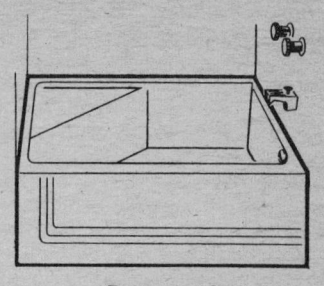

Receptor tub.

Bathroom Floors. Today's bathroom floor finishes are of two main types—(1) nonresilient floor finishes, such as ceramic tile and concrete, and (2) smooth-surface resilient floorings, such as linoleum, asphalt, rubber, and vinyl. Wood floors are rarely seen in bathrooms now. They will give satisfactory service, however, if they are refinished periodically with a water-resistant seal or varnish.

No one floor finish has all the properties desirable in a bathroom flooring; it is up to you to decide what properties you want most and choose accordingly. Necessarily, installation requirements and cost will help determine your choice. Other considerations include durability, appearance, ease of installation and upkeep, resistance to soil, moisture, and indentation, dimensional stability, and quietness. (See NON-RESILIENT TILE FLOORS, RESILIENT TILE FLOORS.)

Cleaning Tip. For a badly soiled bathroom tile floor, a gallon of water to which a tablespoon of turpentine has been added does a marvelous cleaning job.

Bathroom Heating. Remember to plan for heat in your bathroom. If you do not have a central heating system, you will need to install either gas or electric wall space heaters. Plan the location of these carefully. Place the wall heater where there is no possibility of a person being burned on it or of towels or curtains catching fire from it.

Make certain that an electric heater is properly grounded and equipped with a thermostat, and that a gas heater is vented and has safety pilot shut-off features.

Portable heaters are not recommended as the general source of heat for the bathroom. For small areas, ceiling radiant heaters combined with a light or a fan or both are often used for general or for auxiliary heat.

Bathroom Lighting. The well-lighted bathroom has good, glare-free, general illumination and properly placed area lights at the lavatory or dressing counters. The lights at the lavatory or dressing counter should be located so the light shines on the face, not on the mirror.

If proper fixtures are used in the small bathroom, the lights at the lavatory generally give enough illumination for the entire area. To provide good lighting for grooming at the mirror over the lavatory, place one light in the ceiling and one light on each side of the mirror.

Place the lavatory side lights 30 inches apart with the center of the light bulb 60 inches above the floor. Center the ceiling light above the front edge of the lavatory.

In a large bathroom general illumination will be needed in addition to area lights. You may need extra light in your shower. Select a vapor-proof fixture.

Because it is easy to touch water and metal while switching on lights in the bathroom, make certain that lights are controlled by wall switches out of reach of anyone in the bathtub or shower, or anyone using a water faucet. Defective wiring and frayed cords on electrical equipment can result in severe electrical shock. Locate a grounded convenience outlet near the lavatory at a comfortable height for electrical appliances used in the bathroom. (See also LIGHTING FIXTURES.)

Bathroom Painting, see PAINTING, INTERIOR.

Bathroom Planning. You can have bathroom areas in your new or remodeled home that provide maximum family convenience and give satisfactory service for many years. They can be practical and pretty, too. It's all possible if you plan carefully, insist on good workmanship and use the best materials you can afford.

Installation Tips.

1. Comply with plumbing codes, regulations, and guides that will insure a safe and satisfactory installation.

2. Choose an experienced person to install your bathroom.

3. Have an agreement in writing with whoever is installing your plumbing fixtures. This agreement should include price, general descriptions of fixtures and materials to be furnished, and a statement that places the liability for an unsatisfactory installation or damaged fixtures on the installer.

Location.

1. **Single Bathroom, One-Story House.** The bathroom can be reached from the back door without going through the work area of the kitchen and from the kitchen without going through the living room. It is located next to the utility room for a compact, economical plumbing arrangement that requires a short run of supply and waste pipes. The bathroom is accessible from all rooms through the hall. Another desirable feature is that the bathroom door is not visible from the living room or the front entrance.

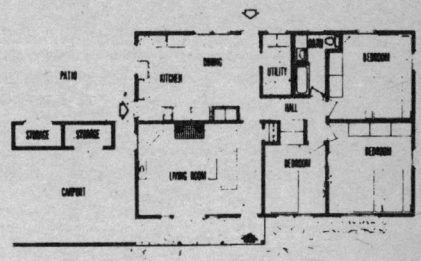

2. **Upstairs Bathroom.** For safety, avoid placing an upstairs bathroom at the head of the stairs or next to the stairs. If, however, this is the only possible location for the bathroom, install night lighting on the stairway, or a gate at the top of the stairs.

3. **Master Bathroom.** When more than one complete bathroom is planned for a home, the second frequently opens from the master bedroom. Such a bathroom can be located to serve a dual purpose. The sketch below illustrates an arrangement in which the master bathroom, located conveniently near the rear entrance, is also the wash-up area. Note how the family bathroom, master bathroom, and laundry area are grouped together for an economical installation of plumbing.

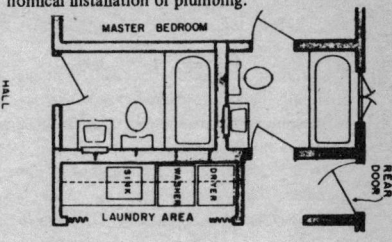

BATHROOM STEAM

Usage.

1. **As a wash-up area.** In the small house the family bathroom also serves as a wash-up area for men coming in from outdoor chores or sports and by children coming in from play. Locate it so it can be reached from the rear entrance without going through other rooms of the house.

2. **For the care of infants and small children.** If the bathroom is to be used for the care of infants and small children, make it spacious enough for the extra equipment needed. If you use a folding bath table to bathe and dress a baby, keep in mind that such a table is approximately 3 feet long and 20 inches wide.

A large lavatory with swing-away faucets or a small kitchen sink set in a counter will be more convenient for bathing a baby than a regular-sized lavatory. An adjoining counter can be used for dressing the baby. A storage cabinet for baby clothes and supplies is an added convenience. Use sliding doors or eliminate the doors on the cabinets above the lavatory and counter for safety and convenience.

3. **By several persons** getting ready for school or work at the same time. The large family with a number of individuals getting ready for school or work at the same time may want to consider the convenience of additional fixtures—an extra lavatory or toilet—a stall shower in addition to the tub.

4. **For the care of family members** who are ill or need assistance. If your household includes elderly or ill persons who need assistance in the bathroom, plan sufficient space for the person who is to help. If a family member is confined to a wheel chair, see that the door to the bathroom is wide enough so the wheel chair can be pushed through. The bathroom should be large enough to accommodate the wheel chair and to permit someone to help the invalid from the chair.

5. **For a dressing room.** Counter areas, generous mirrors, good lighting, and ample storage space are desirable appointments in the bathroom that is also used as a dressing center.

6. **For hand or machine laundering.** In the small home without a basement or separate workroom the most convenient location for laundry equipment may be in the bathroom.

Bathroom Steam.

1. If your bathroom has gotten steamed up from a shower, turn on the cold water full force to quickly clear up the steam.

2. If you will fill your bathtub with a couple inches of cold water before running your hot water, you will avoid steaming up the bathroom.

Bathroom Tile Stain, see STAIN REMOVAL.

Bathroom Ventilation. Every bathroom or wash-up area should be ventilated either by a window or an exhaust fan. Natural or forced ventilation is necessary to comply with local building codes and to meet requirements of lending agencies.

If your bathroom is ventilated by a window, avoid, if possible, locating the tub under the window. If there is no other location for the tub, a window that opens with a crank is easier to operate than a double-hung window.

To help prevent excessive humidity in the house, exhaust fans vented to the outside can be installed in all bathrooms whether or not they have windows. Fans are particularly necessary in humid climates. Exhaust fans in combination with lights and heater are good choices for small bathrooms. Lights and exhaust fans can be installed with one wall switch, but separate switches are preferred if such an installation is permitted by codes and ordinances.

Bathroom Walls. The varied materials used to finish bathroom walls today are pleasing to the eye, remarkably practical, and easily cleaned. Some of these decorative wall materials will last many years, others will need to be renewed from time to time.

You have a choice of paint, ceramic or plastic tile, plastic-coated hardboards, plastic laminates, wallpapers, or fabric-backed wall coverings. The kind of wall finish you select will depend on how much money you want to spend, your personal taste, and the way the bath area is used.

The performance of any wall finish depends on the care with which it is installed and maintained. *Always follow the manufacturer's recommendations exactly for type of adhesive and backing material, and for the method of installation.* Backing material around tubs and showers should be thoroughly sealed with waterproofing materials prior to application of the wall finish.

After installation, protect the beauty and durability of wall finishes by cleaning only with mild detergent solutions and nonabrasive cleaners. With periodic care—wiping with a damp cloth—all finishes can be kept in acceptable condition without the use of harsh cleansers. Abrasive cleansers cause color fading and loss of gloss, particularly on plastic materials. Grout lines between tiles tend to darken with age, but can be cleaned with a small brush and a slightly abrasive cleanser.

Cleaning Tips.

1. If the joints between the tiles on your bathroom wall become so dirty that no amount of scrubbing seems to do any good, use a laundry bleach to solve the problem. Scrub vigorously with a small, stiff-bristled brush, such as an old toothbrush and let it soak on the surface for several minutes. Rinse thoroughly, and repeat if necessary.

2. The appearance of the bathroom wall tile is often marred by the dinginess of the mortared joints between the tiles. You can clean these very nicely and restore them to their original whiteness with a cloth moistened in kerosene. Wrap the cloth around a pointed instrument, or just around your thumbnail.

3. Bathroom tiles can also be cleaned with a solution of sal soda. For stubborn cracks between the tiles, apply the sal soda dry with a stiff brush. For the removal of extra-stubborn spots on the tiles, try using steel wool dampened with a liquid wax.

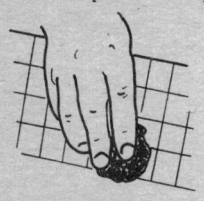

Bathtub Mat.

1. You can make your own bathtub mat, both durable and efficient, simply by lashing a number of rubber fruit-jar rings together with strong thread or fishing line. Let them overlap to make the mat strong, and tie them together until you end up with a rectangular mat.

2. If you have no regular bath mat, use a turkish towel as a substitute. Just lay the towel on the bottom of your tub. Or, fashion some slippers out of a discarded turkish towel, and wear these in the tub to prevent dangerous slipping.

Bathtub Sealer. If the sealer between your bathtub and the wall has crumbled away, leaving an unattractive open place, make your own sealer out of white tile cement. Simply mix this until it forms a paste, then apply.

Batten Doors, See DOORS.

Batteries, see FLASHLIGHT BATTERIES.

Batt Insulation, see INSULATION.

Beads, see JEWELRY.

Bean Bag Chair, see CHAIR MAKING.

Beans, see FOODS.

Bedroom Fixtures, see LIGHTING FIXTURES.

Beds.
   Brass. Clean with a dry cloth and rub with lemon oil.
   Enameled Metal. Clean with soap and water. Remove any spots with a paste of soap, water and whiting.
   Squeaking. If you are annoyed by squeaking wooden beds, pour a small quantity of melted paraffin into all the corners. When the paraffin solidifies, it will act as an effective lubricant.
   Studio, see STUDIO BEDS.
   Varnished. Clean varnished beds with cloth dampened with lemon oil.
   Wooden. Old beds which have cracks should be wiped with citronella on a regular basis.

Bed slats have a way of working into diagonal positions when the bed is shifted about often...and if the slats are not straightened out, they'll drop right out. Keep them in their correct position, by drilling an oversized hole through the end of each slat and

BEEF

into the rail cleat on the bed itself—then drop a nail of proper size into these holes.

Beef, see FOODS.

Beer-Can Opener. A beer-can opener has other uses as well. For instance, its point makes a good scraper for cleaning out corners and may also be used to apply putty. At the other end, the handle when filed off serves as a screwdriver.

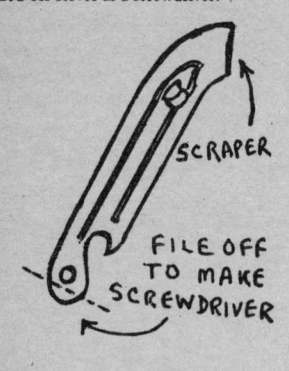

Beer Stain, see STAIN REMOVAL.

Bellows. You can improvise a very efficient bellows from an empty plastic "squeeze" bottle, such as the kind used to dispense catsup. This comes in very handy for blowing sawdust and chips out of blind holes and other awkward locations. Be sure, when using a bellows of this kind, to protect your eyes from the flying particles!

Belt Hanger, see CLOSET ACCESSORIES.

Belt Sander, see TOOLS, POWER.

Bench Grinder, see TOOLS, POWER.

Bench Plane, see TOOLS, HAND.

Bench, Tree, see TREE BENCH.

Bench Vises, see TOOLS, HAND.

Berries, see FOODS.

Bicycle.

Parking Aid. For good solid, "fall-proof" parking of the bicycle at home, try fastening an ordinary broom clip to the rear porch, to a convenient lamp post or fence post—at the height of your bike's handle bars. Then, when the vehicle is parked, all you have to do is snap one of its handles into the clip and it will be securely held on an upright position.

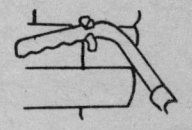

Repair. If the handlegrips on a bicycle have become loose and are continually slipping off, remove them from the handlebar and roughen the bar with an emery cloth. Then coat the bar with rubber cement, also apply cement to the inside of the grips, and push them back into place.

Safety Aid. One way to provide added safety to nighttime bicycle riding is to apply some reflective tape to both the front and rear edges of the bicycle pedals. In this way, the moving reflective qualities of the pedals will be more apt to catch the eyes of approaching motorists.

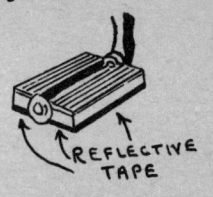

Wheel. If a bicycle wheel is out of round—flat at one point and has a bump at another—remove the wheel from the bicycle and take off the tire. With a spoke wrench and screwdriver, loosen the spokes at the flat point and tighten them at the bump. Then, to check the roundness of the wheel, tie a string to a nail and, holding the nail in the center of the axle hole, sweep the string around the rim.

BIRDHOUSES

Bifold Door, see CLOSET DOORS.

Binder, see PAINT COMPONENTS.

Birdbath. To attract birds to your outdoor birdbath, drop in a few colored marbles.

To clean off the green fungus that grows in the bottom and on the sides of the birdbath, pour out any excess water, then wet some paper towels, stick them to the bottom and the sides of the bath, then pour some household bleach on the paper and let stand for fifteen or twenty minutes, after which remove the paper and wash out the bath. This treatment often proves an effective dispeller of fungus for as long as a month or six weeks.

Bird Feeder. Here's a quickly-constructed bird feeder which you can install eight or ten feet above the ground for easy refilling. Take a small tin can, with the cover still attached, and bend the cover to form a perch. Perforate the underside of the can to drain rainwater, and nail the can to one end of a lath three or four feet long. This same end of the lath is drilled so it can be hooked over a nail driven into a tree or post, allowing the lower end of the lath to hang within easy reach.

Birdhouses.

Cleaning. You can make the job of cleaning out the birdhouse much easier if you'll make the floor of the house removable, fastened by two screw hooks. Just saw two slots opposite each other in the floor cut from 1/8-inch tempered hardboard, which has less tendency to warp than wood. Drive one-inch brass screw hooks into the ends of the house so that the L-shaped ends of the hooks can be turned sidewise to lock the floor of the house into position. Most birds prefer nesting in clean houses, and they'll appreciate your thoughtfulness.

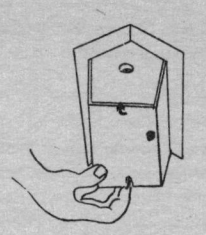

Location. You can fasten a birdhouse firmly to the top of a pole by making use of a large tin can. Screw the house to the bottom of the can, slip the can over the top of the pole, and nail it solidly into place.

Number. Don't go overboard on the number of bird houses you install around your grounds... unless your yard is unusually large. Birds, as a rule, don't care to have their nests close together. Remoteness is more to their liking.

Weatherproofing. One quick and easy way to roof and weatherproof your birdhouse is simply to apply ordinary black friction tape to the roof, as shown. Start at the bottom roof edge of each side, and work up to the top.

BIRDSEED

Birdseed. Wash, dry and store all seeds from melons, squash and pumpkins. The birds will eat every one and sing for more.

Birds' Eggs. Nature hobbyists who make collections of birds' eggs usually puncture the ends of the shells and blow out the fluid contents so that the shells may be preserved without decay. One such hobbyist we happen to know uses a hollow rubber ball with a hole cut to receive the large end of the shell, then slow squeezing of the ball expels the contents of the egg.

Biscuits, see FOODS.

Blackboard. Parents can provide very usable large blackboards for their youngsters from any smooth sheet of hardboard or any large flat wall surface. Just paint with two coats of flat black enamel (available at all paint stores) or ask for special blackboard paints which are also available. These paints can be applied to any paintable surface after a suitable primer has been used.

Blanket Insulation, see INSULATION.

Block Plane, see TOOLS, HAND.

Blood Stain, see STAIN REMOVAL.

Blue Jeans, see CLOTHES CARE.

Board Foot, see LUMBER.

Board Insulation, see INSULATION.

Board Joints, see JOINTS.

Boat Anchor, see ANCHOR.

Boat Oars, see OARS.

Boat, Small Item Storage. Here's a quick and effective idea for keeping small items, such as matches or cigarettes, dry in an open boat. Use a small screw-top jar for holding these articles, and screw its cover with two small screws to the underside of one of the seats.

Boiler Insulation, see INSULATION.

Boilers, see HEATING.

Bolt Measuring, see TOOLS, MEASURING WITH.

Bolts. A bolt is distinguished from a wood screw by the fact that it does not thread into the wood, but goes through and is held by a nut threaded onto the end of the bolt. The four common types of bolts used in woodworking are shown below. Stove bolts are rather small, ranging in length from 3/8 in. to 4 in., and in body diameter from 1/8 in. to 3/8 in. Carriage and machine bolts run from 3/4 in. to 20 in. long, and from 3/16 in. to 3/4 in. in diameter. (The carriage bolt has a square section below the head, which is imbedded in the wood to prevent the bolt from turning as the nut is drawn up.) The machine bolt has a hexagon or square head which is held with a wrench to prevent it from turning.

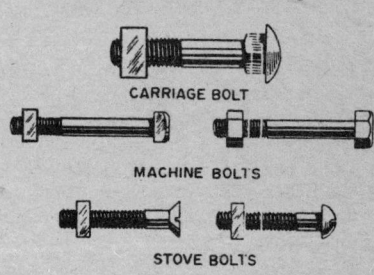

CARRIAGE BOLT

MACHINE BOLTS

STOVE BOLTS

Installation. Whenever possible, install a bolt with the head UP. This way, if the nut has been improperly secured or is shaken loose by vibration and falls off, the bolt will remain within the part and continue to retain its holding capability although the nut is missing.

Be certain that the grip length of the bolt is correct. The grip length is the length of the unthreaded portion of the bolt shank. Generally speaking, the grip length should equal the thickness of the material which is being bolted together.

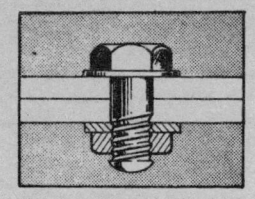

BOLT GRIP LENGTH CORRECT

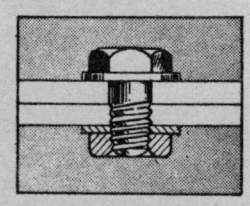

BOLT GRIP LENGTH TOO SHORT

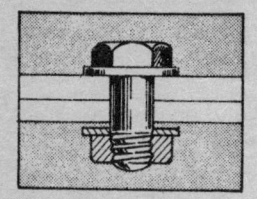

BOLT GRIP LENGTH TOO LONG

Nuts, see NUTS.

Rusted. When a nut has become rusted fast on a bolt and is in a restricted place which prevents the use of a wrench, and a chisel and hammer cannot be used, try splitting the end of the bolt lengthwise with a hacksaw. Cut down through the bolt until the nut is also cut in half. Then drive out the bolt with a hammer and punch.

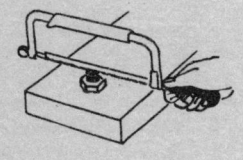

You can often easily loosen a rusted bolt or nut by applying cloths soaked in any carbonated beverage.

Rust Prevention, see RUST PREVENTION.

Shortening. When a bolt needs shortening, thread a nut over the end before hacksawing it off to the desired length. Run the nut down past where the cut is to be made so that the damaged threads near the end can be retreaded simply by unscrewing the nut after the cut is made.

Toggle. A toggle bolt is a type of screw for use with drywall construction, when you want strength where an ordinary wood screw would pull right out of the plasterboard. You insert the toggle into a hole drilled in the drywell, s spring flips the wings of the toggle open inside the wall as a kind of anchor, and you then screw the bolt into the anchor behind. (See also WALL PLUGS.)

Book Care.

1. If you accidentally spill water onto a book page, you can remove it by placing a blotter on each side of the page, then pressing with a medium-hot iron until smooth and dry.

2. A piece of charcoal placed in a bookcase will absorb dampness and protect your books from mildew.

3. A few drops of oil of lavender in the bookcase will help greatly in keeping your books free of mold. Leather bindings that have become moldy should be rubbed with a soft cloth moistened with ammonia, and then wiped dry with a cloth or chamois. (See also MILDEW.)

4. If you have otherwise good books that have become somewhat warped, set them on a flat surface in the humid atmosphere of your bathroom, place a board on top of them, and keep them weighted down for several days.

Bookcases.

Children's. Record racks make convenient and easy to reach bookcases for children. The books are much easier for children to remove than if they are stored in a stack on a shelf.

Homemade. Here's a bookrack which is novel, attractive, and practical, and which can be very easily constructed of some scrap lumber. The books it holds will slip right into place, and they will never tip over. Cut several boards to a length of 16 inches and a width of about seven inches, and glue enough of these boards together to make a rack of from five to six inches in thickness. When the glue has dried, saw the block as illustrated diagonally from one

BOOK CLEANING

upper corner to within one inch of the bottom and 2-1/2 inches from the opposite end. You can then stain or paint the finished product, and glue some felt underneath as a protection to your furniture.

Modern. Here is a good-looking bookcase, with a "modern" motif, which you can cut and assemble quickly and easily. The shelves are nine inches deep, with the top one being 24 inches long, the center one 36 inches long, and the bottom shelf 48 inches long. The two end pieces are nine inches square, while the feet of the bookcase are sections of two-by-four stock. The open ends of the shelves are supported by pairs of 3/4 by 10-inch dowels, which are located about 18 inches from the ends and set in 1/2-inch deep holes drilled into the shelves. Sand all pieces well before assembling with glue and clamping.

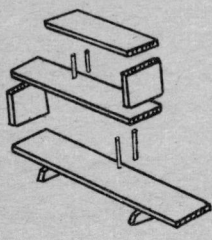

Portable. A very efficient, portable bookrack can be constructed out of an ordinary wooden box. After removing one side of the box, and with the rest of the box left intact, saw the ends in half diagonally—thus producing the trough part of the rack. Screw the triangular shaped waste pieces left from the ends previously sawed off to the ends of the trough to serve as stands. Then you can paint or shellac and varnish the finished product.

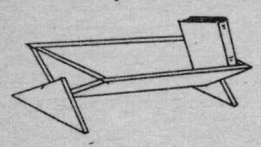

Book Cleaning.

1. The badly-soiled edges of books can be cleaned very nicely by using some fine grade of sandpaper, fitted around a curved sanding block, as illustrated. Use a block which has about the same curvature as the book edges. Sand with light pressure, just enough to remove the stained portion of the paper.

2. For cleaning soiled edges of seldom-used books, try using modeling clay. Simply press a lump of this clay repeatedly over the same spot, kneading it frequently to present a fresh surface. Clean one small area at a time, and be careful not to rub.

Book Covers.

1. Imitation-leather and plastic book covers can be protected against cracking by coating them thinly with some petroleum jelly. Also, coating the bookcovers with clear shellac will make the wiping off of dust much easier. A clean wide paintbrush is ideal for dusting the tops of the books.

2. Book covers will last much longer under heavy wear if they are given a coat of white shellac. Also, the heavy-paper jackets wrapped around school books give a better protection when they are coated with shellac. Thin the shellac before applying.

3. When the leather bindings on books have become scuffed or powdery, rub them smooth with a very fine emery cloth. Then heat two parts of lanolin in a double boiler until it melts, after which mix in three parts of neat's-foot oil. Rub this rapidly and evenly over the entire leather surface, rubbing in

well. Let stand overnight, then polish with a soft cloth. The leather can also be given an extra dose of protection by brushing on some bookbinder's lacquer a couple of days after the oil treatment.

4. Moldy leather book bindings should be gone over with a cloth dampened in ammonia.

Book Ends.

Adjustable. Here is a base for a set of bookends which not only provide expansion or contraction for accommodating various-sized sets of books, but also eliminates the tipping over of the ends from the weight of the books. The base is scroll-sawed from a single piece of stock in a finger-fit pattern. The dowels at either end of the base provide places for setting on your ends and you can scroll-saw these in whatever shape or pattern suits your fancy. You can glue some felt to the underside of the base as a protection to your furniture tops.

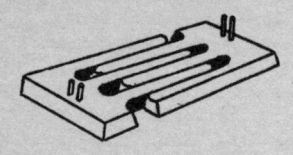

Brick. Need an extra pair of efficient bookends for your young student's room? You can fulfill this need quickly and easily by using a couple of ordinary house bricks. Pad and cover these bricks with material matching or contrasting the draperies and bedspreads, slip-stitching the material in place.

Homemade. Here are some easily-made book ends that will add a pleasing and novel effect to the desk or library table, especially if they are fashioned of some nicely grained hardwood. The arrow gives the appearance of piercing your books and holding them solidly in place. Cut the bases and uprights, and chamfer the ends. Suggested measurements for the bases are 3 by 4 by 1/2 inches, and for the uprights 3 by 5 by 1/2 inches. Take care, when spotting your holes for the 3-inch dowel that forms the arrow shaft so that these holes are perfectly aligned, in order not to spoil the illusion of a nice, straight arrow. The holes are 1/4-inch in diameter and 1/4-inch deep. Taper the stock for the arrowhead only at top and bottom, there being no need to bring it to an actual point. The three slots for the feathers in the nock end of the shaft may be routed in the drill press with a 1/32-inch bit—but saw kerfs will serve if they are cut a bit long and the tapered inside ends plugged with filler.

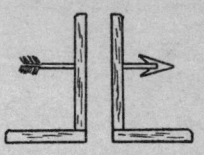

Kitchen. You can easily make a novel and attractive set of bookends, in the shape of a pair of irons, for holding your kitchen cookbooks. Simply scroll-saw out the pieces, as in the illustration, from one-inch stock. Glue some rubber under the pieces, both as a protection to furniture tops and to retard slipping of the bookends.

Non-Skid. If one of your pairs of bookends is always sliding and skidding all over the place, you can usually immobilize them by gluing some wide rubber bands on their bottoms.

Book Jackets. The metal-foil covered, moisture-proof bags supplied by some markets to carry home frozen foods can be used as waterproof book jackets. Straighten out the bag and cut the same size as the book. With the book partly open, fold the edges over and fasten with paste or cellophane tape. Closing the book will tighten the cover, and will aid in smoothing out most of the foil wrinkles.

Book Repair. Here's a good repair for torn pages in books. Place a sheet of waxed paper under the tear, put a little white paste on the torn edges and bring together. Then rub a strip of white tissue paper into the paste so that the entire length of the tear is covered and weight down until the paste dries. Then tear off the excess tissue, pulling toward the tear from both sides. This is easy and it doesn't become soiled or discolored as is the case with cellulose tape.

BOOK SHELF STOP STRIP

Book Shelf Stop Strip. We all know that it is difficult to keep books that are constantly in use from getting woefully out of line on their shelves. You can easily provide a means of keeping them in neat alignment with the front edge of your shelves by means of a stop strip. This strip of wood is cut as wide as the space between the books and the back of the shelf, and just long enough to accept a set of books which are all of one size. You don't have to fasten this strip down in any way, unless of course the shelf has no back—then you'll have to nail or screw the stop strip to the shelf.

Boots, see SHOE CARE.

Bottle Caps. Glue, shellac, and other sticky materials contained in bottles or jugs with screw caps create a sticky problem when it comes to preventing the caps from sealing themselves. You can overcome this by applying a little petroleum jelly to the glass threads at the top of the bottles.

Bottle Opener, see OPENER.

Bottle Cleaning.
 1. To clean out the hard to remove sediment that often clings to the bottom of a bottle or glass vase, fill the vessel half full of warm soapsuds, add a handful of carpet tacks, then shake vigorously.
 2. Try cutting lemons into small pieces and dropping these into the bottle or decanter, half filling with water, then shaking the whole business vigorously.
 3. Discolored or chalky bottles, can be cleaned by putting in crushed eggshells, silver sand or ordinary ashes and shaking well with a little hot water, use a mop if possible to remove marks; if not, raw cotton wound around a narrow wooden stick.
 Repeat process using a nut of washing soda with hot water.
 Finally, shake in a soapy lather, rinse several times in warm water—stand to drain; polish.

Brads, see NAILS.

Bottle Spray Extension. If the plastic pump that hangs in the bottom of your window cleaner or hand cream doesn't reach the bottom of the bottle, you can provide an extension for the tube with waterproof adhesive tape.

Box Nails, see NAILS.

Box Wrench, see TOOLS, HAND.

Brace and Bit, see TOOLS, HAND.

Bracket Lighting, see LIGHTING, STRUCTURAL.

Brackets, Wall. A pair of attractive, matching wall brackets for small potted plants, figurines, or plates can be fashioned from an old, discarded wooden lamp base. Just cut off the standard, then round the end, and saw through the whole thing vertically, as illustrated. Refinish the two halves and mount them on a wall, using the underside of the bases as shelves.

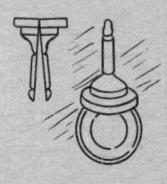

Brass.
 Cleaning. Try washing brass in water in which potatoes have been boiled. It will come out bright and new-looking. Then, to preserve that brightness longer, rub a little salt and vinegar over it. (See also COPPER CLEANING.)
 Lacquer. When the lacquer has worn off brass, rub off the remaining lacquer with lacquer thinner, clean the brass thoroughly with a brass polish, rinse in water and dry, then apply one or two thin coats of spray lacquer.
 Polish. Brass and copper articles that have become dirty and badly tarnished can be cleaned with a solution of salt and vinegar.
 Dissolve in the vinegar as much common salt as the liquid will take up, and wash or swab the tarnished articles with the solution.

For very badly tarnished articles, mix the solution with flour to a paste, spread it on the metal and leave for several minutes, then wash off with clean water.

After wiping dry with a cloth, polish with a good metal polish.

Another very easy and effective method of polishing brass ornaments is to rub them over with the juice of a boiled onion. Worcestershire sauce also makes a good brass polish.

Repair. Usually in the case of broken brass articles, welding is the best answer. However, it is possible sometimes to do an acceptable job by coating the broken edges with epoxy glue and pressing together.

Small holes and cracks in brass articles can usually be repaired by heating the metal and running in some solder. Fill from the reverse side, if possible, and touch up the visible solder joints with metallic paint.

Brass Screws, see SCREWS.

Bread Box. Remove rust with sandpaper or emery cloth, followed by a coat of lard.

Bread Crumbs, see FOODS.

Breast Drill, see TOOLS, HAND.

Bricks. Of all the different kinds of masonry materials, bricks are probably the most familiar to the average person. They are made of baked clay, and are joined together in walls or slabs with mortar the very same way masonry blocks are. Since bricks are smaller than masonry blocks, you will have many more mortar joints in a brick wall, and therefore more chance for trouble if the mortar has been improperly mixed.

There are three basic kinds of bricks: common, face, and firebrick. *Common brick* is 8 inches long, 3¼ inches wide, and 2¼ inches thick. Common brick can be used for most kinds of home jobs except *inside* a fireplace where there is intense heat. *Face brick* is decorative and comes in many different shapes, sizes, and colors. *Firebrick* measures 9 inches by 4 inches by 2½ inches, and is used to line fireplaces and cooking units because of its extraordinary resistance to extreme heat.

Mortar. The best mortar to use with bricks that will be exposed to weather or are set below ground level is made with 1 part cement to 3 parts clean sand. For other bricks, use a mortar of 1 part cement and 3 parts sand, with almost 10 percent of the Portland cement replaced by hydrated lime. The lime makes the mortar buttery and easy to handle. For small jobs, use ready-mixed mortar.

Tools. Along with a trowel, you'll need a hammer and cold chisel to cut bricks, a level, a rule and a cord to lay out the work and keep each course straight and level.

Laying brick. Bricks should be moist when they are laid. Soak them in a bucket of water. Make the mortar joints between bricks from 3/8 inch to 1/2 inch. Every horizontal layer of brick is called a *course.* Bricks laid lengthwise are called *stretchers* and bricks laid at right angles to the wall are called *headers.* The minimum thickness for a brick wall is 8 inches. Two rows of stretchers, with mortar between, will give you an 8 inch wall, and so will a header course where 8 inch bricks run at right angles to the wall.

Mortar joints. The best kind of mortar joint is the flush joint, in which the mortar is cut off flush to the brick face. You can lay a brick wall on a concrete foundation. Apply only as much mortar as can be covered by 3 or 4 bricks at one time. Then lay the bricks and tap them in to produce tight-fitting end joints. The success of any brick wall depends on getting all the joints packed with mortar.

Like most jobs, working with brick takes practice, and you should not expect to turn out a perfect job the first time. Start with a minor project, and work up to harder ones as you perfect your skill.

Discolored.

1. One effective way of dealing with discolored brick walls is to dissolve an ounce of glue in a gallon of hot water, add a piece of alum the size of an egg, plus a half-pound of Venetian red and a pound of Spanish brown. Apply this mixture to the brick surface with a brush. Does a fine brightening job.

2. Discolored brickwork may be brightened by applying a mixture of Venetian red, turps, and just a little varnish to act as a binder. Use fairly thin, two coats if necessary.

Fireplace, see FIREPLACE.

Inside. If you have a real brick wall inside your home, you can help keep these bricks clean and

BRIDLE JOINTS

prevent stains from penetrating them if you'll apply a thin coat of clear penetrating wood sealer, mixed half-and-half with turpentine. Be sure, of course, that the bricks are clean and dry beforehand.

Stain Removal. An unsightly whitish-looking stain called efflorescence which sometimes appears on brickwork can be removed with a solution of spirits of salt (hydrochloric acid).

A suitable mixture is one part of the acid and about five parts of water, put on with an old brush.

First spray the brickwork with water to prevent it absorbing the acid mixture. Keep the mixture off the mortar joints as much as possible. After a few minutes hose the brickwork to remove excess acid.

Wear rubber gloves while using the mixture and keep it away from skin and clothes as spirits of salt is a strong, poisonous acid.

A coat of clear silicone waterproofing after this treatment will help to prevent the efflorescence reappearing, and will restore the bricks to their natural color.

Bridle Joints, see JOINTS.

Broccoli, see FOODS.

Bronze.

Cleaning. Do not wash bronze ornaments. Dust carefully and wipe with a soft cloth moistened with paraffin oil. Then polish with a chamois.

Repair. A broken bronze article can be repaired by welding. But, if you'd like to attempt a mending job yourself, apply some epoxy glue to the broken edges and press firmly together.

Broom Care.

1. To increase the life of a broom, cut off the foot of an nylon stocking, double the leg section, and pull it over the broom straws, leaving just a few inches of the broom for sweeping. This not only prevents the straws from falling out, but keeps the broom in perfect shape.

2. Even an old broom sweeps clean if given a chance. When it is worn short and stiff, cut the bottom stitches loose and trim the edges a little. The broom will spread and be usable for quite a while longer.

3. If you have a broom whose bristles have become somewhat flabby and are in a wild disorder, you can pull these spreading bristles together again and give your broom a new lease on life by slipping a band cut from an old automobile inner tube over the broom.

4. An old broom with frayed and spreading bristles can be renewed if you just soak the bristles in water for a few minutes, then snap a couple of heavy rubber bands around them below the stitching. After the bristles are dry, remove the bands, and your broom should then be practically as good as new.

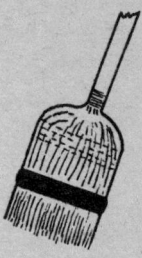

Broom Holder. A screen-door pull or drawer handle, used as illustrated, is fine for hanging the broom on the wall to keep its bristles straight in storage. Mounted at an angle, the handle bears against the opposite sides of the broom's handle to support its weight.

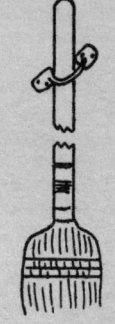

Brown Sugar, see FOODS.

Brushes, Paint, see PAINT BRUSHES.

Brussels Sprouts, see FOODS.

Bubble Gum Removal, see CHEWING GUM REMOVAL.

40

Bucket Handle

1. The narrow steel handle of a heavy pail or bucket often makes for great discomfort to the hands. You can improvise a very comfortable handle by slitting down a four-inch length of old garden hose, and slipping this over the steel handle of the bucket.

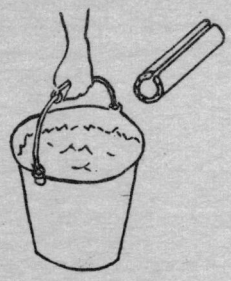

2. Wire-handled buckets with heavy contents are sometimes very painful on the fingers of the carrier. Try slipping a wooden clothespin across the handles to give you a smoother and less painful grip on the situation.

Buckskin Shoes, see SHOE CARE.

Buffer. You can make a buffing wheel for use with your 1/4-inch drill motor just with an old felt hat, a 1/4-inch bolt, and two washers. Cut a number of disks from the hat, using a water tumbler or other round-shaped object as a pattern. Punch a hole in the center of each disk and slip them onto the bolt, with a washer on each side of the assembly. Use a lock washer or locknut to insure your assembly's staying tightly in place when it is rotated at high speed.

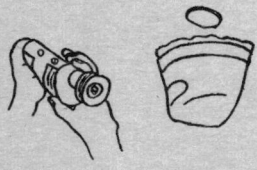

Building Site Selection. An important consideration in selecting the site for a new house is proper drainage. This includes not only drainage of surface water, but also drainage of any subsurface or ground water that may be present or that may accumulate over a period of time and be blocked from its normal course of flow by the new construction.

The highest point on the property is often the best site (A). It will provide the best surface drainage away from the house in all directions, and the subsurface or ground water will be at the greatest depth.

Second choice might be a hillside (B). **The advantage of such a location is that drainage water can be routed around the high side of the house for runoff at the ends and low side.**

If the site is flat, the ground around the house must be built up or graded to drain surface water away from the basement walls (C).

The surface soil and subsoil should be open and porous so that air and water are admitted readily. Desirable soils include sands, loams, and gravels, all of which provide good, deep, natural drainage. Under ideal conditions, the soil is so well drained that during the rainy season the subsurface or ground water level is at least 10 feet below the finished grade. Water at that level is well below the level of the average basement floor.

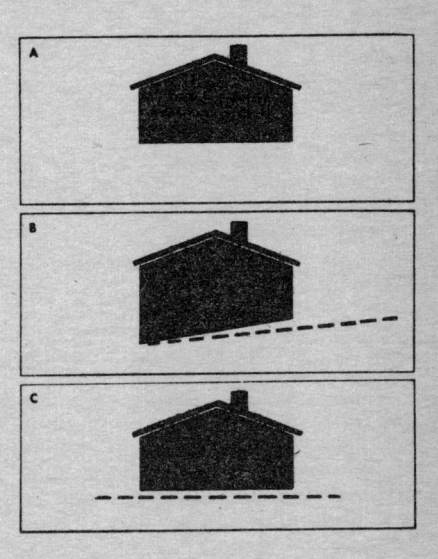

Built-Up Roofing, see ROOF SURFACES.

Bulbs, see LIGHT BULBS, INCANDESCENT.

BULLETIN BOARD

Bulletin Board.

Cork. A cork bulletin board that has become somewhat discolored and unsightly looking can be made to look like new. Merely use some very fine sandpaper to take off all that dirty surface and then, when it is clean, wipe off any dust and apply a thinned coat of fresh, white shellac.

Pegboard. A square pegboard makes a very attractive bulletin board for your kitchen. Use colorful, waxed golf tees to hold your memos in place on this board.

Burglar Alarms. There are four distinct types of burglar alarms: perimeter, spot, area, and comprehensive. Perimeter alarms protect at doors and windows. They must be installed and wired which can sometimes be done by a handy man but could require professional installation. Spot alarms protect a small area and are mostly activated by invisible light. A merchant for instance might want one in front of the safe or across a skylight. Area alarms might cover a room or hall AFTER the intruder gets in. Comprehensive alarms use a number of different sensors including door mats, hall rugs, window and door actuating switches, fire and smoke sensors; even a ground installed system that will alert the resident to anyone approaching the house from any direction. Some even have emergency sensors so that in case of a heart attack for instance, help can be summoned. These are generally wired into a central clearing depot which is manned 24 hours a day and they will tell the operator on duty just what is happening. These are expensive.

The perimeter alarm of course signals before the intruder gets in which is an advantage. Disadvantage of course is installation cost. An area alarm might be more practical for the home owner as it requires no installation and in fact can be taken along on vacations and is usable anywhere there is an electric outlet. It works by ultrasonic vibrations and can be set to sound an alarm and turn on a light anytime anything moves in its active trap zone. If an intruder is frightened off by the alarm it resets itself in a minute or so. Also most of them have a delayed action enabling you to set the alarm and get out of the house or come in with 15 seconds to turn off the set.

Burglar-Proofing Valuables. One of the best ways to protect valuables is to engrave your driver's license number on some non-removable part of valuables. If stolen and sold the police can identify the owner in a matter of minutes and most thieves won't touch items so marked. Your local law enforcement branch may have the electric engraving tools to loan. Be sure to ask. Frequently when the tool is returned you will get decals to place on or near doors notifying that items are marked for quick identification.

Burlap Repair. To make a neat repair of holes or tears in a burlap wall covering or drapery, unravel strands from a scrap piece of burlap and weave into place with a needle.

Burn Repair, see CARPET CARE, FURNITURE REPAIR, LEATHER CARE, UPHOLSTERY CARE.

Butt Joints, see JOINTS.

Buttons, see SEWING TIPS.

BX Cable, see ELECTRIC CABLE.

C

Cabbage. see FOODS.

Cabinet Doors.

1. Here's one good way to insure a perfect fit when you are installing the double-hung, flush-type of doors on your completed cabinet: First, cut a single piece of plywood to fill the entire opening of your cabinet, allowing 1/16-inch for clearance. Draw a guideline down the center of the piece and cut two saw kerfs a third of the way in at the top and bottom. Then hang the entire piece of plywood, and finally saw the doors apart.

2. If your kitchen cabinet doors won't stay shut, try placing a small piece of adhesive tape on the top edge of the door. The tape will not show, and it may be just the grip you need. If the door is terribly loose, try two pieces of tape.

3. If one of your cabinet doors persistently sticks, try rubbing some paraffin on the guilty edges. This often solves the problem nicely, but if it doesn't, sand down the edges that bind.

Cabinet Handles. You can fashion some unusual, attractive, and serviceable handles for your kitchen cabinets with some stainless steel teaspoons — or from long-handled iced tea spoons if a wider grip is needed. Increase the curve in the spoon handle to allow an easier grip, then drill a hole in the center of the spoon's bowl and one in the end of the handle, and attach to your cabinet doors with stainless steel screws.

Cabinet Repair. If there are open spaces between the tops of kitchen cabinets and the ceiling, or between the sides and the walls — and if these cracks remain open winter and summer — fill them with spackle, sand off smooth, and paint. If these cracks open and close with cold and hot weather, you can conceal them by tacking strips of quarter-round over them.

Cakes, see FOODS.

Calcimine, see PAINTS.

Calking.

Compound Thinner. If your calking compound is too thick, or gummy, you can thin it to a proper consistency by placing it on a piece of metal or glass and working in a little paint of the same color as that used on the house. Boiled linseed oil is also a good thinner for a calking compound.

Gun. You can prevent the contents of your calking gun from hardening if you'll seal the tip of the gun after each using. Insert a piece of dowel, pencil stub, or anything that fits snugly.

Preservative. The contents of your calking gun will

CAMERA TIP

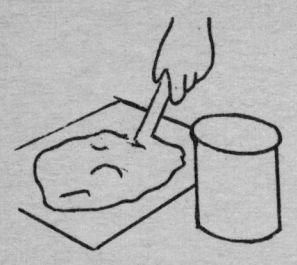

be prevented from hardening if you will seal the tip of the gun after using it. Just insert a piece of dowel, a pencil stub, or anything that will fit snugly.
Tip. Sometimes it is a difficult matter to eject the calking compound from the nozzle of your calking gun into deep and narrow openings. In this situation, try force-fitting a length of brass or copper tubing over the nozzle of the gun, then flattening the other end of the tubing so that its opening is about 1/8-inch wide, and this will aid you considerably in packing your calking compound into the narrow crevices.

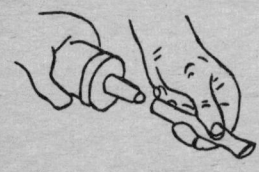

Camera Tip. Sometimes the press-type of camera tends to wobble when mounted on a tripod. You can eliminate this wobble by mounting a T-shaped bracket between the camera and the tripod, as illustrated. Drill a hole through the bracket and fit it over the tripod screw. If the front bed of the camera is higher than the main body, bend up the front flange of the bracket to support it.

Camp Lantern, see LANTERN, CAMP.

Cane Furniture, see FURNITURE CARE.

Candle Holder. A piece of aluminum foil wrapped around the base of a candle being stuck into a decorative liquor bottle will prevent the bottle from overheating and cracking.

Candles.
Care of. Those tall decorative candles often droop and lose their shape during hot weather. You can prevent this by dipping the entire candle into thinned shellac, and then hanging by its wick to dry. The shellac will stiffen the candle and prevent its drooping, but will not affect its burning property.
Cleaning. If some of your candles have gathered dust over a period of time, you can clean them very nicely by wiping over lightly with a cloth dipped into alcohol. The alcohol softens the surface of the candle and effectively removes the dust accumulation without injuring the candle in any way.

Coloring. If you like to melt down old candles and mold the wax into new candles, a lipstick provides a splendid way of coloring your new candles a deep red for use on festive occasions. This is an ideal way, too, of putting lipstick odds and ends to practical use. After your old candle stubs have been melted down, shave the lipstick into the solution.

Dripless.
1. Candles can be made drip-proof if you'll soak them in salt water. Use two tablespoons of salt for each candle and just enough water to cover. They will also burn with less smoke and drip if first dipped into soapsuds.

2. If candles are covered with a good, clear white shellac, or white varnish, this will prevent their dripping and at the same time add to their attractiveness. After shellacking, put away for a day or two before using.

Fragrant. By coating lightly some of your festive candles with cologne, when they are burned later they will exude a pleasant fragrance into your room.
Longer-lasting. If you would like to make your candles longer-lasting and non-smoking, just soak them in thick soapsuds — being careful not to wet the wick. Let them dry in their holder before lighting, and they will burn more slowly, releasing no smoke at all.

A thin coat of white shellac will also prevent dripping and smoking.

Or, chill the candles for twelve hours before using them.
Too large. When candles are a little too large to fit into your candleholders, don't try to cut or chop, or the candles will chip. Instead, take steel wool and twirl it around the end of the candle until it has been whittled to the correct size.
Too small.

1. To avoid wobbly candles in their holders, melt some paraffin and pour this into the socket of the candleholder, then set the candle in while the paraffin is still hot.

2. When candles fail to fit your candle holder, never cut or chop, or the candles will chip. Fill an old can with water and bring it to a boil on the stove. Then hold the butt end of the candle in the water until it is partly soft and warm. Quickly press the candle into the holder and hold it for a second until it is set.

3. When a candle holder is too large for a candle, try burning down an old candle stub — or a bit from the bottom of the new candle — into the hole in the holder. Then, while this stub is still burning, press the heat-softened bottom of your new candle firmly down on it and it will fit tightly and safely in the base.

CARD TABLES

Used. After the candles used for the dinner table have burned down low, cut them down to one and a half inches long and use as candles under your carafe, chafing dish, casserole, and any dish that uses a warming light.

Candle Wax Stain, see STAIN REMOVAL.

Candy Stain, see STAIN REMOVAL.

Cane Chairs, see FURNITURE CARE.

Can Opener, see OPENER.

Canned Food Storage, see FOODS.

Canoe Paddle. To repair a cracked canoe paddle, first dry the wood thoroughly, then apply some epoxy glue to the broken edges, and clamp together for at least twenty-four hours.

Canvas Repair. Repair holes or short tears in canvas by using rubber cement to apply your patching material. Weight the patch down for several hours to insure a good bond.

Canvas, Stained, see STAIN REMOVAL.

Carbon Paper Stains, see STAIN REMOVAL.

Card Tables. When you find it necessary to put two card tables together to form one long table, you can keep them from separating by placing two large rubber bands over a leg of each table. They cannot be jostled apart accidentally and can be treated as one unit.

If you'd like to form two or more card tables into one long table for a family gathering or picnic,

CARD TABLE STORAGE

you can lock these tables together very nicely just by setting the adjacent pairs of legs into tin cans, as illustrated. Use cans which provide a snug fit for the two legs and which are high enough to keep the entire lengths of the legs together.

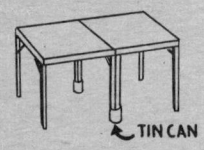

Card Table Storage. An idea for storing that card table. You can make a very handy holder for this table behind a chest of drawers, as in the illustration. Take two 30-inch lengths of 2-by-2 inch wood, and rabbet these like drawer guides. Fasten these with screws parallel at the top and the bottom of the back of the chest. Then all you have to do is slide your table in and out when it is needed.

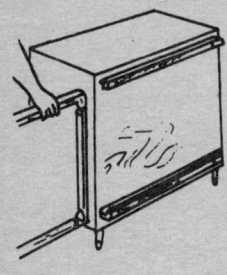

Card Tray. You can easily make your own playing card tray for canasta and other card games out of some scrap stock. The sides are fashioned of one-half-inch stock, beveled on the inner surface and mounted on a one-fourth-inch base with glue and brads. Glue the one-fourth-inch by one and one-fourth-inch dowel pegs into holes which are drilled through the base at a slight angle. After you have painted or finished the tray as desired, glue some felt to the underside.

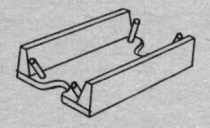

Carpenter's Square, see TOOLS, MEASURING.

Carpentry. Clear thinking and practical planning are important when designing a job of carpentry. But it is the actual marking out which determines the success or failure of a piece of work.

The only way to get off to a good woodworking start is to insure that one surface is flat.

It must have no kinks, curves or ridges and it must be straight and level.

Slide a rule over the surface and look very carefully between its lower edge and the wood. See if there are points where light or ridges are showing.

Use a plane to insure that the surface of the wood is perfectly level before it is marked off.

The best procedure for marking out is then as follows:

- Mark off the face side of each piece of wood.
- Square one edge to face side and mark this as the face edge.
- Only use the face side and face edge for all other marks and measurements.
- When two or more pieces of the same length are required — table legs, for instance — mark them grouped together for the sake of both speed and accuracy. Do this by clamping them in a vice or by using G-clamps.
- Always remember the motto: "It is wise to measure twice and cut once."

Bending. When the saw-kerf method is used to allow a board to be bent, the spacing of the kerfs is of the utmost importance to insure a uniform curve. To find the correct spacing, it is, of course, necessary to know the radius of the bend or curve to be made. Clamp the board to be bent to the workbench, as shown in the illustration, and make the initial saw kerf, which should be about 5/8-inch deep on a 3/4-inch board. Now measure from the initial kerf a distance equal to the radius and make a mark. Raise the loose end of the board until the saw kerf just closes at the top. Measure distance "A" between the top of your workbench and the lower edge of the board at the radius mark. This distance will give you the space between saw kerfs.

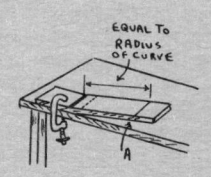

46

CARPENTRY

Concealing Plywood Edges. If you are using plywood to make some article of home furniture, you can conceal the layered edges of the plywood with strips of smooth, thin masking tape, light tan in color and waterproof. Lay this tape on, rub it firmly into place, then shellac, lacquer or varnish over it.

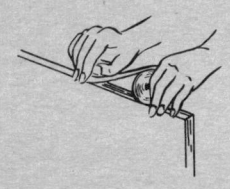

When you are using plywood to make trays and other similar articles, you can finish off the edges very neatly without additional trim by covering them with cellulose ribbon of the proper width. Sand the edges smooth and square before gluing the ribbon into place. After one or more finishing coats of varnish or lacquer, the ribbon, if of the usual striped variety, will have the appearance of a band of colored inlay.

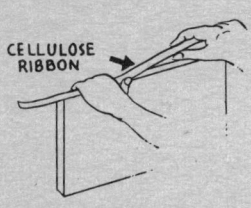

Constructing Crates. Whenever you are constructing wooden boxes or crates, in order to make them strong and impervious to rough handling, you should avoid driving any nails into the end grain of any of your wood pieces. Plan your construction project so that all nails will be anchored in edge grain — as shown in the illustration. The corners formed this way will be much firmer and will resist any tendency to pull apart.

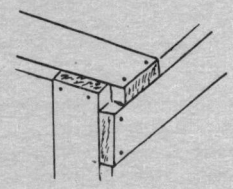

Joints, see JOINTS.
Locating Studs, see STUDS, LOCATING.
Marking Woodwork. In woodworking, marking out for joints and other construction details is done either with a marking knife or a pencil used in conjunction with a marking gauge where necessary.

A marking knife is used for accurate layout work where exactness is demanded.

Pencil lines are used in marking out stock when exactness is not so essential, or on rough surfaces where knife lines may not show clearly.

Pencil lines should also be used when the wood is not to be cut to a line. A knife or gauge line would mar the surface in such cases. Pencil lines can, of course, be removed by erasing or sanding.

Knife lines are usually used across the grain or at an angle to an edge. The marking gauge is used for lines parallel to edges and faces.

This is shown clearly in detail (A) which is the layout of a mortise. The sides of the mortise are gauged and the ends are marked with a knife.

The shoulders of the tenons in a mortise and tenon joint are also cut with a marking knife.

Besides being more accurate than pencil lines, one of the decided advantages of the knife is the shoulder left as it cuts through the wood.

Another typical example is shown in detail (B). Here the knife cuts made for housing joint provide a positive guide for the panel saw after some of the waste timber has been pared away to bottom of cuts.

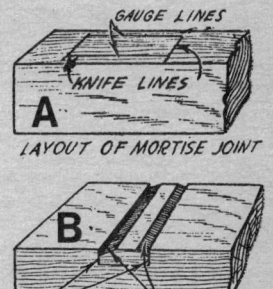

Miter Block. A miter block is an essential tool in the workshop and it is also handy to have a miter clamp to hold joints together for gluing or nailing.

47

CARPENTRY

Shown here is an ingenious appliance which does both these jobs. With it such jobs as picture frame making are simplified. It can easily be made in a few minutes, and the material cost is practically nothing.

To make the block you will require a block of hardwood about 6-inch square by 2-inch thick and another piece about 5-inch long, 1¾-inch wide and 1-inch thick from which to cut the wedges. The base piece of 5/8-inch thick plywood will also be needed.

The drawings show how the wood is cut.

The grooves (Fig. 1) and also the cutting guide, are cut down square to half the thickness of the block.

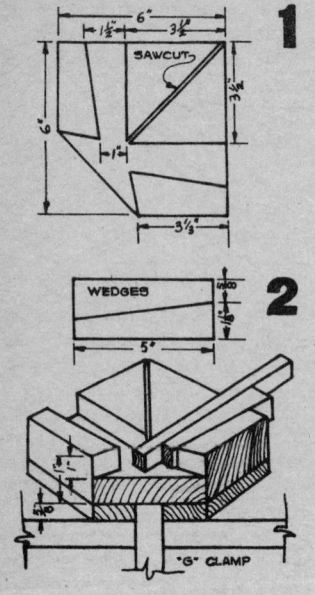

The cutting guide should be cut with the saw — preferably a tenon saw — which is to be used when actually cutting the miters.

Care must be taken to cut the channels square up and down and level at the bottom. If this is not done, the picture frames will tend to be twisted.

Fig. 2 shows the general method of holding molding in position for cutting.

Note that in this particular case a small packing strip of wood has been fitted into the molding rebate to ensure that molding strip is held upright. With solid moldings of course, this is not necessary.

For nailing or gluing the two pieces of molding, they are placed in the positions in which they were cut and are held there firmly by the wedges. The cutting sizes of the wedges are shown in Fig. 2.

If on placing the mitered ends together in position for nailing it is found that the joint does not fit well, run the saw down through the joint and it will then close up perfectly.

Always try to use a tenon saw with very fine teeth and as little set as possible on the teeth.

Fig. 2 shows how the 5/8-inch thick plywood base block is notched on the front edge to house the top jaw of a "G" clamp which is used to attach the miter block to bench or table.

Miter Box Tip. If your wooden miter box is so small that it doesn't permit you to make a miter cut on very thick stock, you can add some needed height to your miter box with this simple little device: Screw two lengths of angle steel to the top of your box at the angle you wish to make your cut, and this will give your saw the required extra guidance.

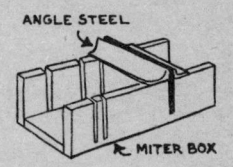

Holding a wooden miter box firmly on a workbench top can sometimes prove a real problem. You can solve this quite easily, however, by using a pair of butt hinges with removable pins. Screw the hinges to the miter box and to the front edge of your bench at a desirable location. You can use cotter pins, instead of the usual hinge pins, to facilitate the installation and removal of the miter box.

Preventing Wood Splitting. When nailing the corners of small boxes or drawers, where the thin wood is likely to split, a C-clamp will come in handy. Clamp two small pieces of wood to the corner, as illustrated, before nailing. By doing this, you will not only avoid splitting of the thin wood, but you will also align your corner better and make a neater job.

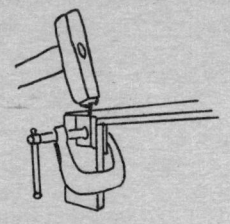

Sawhorse, see SAWHORSE.
Tongue and Groove Boards. When using tongue and groove boards for making a door or any other articles that may be exposed to the weather, always paint the tongues and grooves before assembly. The same applies to the rebate and top edges of weatherboards where they join.
Tools, see TOOLS, HAND; TOOLS, MEASURING; TOOLS, POWER.

Carpet Beetles, see INSECTS.

Carpet Care.
  Brightening. Brighter-looking rugs will usually result if you sprinkle them with salt, let stand for an hour or two, then vacuum them.
  Burn Repair.
  1. You can often camouflage a small burn in a carpet by first scraping out the discolored fabric with a knife, then snipping some pile from a hidden area of the same carpet, spreading this pile in the palm of one hand and dabbing some glue over it, then pressing the whole business into the damaged spot.
  2. Cigarette burns in carpeting are a familiar problem. To remove them easily (if the burns aren't too deep), rub lightly with fine, dry steel wool. If the burn goes deeper, then the ends of the burnt tufts should be clipped carefully with a scissors first. Then scrub again with the steel wool until all black marks disappear.
  Chewing Gum Removal, see CHEWING GUM REMOVAL.
  Cleaning. The worst enemy of carpets and rugs is dirt! How efficiently and thoroughly these carpets are cleaned plays a vital part in how long they will appear fresh and new-looking, and how durable they will be. Ineffective cleaning methods are very hard on the average carpet.
  To clean carpets that are only slightly soiled, try using cornmeal. With a stiff brush, work the cornmeal into the pile of the carpets, then remove it with your vacuum cleaner.
  Cleaning New Carpet. Never use a vacuum cleaner on a new carpet or on new felt until it has been down for about three months. This allows the carpet pile to settle down. During this period, cleaning the carpet or felt should be done with a carpet sweeper.
  Color Restoration.
  1. Try restoring some of the color and life to your faded or dingy-looking carpets by sponging them, a small section at a time, with hot water to which a little ammonia had been added. Rub the area dry after each scrubbing.

  2. Wring a cloth out of water, to which a cupful of vinegar and a half-teaspoon of ammonia have been added, and go over the rug with this. Usually brings out the colors beautifully.
  3. Dull spots on a carpet caused by the weight of furniture can be brightened if you rub some French chalk into them with a stiff brush and then vacuum.
  4. When one of your rugs has acquired some worn sections on it, the appearance of these parts can often be greatly improved with some dye. Applied with a window spray, the color goes on evenly and makes the signs of wear on the rug practically invisible.

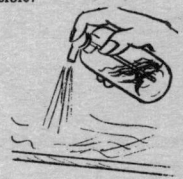

  Curling. Corners on mats and floor rugs may be kept perfectly flat by means of small angle pieces cut with tinsnips from lightweight sheet lead.

CARPETING STAIRS

Pierce the lead for sewing, and then use a needle and strong thread to attach the angle pieces to the underside of the carpet or mat corners at a distance of about one inch in from the edges.

With the angle pieces in place, not only will the corners remain flat, but the mats are not so likely to slip and slide on highly polished floors.

You can also flatten them by dampening with a little warm water and weighting them down with heavy objects until dry.

Frayed Edges. If the edges of your rug have frayed but the rug is otherwise in good condition, you can repair it with fine twine, using a buttonhole stitch. When you have finished, color the twine with crayons in shades that blend with the rug pattern and press with a hot iron. This makes a neat finish and the rug will be serviceable for a long time.

When a rug is continually fraying out on its ends and will not stay sewed, try glue. Work some liquid glue into the rug to about a half-inch from the end with your fingers, let dry on a flat surface, and your rug should then stay "mended."

Nap Lifting. To remove marks left in carpeting by heavy furniture, hold a hot steam iron about two inches away from the rug, and then brush up the nap. Or, go over the marks with a vacuum cleaner. Or, dampen with warm water, then rub with the edge of a coin. Or, pour a little water into the marks and let stand overnight. A damp chamois placed over the depression for a few hours will also restore the nap.

Raveling. You can keep a carpet from raveling by spreading clear plastic cement glue along the edge below the nap. When the glue dries, trim a bevel in the nap. The carpet will not ravel and you will have a professional looking job.

Renovating. If your carpet is wearing in spots, try soaking a clean sponge in dye the color of your carpeting and touching up all the thin spots. Thin spots look darker when wet, so make allowances for this when mixing your dye. When the first application wears off, repeat.

Rotating. In addition to cleaning rugs and carpets frequently, it is advisable to rotate them occasionally. Rotation is important because insects usually feed under heavy pieces of furniture where cleaning is difficult, rather than in the open where regular cleaning, light, and movement of people keep down infestation.

Stain Removal, see STAIN REMOVAL.

Stiffening. If a rug has lost its stiffness, try the following cure: Buy sizing from a rug supply dealer, this coming in powder or grain form, and to be mixed either with hot or cold water according to the brand. To apply it, turn the rug upside down on the floor, pour the sizing on liberally, then spread evenly with an ordinary broom. Wait for at least two days before turning the rug over and using again.

Carpets sometimes lose their sizing after drycleaning or other types of cleaning, and as a result they do not stay in place as well as originally. In this case, try a couple of coats of shellac on the underside of the carpet and see how much this helps.

See also RUG CARE.

Carpeting Stairs. Most stairs look better, sound better and are easier to clean when they have been carpeted. In no time at all the carpeted stairs add warmth and color and quietness to a home. You can save money by doing the job yourself and it isn't difficult. You don't need any expensive tools, just the right battens, underfelt and good carpet.

Before you can do anything, you must check to see that your stairs are either well-rendered concrete, wooden, or wooden encased. These are the only suitable surfaces, for bare concrete will cut through the carpet and must be rendered first. If your stairs are wooden and either warped or worn, you are advised to fill any undulations with wood filler, or to replace the wood. Paint or varnish the skirting board or any part of the tread.

Measure the stairs and the landings, take care to measure each step separately as they may vary up to an inch in height and depth; the width is generally fairly even all the way down, but if you have reason to suspect that one step may be wider, then buy the carpet at that width and then trim it.

CARPETING STAIRS

It is possible to buy haircord carpets in 27 in. and 40 in. lengths if you are lazy about cutting up carpets, but these don't really have the advantage over the looser pile that they were once thought to have. Modern nylon and woolen carpets have every bit of strength and wear needed for stair use, are easier to clean and are softer in texture.

The wisest way to guarantee the life and quality of your carpet is to get a good quality super-underfelt. There are many on the market which are quite inexpensive.

If your floor is wooden, you will need hammer, nails and wooden battens; if you have concrete, you will need metal battens, a drill, plugs, screws and a screwdriver. In either case you will need strong scissors to trim the carpet, and latex adhesive.

Step 1: Place underfelt and batten on stairs; felt should extend at least 2 inches over nose of stair. Lengths of batten can be cut to fit stair length. Or, if you are using metal grips you may need to join two together, to grip the carpet right across. Put landing underfelt in place. Attach one batten on the tread (horizontal area) and one on the riser (vertical part of step).

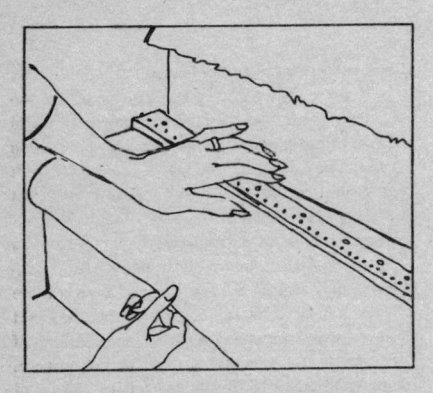

Step 2: Wooden stair: With 1-inch nails fix battens on to both tread and riser. To avoid flattening grips with hammer drive nail home with a puncher or a straight piece of metal.
Cement stair: Using metal battens, drill holes through guide holes, plug them and screw battens down using 1-inch screws.

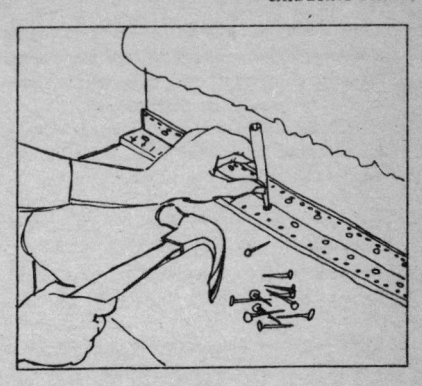

Step 3: Trim carpet (if necessary) to fit width of stairs and paint cut edge with latex adhesive to prevent fraying.

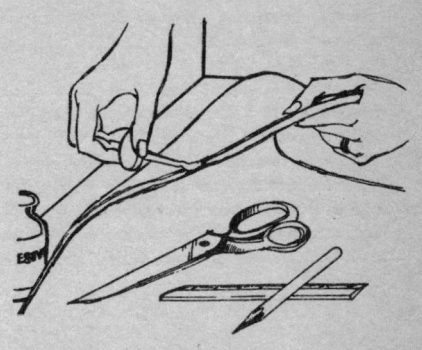

Step 4: Starting at top landing, making sure carpet is perfectly in line with stairs, tack top edge of carpet in position around landing. Leave carpet on stair edge loose.

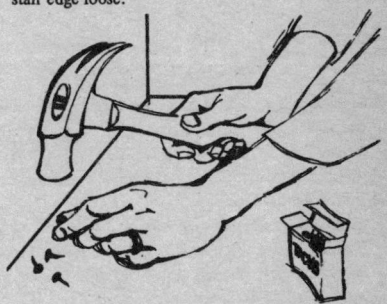

CARPET SWEEPER TIPS

Step 5: Now smooth carpet down over the nose of top stair, taking care not to displace underfelt. Press carpet into crease of stair until nails or gripper teeth bite into it. Using a wedge-shaped piece of wood, hammer down into the crease, to ensure that the carpet backing is firmly held by the gripper. Repeat down the entire length of the stairs.

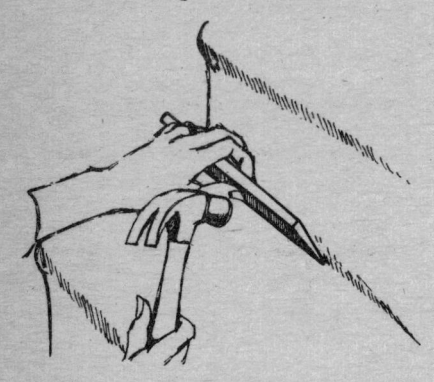

Step 6: At the bottom step, turn under surplus carpet and pulling the carpet taut, tack through both thicknesses along the bottom edge. If the carpet is not too thick, and there is sufficient length, the surplus can be folded under and used instead of underfelt on the bottom step. But make sure this is neat and safe.

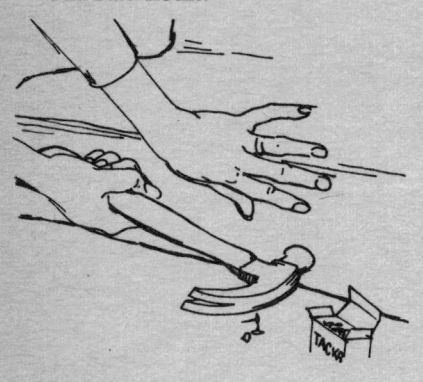

Carpet Sweeper Tips.

1. Dampen the brush on your carpet sweeper before using it and it will pick up ravelings and lint without any trouble.

2. If the bristles of your carpet sweeper are beginning to wear short and don't pick up all the dirt, try winding adhesive tape around the rollers, sticky side down, facing the floor. This lets the brush down and the sweeper works efficiently again.

3. When cleaning the hand carpet sweeper, remove the brush and, after taking off all hair and lint, rub well with a cloth wet in kerosene. Let the brush remain in the air until the odor has evaporated.

Carrots, see FOODS.

Carry-all. A soft drink carton makes an excellent carry-all for assorted cleaning supplies ... such as your furniture polish, window cleaner, spray for the dust mop, upholstery and rug cleaner, as well as a clean cloth or two.

Carving Blade. Old injector-type razor blades make excellent replacement blades for chuck carving tools. Grind the blade on a fine wheel, being careful not to overheat the blade and draw its temper, then hone it on a fine stone. These blades can be ground into a variety of special-purpose shapes to suit particular jobs.

Carving Tips, see COOKING TIPS.

Casein Paint, see PAINTS.

Casement Windows, see WINDOWS.

Caster Marks, see LINOLEUM MARKS.

Caster Repair.

1. If you have a piece of furniture that loses its casters every time it is moved, remove the casters, then fill the openings with plastic wood. As this sets, force the casters into place. Then allow the plastic wood to harden thoroughly before standing the furniture on its feet.

CEILING PANEL BRACE

2. One very easy, but effective, way to remedy a loose caster in a piece of furniture is to wrap the shaft of the caster with some aluminum foil, then force it back into its socket.

ALUMINUM FOIL WRAPPED

3. One of the pet annoyances around a household is the caster which keeps falling out of a piece of furniture everytime you attempt to move it. You can remedy this situation by hacksawing a slot about 1/4-inch deep in the end of the caster post, and then wedging the cut slightly apart.

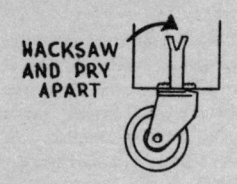

HACKSAW AND PRY APART

4. To repair a loose caster, remove it, fill hole with putty, replace caster and scrape off any excess putty.

Cast Iron Repair. If a cast-iron article is cracked or broken, clean the metal thoroughly with steel wool, then coat the edges liberally with plastic steel or epoxy glue, and clamp together. Applying a coat of plastic steel on the outside of the break will add strength. Nevertheless, don't count too much on this mend's ability to withstand extremely hard abuse.

Cast Iron, Rusted. If cast-iron furniture or other articles are rusted, clean the metal with a wire brush, steel wool, and a liquid rust remover. Then apply a rust-inhibiting primer paint, and finish off with a final paint in the color you desire.

Cat Care. When your kitten needs doctoring and refuses to take the medicine, try spilling the medicine liberally over her fur. She will lick it off and improve.

Catsup Bottle. An easy way to start a new bottle of catsup is to insert a soda straw into it. This permits air to get into the bottom of the bottle, which will encourage it to flow easily.

Catsup Stain, see STAIN REMOVAL.

Cauliflower, see FOODS.

C-Clamp, see TOOLS, HAND.

Ceiling Application, Drywall, see DRYWALL.

Ceiling, Basement, see BASEMENT FINISHING.

Ceiling Installation, see TILE, CEILING.

Ceiling Panel Brace. Make an improvised brace to raise and hold ceiling panel from pieces of 2 x 4 lumber.

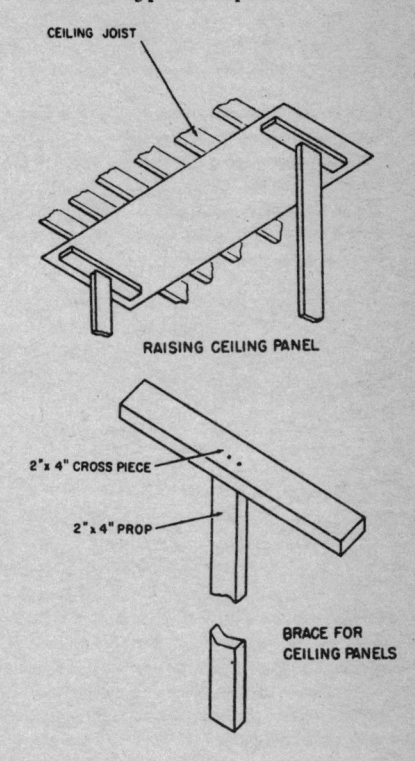

CEILING JOIST

RAISING CEILING PANEL

2" x 4" CROSS PIECE

2" x 4" PROP

BRACE FOR CEILING PANELS

CEILING PAINTING

Ceiling Painting, see PAINTING, INTERIOR.

Ceiling Tile, see TILE CEILING.

Celery, see FOODS.

Cellars, see BASEMENT FINISHING; BASEMENTS, DAMP OR WET.

Cement, see ADHESIVES.

Cement-Asbestos Shingles, see ROOF SURFACES.

Central Air Conditioner, see COOLING.

Ceramic Tile, see TILE, CERAMIC.

Cesspool, see PLUMBING.

Chair Making.
    Bean Bag. *Materials:* 5 yards of 36 in. wide hard-wearing fabric, for example, denim, canvas or vinyl; an old sheet of 5 yds. of unbleached calico or other strong, cheap fabric; 2-inch matching buckle; 5 yds. 2-inch belt backing; eyelets for belt; approx. 12 lbs. soft filling like kapok; 2 size 54 buttons to cover.
    Directions: Cut out pattern carefully following the diagram, using two large sheets of newspaper pasted together. Use pattern to cut out four sections of the cover fabric and four sections of lining.

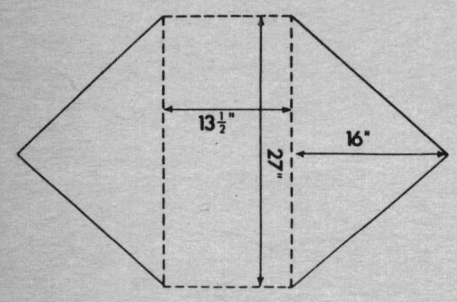

Sew the four cover sections together at the sides, continuing in a clockwise direction until all sides are enclosed. The sections piece together like the segments of a cake, but on one side leave the seams open about 4 in. from where the points come together at the center, forming a hole for turning and filling the ottoman. Turn the cover right side out.

Following the same directions make up the lining and then turn this right side out. Now push lining inside cover making sure seams correspond. Pin lining and cover together around the opening so filling will not pass between the layers. A pin placed at each seam will also keep the lining in place while filling.

Cover two size 54 buttons in the same fabric as the ottoman, following the given directions. Sew one button securely at the center on the enclosed side. Then using strong upholstery cotton or twine sew a few stitches behind the button from the inside, leaving two long threads drawn out through the top opening which, after the cushion is stuffed, are drawn in tautly with another button.

If you are using kapok just push it gently through the opening. Stuff the ottoman until it is about three-quarters full. Before closing the hole with hand sewing, thread the two free ends of cotton and draw them up through the material near the center. Close the seams in the lining and cover with hand sewing.

Draw the threads in as tightly as possible, anchor with a few small stitches, then sew on the second button securely. Make a belt using 2-inch thick belt backing and a 2-inch buckle. Make holes with eyelets just as you would for a normal belt. Place around ottoman as in picture, pull in tightly and fasten . . . and there's the finished product!

Using the measurements in our pattern the finished ottoman is approximately 3 ft. square and 11 in. high. To make it smaller just reduce the pattern, carefully keeping it to scale.

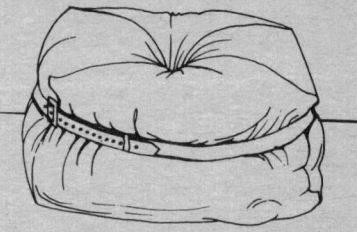

Lawn, Arm for. If you happen to have some lawn chairs of the type illustrated, you can add greater convenience to them, and also permit more elbow room, if you will install a concealed, pivoted arm below the regular one. Bolt this new arm to the rear of the original arm. Partially-drilled holes in this new swinging arm will hold drinking glasses.

CHAIR MAKING

ool. To make the pool chair you will need the ollowing materials; approximately 70 ft. of 2 in. x 1 . dressed lumber (this depends on the length of e chair); about 120 1¼ in. x 14 nails, 4 1¼ in. x 8 crews; 2 small ½ in. wide hinges, and screws; under- at and exterior enamels.

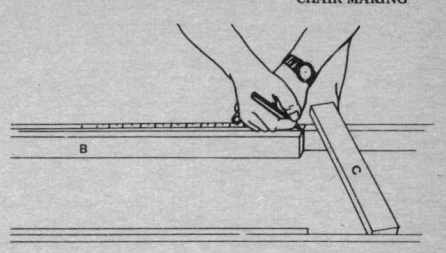

Glue and nail third C piece 25 in. in from one end. The back rest will fit into this end.

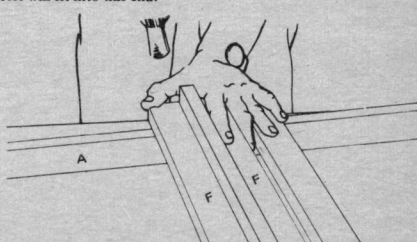

Fit F stays, glueing and nailing them from the seat end with about ¾ in. space. Each F piece is fitted with a 1¼ in. overhang on each side of the frame AC. (An easy way to space the F slats is to use one on its edge.).

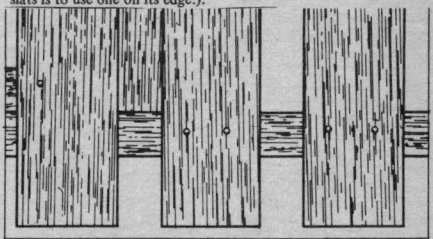

cut parts for the chair. Two 5 ft. lengths for A; two 24 in. s for B; three 14 in. pieces for C; two 12 in. lengths for D; ¼ in. piece for E; and for F 24 x 18 in. pieces.

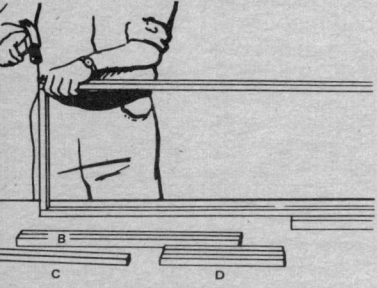

When fitting the slats to the back rest frame pieces B make sure the nails are placed correctly.

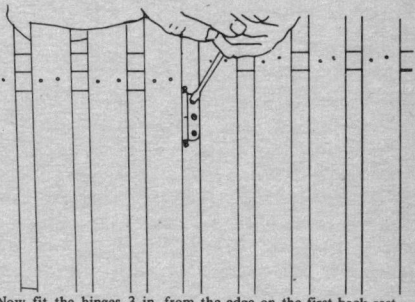

lue and nail the lengths as follows: Fit parts C betwsen , one at each end, to form a rectangular frame.

Now fit the hinges 3 in. from the edge on the first back rest slat and then center piece C.

55

CHAIR RAIL REMOVAL

Drill a hole in each D piece about ½ in. from the top and in the center. This would be at the open end of the U support. Now fit the screw in D, screwing into B.

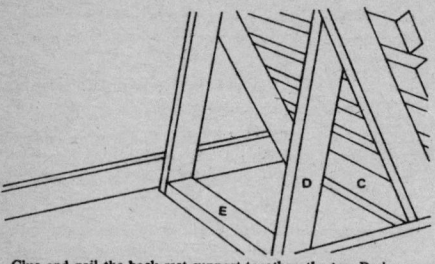

Glue and nail the back rest support together, the two D pieces with E glued and nailed to them to form a "U". This support is then fitted 12¾ in. from the top of the back rest just tight enough to hold the support firm.

To finish, sand off rough edges, paint with undercoat and finish with an exterior enamel.

Chair Rail Removal. The job of getting rid of chair rails is not difficult, but care is needed to avoid unnecessary damage.

The first point to remember is not to use a claw hammer, pinch bar, or chisel to pry the molding from the wall.

This practice invariably results in the hammer or chisel being squeezed into the plaster, causing it to break away and leave large holes.

This only leads to excessive patching up afterwards.

One method of removing chair rails is to locate the nails and punch them deeper into the molding, which is usually not very thick.

If this is possible, then you find that the rails will pull away quite easily, leaving the nails in the wall protruding only a short distance.

It is then a simple matter to extract them with a claw hammer because the bond between the nails and the plugs — or studs in a wood frame — will be broken.

Remember, however, to lay a piece of sheet metal or sheet plastic on the face of the wall when withdrawing the nails to prevent the hammer head digging into the plaster.

Sometimes it may be difficult to locate the position of the nails; then an alternative method of removal is to use an old chisel to split the molding lengthwise along the normal center nailing position.

Although this may appear wasteful at first sight there is not much use for the old molding even if removed intact.

Once the rail is split away the nails will be left protruding, but before extracting them it is a good idea to hammer them into the plugs or studs a little to break their bond.

Chair Repair.
Glue Removal.

1. Before gluing a chair rung back in its hole, always be sure to remove all the old glue, so that the new can take hold. Sand the old glue off the rung, and use a round file or rasp to remove it from inside the hole. Try to remove the old glue without taking off any wood, in order to retain a tight fit.

2. The stub of a broken chair rung which is resisting your efforts to remove it because of the glue, will often be easier to remove after you have applied a little vinegar to the joint.

Loose Frame. Even though chair rungs and legs are tight, you may get wobble from loose frames or rails around the bottom of the chair seat. The best way to cure this defect is to install corner braces diagonally across the leg. If the seat already has corner braces and if they are loose, remove them and replace the screws with larger ones. Then reglue. You can also strengthen corners with metal corner irons.

Loose Legs and Rungs. Trouble usually develops in chairs when the rungs no longer fit into the legs, or when the legs no longer fit into the holes cut in the chair seat. Shooting wood glue into the hole may

CHAIR REPAIR

give you temporary relief, but it seldom cures the problem permanently. You should remove the leg or rung and scrape off all the old glue from the surface of the rung or leg and also from the hole it fits into. When both surfaces are clean, apply fresh glue liberally and force the rung back into the slot.

The trick of gluing successfully is in the amount of pressure exerted while the glue is drying. You must apply a great deal of force to these joints after spreading on the glue. You can use long bar clamps or cabinet-maker's clamps, if you wish. If you are working with chair rungs and legs, you can use a belt-type webbing that encircles all four legs and cinches up tightly when buckled. If you don't have clamps, tie a rope loosely around the outside of the legs in a loop, and then insert a stick in the loop and twist the rope tightly enough to get the proper tension. Be sure the glue is dried before you remove the clamp or rope.

You can add a small amount of sawdust to the glue you are going to use to repair the chair. This will hold better and longer.

To repair a loose chair rung caused by a shrunken tenon, wrap the tenon with glue-saturated bandage gauze before forcing back into the hole. The gauze provides a snug fit and also prevents the glue from oozing out.

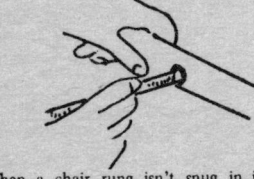

When a chair rung isn't snug in its hole, no amount of glue will hold it in place. One effective remedy for this little problem is to saw a slit in the end of the rung, not quite so deep as the tenon part of the rung. Then tap a slender wood wedge very lightly into this slit — not too far or you'll split the rung. Cut off the wedge so it extends slightly beyond the end of the tenon. Apply some glue to the tenon, fit it into the hole, and clamp until dry. Pressure forces the wedge deeper.

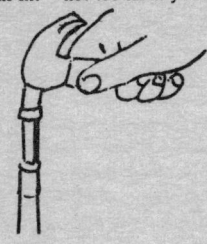

Re-covering Deck Chair. If you are re-covering a deck chair, wrap a piece of felt or other hard-wearing material around the front rail before nailing on the new material and you will find that it will remain serviceable for a much longer period.

Sagging Cane. When cane-bottomed chairs have begun to develop a sag, wash them thoroughly with hot water, then dry them outdoors so they'll shrink up tightly. To preserve the cane, it's a good idea to give it a good coat of clear varnish when it's almost dry.

Split Seats. For bad splits or breaks in chair seats or table leaves, install wooden cleats on one side with glue and screws. Fasten them in place against the bottom of the chair seat or table leaf.

In most cases, glue and screws will make the joint tight and will give added life to a dying chair.

Squeaking Joints. Try dropping some melted paraffin into the joints of any piece of furniture or chair whose constant squeaking is getting on your nerves.

Squeaking Upholstered Seats. When the upholstered seats of some of your dining-room chairs squeak annoyingly, you can silence them very easily. First remove the seats from the chair frames, then staple some waxed paper, folded to form 1-inch-wide strips of two or three thicknesses, all around the undersides of the seats. Then, when you have replaced the seats on the chairs, you will be pleased at how quiet they have become.

Uneven Legs.

1. If one of your chairs or a table wobbles because of a short leg, you can lengthen the guilty leg with some wood putty. Just squeeze some putty onto a piece of waxed paper on the floor, then set the short leg on the putty, forcing it down until the piece of furniture is sitting level. After the putty has completely dried, trim off the excess putty with a

CHAIR STORAGE

knife, then file and sand it smooth. You can then paint or stain this to match the rest of the finish.

2. Here's one little trick for evening up or shortening the legs of a table or chair uniformly. Cut a slot in a cardboard mailing tube, slip this over each leg in turn, and use it to scribe a sharp mark or as a saw guide.

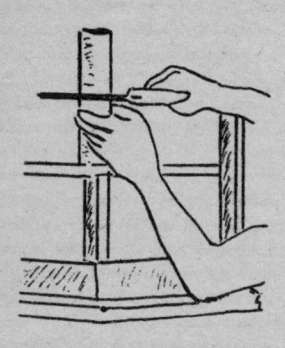

Chair Storage Folding chairs that are stored against a wall in a closet have an annoying habit of sliding and clattering to the floor. Prevent this by placing a rubber stair tread on the floor under the legs of these chairs.

Chalk Holder If you must carry chalk or soft crayon around in your clothing, you can prevent soiling of your pockets by using a discarded lipstick case. Then raising the lever on the case raises the chalk or crayon into working position for easier handling.

Chamois.
   Cleaning. Wash in warm soapsuds. Rinse several times in warm water, adding a small eggcupful of olive oil to the final rinse; press out the liquid and stand to dry in the open.
   When absolutely dry rub the leather between the hands and pull into shape.

The oil will keep the skin both supple and durable.
   Wash chamois in warm, soapy water, to which pinch of baking soda has been added.
   A chamois will always harden and stiffen if washed in water that does not contain a good suds of gentle soap. Never wring it or let it hang up to dry. Instead, press it dry in a towel.
   Stiffened. A stiffened chamois cloth can be softened by rinsing it in two quarts of water with a tablespoon of olive oil added.

Cheese, see FOODS.

Cheese Stain, see STAIN REMOVAL.

Chemicals, Stain Removing, see STAIN REMOVING CHEMICALS.

Chenille Spreads. If you are in need of patching material to repair a chenille or tufted bedspread round off the foot corners, then rehem them. This will give you two sizeable triangles of material. Sew in the pieces so that the tufts match, and you will have an almost invisible repair job.

Chests. A chest is basically a storage box with a lid that opens at the top, like a pirate's chest.
   Most chests are portable pieces—hope chests silver chests, and trunks. Occasionally they are built into the house itself, under a window seat, or under a bench. Such a chest should have a front opening door rather than a lid on the top for your own convenience.
   You should have no trouble building any kind of chest you like. But be sure to hinge the lid far enough forward from the back of the chest or far enough in from either end so that when it is opened it will tilt away from the chest and you do not have to hold it up to keep it from banging down on your head or fingers.

Chewing Gum Removal.
   from Carpeting. A few ice-cubes do a splendid job of removing a wad of chewing gum from your carpeting. Just press the ice against the gum, and it will become brittle and break off. Cleaning fluid will remove the last traces of gum.

from Fabrics.
1. One method of removing bubblegum from fabrics — chew another piece of bubblegum until the sweetness is all out of it, then use this piece of gum to pick off the gum in the fabric. The fabric should be chilled beforehand.

2. To remove chewing gum that has stuck to washable materials, first pick off as much of the gum as possible. Then soften the remaining residue with some egg white, and launder in the usual way. Or, scrape off and soak the article in turpentine, mineral spirits, or kerosene before washing in warm suds.

from Hair. To remove chewing gum from a child's hair, saturate the hair strands with a washcloth dipped in witch hazel. Olive oil applied to the scalp, or egg white, will also remove chewing gum.

Chicken, see FOODS.

Chimneys. Any kind of heat-producing unit at all must have a chimney or vent pipe that lets out excess heat into the outdoors. Such a chimney must have a good flue, be tight its entire length, and preferably be lined with fire-clay flue lining. A flue for a small-house heater should have a cross-sectional area not less than 8 by 12 inches, and the top of the chimney should be more than 4 feet above a flat roof and 2 feet above the peak of a gable roof.

If you are troubled with a chimney that does not draw properly, use this check list to locate the problem:
Obstruction of some kind in the chimney.
A *break* in the chimney lining that lets air in.
An *air leak* around the cleanout door at the base.
Two or more *pipe openings* in one flue.
Small-size pipe extension; flue should be the same at the top.
Top of *chimney below high point* of roof, or blanketed by a tree or building.
Flue clogged with soot or dust, especially at a bend.
(See also FIREPLACE.)

Cleaning. Chimney cleaning usually is not necessary in the average home. But should it become necessary, vacuuming by a commercial cleaning firm is the best and cleanest method.

If there is not too great an offset in the chimney, you can dislodge soot and loose material by pulling a weighted sack of straw up and down in the flue. Seal the front of a fireplace when cleaning the flue to keep soot out of the room.

Chemical soot removers are not particularly recommended. They are not very effective in removing soot from chimneys and they cause soot to burn, which creates a fire hazard. Some, if applied to soot at high temperatures and in sufficient quantity, may produce uncontrollable combustion and even an explosion. Common rock salt is not the most effective remover, but it is widely used, because it is cheap, readily available, and easy to handle. Use 2 or 3 teacupfuls per application.

Creosote may form in chimneys, especially when wood is burned and in cold weather. It is very hard to remove. The only safe method is to chip it from the masonry with a blade, and you must be careful not to knock out mortar joints or damage the flue lining.

To clean soot from the chimney over your fireplace, one good way is to place a piece of zinc on a smoldering fire in your fireplace, and the vapors that arise will clean the soot by decomposition.

Maintenance. Chimneys should be inspected every fall for defects. Check for loose or fallen bricks, cracked or broken flue lining, and excessive soot accumulation by lowering an electric light into the flue. Mortar joints can be tested from the outside by prodding with a knife.

If inspection shows defects that cannot be readily repaired or reached for repair, you should tear the masonry down and rebuild properly. Do not use the old bricks that have been impregnated with soot and creosote in the new work, because they will stain plaster whenever dampness occurs.

Soot and creosote stains are almost impossible to remove.

Test for Tightness. You can test a chimney for tightness by building a fire and then placing a wet blanket over the top of the chimney. The smoke in the flue will come out through any leaks.

China Care. With proper care, the life and beauty of your fine chinaware can be greatly prolonged.

Its greatest enemy is heat — unwisely applied. Don't place china in a hot oven or under a griller to warm.

Put the dishes in hot water and dry them just before using.

Don't use steel-wool, soda, or abrasives for cleaning.

Cleaning Gold or Silver Borders. The gold or silver borders on dinner plates can be cleaned with a toothbrush dipped in bicarbonate of soda. Or, dip a moist toothbrush into powdered alum and scrub with that. Let the alum stay on for a couple of hours before washing the plate.

Cracked. Boil cracked chinaware in sweet milk for 45 minutes. The crack will be only slightly visible and the dish strengthened.

Mending.

1. When mending chinaware or glassware, try using some modeling clay to hold the broken pieces together while the mending cement is hardening and doing its work.

2. You can make your own strong and very handy cement for mending broken dishes just by melting powdered alum in a spoon over a gas flame. While this is still soft, rub it over the edges of the two places that you want to stick together, and let dry. Dishes mended in this way can be washed in hot water without danger of loosening the joint.

3. One good cement for broken chinaware consists of a thick solution of gum arabic in a little boiling water. When this is cold, mix with sufficient plaster of Paris and apply immediately to the broken edges of the china. Keep the pieces firmly pressed together, and your chinaware will be well mended.

4. Broken chinaware or glass, such as vases, powder boxes, and the like, may be successfully and almost imperceptibly mended by applying white lead oil paint from your paint box tube, to both edges, and then pressing the pieces firmly together and placing carefully away to dry for a week. The mended articles will even hold cold water without having the "mend" dissolve.

5. One often-effective method of mending broken chinaware or glass is with colorless fingernail polish. After washing the broken item, dry thoroughly, then apply the nail polish and press the parts together. Subsequent washing in hot water will not melt this adhesive, and it will stand fairly hard usage.

Washing. Chinaware should be washed as soon as possible after use. Avoid strong cleaning agents, since any decorations on the china may be softened by ammonia, steel wool, scouring pads, hard rubbing, or prolonged soaking. Some manufacturer recommend using a plain, hot water rinsing action when possible.

China, Drilling. If you'd like to convert a china vase into a lamp, the drilling of the hole in the bottom of the china vase usually proves a hazardous undertaking. However, if you have the courage to attempt it, you must arm yourself with a little turpentine, a small three-sided file, and a large amount of patience. Place the vase upside down on a soft surface, mark the spot to be drilled, put a few drops of turpentine on it, set the pointed end of your file on the spot, then rotate it slowly between the palms of your hands. Your progress should be steady, but it won't be fast. Keep adding turpentine at intervals and keep rotating . . . with extreme caution.

Chips and Nicks, Furniture, see **FURNITURE REPAIR.**

Chisel, Chiseling, see **TOOLS, HAND.**

Chocolate Stain, see **STAIN REMOVAL.**

Christmas Ornaments.

Hangers. If the hanging hooks of some of your Christmas tree ornaments are missing, paper clips are a very good substitute.

Repair. If some of your Christmas tree ornaments have become chipped in packing, some red nail polish is a quick fixative, even on ornaments of different colors. It is more effective than a blank spot on an ornament.

Storage. It's a good idea to begin saving your empty egg cartons now. These will make ideal containers for storing your Christmas tree ornaments this year, after you have finished with them.

Christmas Tree, Flocking. Ordinary Christmas trees can be painted white with casein paint — the kind of water paint used on papered walls. Daub the tree thickly with the paint and sprinkle artificial snow on while the paint is still wet. Or, combine a cupful of soap flakes with half a cup of water, and beat the mixture with an egg beater until it gets thick and stiff like egg whites for a meringue. Throw the bubbly stuff all over the tree. It will stick and harden to whiten the branches with a real fairyland effect.

Chrome Care.
1. When chromium plate has become scratched and rusted, clean with a chrome cleaner available at auto supply stores, and if any rust remains in the deeper scratches, carefully scratch it out with the point of a knife. Don't use steel wool or emery cloth for this job. Then, to improve the appearance and protect the chrome, spray on a chrome protector, also available at auto supply dealers. You can fill the deeper scratches with plastic chrome.

2. If you'll apply some paste wax to the chrome fixtures in your shower stall or bathtub, the chrome will stay spot-free. The water beads beautifully, rolls off, and will not streak. This is especially good for those who live in hard water areas, or have lots of soap film in their shower stalls or bathtubs. (See also AUTOMOBILE.)

Cinder Blocks, see CONCRETE BLOCKS.

Circular Saw, see TOOLS, POWER.

Clamp Base Vise, see TOOLS, HAND.

Clamps, see TOOLS, HAND.

Claw Hammer, see TOOLS, HAND.

Clay, see MODELING CLAY.

Cleanser. Leftover club soda is excellent for wiping off counters, refrigerators, and laminated plastic tops on tables. It cleans and polishes in one application, and the surfaces thus cleaned have a satiny feeling.

Clean Cement, see ADHESIVES.

Clipboard. Sometimes papers held on a clipboard will curl and blow about in a wind. One way to prevent this is to cut small notches on two sides of the board, about two inches from that corner, then use these notches to hold a large rubber band. This rubber band, snapped over the corners of the papers held in the clipboard, will hold them down securely, while still permitting their easy removal.

Clock Cleaning. Saturate a large piece of raw cotton with kerosene and place it below the works — be careful not to touch them.
Remove cotton after three days, when the kerosene will have attracted all dirt particles from the works.

Clock Muffler. To silence an electric clock that vibrates from worn bearings, mount the clock on a 1/4-inch pad of foam rubber. Motors transmit vibrations to table or chest tops which act as sounding boards. The rubber tends to muffle the effect.

Closet Accessories.
Belt Hanger. A very simple and useful hanger to hold your belts can be made from cardboard to fit over a wire clothes hanger. It is especially good for storing matching belts with a suit or skirt. Note that square openings are cut in the cardboard and slits are made from the bottom corners of the opening to the edges.

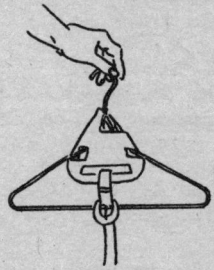

Organizer. Hang a shoe bag on the door of your broom closet. You will find the compartments handy for dustcloths, brushes, and assorted cleaning apparatus, and the closet will look much neater.

CLOSET ACCESSORIES

Pants Hanger. Sometimes when a newly-pressed pair of trousers or slacks are hung over a wire hanger, their appearance becomes spoiled by an unwanted crease. You can avoid this simply by cutting a mailing tube to the proper length of the wire hanger, slitting this along its full length, and then slipping it over the bottom wire of the hanger. You can also achieve the same results by rolling some newspaper around the wire and securing it with some cellophane tape.

Shoe Rack.

1. Make your own handy shoe rack by nailing a metal curtain rod on the back of your closet door. Hang your shoes by their heels over this rod. If necessary, use the whole back of the closet door, nailing several rods one below the other, and allowing sufficient space between the rows, so your shoes won't touch.

2. Here's a simple and quick little project for the home handyman... one that will add no end of convenience and neatness to the clothes closet. This is the rack for the shoes. All you have to do is saw a piece of 10 by 6-inch plywood board diagonally, as in the illustration. Then drill, and fit the ends of two lengths of 1/4-inch or 3/8-inch dowel rods into the holes.

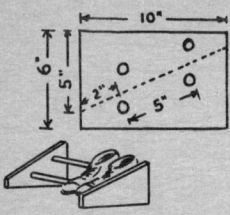

Tie Rack.

1. You can make a nifty tie rack for clip-on ties out of an old tennis racket. Paint the racket to match the door of the closet or room.

2. A discarded ladder from a birdcage makes a handy and useful rack for a man's ties. Fasten one end to a wall with screw eyes, and the rungs will provide good holders for the ties.

Trouser Hanger. A good, efficient wall hanger fo four or more pairs of trousers or slacks can be mad very easily. Just saw out a wall bracket from som solid stock in a series of steps. Screw a strip arm t each step, using flat-headed screws, countersunk throughout. You can then paint or stain the hange to match the woodwork in your closet.

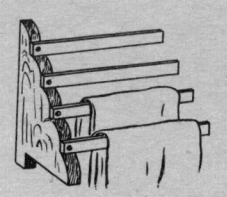

Closet Door Repair. If you have a closet door tha persists in swinging half closed when you want it t remain open, you can easily remedy this little annoyance by making a small coil spring of .03 diameter wire, and installing this over the top knob of the door hinge, as in the illustration. This spring will have sufficient strength to hold the door in an open position, but at the same time will not prevent your closing or latching the door.

Holds Door Open

Closet Doors.

Accordion. These are folding doors made of heavy vinyl mounted on a steel frame. They got their name from the obvious resemblance to the folds of an accordion.

Bifold. The bifold door is a two-panel door built like a huge hinge. The open edge of the panel is pivoted close to one of the door jambs. The open edge of the other panel has a roller that moves in a track. To open the door, you give the roller edge a sideways shove, or pull the knob that is mounted to the center hinge. The two panels fold together back to back. You can get bifold doors in ready-to-hang units, or you can make your own by hanging together 2 ordinary doors.

Use single (2-panel) doors in openings of 2 to 4 feet. Use two (4-panel) doors to fill openings from 3 to 8 feet.

Folding. A folding door is made of long narrow strips of wood or metal hinged together along the vertical edge. It hangs from a track in the doorway header. You can use a folding door in a small closet, or in a large 25-foot wide opening. The best folding doors are made of wood strips about 4 inches wide. The advantage of a folding door is that it does not stick out into the room. The disadvantages are: it doesn't look like a door; it doesn't fit tightly in the opening; you cannot hang clothes as far forward as you can with hinged or bi-fold doors; the doors tend to wave back and forth in a heavy draft.

Hinged. The main value of a hinged door is that you can hang a full-length mirror on the back, or you can use it for storing things on hooks, shallow shelves, or cabinets. The main disadvantage of any hinged door is that you must allow plenty of floor space in front of the closet for the door to swing out.

Pivot. You can use the back of the door for storage. In fact, you can install it so it pivots on the right, on the left, or in the center. Pivoted in the center, the door spins all the way around so that the inside is outside. The disadvantage of the pivot door is that you use up a great deal of valuable closet space in the pivot area.

Sliding doors come in pairs, with the two doors sliding back into slots built into the walls. The cost of this type of installation is extremely high. For that reason, most closets have sliding doors that hang in parallel tracks between the jambs. Disadvantages of this type of installation are two: the doors sometimes jump the track; and you can never see into more than half of the closet at one time.

Closets.

Cedar Freshening. A well-aged cedar closet can be made as fresh and fragrant as new if you'll give those cedar boards a good sanding. Another method is to paint the closet with oil of cedar, obtainable at the hardware store.

Damp. If you have a damp closet, you can cut down on the mildewing if you take some six to twelve pieces of chalk, tie them in a bundle, and hang them in the damp closet. The chalk will absorb a good deal of the moisture.

(See also MILDEW)

Deodorizing. If humid weather has left a closet with the aroma of mildew, hang your clothes outdoors to air and scrub the interior of the closet with a strong solution of one cup of baking soda to a bucket of hot water. You can also dispel mustiness in a closet by placing a pan of water with household ammonia in it inside the closet overnight.

Hanger. Often better than the usual rod is a length of chain fastened across a crowded clothes closet. By hooking the clothes hangers into the links of the chain, you can prevent your clothes from becoming pushed together and crumpled into wrinkles.

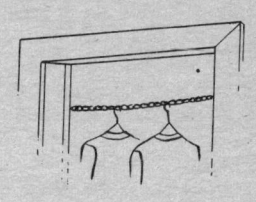

Pomander You can add a very pleasing scent to garments in your closet if you'll take a firm orange and push about 25 or so cloves into it, then put the orange aside in a warm, dry place so that it can dry slowly and thoroughly. As the rind shrinks, it will grip the cloves more firmly, and then you can hang this in your closet where it will give forth an agreeable aroma to permeate your garments.

Prefabricated. Actually this type of closet is a wardrobe about 6 feet high, 21 inches deep, and 4 feet wide. Made of plywood, hardboard, steel or corrugated board, they come knocked down for rapid assembly. You can use them as free-standing units, or build them into wall spaces.

Rods. If a rod in your clothes closet is sagging badly, either replace it with a new one, or twist a strong wire around the center of the old rod and attach to a screw-eye in the ceiling.

If you'll give the hanging rod in your closet a hard coat of paste wax, then polish it, you'll find that your hangers will slide more easily and you'll have less trouble hunting for that dress or coat.

Closet Shelves, see SHELVES.

CLOTHES CARE

Clothes Care.

Blue Jeans, Lengthening. You can lengthen your children's blue jeans without having that horrible white line, if you will take a blue crayon and write over the line, then press.

Boot Care, see SHOE CARE.

Brushing. Brush clothing frequently; always brush in direction of the nap.

Chewing Gum Removal, see CHEWING GUM REMOVAL.

Corduroy, Laundering.

1. Corduroy, as you all know, has the annoying habit of picking up lint from other washables in the same laundry load. One simple way to forestall this is by turning the corduroy garment inside out before washing.

2. Corduroy garments should never be wrung out after washing. Hang them up soaking wet and they will need no ironing.

3. To keep corduroy material soft, turn garments inside out and spray with starch before ironing.

Dog Hair Removal.

1. To get dog hairs off woolen materials (furniture or clothing), take the crust end from a fresh loaf of bread, and rub gently with the soft side of the bread. Then brush well with a whisk broom.

2. Animal hairs can be easily removed from dark suits, coats, and dresses by wrapping a length of masking tape around your hand and brushing over the entire garment with the sticky side of the tape. The animal hair and lint will stick to the tape. This method is also good for cleaning the upholstery of your car after the pet has had a ride.

3. A damp towel placed in your automatic dryer with the garment will also remove hair and lint.

(See also **Lint Removal,** below.)

Furs, see INSECTS.

Grease Stain Removal, see STAIN REMOVAL

Handbag Cleaning, see Pocketbook Cleaning, below.

Handkerchief Whitening. Your handkerchiefs will come out of the laundry much whiter, and will stay fresh longer, if you'll add a little borax to the wash water. This gives the fabric just enough extra body to help it withstand soiling too quickly.

Hat Care, see HATS.

Hosiery Drying. In order to dry your stockings more quickly, wring them out as dry as possible and roll them tightly in a turkish towel for about five minutes. Then hang them in an airy place and they will dry quickly.

Hosiery Matching. Put all the mismates of hosiery which you might otherwise throw away because their mates have acquired runs, into some boiling water, and they will all emerge from this treatment the same shade.

Knits, Wrinkle Removal. Remove wrinkles from a knitted dress by spreading the garment over a large heavy bath towel that has been wrung out of warm water. Cover with another bath towel and leave it overnight. In the morning the wrinkles will have vanished.

Lace, Whitening. Washing lace articles in sour milk whitens them.

Leather Glove Cleaning. One effective method of cleaning unwashable leather gloves is with milk. Soak a flannel cloth in milk, rub it on a cake of soap, then rub over the gloves vigorously.

(See also LEATHER CARE.)

Lint Removal.

1. A rubber sponge makes an excellent remover of lint, fuzz or hair from woolen clothing. First moisten the sponge with water, then squeeze dry before using.

2. Remove lint and hair from a dark dress or suit by rolling up a magazine, wrapping some wide adhesive tape around it, sticky side out, then rolling this over the garment. Usually works like magic.

Moth Prevention, see INSECTS.

Nail Polish Warning. Be careful when doing nails. Some nail polishes and polish removers will permanently damage cellulose acetate rayon.

Necktie Cleaning. You can dry-clean soiled neckties and other small articles very easily in a fruit jar. Fill the jar to within two or three inches of the top with some cleaning fluid or solvent, drop in the tie, screw the cover on tightly, then shake vigorously for several minutes to loosen the dirt. Finally, remove the tie and hang it in a well-ventilated place to dry.

CAUTION: Be sure to remember, when working

with cleaning fluids, that some of them are flammable and others are not good for excessive inhaling... so, use them in a well-ventilated place.

Necktie Pressing. Pressing a necktie without having the seams show through on the right side isn't nearly as difficult as it sounds. First, cut a strip of lightweight cardboard 18 to 20 inches long and shape it to fit snugly between the lining and the face of the tie. Then, press as usual under a damp cloth and you will have a professional-looking job.

Nylon Care.

1. One often-successful method of preventing yellowing of white nylon fabrics is the addition of baking soda to both the wash water and the rinse water.

2. Add a few drops of vinegar to the rinse water to prevent nylon curtains and undergarments from becoming gray and dingy-looking.

3. To restore white or pastel nylon materials that have become dingy looking, try steeping in a bath of color remover... the kind sold to strip color from materials. Follow this by soaking in a chlorine bleach solution, using the proportions advised on the label. Then, after rinsing and drying, you should see a gratifying new brightness.

Patent Leather, Cracked. For cracked patent leather, there's nothing you can do so far as mending is concerned, but you can conceal the crack as best you can by dyeing the fabric underneath... and in the future prevent such cracking by treating the leather with petroleum jelly and avoiding exposure to heat.

Patent Leather Polishing.

1. To keep patent leather sleek and shiny, clean it with ordinary window cleaner. Simply spray on the cleaner, then polish to a high luster. Never use shoe polish... it will destroy the shine!

2. To clean patent leather articles, such as shoes or belts, mix up a solution of two-thirds vinegar and one-third water, apply to the leather with a soft cloth, then polish with a dry one. Petroleum jelly used in the same manner also does a fine job.

3. Sweet oil makes a fine dressing for patent leather. Apply it with flannel, then polish with a soft cloth.

Perfume Use. Perfume and toilet water must never be applied directly to clothing.

Pocketbook Cleaning, Leather or Plastic. Try cleaning leather or plastic handbags with cleaning fluid. Even paint will come off your handbag, and the cleaning fluid will make the bag look like new.

Pocketbook Brightening, Straw. If you have an old, faded and slightly beat-up straw purse, you can often resurrect it by spraying it with black or any brightly-colored enamel, and then stapling bright artificial flowers on it.

Pocket Reinforcing. If a person is in the habit of carrying a lot of keys, coins, or other heavy items in his trouser pocket, the pockets may be reinforced by lining the lower parts with good, strong chamois.

Polished Cotton, Laundering. If borax water is used to launder polished cotton or sateen dresses, it will restore the gloss.

Preserving Color. If the supposedly fast colors in a garment aren't so fast as they might be, you can make them more fast by adding a little vinegar to your rinse water.

Rayon Brightening. To brighten dull spots in black rayon, rub lightly with mineral oil. Black rayon may be redyed.

Scorch Removal. If you inadvertently scorch an article while ironing it, wet the affected area thoroughly and apply some cornstarch freely. Let dry and oftentimes the scorch will be gone. (See also STAIN REMOVAL).

Seersucker Pressing. To make seersucker look like new, place the garment on a turkish towel and press with a warm iron.

Shine Removal. To remove shine from trousers or skirts of serge or other similar materials, dampen a cloth in a solution of one-fourth cup of vinegar to one cup of water. Wring the cloth dry, and press the garment with it as a pressing cloth. Finish off by brushing with a stiff brush or fine sandpaper.

Shoe Care, see SHOE CARE.

Silk, Ironing. White silk is yellowed by ironing; therefore iron inside out with a damp cheesecloth press-cloth and a cotton-cool iron.

Silverfish Repellant, see INSECTS.

Soiled Clothing. Never let uncleaned clothing hang in a closet from one season to the next. Stains set with age. Dirt attracts moths.

Stockings, Nylon, see Hosiery above.

Suede Brightening. Suede articles can be brightened with a wire brush — and it will help if you first go over the suede with a cloth dipped in vinegar.

Suede Cleaning. If your suede article is of any considerable value, it's best not to attempt the job of

CLOTHESLINE

cleaning it yourself. So far as can be determined, there is no home method that doesn't carry with it the risk of streaking or discoloring your suede. Best to send these articles to a reliable leather cleaner — and there are many of these who specialize in the restoration of suede.

Suede Freshening. One very easy method of freshening up articles of suede — shoes, handbags, belts, and the like — is to brush over them with an old nylon stocking. Usually does an effective cleaning job.

Suede, Rain Spots. Rain spots on suede shoes, bags, or jackets will disappear quickly if you'll rub them gently with a manicuring emery board.

Suede Renewal. You can do nice things to your suede jacket, shoes and purses if you'll apply vinegar to them with an old toothbrush, let dry, then brush with a soft suede brush.

Sweater Shaping. If the cuffs on one of your woolen sweaters have stretched out of shape, dip the ends into hot water to shrink them back to normal. This tip also works well in the case of a stretched waistband.

Sweaters, Pilling. Those unattractive knots on sweaters can be easily removed by gently rubbing over them with a piece of fine sandpaper. And, for prevention of these knots in the first place, try turning the sweater inside out and buttoning it before laundering. This keeps the outside of the sweater from rubbing against other materials, the usual cause of the knots.

Taffeta, Laundering. Iron while wet with cool iron. Never squeeze or twist.

Velvet, Bruised. To heal bruises on velvet or velveteen, place the crushed area, pile down, over the bristles of a brush. Then hold a steam iron just above the back of the fabric, letting the steam pour down through the pile. Then shake the fabric until partially dry ... then leave it alone until entirely dry.

Velvet, Restoring. Restore any velvet item by brushing well to remove dust and lint. Then steam on the wrong side with a steam iron, or by hanging in a steamy bathroom. Hang up to dry.

Wet clothes should never be hung in a closet. Allow them to dry thoroughly first.

Woolens, Laundering. Ammonia should be used to soften the water in which woolens and knitted garments are washed. Only a little is needed.

Woolens, Protection from Insects, see INSECTS.

Woolens, Shrinking. If you want to shrink a woolen garment deliberately before the first time it's washed, soak it in cold water for about two hours, then spread it out to dry without stretching it in any way.

Clothesline. To clean a dirty clothesline wrap it around a board and scrub it with a brush and soapsuds.

Clothesline Reel. A very efficient, easy-to-use clothesline reel that will eliminate the annoyance of twisted lines can be made very quickly from some scrap lumber. The reel rotates around a center handle on which it is held with washers and cotter pins.

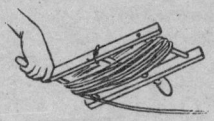

Clothes Marking. An ordinary crayon will put a permanent label on a garment. Write the name or identification with the crayon, then press over the writing on the wrong side with a medium iron. The color will be set and not wash out.

Clothes Moths, see INSECTS.

Coal, see HEATING.

Coated Nails, see NAILS.

Coconut, see FOODS.

Cod Liver Oil Stain, see STAIN REMOVAL.

Coffeemaker, Electric. Keep coffeemakers scrupulously clean, because even a hint of old coffee will spoil the flavor of the fresh brew. After using, wash the inside thoroughly with clean, soapy water, then scald to remove all trace of soap. Dry and air the parts. When the coffeemaker is not in use, leave the parts unassembled to facilitate airing. If you have an electric percolator or urn, you should use a small brush to clean the inside of the tubes, and thoroughly clean the pump every two or three days.

Coffeepot. If you want to keep your coffeepot clean and sweet, put in a teaspoonful of bicarbonate of soda, fill the pot almost to the top with water, boil for awhile, then rinse thoroughly, or scour with equal parts of salt and baking soda.

Coffee Stain, see STAIN REMOVAL.

Coffee Table. A modern-looking coffee table can be very easily made just by fastening four hardwood legs to a flush-type door. Especially suitable for this purpose is the narrow type of closet door which you can procure from almost any lumber dealer. You can use some two-by-two inch stock for the legs, about ten inches long. Fasten these to the underside of the door with two-inch angle irons, or screw and glue them into place.

Coins, Bent. If you are a coin collector and have a few bent coins in your rare collection, straighten without danger of defacing by sawing off two short segments from a broom handle, placing the coin between these, and then striking the top segment with a hammer. Turn the coin after each stroke, and it should flatten out perfectly.

Combination Square, see TOOLS, MEASURING.

Combination Wrench, see TOOLS, HAND.

Common Brick, see BRICK.

Common Nails, see NAILS.

Compass, Improvised.

1. A very handy improvised compass can be fashioned from a strip of screen wire, secured at one end with a thumbtack. The mesh of the screen permits your pencil point to be inserted at any desired opening in the strip. This compass will also permit you to scribe circles much larger than the ordinary kind of compass. Be sure to keep the wire of the screen tight against the shank of your thumbtack as you scribe your circle, since the openings in the screen are larger than the diameter of the tack.

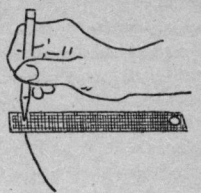

2. For a special job requiring the outline of a large circle, an ordinary extension curtain rod will provide you a fine compass. Tape a pencil to one end and your pivot nail to the other end, as in the illustration. Should you require a circle with a radius smaller than the length of your curtain rod when it is completely closed, you can get down to this smaller radius by cutting off some of the longer, or outer, section of rod.

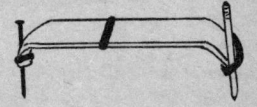

Compass Saw, see TOOLS, HAND.

Compost Container, see GARDENING.

Concrete is simply a mixture of Portland cement, sand, and gravel. When mixed with water, Portland cement undergoes a chemical reaction and becomes a strong binding agent, and when mixed with sand and gravel, it forms a rock-like substance called concrete. Concrete is used for floors, foundations, driveways, and swimming pools.

The proportions of the mixture in concrete combinations are extremely important. Usually most home jobs run about 1 part Portland cement, 2 parts sand, and 3 parts clean gravel. A sack of cement contains 1 cubic foot. Note that if you use 1 cubic foot of cement, 2 cubic feet of sand and 3 cubic feet of gravel, you'll wind up, when mixed and poured, with only 5 cubic feet of concrete.

Strong concrete must have clean sand and gravel in it, for dirt particles produce flaws.

Binding. If concrete is improperly cured or mixed, you may get the appearance of sand and dust when it hardens. Coat the surface with concrete hardener which flows into the concrete pores and binds it.

Cast in situ is the term applied to concrete work which is cast in the actual position it is to occupy in the building.

CONCRETE BLOCKS

Generally speaking, it is more economical to precast concrete units which are fairly small and easily lifted and placed in position.

They can be cast on the building site or in the builder's yard, and fixed as and when required, thus avoiding any possible waste of time on the job.

Forms. Ordinary ¾-inch tongue-and-groove boards are good to use for forms, and so is ¾-inch plywood. You should put supports about every 2 feet with pieces of 2 by 4's, and build the forms so they can be taken apart without damage to the set concrete. You can pound in nails only part way to insure easy removal with a claw hammer.

Don't remove the forms for 2 weeks or so. If you are pouring concrete in a hole in the ground, you may not need forms, especially if the earth is firm and holds its shape. However, you should line the earth with building paper to keep the water in the mixture from soaking into the earth.

Laying New over Old. New concrete can be laid successfully right on top of old concrete. But be sure to get the old surface perfectly clean with soap and water, and have it thoroughly wet when the new concrete is applied.

Mixing. You can mix concrete for small repair and improvement jobs by hand. Use a small wheelbarrow or a wooden platform. Pour out the required amount of sand in the form of a ring. Pour the Portland cement into the center of the ring and mix cement and sand together with a hoe or shovel. Spread the mix into a new ring and mix in the gravel the same way. Once again form a ring, and pour water in the center, very slowly. Use a hoe to mix water and dry ingredients, making sure that you don't get too much water in. Concrete is the right consistency for pouring when you can squeeze it into a ball with your hand so that it stays in that shape.

Pouring. You should pour fresh concrete into forms within a half hour of mixing. As soon as the concrete is poured, cover it with burlap, building paper, or straw, and keep it damp for a week to ten days.

Pre-Cast. A pre-cast lintel or beam is one which is cast in a "form" or box, on a bench or platform and placed in its position later as a completed unit.

Resurfacing. When the concrete surface of a driveway or walk has low spots where water collects, you should resurface the concrete. First of all, remove all grease, oil, and paint, and then roughen the surface by going over it with a hammer and cold chisel. Then sweep the surface clean and coat it with grout of 1 part Portland cement and 1 part clean fine sand mixed to the consistency of thick paint. Work on only a few square feet at a time. Apply new concrete, as described above to the grout quickly before it dries. Trowel on a 2-inch coat of concrete over the grouted area, and then apply grout to the adjoining section and then pour concrete on it immediately. Continue until the whole surface is grouted and poured.

Sealing. When a sidewalk is laid directly against a masonry wall, it will usually begin to tilt towards the wall after a few years of exposure to water, or if the ants do some excavating underneath. You can prevent this by keeping the joint between the two constructions tightly sealed with calking compound, which will remain flexible enough to permit movement due to frost-heaving and expansion and contraction. Before applying the compound, remove the debris from the joint to a depth of one inch. When the joint is dry, tamp some oakum into the joint to a depth of one-fourth inch below the surface of the walk, and follow with a layer of calking compound, allowing this to project slightly above the surface. Remember — it is important that the crack between walk and wall be dust-free if you are to have a good seal.

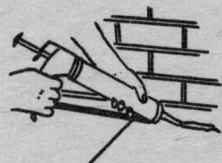

Surface Finishing. For driveways, walks, terraces, and floors, you must smooth the poured concrete surface with a trowel or wood float. As soon as the concrete is poured, level the surface by laying a 2 by 4 across the work and moving it from one end to the other. Then, two hours later, work over the surface with a steel trowel, which will make it compact and give it a smooth hard finish. On walks and driveways, leave a rough surface to give traction and eliminate slipperiness in wet weather. Work with a wood float instead of a trowel.

Concrete Blocks. Concrete or masonry blocks usually measure 8 inches high by 16 inches long. Cinder blocks are the same size, and so are pumice blocks. Concrete blocks are heavier and stronger, but are less porous. These large blocks are used for foundations and basement walls, for outside walls, and for steps, retaining walls, and fences. All these blocks are laid with cement mortar.

Bulging Walls. Sometimes a basement, foundation, or retaining wall of block will bulge, and some blocks may crack. This situation is serious. Call in a competent mason rather than tackle the job yourself.

Cracked Mortar Joints. When a crack shows in a masonry-block mortar joint, cut out all the old mortar with a cold chisel, dampen the masonry, and pack in fresh mortar.

Pointing Up Mortar Joints. Inspect any wall of blocks for cracked or shrunken mortar joints. With a cold chisel, cut out the faulty mortar to the depth of an inch. Replace it with fresh mortar, applied in thin layers with a small masonry trowel.

Porous Mortar Joints. Sometimes the mortar used is so poor in quality that water will seep through it even if there are no cracks. Do not remove all the mortar, but rather coat the joints with waterproofing compound that you can get at a hardware or masonry supply store.

Concrete Floor Care.
Cleaning.
1. To prevent an unsightly, greasy mess on your garage floor where oil drips down from your car engine, place a long flat metal pan on the spot and leave it there at all times. Keep this pan half-full of sand or fine sawdust so as to absorb the drippings, and clean it out whenever the sand or sawdust becomes saturated.

2. Mix about 2 lbs. of tri-sodium phosphate in 1 gallon of water. Scrub the concrete with it, making sure to wear rubber gloves. When the area has been cleaned, hose it down.

3. To clean and freshen a concrete floor — and this holds true also for outdoor pavements and driveways — scrub with soap and water. Then, while the concrete is still wet, sprinkle some dry cement powder over it. After about ten minutes, sweep off the excess powder with a stiff broom.

4. Clay and other dirt that has hardened on the garage or basement concrete floor can be removed easily with the aid of a scraper, made of heavy sheet metal, which can be attached to the broom. Such a scraper is also a big help in stores and public halls where chewing gum is often tramped on the floor.

Dust Prevention.

1. For a concrete floor that has begun to get powdery, try this: Wash the surface thoroughly, then apply some boiled linseed oil liberally with a paint brush. After two days, wash the floor again, and give it another dose of boiled linseed oil. A third treatment may be necessary in two more days.

2. One easy way to prevent a concrete floor from becoming dusty is to give it a coat of wax. This is usually very effective in keeping the dust down. If, however, you don't want to apply wax or if the waxing proves ineffective, a hardener can be applied. There are commercial hardeners on the market for this purpose but you can also make your own by mixing one part of water glass to four parts of water. Apply this mixture in two coats, allowing the first to dry for at least 48 hours before applying the second coat.

Removing Stains. Liquids and substances tend to seep into concrete, and are difficult to remove. Seal the concrete with a sealer, hardener, decorative stain or paint to keep it free of discoloration.
(See also STAIN REMOVAL.)

Concrete Repair. You can repair cracks in concrete with cement mortar or prepared packaged concrete patching material. Mix patching concrete mortar, 1 part cement and 3 parts fine sand. Widen all cracks in the broken concrete so that they are wider inside than at the surface. Use a cold chisel and a hammer. Then dust out the crack with a bicycle pump, wet the inside of the crack, and pack in the wet mortar.

Drives and Walks. You repair cracks in drives and walks the same way you do a concrete wall. Cut the crack first with a cold chisel, widen it inside, dust it, and wet it down. Do not use tar or calking compound in concrete drives or walks: the tar will be picked up by tires and shoes.

If the concrete slab has broken, remove the pieces or break them up into smaller ones for base.

CONDENSATION

Use a heavy cold chisel and hammer. The patch should be at least 4 inches thick on a walk and 6 inches thick on a driveway.

Cut the edges of the surrounding concrete in a straight vertical manner and wet the base and edges. Fill in with concrete or packaged gravel mix concrete. The patch should rise about 1/8 inch above the rest, for it will shrink and fall as it hardens. Keep the patch damp and cover it with a piece of burlap, cloth or straw for about a week for proper curing.

If an entire section of a walk or drive is damaged, break it all up and put in a new section. Use a cold chisel to trim off the edges of the good part, and cover the edges where new and old will join with a sheet of roofing paper. Set wood forms along the borders to hold the concrete in place. Use 2 by 4's or 2 by 6's supported by stakes driven into the soil.

Foundation Walls. Cracks in foundation walls are usually not harbingers of collapse, but they do sometimes allow water to seep into the basement or crawl space. Repair them as soon as the foundation has settled and the cracks stop enlarging. It's best to repair the crack on the inside *and* outside surfacing if practicable, but since this necessitates digging up dirt around the outside of the house, you can usually get away with patching only the inside. You can sometimes use calking compound or tar in place of mortar. These will repel insects and keep out moisture. If there is a serious water problem, use cement mortar, or even waterproof with epoxy waterproof compound.

Pools. Treat cracks in poured-concrete swimming pools the same way you treat concrete wall cracks: cut the crack with a cold chisel, widen it inside, dust it out and wet it down. Fill with cement mortar made with 1 part Portland cement and 2 parts sand. As soon as you have the patch in place, fill the pool and cover the patch with water for at least 10 days. Curing the patch slowly will insure its waterproofing.

Condensation, see BASEMENTS, DAMP OR WET.

Condensers, Air Conditioner, see COOLING.

Conduction, see HEAT THEORY.

Conductors, see ELECTRICITY, THEORY OF.

Conduit, Electrical, see ELECTRICAL CONDUIT.

Contact Cement, see ADHESIVES.

Container, Improvised. It's often difficult to find a suitable container for mixing small amounts of glue, paint, and such. However, by bending up four sides of a small piece of aluminum foil, you can fashion a small leak-proof container of any size desired — and it's disposable, too, after the job is done.

Containers for Small Items. Instead of throwing away those transparent plastic containers in which new toothbrushes come, use them as ideal holders for small nuts, bolts, screws, paper clips and the like.

Contour Sheets, see SHEETS.

Control Outlets, see ELECTRICAL OUTLETS.

Convection, see HEAT THEORY.

Convenience Outlets, see ELECTRICAL OUTLETS.

Cooking Tips.
  Boiling. Put three or four marbles in the bottom part of your double-boiler before putting it on the fire. Then when the water gets low, they will warn you by bouncing about noisily. This idea will lengthen the life of your double-boiler, to say nothing of saving your temper, time and food.
  Cake Pans, Hot. A clip-type clothespin makes an excellent handle to steady a hot pan when removing a cake.
  Cakes, Cutting. Try using thread when cutting a hot cake.
  Carving Tips.
    1. Always use a sharp knife when carving, being sure to cut across the grain. Cutting with the grain results in stringy texture. The exception is steak.
    2. A large roast carves more easily if allowed to stand 30 minutes.
    3. Do not over-garnish. Be sure to leave space for carving.
  Cutting Board.
    1. Wooden cutting boards in the kitchen often become so dark and stained that no amount of washing seems to do any good. One way to clean and whiten them is to bleach them — by use of a slice of lemon and ordinary table salt. Squeeze the

lemon into the salt, rub this mixture vigorously over the board, then rinse off with clean water. If necessary, repeat the process.

2. Remove strong odors, such as onion, from your kitchen chopping board by rubbing over it with a damp paper towel sprinkled with baking soda.

Deodorizing.

1. Unwelcome cooking odors in a room can be dispelled by boiling three teaspoons of brown cloves and two cups of water for about fifteen minutes. Or, heat some vinegar on the range.

2. To rid your hands of the odor of fish or onions, rub them with a little butter.

3. Cabbage and cauliflower cooking odors can be prevented from permeating the house if you'll drop a few walnuts, shells and all, into the pot while cooking.

4. To absorb the odor from cooking cabbage, place a tin can half full of vinegar near the cabbage.

Drippings Container. Paper cups make excellent containers for drippings. They take up little refrigerator room and are disposable when empty.

Egg Poacher. Using an opener that leaves a smooth edge, remove both ends of a tuna or similar size can for an excellent egg poaching mold.

Frying. Sprinkle salt into frying pan before adding fat to prevent spattering.

Grater Cleaning. Before washing a grater on which you have shredded soft cheese, onions, or whatever, rub a hard, dry crust of bread over it.

Liquids, Straining. To strain almost any liquid in your kitchen, place a wad of sterile absorbent cotton in a funnel and pour the liquid through this. It will come out clear.

Lubricant. Glycerin is an excellent lubricant for small kitchen appliances. e.g. egg beaters. Apply with a medicine dropper.

Measurements.

All measurements are level.

Frequently used food measurements are given below.

1 tablespoon	=	3 teaspoons
1 fluid ounce	=	2 tablespoons
1/4 cup	=	4 tablespoons
1/3 cup	=	5-1/3 tablespoons
1/2 cup	=	8 tablespoons
2/3 cup	=	10 2/3 tablespoons
3/4 cup	=	12 tablespoons
1 cup	=	16 tablespoons or 8 fluid ounces
1 pint	=	2 cups
1 quart	=	2 pints or 4 cups

Part of cup. – Use tablespoons or small measures – 1/2, 1/3, 1/4 cup – for greater accuracy.

Oven-Cleaning. When juices from apple pie runs over in the oven, sprinkle with salt. The juice burns to a crisp and is easily cleaned up.

Try cleaning the glass in your oven door by wetting a cloth, wringing it out thoroughly, and then using a bit of baking soda as you would any scouring powder.

Salt Storage.

1. Salt is a problem to pour during damp or muggy weather. Overcome this by wrapping a small piece of aluminum foil tightly around the top of the salt dispenser. Moisture-proof, it will keep the dampness out of the salt, allowing it to flow freely.

2. To prevent salt from becoming damp, put a half-teaspoonful of raw rice into the salt shaker – or, tear up an ink blotter and put the fragments into your shaker. Either one, rice or blotter, will absorb the moisture and keep the salt flowing freely.

Storage. Wrap odorous foods, such as cheeses and onions, in aluminum foil when storing them in refrigerator, and you'll prevent them from contaminating the other foods. The foil is odor and moisture proof.

Cooling. There are four ways to cool your home: with fans; with an evaporative cooler (cooling by water evaporation); with an air conditioner; with a heat pump. The way you choose will depend on how much you can invest, both initially and in operating expense, and on your climate.

Good design and construction are as necessary to keeping your house cool in the summer as they are to keeping it warm in the winter. The house should be tightly constructed and well insulated. In the summer, the windows should be shaded from the direct rays of the sun.

(See also INSULATION.)

Air Conditioner. Certainly an air conditioner is the best way to keep your house at a constant, cool temperature. But it is also more expensive than other methods of cooling.

There are two types of air conditioners: room units; and central-system units. The cooling opera-

COOLING

tion of both is the same. Air passes through filters that remove large dust particles, and over a series of refrigeration coils where it is cooled and dehumidified. A fan then blows the cooled air into your home. Most air conditioners have either built-in thermostats or provisions for wiring the conditioners to remote temperature controls. Some of the small units are not thermostat equipped but you may be able to purchase an optional thermostat.

Air Conditioner, Central. Central air-conditioning systems can be separate systems with their own ducts, or they can be combined with forced-air heating systems. Since cooling requires a greater amount of air flow than heating, if you choose an add-on system it will probably be necessary to increase the fan capacity of your furnace, and it may be necessary to enlarge and even relocate the distribution ducts. Larger ducts also decrease the velocity of the cooled air and reduce the noise of air conditioning. For greatest uniformity of comfort, cold air supply grilles should be high in walls or in the ceiling and hot air supply grilles should be near or in the floor. If economy dictates use of only one grille for both heating and cooling, the near floor location is preferred. The cost of purchasing and installing a central air-conditioning system will depend on whether you choose a separate central system, or a system to be added to your heating system.

Air Conditioner, Room. Room air conditioners cool one or more rooms. They range in output from about 5,000 to 32,000 B.T.U.'s per hour. They operate on electricity only, and should have separate electrical units (this may require adding a circuit, particularly if you live in an apartment). You can choose from many available models — for conventional double-hung windows, for casement windows, for in-front-of-window consoles, for special wall openings.

Condensers. Most room air conditioners have air-cooled condensers. This means that the condenser must be outside the cooled room, that it must have unrestricted air circulation over the condenser coils, and that it should be shaded from the sun. Some air conditioners have water-cooled condensers. They require large quantities of water to disperse the heat, approximately 75 to 150 gallons per hour for each 12,000 B.T.U.'s of cooling capacity. This water can be cooled in a cooling tower and reused. Locate the tower outdoors, away from your house; it is noisy.

Air-cooled units require more electrical energy than water-cooled units. This increased cost is usually offset by water supply and disposal (or cooling tower) costs.

Dehumidifier. Not all air conditioners dehumidify adequately during humid, muggy weather. The result is that the cooled air they put out feels clammy. This clamminess can be reduced, to a certain extent, by operating a dehumidifier when you operate your air conditioner.

Fan Disadvantage. Cooling with fans has some disadvantages. Dust and pollen are likely to be drawn into your home. Fans are noisy. The cost of a good attic fan plus installation may be as much as a room air conditioner. While the attic fan may cool the entire house in some areas at night, it may not help much during the day because of high outside air temperatures. And remember, a fan will cool your house to only approximately the temperature of the outside air.

Fans, attic and window, exchange inside air for outside air. You can use them for night cooling, or whenever the temperature inside your home is greater than the temperature outside. A time switch can be installed in the electrical circuit to your fan to cut it off automatically at any time you desire. When you have cooled your house at night, keep the windows and doors closed during the next day as long as it is cooler inside than out.

You will find that window fans are easier to install than attic fans—no construction is required—but you will also find that they are usually noisier.

When cooling with a fan, you should close off any portion of the house that you do not wish to cool; otherwise, the fan will not provide the proper number of air changes per unit time.

You can also remove accumulated attic heat during the day with an attic fan. Often an attic is 25° or more hotter than outside; even if the ceiling of your house is insulated, this additional heat will warm your house.

When you remove attic heat with an attic fan during the day, close the attic off from the rest of your house. Otherwise the fan will draw hot outside air into your house.

Fans, Room. A good room fan has large blades, turns at about 1,000 rpm (it may have a speed adjustment), operates quietly, and has an oscillating mechanism. Sizes range from small table model sizes to 7-foot pedestal floor models. These fans stir up the air, making it seem several degrees cooler than outside. Also, air movement increases moisture evaporation, and moisture evaporation cools the body, or skin surfaces.

Heat Pump. This is a single unit that replaces the conventional furnace air conditioner system. It removes heat from your home in the summer and supplies heat to your home in the winter. The heat removed in the summer is discharged to the outside air.

Usually the heat pump is sized to handle your summer cooling load and is supplemented with an auxiliary heater to handle part of your cold-weather heat load. A heat pump may cost more than a central furnace-air conditioning system. Operation costs over a year's time will depend on how much supplemental resistance heat is needed in the winter. In areas where little supplemental heat is needed, or where the cost of electricity is low, operation costs may be less than for conventional central furnace-air conditioning systems. In other areas, it may be higher.

Water Evaporation. The most common and effective method of cooling with water is the water-evaporation method. Of course, cooling by water is satisfactory only when the humidity is low. It is used extensively in hot, dry climates.

Water is sprayed on excelsior (or some other good water-absorptive material). A fan then draws air through the excelsior. The water in the excelsior evaporates and cools the air; the cooled air, in turn, cools your home.

An air velocity of 150 feet per minute through the excelsior provides maximum cooling. Slightly higher velocities keep the circulated air from becoming saturated. Twenty to 40 house-air changes per hour are necessary. Water-evaporation cooling requires 5 to 10 gallons of water per hour to cool an average-size house.

Coping Saw, see TOOLS, HAND.

Copper-Bottom Pans. It's easy to keep copper-bottom pans shining brightly by using a little white vinegar and salt. Merely coat the copper with the vinegar, sprinkle over with salt, and rub the mixture over the metal with a cloth.

Copper Cleaning.

1. You can clean copper items nicely with a cut lemon rubbed with salt. Don't use steel wool on them, since steel particles might possibly become embedded in the copper and later rust.

2. One easy and effective way to polish copper and brass articles is to rub them thoroughly with some crumpled sheets of newspaper. This does a surprising job of erasing stains and bringing out the natural luster of the metal. Another fine method is the use of very fine "00" steel wool pads (without soap), which does a wonderful job of highlighting embossed surfaces on copper and brass.

3. Copper and pewter may be cleaned successfully by applying a paste made with equal parts of flour, vinegar, and salt. Let the paste remain on for about an hour, then rub off, and wash the metal with warm water before polishing.

4. A good home-made polish for copper consists of a paste made by mixing equal parts of salt, vinegar, and flour. Rub the copper with this until it is perfectly clean, then wash in hot suds, rinse, and polish. Or, you can use whiting or rottenstone mixed to a paste with olive oil.

(See also STAIN REMOVAL.)

Copper Tubing, see TUBING, COPPER.

Copper Wire, see ELECTRIC CORD, ELECTRIC WIRE.

73

Cork Bulletin Board, see BULLETIN BOARD.

Cord, Non-Fray. You can prevent a nylon cord or twine from fraying at a cut end if you'll heat the end over a small flame. The nylon will melt and the strands will bond into a solid unit. Knots can be kept from working loose by this same method.

Corduroy Care, see CLOTHES CARE.

Cork.
   Removal.
   1. One effective method of twisting out a stubborn cork from a bottle is to push in two safety pins from opposite sides of the cork, as in the illustration, then twist and pull out the cork.

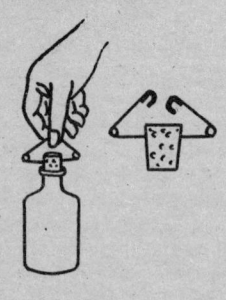

   2. Stubborn corks can be removed from bottles if you insert a screw into the top of the cork, tie a string around the screw, and then tug on the string.
   3. When a cork has dropped down inside a bottle and defies all your attempts to remove it, pour some straight household ammonia into the bottle, let this stand for a few days, and the cork will disintegrate. You can then pour it out.
   Substitute. A satisfactory substitute for a lost cork is an inch or two of candle. Soften up the wax by heating it and your candle stub is sure to fit.
   Too Small. When a vacuum bottle cork has become too small after repeated usage, and fits too loosely into the neck of the bottle, you can bring it back to normal by boiling it in water in a covered pan. This treatment sterilizes it, too.

Cork Floor. Cork flooring consists of cork curlings and granulated cork compressed in molds. When properly installed, it is treated with a sealer and finished to obtain surface protection.

When the seal and finish are worn through, the floor becomes porous and subject to deterioration.
   Cork floors are susceptible to damage from *water, oils, and grease.*
   Burn Repair. If a burn spot on a cork floor cannot be remedied by sanding, cut it out with a sharp knife and try filling it as follows: Cut a bottle cork into tiny slivers (use a kitchen grater if you wish), mix these slivers with some white shellac or clear lacquer, and press immediately into the hole. Sand smooth when the patch has dried.
   Stained. If there are some stains on your cork floor that seem to resist ordinary soap-and-water cleaning, try sanding them out with some No. 1/2 sandpaper.

Corn, see FOODS.

Corner Bridle Joints, see JOINTS.

Corner Seating.
   Materials: 3/4-in. pineboard (the amount needed depends on the length of the seating required. Work out the amount from the diagram); 1¼-in No. 14 nails; glue; and undercoat-sealer; enamel paint.
   First cut three sides A, 24 in. x 24 in. (two are used for the larger unit and one for the smaller). Next cut the back rests B. These two pieces will be 24 in. high by the length required. The seat bases C are cut 23¼ in. wide and the same length as the back rests. The seats are 3/4-in. shorter in width so that when the back rests are fitted to the seats they make 24 in., fitting neatly on to the sides. Next cut the front pieces D 9 in. high and the same length as the seats. Now cut out supports E. These are fitted at least 2 ft. apart and are 9 in. x 22½ in.
   To assemble the unit: Start by glueing and nailing sides A to D and B. Then fit in supports E and finish off by fitting seat base C. Then undercoat and paint.
   To make the cushions, work out how many you will need. This depends on how long your seats are. For each cushion you will need two pieces of fabric about 23 in. square, (or if a rectangular shape is needed, one side should be 23 in.), leaving a seam allowance of ½-in. all round. Then for square cushions you will also need a length of fabric 7 in. wide and 7 ft. 9 in. for the sides of each cushion. Sew the top and bottom to the long side sections, leaving a space for filling. If you empty the odd

pillows you don't use into the cushions and add bits of raw cotton and any soft stuffing you can find, you have perfectly adequate cushions at a reasonable price. It is best to make the cushion in its own bag, then put this into a cushion cover which is complete with piping; 15 ft. 6 in. of piping cord will be needed for each cushion — this is covered with the fabric of the cover and stitched in with the main seams. You will need slightly more of course for rectangular cushions.

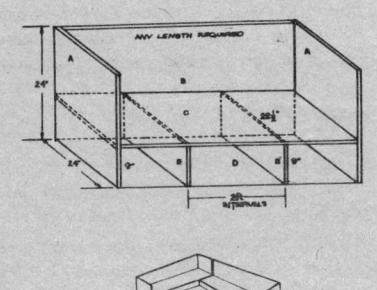

Cornice Lighting, see LIGHTING STRUCTURAL.

Cornish Game Hens, see FOODS.

Corsage. If you'd like to preserve a corsage for a week or more, remove its ribbon, sprinkle the flowers with water, insert into a cellophane or freezer bag, and keep in the refrigerator.

Cotton, see FIBERS, NATURAL.

Cotton Removal. If cotton is stored in a bottle to keep it clean and dry, but you find it difficult to remove the cotton, try removing the cotton with a coping saw blade fastened to a cork stopper.

Crack Filler, see SAWDUST.

Cracks, see CHINA CARE; CONCRETE REPAIR; PLASTER, PLASTERING; WOOD CARE TIPS.

Crate Construction, see CARPENTRY.

Crayon Marks, see STAIN REMOVAL.

CURTAINS

Crazed Surfaces, see FURNITURE REPAIR.

Creosote. Creosote has for generations been employed as a preservative for telephone poles, railroad ties, fence posts, and pier foundations. Long-lasting and insoluble in water, creosote is very effective, particularly for wood touching the ground. The most practical way for the home handyman to apply creosote is by soaking it into the wood. Merely brushing creosote on wood that is to be buried in the ground is unsatisfactory, because creosote will not soak deeply into wood fibers.

Crescent Wrench, see TOOLS, HAND.

Crosscut Saw, see TOOLS, HAND.

Crossrails, Rails, see DOOR REPAIR, DOORS.

Cucumbers, see FOODS.

Curled Picture, see PICTURES, CURLED.

Curtains.
 Faded. Most window curtain fabrics deteriorate in constant sunshine. But rather than rob your house of sunshine by pulling the blinds, alternate your curtains as much as possible between sunny and shady sides of your house to prolong their life.
 Repair. If one of your good curtains has torn, you can effect a good job of invisible mending by covering the hole with a piece of white paper, then running it back and forth under the sewing machine needle. Subsequent laundering will dissolve the paper, and your repair job will be hard to detect.
 Ruffled. Sometimes, when ruffled curtains are freshly laundered and starched, one of the ruffles at the top of the window refuses to stay in place. In this case, use a small piece of tape and tape the outer edge right to the window casing. It will stay there and look fine.
 Snag Prevention. The job of slipping a rod through a freshly washed (and starched) curtain hem can be made easier in several ways without snagging the

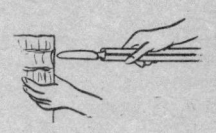

75

material. For flat rods, try inserting the blade of a kitchen knife, as illustrated, into the rod and let the handle act as a guide. For round rods, cap the end with a thimble.

Tie Backs. Try using the gummed picture hangers that have a little metal hook on their backs to anchor your tie-backs for curtains and draperies. Then you can change your curtains when you like, because with this method you'll never mar your woodwork or walls with nail holes.

Cushion Filling. Some light, fluffy fillings for cushions can be made by cutting up a roll of cotton into small squares, then heating these in the oven for a half-hour. Don't let them scorch. Each cotton square will swell to twice its original size.

Custard, see FOODS.

Cut Glass Care.

1. Cut glass can be given a high polish by washing it first in hot water and then dipping it into cold water to which has been added a handful of starch. Let the starch dissolve completely before the glass is dipped. The cut glass is then allowed to stand and dry, after which it is polished with dry linen. When washing cut glass or fine china, it's a good idea to put a towel in the bottom of the dishpan to prevent chipping.

2. Ornamental cut or etched glassware that is deeply cut can be cleaned and brightened by a scrubbing with a soft brush dipped in a baking soda solution. Rinse, then dry with a soft cloth.

Cut Nails, see NAILS.

Cutting Out Pages. To cut pages cleanly out of a magazine or book, a very sharp knife or razor blade is ordinarily used. However, unless extreme care is used, the blade will usually cut through pages below, remove sheets that you did not want to damage. To prevent this, slide a sheet of stiff cardboard under the page before slicing. This will provide a firm backing which assures a neat cut and will prevent damage to other pages.

D

Damper, see FIREPLACE.

Dart Game. You can have a load of fun, not only out of playing the popular dart game, but by making your own set. All the materials you need can be found around the house — a large cardboard box, some corrugated cardboard, some clothespins, and some nails. Paint some concentric rings on the bottom of the box with water colors, and number them for your scoring marks. For the body of your darts, use wooden clothespins with the knob portions cut off. Snip off the heads of some nails, and after filing to form dart points, drive them halfway into the ends of the clothespins. Cut the dart fins from the corrugated cardboard, and cement them into the slots of the clothespins.

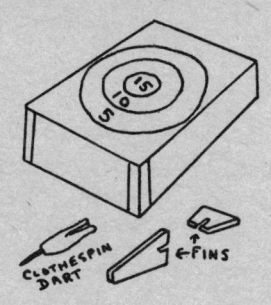

DC (Direct Current), see ELECTRICITY, THEORY OF.

Decal Removal. One method of removing decals from furniture surfaces is to apply some cellophane tape over the decal, then peel it off, and often the decal will slip off with the tape.

Decals can also be removed without damaging the finish underneath by covering them with a wet washcloth and running a hot iron over the cloth.

Decorating Tips.
(See also LIGHT AND COLOR, LIGHT REFLECTANCES.)
Decorative Pulls. New pulls for your window shades or pull-chain light sockets can be provided with toothpaste tube caps. Simply drill, thread the cords through, and knot the ends, and you'll have some pulls with a modern look and a classic decor.
Low Ceilings. When the ceiling in a room seems too low to you, an illusion of height will be added if you hang floor length draperies high and top them with a cornice.
Paint Matching. While you are repainting the rooms in your home, it's a good idea to brush a bit of the color on different wooden clothespins. Then you can take these with you while you are shopping for fabrics for draperies, or curtains or wallpaper to help in matching and contrasting.
Playing Card Mobile. Old playing cards that have outlived their "playtime" use can be improvised into a decorative function. Spray them with shellac from a pressurized can, then make a mobile out of them for your family room. The picture cards, of course, are the most colorful for this purpose.

DEHUMIDIFIER

Dehumidifier, see COOLING.

Dents, Furniture, see FURNITURE REPAIR.

Deodorizers, Cooking, see COOKING TIPS.

Deodorizing.
Bathroom Odors. If you'll keep a ball of ordinary twine in your bathroom, and burn an inch of this occasionally, it will absorb all bathroom odors. Lighting and burning an ordinary kitchen match will have the same effect.
Bottle Odors. If you have some glass tumblers, jars or vases which are badly in need of deodorizing, you can accomplish this easily by the following process: After washing the container in soapy water, fill it about half-full with clear water. Then add a teaspoonful of dry mustard and stir thoroughly. Allow to remain for about an hour or so, then rinse with clear water.

You can remove the scent from an empty perfume bottle by pouring a solution of water and dry mustard into it and letting it stand for several hours. Or, fill it with warm water and baking soda and leave overnight.

Also you can fill the bottle with rubbing alcohol and let stand for an hour or so, then wash with warm water.

To remove the musty odor in bottles or jars you wish to use for preserving, fill them with cold water in which baking soda has been dissolved. This will freshen them. Then wash in hot, sudsy water and rinse well.

Cooking Odors. To remove cooking odors from a room, when a deodorizer is not at hand, try placing a little perfume or cologne on the light bulbs of your table lamps. By the time your guests arrive, the heat from the bulbs will have given off a pleasant aroma to counteract the cooking odors.

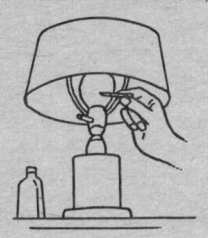

Garbage Disposer Odors. Drop a slice of lemon, orange, or grapefruit peel into your electric kitchen garbage disposer now and then. The pleasant fragrance of the rinds expels any possible unpleasant odors.

Plastic, Odors on. Odors that cling to plastic tablecloths and mats and defy soap-and-water washings will respond quickly to a soaking in a baking soda solution. This also works for dishcloths, sponges and towels.

Refrigerator Odors. An open box of baking soda placed on a refrigerator shelf is a good deodorant.

Another way to eliminate odors from your refrigerator is to take a small ball of cotton, dip it into vanilla, and place it in a sauce dish in the refrigerator.

Smoke. If you're giving a party and want to prevent the room from getting stale with cigarette smoke, place a bowl of vinegar in an inconspicuous place.

Desk, Mobile, see MOBILE DESK.

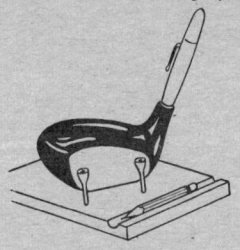

Desk Set. For the golfing enthusiast, here's a novel and good-looking desk set that's easily made. Use the head of a discarded driver, brassie, or spoon — the head of the club providing the holder for the pen, while two golf-ball tees set slightly away from the face of the club provide a letter rack. A groove in the base holds a pencil. You'll have to enlarge the hole in the shank of the club head to accommodate your pen, and it should be drilled somewhat deeper to prevent the pen point from touching bottom. If your club head is badly scarred, you can remove the old finish, fill in the dents and nicks with some plastic wood, and rescore the original grooving in the face. Stain the whole thing, except the face, then shellac it. The club head is then attached to a 3/4-inch base, as illustrated, with flathead screws from the underside. Force the tees into undersized holes. Finally, glue a piece of felt to the bottom of the base as a protection to your furniture.

Desk Stand. A single sheet of 1/16-inch clear plastic can be formed into a crystal-like desk stand to hold your name on a one-by-seven inch strip of cardboard. Bend the plastic at two places over a 1/8-inch thick strip of wood. Sand the edges smooth and remove the masking paper. The heating may be done in the oven at 250 degrees or, perhaps easier, it may be done along a strip 1/2-inch wide where the plastic is to be bent. The latter can be accomplished by masking with asbestos and using a heat lamp.

Dial Markings. Obscure dials, figures that have worn thin on appliances, such as your TV, radio, oven, steel ruler, or your typewriter keys, can be brought back to light if you'll rub a child's crayon across the dial, rubbing off the excess. A little white shoe polish can also be used in the same manner.

Diamond Care, see JEWELRY.

Diffusers, see LIGHT DIFFUSERS AND SHIELDS.

Dimmers, see LIGHT DIMMERS.

Dining Room Fixtures, see LIGHTING FIXTURES.

Direct Current , (DC), see ELECTRICITY, THEORY OF.

Dish Drainer. If your rubber covered dish drainer has become sticky, clean and dry it, then apply some white shellac. This hardens the rubber and eliminates the stickiness.

Dish Repair, see CHINA CARE.

Dishwasher, see APPLIANCES.

Disk Sander, see TOOLS, POWER.

Document Storage, see STORAGE, DOCUMENT.

Dog Care.
  Appetite Stimulant. If your dog will not eat, to the degree of becoming undernourished, try feeding him some stale beer. This has been known to whet the appetite.
  Bathing. Here's a handy little tip for easing the chore of washing your dog. Make yourself a bag of about 6 by 12 inches out of some nylon netting. Then cut up a bar of dog soap into from eight to ten pieces, put these into your bag, and tie the open end securely. Use this to scrub your dog . . . it's wonderfully efficient, leaving one hand free to hold the dog, requires no sponge, and there's no lost soap.
  Discipline. Does your dog insist on tearing up the footmat ouside the door? You can break him of this undesirable habit in short order by sprinkling the mat VERY LIGHTLY with cayenne pepper.
  Drinking Pan. An ideal outdoor drinking pan for your dog is provided by a discarded angel food cake pan. You can drive a stick through the center hole in this pan into the ground, which will prevent its being tipped or overturned.
  Feeding. If you really want a happy, healthy dog, save all your vegetable waters (including potato) and mix them (instead of tap water) with your pet's dry dog food.
  Fleas. Many veteran dog owners have claimed that pine needles in the dog's house will keep the animal free of fleas, and that pine needles in the dog's bed work the same little wonder.
  Shedding. If your dog is a constant "shedder" lubricate his coat with some olive oil, coconut oil, or lanolin every ten days or so. Three egg yolks weekly will help the canine have a healthier and shinier coat.
    If you own a shaggy dog — or any sort of dog that sheds a lot — it's a good idea to hand-vacuum him frequently. Then you won't have to vacuum the floors and furniture quite so often. Dogs usually like it, and so do your dark-suited guests.

Door Hardware. Hardware involved in door repair includes: hinges, fastened at the top and bottom of the inside stile of the door and the jamb; locks, latches, and handles or knobs that fasten the door,

DOOR HOOK

set into the outside stile and the door frame. See **DOOR REPAIR**, below.

Door Hook. Fasten a coathook on a very thin door panel, or on one of the newer cored-style doors with a sheet metal screw, threaded all the way to its head. Punch the starting hole with a heavy brad awl and tighten the screw only until it makes firm contact. Further tightening will endanger stripped threads.

Door Pulls. You can add a touch of modern decor to your cabinet or closet doors by using some black keys from your old piano. These prefinished ebony handles will add no end of attractiveness to your doors, and can be attached with some glue and wood screws. To remove the keys from their wooden bases on the piano, just insert a thin knife edge, and the keys will usually snap loose. Any wood fibers that may cling to the bottoms of the keys can be removed by a little sanding.

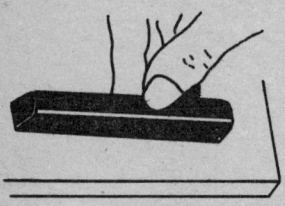

Door Repair.

Accordion. If you have an accordion door that works rather stiffly, try cleaning the overhead rack and coating it very lightly with petroleum jelly.

Hinges, Faulty. Unscrew all the screws from a loose, bent, or faulty hinge. If the loose leaf is in the door stile, measure the screws to see if you can replace them with longer ones. Use thicker and longer ones, but not so much thicker that the heads will not sink flush to the hinge leaf. If you cannot use the larger screws, that is, if the screw hole is torn beyond repair, fill up the old screw hole as directed below. Then refasten the hinge with new screws and rehang the door, reversing the procedure above.

Hinges, Squeaking.

1. A door hinge that persists in squeaking, even though oiled, because the oil does not penetrate the full length of the pin, can be permanently silenced as follows: Remove the hinge pin and rub the length of it with emery cloth to remove the rust, then file a flat surface the full length of the pin. Coat the pin with petroleum jelly and replace it in the hinge. The flat surface stores the lubricant and keeps the hinge quiet.

2. If some of your inside doors are squeaking annoyingly, you can put a silencer on them very easily. Lift off the hinge pins, one at a time, and rub their surfaces well with a soft lead pencil. This is a "graphite" method of lubrication, and it usually puts an effective end to the squeaking.

Knob Removal.

1. *No lock.* Unscrew the knob from its stem, then take the stem side out from the opposite side. If the spring is broken, replace it. If the trouble is dust and dirt, clean it. Never use oil—always use powdered or jellied graphite.

2. *With lock.* Unfasten one knob, and then remove the knob containing the knob stem. Release the lock by unscrewing the two exposed screws. One side of the lock is a loose plate. When you withdraw this loose plate, you expose the mechanism. Clean it out with powdered graphite.

Knobs, Slipped or Sagging. Door knobs slip and sag if the knob pin is bent or if the spring is broken. The knob may also be clogged with dust and rust. First shoot powdered graphite into the knob pin to make it turn more easily. If that doesn't help, remove the knob and clean it.

Latch, Off-Center. If the latch does not hit the center of the strike plate, check the door to see if it is hanging correctly. If not, readjust the hinges, if the door is hanging to your satisfaction, remove the strike plate and reset it in the jamb.

Lifting. A washer inserted between the plates of each hinge will often serve to lift and correct the door that persistently sticks at the bottom.

DOOR REPAIR

Locating the Problem Spot.

1. Before planing a door that persistently sticks at a certain spot, use a chalk to coat the inside of the door jamb. When the door is closed, the chalk will rub off on the door wherever it binds, thus marking the spot that needs planing.

2. Ordinary carbon paper, carbon side toward the door, will give the same results.

Locks, Frozen. Locks on doors sometimes freeze in the winter if water accidentally creeps in and turns to ice. You can squirt a graphite lubricant into the key hole from the outside to coat the tumblers and key opening. This will cause the water to run out before it can freeze.

Non-Latching.

1. If the door shrinks enough with seasoning so the latch does not catch in the plate, use shims under all the hinges in the jambs, and, if necessary, in the door stile. If the door latch will not meet the plate then, you may have to replace the door, or add on a strip of wood to build up the jamb.

2. When the latch on a door refuses to snap into the opening in the strike plate, quite often this little problem can be corrected just by filing the edge of the plate facing the door. Be careful to file only enough metal off to do the job, because if too much is filed away you could have a loosely-engaged, rattling door. Sometimes, of course, the plate is too far out of line to be corrected by filing — and in this case the only thing to do is to remove the screws from the plate and relocate it.

Rattling. The latch of the door is slipping into its catch hole in the strike plate too soon before the door closes against the stop molding. In a well-hung door, the latch should not close in the catch hole until the door is pressing firmly against the stop. Shift the strike plate slightly toward the stop molding by unscrewing the strike plate, removing it from the frame, and chiseling out the hole a bit in the direction you want to shift it. Move the strike plate and insert wood screws in fresh holes. Test it until the latch does not catch before the door solidly presses against the stop.

Removing. Open the door and prop up the outer corner at the bottom with something like a thin book or magazine. When you prop up the end, you take the weight off the top hinge. Now remove the pin from the bottom hinge. Indoor hinges are made with a pin connecting two leaves, one fastened to the door and the other to the jamb. To withdraw the pin, lift it out from the top, or hammer with a nail or cold chisel hard against the underside of the top knob of the pin. Remove the pin from the top hinge the same way and lift the door off.

Sanding Bottom Edge. If one of your doors stick annoyingly at the bottom, you can eliminate the necessity of removing the door and planing off the stubborn area. Try slipping some sandpaper, padded underneath by newspapers, under the door at the spot where the sticking occurs. Then open and close the door over the sandpaper, which should smooth off the rough spots nicely.

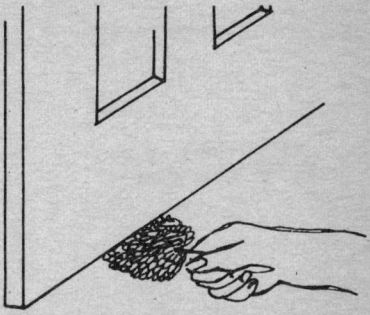

Screw Holes, Damaged.

1. You can force plastic wood into the damaged screw hole, and wait for it to dry. Then use a new screw.

2. You can effect a good repair by use of dowels or wooden pegs. Drill out the screw hole to a

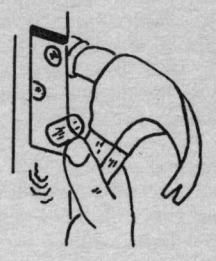

generous oversize, wipe the inside surface with glue, and hammer in a short length of dowel. When the glue has set thoroughly, use a file or knife to cut off the plug flush with the surface. Drill a pilot hole into it, and then insert a new screw.

3. When the hinge or lock areas of old doors are so worn that they refuse to hold the necessary screws, you can try salvaging these areas by fitting them with dovetail insets of new wood, as in the illustration. Saw and chisel a dovetail slot of sufficient size to remove all the damaged wood in the area. Then cut and trial-fit a dovetail inset of new stock to match that of the door. Spread some glue on the contacting surfaces, and press the piece into place, allowing plenty of time for the glue to set before sanding the piece flush. Then screw your hardware to the new wood.

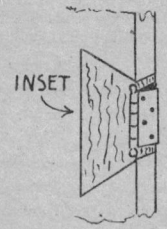

Sliding Glass.

1. If you have a sliding glass door that doesn't slide as easily as it might, clean out the tracks with your vacuum cleaner, then scrape out any accumulation of hardened paint, wax, grime, or the like. Polish the track lightly with steel wool, and finally rub a light film of oil on the track.

2. Another method is to remove the doors, thoroughly clean tracks and apply a coat of thin shellac to the grooves and sliding parts. When dry, rub some paste wax over the shellac.

Sticking or Binding. If the door top catches against the jamb, try tightening up the top hinge where it is fastened into the jamb. If the bottom door rail hits the threshold, try tightening the upper hinge. If the bottom of the door hits the bottom of the jamb, try tightening the bottom hinge. If the top rail hits the top jamb, try tightening the lower hinge. In any case, if the hinges are in as tight as they will go, unfasten the *other* hinge, and insert a cardboard shim in the cut and screw the hinge in on top of the shim. This will push the hinge out from its sunken position.

If these remedies do not work, mark the portion of the door that scrapes against the jamb, remove the door, and plane the surface until it does not strike on the jamb.

Stiles and Crossrails. Sometimes, because of moisture, the stiles and crossrails of a door will begin to part company. This condition can be righted by installing dowels diagonally through the door corners, as in the illustration. Remove the door from its hinges, wipe the opened joints with glue, and pull the stiles against the crossrails with bar clamps. Drill 1/2-inch or 3/4-inch holes diagonally through the door corners and drive in the dowels. Wipe the dowels and inside the holes with glue before assembling. Then cut the projecting ends of the dowels flush with the door edges and sand smooth. After the glue has had time to set, rehang the door.

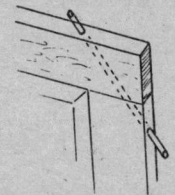

Striking Latch Jamb. If one of your doors refuses to close because it strikes the jamb on the latch side, first check if there is too wide a clearance on the hinge side of the door. If there is, try screwing the hinges down tighter. If this doesn't work, loosen the hinges from the jamb and insert under their inner edges some thin strips of cardboard (shims). On the other hand, if there isn't any appreciable clearance on the hinge side, your door has swelled and the only solution is to plane down the hinge-side edge of the door.

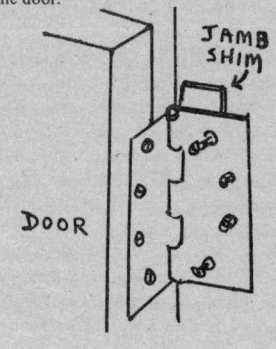

DOORS

Trimming Bottom Edge. Here is a simple and quick way to make a shallow cut across the bottom edge of a door, without the trouble of removing the door from its hinges. Just tape a hacksaw blade to a thin ruler and work this across the sticking part of the door edge. The blade will do a good job of cutting, while the ruler will protect the floor from marring.

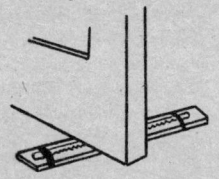

Warped.
1. Exposure to damp air on one side of a door and dry air on the other can cause it to warp. Remove the door and lay it on sawhorses or wooden blocks with the dry side up; that will be the concave side. Place weights of 50 pounds on the ends of the door, past the props or horses, using large books, or rocks, or pails of rocks. In several days the door should straighten out. Before you hang it again, paint or varnish the surface, particularly the edges, bottom, and back border. Then rehang the door.

2. Wide doors and cabinet doors that are warped can often be straightened out by applying heat from an ordinary heat lamp on the convex side. Avoid holding this so closely that the surface finish is scorched, and remove the source of heat as soon as the warp disappears. Then immediately coat both sides and edges with sealer to prevent the re-entry of moisture.

Doors. Doors can be batten, solid, panel or flush in type. Most of the doors in use in the average home are either panel doors, solid doors, or flush doors, although some cellar doors, shed doors, and storerooms doors are batten doors. *Batten doors* are made of vertical boards fastened together with horizontal and diagonal wooden strips. *Panel doors* are made of panels of wood or glass inset in solid borders. *Flush doors* are made of lumber core plywood, and because of their great versatility are the most popular kind of door now in use.

Most doors vary in thickness from 1-1/8 inches to over 2 inches. Interior doors are usually 1-3/8 inches or thinner, exterior doors, thicker. The vertical pieces are called *stiles*; the horizontal pieces *rails*; the sheets of wood or glass enclosed by stiles and rails are called *panels*; strips that seal the joints are called *moldings*. The strip of wood that covers the joint between frame and wall is a *casing*; the interior face of the door opening is called the *jamb*; the strip of wood against which the door closes is the *stop*. At the bottom of the door there may be a strip of wood called a *threshold*.

Accordion, see CLOSET DOORS.
Bifold, see CLOSET DOORS.
Cabinet, see CABINET DOORS.
Closet, see CLOSET DOORS.

Fitting. When you are buying a strong door for your house, make sure it is a strong, good quality one that will improve your home's appearance, and withstand weather conditions.

Most houses have standard size doors 6-ft. 8-in. x 2-ft. 8-in., but doors are available in a range of sizes from 1-ft. 3-in. x 2-ft. 8-in. wide. The most important thing to do before buying a new door is to measure not the old door but the inside measurement of the frame and make an allowance to be sure of easy fitting.

If a standard size is not available, a special size can be ordered. A door frame can be built up on the hinge side of the door or a larger door can be cut down.

Hanging. When you are sure that door and frame fit properly you are ready to hang the door.

Make sure that an even space is obtained all around the door—tape a few quarters on both sides and at the top, or tack on a wooden shim of about the same thickness. Fit the door in position, making sure the bottom is parallel with the floor and leaving enough space for the door to open over any type of floor covering. If this is only the replacement of a door, fit the new door in place and drive a wedge in at the base to hold it in place. Next mark in pencil where the hinges are to go and what size they are, and remove the door. Chisel out a depression in the door to the thickness of the hinge, then screw the door in place. Remove the shims and wedges and the door should swing free. Now fit locks by following the instructions supplied with the particular lock to be fitted.

When you have had to add to the door frame, re-fit hinges to the new frame with the additions made on the hinge side of the door for appearance. The top hinge should be fitted between 6 and 7

DOOR STOP

inches from the inside of the jamb and the bottom hinge about 8 to 9 inches from the floor. When fitting hinges, the frame and door should be marked with pencil and wood chiselled out to the required size and depth. This will give you a flush fitting door.

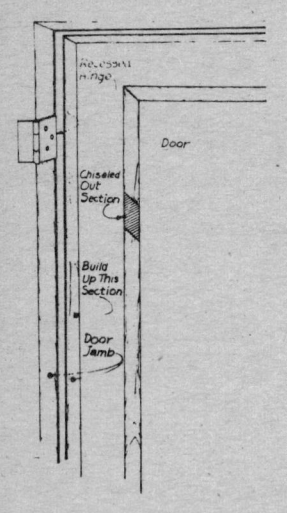

Hanging Tip. If you're hanging a brand new screen door—or any any other kind of door for that matter — here's a little tip that should help you. Before screwing your hinges into place, rest the bottom of the door on several thicknesses of newspaper laid between it and the threshold, and this will insure you plenty of clearance after the door has been attached.

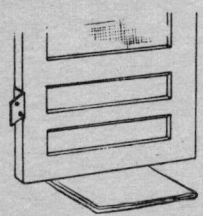

Improvised. A venetian blind of the proper width works wonderfully when you want a good "door" to hang in front of a doorless closet or cupboard which you want to cut off from view while still providing ventilation.

Matching. When building a pair of matching hinged doors, here is a simple method of assuring that both doors will meet perfectly in the middle after they are hung. Fabricate the two doors as one piece, then saw them apart in the middle, as in the illustration. This will assure their meeting in a perfect fit at the center joint, and furthermore the width of your saw kerf will provide just the right amount of clearance necessary to prevent rubbing or binding.

Painting, see PAINTING TIPS.
Pivot, see CLOSET DOORS.
Sliding, see CLOSET DOORS.

Sliding Glass Doors, work on the same principle as sliding windows.

Weatherstripping, see WEATHERSTRIPPING.

Door Stop. Here's one practical use for an empty thread spool. Use it as a door stop. Apply thin coats of fresh, white shellac to the spool and, when dry, fasten it to the floor or baseboard where you want a certain door to stop.

Double-hung Windows, see WINDOWS.

DRAWERS

Dowel Centering. When making some doweled joints, you can mark the centers for the holes by driving brads into place and clipping them short. In order to insure correct positioning, the marking should be done with the members laid out on a flat surface, or with a flat surface held against them. The clipped brads are easily removed with a pair of pliers after you have completed your marking.

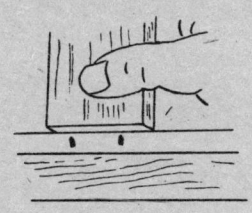

Drain, Drainpipe Repair, see PLUMBING.

Draintile, see BASEMENTS, DAMP OR WET.

Draperies, see CURTAINS.

Drapery Hooks. When drapery hooks just won't pin through material easily, run each hook through your hair as you tackle each pinning. Your hair oil usually provides enough lubrication to do the trick.

Drapery Supports. If your drapery cranes are sagging under the weight of the drapery material, one easy way to support the cranes is by means of wire coat hooks turned into the window casing near the outer ends of the cranes. Your draperies will conceal these hooks.

Drawer Cleaning

Desk. It isn't necessary to empty and turn over a desk drawer to get it clean. Brush all the dust and dirt into a small pile, then press a small piece of cellophane tape over it, and lift all the dirt out.

Dresser. Empty your dresser drawers ever so often and clean them by wiping over the inner surfaces with a soapy cloth and rinsing with a clean damp cloth. Then, when dry, line the drawers with waxed paper or with plastic sheets.

Drawer Pulls. If you are unable to pull out a drawer in a chest or bureau because one of the knobs has come off, try using a suction cup or rubber plunger against the drawer. This will give you the needed pull to open that stubborn drawer.

Drawers. A drawer is simply an open box or lidless chest that can be used to store material. The main point to remember about a drawer is its versatility—in position, in size, and in installation.

A drawer should be placed so that you can stand almost directly in front of it and open it to its full depth. And the drawer should be placed so that you can see into the bottom when it is open.

The size of a drawer is extremely important in judging its usefulness. Here are some rules of thumb to follow when you begin to construct your own drawers.

A drawer should be 12 inches high or less.

A drawer should be 30 inches deep or less.

A drawer should have handles near the sides, but no more than 3 feet apart.

A heavy drawer should not be installed at the top of a cabinet without making sure the cabinet will remain upright when it is opened wide.

A drawer should have stops installed so that it cannot be pulled out too far. *All* drawer slides with rollers should be equipped with stops.

Usually you find drawers built into cabinets or chests. You may also find them suspended under counters, tabletops, desk tops, and so on. And there are small drawers that slide into racks screwed on top of shelves in kitchen cabinets.

You can get complete chests of drawers or drawer cabinets that are built into walls of the house. Made of metal or wood, they usually have sides and a back. The sizes of the drawers vary considerably.

You can get stacking drawers, too. These are individual wooden drawers, each in its own frame; the frames have sides, but neither top nor bottom. They

85

DRAWERS

are built so that one can be interlocked on top of another. You can build your own chest of almost any number of drawers without using any nails or screws. And you can take apart the drawers anytime and use them in some other combination. You can even set them up side by side.

Drawers come without frames, too. They are made of wood and molded plastic. You can build these in almost anywhere, either individually or in chests. You can suspend them under counters, too. Wood drawers can be built into a frame like a bureau where the bottom edges of the drawers slide on wood runners attached to the frame.

Drawer operation is vastly improved if you mount them in metal slides equipped with rollers.

Plastic drawers are designed with lips that flare out from the top edges. These lips slide in grooves in the frame. You can get light steel framework, too, or you can make your own out of plywood or hardboard.

Sticking. Drawers usually jam because damp weather swells up the wood. You can sometimes correct this defect by a simple application of paraffin, or ordinary candle wax, or a silicone lubricant. Remove the drawer and wipe all dust off. Clean the guide strips and apply lubricant to the guides as well as the edges of the drawer itself.

Overloaded dresser drawers sometimes are very difficult to slide in and out. You can remedy this situation simply by use of ordinary thumb tacks, forced into the slides a short distance back from the front edge of the dresser.

When drawers stick there are probably several "high spots" on the drawer sides. These should show up as slightly rubbed areas, which can be planed or glass-papered.

To pinpoint these spots it sometimes helps to place sheets of carbon paper in the drawer opening, then open and close the drawer several times.

The carbon paper leaves a distinct mark on the drawer sides at tight spots.

Where the trouble is not severe, rub a candle along the runners and drawer sides.

If the drawers in a cabinet or bureau persist in sticking because of dampness, screw an electric light bulb into the plug on an extension cord and put this inside the drawer. The heat will dry out the wood in a short time and the drawer should open easily. Be sure to avoid the danger of scorching or fire by removing paper and other inflammable material from the drawer, and the light bulb should be placed on an asbestos hot pad or other fireproof surface. Once the drawer is opened, places where it has rubbed should be planed slightly. Also, paraffin, or paste wax, rubbed on the bottom and sides, will help to keep it from sticking again.

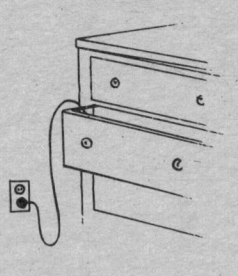

If lubrication and heating fail, sand or plane down the side or edges of the drawer. Check the surfaces of the drawer to find out where the most rubbing occurs and try to trim down those spots. Medium grade sandpaper wrapped around a wooden block will do the trick. Or use a sharp plane.

In a large chest or dresser, a sticking drawer may be caused by the fact that the entire framework of the piece may be out of plumb. Check the level of the dresser with a carpenter's level. To correct a tilting bureau, wedge thin strips of wood or folded cardboard under the low side until the top is level.

Drawer Stop. You can make a simple, but effective, limit stop for a drawer from a two-inch length of coil spring. Pass a wood screw through an eye on one end of the spring and drive this into the inside surface of the drawer back. Allow the spring to project about a half-inch or so above the top of the drawer. This short projection is rigid enough to prevent the drawer from being pulled all the way out accidentally, but the spring can always be bent forward easily to permit installation or removal of the drawer.

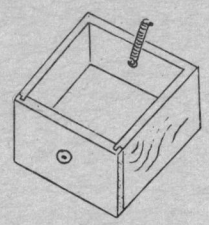

Drawing Board Resurfacing. If your drawing board has become pitted with thumbtack holes, here's one method of renewing the surface. Dip some round toothpicks in glue, and force them into the tack holes. When the glue has set, break off the toothpicks and sand flush with the surface of the board. Then an overall sanding will remove any minor irregularities, and smooth off the picks.

Drawing Ink Stain, see STAIN REMOVAL.

Drier, see PAINT COMPONENTS.

Drill, Drilling, see TOOLS, HAND.

Drill, Electric, see TOOLS, POWER.

Drill Press, see TOOLS, POWER.

Drinking Glasses, see GLASSES, DRINKING.

Drinking Straws. Glass drinking straws can be nicely cleaned on the inside simply by running pipe cleaners through them.

Dripless Paint, see PAINTS.

Driveway Markers. Here's one way to manufacture your own stone markers to border your driveway and protect your lawn. Use some discarded aluminum cooking pans as forms and, if you wish, you can hammer the bottoms and sides of these containers to make irregular shapes. After filling these containers with concrete mix, force a large bolt or length of steel rod into the middle of the concrete, allowing about four inches to project. After your concrete has set, a few light taps will cause the stone to drop out of the form. The projecting bolt or rod is forced into the ground along your driveway to anchor the stone marker in place.

Driveway Repair, see CONCRETE REPAIR.

Drop Cloths, see PAINTING TIPS.

Drywall is also called "sheetrock," "rockwall," "gypsum," "plasterboard," and by a number of brand names. The principle of drywall is simple: it is a prefabricated plaster wall, except that the plaster is covered on both sides by smooth, tough sheets of cardboard to give the plaster rigidity and strength. Drywall has the insulation properties of plaster, and the excellent surface properties of plaster. The advantage of working with drywall is that the very messy business of plastering with wet plaster is bypassed. You simply nail up the drywall as it comes, after, of course, shaping it to fit.

Drywall is manufactured in "modules," or set sizes, for convenience. The average module for drywall is a sheet 4 feet by 8 feet. Manufacturers also make it in 4 by 10 and 4 by 12 and other lengths for special purposes. The 8-foot module is a natural because most ceilings are 8 feet from the floor. Since studs inside walls are conventionally arranged with their centers set exactly 16 inches apart, you attach the 4-foot width—48 inches—at the edge to the middle of Stud 1, to Stud 2 and Stud 3, and the other edge to the middle of Stud 4. The 8-foot height fits snugly between floor and ceiling.

Most drywall comes in quarter-inch thickness, but it is also available in 3/8-inch thicknesses, as well as half-inch thickness. Sometimes builders join two quarter-inch sheets for greater rigidity. Many types of drywall come with a vapor barrier on one side — it's a sheet of metal foil that prevents moisture from seeping through the drywall.

Drywall, like a plaster surface, is excellent for all kinds of paint, and for wallpaper as well.

Application, Ceiling. Normal ceiling joist spacing of 16 and 24 inches on center is sufficient for nail

DRYWALL

support. Plywood joints may be exposed, covered with wood molding, bevel edged or metal divider strip mounting may be used.

The size and shape of the ceiling will largely determine which of three methods of applying wallboard will be used. In all cases, the facelayer is applied at right angles to the direction of the first layer. When the number of pieces and their sizes have been determined proceed as follows:

1. Even if the walls are to be covered, start by applying the first piece of base wallboard to the ceiling.

2. Nail on the first layer parallel to the nailing joists. Span the entire width of the room with one piece if possible. If this is not possible, stagger the end joints.

3. Start the application of the face layers. Nail all face layers on at right angles to the base layers. Special adhesive, usually supplied with the boards, is mixed and spread on the backs of the face layers with a notched trowel. This "buttered side" is then placed against the base coat and nailed.

4. Use only enough nails in the face layer to hold it in place. Drive the nails in so that the heads are slightly below the surface of the wallboard.

5. Seal all joints and nail holes.

CEILINGS WHERE NEITHER DIMENSION EXCEEDS 12 FT

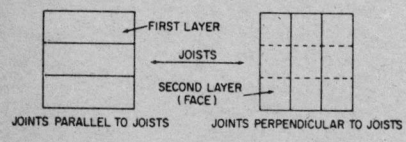

JOINTS PARALLEL TO JOISTS   JOINTS PERPENDICULAR TO JOISTS

CEILINGS NOT MORE THAN 12 FT WIDE BUT LONGER THAN 12 FT.

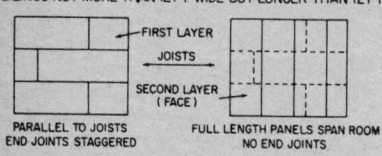

PARALLEL TO JOISTS
END JOINTS STAGGERED

FULL LENGTH PANELS SPAN ROOM
NO END JOINTS

CEILINGS WITH BOTH DIMENSIONS GREATER THAN 12 FT

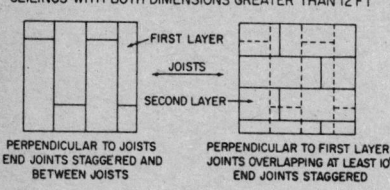

PERPENDICULAR TO JOISTS
END JOINTS STAGGERED AND
BETWEEN JOISTS

PERPENDICULAR TO FIRST LAYER
JOINTS OVERLAPPING AT LEAST 10"
END JOINTS STAGGERED

Application, Double Thickness Walls. The double thickness dry wall system calls for two layers of wallboard, each 3/8 inch thick. The base layer is nailed vertically to the studs and the face layer is applied horizontally over the base layer with an adhesive which makes the two adhere to each other. The joints are sealed with a reinforcing tape and a cement especially designed for this purpose.

WHERE WALLS ARE NOT MORE THAN 8 FT. HIGH

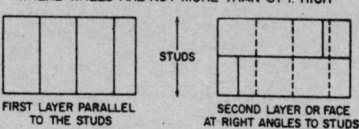

FIRST LAYER PARALLEL
TO THE STUDS

SECOND LAYER OR FACE
AT RIGHT ANGLES TO STUDS

WHERE WALLS ARE MORE THAN 8 FT. HIGH

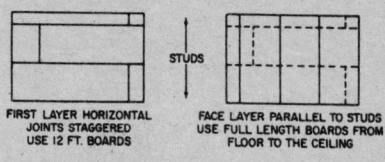

FIRST LAYER HORIZONTAL
JOINTS STAGGERED
USE 12 FT. BOARDS

FACE LAYER PARALLEL TO STUDS
USE FULL LENGTH BOARDS FROM
FLOOR TO THE CEILING

THE SKETCH AT THE RIGHT SHOWS PROPER CUTTING AND FITTING OF THE FACE LAYER WHERE DOORS AND WINDOWS ARE IN WALL. WHEREVER PRACTICAL, VERTICAL END JOINTS ON SIDE WALLS SHOULD BE PLACED ABOVE DOOR AND WINDOW OPENINGS, TO REDUCE THE JOINT TREATMENT TO A MINIMUM.

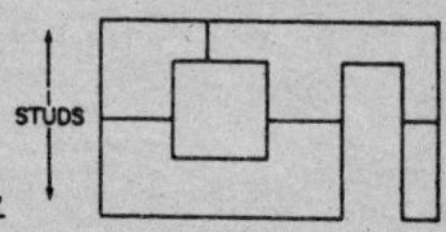

Application, Single Thickness Walls.

1. Start in one corner and work around the room, making sure that the joints break at the centerline of a stud.

2. Use 1/2 inch thick recessed-edge wallboard and span the entire height of the wall, if possible.

3. Using 13-gauge nails, 1-5/8" long, start nailing at the center of the board and work outward. Space the nails 3/8 inch from the edge of the board and about 8 inches apart. Dimple nails below surface of the panel with a ball peen hammer. Be careful not to break the surface of the board by the blow of the hammer.

Application to Uneven Wall.

1. Place a piece of scrap material in the angle as shown and scribe it to indicate the surface peculiarities.

2. Place the scribed strip on the wallboard to be used, keeping the straight edge of the scrap material parallel with the edge of the wallboard.

DRYWALL

3. Saw both the scrap and the wallboard along the scribed line. (See also SCRIBING.)

SCRIBED LINE FOLLOWING CONTOUR OF WALL

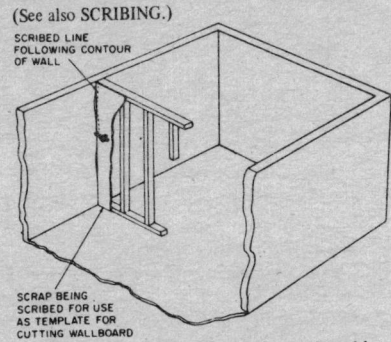

SCRAP BEING SCRIBED FOR USE AS TEMPLATE FOR CUTTING WALLBOARD

Cutting. Cut panels by sawing, or by scoring with an awl and snapping over a straight edge. Cut with finish side up to avoid damaging surface. Cut openings for pipe and electrical receptacles with a keyhole saw.

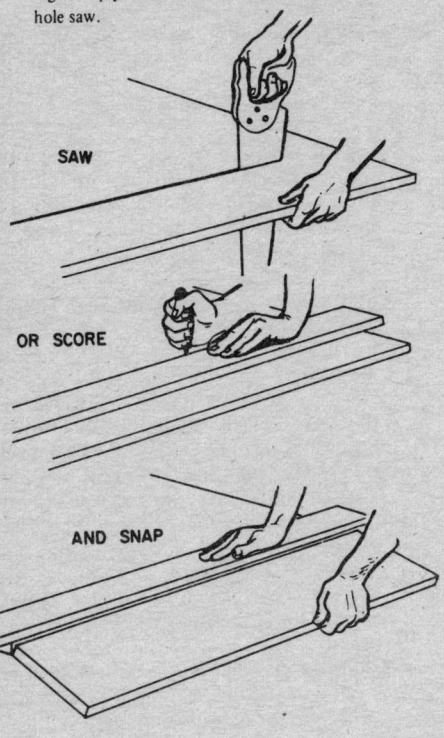

SAW

OR SCORE

AND SNAP

Joint Filler. Cracks of seams where wallboard or hard-pressed panels are joined can be smoothed off with this filler: Mix two parts of soft paste white lead (in oil), three parts of Spanish whiting, and one part of plaster of Paris. If too stiff, add boiled linseed oil, a little at a time. Paint the cracks first and apply the filler with a broad putty knife. Smooth it off evenly, let dry, then sandpaper lightly for a nice finish.

Joint Treatment. Joints may be left open, beveled, lapped, filled, covered with battens or moldings, or treated with cement and tape. The treatment of joints varies slightly with different materials. Generally, all cracks over 1/8 inch must be filled with special crack filler before joint cement is applied. The cement is spread over joints with a plasterer's trowel. Apply the cement evenly and thin (feather) edges on surface of wall panel. Fill channels in recessed edges with cement, carrying it 1 inch past channel edges. At corners, apply cement in a channel-wide band and feather edges. Press perforated tape into wet cement and smooth down with the trowel. Clean off excess cement. At corners, fold tape down center before applying, and smooth each side of corner separately when applied. When cement is dry, apply a second coat of thinned cement to hide tape. Feather the edges carefully to preserve flat appearance of wall. When the final coat is dry, smooth the joint with sandpaper.

Nailing. Nail panels to wall studs with 13-gauge nails, 8 inches on centers. All panel and joints must center on studs. Cover nails with cement.

Nailing Tip. One way to protect your wallboard from an inadvertent slip of your hammer while you are countersinking the nails is to place the round end of your ball-peen hammer against the head of each partly-driven nail, then strike the flat end of the hammer with another hammer to set the nail. The slight indentation or dimple created by the ball of the hammer makes for easy spackling and resultant concealment of the nail heads.

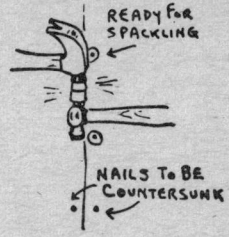

READY FOR SPACKLING

NAILS TO BE COUNTERSUNK

DUCKS

Nails, see NAILS.

Section Replacement. Let's assume that you have somehow managed to drive a rocking chair or a poker through a section of drywall so hard you have torn a great piece out of it right where the edge of the sheet is attached to the stud. There is no way to repair it but to replace the entire 4 feet by 8 feet section.

First remove the ceiling molding carefully, being sure not to split the stripping. Leave the finish nails exactly where they are. Do the same with the baseboard molding.

Remove the covers to the electric outlets and wall switches in the section.

Locate the studs and find both ends of the 4 by 8 sheet. Where the drywall sheet joins its neighbor, cut through the spackling tape with a sharp utility knife, until you have a sharply defined cut.

With a claw hammer remove all the nails. Since you are going to throw away the drywall sheet, don't bother about marring the surface. Pull off the broken sheet.

Put up the new sheet of drywall and see if it needs any trimming to fit into place. If it's a corner piece, you may have to do some cutting, for corners of rooms are almost never really true. While you have the sheet in place, mark slots for the electric outlets and for the wall switches; mark and cut the openings so that the drywall will slip over the corners easily, and yet make a fairly tight fit.

When the board is properly prepared with all cuts made, nail it in place, using drywall nails at 10 inch intervals along the studs.

Tape the joints between the new drywall and its neighbors and prepare for spackling.

Mix spackling compound with water according to directions. Apply to the tape with spackling knife or similar tool. Allow to dry.

When spackling compound is thoroughly dry, put baseboard and molding back in place.

Paint the entire wall and allow to dry.

Replace electric outlet covers and switch covers.

(You can use the above step-by-step procedure for putting up prefinished plywood paneling. To cut drywall, of course, you use a sharp knife or a keyhole saw to cut out portions over electric outlets. To cut paneling you use a crosscut saw and a drill and keyhole saw to cut for outlets.)

Ducks, see FOODS.

Ducts, see HEATING.

Dustcloth. To make a good furniture duster soak old pieces of flannel in paraffin oil overnight, then the next day wring tightly, wash in lukewarm water, and allow to dry. These cloths will pick up dust efficiently, and also produce a gloss on the furniture and woodwork.

Your dustcloth can be kept slightly oiled if you'll add a spoonful of lemon oil or any furniture oil to the rinse water when you wash it.

For dustcloths, try using ordinary paper toweling. First wet your hands, then dry them on two sections of the paper toweling. Next apply a little furniture polish on one of these sections of paper, and polish your furniture piece. Buff over this with the other section of paper. Does a fine job — and no dirty cloths to wash either!

Dust Mop. Freshen your dust mop by boiling it in water to which you've added a tablespoon of baking soda and two of paraffin. To the rinse water add about ten drops or so of furniture polish.

Dustpan. If you're making use of a newspaper as a substitute dustpan, you can prevent the usual annoyance of part of the sweepings being pushed under the paper if you wet the edge of the paper so that it adheres to the floor.

Dutch Oven. A new dutch oven or pot, which has already been preseasoned to prevent rusting, should be scoured, then washed thoroughly in hot soapsuds, rinsed, and dried well. Grease the inside and lid with an unsalted fat and store away. Grease it again lightly before putting food in to cook. This procedure, followed for the first month or so, will put your new dutch oven in Grade A working order.

Dyeing Hint. When dyeing a dress, run several lengths of white thread through the material before you dip it into the dye. Remove the thread before you press the garment. Then you will have matching thread for mending and sewing on buttons.

Dye Stain, see STAIN REMOVAL.

E

Earrings, see JEWELRY.

Earthenware Repair. After washing the edges of some broken earthenware and letting them dry thoroughly, coat both edges with some epoxy glue and press together for at least twenty-four hours. The epoxy repair job will withstand water and oven heat.

Ebony Polishing. Ebony articles that have become dull-looking can be brightened up by rubbing with a soft cloth and white petroleum jelly. Rub until the wood has absorbed all the grease and acquired a gloss.

Eggs, see FOODS.

Egg Stain, see STAIN REMOVAL.

Electrical Conduit. Have you ever had lots of trouble maneuvering that heavy electrical conduit around a sharp 90-degree corner in a limited space? One easy way to do this is to combine two gradual curves, as illustrated. Holding the conduit flat against the wall, bend it down gradually into the corner, then out from the corner flat against the other wall. In this way, your conduit will negotiate the right-angle turn without any strain, and the cable can then be covered with paneling without a break.

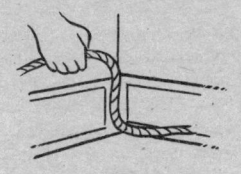

Electrical Fuses. Screw-type fuses come in capacities up to 30 amperes. Fuses of 60 to 100 amperes are of the cartridge type.

① PLAIN CARTRIDGE FUSE ② PLUG FUSE ③ KNIFE-BLADE CARTRIDGE FUSE

Blown. When a fuse blows out, it means that an electrical circuit in your house has been overloaded. Each circuit can carry a certain amount of current—15 amperes or 20 amperes of power usually—and if the appliances and lights draw too much current—over 20 or over 30—the fuse blows to prevent the wiring from heating up with the excessive current and starting a fire. Overloading can come from a short in a faulty appliance, a bad wire in a fixture, a broken switch, or too many appliances for the fuse load.

Check first to see that you do not have an overload on the circuit. Simply add up the amperes each light and appliance pulls and be sure that the total is well within the circuit range. For instance, a 60 watt light on house voltage of 120 pulls ½ an ampere.

If the trouble is not a simple overload, disconnect all lamps and appliances in use when the fuse

ELECTRICAL INTERFERENCE

blew. Check them all for any exposed wires. If you find any, tape them so hot wire and ground wire do not touch. Check next to see that the connections in the plug itself are tight and that the two wires do not touch.

Remove the cover of the wall switch and work the toggle up and down. Be sure the wires are securely connected. Sometimes the toggle itself is broken.

If you are sure all the lights, appliances and fixtures are safe, insert a circuit breaker in the fuse box, making sure it is the same amperage as the blown one. Proceed one by one to reconnect all the appliances and lamps in use. You can isolate the trouble in this manner. When you have found the guilty one, reset the circuit breaker, or replace it with a regular fuse. Throw out the bad appliance or lamp. (See also ELECTRICITY, THEORY OF.)

Fustats are protective devices somewhat similar to common plug fuses. They also protect appliances and circuits from high currents or continuous overloads. A fustat is made so a small block of solder melts when heated by a continuous overload of high current. After the solder has melted, a spring attached to the fuse strip pulls the circuit open. With each different size of fustat, a different adapter is used. The adapter is screwed into a plug fuse socket. The adapter is constructed so that when it is once placed in the socket, it locks in place and cannot be removed. This prevents the insertion of fuses that are too large.

Locating Short Circuit. One easy method of locating the short that blew out a fuse is first to replace the blown fuse with a 75- to 100-watt light bulb. This bulb will light brightly as long as the short exists. Then, while someone watches the bulb, quickly unplug each gadget or lamp on that circuit. When you hit the item that is defective, the light will dim and you'll know where the repair is needed.

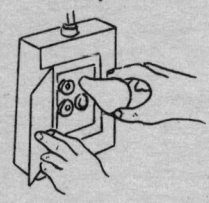

Electrical Interference. You can do something about the radio interference caused by your electric tools or an electric razor, if you'll wire a condenser across the line that carries the current to the tool or accessory. One good method is to bend the pigtails of a .01-mfd. 600-volt capacitor (condenser) to fit into one side of a three-way plug. After the pigtails have been inserted into the plug and make contact, the condenser is taped into place. The three-way plug is then used, as in the illustration, between the tool cord and the outlet.

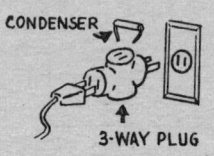

CONDENSER
3-WAY PLUG

Electrical Outlets. There are four types of outlets in the home: control, convenience, fixed-light and special purpose outlets.

Control outlets for switches are used for complicated types of wiring, and may sometimes serve for tools and heavy motors that will burn out any ordinary circuit.

Convenience outlets are usually placed in the walls, about a foot above floor level. In a typical convenience outlet, there are two sockets where cords can be plugged in. Outlets may be controlled from a wall switch, or they may be "hot" outlets that work immediately when you plug in a device.

Fixed-light outlets are built into the walls or ceilings. You simply screw in light bulbs and operate the lights from a wall switch or from the light itself.

Outdoor Sockets. Light bulbs on outdoor porches and other exposed areas sometimes corrode at the base and tend to "freeze" in their sockets. To prevent this, smear a very thin coat of grease or petroleum jelly over the metal stub of a new bulb before inserting it in an outdoor socket.

Special purpose outlets may be combinations of convenience outlets and switches combined.

Socket Repair. Socket assemblies can easily be taken apart and fixed. Quite frequently the trouble involves the electrical connections where the wire is screwed into the terminal.

Let's take a look at the socket assembly, and remove the pieces one by one. At the bottom of the socket, where the light screws in, there is a brass shell that covers the whole works. It is usually secured to the socket body by crimps in the top of the brass. Simply pull this shell off.

ELECTRIC BULBS

Inside the shell there is an insulating paper shell made of cardboard. Slip that off. It is an insulating device. Now the socket body is visible, along with the brass screw unit. It is into this that the light bulb fits.

You can now see the terminals where the wires are fastened to the socket body. Check these screws carefully. It is usually here that loose connections occur.

There may be broken insulation inside the cap, which is placed over the socket body, or breaks in bushing, which is the protective unit that keeps the cap from cutting the wire cord. Be sure the insulation is perfect in all these places.

Tighten all screws and terminals. Then reassemble the socket. If it doesn't work, throw it away and get a new one.

Incidentally, broken switches are a commonplace problem. It is useless to try to repair them. Just get a new socket.

Electrical Safety Tips.

1. Eliminate all multiple connections.

2. Use only a 15 ampere fuse. If the fuse burns out frequently, have an electrician check your wiring.

3. Inspect appliances for frayed cords, cracked plugs. Replace defective parts immediately.

4. Disconnect electric irons when not in use.

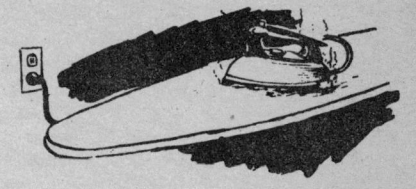

5. Never run wire under rugs, through doorways, over nails or hooks. Worn or broken cords cause short circuits and fires.

6. Remove cord from socket by grasping the plug, not the wire.

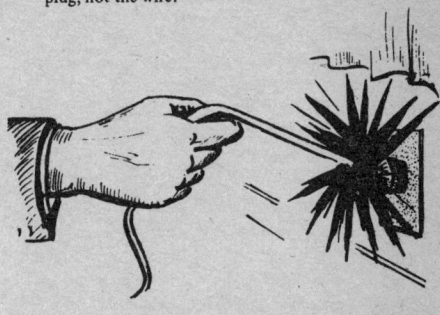

Electric Blankets should be folded end to end, or from side to side when storing them, in order to avoid creasing on the thermostats inside. Use moth preventive. Don't place heavy objects on these blankets, or attempt to pin them. Dry cleaning is not recommended since the solvents used have a tendency to destroy the insulation of the wires. They should be washed.

Electric Bulbs, see LIGHT BULBS, INCANDESCENT.

ELECTRIC CABLE

Electric Cable. BX cable, a construction wire, is doublestrand wire covered with a thin, flexible metal covering, and is used for wiring installations. The BX cable in your home is probably covered up inside the walls.

Electric Circuits. Each electric circuit in a house, is constructed to deliver power to a certain number of appliances. If too much power is drawn by these motors, too much current will flow through the wire. Since the wire would overheat and start to burn, fuses are placed in the fuse box to prevent overloading. At its maximum capacity, a circuit will serve an amount totaling its fuse designation.

You can find out how much a circuit will serve simply by adding the number of watts listed on the appliances and dividing by the house voltage. The answer will give you the number of amperes drawn. If the total amperes is less than the fuse rating, you will be safe in using all appliances listed.

For instance: an iron usually draws about 1650 watts; a vacuum cleaner 125 watts. Together they draw over 14 amperes (1775 divided by 120). If you were running both of them at once, you couldn't plug in anything else on the same circuit. (See also APPLIANCE WATTAGE CHART.)

Electric Cord.
Care.

1. Rubber-covered electric cords can be protected from premature drying out and cracking if a thin coat of wax or paraffin is rubbed over them periodically. Wipe on with one cloth, then draw the cord through a second dry cloth several minutes later to remove the excess stickiness.

2. All cords on electric appliances should be wound loosely. The fine wires inside the cord may break if pulled too tight.

Copper Wire. Insulated copper wire is the standard type of wire used for conducting current in the home. Each size of wire has a specific capacity. Wire size 14 (that which is most commonly used in the home) carries a maximum of 15 amperes before it begins to heat and burn; size 12 can carry 20 amperes; size 10 can carry 30; and size 8 can carry 40 amperes. The smaller the number of the wire, the bigger it is.

Insulation can be of many different kinds, particularly on cords that plug into outlets. Radios, lamps, and other low-power equipment can have fabric-covered or all-rubber lamp cords. Refrigerators, vacuum cleaners, power tools, sewing machines, and so on, usually have rubber-covered wires, and are larger and better insulated; the reason for this is that they pull more current and need greater protection. Heater cords used in heat-producing appliances are thickly insulated with asbestos to keep the heat from scarring or burning the outer fabric.

Insulation Repair. Insulation is the most important part of any electric cord. The slightest break may cause a short. Sometimes the break is so minute that it is invisible to the naked eye. You must thoroughly inspect a cord to see if it has a break in it.

When insulation is broken, unplug the cord from the outlet and peel back the break to be sure there is no damage to the wire itself. Then separate the two wires and cut the wire back a half inch or so from the break to be sure the wire is all right. Then tape up each bare wire separately with friction tape or with rubber electric tape. Be sure when you finish taping that no bare wire is visible anywhere.

Proper Functioning. In order to insure proper functioning of any light or appliance, the cord that carries the power to it must be completely insulated and unbroken. Bad insulation can result in short circuits. Broken wire can result in lack of operating power of the appliance itself.

Shortening.

1. If one of your lamp cords is too long, wrap it tightly around a broom handle for a day or so. This will cause the cord to spiral, thus shortening it.

2. Is the cord on one of your lamps too long and continually getting in your way? If the base of your lamp is of the concave type, you can cut down the length of the cord easily by pulling the excess cord inside the base and taping it in flat loops. Besides effecting a neater appearance, the hidden loops can be quickly unwound, should the lamp be moved to another location that requires a longer cord.

3. You can increase the utility of a trouble lamp by cutting the cord about a foot from the lamp and fitting the short cord with a male plug and the longer cord with a female plug. This converts the longer section of cord into an extension cord for use with an electric drill or other power tool—and you can still always use your trouble lamp by plugging the two sections of cord together.

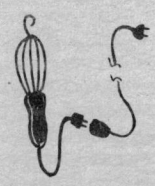

4. If you will loop the cord of your extension lamp through a large washer, as in the illustration, the lamp will then be easily adjustable to any height you may desire.

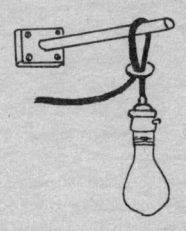

Electric Heating, see HEATING.

Electricity, Theory of. Electric power is brought into your home by means of wires that are attached to a power supply. Once inside the house, electricity can be tapped for use by plugging in cords to a wall convenience outlet. A cord is a double wire, one of which carries electricity from the source to the appliance; the other wire carries the current back to the source.

Circuit. Electricity travels in a complete circle from source to motor and back to source, a path called a "circuit." Because the earth is as good a conductor of electricity as the best copper wire, the earth itself acts as the second "wire" back to the original source; therefore, the second wire can be dispensed with and the line back can simply be attached to the "ground"—the earth itself. (See **Short Circuit** below.)

When electric power comes in from the street source, it is broken in your fuse box and delivered to various areas of the house. Each area controls a number of outlets and collectively is a "circuit." Each circuit controls a specific part of the house. Each circuit is protected by a specific fuse in the fuse box. Some fuses are 20 amp fuses and others are 15 amp fuses. Always replace a blown fuse with one exactly the same value! Other circuits of 220 and 240 volts will control stoves, heating devices and air-conditioning units.

Conductors. Copper wire has little resistance to electricity; because of that, it is used to conduct, or carry, power. Copper, silver, iron, and so on are excellent conductors of electricity. So are other kinds of metal. Other substances have excellent conductivity—for example, water.

Current. There are two kinds of electric current: AC and DC.

In Alternating Current (AC) the current is produced by a generator, and every half-rotation of the generator changes the direction of the current. A complete rotation from plus to minus and back to plus is called a cycle. Commercial AC is normally delivered to the home at the rate of 60 cycles a second (the current changes direction 120 times a second). The reason house current is delivered in AC rather than DC is that it has been found that the change of direction in current allows electric motors to run better over a long period of time since each reversal clears up all the excess charges that might tend to remain in the machinery.

In Direct Current (DC) the flow of electricity goes from the power source through the appliance motor and back to the source in one direction continuously. A battery supplies Direct Current in a flashlight.

Cycles. Most appliances and light bulbs are made to operate on a 60-cycle, 120-volt AC current, and residential areas are supplied with electric power in this manner. Big appliances like electric stoves and electric heating units use a 220 or 240 volt AC current. This power is delivered on a circuit separate from the circuit your lights and small appliances are hooked into.

Fuses. In a short circuit, the electricity rushes back through the ground wire before reaching the appliance for which it was intended. In the appliance a specified amount of resistance is built into the circuit. When the resistance is by-passed, the current

ELECTRIC LIGHTS

traveling back is too great for the ground wire to handle. That is why a short circuit can cause a wire to heat up and burn. To protect you from such fires, fuses are used in the circuit to prevent overloading. A fuse is simply a wire of a known resistance that has a low melting point; when too much current flows through it, the wire melts and breaks, thus cutting off all flow of electric current.

High-Resistance Wires. Certain types of wire have a high resistance to the flow of electricity. When current can't flow through a particular kind of wire, the wire itself begins to heat up. The wire that makes up the filament of an electric light is such a high-resistance wire. When it heats up it begins to glow, which gives us our light. High-resistance wires all heat up; conductive wires do not. However, if a conductive wire is too small to handle the amount of current traveling through it, it too will begin to resist the flow and heat up and eventually burn.

Insulators. Many substances have great resistance to the flow of electricity. These are used as insulators to keep electricity from flowing through. Rubber, plastic, and ceramic are used as insulators. So is cardboard.

Measurement. Electric current, analagous to the amount of water flowing in a river, is measured in "amperes." Electric pressure, analagous to the pressure of water in a waterfall, is measured in "volts." Electric resistance, analagous to sluice gates in a dam, are measured in "ohms."

Measurement, Amperage. Circuits in the home are usually measured in amps—short for amperes. That is, the size of the wire carrying the power from the fuse box to the appliance will be capable of carrying a certain current at the prescribed voltage. In other words, all appliances attached to a certain 15 amp circuit, running at 120 volts, must not draw a total wattage of over 1800; 1800 watts would pull 15 amperes of current through the circuit at 120 volts. You could plug in 15 120-watt light bulbs, but that is all; or you could run two 900 watt appliances at once.

Measurement, Kilowatt Hours. For purposes of measuring the consumption of electrical current, power companies charge consumers by the "kilowatt hour." A kilowatt is 1000 watts. A kilowatt hour is simply the amount of 1000-watt units used over the period of an hour. Power consumption is measured by electric meters in kilowatt hours. Two amperes delivered at 120 volts for an hour would equal 240 watts, or a KWH consumption of .240 KWH (240 divided by 1000).

Measurement, Voltage. To find out how many amperes a specific wattage draws, simply divide the wattage (240) by the voltage (120) to ascertain the amperage (2). Except for certain air-conditioning units, dishwashers, and stoves, home circuits deliver current at 120 volts pressure. Although voltage listed variously as 110, 115, and 120, you generally figure you get 115-120 volts across your wires.

Measurement, Wattage. We have a simple formula: volts (pressure) times amperes (current) equals ohms (resistance). Most home appliances and light bulbs are designed for a specific amount of current at a specific voltage. The amount of current driven through a light or motor for a certain amount of time is measured in the amount of resistance built in to the appliance; although resistance is measured in ohms, the work performed by electric power is measured in "watts." In the above formula, watts is substituted for ohms. Watts (work) equals volts (pressure) times amperes (current).

A 120-watt light bulb will draw exactly 1 ampere of current though a 120-volt circuit. A 60-watt light bulb will draw exactly ½ ampere of current through the same circuit.

Short Circuit. A charge of electricity travels with the speed of light back to its source along the path of least resistance. If hot wire and ground wire in a cord are not properly insulated from each other they may touch and allow the current to "short" across the two wires and rush back to the source—the ground—before it reaches the motor and does its work.

Electric Lights, see LIGHT BULBS, INCANDESCENT LIGHTING FIXTURES; LIGHTING, FLUORESCENT.

Electric Mixer, see APPLIANCES.

Electric Plugs.
  Lubricant. If you have a stubborn electric plug that refuses to pull out of the socket easily, try rubbing the prongs with a lead pencil. The graphite contents act as a lubricant.
  Repair. If the insulation and the wires are all right, the next trouble spot to inspect is the plug itself. A plug is the fitting that carries the power from the

outlet to the cord wires through prongs that fit into the outlet socket. First examine the prong side of the plug. Many times the screws that hold the wires to the prong are loose. Be sure that the wires are wound tightly around the screw head, and that the screws are good and tight. If you have to, clean off the ends until you have enough wire to get a good connection with the terminal.

Then check the cord end of the plug, making sure that there are no breaks in the wire where it enters the plug. If there are, cut the cord just past the plug, strip the ends, insert the bare wires into the plug, and attach the bare wires to the terminal connections, making sure the screw is tight.

Temporary Repair. It is a good and safe idea to inspect the plugs on your appliance cords now and then for exposed wires. And if the cardboard seal is badly torn or is missing, you can improvise a seal by crisscrossing the open end of the plug with some plastic tape, as illustrated. Trim off the excess tape.

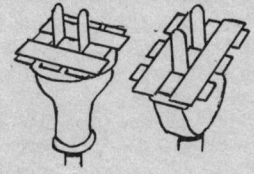

Electric Sockets, see Electrical Outlets.

Electric Switches. A switch may be operated by a push button or a key, but the interior mechanism is the

TUMBLER-FOR BOX MOUNTING

TUMBLER COVER

ELECTRIC SWITCHES

same. To replace a switch remove the cover plate on wall, remove the screws which keep the switch in place, then pull out the switch in order to detach the old wires. *Before detaching the wires, remove the fuse or throw the circuit breaker for the circuit involved.* Then disconnect the wires, remove and replace the old switch. After the switch is in place, replace the cover plate. The circuit supplying the switch may then be closed.

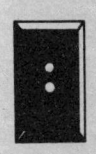

PUSH BUTTON— FOR BOX MOUNTING

PUSH BUTTON COVER

Three-way switches are available to control a light from two different locations, such as a light at the head of the stairway which can be turned off and on from either floor.

Automatic. You can make your own automatic switch for turning on a light, a radio, or turning off or on any other electrical device. This can be fashioned from a spring-wound alarm clock and a pull-chain light socket, as illustrated. Add an extension to the alarm-winding key on the back of the clock to take care of the string which is attached to the chain on the socket. Drill a hole crosswise through the extension to prevent the string from slipping on the shaft. Then screw a light bulb into the socket or a receptacle plug for whatever appliance you wish to be turned on or off.

Dimmer, see LIGHT DIMMERS.

Luminous. Try putting a few dabs of luminous paint on your electric light switch, and you'll be able to see it in the dark. This puts an end to smudges on the wall caused by feeling around for the switch.

Mercury. If you find, after installing a new, quiet-working electric mercury wall switch, that it does not work—turn it around. This type of switch does not function properly if installed upside down.

ELECTRIC TOOLS

Repair. To check out a broken wall switch, first remove the fuse that controls the electric circuit in which the wall switch is located. If you are not sure which fuse is the right one, take them all out. Now remove the switch plate by unscrewing the machine screws that hold it to the wall box. The toggle, or off-and-on switch, is mounted on a strip screwed to a box of wires and connectors. Unscrew the toggle strip and pull it away so you can check the screws holding the power wires, making sure they are tight and that the wires curve around the screw for a perfect fit. If you find that the solderless connectors are tight and all connections to the switch are tight, the toggle switch itself may be broken. If so, replace it. Attach the power wires to the switch, and push the toggle strip back in place, working the wires in to fit. Refasten the toggle strip and switch plate.

Electric Tools, see TOOLS, POWER.

Electric Wire. The wire that carries the current to the motor is the "hot" wire; the wire that carries it back is the "ground" wire. The hot wire is usually black; the ground wire, white or red. (See also ELECTRIC CORD.)

Center Tap Splice. When it is necessary to attach any additional wire to a continuous one, make a center tap splice:

1. Remove about 1-1/2" insulation from the main wire.
2. Remove about 1-1/2" insulation from the second wire.
3. Scrape both wires clean with a knife.
4. Using pliers, twist the second wire firmly around the main wire as shown.

CENTER TAP

End Tap Splice. The end tap splice is used to connect a small feeder to a larger wire or to several wires previously joined with a pigtail splice.

1. Remove insulation: 1-1/2" from the end of the larger wire, 2" from the end of the small wire.
2. Clean both wires by scraping with a knife.
3. Starting from the middle of the exposed larger wire, wrap the smaller wire. Using the pliers, clamp the larger wire back over the smaller wire.

Pigtail splice is used for attaching fixture leads in outlet boxes or in other places where there is no pull on the wires. Proceed as follows:

1. Remove about 1-1/2" of insulation from both wires to be spliced.
2. Scrape the wires clean with a knife.
3. Cross the wires and using lineman's pliers twist them together, turning up the ends.

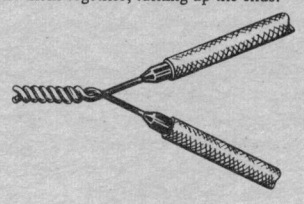

PIGTAIL SPLICE

Screw-type Terminal Connections. When attaching a wire to a switch or a receptacle, an eye or a hook should be made on the end of the wire. This will provide ample contact between the surface of the wire, the screw and the base.

To form a hook or eye:

1. Remove 1/2 or 3/4 inch of insulation. Using a knife, pare away the insulation in the same way you would sharpen a pencil. Care should be taken not to damage the wire. If lineman's pliers are available, insert the wire through the handle side of the pliers next to the jaw, and break the insulation by pressing on the handles of the pliers.
2. Clean the wire by carefully scraping off the insulation.
3. Make a right angle bend in the wire and use long nose pliers to draw the end of the wire around to form a hook or completely around to form an eye. Note that the wire is turned *clockwise*. When placed under a screw head, the wire will pull tighter as the screw is tightened.

RIGHT
TURNING SCREW CLOSES LOOP

WRONG
TURNING SCREW OPENS LOOP

ELECTRIC WIRE

Soldering Spliced Wire. Soldering of splices is an important part of good splicing. If electricity is available, an electric soldering iron can be used. If not, use a blow torch to heat the soldering coppers. To solder:

1. Thoroughly clean the wires to be soldered.
2. If wire solder with flux core is used, be sure it is rosin-core solder. Acid-core solder has a tendency to corrode, and weaken the splice causing a poor electrical contact.
3. If bar solder or solid wire solder is used, it is necessary to apply flux of the proper type to the surfaces to be soldered. Flux prevents the formation of oxides which keep the solder from sticking.
4. Use the soldering copper to heat the wires to be spliced until they melt the solder.
5. Apply enough solder to fill the space between the spliced wires and to give the entire joint a thin even coating. *Warning: Excess solder that may drop off is hot. Be careful!*

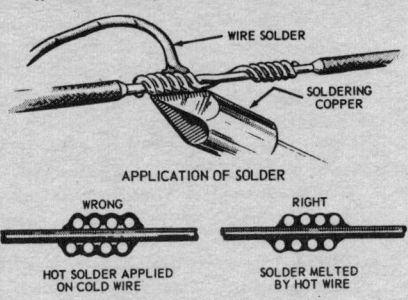

APPLICATION OF SOLDER

WRONG — HOT SOLDER APPLIED ON COLD WIRE
RIGHT — SOLDER MELTED BY HOT WIRE

RIGHT AND WRONG SOLDER JOINT

Solderless Connector. A solderless connector is used principally for attaching fixture leads. The ends of the wires are cleaned and twisted together. Then they are inserted into the connector which is screwed on clockwise until no bare wire shows.

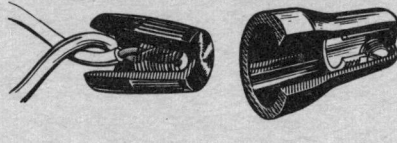

CONNECTOR

Stripping Insulation.

1. One quick and easy way to remove the rubber insulation from an electric cord is to make use of a claw hammer. After pulling the two strands of wire apart, remove the rubber from them in bites of about two inches long.

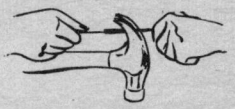

2. For removing insulation from small-gauge wire, a "pinch-type" nail clipper proves an excellent tool. First, however, remove the pressure handle to avoid exerting too much force and cutting right through the wire.

3. You can make yourself a very useful and efficient tool for stripping the insulation off electrical wires. This stripper is easily made from a pair of blunt-end tweezers. All you have to do is file the tips of the tweezers as shown in the illustration, then bend them inwards at right angles so that the jaws just overlap. Then to use this little gadget, you press the cutting edges over the wire, twist to cut through the insulation, and then pull.

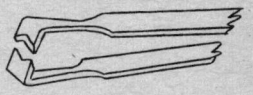

Taping Splices. In taping splices, rubber tape and friction tape should both be used. Rubber tape, which is applied first, serves as the primary insulator. Each layer of tape should overlap the preceding layer by one-half the width of the tape. Start the application of the rubber tape at a point where it overlaps the original insulation. Stretch the tape a little as you wind it around the exposed wire. Next apply friction or plastic tape. This serves as a binder for the rubber tape and as additional insulation. Wrap it tightly as for the rubber tape. Friction tape should not be used directly on the wire because it has a tendency to loosen with age.

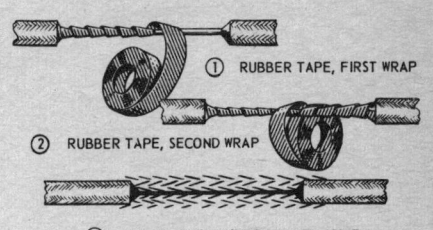

① RUBBER TAPE, FIRST WRAP
② RUBBER TAPE, SECOND WRAP
③ RUBBER AND FRICTION TAPED JOINT

ELECTRIC WIRING

Underwriters Knot. In a lamp socket, under the socket cap an Underwriters Knot is made. This is a double knot in which the two wires are tied together. It serves to ease the strain of the weight of the connection and it fits snugly into the socket cap.

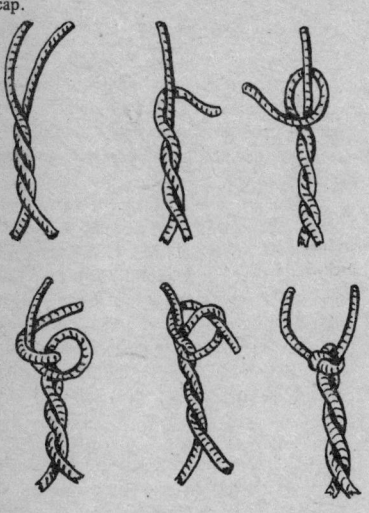

The Underwriters knot.

Western Union Splice. To make a common or Western Union splice:

1. Remove about three inches of insulation from the ends of both wires.
2. Clean the wires by scraping with a knife.
3. Using pliers, make a right angle bend on each wire (A).
4. With pliers hold the wires tightly together at the point. Using a second pair of pliers, wrap the loose ends to form a finished splice. (B).

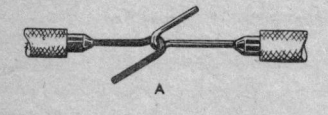

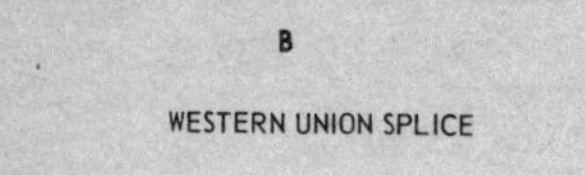

WESTERN UNION SPLICE

Electric Wiring. Good-quality, adequately protected wiring makes it possible to light your home well. It also provides for convenient use of electrical equipment.

Safety is assured by careful inspection and follow-up maintenance. Make certain that all wiring complies with the National Electrical Code, and meets local and area requirements. Each fixture, control, or electrical part should carry the label of the Underwriters' Laboratories (UL).

Efficient wiring has outlets located so that no point along the floor line in any usable wall space is more than 6 feet from an outlet. Wire size is large enough to prevent excessive voltage drop that results in poor lighting (a 5 percent voltage loss produces a 17 percent loss of light from an incandescent bulb).

Install enough circuits to provide electricity where you want it without overloading any one circuit. Locate switch controls at all principal doorways. Modern wiring systems generally use standard switches, but low-voltage relay switching for multiple-point light and equipment control is on the increase. Special controls—dimmers, timers, and photocell units—all have a place in the effective performance of equipment and lighting.

A service entrance geared to present and future family needs is essential. A 100-ampere service entrance—the minimum code requirement—provides for modern living in a small home. If you have a large house or expect to add large electrical appliances, consider installing a 150- or 200-ampere service entrance. The 200-ampere service provides for electric space heating and other possible applications.

Help in planning wiring is available from your electric power supplier, from experienced electrical contractors, or from county extension agents.

Lamp Rewiring. The feeding of a new wire through a lamp column which has a number of sharp bends or curves in it sometimes presents quite a problem. One solution is as follows: Tie a length of thread to a small bit of cotton and push the cotton into the lamp column with a match or toothpick. Now, blow into the column so that the cotton is forced through to the other end, carrying the thread with it. Then tie a length of heavy twine to the thread and pull

100

this through the column, after which the twine can be used to pull your wire through the column of the lamp.

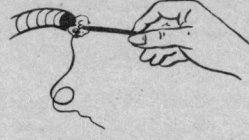

Emery Board. The striking part of the back of a paper match book is very effective in an emergency for smoothing the roughened edge of a fingernail.

Enamel

Cleaning. White enamel finishes can be cleaned nicely with turpentine or mineral spirits. Simply rub with a cloth moistened in either of these, then wipe off with a dry cloth.
Paint, see PAINTS.
Scratch Repair. The best way to repair a scratch in an enameled surface is with some of the original enamel, dripped in with a toothpick. After the enamel dries, rub it down with some rottenstone. An easier treatment is to fill the mar with a wax crayon matching the enamel color, following this with a wax polish.

Enamel, Porcelain, see PORCELAIN ENAMEL REPAIR.

Enamelware Cleaning. Try cleaning your discolored enamelware with a paste made of salt and vinegar.

Envelope.

Moistener. If you have a large amount of correspondence at home and have become tired of running your tongue over the flaps of the envelopes, you can make your own sealing machine. All you need is a length of broom handle or a dowel for a roller, two nails, and a small, shallow, square can (perhaps of the sardine variety). Cut your roller to the proper length for fitting lengthwise inside the can, drive a small nail into each end for the shaft, then file a notch into the center edge of each end of the can, insert your roller, fill the can with water, and run your envelope flaps over the roller.

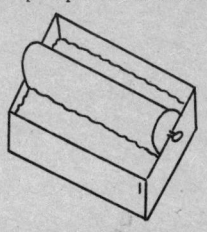

Opener. Most of us have at one time or another sealed a letter only to discover we had forgotten to include something else in the letter or in the envelope itself. In a case like this, one easy way to open the sealed envelope is to pull the sealed part back and forth over a hot, lighted electric bulb.
Sealer. One way to seal an envelope so that it cannot be steamed open is by use of the white of an egg.
Envelopes, Stuck. If a whole package of envelopes has become glued together in hot, sticky weather, don't throw them out. Put them into your freezer for a few hours, then slide an ordinary table knife under the flaps. The glue will be as good as new and you will have saved all the envelopes. This trick also works well with stamps that are stuck together.

Epoxy. is an almost impervious plastic material that forms a hard film resistant to alkalies, acids, and moisture. Epoxy resins come in clear waterproofing compounds, opaque-colored compounds, and opaque-colored, with sand added. The sand adds the extra bulk needed for patching foundations or floor cracks, or for laying a new floor surface over an irregular one or over one broken by flooding.

Like all epoxies, this compound comes in two parts—one the resin and the other the hardener. You buy it in two containers, and as soon as you mix the two, the hardening process begins almost immediately.

Epoxy bonds an infinite number of materials, but will dissolve some plasters. It sets at lower temperatures than other glue, and in wet conditions, no clamping is necessary. (See also BASEMENT, WATERPROOFING.)

EPOXY GLUE

Epoxy Glue, see ADHESIVES.

Epoxy Resin, see PAINTS.

Eraser. If you have to erase mistakes when writing a letter with pen and ink, try using an emery board to sand off your error. The small size is the handiest for this purpose and works marvelously well.

Escutcheon Pins, see NAILS.

Evaporative Cooling, see COOLING.

Evergreens, see GARDENING.

Extension Cord.
   Reel. Make your own reel for keeping in order long extension cords of the type used with electric lawn mowers, hedge clippers, home appliances, and the like. First, cut two disks six inches or larger in diameter from 1/4-inch hardboard or plywood and drill or saw a two-inch hole in the center of each. Cut a notch in one of the disks for fastening one end of the cord on the reel. Then force the disks over a small frozen-juice can after cutting off the rim from the opened end. Peen over the cut edge of the can so that the disk on that end cannot slip off, then fix both disks into place with household cement and paint the entire thing.

   Storage. To prevent long electrical extension cords from knotting up or kinking badly when storing them away, try wrapping them around an empty tin can, such as a large juice can—tucking the last turn under itself to keep the cord from unraveling.

Extension Wiring, see WIRING, EXTENSION.

Exterior Painting, see PAINTING, EXTERIOR.

Exterior Wall, see WALLS, EXTERIOR.

Eyeglass Cleaner. The tissues separating the pages in a stamp book make an excellent cleaner for eyeglasses. You can carry them in your pocket or purse, making them always available.
   An occasional soap-and-water bath for your eyeglasses is recommended, especially for removing that inevitable film of oil that is present from your skin.

Eyeglasses, Prevention of Steaming. You can prevent your eyeglasses from steaming up in cold weather if you'll rub both sides of each lens with soapy fingers, then polish with a soft cloth.

Eyeglass Repairing. One emergency method of mending plastic frames on your eyeglasses is to hold the break together with softened paraffin, then add a drop of acetone to the break before the paraffin hardens.

Eyeglass Screws. One way to avoid having the small screws in your eyeglass frames work loose and possibly fall out is to place a small drop of clear fingernail polish on the top of each screwhead. This will keep them tightly in place.

Eye Protection. If you will rub a little mineral or olive oil over your lashes before swimming in a pool, it will prevent the chlorine in the water from stinging your eyes.

F

Fabrics, see FIBERS, MAN-MADE; FIBERS, NATURAL.

Facebrick, see BRICKS.

Fan Belt, see AUTOMOBILE.

Fans, see COOLING.

Fats, Cooking, see FOODS.

Faucet Handle, Outdoor. If the handle on one of your outdoor faucets has disappeared or broken, one good replacement for it is an old door knob you may have lying around. Simply secure it with its set-screw to the shank of your faucet.

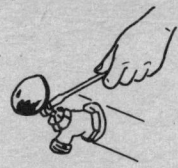

Faucets, see PLUMBING.

Feathers, Stuffing. One quick and easy way to stuff feathers into a pillow is by using your electric vacuum cleaner. Merely substitute the tick for the cleaner bag, dump your feathers on a paper, and draw them into the casing through the vacuum cleaner.

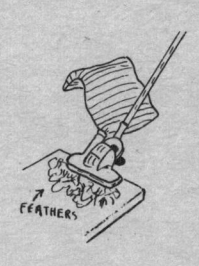

Felt. Steel wool, rubbed gently over soiled felt in the wrong direction of the material, will usually do a nice cleaning job.

Fence, see SCREEN, OUTDOOR.

Fence Posts.

Erecting. When erecting fence posts, the aim at all times should be to make them as firm as possible.

Two methods often used to insure this are to concrete around the base of each post, or to fix braces above ground level.

Both methods, however, have disadvantages. Concrete makes the job more costly, and the braces look unsightly.

Here, however, is a simple way to insure that a post remains firm and secure in the ground.

Allow that each post will go at least 2½ feet into the ground.

Obtain two pieces of scrap hardwood — say 4 in. wide, 2 in. thick — and cut them about 2 ft 6 in. long.

FERRULES

Nail these two 2 ft. pieces to the post at right angles to each other, keeping the first piece about 6 in. above the bottom end of the post, as shown in the sketch.

The post should then be lowered into the hole, and broken bricks packed tightly around the supporting ledges.

Finish off by filling in the remainder of the hole with earth in 4 in. layers, taking care to compact each layer tightly by ramming before laying the next.

If the supporting ledges are well nailed to the post and the earth is fully compacted around the base, the post will remain firm.

It is advisable to apply two coats of creosote to the bottom of the post and also to the ledges before placing in the hole.

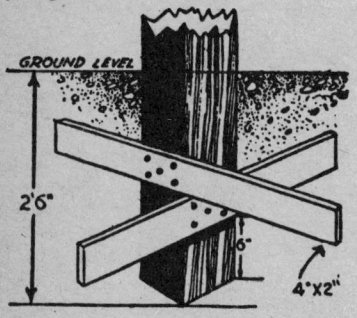

Repairing. Dig a hole alongside the rotten post at least 24 in. deep. Get a post about 4 ft. long in a durable hardwood. Put it in the hole and fill it with concrete. Using a hardwood bit drill three holes through the broken and the new post. Then bolt them together with coach bolts.

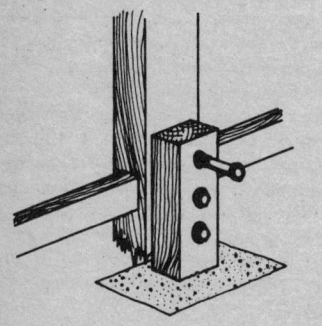

Ferrules. If you'd like to add something attractive to the short, plain, round legs on some of your furniture pieces, try providing each leg with a thread "ferrule" at the bottom. Thread, such as used on fishing poles, is ideal and comes in many fetching colors. Wind it tightly and closely, and then coat it with some clear shellac or lacquer.

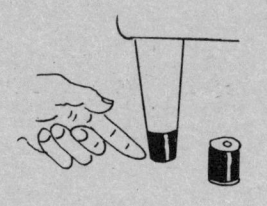

Fertilizer, see GARDENING.

Fiberglass, see FIBERS, MAN-MADE.

Fiber Rugs, see RUGS.

Fibers, Man-Made.
Acetate. Although acetate is made from cellulose, it is considered a man-made fiber because in production the cellulose is changed by chemical means. It is closely related to rayon; in fact, it was called acetate-rayon until a 1952 Federal Trade Commission ruling separated the two fiber groups into "acetate" and "rayon."

Acetate is produced in both filament and spun yarns, and combines well with a large number of other fibers. Its luster, silkiness, body, good draping qualities, and crisp "hand" have made fashion fabrics such as bengaline, taffeta, satin, faille, crepe, brocade, double knit and tricot the major uses of acetate.

Solution-dyed or spun-dyed acetate has excellent colorfastness to light, perspiration, atmospheric contaminants, and washing.

PROPERTIES

appearance (silk-like)	
dimensional stability (if dry cleaned)	
drapability	good to excellent
hand (crisp or soft)	
resistance to: mildew moths	

absorbency
colorfastness
pressed-in crease
   retention
resistance to:
   abrasion
   wrinkling
strength, dry and wet
washability
wash-and-wear qualities
} fair to poor

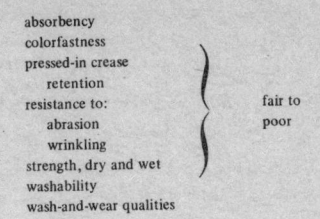

Acetate ignites readily and is not self-extinguishing, but it can be made flame resistant, with some loss of other properties. Effect of heat: sticks at 375-400° F, softens at 460-490° F, and melts at 500° F

CARE
Acetate can be:

hand laundered, in some constructions, using warm water and gentle agitation. Garments should not be soaked, wrung out, or twisted.

dry cleaned.

ironed with a cool iron: acetate fibers melt at high temperature. A safe ironing temperature is 250-300° F.

Garments made of acetate should be protected from nail polish, paint remover, and some perfumes since these substances dissolve the fibers.

USES
apparel
home furnishings
linings
tricot-bonded fabrics

Acrylic. Wool-like qualities and easy care are acrylic's major contributions to textiles. Although acrylic fibers can be made into crisp fabrics, they are associated mainly with the soft, high bulk, textured yarns used in sweaters and fur-like fabrics.

In comparison to wool, acrylic fabrics are stronger, easier to care for, softer, do not felt, and provide more warmth for less weight. The versatility of this fiber is illustrated by the fact that while it is more durable than rayon or acetate, it can be made to perform more like wool than can nylon or polyester.

Acrylic is not harmed by the common solvents and is resistant to weathering, bleaches, and dilute acids and alkalis. Because of these qualities, its use—alone or in blends—ranges from fine fabrics to work clothing and chemical-resistant fabrics.

FIBERS, MAN-MADE

PROPERTIES
colorfastness
dimensional stability
hand (wool-like)
moth and mildew
   resistance
pressed-in crease
   retention
resiliency
sunlight resistance
warmth
wash-and-wear qualities
wrinkle resistance
} good to excellent

abrasion resistance
pilling resistance
strength
} fair to poor

Acrylic ignites and burns readily. Effect of heat: sticks at 420-490° F. Acrylic can be heat set (pleats and creases), has low absorbency, and is subject to static buildup.

CARE
Acrylic can be:

machine washed and tumble dried at low temperatures.

dry cleaned.

ironed. A safe ironing temperature is 300-325° F.

bleached with either chlorine or peroxide bleaches.

USES
apparel (a major use is in sweaters)
blankets
carpets
fleece and fur-like fabrics
home furnishings
work clothing

Anidex is the newest of the elastic fibers. Its exceptional resistance to chemicals, sunlight and heat, excellent "hand," and ease-of-care properties make it possible to combine anidex successfully in blends with both natural and man-made fibers. For example, wool, cotton, linen, nylon, or silk may be blended with anidex without changing the natural look and feel of the basic fabric.

A major application of these fabric blends is in woven and knit fabrics where anidex contributes properties of stretch and recovery. In apparel, the blend fabric permits freedom of body movement while reducing or eliminating sagging or bagging. When used in upholstered furniture, anidex blends provide greater freedom of design because the fabric can stretch to conform to the contours of the furniture.

FIBERS, MAN-MADE

PROPERTIES
flexlife
resistance to:
  aging
  body oils
  chlorine bleaches
  cosmetic lotions
  drycleaning solvents
  heat } excellent
  household detergents
  light
  normal atmospheric fumes

holding power
strength } moderate

Anidex fibers retain their color and physical properties with age unless exposed to temperatures above 325° F for long periods of time.

Anidex does not ignite readily but will burn when ignited. Since anidex is usually 5 to 10 percent by weight of the fabric being considered, its flammability and heat effects are largely dependent on the fibers with which it is combined.

CARE
Anidex can be:
machine washed and tumble dried at "normal" settings.

bleached with chlorine bleaches (recommended by fiber manufacturer).

pressed at temperatures up to 350° F if in the core-spun form. (Recommended safe ironing temperature, 320° F.)

USES
hosiery
knit and woven outerwear
lingerie
stretch fabrics
upholstery fabrics, knit and woven

Fiberglass Repair. To repair holes in fiberglass fabrics, darn with some fiberglass yarn, or sew on a patch of matching fabric with cotton thread. Patches can also be glued to the fabric, but you must use methyl methacrylate "invisible" glue.

Glass fibers have many properties which make them particularly suitable for industrial and home furnishing products; however, because of their heavy weight, low abrasion resistance, and poor bending strength they are not suitable for apparel textiles.

In batting form, glass fibers provide excellent insulation. Fabrics made from glass fibers are used as reinforcement for molded plastics in boats and planes, and for curtains and draperies where fire resistance and easy care are important.

The most important recent advance in the glass fiber industry has been the development of ultra-fine, continuous filament "Beta" yarns. These yarns are stronger than regular glass yarns, and can be bent in a sharper angle without breaking. They are soft and pleasant to the touch, yet durable.

PROPERTIES
Colorfastness
dimensional stability
resistance to:
  chemicals
  heat
  mildew } good to excellent
  moths
  sunlight
  weather
  wrinkling
strength

resistance to abrasion
(except for the new
continuous filament } fair to poor
yarns)

Glass fibers are non-absorbent and naturally non-flammable except when they are treated with flammable resinous finishing materials.

CARE
Glass fiber cloth can be:

machine washed if agitated gently, but hand washing is safer. It should not be spin dried, twisted, or wrung out. No ironing necessary. If machine washed, rinse out washer thoroughly before loading with apparel.

drip dried until most of the moisture is removed, then hung on rods to complete drying.

Dry cleaning is not recommended. Draperies should be hung so that they do not touch the floor or the window sill.

USES
curtains
draperies

Metallic as defined by the Federal Trade Commission, is any manufactured fiber composed of metal, plastic-coated metal, metal-coated plastic, or a core completely covered by metal.

The history of pure metal yarns goes back for thousands of years, but their uses were restricted because they were heavy, brittle, expensive, and easily tarnished. New processes, developed to overcome these characteristics, generally consist of covering metallic threads with plastic, or the use of heat or adhesives to bond thin layers of metal foil between two sheets of plastic film.

These lustrous yarns are finding increasing use in many types of apparel and household furnishings, and in some industrial fabrics.

PROPERTIES

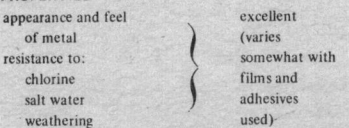

appearance and feel of metal	excellent (varies
resistance to:	somewhat with
chlorine	films and
salt water	adhesives
weathering	used)

Metallic yarns and fabrics are non-absorbent and non-tarnishing. They are extremely sensitive to heat because their plastic components cause them to soften and shrink.

CARE

Metallic fabrics can be:

washed, when the amount of metallic yarns is small, the other fibers present in the fabric, and the construction of the garment permit.

cleaned, generally when used as a decoration for another material, by the same methods used for the base material.

ironed at a temperature low enough to keep the plastic coating from melting (a "cool" iron unless otherwise specified by the manufacturer).

Read hang tags and labels for specific care instructions.

USES
apparel
braid
decorations
home furnishings
hosiery

Modacrylic as its name indicates, is modified acrylic fiber. It possesses many properties in common with acrylic. The heat sensitivity of modacrylic fibers permits them to be stretched, embossed and molded into special shapes, and to be used in fabrics or fabric blends which require no ironing.

Dense, fur-like fabrics are also possible because of its heat-sensitivity. The fibers may be produced with different heat shrinkage capacities. When such fibers are combined in the surface of a pile fabric and heat is applied, the fibers shrink to different lengths forming a surface pile which resembles the hair and undercoat fibers of natural fur.

Since modacrylic fibers are self-extinguishing, they are often blended with other fibers to reduce the flammability of carpets and other textile items.

PROPERTIES

colorfastness	
resiliency	
resistance to:	
chemicals	
moths and mildew	good to
sunlight	excellent
wrinkling	
softness	
warmth	
wash-and-wear qualities	

dimensional stability	
resistance to:	
abrasion	fair to
pilling	poor
strength	

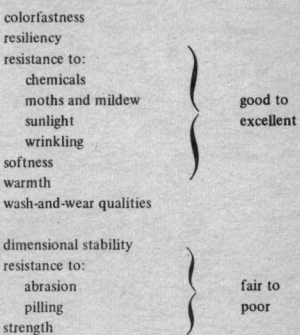

Modacrylics are flame resistant and generally self-extinguishing. Effect of heat: soften at comparatively low temperatures, shrink at 260° F, stiffen and discolor when exposed to pressure and temperatures above 300° F.

CARE

Modacrylics can be:

machine washed in warm water and tumble dried at low temperatures. Remove article from machine as soon as tumble cycle stops.

ironed, if necessary. Safe ironing temperature: 200-250° F.

dry cleaned. The fur cleaning process is recommended for deep pile fabrics.

USES
blankets
carpets
dolls' hair
draperies
fur-like pile fabrics
knitwear
wigs

Nylon the strongest of all man-made fibers in common use, was the first truly synthetic fiber to be developed. Since 1939, when nylon was first introduced in women's hosiery, many different forms have come on the market.

Nylon's outstanding characteristic is its versatility. It can be made strong enough to stand up under the punishment tire cords must endure, fine enough for sheer, high fashion hosiery, and light enough for parachute cloth and backpacker's tents. Nylon is used alone and in blends with other fibers

FIBERS, MAN-MADE

where its chief contributions are strength and abrasion resistance. (i.e. degree of resistance to surface wear by rubbing)

Nylon washes easily, dries quickly, needs little pressing and holds its shape well since it neither shrinks nor stretches.

PROPERTIES
colorfastness
dimensional stability
elasticity
resiliency
resistance to:
   abrasion
   mildew
   moths
   perspiration
strength
} good to excellent

absorbency
resistance to:
   pilling
   sunlight
   wrinkling
} fair to poor

Nylon can be heat set (pleats and creases). It is not readily ignited but when ignited, particularly in combination with other fibers, it burns, melts, and drips. Effect of heat: yellows and creases slightly at 300° F after five hours exposure, and melts or sticks at 420-500° F depending on the type of nylon.

CARE
Nylon can be:

machine washed and tumble dried at low temperature.

bleached with chlorine bleach.

ironed. A safe ironing temperature 300-375°F, (depending on type).

USES
apparel home furnishings
hosiery
household textile products
rugs and carpets
stretch fabrics
tents
textured yarns

Olefin. The olefin fibers, polyethylene and polypropylene, are petroleum products which are derived from ethylene and propylene gases. They have the lightest weight of all fibers, are non-absorbent and difficult to dye.

The shortcomings of these fibers, namely their sensitivity to light and to heat, and their difficulty in dyeing, have been largely overcome by the use of heat and light stabilizers, and by solution dyeing. More recently, the modification of fiber structure has made it possible to dye olefin by the use of standard techniques.

In general, the properties of polyethylene (first of the olefins) and polypropylene are similar. It is doubtful that you will find polyethylene in apparel products. Polypropylene, however, is used in a variety of textile products, including apparel.

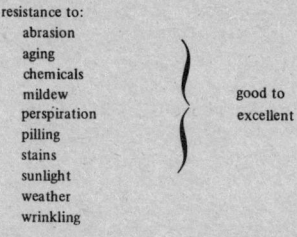

PROPERTIES
resistance to:
   abrasion
   aging
   chemicals
   mildew
   perspiration
   pilling
   stains
   sunlight
   weather
   wrinkling
} good to excellent

absorbency
dyeability
} fair to poor

Olefin is very light in weight and provides better thermal insulation than wool. Olefins which have been given a wash-resistant, anti-oxidant treatment do not ignite readily but, once ignited, they burn, melt and drip. Effect of heat: polypropylene softens at 285-300° F, melts at 320-350° F, and shrinks at temperatures above 212° F; polyethylene is more heat sensitive. It shrinks at temperatures above 225° F, and melts at 230-250° F, depending upon fiber type.

CARE
Olefins can be:

machine washed in lukewarm water.

tumble dried at low temperatures EXCEPT when the fiber is used as the batting or filler in quilted pads and other items and is not treated with a wash-resistant anti-oxidant by the manufacturer. In these forms, the heat from the dryer builds up in the fiber filling and cannot escape. Under these conditions, the temperature may reach the kindling point of the fiber, resulting in fire.

bleached at low water temperatures (below 150° F).

drycleaned.

Articles made of 100 percent olefin cannot be ironed, but blends may be ironed at low temperatures (250° F or lower).

USES
apparel
blankets
floor coverings (including indoor-outdoor carpets)
household textile products
nonwoven products
upholstery

Polyester. With the advent of the polyester fiber, the centuries old dream of "wash-and-wear" ("easy-care") clothing became a reality. Polyester does not shrink or stretch appreciably during normal use. Heat-set pleats and creases stand up extremely well under everyday wear, even when the wearer is very young and very active. Water-borne stains may be quickly and simply removed.

Because of polyester's outstanding wrinkle resistance and dimensional stability, it is used extensively in blends with other fibers, notably with cotton, rayon and wool. The combination produces a fabric which retains the major characteristics of the base fiber, with the added benefits of increased strength and improved crease retention. Currently, a major use of polyester is in cotton blends used in durable-press textiles.

PROPERTIES
colorfastness
dimensional stability
pressed-in crease
   retention
resiliency
resistance to:
   abrasion
   mildew } good to excellent
   moths
   perspiration
   sunlight
   wrinkling
strength
wash-and-wear qualities

absorbency
resistance to:
   oily stains } fair to poor
   pilling (spun yarns)

Polyester can be heat set (pleats and creases). It does not ignite readily, but when ignited, it burns, melts and drips. In blends, particularly with cellulosic fibers, it burns readily. Effect of heat: sticks at temperatures above 445° F, and melts above 480° F, the exact temperature depending on the type of polyester.

CARE
Polyester can be:
machine washed and tumble dried. Articles containing fiberfill may also be machine washed and dried, depending on the cover fabric.
bleached with chlorine bleaches.
ironed. Safe ironing temperature: 300-350° F.
dry cleaned.

USES
apparel,
   including durable-press (permanent-press).
carpets
curtains
fiberfill for pillows, sleeping bags, ski jackets, cushions
home furnishings
thread: filament, spun and core-spun

Rayon was the first of the man-made fibers. Although made from cellulose, the raw materials are converted chemically and then regenerated into cellulose fibers. The two main types of rayon, *viscose* and *cuprammonium*, differ in the way the cellulose is processed and regenerated, but their properties are similar. The cuprammonium process favors yarns of finer diameter used mainly in sheer and semi-sheer fabrics. In recent years several "new" rayons have been developed to overcome some of the limitations of the regular viscose and cuprammonium rayons. The major distinctive feature of these new fibers is greater strength, particularly when wet.

Rayon is one of the least expensive "man-made" fibers, and since it combines well with practically all other fibers, it is used extensively in blends. It has advantages of comfort, efficiency and lustre.

PROPERTIES
absorbency
colorfastness to:
   dry cleaning
   perspiration
   sunlight } good to excellent
   washing
drapability
dyeability
hand and appearance

dimensional stability
resiliency
resistance to:
   abrasion
   mildew } fair to poor
   wrinkling
wash-and-wear qualities
wet strength

FIBERS, MAN-MADE

Rayon ignites readily and is not self-extinguishing, but it can be made flame resistant. Effect of heat: decomposes after prolonged exposure at 300-400° F, depending on fiber type.

CARE

Rayon can be:

washed by hand with lukewarm water, unless manufacturers specify otherwise. Squeeze gently, do not wring or twist.

machine washed and tumble dried.

bleached with chlorine bleach, unless resin finished. Some resin finishes used on rayon discolor in the presence of chlorine bleach.

ironed with a moderate iron. Safe ironing temperature: 300-350° F. Rayon will scorch, but not melt if the iron is too hot.

dry cleaned.

USES

apparel
home furnishings
household textile products
linings
rugs and carpets

Rubber. Natural rubber comes from the latex of certain plants, while man-made rubber is a chemical compound produced from petroleum. Both are defined as "rubber" by the Federal Trade Commission. Rubber fibers are generally used as a core around which other fibers are wrapped to protect the rubber from abrasion. Rubber core yarns are used where stretch or elasticity is required. Either natural or man-made fibers may be used in manufacturing rubber yarns.

Man-made rubber, sometimes called "elastomer," is a synthetic rubber compound which has the physical properties of natural rubber such as high stretchability and recovery. Man-made rubber (see anidex and spandex) can be stretched repeatedly to at least twice its length, yet when the force is removed it will snap back to approximately its original length.

NATURAL RUBBER PROPERTIES

elongation	}	high
elasticity holding power	}	good

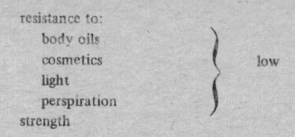

resistance to:
body oils
cosmetics } low
light
perspiration
strength

Rubber does not ignite readily but when ignited, it burns and produces dense smoke. Effect of heat: at 300-400° F, it becomes permanently soft and sticky.

When used in recommended amounts, the effect of bleaches on some rubbers is minimal. When used in high concentrations, however, chlorine will cause some surface embrittlement, and peroxide some surface softening.

CARE

Products made of rubber yarns should be laundered in accordance with the manufacturer's recommendations. If omitted, wash with water at a low temperature. Avoid high concentrations of bleaches, heat, and exposure to sunlight. Do not dry clean or dry in automatic dryers.

USES

elastic webbings, bands, tapes, core threads
elastic fabrics
girdles and other foundation garments
swimwear

Saran has many desirable characteristics, among them: low absorbency, high resiliency, and little reaction to chemicals. However, because of its low resistance to heat, and poor stability, saran's use in apparel fabrics is very limited.

In household and industrial applications, saran is used to produce a variety of products. In multifilament form, it is used for carpet pile, protective clothing, blankets, imitation fur, upholstery, and drapery fabrics. In monofilament form, it is used chiefly in automotive upholstery, curtains, screening, luggage, and outdoor furniture.

Since saran is virtually impervious to weathering, it finds many outdoor uses on the lawn and patio, and in the camp. It is highly resistant to chemicals in the atmosphere.

PROPERTIES

resiliency
resistance to:
abrasion
chemicals
fading
mildew } good to excellent
staining
sunlight
water
weathering

FIBERS, MAN-MADE

absorbency } fair to
resistance to heat } poor
strength
washability

Saran does not support combustion. When combined with flammable fibers, saran acts as a retardant. Effect of heat: softens at temperatures about 212° F and melts at 340° F.

CARE

Saran can be:
washed with soap or detergent.
bleached with chlorine bleach, but the water must be at a temperature of 100° F or below.

USES

awnings
carpets, indoor-outdoor
garden furniture
handbags and luggage
home furnishings
screening
shoes

Spandex is a man-made fiber with great elasticity. Garments containing spandex core-spun yarns retain their holding power better than other garments of similar weight made with covered natural rubber yarns. Foundation garments containing spandex are usually soft, and provide great freedom of movement.

Currently, however, few garments are made of 100 percent spandex, since only a small amount of spandex is required to provide the desired holding power and superior recovery characteristics.

In home sewing on spandex fabrics, there is little danger of damage from "needle cutting." This feature eliminates one of the problems the housewife encounters when she makes her own foundation garments and swim suits.

PROPERTIES

elasticity
resistance to: } excellent
  cosmetic lotions
  and body oils
  flexing
  sunlight

Spandex yellows with age and at temperatures above 300° F. It does not ignite readily, but when ignited, it melts and burns. Effect of heat: it has dimensional stability at 300° F, sticks at 345-450° F, depending on fiber type, and melts at 445-590° F, also depending on fiber type.

CARE

Spandex can be:
machine washed and tumble dried at low temperatures.
bleached, except with chlorine bleaches.
ironed, if necessary. Safe ironing temperature: below 300° F; but iron quickly, and do not leave the iron in the same position too long.
dry cleaned.

USES

apparel
elastic waist bands
form persuasive garments
foundation garments
surgical hose

Stain Removal, see STAIN REMOVAL.

Triacetate. Chemically, triacetate is quite similar to, and has many properties in common with, acetate: lower strength when wet and low resistance to abrasion, but excellent appearance, drapability and resistance to moths and mildew.

Triacetate's chief difference and most valuable characteristic is resistance to damage by heat. This property permits the heatsetting treatments which are responsible for triacetate fabrics' outstanding features of durable crease and pleat retention, dimensional stability, and resistance to glazing during ironing.

Also, because triacetate is comparatively insensitive to high temperature, it can be made into products which launder easily, dry quickly, and require very little special care.

PROPERTIES

appearance
dimensional stability
drapability
hand } good to
resistance to: } excellent
  heat
  wrinkling
wash-and-wear qualities

absorbency } fair to
resistance to abrasion } poor
strength

Triacetate ignites readily and is not self-extinguishing, but can be made flame resistant with some loss of other properties. Effect of heat: melts at 572° F, but will not stick at 560° F.

FIBERS, MAN-MADE

CARE
Triacetate can be:

machine washed and tumble dried.

ironed, if necessary, with a hot iron.

A safe ironing temperature is 450°F.

USES
bonded and tricot fabrics
knits
permanently pleated garments
sportswear

Vinyon is a limited-use fiber. Because of its low strength and high extensibility it is not a good fiber to spin into yarns. However, it may be blended with other fibers in the manufacture of fabrics having a high degree of resistance to chemicals, oils, and some of the solvents.

Because of its low strength and extreme sensitivity to heat, the principal use of vinyon is a binder agent which softens, shrinks and bonds to other fibers under pressure and in the presence of heat and appropriate solvents. These unusual properties have led to the extensive use of vinyon in the manufacture of embossed carpets, pressed felts, bonded fabrics, and rubber-coated elastic fabrics. Some of the more interesting non-woven fabrics owe their existence to vinyon.

PROPERTIES
elasticity
resistance to:
   alcohols
   bacteria
   chemicals
   fungi   } excellent
   gasoline
   mildew
   moisture
   moths
   water

resistance to:
   heat   } poor

Vinyon does not support combustion. Effect of heat: shrinks when heated above 150° F, becomes tacky at 185-215° F, and melts around 260° F.

CARE
Vinyon can be:

washed in warm water with a mild detergent and drip dried. Do not tumble dry or iron.

USES
bonding agent in nonwoven textiles
embossed carpets
pressed felts
shower curtains
waterproof clothing
work clothes

Wash-and-Wear garments tend to retain their original shape and appearance after repeated wear and laundering, with little or no ironing. "Durable-press" (permanent-press) is considered the ultimate in wash-and-wear. Wash-and-wear performance depends on several factors, including the types and amounts of fibers, fabric structure, finish, construction, and washing and drying methods.

Durable-press finishes are also applied to products such as bed and table linens. Fabrics usually are cotton or rayon blended with polyester, acrylic, acetate or nylon, and may be lightweight and sheer like organdy, or heavy like corduroy.

Correct size is important in durable-press garments because alterations are difficult. Original hem and seam lines cannot be removed by home ironing. A "fishy" odor may indicate a finish which has not been fully cured.

CARE
To get the best service from wash-and-wear:

wash frequently, heavy soil is hard to remove.

pre-treat oily stains before washing by rubbing a small amount of concentrated liquid detergent into the spot. Stains that remain after the first washing will generally be removed after repeated laundering.

garments may be laundered in any of the following ways, except that the manufacturer's labeling instructions should be followed when given:

1. *Preferred method*: machine wash and tumble dry; remove from dryer immediately after dryer stops and put on hangers to avoid wrinkling.

2. machine wash and drip dry; remove items from washing machine before spinning cycle; line dry.

3. hand wash and drip dry; remove from rinse water without wringing or twisting; line dry.

4. *Least preferred method*: machine wash and line dry after spinning: the spinning cycle adds wrinkles that are difficult to remove.

A fabric softener added to the final rinse water will decrease static build-up and aid wrinkle resistance.

Fibers, Natural.

Cotton is a natural cellulose fiber obtained from the boll of the cotton plant. Its quality is dependent on fiber length, fineness, color and lustre. Long cotton fibers can be spun into fine, smooth, lustrous and comparatively strong yarns from which the better quality cotton fabrics are made. The short fibers produce coarser yarns for use in durable fabrics which are less fine, smooth, and lustrous.

Cotton is still the world's major textile fiber, and is used alone or in blends in an infinite variety of apparel, household and industrial products. New finishes have extended cotton's usefulness in the "easy-care" field and in many other applications. Some of the most common are resin finishes used in wash-and-wear, and chemical finishes which make cotton fabrics water repellent or fire retardant.

PROPERTIES

absorbency
color fastness
dyeability
resistance to:
   heat
   moths
   perspiration
softness
strength, wet or dry

} good to excellent

dimensional stability
   (ability to retain size and shape)
pressed-in crease retention
resistance to:
   mildew
   sunlight
   wrinkling
wash-and-wear qualities

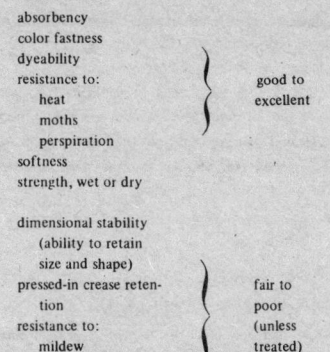

} fair to poor (unless treated)

Cotton ignites readily and is not self-extinguishing, but it can be treated and made flame resistant to some extent, with some loss of durability and aesthetics. Effect of heat: yellows slowly at 245° F.

Resin finishes may improve such qualities as dimensional stability, crease retention and wrinkle resistance.

CARE

Cotton can be:

sterilized.

machine washed and tumble dried.

dry cleaned.

bleached with chlorine or peroxide bleaches, but excessive or prolonged use of bleach may weaken the fabric. Some cotton finishes may cause the fabric to yellow when exposed to chlorine bleach.

ironed (but "easy-care" finishes may not require it.) A safe ironing temperature is 400° F.

Cotton fabrics should be pre-shrunk for home sewing purposes.

USES

apparel
carpets and rugs
home furnishings
household textile products

Linen is produced from the fibrous materials in the stem of the flax plant. These fibers, in a great variety of thicknesses, tend to cling together, giving linen its characteristic "thick-thin" quality. Relative to cotton, linen is expensive due to its limited production and the hand labor still involved in processing it.

The quality of linen is determined by the length and fineness of the fibers and the degree of bleach, if white, or the fastness of the dyes, if colored.

Terms like "silk-linen" can be misleading when they refer to the linen-like appearance rather than the fiber content of the fabric. Labels and hang tags should reveal whether these fabrics are made of pure linen, blends of linen with other fibers, or some other fiber which resembles linen.

PROPERTIES

absorbency
colorfastness
dimensional stability
durability
launderability
resistance to:
   heat
   moths
   perspiration

} good to excellent

pressed-in crease retention
resistance to:
   mildew
   sunlight
   wrinkling

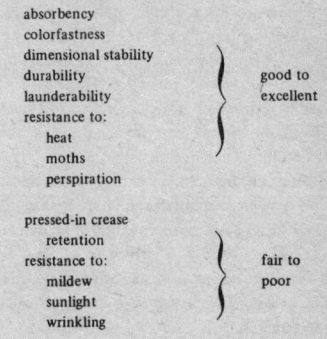

} fair to poor

Linen ignites readily and is not self-extinguishing, but it can be treated to make it flame resistant to some extent with some loss of durability.

Linen does not lint. It has poor resistance to flex abrasion (wear caused by repeated bending and rubbing), and

FIBERS, NATURAL

may crack or show wear along the seams and edges where fibers are bent.

CARE
Linen can be:

machine washed and tumble dried.

dry cleaned.

bleached if white, (although bleaching tends to weaken linen fibers).

ironed, with best results when damp.

A safe ironing temperature is 400° F. Lustre (sheen) can be increased by ironing on the right side of fabric when it is damp. Creases should not be pressed in, and table linens should be rolled on cardboard rollers rather than folded, since sharp angles may cause linen fibers to break.

USES
apparel
handkerchiefs
home furnishings
table linens
towels

Rubber, see FIBERS, MAN-MADE.

Silk the only natural continuous filament fiber, is obtained by unreeling the cocoon of the silkworm. Used alone, "silk" refers to a *cultivated* silk from carefully tended silk worms. *Raw* silk contains the gum which bound the fibers to the cocoon. *Wild* or *Tussah* silk comes from uncultivated silk worms. Uneven in texture and tan in color, it cannot be bleached. *Duppioni* silk comes from two or more cocoons that were joined together. These "thick-thin" filaments are used in making shantung. *Spun* silk is made from pierced cocoons or *waste* silk, the tangled fibers on the outside of the cocoon.

Silk, pure silk, all silk, or pure dye silk must contain no metallic weightings and no more than 10 percent by weight of dyes or finishing materials (black silk, 15 percent). Weighted silk contains metallic salts; labels must indicate the percentage of weighting. It may be cheaper and more drapable but less serviceable.

Silk does not ignite readily, but materials added to silk to change its color or other properties may in some instances create a flammability hazard.

Silk is weakened by sunlight and perspiration; yellowed by strong soap, age and sunlight.

PROPERTIES
absorbency
colorfastness
dimensional stability
drapability   } good to
dyeability   } excellent
hand and appearance
strength, dry
wrinkle resistance

pressed-in crease
  retention
resistance to:
  aging   } fair to
  abrasion   } poor
  heat
  perspiration
  sunlight
strength, wet

CARE
Silk can be:

hand laundered, though certain dyes "bleed" color when washed.

dry cleaned.

ironed with a warm iron. A safe ironing temperature is 250-275° F.

White silk can be bleached with hydrogen peroxide or sodium perborate bleaches, but chlorine bleaches should not be used.

USES
apparel
home furnishings

Stain Removal, see STAIN REMOVAL.

Wool fibers are obtained from the fleece of the sheep or lamb, or from the hair of the **Angora** or **Cashmere** goat, the camel, vicuna, alpaca or llama. Silky Angora hair is called "mohair."

Wool, new wool, or virgin wool is made of fibers that have never been used or reclaimed. It is usually stronger and more resilient. Reprocessed wool fibers have been reclaimed from unused wool products (mill end pieces, for example). Reused wool fibers have been reclaimed from used textile products.

Woolen fabrics are made from wool yarns containing both long and short fibers. Woolen fabrics are soft, resist wrinkling, but do not hold a sharp crease. Worsted yarns, made from the longer fibers, are firm and smooth. Worsted fabrics are more durable. They tailor well, take a sharp crease, but may become shiny with use.

PROPERTIES	
absorbency	
colorfastness	
dyeability	
pressed-in crease retention (worsted)	
resiliency	good to excellent
shape retention	
sunlight resistance	
warmth	
wrinkle recovery	
wrinkle resistance	
pilling resistance to:	
bleaches	
friction	fair to poor
moths	
perspiration	
strong soaps	
wash-and-wear qualities	
water repellancy	

Wool, in some constructions, is not readily ignited and is self-extinguishing. Effect of heat: becomes harsh at 212° F, scorches at 400° F, and chars at about 572° F. Wool may be allergenic.

CARE

Wool can be:

laundered, but only with extreme care using cool water, mild detergent, and gentle action. Never rub. Felting occurs when wool is subjected to heat, moisture, and mechanical action. Laundered garments should be dried on a flat surface, or spread over two or three lines to distribute weight. Wool products should be handled carefully when they are damp or wet.

dry cleaned.

pressed with a cool iron and steam.

Hanging garments over a bathtub filled with hot water will sometimes remove wrinkles.

Garments should be brushed after wearing, and allowed to rest 24 hours before they are worn again. Wool absorbs odors, so garments should be hung where air can circulate around them. Wool articles should be moth-proofed before storing.

USES
apparel
blankets
carpets

Files, see TOOLS, HAND.

File, Wall. The long coil spring from a discarded windowshade roller can be converted into a very handy wall holder for letters, memos, bills, recipes, and the like. Shape the eyes on the ends of the spring and attach it under a slight tension to a strip of wood with small nails. Then screw the whole thing to a wall in a handy location.

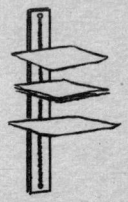

Film Hangers. For the home photography enthusiast, a single saw cut will transform the common variety of spring wooden clothespin into an efficient hanger for drying his films. These slotted hangers have a great advantage in that they cause the films to hang parallel to one another.

Fingernail Brush. A fingernail brush can be made from an old toothbrush, the bristles being stiffened by cutting them down to about one-fourth inch in length. If your fingernails are particularly grimy, dig them into a bar of soap several times before scrubbing them.

Fingernail File. For cleaning the grit from a fingernail file, a piece of adhesive tape does the trick nicely. Simply press the tape firmly over the teeth of the file, then when you pull it loose the grit and dirt will come out, too.

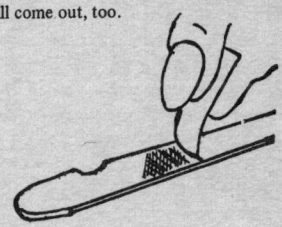

Fingernail Polish, see NAIL POLISH.

Finger Paint. You can prepare some finger paints for your children very easily just by boiling some

FINISHING NAILS

laundry starch and a few soap chips to a paste, tinting it with food coloring, and adding a small quantity of glycerin to keep the mixture moist and workable. Place each color in a separate bowl for your young artists.

Finishing Nails, see NAILS.

Firebrick, see BRICKS.

Fire.

Electrical Fire Prevention, see ELECTRICAL SAFETY TIPS.

Emergency Preparedness. Pre-planning before an emergency occurs is very important, whether you live in a house or an apartment. Make sure your family knows the quickest and safest way to escape from every room. Keep a flashlight in all rooms to help escape at night (check the batteries from time to time to see that they will be in working order should you need them). Make sure your children can open doors, windows and screens to escape routes. Teach them how to use a phone to report a fire if they are trapped. (Emergency numbers should be available at each phone.) If they can get out, they should know where the nearest alarm box is.

Extinguishers. Water may be the handiest and most effective extinguisher. Do not use water on electric, gasoline, and oil fires. Electricity may travel up a stream of water to injure you. Gasoline and oil, being lighter than water, will float and continue to burn.

Every house should have one or more fire extinguishers of approved types.

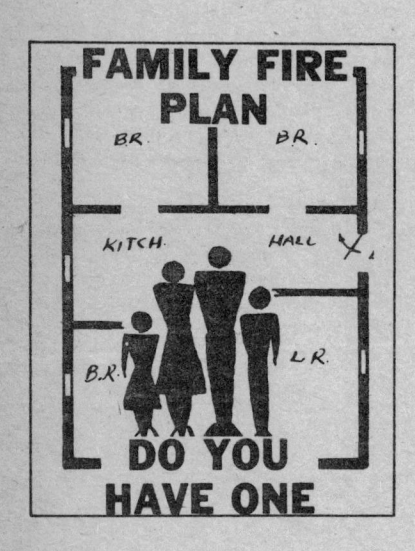

FIRE EXTINGUISHERS

TYPE OF EXTINGUISHER	FOR WHAT KINDS OF FIRE	CONTENTS	HOW TO START	RANGE AND DURATION
SODA-ACID	CLASS A (Wood, paper, textiles, etc.)	Water solution of bicarbonate of soda and sulfuric acid.	Turn over	30 to 40 feet 50 to 55 seconds (2½ gallon size)
PUMP TANK		Plain water	Pump by hand	●
GAS CARTRIDGE	CLASS A ("Loaded stream" model is also good on Class B)	Water and cartridge of carbon dioxide	Turn over and bump	● DANGER: Do not use these water base extinguishers on electrical fires.
FOAM	CLASS A and CLASS B (Oil, gasoline, paint, grease, etc.)	Water solution of aluminum sulfate and bicarbonate of soda	Turn over	
CARBON DIOXIDE	CLASS B and CLASS C (Live electrical equipment) ● NOTE: If nothing else is available, these extinguishers may have some effect on small Class A fires.	Carbon dioxide	Pull pin and open valve	6 to 8 feet about 42 seconds (15 lb. size)
VAPORIZING LIQUID		Carbon tetrachloride and other chemicals. CAUTION: Avoid breathing vapors from extinguisher, especially in small, closed places.	Turn handle, then pump by hand	20 to 30 feet 40 to 45 seconds (1 quart size)
DRY CHEMICAL		Bicarbonate of soda with other dry chemicals and cartridge of carbon dioxide	Pull pin and open valve (or press lever), then squeeze nozzle valve	About 14 feet 22 to 25 seconds (30 lb. size)

FIRE

In Case of fire. If a fire should break out, do the following:

1. Collect your thoughts. Keep your mind on what you are doing. Act quickly. Don't underestimate how fast a small fire can spread. If you cannot cope with it, get out fast.

2. Once you are safely out, notify the fire department or have someone else do this. *Don't go back in.*

3. Summon help if anyone is within sound of your voice.

4. If the blaze is small and you think you can put it out by devices which are available, either

   (a) use a suitable fire extinguisher, or

   (b) use a *woolen* blanket or rug to smother the fire. (Be sure to use woolen items, as many of today's synthetics will ignite readily.) Keep the air from the fire; or

   (c) throw water from a garden hose on the fire if such a hose is available. If it is not, throw water from a pail using a dipper or a broom. *Do not use water on an oil or grease fire*; use sand or earth from flower pots, or baking soda. Water, especially in small amounts, will cause spattering of burning grease.

   (d) Beat down any draperies, curtains, or light materials causing the blaze, using a wet broom or a long pole. Using the bare hands may result in serious burns.

5. Tie a wet towel or any other material (preferably of wool) over the mouth and nose if you are fighting the fire and are exposed to smoke or flames. More people lose their lives by smoke inhalation and/or suffocation than through burning.

6. Place yourself so that you can retreat in the direction of a safe exit without passing through the burning area. Unless you can do something worthwhile, get out of the building fast.

7. If necessary to go through a room full of smoke, keep close to the floor and crawl on the hands and knees, having covered the mouth and nose with a wet cloth. Take short breaths, through your nose. The drafts and currents cause the smoke to rise and the air nearest the floor is usually the purest.

8. If you find smoke in an open stairway or open hall, use another preplanned way out.

9. Head for stairs, not the elevator. A bad fire can cut off the power to elevators. Close all doors behind you.

Prevention. Repair defective chimneys, spark arresters, flues, stovepipes, and heating and cooking equipment.

Store gasoline and other flammables in approved containers and locations.

Remove fire hazards from storage areas.

Be sure electric wiring is safe and adequate ... electric circuits are fused properly ... electric equipment is in good repair.

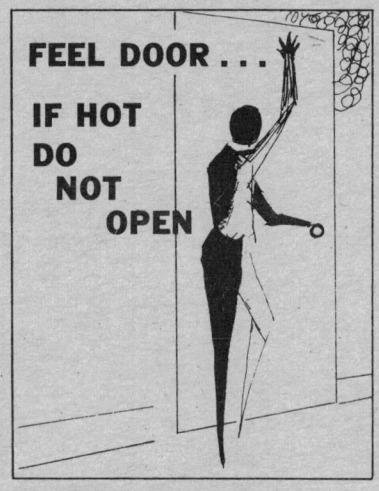

FEEL DOOR ... IF HOT DO NOT OPEN

Close Door IT WILL SLOW SPREAD OF FIRE

FIRE

USE STAIRS NOT ELEVATOR which may stop and trap you

IF TRAPPED OPEN WINDOW at bottom to breathe and at top to let heat and smoke out

WALK QUICKLY DON'T PANIC

TO TRAVEL THROUGH SMOKE KEEP LOW THE AIR IS COOLER

Plan a Meeting Place **OUTSIDE**

DON'T GO BACK FOR YOUR THINGS

SEND THE ALARM

Alert Others — FIRE

DIAL "O"perator

Give Exact Location

PULL HANDLE then Wait to Direct Firefighters

FIRE, OPEN

See that lightning rods are properly grounded. Use properly grounded arresters on radio and television antennas.

Keep matches and chemicals away from children. Have fire-fighting equipment ready.

Fire, Open.

Colored Flames. If powdered chemicals are used you can add different colors to the firewood in your wood-burning fireplace. Copper chloride produces a bluish-green flame; barium nitrate an apple-green flame; calcium chloride an orange flame; sodium chlorate or potassium nitrate a yellow flame; and lithium chloride a purple flame. Tie about a half-ounce of your favorite color of the chemicals in a cellophane bag and toss onto the logs in your fireplace.

Kindling. Here's one efficient way to build up the kindling supply for your wood-burning fireplace. Instead of throwing away the wood shavings and scraps you accumulate in your workshop, save them in paper bags, tie the necks of the bags securely, and stack them neatly near your fireplace. These will make fine kindling when you build your fires.

Starting.

1. One easy method of starting a fire in your woodburning fireplace is with a brick that has been soaked in kerosene. Keep a bucket of kerosene tightly covered somewhere out of children's reach outside, and soak common building bricks in this. When you want to kindle a fire, lay a kerosene-impregnated brick in the grate, pile fuel on it, and light a match. The brick will burn for thirty to forty minutes and save kindling wood.

2. You can start a fire in your fireplace easily by letting some tallow drip from a candle over the kindling. This gimmick works even in the case of damp kindling.

Fireplace.

Andirons, see ANDIRONS.
Brick Care.

1. A brick fireplace is easier to keep clean if its front is coated with liquid wax. The wax gives the bricks a slight gloss and a comparatively smooth finish, filling the porous surface in which dust usually accumulates. In this way, soot and dust are less likely to collect and any that does can be wiped off quickly. A small brush is a handy applicator.

2. If you burn pine wood in your fireplace and want to prevent the gum from collecting on the stones, bricks, or tiles, coat them (after they are thoroughly clean) with boiled linseed oil.

3. Boiled linseed oil does a good job of restoring red fireplace bricks to their original color. After washing the bricks, allow them to dry thoroughly, then apply the oil with a paintbrush. Be sure to use the oil sparingly so that it is absorbed completely.

Cleaning Tips.

1. To clean a stone or brick fireplace, hot water and strong soap, applied with a stiff brush, are often adequate. If they're not, mix up a paste of powdered pumice and concentrated ammonia, and cover the smoked-up areas with this, letting remain for about an hour or so before scrubbing it off with hot water and soap.

2. For the easy cleaning of the sooty bricks around a fireplace, scrub them with a pailful of hot water to which a cup of washing soda has been added.

3. There is no need to scrub the fireplace so often if you throw salt on the logs occasionally. This will reduce the soot by two-thirds.

4. For a good job of cleaning the soot out of a flue, spread a little rock salt in your fireplace when there is a fire burning in it.

5. You can make the job of cleaning out your open fireplace easier if you'll first use a garden sprayer filled with water to moisten the soot that has accumulated. Then scoop this out into a paper bag, and finish cleaning with a vacuum cleaner. If you burn a few zinc jar lids or a handful of salt in your fireplace occasionally, less soot will gather in the chimney.

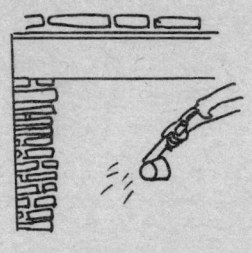

6. If you'll keep some newspaper burning in a back corner of your fireplace while you are removing the ashes, the cloud of dust you raise will be drawn up the chimney in the draft created by the flames, instead of being blown all over the room.

Construction. Proper construction of fireplaces is essential for safe, efficient operation. Therefore, it is recommended that they be designed and built by persons experienced in that type of work.

The homeowner should have a working knowledge of fireplace construction so that he can assist in the designing, follow the work closely, and properly inspect and maintain the completed unit.

Damper. With a well-designed, properly installed damper, you can —

1. Regulate the draft.

2. Close the flue to prevent loss of heat from the room when there is no fire in the fireplace.

3. Adjust the throat opening according to the type of fire to reduce loss of heat. For example, a roaring pine fire may require a full throat opening, but a slow-burning hardwood log fire may require an opening of only 1 or 2 inches. Closing the damper to that opening will reduce loss of heat up the chimney.

4. Close or partially close the flue to prevent loss of heat from the main heating system. When air heated by a furnace goes up a chimney, an excessive amount of fuel may be wasted.

5. Close the flue in the summer to prevent insects from entering the house through the chimney.

Flue. Proper proportion between the size (area) of the fireplace opening, size (area) of the flue, and height of the flue is essential for satisfactory operation of the fireplace.

Function. Fireplaces are not an economical means of heating. And tests indicate that, as ordinarily constructed, they are only about one-third as efficient as a good stove or circulator heater.

However, a well-designed, properly built fireplace can —

Provide additional heat.

Provide all the heat necessary in mild climates.

Enhance the appearance and comfort of the room.

Burn as fuel certain combustible materials that otherwise might be wasted—for example, coke, briquets, and scrap lumber.

Hearth Repair. If some of the mortar joints in the hearth of your fireplace have cracked, chip out the bad mortar and blow out all the crumbs. Then wet the edges of the bricks or stones and pack in some fire clay (available from a building supply dealer) or mortar made of one part cement, one part lime, and six parts of sand.

Location of the fireplace within a room will depend on the location of the existing chimney or the best location from the standpoint of safe construction for the proposed chimney. A fireplace should not be located near doors.

Modified, see HEATING.

New Brick, Cleaning. The new brick fireplace in the brand new home is often in need of cleaning, and a solution of muriatic acid will aid considerably in loosening any mortar that has spilled onto the bricks. Use a solution of 1 part muriatic acid to 4 or 6 parts of water, and be very careful of your hands and clothing while handling this acid. Mix it in a wooden, glass, or earthenware container. This solution will damage metal. After scrubbing it on with a

FIREPLACE, OUTDOOR

stiff brush, rinse thoroughly with clear water. The ease or difficulty of cleaning will depend to a large extent on the texture of the brick. Rough-textured material will tend to collect dust, while a smooth-surfaced material will not. A light application of linseed oil, rubbed over the surface, tends to bring out the brick color.

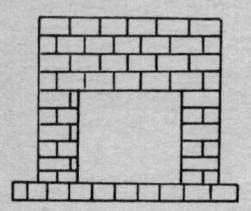

Openings. Fireplace openings are usually made from 2 to 6 feet wide. The kind of fuel to be burned can suggest a practical width. For example, where cordwood (4 feet long) is cut in half, an opening 30 inches wide is desirable; but where coal is burned, a narrower opening can be used.

Height of the opening can range from 24 inches for an opening 2 feet wide to 40 inches for one that is 6 feet wide. The higher the opening, the more chance of a smoky fireplace.

In general, the wider the opening, the greater the depth. A shallow opening throws out relatively more heat than a deep one, but holds smaller pieces of wood. You have the choice, therefore, between a deeper opening that holds larger, longer-burning logs and a shallower one that takes smaller pieces of wood, but throws out more heat. In small fireplaces, a depth of 12 inches may permit good draft, but a minimum depth of 16 inches is recommended to lessen the danger of brands falling out on the floor. Suitable screens should be placed in front of all fireplaces to minimize the danger from brands and sparks.

Second-floor fireplaces are usually made smaller than first-floor ones, because of the reduced flue height.

Outdoor, see BARBECUE.

Prefabricated fireplace and chimney units—all parts needed for a complete fireplace-to-chimney installation—are on the market.

Such units offer these features:
1. Wide selection of styles, shapes, and colors.
2. Pretested design that is highly efficient in operation.
3. Easy and versatile installation — can be installed freestanding or flush against a wall in practically any part of a house.
4. Light in weight.
5. Lower cost than comparable masonry units.

The basic part of the prefabricated fireplace is a specially insulated metal firebox shell. Since it is light in weight, it can be set directly on the floor without the heavy footing required for masonry fireplaces.

Smoking. If your fireplace begins to smoke or puff out into the room, it is possible that you are building your fire too near the front of the opening, instead of against the back. Stubborn smoking may be checked by blocking off part of the opening to increase the draft. Experiment with a board by holding it across the top of the opening (as in the illustration). Lower it until the smoke draws properly. Then build (or have built) a metal hood or a masonry fill-in to that level.

Smoky. Fallen bricks in the chimney blocking the flue, loose mortar joints, or nearby trees or tall structures causing eddies down the flue may cause a smoky fireplace.

An undersized flue may also cause a smoky fireplace. Installation of a metal hood across the top of the fireplace opening so as to reduce the area of the opening may eliminate the smoking.

Fireplace, Outdoor, see BARBECUE.

Fish, see FOODS.

Fishhook Storage. To keep fishhooks from rusting when not in use, stick them in a cork and store the cork in a jar of baking soda.

FLASHLIGHT BATTERIES

Fishing Bobber. Some very efficient fishing bobbers can be improvised from your burned-out miniature flash bulbs. Merely split the solder on the end contact with a knife, insert your line, and then close the solder with a pliers. These bulbs will not become water-logged, can be used for a long time, and their white appearance makes them readily visible on the surface of the water.

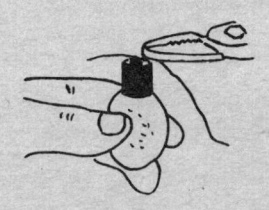

Fixed-Light Outlets, see ELECTRICAL OUTLETS.

Fixed Windows, see WINDOWS.

Fixtures, see LIGHTING FIXTURES.

Flares, see AUTOMOBILE.

Flashing, see ROOF FLASHING.

Flashlight.
  Corrosion. If you will insert a wad of aluminum foil between the spring and the end cap of your flashlight, this will prevent the usual corrosion that comes from electrolytic action. Remove any corrosion on the parts with an emery cloth before inserting your foil.
  When flashlight cells corrode and stick to the case, invert the case and pour in a solution of two tablespoons of baking soda and one-half cup water. Soak, then tap the case lightly and the cells will come out. Then dry the case thoroughly.
  Emergency. You can quickly improvise an emergency flashlight with one dry-cell battery, a strip of tin, and a one-cell flashlight bulb. Cut the tin strip to a point at one end and punch a hole near the opposite end, into which you screw the bulb. Bend the strip at right angles in the center and force the pointed end between the dry-cell case and the cardboard cover. Then, simply by bending the tin strip so that the bulb touches the dry-cell contact, you will have a light.

Maintenance. Keep a flashlight from being turned on accidentally and burning out when in a drawer by sealing the switch in the "off" position with some cellophane tape.

Flashlight Batteries.
  New Life. You can revive apparently dead flashlight batteries to some extent by keeping them in a warm oven overnight. Or, much better, remove the paper covering from the batteries, punch a few small holes in the base of the batteries with a nail, and then put them into a strong salt water solution for three or four hours. When you take them out, dry them and dip them into melted wax, then replace their paper covers when they have cooled.

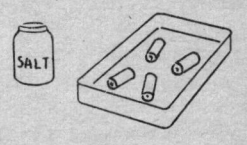

  Protection. If you will press a strip of adhesive tape tightly over the center terminal of a flashlight battery, this will prevent excessive drain of juice from the battery, should the terminal come into contact with any metallic objects while the battery is stored.

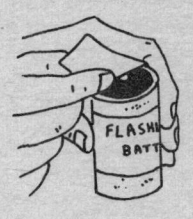

  Storage. You can prolong the life of flashlight batteries by storing them in a cool place.

FLAT ROOF

Flat Roof, see ROOF, FLAT.

Fleas, see INSECTS.

Floor, Cork, see CORK FLOOR.

Floor Creaking, see WOOD FLOOR REPAIR.

Floor Drain Repair, see PLUMBING.

Flooring Nails, see NAILS.

Floor Insulation, see INSULATION.

Floor Lamps, see LIGHTING, PORTABLE.

Floor, Linoleum, see LINOLEUM CARE, LINOLEUM INSTALLATION, LINOLEUM RENEWAL, LINOLEUM REPAIR.

Floor, Sagging, see WOOD FLOOR REPAIR.

Floors, Non-Resilient Tile, see NON-RESILIENT TILE FLOORS.

Floors, Resilient Tile, see RESILIENT TILE FLOORS.

Floor Support. Wooden floors are held up by heavy beams of framing timber called joists that run from foundation to foundation, supported there by plates, strips of timber bolted to the foundation. It is to these joists, usually 2 by 10's or 2 by 12's separated by 16-inch intervals, that flooring material is attached. Cross strips of wood or non-rusting metal X's bridge or brace the joists, keeping them apart and upright.

Immediately on top of the joists rests the subflooring, a sheathing either of 1/2, 5/8, or 3/4 inch plywood, or of strips of 1-inch wood. In some floors the finish floor is applied directly to this subflooring; in others a thickness of wood, usually 3/8-inch material called underlayment, is laid to take such finish floors as tile, carpet, or linoleum. Finish floors of wood can be laid directly on the subflooring. In some inexpensive construction, the actual finish flooring is nailed directly to the joists. Usually, a layer of building paper separates the subfloor from the finish floor.

The most common kind of finish floor in use today is tongue-and-groove hardwood, laid parallel to one of the walls of the room. It is attached to the subfloor with flooring nails driven in diagonally through the tongues.

Some wooden floors are laid on a "diagonal" subfloor, strip sheathing applied diagonally to the walls of the room. With the joists running north and south, and the finish floor running east and west, the diagonal subfloor running northeast and southwest, gives added rigidity and strength.

Other types of finish floors now used include resilient tiling (including asphalt tile), linoleum of all kinds, parquet floors, vinyl types of tile. These are usually attached to an underlayment rather than subflooring.

In addition to wood flooring or tile flooring attached to subflooring and joists, there are floors made of solid concrete slabs. The cement slab takes the place of joists, subflooring, and underlayment. Finish floors on cement slabs are usually resilient tiling, vinyl, or some types of carpeting, attached by mastic adhesive.

Floor, Wood, see WOOD FLOOR CARE, WOOD FLOOR RELAYING, WOOD FLOOR REPAIR, WOOD FLOORS, WOOD FLOOR SANDING.

Flower Arranging.

1. If cut flowers are being used in a glass bowl, cover the bottom thickly with small, colorful pebbles and use these as supports for the flower stems. They add a decorative touch to the whole arrangement.

2. When making any cut-flower arrangements, be sure always to take off all leaves below the water line. Otherwise, they will sour the water.

3. Freshly cut rosebuds will remain buds in a flower arrangement for several days if their stems are singed with a match before they are placed in the water.

4. To make a floating-flower table arrangement, try inserting the stem of each flower through a disc of waxed paper cut to the size of the blossom. Your blooms will last much longer, because the waxed paper protects them from the water.

Flower Boxes. Cover the tops of your flower boxes which contain flowers planted in soil with about a half-inch of gravel, and this will prevent the soil from splashing when watered and also prevent its drying out as quickly.

Flower Frogs.

Chicken Wire. Flower frogs from discarded chicken wire, can be cut and bent to fit each individual container. The large mesh of the wire accommodates flower stems much more easily than the standard frogs. And if you want even better positioning of your flowers, you can place a frog an inch off the bottom of the container, as well as the one at the top.

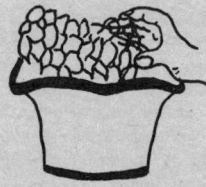

Clay. You can make a very efficient, self-anchoring flower frog of any size or shape you need from a large lump of green or brown modeling clay. Simply roll the clay into a ball in your hands, then press and flatten it to the center of a dry bowl, then punching holes of the required size and depth with a skewer or manicure stick.

Flowerpot.
Anchors.

1. One effective way to prevent flowerpots from toppling or being blown off the ledge on your porch or other outdoor location is to hammer a long, thin nail into the ledge, letting most of it protrude above the ledge...then fit the hole in the bottom of your flowerpot over the nail. This little trick holds the plant quite securely.

2. Drill a 1/2-inch hole in the sill and inset a short length of wood dowel. Then set the flower pot over this peg which extends up through the drain hole in the bottom of the pot.

Holder. If the usual type of flower box presents a too-bulky appearance for a particular window or house, you can fashion an attractive and practical flowerpot holder from one-half-inch metal rod. The rod can be steel or brass — steel, of course, requiring paint to rustproof it. When bending the holder, make the center circle larger than the two side circles, so as to produce a balanced look. The vertical portions of the holder are drilled so wood screws can be passed through them and driven into the house siding. Further rigidity is assured if the points at which the rod crosses are riveted or welded together.

Painting. Paint sometimes blisters and peels off red clay flower pots. To remedy this, be sure the pot is absolutely clean and free of moisture. Then paint the inside of the pot with aluminum paint, and let dry hard. Finish the outside of the pot with a high grade of enamel, and let this harden before filling the pot with earth.

Shelf. You can make a very attractive, usable, and safe flower pot shelf to attach outside one of your windows. Supported by sturdy brackets and bordered with a scroll-sawed valance, this shelf should add interest to the plainest window. Use stock material throughout, 3/4 inch for the shelf and valance, mitering the latter at the corners, and two-inch stock for the brackets. Attach the shelf to the brackets with four 1-1/2 inch flathead screws, and fasten the valance to the edge of the shelf with finishing nails. Cut holes through the shelf to fit the size of the pots it will be accommodating.

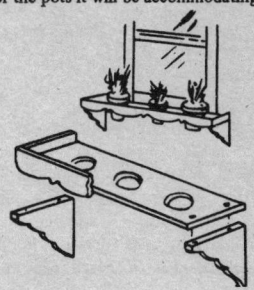

FLOWERS

Flowers.

Artificial flowers can be kept in a fixed position in their vases if the stems are placed in sand and hot paraffin is poured over the sand.

To clean artificial flowers, place inside a large paper bag with half a cup of salt and shake.

Cut. To preserve a short-stemmed flower in a deep vase, slit the stem and wrap one end of a wired pipe cleaner around it to serve as a wick and extend into the water.

Fresh. Aspirin tablets, pennies, or ice cubes in the water are all said to lengthen the lives of freshly-cut flowers. Or, add a teaspoon each of vinegar and sugar to each pint of water used. Or, some weak tea may be added to the water. Or, flowers stay fresh if a thin slice of soap or a teaspoon of salt is added to the water in the vase.

One way to prolong the life and beauty of cut flowers is to give them a hairspray treatment.

Flue, see FIREPLACE.

Fluorescent Lighting, see LIGHTING, FLUORESCENT.

Flush Doors, see DOORS.

Fluxes, see SOLDERING.

Foam Rubber.

Cushions. To wash foam rubber cushions, remove the covers, dunk them into clear, lukewarm water (no soap), and slowly squeeze to remove the water. Keep repeating this operation until your water runs clear.

Cutting. As you probably already know, foam rubber is awkward to cut neatly with an ordinary knife or scissors. But if you compress it tightly beforehand by pressing down on it with a flat board, it will slice easily with a sharp knife. Dip the blade in water to lubricate it if it tends to bind.

Folding Door, see CLOSET DOORS.

Food Measurements, see COOKING TIPS.

Foods.

Apples. Good color usually indicates full flavor.

Apples, Baked. Peel a 1-inch band around the middle of the apple. This will keep the skin from cracking while the apple bakes.

Asparagus. Stalks should be tender and firm; tips should be close and compact. Choose the stalks with little white—they are more tender. Use asparagus promptly—it toughens rapidly.

Bananas. Should be firm, fresh in appearance, and unscarred. Yellow or brown-flecked ones are ready for immediate use. Select slightly green-colored bananas for use within a few days.

Beans, Dry. Dry beans need soaking before cooking. Use 2½ cups water for 1 cup of blackeye beans (blackeye peas, cowpeas), Great Northern beans, and lima beans. Use 3 cups water for 1 cup of kidney beans, pea (navy) beans, and pinto beans.

To soak them quickly, boil beans 2 minutes, remove from heat, and let stand 1 hour. Or if you prefer, boil beans 2 minutes and let them stand overnight.

Cook the beans in the soaking water. Add 1 teaspoon salt for 1 cup of beans; boil gently for the time given below. One cup of uncooked beans yields about 2½ cups cooked beans.

Dry beans will cook more quickly if you add baking soda to the water before soaking. If tap water is of medium hardness, adding 1/8 teaspoon soda to the water for each cup of dry beans reduces cooking time about one-fourth. Measure soda exactly; too much soda affects flavor and nutritive value of beans.

To reduce foaming when cooking dry beans, add 1 tablespoon meat drippings or other fat to the cooking water for each cup of beans.

Cooked dry beans may be seasoned and eaten without further cooking, or they may be baked, or combined with other foods.

If acid ingredients like tomatoes, catsup, or vinegar are included in the recipe, add them after the beans are tender. Acids prevent softening of the beans.

Kind of beans	Approximate cooking time (hours)
Blackeye (blackeye peas, cowpeas).	1/2
Great Northern	1 to 1½
Kidney	2
Lima	1
Pea (navy)	1½ to 2
Pinto	2

Beans, Snap. Choose slender beans with no large bumps (bumps indicate large seeds). Avoid beans with dry-looking pods.

Berries. Select plump, solid berries with good color. Avoid wet or leaky berries. Blackberries and raspberries with clinging caps may be underripe. Strawberries without caps may be too ripe.

Biscuits. After mixing baking powder biscuits, knead dough for a half minute to improve texture.

Biscuits, Cutting. Use an ice tray to cut biscuits. Shape the dough to the size of the divider and cut. The biscuits will separate at the dividing lines after baking.

Bread Crumbs. Make bread crumbs by using the fine cutter of a food grinder. Cover the spout with a paper bag to prevent flying crumbs.

Broccoli. Look for small flower buds on compactly arranged heads with good green color. Avoid yellowing, soft, or spreading heads.

Brown Sugar. To measure, pack brown sugar firmly and level off top.

Brussel Sprouts. The heads should be firm with good green color. Yellowing outer leaves and softness indicate aging. Smudgy, dirty spots may indicate insect damage or decay.

Cabbage. Choose heads that are firm and heavy. Outer leaves should be fresh, green, and free from wormholes.

Cake-Baking Tips.

1. Fill cake pans two-thirds full, spreading batter to corners and sides. Leave a slight depression in center.

2. Tests for doneness.

Cake is done when a toothpick is inserted and comes out clean.

When cake shrinks from the sides of the pan it is done.

Press cake gently with a finger. If it springs back it is done.

3. Cake should be cooled in pan on a rack for five minutes and then turned out on a rack to finish cooling before frosting.

Cake Problems.

Heavy: Oven too slow; too much sugar or too much shortening.

Coarse-Grained: Too much leavening; oven too slow; insufficient creaming of shortening and sugar, or underbeating before adding egg whites.

Coarse Angel Cakes: Insufficient blending of egg whites with other ingredients, too little sugar or too fast an oven.

Fallen Cakes: Insufficient quantity of flour or leavening ingredients, excessive temperature or moving cake after it has risen but before the cell walls have become firm.

"Bready" Cakes: too much flour.

Uneven Cakes: too much heat.

Loaf Cake: with heavy streak at bottom; too many egg yolks or too slow oven.

Carrots. Removing tops before storing reduces wilting.

Cauliflower. Choose heads that are compact, firm, and white or creamy white. Avoid discolored heads and those with soft spots.

Add small amount of milk to water when cooking cauliflower to keep the vegetable white.

Celery. Best-quality celery is fresh and crisp. It is clean and has leaves that appear fresh; stems do not have black or brown discoloration. Avoid pithy, woody, or very stringy celery.

Cheese. Chill cheese for easier grating.

Coconut. To freshen shredded coconut, soak in fresh milk to which you've added a dash of sugar. Let it soak for several minutes before using. Another method is to place it in a sieve over boiling water, and steam it until it is moist.

Corn. Good-quality fresh corn has husks that are fresh and green. The ears are well filled with plump, firm, milky kernels. Immature ears of corn have small, undeveloped, watery kernels. Overmature ears have very firm, large, starchy kernels, often indented.

Sweet corn keeps best if refrigerated uncovered in husks. Use it promptly.

Cucumbers. Choose firm, slender cucumbers for best quality. Avoid yellowed cucumbers and those with withered or shrivelled ends.

Custard. When the custard mixture coats the spoon, the cooking is finished. Pour it into a bowl to cool.

Custard, Baked. An inserted knife will come out clean with just a bit of custard on it when it is time to remove it from the oven.

Egg Mixtures. Before adding eggs to a hot mixture, stir a little of that mixture into the slightly beaten eggs.

Egg Quality. U.S. Grade AA (or Fresh Fancy) and Grade A eggs are excellent for all purposes, but are especially good for poaching and frying where the appearance of the finished product is important. Grade B eggs are satisfactory for use in cooked dishes.

The grade of the egg does not affect its food value; lower grades are as high in nutrients as top grades. Buy either white or brown eggs. The color of the shell does not affect the nutritive value or quality of the egg.

Eggs, Cracked. When boiling eggs crack, add vinegar to the water to help seal the eggs.

Egg Selection. Buy graded eggs in cartons at a store that keeps eggs in refrigerated cases.

Eggs, Green Discoloration. The green discoloration that sometimes appears between the white and the yolk of a hard-cooked egg results from a chemical reaction, which is harmless. To help prevent this discoloration, cook eggs at low temperature, avoid overcooking, and cool promptly.

Egg Size. Eggs are also classified by size according to weight per dozen. Size is independent of quality; large eggs may be of high or low quality and high-quality eggs may be of any size. Common market sizes of eggs and the minimum weight per dozen:

U.S. Extra Large — 27 ounces.
U.S. Large — 24 ounces.
U.S. Medium — 21 ounces.
U.S. Small — 18 ounces.

The substitution of one size egg for another often makes little difference in recipe results. However, in some recipes—for example in sponge and angelfood cakes—the proportion of egg to other ingredients is very important. For these recipes, it may be necessary to increase the number of eggs if you are using a smaller size.

Eggs, Omelet. Press omelet gently with a finger. If it springs back it is done.

An inserted knife will come out clear when an omelet is done.

Eggs, Peeling. Crack the shell of hard boiled eggs over the entire surface. Roll them between your hands, peel, starting where the air pocket is.

Eggs, Soiled. Cracked or soiled eggs may contain bacteria that can produce food poisoning. For your protection, use cracked or soiled eggs only when they are thoroughly cooked or when the foods in which they are an ingredient are thoroughly cooked.

Egg Storage. To help maintain quality, store eggs in the refrigerator promptly after purchase—large end up.

For best flavor and cooking quality, use eggs within 1 week if possible. Eggs held in the refrigerator for a long time may develop off-flavors and lose some thickening and leavening power.

Cover leftover yolks with cold water and refrigerate in a tightly covered container. Refrigerate leftover egg whites, too, in a tightly covered container. Use leftover yolks or whites within 1 or 2 days.

Egg Whites. If you need just the white of an egg, try pricking a hole in the shell with a pin, then turning it upside-down over the mixing bowl until the white runs out. Then the yolk, in its natural container, can be refrigerated until some future need for it arises.

Egg Yolks. Preserve leftover egg yolks by placing in small container and adding two tablespoons of salad oil.

Fish, Market forms. *Whole.*—Fish marketed just as they come from the water. Ask your dealer to scale, eviscerate, and remove head, tail, and fins.

Dressed or pan-dressed.—Fish with scales and entrails removed, and usually—head, tail, and fins removed. Small fish are called pan-dressed and are ready to cook as purchased. Large dressed fish may be cooked as purchased, but often are filleted or cut into steaks or chunks.

Steaks.—Cross-section slices from large dressed fish cut 5/8 to 1 inch thick. Steaks can be cooked as purchased.

Fillets.—Sides of the fish cut lengthwise away from the backbone. They may be skinned or the skin may be left on. Fillets are ready to cook as purchased.

Chunks.—Cross sections of large dressed fish. A cross section of the backbone is the only bone in a chunk. They are ready to cook as purchased.

Raw breaded fish portions.—Portions cut from frozen fish blocks, coated with a batter, breaded packaged, and frozen. Raw breaded fish portions weigh more than 1½ ounces. They are ready to cook as purchased.

Fried fish portions.—Portions cut from frozen fish blocks, coated with a batter, breaded, partially cooked, packaged, and frozen. Fried fish portions weigh more than 1½ ounces. They are ready to heat and serve as purchased.

Fried fish sticks.—Sticks cut from frozen fish blocks, coated with a batter, breaded, partially cooked, packaged, and frozen. Fried fish sticks weigh up to 1½ ounces. They are ready to heat and serve as purchased.

Frozen Foods. Buy only packages that are frozen solid. Avoid partially thawed packages that feel soft or are stained. Thawing and refreezing lower quality.

Grapes should be plump, fresh in appearance, and firmly attached to the stems. Red or black varieties should be well colored for the variety. Most white or green varieties should have a slightly amber tone.

Ingredient Substitutes.

For these	You may use these
1 whole egg, for baking or thickening	• 2 egg yolks.
1 cup butter or margarine for baking	• 7/8 cup vegetable or animal shortening plus 1/2 teaspoon salt.
1 ounce unsweetened chocolate	• 3 tablespoons cocoa plus 1 tablespoon fat.
1 teaspoon double-acting baking powder	• 2 teaspoons quick-acting baking powder.
	• ¼ teaspoon baking soda plus ½ cup sour milk or buttermilk instead of ½ cup sweet milk.
1 cup buttermilk or sour milk, for baking	• 1 cup fluid whole milk plus 1 tablespoon vinegar or lemon juice.
	• 1 cup fluid whole milk plus 1¾ teaspoons cream of tartar.
1 cup fluid whole milk	• ½ cup evaporated milk plus ½ cup water.
	• 1 cup fluid nonfat dry or skim milk plus 2½ teaspoons butter or margarine.
1 cup fluid skim milk	• 1 cup reconstituted nonfat dry milk.
1 tablespoon flour, for thickening	• ½ tablespoon cornstarch.
	• 2 teaspoons quick-cooking tapioca.
1 cup cake flour, for baking	• 7/8 cup all-purpose flour.

Leftovers. Don't throw good leftover food away. Use your cooking skill—and your imagination—to make leftovers tasty.

Some leftovers make good second meals merely by reheating. Others are better prepared in a new way—with seasonings, sauces, crisp toppings. Try leftover fruit in muffins, vegetables in omelets. Substitute 2 leftover egg yolks for 1 whole egg in baked custard. And soups often become richer, more delicious when leftovers are added.

Bread
    Bread pudding
    Croutons
    Dry crumbs for breading meat, poultry, or fish
    Fondues
    French toast
    Meat loaf, salmon loaf
    Sardine puff
    Stuffings

Buttermilk
    Cakes, cookies
    Quick breads

Cooked or canned fruits
    Fruit cups
    Fruit sauces
    Gelatin desserts
    Prune cake
    Quick breads
    Salads
    Shortcake
    Upside-down cake
    Yeast breads

Cooked leafy vegetables, chopped
    Creamed or scalloped vegetables
    Omelets
    Souffles
    Soups

Cooked meats, poultry, fish
    Casseroles
    Creamed foods
    Curries
    Hash
    Patties
    Potpies
    Salads
    Sandwiches

Cooked potatoes
    Fried or creamed potatoes
    Meat or potato patties
    Meat-pie topping

FOODS

- Potatoes in cheese sauce
- Salads
- Soups, stews, or chowders

Cooked rice, noodles, macaroni, spaghetti
- Baked macaroni and cheese
- Casseroles
- Macaroni salad
- Meat or cheese loaf
- Spanish rice

Cooked snap beans, lima beans, corn, peas, carrots
- Casseroles
- Creamed dishes
- Meat, poultry, or fish pies
- Salads
- Sauces
- Scalloped vegetables
- Soups
- Stews
- Vegetables in cheese sauce

Cooked wheat, oat, or corn cereals
- Fried cereal
- Meat loaf or patties
- Souffles
- Sweet puddings

Cookies or unfrosted cakes
- Crumb crust for pies
- Ice cream sandwiches
- Refrigerator cake (cake strips or cookies layered with pudding or whipped cream and chilled)
- Toasted cake slices, served with fruit or ice cream

Egg Whites
- Cakes
- Meringue
- Souffles

Egg Yolks
- Baked custard
- Cakes, cookies
- Homemade noodles
- Mock hollandaise sauce
- Scrambled eggs

Fruit cooking liquids or fruit syrups
- Fruit cups
- Fruit sauces
- Fruit drinks
- Gelatin mixtures
- Tapioca puddings

Hard-cooked egg or yolk
- Casseroles
- Egg sauce
- Garnish
- Salads
- Sandwiches
- Thousand island dressing

Meat or poultry drippings and broth
- Gravies
- Sauces
- Soups
- Stews

Sour cream
- Beef stroganoff
- Cakes, cookies
- Salad dressings
- Sauce for vegetables

Vegetable cooking liquids
- Gravies
- Sauces
- Soups
- Stews

Lemonade. Try using your grinder when making lemonade. Put the whole lemon through and achieve far greater strength in your final product.

Lemons. You can get more juice from a little, dried up lemon if you heat it for about five minutes in boiling water before you squeeze it.

Lettuce. Select heads that are green, fresh, crisp, and fairly firm to firm. Head lettuce should be free from rusty appearance and excessive outer leaves.

Use a plastic knife when cutting lettuce to prevent lettuce from browning.

Meal Planning.

1. Include a variety of foods each day and from day to day. Introduce a new food from time to time.

2. Vary flavors and textures. Contrast strong flavor with mild, sweet with sour. Combine crisp textures with smooth.

3. Try to have some meat, poultry, fish, eggs, milk or cheese at each meal.

4. Make a collection of nutritious recipes that the family enjoys and serve them often.

5. Brighten food with color—a slice of red tomato, a sprig of dark greens or other garnish.

6. Combine different sizes and shapes of food in a meal, when possible.

Measurements.
Baking powder, cornstarch, cream of tartar, spices. Dip spoon into container and bring it up heaping full. Level off top with straight, thin edge of spatula or knife.

Brown sugar. Pack firmly into cup or spoon and level off top with straight thin edge of spatula or knife.

Dry Milk. Pour dry milk from spout or opening in package, or spoon lightly, into measuring cup until measure is overflowing. Do not shake. Level off top with straight, thin edge of spatula or knife.

Fine meal, fine crumbs. Stir lightly with fork or spoon. Measure like flour.

Flour. Spoon flour lightly into measuring cup until measure is overflowing. Do not shake or tap cup. Level off top with straight, thin edge of spatula or knife.

Solid Fats. Pack fat firmly into cup or smaller measure and level off top with straight, thin edge of spatula or knife.

For solid fat in sticks or pounds, cut off amount needed. A 1-pound form measures about 2 cups; a ¼-pound stick of butter or margarine measures ½ cup.

To measure less than 1 cup, you can also use the water method: Partly fill a cup with cold water, leaving enough space for the amount of fat needed. (To measure 1/4 cup of fat, for example, fill cup with water to 3/4 mark.) Spoon fat into cup, push under water until water level reaches 1-cup mark. Drain thoroughly before using fat.

Meat. Use a potato masher to separate ground beef when browning it for spaghetti sauce.

At the meat counter, consider the amount of cooked lean meat you will get for the money you pay.

Meats. When barbecuing spare ribs or chicken, baste with a paint brush or pastry brush.

Melons (except watermelons).—Ripe cantaloupes have a yellowish surface color; honeydews, a creamy color; crenshaws, a golden-yellow color mottled with green; casabas, a yellow color; and Persian melons, a dull gray-green color. Ripe melons of these types usually have a fruity aroma and a slight softening at the blossom end. A ripe cantaloupe has no stem; other melons may have stems attached.

Milk Cubes. It's a good idea to keep one of your ice cube trays full of frozen sweek milk to use in milk or cold milk chocolate drinks. These cubes will chill the drink without weakening it.

Nuts, Blanched. Nuts are blanched by immersing in boiling water for two minutes, then in cold water. Drain and remove the skins, then spread thinly in pans and put in a warm oven to dry for a few hours. The crispness of the nuts depends on their dryness.

Olive Oil. A small pinch of salt added to olive oil, if the taste is considered unpleasant, will make it agreeable.

Onions. Size and color do not affect flavor or quality of dry onions. Clean, hard, well-shaped onions with dry skins are usually of good quality. Moisture at the neck may be a sign of decay. Mild-flavored onions, which are often large, may be elongated or flat. Stronger-flavored onions are usually medium size and globe shaped.

Onions, Peeling. The very old method of peeling onions without having to resort to the crying towel is still good. Put two kitchen matches between your teeth, sulphur tips on the outside, while paring the tear-jerkers. The sulphur absorbs the onion vapors.

Oranges, grapefruit and lemons. Choose those heavy for their size. Smooth, thin skins usually indicate more juice. Most skin markings do not affect quality. Oranges with a slight greenish tinge may be just as ripe as fully colored ones. Light or greenish-yellow lemons are more tart than deep-yellow ones.

Pancakes are ready to turn when the bubbles have burst and the underside has turned golden brown.

Paste. Add olive oil to water when cooking pasta to prevent sticking to pan.

Peaches. Best quality peaches are fairly firm, not bruised, with yellow or red color over the entire surface.

Pears. Some pears, especially winter varieties, are marketed when slightly underripe and need to be ripened at home—at room temperature. Pears are ripe and ready to eat when they yield slightly to moderate pressure.

Peas and lima beans. Select pods that are well filled but not bulging. Avoid dried, spotted, yellowed, or flabby pods.

Pie. Fold the top pie crust over the lower crust before crimping to keep juices in the pie.

Pie Crust. Be sure all ingredients are chilled for an easier to roll pie crust.

Pies, Custard. Bake at high temperature for ten minutes to prevent a soggy crust. Finish baking at low temperature.

Pineapple varieties vary greatly in color. Ripe pineapples have a fragrant, fruity aroma. Usually, the heavier the fruit for its size, the better the quality. Avoid pineapples that have decayed or moldy spots.

FOODS

Popcorn. Here's a little tip for better popping. Sprinkle the kernels of popcorn lightly with warm water an hour or two before popping. Then, regardless of your method of popping there will be a reduced number of unpopped kernels, and the flavor will be much improved, too.

It's hard to beat freshly-popped corn that is topped with melted butter, but for a different flavor, try adding a spoonful of peanut butter to the melted butter just before pouring it over the corn. Then, salt to taste.

Potatoes. Best-quality potatoes are firm, smooth, and well shaped. They are free from cuts, blemishes, and decay. To judge quality more easily, look for potatoes that are reasonably clean. Avoid potatoes with wasteful deep eyes. Potatoes with green skins may be bitter. If you plan to buy a large quantity of potatoes, buy a few first to see if they are the kind you want. Early-crop potatoes, harvested in spring and summer, tend to be less mealy when cooked than those harvested later.

Potatoes, Baking. The baking time of potatoes may be shortened by letting them stand in boiling water about 15 minutes before baking.

Wrap potatoes in foil before baking for tender skins.

Potatoes, Peeling. A strawberry huller makes an excellent peeler for boiled potatoes.

Poultry. Serve poultry often—it's versatile, flavorful, and economical. You can buy chicken and turkey in convenient sizes—chilled or frozen—any day of the year. And for variety, try duck and goose.

Poultry, Cooking Guide. Most poultry sold whole can be roasted. Stewing chickens and mature turkeys, however, are more tender if braised or stewed. They are good for stews, or to provide cooked meat for casseroles, sandwiches, and salads.

Broiler or fryer chickens can be roasted, oven-baked, barbecued, or cooked on a rotisserie as well as broiled or fried. Fryer-roaster turkeys weighing 4 or 5 pounds can be roasted whole, or can be cut into parts and fried or broiled.

Rock Cornish game hens can be cooked like broiler or fryer chickens. Small ducks are suitable for broiling or frying; larger ones, for roasting or rotisserie cooking. Geese roast very well.

Roast poultry uncovered for best color and to reduce splitting and shrinkage. Poultry can be roasted with or without stuffing; unstuffed birds take slightly less time to cook. Cook poultry until tender and juicy; do not overcook.

To roast poultry, place breast side up on a rack in a shallow pan. Do not cover pan and do not add water.

A meat thermometer is the best guide to doneness of turkeys. Insert the thermometer into the center of the inner thigh muscle. Make sure it does not touch the bone.

Salt the giblets and neck, seal them in aluminum foil, and roast along with the poultry. Or simmer them in salted water until tender.

You can baste poultry with pan drippings or a little fat if you like.

If poultry browns early in the roasting period, cover the breast and drumsticks lightly with aluminum foil or with a thin cloth moistened with fat. After poultry is partly roasted, cut band of skin that holds legs together.

Poultry, Frozen. Keep *frozen poultry* frozen until time to thaw or cook. Frozen poultry usually is thawed before cooking, but poultry parts or whole poultry frozen without giblets can be cooked without thawing. Cooking time will be longer than for unfrozen poultry. Do not thaw commercially frozen stuffed poultry before cooking.

To thaw poultry in the refrigerator, place frozen poultry on a tray or shallow pan to catch the thawing drip; if unwrapped, cover lightly. Remove giblets from cavity when bird is pliable.

If it is not practical to thaw poultry in the refrigerator, immerse poultry in a watertight wrapper in cold water. Change water often to hasten thawing. Or you can partially thaw poultry in the refrigerator and partially in cold water. It takes 1 to 8 hours to thaw poultry in cold water, or 1 to 3 hours in a refrigerator.

Cook poultry promptly after thawing. Stuff poultry just before roasting.

Poultry, Ready-to-cook. Ready-to-cook poultry needs little preparation before cooking. Inspect for pinfeathers. Wash and drain poultry.

Poultry, Precaution. Do not partly roast poultry on one day and complete roasting the following day.

Poultry, Salting. Salting the skin causes it to blister. Salt will not penetrate the skin.

Poultry, Testing for doneness. Use any one or more of the following ways to tell if poultry is done:

A meat thermometer inserted in the center of the inner thigh muscle of a turkey reaches 180° to 185° F. If turkey is stuffed, also check stuffing temperature by inserting a thermometer into the body cavity for 5 minutes. Temperature should reach 165° F.

Drumstick feels soft when you press meaty part with protected fingers.

Drumstick moves up and down easily and leg joint gives readily.

Pumpkin Pie is done when no ripples appear on surface as the pan is moved.

Radishes. Removing tops before storing reduces wilting.

Rice. Add small amount of vinegar to water when cooking rice to prevent sticking.

Rolls. Press a yeast roll gently with a finger. If it leaves a slight dent, the roll has risen enough and is ready for the oven.

Root Vegetables. Choose smooth, firm vegetables. Very large carrots may have woody cores; oversized radishes may be pithy; oversized turnips, beets, and parsnips may be woody. The size and condition of the tops on root vegetables do not necessarily indicate the eating quality.

Salad Dressings. Main-dish salads made with meat, fish, poultry, eggs, beans, cheese, or potatoes usually call for a mayonnaise-type dressing, but some are good with French or Italian dressing.

On vegetable salads and vegetable-fruit combinations, try French, Italian, Thousand island, or Roquefort or Blue cheese dressing. Fruit salads taste best with sweet dressings—sweet French, orange-honey, or celery seed dressing.

Prevent sogginess and wilting by using just enough salad dressing to moisten ingredients. Add dressing to raw vegetable salads at the last minute unless your recipe calls for marinated vegetables.

Salad Making Tips. Selecting top-quality fruits and vegetables is a good start toward a good salad. Fresh food has eye and taste appeal.

FOODS

Give salad foods the best care to avoid damage and to keep them fresh. If you prepare salad ingredients ahead of time, store them, without dressing, in the refrigerator.

If you plan to use unpeeled fruits or vegetables in a salad, choose those with smooth, tender, colorful skins.

Chill ingredients before you mix your salad.

Always thoroughly drain the greens you use in salads.

Vary your salad greens. Try chicory, escarole, endive, kale, spinach, dandelion greens, romaine, watercress, and Chinese cabbage.

Some salad fruits are likely to turn dark on standing; dip these in a little citrus juice. Drain canned fruits and vegetables before you add them to a salad.

Salmon. To eliminate cooking odor from salmon, cover surface of fish with fresh lemon juice and refrigerate for at least one hour.

Salt, when to add.

1. Soups and Sauces: blend in early in cooking process.
2. Meats: Add just before taking from heat.
3. Cakes: Mix with eggs.
4. Vegetables: Add to cooking water.
5. Fish: Salt while frying.

Servings and Pounds. To avoid waste and to make the most of your food dollar, you also need to know how many servings you get from a market unit, such as 1 pound of fresh carrots or a 10-ounce package of frozen peaches.

Meat, poultry, and fish. The amount of meat, poultry, and fish to buy varies with the amount of bone, fat, and breading.

Servings per pound[1]

MEAT
Much bone or gristle .... 1 or 2
Medium amounts of bone .... 2 or 3
Little or no bone .... 3 or 4
POULTRY (READY-TO—COOK)
Chicken .... 2 or 3
Turkey .... 2 or 3
Duck and goose 2
FISH
Whole .... 1 or 2
Dressed or pan-dressed .... 2 or 3
Portions or steaks 3
Fillets .... 3 or 4

[1] Three ounces of cooked lean meat, poultry, or fish per serving.

FOODS

Vegetables and fruits. For this table, a serving of vegetable is 1/2 cup cooked vegetable unless otherwise noted. A serving of fruit is 1/2 cup fruit; 1 medium apple, banana, peach, or pear; or 2 apricots or plums. A serving of cooked fresh or dried fruit is 1/2 cup fruit and liquid.

FRESH VEGETABLES

	Servings per pound[1]
Asparagus	3 or 4
Beans, lima[2]	2
Beans, snap	5 or 6
Beets, diced[3]	3 or 4
Broccoli	3 or 4
Brussels sprouts	4 or 5
Cabbage:	
Raw, shredded	9 or 10
Cooked	4 or 5
Carrots:	
Raw, diced or shredded[3]	5 or 6
Cooked[3]	4
Cauliflower	3
Celery:	
Raw, chopped or diced	5 or 6
Cooked	4
Kale[4]	5 or 6
Okra	4 or 5
Onions, cooked	3 or 4
Parsnips[3]	4
Peas[2]	2
Potatoes	4
Spinach[5]	4
Squash, summer	3 or 4
Squash, winter	2 or 3
Sweet potatoes	3 or 4
Tomatoes, raw, diced or sliced	4

[1] As purchased.
[2] Bought in pod.
[3] Bought without tops.
[4] Bought untrimmed.
[5] Bought prepackaged.

FROZEN VEGETABLES

	Servings per package (9 or 10 oz.)
Asparagus	2 or 3
Beans, lima	3 or 4
Beans, snap	3 or 4
Broccoli	3
Brussels sprouts	3
Cauliflower	3
Corn, whole kernel	3
Kale	2 or 3
Peas	3
Spinach	2 or 3

Soup, Clear. To clear soup, strain stock, Mix together the beaten white and crushed shell of one egg and 2 teaspoons water for each quart of stock to be cleared. Stir constantly until boiling point is reached. Remove from heat, let stand for 20 minutes. Strain.

Soup, Color. The color of vegetables in cream soup can be intensified by adding 1/4 teaspoon baking soda.

Soup, Grease Removal. To remove grease from the top of soup drop a lettuce leaf into the pot. Discard after grease is absorbed.

Storage, Canned Foods. Store in a dry place at room temperature (not above 70°F.).

Storage, Dry Milk. Store *nonfat dry milk* in a closed container at a temperature of 75° F., or lower. Because of its higher milkfat content, *dry whole milk* does not keep as well as nonfat dry milk. Keep dry whole milk in a tightly closed container in the refrigerator. Refrigerate *reconstituted dry milk as you would fresh fluid milk.*

Storage, Dried Foods. Store *dried fruits* in tightly closed containers at room temperature (not above 70° F.). In warm humid weather, refrigerate.

Storage, Fats and Oils. Refrigerate lard, butter, margarine, drippings, and opened containers of cooking and salad oils. You can store most firm vegetable shortenings (those that have been hydrogenated), covered, at room temperature. Refrigerate opened jars of salad dressing; do not freeze.

Storage, Fresh Fruits and Vegetables. Fresh fruits should be ripe when stored in the refrigerator. Some unripe fruits will ripen if left for a time at room temperature—preferably in a cool room between 60° and 70°F.

Keep bananas at room temperature. They will turn dull brown if refrigerated. Sort berries and cherries; then refrigerate, unwashed. Use promptly. Refrigerate ripe pineapples.

Sweet corn keeps best if refrigerated uncovered in husks; use it promptly. Removing tops from carrots, beets, and radishes reduces wilting. Storing potatoes in a cool, dark place prevents greening.

Storage, Frozen Foods. Can be stored in freezing unit of refrigerator up to 1 week. For longer storage, keep in a freezer at 0° F.

Storage, Meat, Poultry, Fish. All meat should be promptly refrigerated.

The transparent wrap on prepackaged meat,

STORAGE GUIDE FOR FRUITS AND VEGETABLES

Hold at room temperature until ripe; then refrigerate, uncovered:

Apples	Grapes	Peaches
Apricots	Melons, except	Pears
Avocados	watermelons	Plums
Berries	Nectarines	Tomatoes

Store in cool room or refrigerate, uncovered:

Grapefruit	Limes
Lemons	Oranges

Store in cool room, away from bright light:

Onions, mature	Rutabagas	Sweet Potatoes
Potatoes	Squash, winter	

Refrigerate, covered:

Asparagus	Cauliflower	Parsnips
Beans, snap or wax	Celery	Peas, shelled
	Corn, husked	Peppers, green
Beets	Cucumbers	Radishes
Broccoli	Greens	Squash, summer
Cabbage	Onions, green	
Carrots		Turnips

Refrigerate, uncovered:

Beans, lima, in pods	Corn, in husks	Pineapples
	Peas, in pods	Watermelons

poultry, or fish is designed for refrigerator storage at home for 1 or 2 days.

Meat or poultry wrapped in meat paper when brought from the store—or prepackaged roasts and steaks that may be stored in the refrigerator for 3 to 5 days—should be unwrapped, placed on a platter or tray, and loosely covered before refrigerating. Wrap and store fish separately from other foods. Poultry giblets should also be wrapped and stored separately.

Keep cooked meat, poultry, and fish, and the gravy or broth made from them, in covered containers in the refrigerator. Use within 1 or 2 days.

Cured and smoked meats—ham, frankfurters, bacon, sausage—can be stored in their original containers in the refrigerator. Mild-cured hams are similar to fresh meats in keeping quality. Use whole hams within a week, half hams and slices within 3 to 5 days. For best flavor, use bacon, franks, and smoked sausages within a week.

STORAGE GUIDE

	FROZEN FOOD	FREEZER AT 0° F.
FRESH MEAT, POULTRY, FISH Loosely wrapped Roasts, steaks, chops— 3 to 5 days Ground meats, variety meats, poultry, fish— 1 to 2 days	**MILK, CREAM, CHEESE** Tightly covered Milk, cream, cottage cheese, cream cheese— 3 to 5 days Hard cheese— Several weeks	COLDEST PART OF REFRIGERATOR
BUTTER, MARGARINE Tightly covered — 2 weeks	**EGGS** Covered — 1 week	
MAYONNAISE AND OTHER SALAD DRESSINGS—Covered Refrigerate after opening		
OPENED CANNED FOODS, FRESH OR RECONSTITUTED JUICE Tightly covered	**NUTS** Tightly covered **PEANUT BUTTER** Refrigerate after opening	
FRESH FRUITS, RIPE—Uncovered		
Apples—1 week Berries Cherries } 1 to 2 days	Apricots Grapes Pears Peaches Plums Rhubarb } 3 to 5 days	OTHER PARTS OF REFRIGERATOR
SOME FRESH VEGETABLES—Uncovered		
Ripe tomatoes Corn in husk	Lima beans Peas } In pods	
MOST FRESH VEGETABLES Leafy green vegetables Asparagus Brussels sprouts Cauliflower Summer squash	Beets Cabbage Carrots Broccoli Celery	Cucumbers Green onions Peppers Radishes Snap beans	CRISPER AND/OR PLASTIC BAG

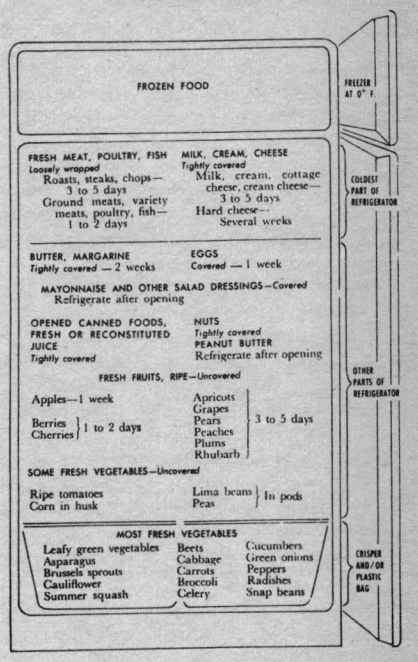

Sweet Potatoes. Choose sweet potatoes that are clean, smooth, well shaped, and firm. Damp or soft spots may indicate decay. There are two types of sweet potatoes. The moist type has soft, moist, orange-colored flesh and bronze or rosy skin. The dry type has firm, dry, somewhat mealy, yellow-colored flesh and yellow or light-brown skin.

Tea. You can prevent leftover tea from becoming cloudy and help it to retain its refreshing flavor if you put the extra lemon slices in the pitcher of unused tea.

Tomatoes. Choose tomatoes that are plump, firm, and uniformly pink, red, or yellow in color. They should be free from growth cracks, scars, and bruises. The best flavored tomatoes are ripened on the vine.

Vegetables. Knowing how to prepare vegetables to retain their nutritive value and appetite appeal is a test of any good cook. To help you improve your skill with vegetables, here are some cooking tips—

Boil vegetables in as little water as possible; losses in vitamins and minerals will be less, the less water you use. Serve the cooking liquids with your vegetables, or make them into sauces, gravies, or soups.

Cook vegetables until just tender, and serve them immediately; they will taste better and retain more nutrients.

Trim leafy vegetables like lettuce and cabbage sparingly. Use the dark outer leaves—they are especially rich in nutrients. Remove woody midribs from kale leaves—there is little nutritive loss and the kale cooks more uniformly.

Vegetable, Cooking Tips.

1. Add a little vinegar or lemon juice to beets and red cabbage to help keep the color.

2. Small amount of sugar added after cooking to carrots, peas, corn, beets helps to retain their flavor.

3. Addition of baking soda to vegetables destroys some of the vitamins.

Watermelons. Ripe watermelons have a somewhat dull surface and a creamy color underneath. The interior should be fully red and firm, and should have few immature seeds.

Footing Drain, see BASEMENTS, DAMP or WET.

Force Pump, see TOOLS, PLUMBING.

Formica. In some cases you can install new Formica right over old if the old surface is sound. On table tops this is fairly simple — that is, as simple as any Formica work. All of this is a bit complicated because of special equipment required for trimming the edges of top surfaces. But first get a power sander of the orbital type and some medium grit garnet paper. Go over the entire surface including edges if they are covered to remove the high gloss. If edges are to be covered they should be applied first. Cut the edge strips about 1/16 inch wider than the edge and if you have any way of clamping you can put these on with white glue, otherwise use contact cement by coating the edge and also the strip and allowing both to dry. Then place the strip in position and tap all over the surface thoroughly with a rubber mallet or a block of wood under an ordinary hammer. Next, you'll have to cut the top edge of this strip down flush with the table top and this can be done with a file or a regular laminate bit in a router. The top sheet should be cut a quarter inch all around bigger than the area it is to cover and contact cement is the only adhesive to work on tops. After coating the table top and the sheet and they have dried to the touch, lay several thin strips of wood like yardsticks on the table and position the top sheet on these so it doesn't touch as contact cement clings at the slightest touch. When you get it just where you want it gently pull out one of the end strips of wood and press the sheet into contact after which you can pull the remaining strips and go over the entire top several times with the mallet or wood block and hammer. The tricky part comes in trimming back the edge which has to be done with either a router equipped with a regular carbide laminate bit or a special power tool called a laminate trimmer. This can usually be rented. Formica can best be cut on a table saw using a very fine tooth blade but can be cut by scoring along a straightedge with a sharp instrument such as the corner of a sharp chisel. After the score has been gone over several times to cut thru the tough outer surface, you can snap the sheet much like breaking crackers apart.

Formica work is generally a bit beyond the average do-it-yourselfer because of the specialized equipment needed.

Regarding contact cement, there are a number of kinds and some of them are extremely flammable.

On kitchen cabinet tops that have a coved section where the top meets the back spash, these have to be factory made and there is no way they can be remodeled in the home. What is involved in this case is to disconnect the sink and remove the entire cabinet top and have a new one made to order. This gets entirely out of the field of do-it-yourself.

Foundation Wall Repair, see CONCRETE REPAIR.

Foundation Waterproofing. There are, of course, many commercial products on the market that are applied on the inside basement walls and do a very good job of preventing moisture from coming through. However, it is still a good practice to apply that well-known black waterproofing to the OUTSIDE surfaces of your foundation, if at all possible, in order to prevent the moisture from getting into your wall and building up hydraulic pressure.

FRAMES

Frames.

Construction. The making or repairing of a picture frame itself may have been straightforward. The difficulties arise when the frame has to be assembled and no picture frame clamp is available.

The method suggested here is practical and inexpensive.

From an eight-inch length of two-inch square softwood cut a one-inch rebate as shown in Fig. 1.

This can be done very easily with a portable electric saw, or by hand with a tenon saw.

The rebated length of wood should now be sawed into four pieces across the dotted lines, each piece being a block two inches long.

The sawed angle of the rebate should be trimmed up with a chisel to insure that it is a good right angle.

The next step is to chisel a notch in each of the four blocks as indicated in Fig. 2.

The picture frame can now be assembled by this method:

The faces of two of the mitered corners of the frame should be lightly smeared with a cold glue, preferably of the synthetic resin type.

One piece of the frame is held in the vice and the other placed over it with a panel pin already in position (Fig. 3).

The action of tapping home the panel will bring the two edges nicely into line.

The other corners of the frame are dealt with in a similar way. Do not worry too much about the job being tight or square at this stage.

The four blocks should now be placed over the corners of the frame and a double length of stout string or cord wound around the blocks and arranged in the notches to prevent slipping.

A short length of light wood is inserted between the two cords in the middle of each of the four sides of the frame.

Turning these pieces will twist and tighten the cord, a similar action to that of a tourniquet, and the frame will be clamped tight.

The cords are locked tight by allowing the tourniquet level pieces to rest on the sides of the frames as in Fig. 4.

Test the frame for squareness by measuring the diagonals, and make any necessary adjustments by tightening the tourniquets on the appropriate sides.

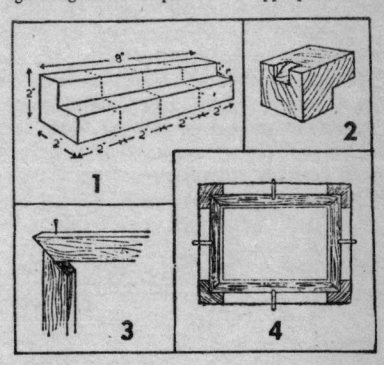

Gilded. Gilt mirror or picture frames usually need nothing more than dusting so long as they are supposed to look antique. But if you want to clean them and forget the "antique" part, this can be done by coating the frame with petroleum jelly, letting this stay on about ten minutes, then rubbing off with a clean cloth. Or, boil a few onions and douse the frame with a cloth dipped in the onion water. Rinse off with clear water. A brush dipped in onion juice will clean out deeper places.

The appearance of gilded picture or mirror frames can be much improved by rubbing gently with a cloth wet with alcohol, turpentine or mineral spirits. If the gilt feels sticky after this treatment, don't touch it. Let dry for a day or so.

Beer also makes an effective cleaner.

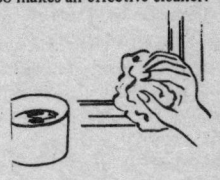

Gold leaf picture or mirror frames should never be cleaned with gritty powder. Cut an onion in half, rub gently over the surface, and then wipe the re-

FRAMING TIPS

sulting moisture from the frame with a soft, lintless cloth. A brush dipped into onion juice will clean out the deeper ridges.

Maintenance. Masking tape or surgical adhesive tape, placed along the joints between the backing and the frame of a picture, will prevent dust from seeping in and ruining the picture itself.

Repair. When the ornamental moldings on picture frames, furniture, or other woodwork, has been chipped, it can be easily repaired by building up the missing sections with some wood putty. This wood putty comes in powder form and when it is mixed with water, it dries into a hard, wood-like substance that can be sanded, carved, or sawed.

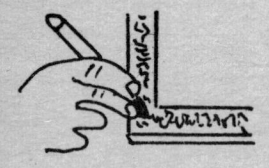

Staining. One easy and effective method of staining unfinished picture frames is with paste shoe polish. Just rub it on evenly, let it dry, then shine it with a soft cloth.

Framing Tips.

1. When framing pictures, a pair of slip-joint pliers makes a handy device for forcing in the brads or glaziers' points that hold the picture and mat in place. Use a backing block to protect the edge of the frame.

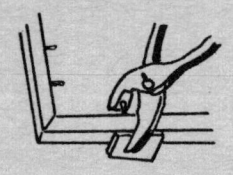

2. You can make prints and magazine covers look like oil paintings by pasting the pictures wet on burlap, and then applying a coat of shellac. Frame them in natural color wool, without glass.

3. You can make some very nice and efficient staples for framing pictures out of paper clips. Snip each clip near its center to make three staples, cutting them at an angle in order to produce sharp ends for nailing into your frame.

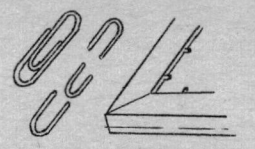

4. The next time you go into the chore of framing some pictures, try the idea of using some of your worn-out phonograph needles for holding the picture backs securely in their frames. The absence of heads on these "tacks" permits them to lie flat against the backs of the pictures.

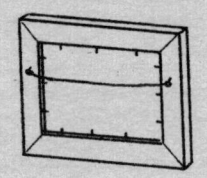

Frozen Foods, see FOODS.

Frozen Pipes, see PLUMBING.

Fruit, see FOODS.

Fruit Stains, see STAIN REMOVAL.

Frying Tips, see COOKING TIPS.

Fuel, see HEATING.

Fungus Growth, see PAINTING, EXTERIOR.

Fur Care, see INSECTS.

Furnaces, see HEATING.

Fuses, See ELECTRICAL FUSES; ELECTRICITY, THEORY OF.

Furniture Brake. When a typewriter table, a tool stand, or any other caster-mounted piece of furniture persists in inching away from you as you work on it, you can immobilize it by pressing a small wedge of wood between the roller and frame of two or more of the casters. Then later, when you wish to restore the caster action, it's a simple matter to knock the wedges free.

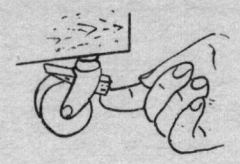

Furniture Care.

Aluminum. To restore original luster to outdoor aluminum furniture, rub it vigorously with a dry pad of fine steel wool, following this with a light coat of paste wax. Allow this wax to dry for about 20 minutes before buffing. By renewing this wax coating at least once or twice a year, you'll protect the aluminum from the elements and will help keep dirt from sticking to it and causing pitting.

Bamboo, cane, reed, wicker, and rattan furniture should be dusted with untreated cloth, or with a cloth dampened with water. Or, you can use the dusting attachment of your vacuum cleaner, which is ideal for the crevices. To prevent drying out and splitting, this type of furniture should be wet thoroughly about once a year, placing it outside and treating it with the fine spray from your garden hose. If such furniture needs washing, use mild suds containing a little ammonia, then rinse with clear water. Once a year, it's a good idea, too, to treat it with a coat of shellac.

Outdoor. Give your outside lawn furniture a generous coating of paste wax. This prevents the hot sun from blistering the paint, and also keeps the metal parts from rusting in damp weather.

Rustic. Your outdoor rustic furniture should be treated annually to a coating of spar varnish to safeguard it against damage from weather and insects. A coat or two of spar varnish will also prevent peeling. **Wicker** or rattan furniture can be cleaned nicely by scrubbing with a stiff brush moistened with salt water. The salt prevents the wicker from yellowing. **Wrought Iron.** If some of your wrought iron furniture or railings have become badly pitted, clean out the pits with some steel wool, then smooth in some plastic steel, which you can procure at the hardware store.

Furniture, Cleaning and Polishing.

Cleaner. Weak tea makes a good furniture cleaner. Rub the furniture with a cloth saturated with tea, then wipe dry.

Dusting Tip. For efficient, "double-quick" dusting, try dampening a pair of old socks with furniture polish, slipping these like gloves over your hands, then proceeding with your dusting ... with both hands.

Polish.

1. If you'd like a really high polish on your furniture, saturate a cloth with equal parts of lemon oil and turpentine, and go over the entire surface of each piece. Wipe off the excess oil with a damp cloth, then polish with a woolen cloth until you've achieved what you're looking for.

2. If you'd like to give a higher polish to your mahogany, first rub the surface with lemon oil and clean it off. Then use a soft cheesecloth which has been treated with alcohol and patted until only the vapor remains, and rub this quickly over the surface of the wood. It will produce a clear, lustrous finish.

3. Old furniture that has become dirty or discolored will be greatly improved in appearance by cleaning with a solution of vinegar, sweet oil and turpentine, mixed in equal parts. This solution is applied by rubbing vigorously on the wood with a soft cloth. The polish should be shaken before using to assure an even mixture.

4. A polish recommended especially for genuine old mahogany is made from boiled linseed oil (cold), to which a little vinegar has been added. Rub the oil well into the wood with one cloth, wipe off the excess with another cloth, then polish with a third cloth.

Polish Remover. To remove furniture polish, mix one-fourth cup of vinegar, one-half cup of water, dip a soft cloth into this, wring out, then rub the furniture with it. Dry immediately with another soft cloth.

Soapless Wash. You can prepare a soapless furniture wash by adding two tablespoons of linseed oil and two of turpentine to a quart of hot water. After mixing this well and allowing to cool, apply to the furniture with a soft cloth, well wrung out, and covering a small area at a time. Wipe each part dry as you proceed. Polish the furniture afterwards.

Furniture Making Tips. Furniture making is largely a matter of patience, using common sense, and following a few basic rules.

FURNITURE MARK REMOVAL

Here are some of those rules that will enable you to turn out a good job:

1. *Measure twice.* Don't rush into a job and start cutting your materials before planning the job carefully.

Materials can be expensive, and a wrong cut often means a piece of wood wasted. So after marking out, always check your measurements again just to make sure.

2. *Mark out with fine lines.* Use a hard pencil with fine point, and keep it sharp as you work.

For really fine lines and accurate work, as in making joints, use a marking knife, a tool with a chisel-like edge.

3. *Use good tools.* It's much easier to produce good workmanship with good quality tools than cheap ones. Good tools cost more, but last a lot longer.

4. *Keep tools sharp.* You can't produce good results with blunt cutting tools. They are more dangerous too, because the extra pressure that has to be used with them increases the danger of slipping.

5. *Use fillers sparingly.* Wood fillers are necessary for filling small cracks and splits, but should never be used as a camouflage for bad workmanship.

Large cracks and knotholes should be repaired with glued-in wooden plugs.

6. *Use a sanding block.* In rubbing down the work with glasspaper to a fine finish before polishing, always use a sanding block with the paper — a cork one is best — to get a smooth surface.

Always rub in the direction of the grain when using the glasspaper, start with a fairly coarse grade and finish with the finest grade available.

7. *Use your nail punch.* Nothing mars the appearance of a job more than to see nail heads protruding through a finished surface.

Always punch nail heads well below the surface, and fill them with plastic wood or putty — depending on the type of finish to be applied.

Remember that nail punches — or nail sets to give them their correct name — are made in various sizes to suit different nail gauges.

8. *Use correct screwdriver.* Always use the correct screwdriver. Driving in a large-headed screw with a small screwdriver damages the screw-slot and the blade.

It also makes the work harder and more difficult. On the other hand, using a larger screwdriver than necessary will damage the surface of the work.

Always drill pilot holes for screws, and where a number of screws are visible, always dress the heads — that is, have all slots running in the same direction.

Furniture Mark and Stain Removal.
Adhesive Tape Marks. Rub the marks with kerosene, which will dissolve them. Then rub with a cloth moistened with water containing a little vinegar, dry well and polish with furniture cream (not wax polish).

This removes the smeary look and smell left by the kerosene.

Marks left by cellulose tape on windows or mirrors can be removed with either kerosene or amyl acetate (used for thinning lacquer).

Finger Marks.

1. The varnish on some furniture is so hard and smooth that fingermarks and soiled places may be removed with a cloth wrung out in lukewarm suds made with white soap and the finish restored by rubbing with a cloth on which a few drops of light lubricating oil or furniture polish has been sprinkled. Especially good for dining tables.

2. Finger marks on furniture can be easily removed with a cloth saturated in olive oil. When applying wax polish, use just as little as possible, and rub until the surface is free of film. If you do this, your furniture will increase in loveliness and luster.

3. Before attempting to remove fingermarks from mahogany by polishing, go over the woodwork with a cloth dampened in a hot solution of vinegar and water. Then follow immediately with the polish, and rub until dry. All the marks will vanish.
Heat Marks. Rub those unsightly white heat marks on tabletops with a hard paraffin wax candle. Then cover with blotting paper and press with a warm iron. Repeat this process if necessary. Afterward, rub well with a soft cloth to restore the finish. (See also **White Stains,** below.)
Perfume Stain. Providing that perfume damage is not too severe, rub a little nail varnish remover very gently over the stains.

Use a soft cloth or paper tissue for rubbing.

Stuck Newspaper. In humid weather, when varnished furniture surfaces become sticky, a newspaper laid on a table may adhere to it. If this happens, don't mar the finish by applying water. Instead, rub the stuck paper with olive oil.

FURNITURE PAINTING TIPS

Surface marks on fine furniture that resist cleaning with a mild cleaning solution will usually yield to a rubbing with an ordinary ink eraser. Follow this with an application of polish to restore the original luster.

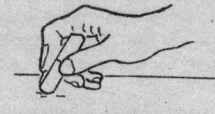

White stains. Sometimes wet glasses, hot dishes, alcohol, whiskey, perfume cause white rings to appear on finely finished table tops.

1. To get rid of white stains on mahogany furniture, spread a thick coating of petroleum jelly over the spot, let stand for 48 hours, then wipe off the jelly, and the stain should have vanished.

2. For restoring the original color to furniture that has turned white from water or other liquids, use 2 parts of alcohol, 2 parts of turpentine, and 1 part of olive oil, and rub well.

3. Stains and rings left on furniture surfaces by drinking glasses can be removed if you'll make an abrasive consisting of oil mixed with cigarette or cigar ashes. Merely dip an oil-moistened cloth into the ashes, then gently rub this over the stains and spots.

4. To deal with white marks left on furniture surfaces by water or hot dishes, rub lightly with a piece of flannel dampened with spirits of camphor or essence of peppermint . . . or you can use, very sparingly, a drop or two of ammonia on a damp cloth. Then cover with furniture polish.

5. White rings and stains left on furniture by glasses or dishes can often be removed by using vegetable shortening and salt. Sprinkle the stains with the salt, then rub gently with a clean cloth dipped into the shortening. When the stain has been removed, wash the surface immediately and rewax. In cases where the stain is extremely stubborn, probably the only solution is to sand and refinish the surface.

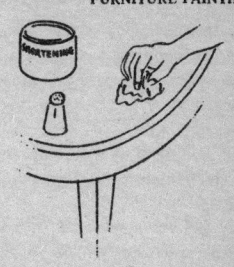

6. Ammonia will oftentimes remove alcohol, perfume, or water stains from furniture if it is applied quickly after the liquid has been spilled. Just put a few drops of ammonia on a damp cloth, rub over the spot, then follow immediately with an application of wax.

Furniture, Musty. If old furniture has a musty odor in it, stick some cloves in a green apple and place in the drawer. This will freshen it.

Furniture Painting Tips.

Legs. If you'll drive a nail into the bottom of each leg of a table or chair, and stand the furniture on these nails, it will make the job of painting the legs much easier and avoid the annoyance of their sticking to the floor as they dry.

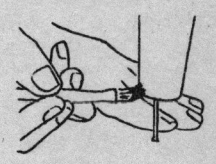

Metal. When repainting metal furniture, be sure first to remove all rust spots either with steel wool or sandpaper. Touch these spots up with red lead or the same paint you will be using to refinish the furniture. Then, when thoroughly dry, apply the final coat of exterior paint.

Outdoor. Before repainting outdoor furniture, scrub it well with a strong solution of sal soda concentrate, to remove all traces of greasy soil. If any soil is allowed to remain, the fresh paint won't form a firm bond and will peel or chip away.

Small Pieces. When painting small pieces of furniture, turn them upside down and paint the underneath portions first. Much more convenient and efficient.

FURNITURE REFINISHING

Unpainted. Always be sure to sandpaper new, unpainted furniture before painting it. This removes unseen dirt and grease, and provides a better base for your paint.

Furniture Refinishing. A great way to save money in furniture is to keep the old piece, no matter how bad it looks and refinish it.

First remove the old finish, which will take some muscle and patience. Whether it is paint, varnish, or shellac, the only way to do the job right is to use a paint-and-varnish remover. You must follow the directions on the can. It's a tough job, usually, and you must keep working until the last trace of the original finish is gone. Use remover, sander, and steel wool and sandpaper if necessary.

Once you are down to the base wood, you can tell if you need bleaching or not. Avoid bleach if possible, because it will make the wood rough and necessitate sanding. You must bleach, however, if there are dark spots in the wood.

Go over the work and make any needed repairs to the surface. Fill holes with wood filler or wood plugs. Reglue and/or reinforce loose joints as described above. Then apply desired finish according to directions.

Antique. One excellent antique stain for pine wood is provided with strongly brewed tea. After applying, cover it with two coats of fresh white shellac, then wax for a fine finish.

Antique Knotty Pine. If you'd like to achieve an antique appearance on your knotty pine woodwork, one way to do this is to sponge its surface with a fairly strong solution of ammonia, then apply two thin coats of fresh white shellac.

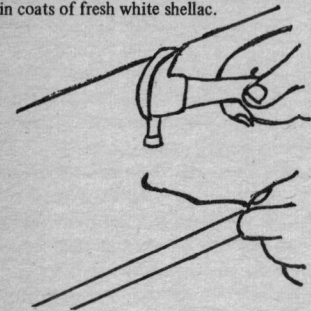

Antique Look. You can give an antique look to unfinished pine furniture by first applying an antique pine stain, then by scarring and denting the surface. These scars and dents can be made by pounding on a piece of wire, then rubbing some raw umber in the dents.

Finish Removal.

1. When removing the old finish from an antique, do as many of the cabinet makers do — scrub it with a strong solution of sal soda concentrate.

2. If some of your furniture pieces have soft finishes, these are easy to remove with steel wool that has been soaked in paint remover. Always use steel wool on the softer woods where a scraper's blade might possibly mar or damage the surface while removing the finish. This is especially good for grooves and corners.

3. When removing the finish on furniture, use plenty of paint remover. Spread it on with a brush. You'll know the remover has done its job when bubbles appear or when you can rub down to the bare wood with a finger. Use a scraper to take off most of the remover and paint. You can use steel wool if the paint isn't too thick. Wear rubber gloves to protect your hands. When all the old finish is off, rinse the surface with some water, wipe it off with a clean cloth, and allow to dry completely before sanding.

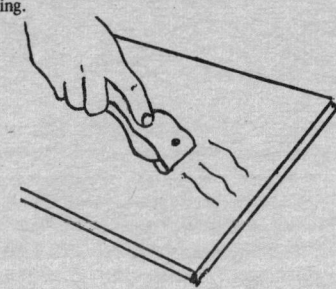

FURNITURE REFINISHING

Hand Rubbed. To produce a hand-rubbed finish on furniture pieces, you can use either powered pumice or rottenstone. Rottenstone cuts more slowly than pumice, but it produces a higher finish. Apply the powdered abrasive with a felt pad dampened with linseed oil, and be sure to check frequently to be sure you aren't cutting the finish.

Limed-Oak. One way to create a smart looking and attractive limed-oak finish is by stirring a pound of unslaked lime into two quarts of water, rubbing this across the grain of the wood, and wiping when partly dry (to prevent accumulation of excess lime). Seal with two coats of thin white shellac, and finish off with a thin coat of paraffin wax.

Mahogany Stain. A very versatile and economical mahogany stain can be made by mixing permanganate of potash and epsom salts with water. The depth of the color obtained depends on the strength of the solution.

Oil. You can use prepared oil finishes on furniture if you wish. You just brush on the oil, let it soak in, and then wipe off the excess. Apply several coats until the oil no longer soaks into the wood. Oil finishes take a lot of abuse, and if they begin to show signs of wear, just brush them up with more oil. You can make homemade oil finish by thinning linseed oil with turpentine, but the prepared finishes on the market are superior to anything you can mix yourself.

Paint, see FURNITURE PAINTING TIPS.

Sealer. A sealer gives you a durable finish that is easy to apply. You can get sealer clear or with stain added. For furniture that will get heavy-use, a sealer is ideal. A sealer resists heat and liquid. If a sealer finish is damaged, you can apply a thin coat or two of fresh sealer to the spot that is damaged. When using sealer, you need only apply two coats. After each coat buff it with steel wool. Let it dry for 15 minutes, and then wipe off the excess sealer with a cloth. Let the sealer dry overnight and rub with #000 steel wool. Apply paste wax over it as a final coat.

Semi-Gloss. When finishing furniture with varnish or enamel, it's usually better to use a semi-gloss varnish or enamel, rather than a high-gloss finish. The semi-gloss has a pleasing, satiny look which simulates hand rubbed furniture, and it is less likely to show brush marks or other defects when dry.

Shellac is a quick-dryer, and is easy to put on. It does not take the most rugged of treatment, but it is adequate for average use. Plan on using 2 or 3 thin coats, and after each coat is dry, rub with #000 steel wool. Put paste wax over the final coat. Use white shellac on light-colored wood, and orange shellac on dark-colored wood.

Stain. If you want to change the color of the wood and emphasize the grain, you should apply a coat of stain. Usually you don't have to stain a refinishing job because the wood has enough natural tone and color. And certain kinds of finishes will add color as they go on. New wood, especially a soft wood, can be improved, however, by staining. But don't try to make a piece of pine into a piece of walnut by putting on a walnut stain.

If you are unsure of whether or not to stain, try some of the prospective stain on the piece in an inconspicuous spot and then you'll be sure whether or not it actually does improve the appearance of the wood. Don't forget that a stain is simply a coloring layer and does not give any protective finish whatsoever to a piece of wood. You must have a protective finish on top of that in order to prevent dirt from discoloring the surface.

Varnish is one of the most popular finishes for furniture ever devised. Preparation of a surface to take a finish of varnish is one of the most exacting in painting. You must always sand the surface as smooth as possible and remove any stains or blemishes in the material before beginning, then dust the surface carefully and thoroughly.

Use a good quality bristle brush. Dip the brush into the varnish one-third of its length, and remove any excess by tapping against the inside of the container. Flow the varnish on liberally with long strokes going with the grain.

FURNITURE REPAIR

Do not press down too hard on the brush, or you will get air bubbles in the finish. After covering the surface in one direction, cross-stroke immediately by brushing across the grain at right angles to the original strokes. Finish off by stroking lightly with the grain using an almost dry brush.

Never varnish in a dusty location. When possible, lay all pieces horizontal for painting. Remove all knobs and hardware before starting. Varnish chests and drawers with the drawers removed. Stand each up with its front in a horizontal position and then apply varnish.

If you use more than one coat of varnish, thin the first with 10 percent turpentine. To get a smooth finish, sand lightly between coats, with #2/0 very fine sandpaper. Dust thoroughly.

To get a good rubbing finish, use cabinet rubbing varnish. Allow the final coat to dry till hard, and make a paste of pumice stone and crude oil. Mix these together on the surface itself. Then make a pad out of a heavy cloth. Press the pad in the paste and rub over the surface with straight strokes parallel to the grain.

Next use a clean dry cloth to wipe off all pumice. Use another cloth moistened with turpentine to clean off the residue, then wipe again with a clean cloth. The surface will now be cloudy.

Rub a second time with powdered rottenstone and crude oil. Mix the paste as before, then rub with a pad of clean felt—straight, with the grain. When the surface is polished as you want it, wipe off the paste with a clean cloth and polish with a soft dry cloth. Then put on any good furniture polish after waiting a day or two.

Varnishing Tips.

1. While working with varnish, fill a shallow pan with hot water and place the container of varnish in it. The heat will make your varnish flow much easier, and it will also dry in a shorter time.

2. If someone's clothing has left lint on a freshly-varnished surface that has not yet fully hardened, rub these spots with a cloth moistened with turpentine or mineral spirits, then follow with some furniture polish.

Varnish Removal.

1. To remove old varnish from furniture, woodwork, or floors, make a strong solution of baking soda and water, and apply to the surface. Let stand for a few minutes, then scrub with a coarse cloth until the varnish or paint is removed. Continue this routine until the surface is clean. Steel wool may also be used if not injurious to the wood.

2. To remove varnish from furniture, use ammonia and water in equal parts.

Furniture Repair.

Blistered Veneer. When veneer on furniture blisters up, repair it by first slitting the blister with a razor blade, cutting parallel to the grain, then covering with a cloth pad that has been moistened in hot water and letting this soak on the surface until the veneer softens. Then remove the cloth and immediately work fresh stainproof glue under the blistered surface with a thin spatula or knife blade. Press flat, cover with waxed paper, and weight it down until the glue has dried. Any glue that oozes out may be carefully scraped off, and a fresh coat of wax or furniture polish applied over the repaired area.

Broken Veneer. If the veneer on some article of furniture is broken or gouged, cut it out with a very sharp knife. Then cut a matching piece from a new piece of veneer, clean out the hole very thoroughly, and glue in the new piece. Weight this down for at least 24 hours.

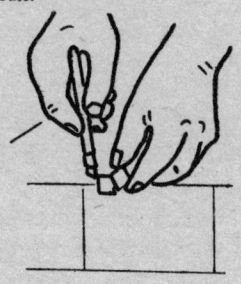

Burns.

1. With cigarette burns and other bad scars, you may have to remove all the finish around the damaged area. Scrape the scarred surface with a knife blade held as right angles to the surface. Rub the scar with a small piece of #0000 steel wool or fine sandpaper. Use colored wood plastic or wood filler to fill the area. If the scrape is shallow, build it up with several coats of colored varnish. Then brush on a thin coat of clear varnish or shellac. After this

FURNITURE REPAIR

has dried, polish with powdered rottenstone or crude oil. Finish with a wax coating.

2. Burn marks that are not too deeply embedded will sometimes disappear when rubbed with your usual furniture polish. If this fails, try using rottenstone or finely powdered pumice, mixed to a thin paste with raw or boiled linseed oil. Rub in the direction of the grain, wipe with another cloth moistened with plain linseed oil — repeating as often as may be necessary — then polish.

Chipped Veneer. Veneers on furniture that have chipped, cracked, or peeled, can be mended more easily if you'll use cellophane tape as a clamp for holding the new or repaired veneer in place while your glue is setting. This tape is especially good for repairing corners where the veneer has pulled away.

Chips and Nicks. Small chips and nicks in painted surfaces can be camouflaged very nicely by using wax crayons. These crayons, which come in an almost endless variety of colors and hues, can be selected to match any paint color. Rub the crayon lightly over the marred area, and this will both fill in and color the damaged spots in the painted surface.

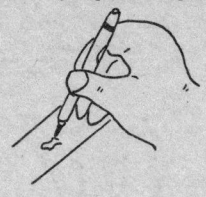

Crazed Surfaces. You can renew checked or "crazed" varnished or lacquered surfaces on furniture just by using a pad of fine steel wool dipped in rottenstone paste. Rub until the surface is smooth to the touch, then wipe off with a rag dipped in thinner, apply two coats of wax, and buff it down.

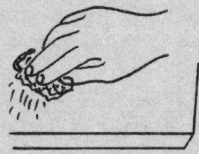

Dents. Disfiguring dents in your furniture can sometimes be raised, and thus avoid the necessity of refinishing. Try this little trick: First place a damp cloth over the dent, then on top of this a bottle cap to concentrate on the dent — then on this rest a warm iron lightly. Often this causes the wood fibers in the dent to swell. But, if after several treatments, the dent refuses to rise, you'll have to remove the finish with some fine sandpaper and try again. Refinish the area, if necessary, and rub it with rottenstone and wax.

Holes left in the wood when an ornament or drawer pull is removed can be hidden. First drill the hole a bit larger to expose fresh wood. Pack this with some wood plastic. Finish the filling job with some stick shellac, rub over with rottenstone, and wax.

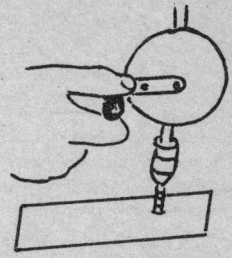

Loose Joints. When the glued joints on chairs, tables, or other furniture begin to loosen, try to repair them by regluing. To avoid the necessity of completely disassembling the article, inject your glue into the joints with the aid of an eyedropper. Spread the joints slightly apart before doing this, and warm the glue beforehand by immersing the container in hot water for several minutes, so that it will flow more easily.

(See also CHAIR REPAIR.)

Loose Veneer. If the veneer on an article of furniture has become loosened, you can repair it as follows: first remove the finish from the loosened area, then give it a steaming with an iron and a wet cloth to make it pliable. After scraping out the old glue with a piece of sandpaper, work some fresh glue in under the veneer with a spatula or wire, then let down your veneer and cover the surface with some newspapers and the weight of several books until

FURNITURE, SCRATCH PREVENTION

the glue has set. Finally, after sanding lightly with fine sandpaper, wipe on some varnish, rub with rottenstone, and wax.

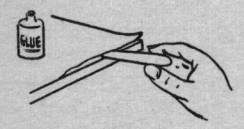

Squeaks. One usually effective way to muffle a piece of furniture that squeaks annoyingly is to drop a little melted paraffin into its joints.

Furniture, Scratch Prevention.

1. Ashtrays, vases, figurines, and other chinaware that might mar or damage the finish of your furniture can be very nicely remedied by cementing to their bottoms the kind of rubber rings that are used to seal fruit jars. These rubber protectors have an advantage over felt, ordinarily used, in that they do not absorb water when the objects to which they are attached are washed. And also, the rubber cement which is used to attach the rubber to the objects does not dissolve in water, as do some of the adhesives used with felt.

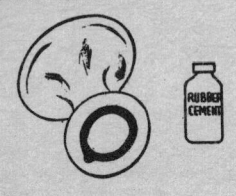

2. Lamps and knickknacks can be padded with cork inserts removed from beverage bottle caps to prevent their marring the table surfaces. Plastic cement will affix the cork to glazed surfaces.

3. Your discarded felt hats can be put to good use if you'll cut them into desired shapes and glue them to the bottoms of ashtrays or other knickknacks that might otherwise scratch your furniture.

Furniture, Scratch Repair.

Deeper scratches need filling and can be fixed by using stick shellac. Heat a knife blade in a flame and melt the end of the shellac stick and press the liquefied material into the crevice. Build up the shellac higher than the surrounding surface, and then shave down the level by using a razor blade. Then polish with powdered rottenstone and crude oil.

Light scratches on dark furniture can be touched up with ordinary shoe polish, colored wax stain, or a wax crayon, particularly on dark walnut or mahogany.

Scratches on dark furniture have a way of standing out, because they look white. For a quick and usually effective touchup, try using some ordinary iodine, applied either with the point of a toothpick or with a fine-pointed brush. You can lighten the color of the iodine if necessary by diluting it with a little alcohol. Let your touchup job dry thoroughly, then give it a good going-over with furniture polish.

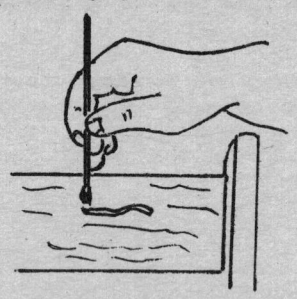

Minor Scratches.

1. Many minor scratches on furniture can be eradicated just by rubbing over them with a little light machine oil.

2. A preparation good for removing scratches from furniture is made from equal parts of salad oil and vinegar. Keep a bottle handy, shake well before using, and rub the mixture well into the wood until the scratches are gone.

3. One way to deal with scratches on natural wood cabinets and woodwork is with mineral oil, which blends nicely into the wood, assuming its shade as well as adding a polish at the same time.

4. The meat of a walnut or pecan is a very efficient material for camouflaging shallow scratches or nicks in the finish of furniture. All you do is rub

FURNITURE SKID PREVENTION

the oily meat over the scratch until it blends with the finish, then wipe the surface lightly with a polishing cloth. The nut meats must be fresh, because stale, dry meats could cause more scratches.

Furniture Skid Prevention.

Metal. You can prevent kitchen step stools and tables with metal legs from skidding, sliding, and slipping all over on waxed floors if you'll slip rubber crutch tips over the bottoms of the legs. These come in all sizes in surgical supply houses and most hardware stores.

Sectional. It's a good idea to hook adjoining pieces of sectional furniture together so that they won't be continually sliding apart. Just attach screen hooks to the backs of the legs.

Sofa. Do you have a sofa that is forever sliding away from its proper position against the wall? Here's one remedy for your trouble: First lay a strip of wood about 2 inches wide on the floor at each rear leg of your sofa, with one end of the wood pressed against the wall, and mark the location of each sofa leg on top of each wood strip. Then drill holes through the strips to accommodate the sofa legs. Then tack the wood strips onto the floor, place your sofa with its legs in the holes, and your slippage troubles will be over.

G

Galvanized Screens, see SCREEN CARE.

Garage Door Repair. Here's one easy way to replace a damaged panel in an overhead garage door. First trim off the edges of the opening into which the new panel is to be fitted, smoothing them down flush with the bottom of the old grooves in which the original panel rested. Cut out a new panel from 1/8-inch plywood and set this into the door in some calking compound which you have spread clear around the edges. Then fasten your new panel securely in place with some quarter-round molding.

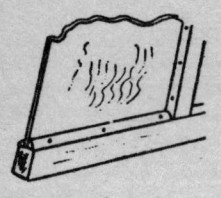

Garage Floors, see CONCRETE FLOOR CARE.

Gardening, see also LAWN.
  Compost Container. A compost pile, of course, is of inestimable value to the home gardener. Oftentimes, however, it proves harder to take the material from one of these piles than to add to it. By constructing a box such as the one illustrated, you'll have a container with an opening at the bottom from which the rotted leaf humus can be removed with a minimum of trouble and effort. The inside corner posts, to which the side boards are nailed, can be made of ripped two-by-four stock.

Evergreens. If the soil around the evergreens in your yard is lacking in acid, bury some of your citrus peels near them.

Fertilizer. Don't throw away the ashes from your wood-burning fireplace. They will make perfect fertilizer for your rose bushes next season.

Grass.
  1. It's always a laborious and tedious job hand-trimming the grass that grows under a fence. You can eliminate this chore if you'll dig a small groove or trough under the fence and make a practice of pouring into it now and then some salt water or crankcase oil. This will discourage the growth of grass, weeds, and other plant life.

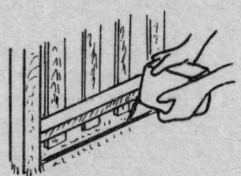

GARDENING

2. Here's a simple little trick to help you make a neat and perfect circle of turned-over soil around your trees and shrubs. Just knot a loop of rope around the tree trunk and the shovel handle, and keep this rope taut and your shovel upright as you work around the edge of your cultivated circle.

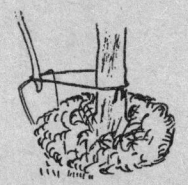

3. If grass persists in growing between the cracks in your walk, try scattering salt into these crevices. It will kill the grass roots.

Icy Bushes. Avoid damage to some of your plantings by using your garden hose to melt off heavy accumulations of ice. This can be done safely when the temperature is not below about 26 degrees. Speed is essential.

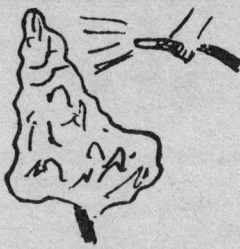

Ivy.

1. English and Boston ivy can be persuaded to climb on brick walls by placing the tendrils in the grooves between the bricks and plastering them in place with some mud. By the time the mud falls away, the ivy will have taken root in the brick.

2. Large hairpins do the trick of anchoring down ivy plants on a bank until they take root. These pins will also secure the ivy in the direction you want it to follow.

Markers. Small glass jars with screw tops make excellent waterproof and windproof markers for the vegetable or flower garden. Simply nail the lid to a stake and insert the empty seed package. You can write the date of the planting on the seed package,

also, if you like to keep a record of the plant growth.

Moss growing on brick or concrete paths can make them very slippery, and dangerous, especially in the winter.

Paint the moss-infected parts with a solution of lime sulphur or an orchard spray for killing fungus disease, sold by most general stores.

Use in the strength recommended on the container.

Mowing Strips. Here's an idea to ponder on for easier and neater mowing come springtime, and this consists of brick edgings around your flower plots or around your favorite shrubs. These mowing strips can be one brick wide (the bricks being buried to proper level in the soil)—or, if you'd like a wet-weather path about 16 inches wide, you can make the strip two-bricks wide, as in the illustration. You can use a cement base for a real permanent job, or you can lay the bricks on a sand base that has been thoroughly tamped down.

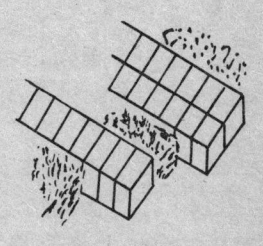

Plant Stakes. Don't be too hasty about throwing away that old bamboo rake. Save the remaining pieces to use for plant stakes for your houseplants

GARDEN TOOLS

or small garden plants. The handle also makes good stakes, as it can be cut in two pieces and split according to the size of the plants that need support.

Plant Support. If you have a tall plant that is in need of support, try using a small brass extension curtain rod. As the plant grows, pull the rod out to the proper height.

Poison Ivy. To clear away poison ivy in an area of your yard, spray with a solution of a gallon of soapy water and three pounds of salt. A few such dousings will kill the stuff.

Potting Plants. Your worn out household sponges can be put to good use the next time you are potting plants. Fit pieces of these sponges into the bottoms of the pots. They provide excellent drainage and help hold moisture in the soil.

Pruning is not done only to small plants. Any plant that grows out of normal proportion should be brought back into line and this applies likewise to seedings. If the plants in the seed flats have to wait a bit longer than anticipated, or if they get leggy because of insufficient light, just nip out the growing point at the top. This will prevent further upward immediate growth and encourage the formation of a bushy, well-formed plant.

Rose Cuttings. You can root rose cuttings by sticking them into a raw Irish potato.

Seedling Protector. A quick and effective method of affording protection for those tender seedlings—avoid their being trampled—is to shield them with a couple of croquet wickets. All you have to do is force the wickets into the ground to form a wire arbor over the plant. You can attach identification tags to the wickets, too.

Trellis. A very fine trellis for small climbing plants can be formed from three or four wire coat hangers nailed one above the other on a wooden upright, as illustrated. Use some small staples to secure the hangers to the upright and apply some wood preservative (such as creosote) to the part of the upright that is to go into the ground. Then paint the completed trellis with some rust-preventive paint.

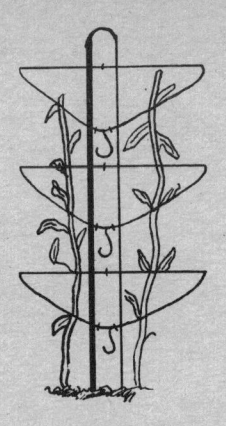

Walkway. One of the easiest methods of making stepping stones for the yard or garden is first to dig a series of shallow holes, the size and shape you like best, and then to pour concrete mix into each of these holes and smooth it over. For concrete economy, you can first throw some stones into the holes as a partial filler. One very good concrete-mix formula consists of: One sack (one cubic foot) of cement, two cubic feet of sand, three cubic feet of gravel or crushed rock, and six gallons of water.

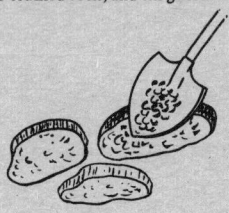

Watering. A canvas hose soaker is the best method of watering flower beds, as it lets the water seep directly into the soil without waste. It is inadvisable to stand and spray the bed with a hose, as the water wets the flowers and foliage, and for some plants this is an invitation to disease.

Weeding. Use an apple corer for digging out all weeds in your garden. It gets down under the roots without disturbing the nearby plants. Use it too for making holes when you transplant seedlings or small plants—it makes the task much more pleasant.

Garden Tools.

Hose Maintenance. Drain after each use. Store in

large loose coils or over a round object. Keep away from heat.

Hose Nozzle. The nozzle of your garden hose won't be misplaced, while not in use, if it is set into a holder near the outside faucet. A broom clamp, obtainable at any hardware store, provides an ideal holder for the nozzle.

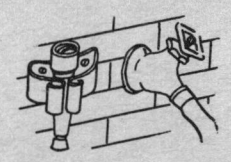

Hose Repair.

1. If your garden hose has sprung a leak and you'd like to make a really good repair job, try using a short piece of BX electrical cable with the wire removed. Cut the hose at the leak, force the cable into one part of the hose, and put a hose clamp on it. Now force the other part of the hose onto the cable, and place a clamp on it. The advantage of using the BX cable is that it permits the hose to bend, whereas a piece of pipe would not. And, therefore, you are still able to coil the hose up on its customary rack.

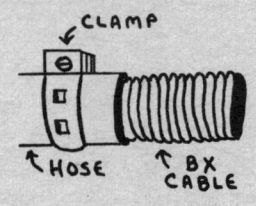

2. Pliable roof paint, applied in one coat to a leaky rubber garden hose, will often restore it to first-class usage.

Hose Sprinkler. When your rubber or nylon garden hose develops several leaks in it, don't throw it out. Just stick some more holes in it and you then have a sprinkling hose for watering the lawn.

Hose Support. From an ordinary wire coat hanger, you can fashion a very efficient support for your garden hose, which will enable you to aim the hose in just the right direction for soaking your plants, bushes or trees. The wire can be bent, as in the illustration, and the finished product will be stiff enough to stay put.

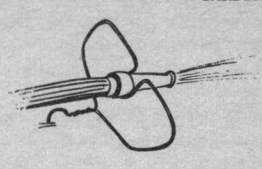

GARDEN TOOLS

Hose Washers.

1. The washers in some hose connections simply refuse to stay put! You can overcome this little annoyance very easily. Take a length of fine wire and force it through the edges of the washer, allowing just a bit to project on both sides. These projections will permit the washer to be "threaded" into the hose connection, and it will then be locked into place.

2. Rubber washers for the garden hose have a way of getting misplaced. To keep them always handy so that they can be instantly located when needed, slip them over a large nail driven into the wall near where the hose is stored. Drive the nail at a slight downward angle so that the washers won't slide off.

Maintenance.

1. Every gardener knows that sharp shovels and spades insure much quicker and easier digging in the yard and garden. You can put a nice, sharp edge on these tools by use of a small mill file—being sure to stroke the file toward the tool's cutting edge. If your tools are rusty, first take off the old rust with a wire brush. Then use a rust remover, such as ammonium citrate (available in most drugstores). It will take about a half-hour for the rust to dissolve.

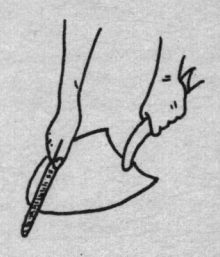

2. Garden tools and other small hand tools that are used around the outside of the house can be kept rust-free by coating them with a thin layer of paste wax. This not only forestalls rusting, but also helps to keep dirt from sticking to the tools.

3. Soak rusty garden tools in kerosene for a while, then use a wire brush and an emery cloth to finish the cleaning.

Pick Handle Repair. If your pick has loosened on its handle, it can be tightened by using a strip of screen wire the width of the pick hub. After first removing the handle, wrap the screen around the end and then drive the handle back into the pick. The screen will bite into the wood and stay in place.

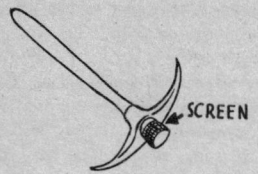

Rack. Two large tin cans having both ends removed, and nailed to a stud in the garage or tool shed, will provide a good rack for storing your handled garden and yard tools. Such a rack also proves ideal for storing rod and pipe—and wonderful, too, for clothesline props.

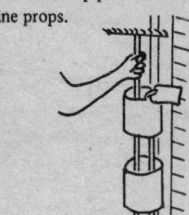

Rake. Here's a little tip for you home gardeners to paste in your scrapbook for future use. A child's toy rake, fitted with a longer handle, makes an ideal special-duty garden tool. It fits in under hedges and into narrow corners where the ordinary kind of "adult" rake can't be used.

Soaker. An empty, discarded, bottle-cap type of beer can can be converted into a very efficient garden-hose soaker. Puncture the can with about 30 small nail holes, and fasten a 1/2-inch hose connector with a washer to the can opening. All you have to do then is to screw the can onto your hose, place it in a strategic position in your garden, and let the seepage of water do its life-giving work.

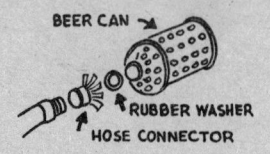

Weeding. A real handy weeding tool can be fashioned from an ordinary table knife. Bend an offset in the steel blade of the knife by clamping it into a vise. This offset permits you to get beneath the roots of the weeds to lift the whole plants out of the ground. For a better grip, wrap some friction tape around the handle.

Gas, Gas Burners, see HEATING.

Gasket, Shrunken. A cork gasket that has shrunk can sometimes be restored to its original size by dipping it into water, and then laying it flat long enough to absorb the moisture and swell. Be sure not to soak it for too long a period of time in the water, as it might come apart and crumble beyond redemption. It's a good idea, too, to lay the slightly-wetted gasket on some paper toweling for the drying-out process.

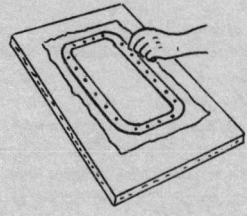

Gas Leak. Never test with a lighted match if you have reason to suspect that a connection in your home is leaking gas... the results might be disastrous. Instead, make a strong solution of soap and water, such as children use for blowing bubbles, and brush this over the connection. If there is a leak, gas will blow bubbles.

Gas Logs. Gas fire logs can be dusted with a cloth or, better still, with the dusting attachment of your vacuum cleaner.

Gasoline Stains, see AUTOMOBILES.

Geese, see FOODS.

Gem Resetting, see JEWELRY.

Glass.
  Broken. An easy way to pick up slivers of broken glass from the floor or table top is by use of a moistened wad of cotton. This will do a thorough job and reduce considerably the danger of your cutting your fingers.

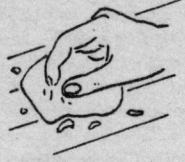

  Cement, see ADHESIVES.
  Chipped. Sharp edges on chipped glass can be rubbed smooth with fine sandpaper, making the glass safer to handle.
  Cleaning.
    1. Stale liquid tea does a splendid job of cleaning windows, mirrors, and other glass surfaces and glassware.
    2. If some of your glassware is spotted, soak it for several hours in buttermilk. Usually makes it sparkle!
  Cutting.
    1. If there is no regular glass cutter at hand, it is possible for you to do the job by holding the glass under water and using tin snips. If you are cutting a particular design, in order to help prevent breaking of the glass while cutting, cement a paper pattern to the glass with some rubber cement. When using the snips, the glass is not actually cut in the normal sense of the word—instead, it is "nibbled" away,

each nibble being no more than about 1/8-inch. Your finished edge, of course, will be rough. Plate glass or heavy window glass usually cannot be cut in this manner.

  2. The first thing to do when preparing to cut a sheet of glass is to use a large, flat working surface, such as a kitchen table, padding it with some old carpeting or thick layers of newspaper. Then before making your cut, wipe a film of oil or turpentine along the path of the cut, as shown in the illustration. This oil will prevent chipping and popping. It is advisable, too, to use a strip of hardwood, instead of a yardstick, as a straight-edge for your glass cutter. This gives you a much better grip for holding it steady along the line.

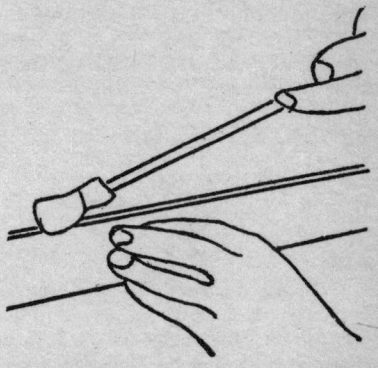

  3. When cutting glass, the job can be made much easier if you'll make some heavy crayon marks on the glass under the straight-edge used to guide your glass cutter. This wax crayon provides good friction to prevent the straight-edge from slipping.

  Frosting Windows, see WINDOWS, FROSTING.
  Polishing.
    1. To clean and polish mirrors and window glass at the same time, add a little starch to your water.
    2. Discarded nylon stockings used as cleaning rags will give your mirrors and windows a bright, lint-free shine.

GLASS BOTTLES

Repairing.

1. Shallow surface scratches in glass can often be removed by rubbing with a mixture of glycerin, water, and red rouge, using a felt pad as an applicator.

2. Small scratches on the glass tops of furniture can often be obliterated just by rubbing on some ordinary toothpaste, then polishing off with a soft cloth.

Glass Bottles, see BOTTLE CLEANING.

Glass, Cut, see CUT GLASS CARE.

Glass Doors, see DOORS.

Glasses, Drinking.

Decorations. You can add an attractive touch to some of the drinking glasses in which you serve fruit juices or other iced drinks at your parties. Procure some chenille pipe cleaners, which are found now, not only in smoking supply stores, but also in arts-and-crafts stores, in a variety of colors. Wrap some of these around your glasses, as in the illustration. They not only add decorative beauty, but also insulate your glasses.

Holders.

1. One way to prevent your refreshment glass from continually sliding off the arms of your lawn chair is by construction of this simple little gadget. Procure some No. 8 or No. 10 insulated electric wire, and bend it in a spiral, as in the illustration, with a tight-fitting sliding clamp on the bottom to fasten to the arm of your chair.

2. A very handy and efficient one-glass lawn "table" can be made with a length of dowel and a shallow tin can. Punch a hole in the center of the can and screw it to one end of the dowel, using a washer under the screw head. Point the other end of the dowel for easy pushing into the ground beside your lawn chair.

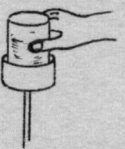

Marking. At a party in your home, you can avoid the risk of getting your guests' glasses mixed up by writing their names or initials on the outside of their glasses with some colored nail polish. These markings are easily removed after the party with a little nail-polish remover.

Monogramming. You can monogram your glassware permanently by applying metallized, gummed letters to their clean, grease-free surfaces. After applying, wash away any of the adhesive that might ooze from the edges, then let dry, then spread some clear epoxy resin evenly over the monograms, letting this extend about 1/16-inch beyond the edges. This coating should be about 1/32-inch thick. After allowing this to harden overnight, use a file or knife to level the coating and to clean and bevel the edges, then scrape smooth with a sharp knife or razor blade. To restore the transparency, moisten a small cloth pad with a little linseed oil and some shellac, then rub this over the monogram for a nice polish.

Repair. If some of your otherwise good drinking glasses have nicked edges that are uncomfortable to the lips, you can often smooth off the rough spots with fine emery cloth.

Stuck.

1. When one of your drinking glasses has become tightly stuck inside another, don't try to force them apart—fill the inside glass with cold water (for contraction) and dip the outside glass in hot water (for expansion)—and the two glasses will usually come apart without strain or breakage.

2. If you have some glasses that are tightly stuck together, place them in a refrigerator for a few minutes. When they are thoroughly chilled, they will usually come apart easily.

Glass Fibers, see FIBERS, MAN-MADE.

Glasspaper, see ABRASIVES.

Glass Tube Cleaner. For cleaning long, curved glass tubes and laboratory piping, a knotted cord does a fine job. Use a cord at least three times as long as the tube. Tie multiple knots at one place to make a ball that fits snugly inside the tubing. Then slip one end of the cord through the tube, fill the tube with water or cleaning solution, and draw the ball back and forth until the tube is clean. You can use a second cord with ball to dry the tube in the same manner.

Glassware.
1. Stains or cloudiness in glass vases, carafes, cruets, etc., will yield to ammonia. Fill them with water containing a teaspoon or two of ammonia and let stand for several hours or overnight. Then wash and rinse. This method works almost as well for mineral deposits. Or, you can try shaking tea leaves, plus vinegar, around in the vessel.

2. Strengthen new glassware by placing in a vessel of slightly salted water, letting it come slowly to a boil, then boiling thoroughly and follow by cooling slowly. The slower this treatment is done the more effective the results.

Gloves, see CLOTHES CARE.

Glue, Gluing, see ADHESIVES.

Glue Stain, see STAIN REMOVAL.

Glycerin, see LUBRICANTS.

Gold, see METALS.

Gold Cleaning, see JEWELRY.

Gold Leaf Frames, see FRAMES.

Gold Paint, see PAINTING TIPS.

GUTTERS AND DOWNSPOUTS

Golf Balls, Practice. Crumpled aluminum foil makes perfect practice golf balls. You can use them indoors or out. They will harm nothing and are lightweight and easy to spot.

Golf Club Care. Wooden golf clubs will keep their luster and finish if occasionally washed with shoe polish.

Grapefruit, see FOODS.

Grapes, see FOODS.

Grass, see GARDENING.

Grass Stain, see STAIN REMOVAL.

Gravy Stain, see STAIN REMOVAL.

Grease Gun. A very efficient grease gun for lubricating small machines and models can be provided from an old mechanical pencil. Remove the inner parts of the pencil, and make a plunger for it out of a brass tube with a leather washer screwed to one end. Fill the barrel of the pencil with light grease or petroleum jelly, insert the plunger, and force your lubricant out of the small end.

Grease, see STAIN REMOVAL.

Grill, Barbecue, see BARBECUE.

Grout, see ADHESIVES.

Gummed Paper. That roll of gummed paper will not stick together if you coat the sides of the roll with a thin layer of melted paraffin, which will seal the edge of the paper nicely and still permit the roll to be unwound.

Gutters and Downspouts. Houses should have gutters and downspouts to take care of roof water from rain and snow. Keep the gutters and downspouts free of debris. Where leaves and twigs from nearby trees may collect in a gutter, install a basket-shaped wire strainer over the downspout outlet. Repair gutters and downspouts as soon as the need appears. Keep them painted.

GUTTERS AND DOWNSPOUTS

Downspouts usually have an elbow or shoe on the lower end to discharge the water slightly above the ground and away from the basement wall. To prevent concentration of water at the point of discharge, use a concrete gutter or a splash block to carry the water away. The gutter or block should slope 1 inch per foot, and its edges should be flush with the grade.

Disposal of roof water as shown below makes it easy to clear clogged downspouts.

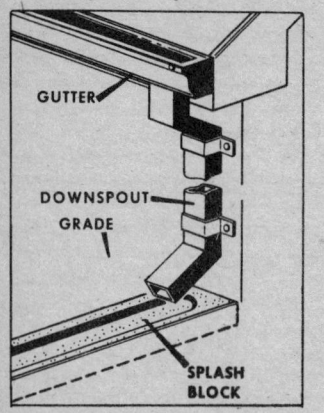

Roof water can also be piped underground to a storm water drain, dry well, or surface outlet, 15 feet or more from the house. The bottom of a dry well should be lower than the basement floor and in earth or rock that drains rapidly.

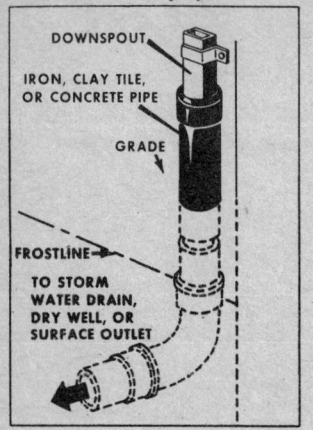

Gutters are semi-circular troughs with open tops that are used to catch drainage water from your roof. They hang on the edge of every roof. In a heavy rain almost 150 square feet of area can be drained by a gutter and leader having 1 square inch of area.

Gutters are made of aluminum, galvanized iron, copper, plastic, or wood. Leaders (downspouts) are usually made of copper or aluminum. Wooden leaders are not too successful; when the wood dries out in warm weather, the joints open up.

Leaders are made in round shapes, rectangular shapes, and corrugated shapes. Those built in corrugated shapes, for some odd reason, tend to freeze less rapidly than any other model.

Bracket Replacement. The gutter is supported by galvanized iron brackets nailed through the fascia boards. The added weight on the gutter could pull rusted nails from their holes. When replacing brackets always push the gutter upwards never pull it downwards, to free the old brackets. Then remove old brackets and replace and nail with galvanized nails through fascia boards into sound rafters. Now lower into place.

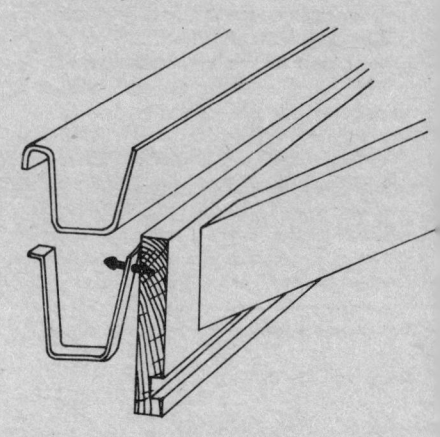

Cleaning. Gutters may be cleaned with a small hand spade or wire brush. Down pipes are cleaned with the aid of a thick dowel rod or a flexible wire, depending on the curve in the pipe. After forcing out the clogging matter, wash the pipe and gutter with the use of the garden hose. If rust holes are found on a section of guttering, it is best to cut that section out and replace it by soldering a new piece in place.

Cleaning Tool. A very efficient tool for cleaning your roof gutters can be fashioned by nailing a piece of rubber belting to a wooden handle. The flexible belt will follow the trough contours, but will not scratch the paint or other coating inside the gutter.

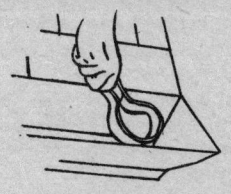

Maintenance. You should inspect your gutters and downspouts at least twice a year. In the fall, remove all the leaves that have fallen into the gutter. In the spring, check for leaks and buckling caused by winter freezing. Check all hangers, making sure none of them have been loosened by ice and snow.

Metal gutters may sometimes come apart where they are fastened in sections; they will leak at the joints. If refastening the sections does not stop the leakage, apply a piece of roofing felt inside, using asphalt roofing cement. Or, you can also repair holes in metal gutters with fiberglass patching kits sold especially for that purpose. Be sure you clean the surface completely before applying the patch.

Leaves and other material can cause clogging in a gutter. When the water stops flowing, it sits in the trough and freezes in the first cold snap. Usually the leader (or downspout) clogs up where it joins the gutter. You can get wire cages to fasten over the intake point where the downspout drains the gutter. You can also get ½-inch mesh wire netting to place over the top of the gutter. Slip one side of the netting under the lowest course of roof shingles; solder the other side to the rim of the gutter.

Painting. Before painting the outside main walls and trim of a house, the gutters must be cleaned out.

Inside surfaces of gutters are best painted with a bitumen-base paint. Downspouts are painted with normal exterior oil paints, but be sure to paint all the way around them.

Repair. One way you can repair a roof gutter which has begun to leak because of rust accumulation, first scrape out as much of the rust as you can with a wire brush or some steel wool. Then cover the inside of the gutter with a good grade of asphalt paint, and let this dry before continuing. Next coat the inside of the gutter with a heavy film of plastic roof cement, and before this sets, cover it with strips of heavy aluminum foil, pressing the foil down tightly with a dry cloth. Be sure to overlap the strips of foil in the direction of the water flow, and cement the edges together.

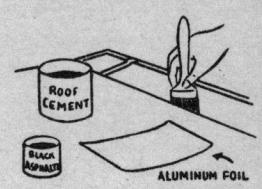

Gypsum, see **DRYWALL.**

H

Hacksaw, see TOOLS, HAND.

Hair Removal. To remove cat or dog hairs from materials, wipe with a damp chamois. (See also CLOTHES CARE.)

Hall Fixtures, see LIGHTING FIXTURES.

Halved Joints, see JOINTS.

Hammer, Hammering, see TOOLS, HAND.

Handbag Care, see CLOTHES CARE.

Hand Care.
   Deodorizing. Baking soda can remove the odor of onions from your hands.
   Dirt Removal. To get your hands and fingernails really clean after a session of housecleaning or gardening, scrub them with a damp nailbrush, sprinkled with dry baking soda. Does a fine job of cleaning and it is gentle and soothing, also.
   Grease Removal. That hard-to-remove grease which has a way of penetrating all the crinkles in the hands, especially after some work on the car, is not at all hard-to-remove if you'll use some cuticle remover. Just pour some of this on, rub and massage into the hands, let remain a few minutes, then wipe off with tissues and wash as usual.
   Manicuring. A teaspoonful of lemon juice in a cup of warm water will remove stubborn stains from your fingernails and fingers prior to your manicure job.

Paint Removal.
   1. If you prefer a commercial brand of sand soap, especially for removing paint from your hands—but it isn't kind to your skin—try adding a little petroleum.
   2. Clean paint-stained hands by rubbing them with cooking oil or with baby oil before scrubbing them with soap and water.
   3. You'll do a better and quicker job of cleaning your hands after painting if, instead of using turpentine or other such solvents, you rub sawdust over the stubborn spots. Finish off by washing the hands as usual with soap and water.
   Perspiration Prevention. Troubled with hands that perspire too freely? You can usually remedy the situation by bathing them with warm water and alcohol.
   Puckering. When the skin on your hands has become all puckered up as a result of long immersion in water, you can relieve the situation by rubbing your hands either with lemon juice or vinegar.
   Resin Removal. If you happen to get resin on your hands from installing the Christmas tree, wet them, sprinkle them with some dry baking soda, rub them together, and rinse. The resin will be gone. This also works for pine pitch.

Hand Drill, see TOOLS, HAND.

Handkerchief Care, see CLOTHES CARE.

Handkerchiefs, Scented. Your handkerchiefs will have a lasting scent of violets if one-fifth ounce of orris

158

root is broken up and placed in a muslin bag, and then boiled with the handkerchiefs for a short time.

Handle, Bucket, see BUCKET HANDLE.

Handle, Cabinet, see CABINET HANDLE.

Handle Repair. If the threaded wooden handle on a floor brush or other such gadget works loose, an emergency repair can be quickly made by unscrewing the handle, wrapping the exposed threads with several layers of cellophane tape, then twisting the handle back into its socket—which will squeeze the tape into the threads and make the handle secure.

Handrail, Rope. If there is no handrail in the enclosed stairway leading to your attic or basement playroom, and if you'd like to add a novel touch of character, try the installation of handrail of rope, as shown in the illustration. You should use a good quality, smooth rope, free of ravelings, and the metal or wooden rings through which it is threaded should be attached firmly to the wall.

Handsaw, see TOOLS, HAND.

Hand Screw Clamp, see TOOLS, HAND.

Hangers.
  Drip-Dry. If you don't happen to have any plastic coat hangers for your drip-dry clothing, you can make an effective substitute by covering a wire coat hanger with some aluminum foil. Cut the foil in one-inch strips and wrap round and round, covering three sides of the hanger and pinching together at the top.
  Repairing. Sometimes wooden garment hangers have cracks or slivers on them that might catch on and damage the linings of your coats and other garments. One quick and easy way of remedying this situation is to smooth out those rough spots with a coat of fingernail polish.

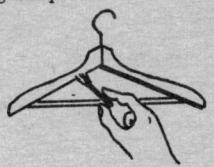

  for Rope, see ROPE HANGER.
  Wire. Do some of your wire hangers cave in under the weight of heavy garments? Double their strength by binding two hangers together with cellulose or adhesive tape.

Hanging Doors, see DOORS.

Hardware is a general word used to describe any kind of device that fastens, hooks, supports, guides, suspends, grips, ties or holds together in any way. The two basic kinds of hardware are nails and screws.

Protect your brass door knobs, escutcheon plates, and other such ornamental hardware from corrosion and pitting by periodically treating them with thin layers of paste wax. Clean these items first with metal polish or scouring powder, then rub on the wax, and buff well when dry. Once or twice a year will insure you of continued protection.

Hardwood, see LUMBER; WOOD, WORKABILITY OF.

Hardwood Floors, see WOOD FLOORS.

Hat.
  Cleaning.
    1. Clean light-colored felt hats with a mixture of two tablespoons of corn meal and one teaspoon of salt. Put this on with a soft cloth, then rub off with a stiff brush.
    2. For cleaning white felt hats, apply a paste made of arrowroot and magnesia, and when this has dried, whisk it off with a soft brush.
  Racks.
    1. Here is a quick and easy way to make a handy rack for a man's hat. Procure the shallow lid of a large cardboard box, cut it out as illustrated, and then tape it to the lower surface of a closet shelf so

that the hat it holds will clear all other articles in the closet and the crown will not be in any way crushed.

2. Hat racks made from ordinary coat-hanger wire and hinged inside a closet door will help keep men's hats in good shape and also leave more space on the closet shelves. Hold the wire with a clip, and screw into place.

Headache Remedy. The juice of half a lemon in a cup of black coffee is a remedy that is often effective for a headache.

Hearth, see FIREPLACE.

Heating.

Area Heating Units, see **Circulator Heaters, Fireplaces, Pipeless Furnaces, Stoves, Vertical Heaters,** below.

Boilers are made of cast iron or steel and are designed for burning coal, gas, or oil. Cast-iron boilers are more resistant to corrosion than steel ones. Corrosive water can be improved with chemicals. Proper water treatment can greatly prolong the life of steel broiler tubes.

Buy only a certified boiler. Certified cast-iron boilers are stamped "I-B-R" (Institute of Boiler and Radiator Manufacturers); steel boilers are stamped "SBI" (Steel Boiler Institute). Most boilers are rated (on the nameplate) for both hot water and steam. Contractors can advise on selecting a boiler.

Circulator Heaters. With proper arrangement of rooms and doors, a circulator heater can heat four or five small rooms, but in many instances heating will not be uniform. A small fan to aid circulation will increase efficiency. The distance from the heater to the center of each room to be heated, measured through the door opening, should be not more than about 18 feet. Doors must be left open; otherwise, grills or louvers are needed at the top and bottom of doors or walls for air circulation.

Coal. Two kinds of coal are used for heating homes—anthracite (hard) and bituminous (soft). Bituminous is used more often.

Anthracite coal sizes are standardized; bituminous coal sizes are not. Heat value of the different sizes of coal varies little, but certain sizes are better suited for burning in firepots of given sizes and depths.

Both anthracite and bituminous coal are used in stoker firing. Stokers may be installed at the front, side, or rear of a furnace or boiler. Leave space for servicing the stoker and for cleaning the furnace. Furnaces and boilers with horizontal heating surfaces require frequent cleaning, because fly ash (fine powdery ash) collects on these surfaces. Follow the manufacturer's instructions for operating stokers.

Controls, Automatic. Each type of heating plant requires special features in its control system. But even the simplest control system should include high-limit controls to prevent overheating. Limit controls are usually recommended by the equipment manufacturer.

The high-limit control, which is usually a furnace or boiler thermostat, shuts down the fire before the furnace or boiler becomes dangerously or wastefully hot. In steam systems, it responds to pressure; in other systems, it responds to temperature.

The high-limit control is often combined with the fan or pump controls. In a forced-warm-air or forced-hot-water system, these controls are usually set to start the fan or the pump circulating when the furnace or boiler warms up and to stop it when the heating plant cools down. They are ordinarily set just high enough to insure heating without overshooting the desired temperature and can be adjusted to suit weather conditions.

Other controls insure that all operations take place in the right order. Room thermostats control the burner or stoker on forced systems. They are sometimes equipped with timing devices that can be set to change automatically the temperatures desired at night and in the daytime.

Since the thermostat controls the house temperature, it must be in the right place—usually on an inside wall. Do not put it near a door to the outside; at the foot of an open stairway; above a heat register, television, or lamp; or where it will be affected by direct heat from the sun. Check it with a good thermometer for accuracy.

Controls, Coal-Stoker. The control system for a coal stoker is much like that for an oil burner. However, an automatic timer is usually included to operate the stoker for a few minutes every hour or half hour to keep the fire alive during cool weather when little heat is required.

A stack thermostat is not always used, but in communities where electric power failures may be long enough to let the fire go out, a stack thermostat or other control device is needed to keep the stoker from filling the cold fire pot with coal when the electricity comes on again. Sometimes a light-sensitive electronic device such as an electric eye is used. In the stoker-control setup for a forced warm-air system, the furnace thermostat acts as high-limit and fan control.

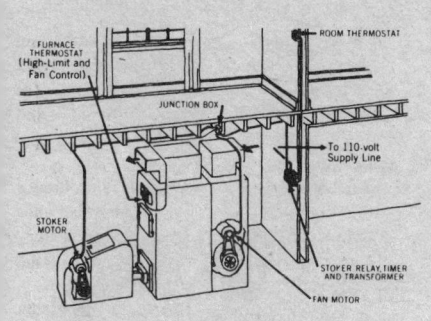

Controls for a stoker-fired coal burner with a forced-warm-air heating system.

Controls, Gas-Burner, see **Gas Burner,** below.

Controls, Heating-System. Warm-air, hot-water, or steam heat distribution systems may be controlled in other ways besides those described in **Oil-Burner Controls,** below. If the furnace or boiler heats domestic water, more controls are needed.

In some installations of forced hot-water systems, especially with domestic-water hookups, a mixing valve is used. The water temperature of the boiler is maintained at some high, fixed value, such as 200°F. Only a portion of this high-temperature water is circulated through the heating system. Some of the water flowing through the radiators bypasses the boiler. The amount of hot water admitted is controlled by a differential thermostat operating on the difference between outdoor and indoor temperatures. This installation is more expensive than the more commonly used control systems, but it responds almost immediately to demands; and, although it cannot anticipate temperature changes, it is in a measure regulated by outside temperatures, which change earlier than do those indoors.

The flow of hot water to each part of a building can be separately controlled. This zoning—maintaining rooms or parts of the building at different desired temperatures—can be used to maintain sleeping quarters at a lower temperature than living quarters. Electric heating is also well adapted to zoning.

Fuel savings help to offset the initial cost of the more elaborate control systems.

Controls, Oil-Burner. The oil-burner controls allow electricity to pass through the motor and ignition transformer and shut them off in the right order. They also stop the motor if the oil does not ignite or if the flame goes out. This is done by means of a stack thermostat built into the relay. The sensing element of the stack control is inserted into the smoke pipe near the furnace or boiler. Some heating units are equipped with electric eye (cadmium sulfide) flame detectors, which are used in place of a stack control.

Without the protection of the stack thermostat or electric eye, a gun- or rotary-type burner could flood the basement with oil if it failed to ignite.

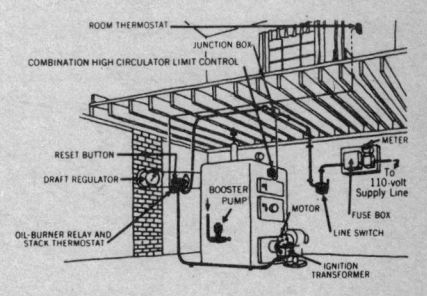

Controls for an oil burner for a forced-hot-water heating system.

HEATING

With such protection, the relay allows the motor to run only a short time if the oil fails to ignite; then it opens the motor circuit and keeps it open until it is reset by hand.

The illustration shows controls for an oil burner with a forced-hot-water system. The boiler thermostat acts as high-limit control if the water in the boiler gets too hot.

Convectors usually consist of finned tubes enclosed in a cabinet with openings at the top and bottom. Hot water or steam circulates through the tubes. Air comes in at the bottom of the cabinet, is heated by the tubes, and goes out the top. Some units have fans for forced-air circulation. With this type of convector, summer cooling may be provided by adding a chiller and the necessary controls to the system. Convectors are installed against an outside wall or recessed in the wall.

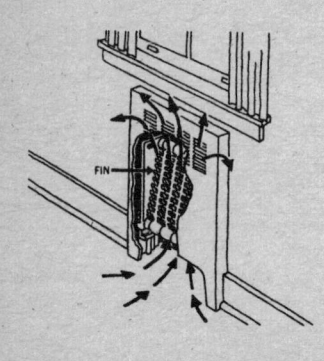

Convectors for hot water or steam heating are installed against the wall or recessed in the wall as shown here.

Converting Units. It is best to buy a heating unit designed specifically for the fuel to be used. Coal or wood burners can be converted to oil or gas but usually do not have sufficient heating surface for best efficiency.

Ducts. Check exposed ducts forced-warm-air systems for too-sharp bends. Eliminate such bends, if practicable and you may be able to increase the cool air intake of the furnace for improved performance. You may wish the advice of a heating engineer concerning changes in ducts.

Electric Heating. Many types and designs of electric house-heating equipment are available. Some are (1) ceiling unit, (2) baseboard heater, (3) heat pump, (4) central furnace, (5) floor furnace, and (6) wall unit. All but the heat pump are of the resistance type. Resistance-type heaters produce heat the same way as the familiar electric radiant heater. Heat pumps are usually supplemented with resistance heaters.

Ceiling heat may be provided with electric heating cable laid back and forth on the ceiling surface and covered with plaster or a second layer of gypsum board. Other types of ceiling heaters include infrared lamps and resistance heaters with reflectors or fans.

Baseboard heaters resemble ordinary wood baseboards and are often used under a large picture window in conjunction with ceiling heat.

Electric heating cable is one of the different types of electric heating used.

The heat pump is a single unit that both heats and cools. In winter, it takes heat from the outdoor air to warm the house or room. In summer, it removes heat from the house or room and discharges it to the outside air. It uses less electricity to furnish the same amount of heat than does the resistance-type heater. Room air conditioners of the heat pump type are especially convenient in warmer climates where continuous heating is not needed or for supplemental heat in some areas of the house.

Either heat pumps or furnaces with resistance heaters are used in forced-air central heating systems. They require ducts similar to those discussed for forced warm-air heating. Hot-water systems with resistance-type heaters are also available.

Wall units, either radiant or convection, or both, are designed for recessed or surface wall mounting.

HEATING

They come equipped with various types of resistance heating elements. The warm air may be circulated either by gravity or by an electric fan.

The better types of electric wall heaters discharge the warm air from the bottom and circulate it by means of a fan.

Each room heated by the equipment just described (with the exception of some central-heating systems) usually has its own thermostat and can be held at any desired temperature. Thermostats should be designed for long life and should be sensitive to change in temperature of ½° F., plus or minus.

Electric heating offers convenience, cleanliness, evenness of heat, safety, and freedom from odors and fumes. No chimney is required in building a new house, unless a fireplace is desired.

For electric heating to be more competitive economically with other types of heating, houses should be well insulated and weatherstripped, should have double-or triple-glazed windows, and should be vapor sealed. The required insulation, vapor barrier, and weatherproofing can be provided easily in new houses, but may be difficult to add to old houses.

Some power suppliers will guarantee a maximum monthly or seasonal cost when the house is insulated and the heating system installed in accordance with their specifications.

The heating equipment should be only large enough to handle the heat load. Oversized equipment costs more and requires heavier wiring than does properly sized equipment.

Equipment. Different types of heating equipment and systems are available for heating the home. Considerations in selecting a unit or system include heating requirements, installation and maintenance costs, and heating costs. Heating-equipment dealers and contractors can assist in determining heating requirements and in selecting the most efficient and economical unit for your house.

For safety and efficiency, have a reputable contractor install your central heating system and inspect it once a year. A less costly system correctly installed will be more satisfactory than an expensive one that is not the right size for the house or that is not properly installed.

Fireplaces are used more for personal enjoyment than for heating efficiency. They are often used to supplement other heating equipment, to take the chill off the house when it is not cold enough to run the furnace, or for emergency heating when the central system fails.

Modified fireplaces are manufactured units, made of heavy metal and designed to be set in place and concealed by brickwork or other masonry construction. They are more efficient than ordinary fireplaces, because warm air is discharged from air ducts surrounding the fireplace. A fan in the duct system will improve the circulation.

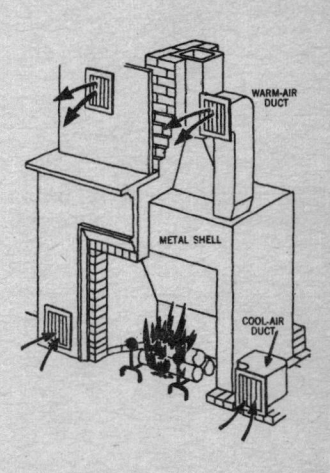

Modified fireplaces heat more efficiently than ordinary fireplaces. Cool air enters the inlets at the bottom, is heated by contact with the warm metal of the fireplace, rises by natural circulation, and is discharged through the outlets at the top. The outlets may be located in the wall of an adjacent room or a second-story room.

HEATING

Forced-hot-water heating systems are recommended over the less efficient gravity hot-water-heating systems.

In a forced-hot-water system, a small booster or circulating pump forces or circulates the hot water through the pipes to the room radiators or convectors.

In a one-pipe system, one pipe or main serves for both supply and return. It makes a complete circuit from the boiler and back again. Two risers extend from the main to each room heating unit. A two-pipe system has two pipes or mains. One carries the heated water to the room heating units; the other returns the cooled-water to the boiler.

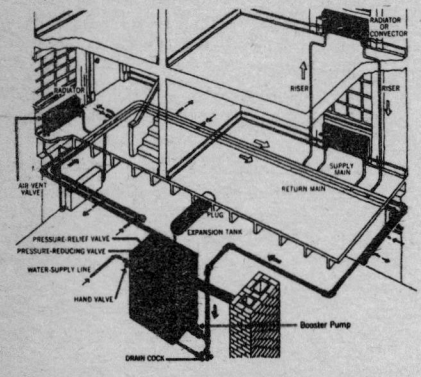

Two-pipe forced-hot-water systems have two supply pipes or mains. One supplies the hot water to the room heating units, and the other returns the cooled water to the boiler.

A one-pipe system, as the name indicates, takes less pipe than a two-pipe system. However, in the one-pipe system, cooled water from each radiator mixes with the hot water flowing through the main, and each succeeding radiator receives cooler water. Allowance must be made for this in sizing the radiators—larger ones may be required further along in the system.

Because water expands when heated, an expansion tank must be provided in the system. In an "open system," the tank is located above the highest point in the system and has an overflow pipe extending through the roof. In a "closed system," the tank is placed anywhere in the system, usually near the boiler. Half of the tank is filled with air, which compresses when the heated water expands. Higher water pressure can be used in a closed system than in an open one. Higher pressure raises the boiling point of the water. Higher temperatures can therefore be maintained without steam in the radiators, and smaller radiators can be used. There is almost no difference in fuel requirements.

With heating coils installed in the boiler or in a water heater connected to the boiler, a forced-hot-water system can be used to heat domestic water year-round. If you want to use your heating plant to heat domestic water, consult an experienced heating engineer about the best arrangement.

One boiler can supply hot water for several circulation heating systems. The house can be "zoned" so that temperatures of individual rooms or areas can be controlled independently. Remote areas such as a garage, workshop, or small greenhouse, can be supplied with controlled heat.

Gas- and oil-fired boilers for hot-water heating are compact and are designed for installation in a closet, utility room, or similar space, on the first floor if desired.

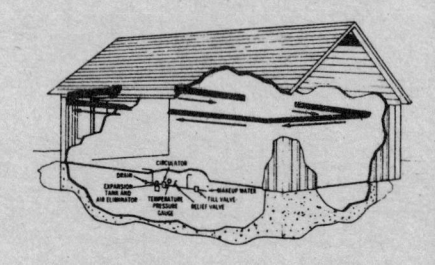

Electrically heated hydronic baseboard systems are made in units so that several units may be connected to form a single-loop installation. Water is circulated through the entire loop by pump. Each baseboard unit has a separate heating element, so that the circulating water can be maintained at a uniform temperature, if desired, around the entire house.

Electrically heated hydronic (water) systems are especially compact, and the heat exchanger, expansion tank, and controls may be mounted on a wall. Some systems have thermostatically controlled electric heating components in the hydronic baseboard units, which eliminates the central heating unit. Such a system may be a single-loop installation for circulating water by a pump, or it may be composed of individual sealed units filled with anti-

HEATING

freeze solution. The sealed units depend on gravity flow of the solution in the unit. Each unit may have a thermostat, or several units may be controlled from a wall thermostat. An advantage of these types of systems is that heating capacity can be increased easily if the house is enlarged.

Forced-warm-air heating systems are more efficient and cost less to install than gravity warm air heating systems.

Forced-warm-air systems consist of a furnace, ducts, and registers. A blower in the furnace circulates the warm air to the various rooms through supply ducts and registers. Return grilles and ducts carry the cooled room air back to the furnace where it is reheated and recirculated.

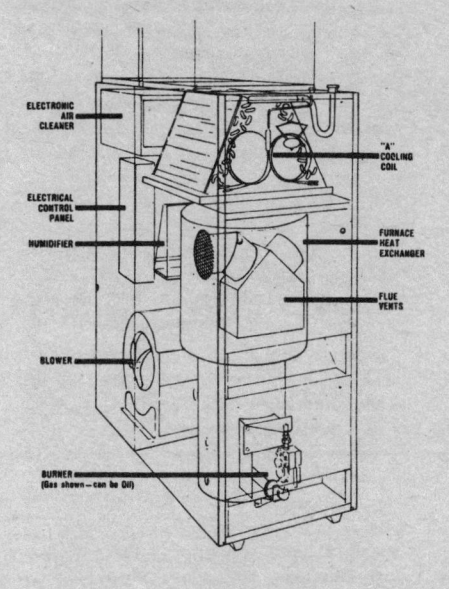

Modern forced-warm-air furnaces may have an electronic air cleaner for better air filtration and cooling coils for summer air conditioning. This is a gas furnace.

Forced-warm-air systems heat uniformly and respond rapidly to changes in outdoor temperatures. They can be used in houses with or without basements—the furnace need not be below the rooms to be heated nor centrally located. Some can be adapted for summer cooling by the addition of cooling coils. Combination heating and cooling systems may be installed. The same ducts can be used for both heating and cooling.

The warm air is usually filtered through inexpensive replaceable or washable filters. Electronic air cleaners can sometimes be installed in existing systems and are available on specially designed furnaces for new installations. These remove pollen, fine dust, and other irritants that pass through ordinary filters and may be better for persons with respiratory ailments. The more expensive units feature automatic washing and drying of the cleaner.

A humidifier may be added to the system to add moisture to the house air and avoid the discomfort and other disadvantages of a too-dry environment.

Warm-air supply outlets are preferably located along outside walls. They should be low in the wall, in the baseboard, or in the floor where air cannot blow directly on room occupants. Floor registers tend to collect dust and trash, but may have to be used in installing a new system in an old house.

High-wall or ceiling outlets are sometimes used when the system is designed primarily for cooling. However, satisfactory cooling as well as heating can be obtained with low-wall or baseboard registers by increasing the air volume and velocity and by directing the flow properly.

Ceiling diffusers that discharge the air downward may cause drafts; those that discharge the air across the ceiling may cause smudging.

Most installations have a cold air return in each room. When supply outlets are along outside walls, return grilles should be along inside walls in the baseboard or in the floor. When supply outlets are along inside walls, return grilles should be along outside walls.

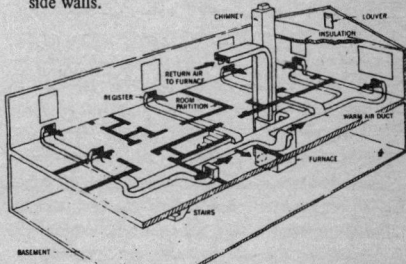

Forced-warm-air systems are the most popular-type of heating systems. Most installations have a cold air return in each room (except the bathroom and kitchen). If the basement is heated, additional ducts should deliver hot air near the basement floor along the outside wall.

HEATING

Centrally located returns work satisfactorily with perimeter-type heating systems. One return may be adequate in smaller houses. In larger or splitlevel houses, return grilles are generally provided for each level or group of rooms. Location of the returns within the space is not important. They may be located in hallways, near entrance doors, in exposed corners, or on inside walls.

In the crawl-space plenum system, the entire crawl space is used as an air supply plenum or chamber. Heated air is forced into the crawl space and enters the rooms through perimeter outlets, usually placed beneath windows, or through continuous slots in the floor adjacent to the outside wall. With tight, well-insulated crawl-space walls, this system can provide uniform temperatures throughout the house. Because this system is relatively new, however, specific recommendations are not available for the most economical installation and operation. See also **Horizontal Furnaces, Perimeter-loop Heating Systems** and **Vertical Furnaces,** below.

Fuel Conservation. You'll waste money if you keep your house too hot. The usual temperature should be about 70 degrees. In many cases, 66 degrees is quite comfortable, and if you keep it at 66° you will save fuel.

Keep a good thermostat in control of the heater. The thermostat should be placed in an "average" spot about 5 feet above the floor. Set it at 70 degrees. If you find that your house is running cold at 70 degrees, set the thermostat up to 72° and see how it feels. Or, if it is too hot at 70°, lower the thermostat setting to 68. You'll find the most equable temperature soon.

Do not place a thermostat near a television set or near a refrigerator—both create a great deal of excess heat.

Fuel Selection. The therms of heat per dollar should not be the sole consideration in selecting the heating fuel. Installation cost, the efficiency with which each unit converts fuel into useful heat, and the insulation level of the house should also be considered. For example, electrically heated houses usually have twice the insulation thickness, particularly in the ceiling and floor, and, therefore, may require considerably less heat input than houses heated with fuel-burning systems. To compare costs for various fuels, efficiency of combustion and heat value of the fuel must be known.

Furnace Cleaning. Although it is a difficult job, you can clean a furnace that has become so dirty it does not function correctly. Disconnect the stove pipes or ducts. Scrub them inside and out with a long-handled brush, removing soot, rust and dirt. Paint them inside and out with stove pipe paint, or rub them with a cotton rag dampened with kerosene. Replace the stove pipes.

Working from the top of the furnace down, open each of the clean-out doors and remove all ashes. Brush out soot, dirt and rust particles with a long-handled wire brush. Give the inside of the furnace a thin coat of light oil, and then do the same to the outside. Oil all the door hinges, using an oil can. Inspect all fire gates, replacing any that are warped. Oil the dampers. Leave the furnace doors ajar so that air circulates freely to prevent moisture condensation. Then close them and start up the furnace.

Gas is used in many urban homes and in some rural areas. It is supplied at low pressure to a burner head, where it is mixed with the right amount of air for combustion.

Three kinds of gas—natural, manufactured, and bottled—are used. Different gases have different heat values when burned. A burner adjusted for one gas must be readjusted when used with another gas.

Gas, Bottled. Bottled gas (usually propane) is sometimes called LPG (liquefied petroleum gas). It is becoming more popular as a heating fuel in recent years particularly in rural areas.

Bottled gas is heavier than air. If it leaks into the basement, it will accumulate at the lowest point and create an explosion hazard. When bottled gas is used, make sure that the safety control valve is so placed that it shuts off the gas to the pilot as well as to the burner when the pilot goes out.

Gas Burners. A room thermostat controls the gas valve. A pilot light is required. It may be lighted at the beginning of the heating season and shut off when heat is no longer required. However, if it is kept burning during nonheating seasons, condensation and rapid corrosion of the system will be prevented.

The pilot light should be equipped with a safety thermostat to keep the gas valve from opening if the pilot goes out; no gas can then escape into the

HEATING

room. (The pilot light of all automatic gas-burning appliances should be equipped with this safety device.)

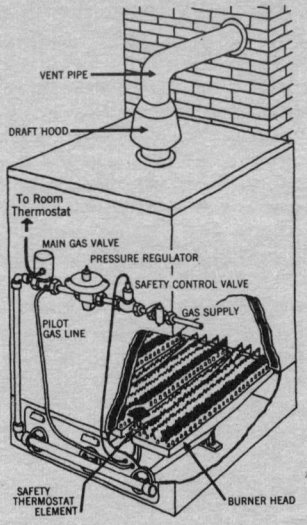

Gas burners vary in design, but all operate on much the same principle. The controls shown are essential for safe operation.

Conversion gas burners may be used in boilers and furnaces designed for coal if they have adequate heating surfaces. Furnaces must be properly gastight. Conversion burners, as well as all other gas burners, should be installed by competent, experienced heating contractors who follow closely the manufacturer's instructions. Gas-burning equipment should bear the seal of approval of the American Gas Association.

Vent gas-burning equipment to the outdoors. Keep chimneys and smoke pipes free from leaks. Connect all electrical controls for gas-burning equipment on a separate switch so that the circuit can be broken in case of trouble. Gas-burning equipment should be cleaned, inspected, and correctly adjusted each year.

Horizontal Furnaces. In houses without basements, horizontal furnaces that burn gas or oil may be installed in the crawl space or hung from ceiling joists in the utility room or adjoining garage. The gas furnaces may also be installed in attics. Allow adequate space for servicing the furnaces. Insulate attic furnaces and ducts heavily to prevent excessive heat loss.

Hot-water and steam heating systems consist of a boiler, pipes, and room heating units (radiators or convectors). Hot water or steam, heated or generated in the boiler, is circulated through the pipes to the radiators or convectors where the heat is transferred to the room air. See **Boilers, Convectors, Forced-Hot-Water,** above and **Radiant Panel Heating, Radiators, Steam Heating,** below.

Insulation, see INSULATION.

Oil is a popular heating fuel. It requires little space for storing and no handling, and it leaves no ash.

Two grades of fuel oil are commonly used for home heating. No. 1 is lighter and slightly more expensive than No. 2, but No. 2 fuel oil has higher heat value per gallon. The nameplate or guidebook that comes with the oil burner indicates what grade oil should be used. In general, No. 1 is used in pot-type burners, and No. 2 in gun- and rotary-type burners.

Oil Burners. For best results, a competent serviceman should install and service an oil burner.

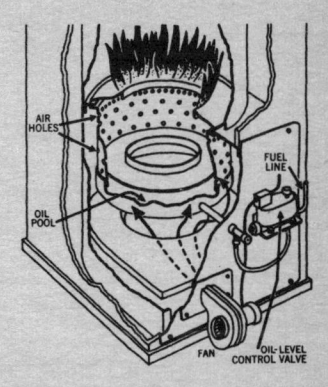

Vaporizing or pot-type oil burners are the least expensive type.

Oil burners are of two kinds—vaporizing and atomizing. Vaporizing burners premix the air and oil vapor. The pot-type burner is vaporizing and consists of a pot containing a pool of oil. An automatic or handset valve regulates the amount of oil in the pot. Heat from the flame vaporizes the oil. In some

167

HEATING

heaters a pilot flame or electric arc ignites the oil pot when heat is required; in others the oil is ignited manually and burns continuously at any set fuel rate between high and low fire, until shut off. There are few moving parts, and operation is quiet. Some pot-type burners can be operated without electric power.

Atomizing burners are of two general types—gun (or pressure) and rotary. The gun burner is by far the more popular type for home heating. It has a pump that forces the oil through a special atomizing nozzle. A fan blows air into the oil fog; and an electric spark ignites the mixture, which burns in a refractory-lined firepot.

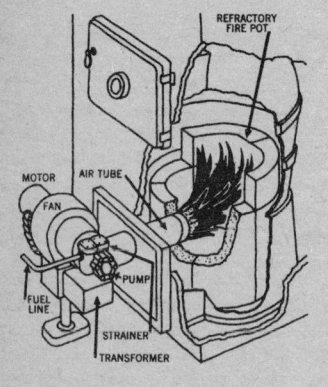

The gun or pressure type oil burner is the most popular for home central heating systems.

Perimeter-loop Heating System. Houses built on a concrete slab may be heated by a perimeter-loop heating system. Warm air is circulated by a counterflow type furnace through ducts cast in the outer edge of the concrete slab. The warm ducts heat the floor, and the warm air is discharged through floor registers to heat the room.

To prevent excessive heat loss, the edge of the slab should be insulated from the foundation walls and separated from the ground by a vapor barrier.

Pipeless furnaces may be used in smaller houses. They discharge warm air through a single register placed directly over the furnace. Units that burn wood, coal, gas, or oil are available for houses with basements. Gas- and oil-burning units, which can be suspended beneath the floor, are available for houses without basements.

Radiant panel heating is another method of heating with forced hot water or steam. (It is also a method of heating with electricity.)

Hot water or steam circulates through pipes concealed in the floor, wall, or ceiling. Heat is transmitted through the pipes to the surface of the floor, wall, or ceiling and then to the room by radiation and convection. No radiators are required—the floor, wall, or ceiling, in effect, act as radiators.

With radiant panel heating, rooms can be more comfortable at lower air temperatures than with other heating systems at higher air temperatures. The reason is that the radiated heat striking the occupant reduces body heat loss and increases body comfort. Temperatures are generally uniform throughout the room.

Underfloor radiant panel heating systems are difficult to design. For instance, a carpeted or bare wood floor might be very comfortable while the ceramic-tiled bathroom floor or the plastic kitchen-floor covering might be too hot for bare feet. An experienced engineer should design the system.

Panel heating in poorly insulated ceilings is not practical unless you want to heat the space above the ceiling. Exterior wall panels require insulation behind them to reduce heat loss.

Radiators. Conventional radiators are set on the floor or mounted on the wall. The newer types may be recessed in the wall. Insulate behind recessed radiators with 1-inch insulation board, a sheet of reflective insulation, or both.

Radiators may be partially or fully enclosed in a cabinet. A full cabinet must have openings at top and bottom for air circulation. Preferred location for radiators is under a window.

Baseboard radiators are hollow or finned units

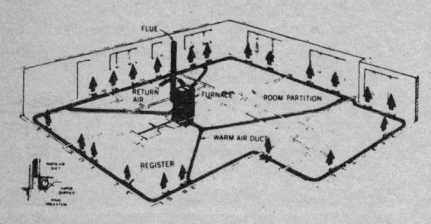

Perimeter-loop heating systems are often used in basementless houses built on a concrete slab. The inset shows duct-slab-foundation construction details.

HEATING

that resemble and replace the conventional wood baseboard along outside walls. They will heat a well-insulated room uniformly, with little temperature difference between floor and ceiling.

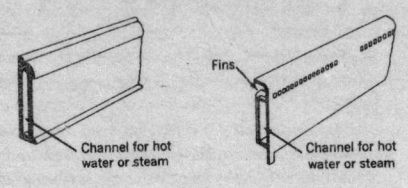

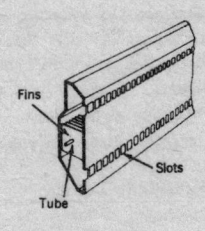

Baseboard radiator units are designed to replace the conventional wood baseboard. In the hollow types, *A* and *B*, water or steam flows directly behind the baseboard face. Heat from that surface is transmitted to the room. In the finned-tube type, the water or steam flows through the tube and heats the tube and the fins. Air passing over the tube and fins is heated and delivered to the room through the slots.

Radiator water level may be too low for proper and efficient heating. To raise the water level, first close the water valve. Put a pan under it, and remove the radiator air valve. Reopen the water valve until the water comes out of the air valve hole. Shut off the water valve and replace the air valve. Repeat this with all radiators, starting with those closest to the boiler.

Reducing Heat Requirements. Much can be done to reduce the heat requirements in a house. This, in turn, can reduce heating costs and increase personal comfort.

New houses may be oriented so that the main rooms and the large windows in the rooms face south to receive maximum sunlight in the winter. (In summer, the sunlight may be shaded out by trees, wide eaves, shutters, awnings, or other natural or artificial shading.)

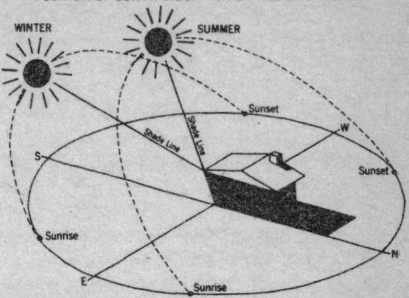

Solar orientation of a house to reduce heat requirements. Large glass areas face south to take advantage of the winter sun which strikes the earth at a lower angle than the summer sun.

Tight construction also reduces heat requirements. Insulate ceilings and outside walls. Calk and weatherstrip joints. Install storm sash or double- or triple-glazed windows to reduce heat loss through the windows. An old house should always be repaired and insulated before a new heating system is installed.

The chimney is a part of the heating plant; proper construction and maintenance are important. Chimneys should extend a minimum of 2 feet above the roof ridge. Manufacturers usually specify the size of flue required for heating equipment. Keep flues clean and free from leaks.

Steam heating systems are not used as much as forced-hot-water or warm-air systems. For one thing, they are less responsive to rapid changes in heat demands.

One-pipe steam heating systems cost about as much to install as one-pipe hot-water systems. Two-pipe systems are more expensive.

The heating plant must be below the lowest room heating unit unless a pump is used to return the condensate to the boiler.

Steam systems can lose efficiency if the air has become stale and too dry in a room. Open the windows for short intervals, or place pans of water on the radiators.

Stoves are one of the simplest heating devices. Although they are cheaper than central heating system, stoves are dirtier, require more attention, and heat less uniformly. If more than one stove is used, more than one chimney may be needed.

Wood- or coal-burning stoves without jackets heat principally by radiation. Jacketed stoves or circulator heaters heat mainly by convection and are available for burning the four common fuels—wood, coal, oil or gas.

Thermostats, see **Controls,** above.

Unit Efficiency. Heating units vary in efficiency, pending upon the type, method of operation, condition, and location. Stoker-fired (coal) steam and hot-water boilers of current design, operated under favorable conditions, have 60 to 75 percent efficiency. Gas- and oil-fired boilers have 70 to 80 percent efficiency. Forced-warm-air furnaces, gas fired or oil fired with atomizing burner, generally provide about 80 percent efficiency. Oil-fired furnaces with pot-type burner usually develop not over 70 percent efficiency.

Vertical Furnaces. Vertical gas or oil furnaces designed for installation in a closet or a wall recess or against a wall are popular especially in small houses. The counterflow type discharges the hot air at the bottom to warm the floor. Some, such as the gas-fired unit shown below, provide discharge grilles into several rooms.

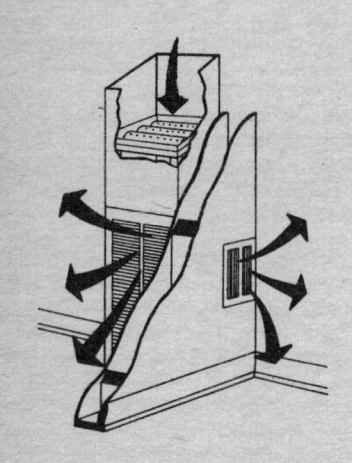

Vertical furnaces installed in a closet or a wall recess or against the wall are popular in small houses. The counterflow type (shown here) discharges the warm air at the bottom.

Upflow-type vertical furnaces may discharge the warm air through attic ducts and ceiling diffusers.

Without return air ducts, these furnaces are less expensive, but also heat less uniformly.

Vertical Heaters. Small gas-fired vertical heaters are sometimes recessed in the walls of the various rooms. Such units may be either manually or thermostatically controlled. Heater vents are carried up through the partitions to discharge the burned gases through a common vent extending through the roof.

Wood. The use of wood requires more labor and more storage space than do other fuels. However, wood fires are easy to start, burn with little smoke, and leave little ash.

Most well-seasoned hardwoods have about half as much heat value per pound as does good coal. A cord of hickory, oak, beech, sugar maple, or rock elm weighs about 2 tons and has about the same heat value as 1 ton of good coal.

Heating Pipe Insulation, see INSULATION.

Heat Pump, see COOLING.

Heat-Sealing. Cellophane or pliofilm wrappings may be heat-sealed with a warm iron. Don't apply the heat too directly to the pliofilm, but iron through cellophane so the pliofilm won't melt or stick to your iron.

Heat Theory. Heat is a one-way traveler: it always leaves an object that is warm in favor of one that is relatively cool. Because no two objects are ever exactly the same temperature, heat is usually on its way from one place to another.

Conduction. Like water, heat flows in the direction of least resistance (on its way to that cooler object). Many materials are excellent conductors of heat; others are poor conductors. Those that do not allow heat to flow through them at all are called insulators. The main problem you will have in keeping a house properly heated is in retaining the warm air inside. If it is cooler outdoors, the heat will travel through walls, ceiling, and floor to escape. If the air outside is the same temperature as the air inside, the heat will stay in the house indefinitely.

When heat passes through the walls of a house or through a window, it travels by "conduction," which is simply the ability of a substance to transmit heat. Air itself is a poor conductor. Pockets of air inside a wall serve as good heat insulation. The wall itself is a good conductor.

Convection. Air itself, like water, tends to rise if it is warm. Warm air always rises to the ceiling and cold air drifts down. Warmed air pushes upward from a heater, forcing down cooler air to the heater where it in turn will be heated and likewise rise.

The current formed by the tendency of warm air to rise is called "convection." It is through a knowledge of convection currents that you can control the heating of your house. Basically, the tendency of warm water to rise and displace cooler water is the theory upon which a radiator system works, and it is also the way water is kept heated in a boiler.

Radiation. Heat also travels by radiation, the transference of heat from one object directly out into the air. Steam and hot-water radiators work on this theory, sending heat from the metal surface directly into the air itself.

Heat Stains, see STAIN REMOVAL.

High Resistance Wires, see ELECTRICITY, THEORY OF.

Hinged Door, see CLOSET DOORS.

Hinges.

Corner irons (sometimes referred to as mending plates) make strong and practical hinges for the cover of a tool box or toy box. To attach these, locate the cover on the box and clamp it in place so that it cannot shift. Then attach the irons to the cover with two screws and to the box itself with one screw each.

Maintenance. One easy and effective way to touch up the black "H" and "L" hinges on cupboard doors instead of removing them or trying to paint them with a brush, is to use a black marker pencil. This does a lovely job of covering up the nicks and scratches and it dries immediately.

Repair, see DOOR REPAIR.

Storing. Safe and easy storing for the hinges and screws which have been removed from discarded furniture can be provided by mounting them on a piece of insulating wallboard. The wood screws can be forced easily into the board, but will hold fast enough to keep the hinges well in place.

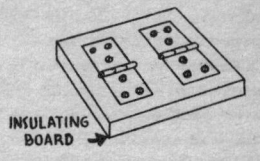

Hobby Storage, see STORAGE, HOBBY.

Hole Punch Tip. Eliminate the nuisance of picking up those little elusive paper punchings, even if your punch is not the type with a built-in "reservoir." Simply fit your punch with a cellulose tape receptacle, as in the illustration. Wedge in a small block of rubber or cork, trim it off flush, then press on a length of cellulose tape over the hollow part of the punch. Since the tape is transparent, you will be able to see when the chamber has filled with punchings.

Home Inspection. Many home owners give attention to the house only when problems arise such as a leaking roof or a burst pipe. Such a practice is neither wise nor safe. Trouble should be anticipated and prevented by making regular inspections and keeping the house in good repair.

Before purchasing a home it is wise to have an inspection made by experienced workman whose training enables him to discover defects which may not be apparent to the average home owner. After a first professional inspection, home owners may wish to make their own inspections. Using the list, below, and the diagram, and beginning with the basement, systematically inspect the essential parts of the house.

HOME MOVIE SCREEN

1. Gravel fill*
2. Basement floor
3. Foundation wall
4. Column
5. Girder
6. Joists
7. Heating plant
8. Waterproofing*
9. Footing
10. Drain tile
11. Bridging
12. Siding
13. Corner Board
14. Window frame and sash
15. Sheathing paper
16. Diagonal sheathing
17. Insulation
18. Studs
19. Shutters
20. Exterior trim
21. Roof sheathing*
22. Roofing felt*
23. Roof valley
24. Flashing
25. Flue linings
26. Shingles
27. Chimney cap
28. Dormer windows
29. Louver
30. Gable end
31. Gutter
32. Downspout
33. Building paper*
34. Ridge board*
35. Rafters*
36. Interior trim
37. Interior wall finish
38. Stairway
39. Subfloor*
40. Finish floor
41. Hearth
42. Fireplace

*These inspections should be made before construction is complete.

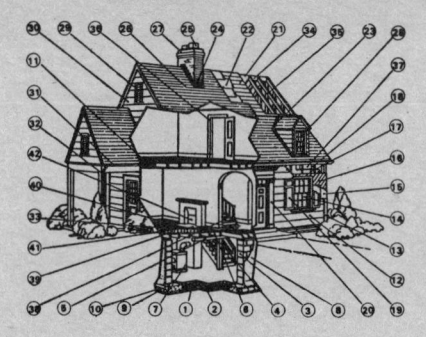

Home Movie Screen. You can improvise a very nice screen for your home movies just by using a card table. Two of the table's legs are extended to hold it on edge. Then, if the top of the table is dark-colored, it may be covered with some white paper or sheeting.

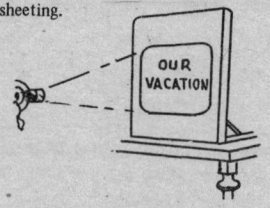

Hose, see GARDEN TOOLS.

Hose Faucet, see PLUMBING.

Hosiery, see CLOTHES CARE.

House Number, see ADDRESS PLAQUE.

HousePaint, see PAINTS.

House Plants, see PLANTS, HOUSE.

Hurricane Lamp, see LIGHTING, PORTABLE.

Hydrant, Frostproof, see PLUMBING.

172

Ice Cream Sticks. Save your children's ice cream sticks, and glue them together as in the illustration to serve as a convenient flowerpot stand, or as coasters for hot plates. After your glue has dried, stain or paint the stand the color you wish. You can use small wire brads, instead of glue, if you wish.

Ice Cube Trays. One way to prevent that annoying sticking of ice cube trays in your refrigerator is to place the trays on sheets of aluminum foil in the freezer compartment. The foil prevents the tray bottoms from freezing to the compartment, and permits their easy removal without the usual tugging or prying.

Ice Traction, see AUTOMOBILE.

Incandescent Bulbs, see LIGHT BULBS, INCANDESCENT.

Indelible Pencil, see STAIN REMOVAL.

Ingredient Substitutes, see FOODS.

Ink Eradicator. One way of producing a homemade ink eradicator is by whipping up a solution of one part chlorinated laundry bleach and ten parts of water. Keep in an old iodine bottle with a rubber stopper to withstand the destructive effects of the bleach, and with a glass rod as an applicator. Use this along with a blotter, just as you would a commercial eradicator.

Ink, Invisible. You can improvise a good "invisible ink" with some lemon juice. Squeeze some into a bottle and use a clean pen for writing with it. When the liquid has dried, it will be invisible. Then, to make it visible again, just apply the heat of an electric iron or lamp bulb to the paper. The writing will appear brown and be then permanently visible. Be sure to stroke your pen lightly when you are writing, so as not to cause any visible scratches on the paper's surface.

Ink Stain, see STAIN REMOVAL.

INLAID DESIGNS

Inlaid Designs. To inlay names or designs in wooden boxes, like the one illustrated, lay out the letters with a sharp knife, then cut the outline about 1/16-inch deep with a sharp knife. Inlay with any constrasting wood, mitering the joints wherever possible, and gluing the pieces into place. When the glue has dried, sandpaper, and finish.

Insecticides, Pesticides, see INSECTS.

Insects.

Ant Extermination. One effective manner of getting rid of ants in your yard is to place flower pots over the ant hills, as in the illustration, then pour in about a teaspoonful of carbon tetrachloride. The fumes will sink and surround the ant hill, shutting out all oxygen.

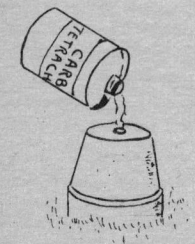

Ant Hill Destruction. Add some clear water to some used coffee grounds, and pour this over and down ant hills in your yard. The inhabitants will disappear after one or two applications.

Ant Repellent. Ants can be prevented from climbing the legs of food cabinets and tables if you will set the legs into caster cups filled with some insecticide. This is a good idea, too, for protecting the legs of tables on which food is served in the yard or on the patio.

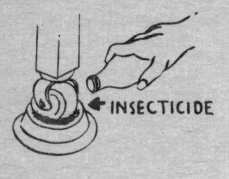

Carpet Beetles, see **Clothes Moths, Fabric Damage Prevention, Moth Preventive Storage,** below.

Clothes Moths and Carpet Beetles. Clothes moths are well-known pests of fabrics in the home.

Not so well known as clothes moths, but just as destructive to fabrics, are carpet beetles, or "buffalo moths." Carpet beetles are more abundant than clothes moths in most localities, and damage that they do often is blamed on clothes moths.

The larvae of clothes moths and carpet beetles damage fabrics by feeding on them. They feed on anything that contains wool or other animal fibers.

The adult moths and beetles do no damage.

The larvae of clothes moths and carpet beetles begin feeding as soon as they hatch. They feed on wool, mohair, hair, bristles, fur, feathers, and down. They attack clothing and a wide range of household furnishings: blankets, comforters, rugs, carpets, drapes, pillows, hair mattresses, brushes, and upholstery.

Clothes moth larvae usually are found on their food material. But carpet beetle larvae crawl from place to place and may be found on cotton goods or other things on which they do not feed. They often live behind baseboards and moldings, in cracks in floors, in corners, behind radiators, in air ducts of heating systems, on closet shelves, or in dresser drawers.

In urban areas some infestations are started by adult carpet beetles or clothes moths that fly from house to house. Such infestations are more likely to be started by beetles than by moths.

Eggs and larvae of the moths and beetles may be carried into homes on articles containing wool or other animal fibers. The articles on which they hitchhike most commonly are secondhand clothing, upholstered furniture, and other home furnishings.

The practice of exchanging woolen scraps for use in making rugs accounts for some infestations. When woolen scraps have lain unprotected for long periods, they often are infested.

Carpet beetle larvae frequently crawl from one room to another. If a hall carpet in an apartment house becomes infested, it is almost certain that some of the larvae will crawl from the hall into rooms that open onto it.

Carpet beetles breed and feed outdoors in places such as bird and rodent nests; adults sometimes enter homes from these places.

Fabric Damage Prevention. The best way to protect your clothing and furnishings against fabric insect damage is to use effective preventive measures. This includes (1) purchasing woolens or woolen-synthetic blends that have already been treated by the manufacturer with a moth-resistant compound, (2) applying protective treatments to susceptible articles, (3) practicing good housekeeping, and (4) when needed, spraying insecticides on surfaces over which the insects are likely to crawl.

If you have a heavy or widespread infestation, it is advisable to get the services of a reputable pest-control firm.

You can rid woolen clothing, blankets, and unupholstered furnishings of insects and their eggs and larvae by brushing and sunning them, or having them drycleaned.

If pillows, mattresses, or upholstered furnishings are infested, you should have them fumigated by a reputable pest-control firm, or you should dispose of the infested articles.

However, these practices give no protection again reinfestation.

To prevent infestation you should mothproof articles with chemicals or store them properly.

Flea Extermination. To rid a house of fleas, wet some pieces of wrapping paper with oil of cedar, scatter these around the floor, under the beds, and on the rugs during the night.

Insecticide Sprays, Aerosol. Aerosol containers deliver a fine spray which does not moisten surfaces as coarse sprays do; aerosol sprays do not give lasting protection. Do not use aerosols for surface spraying.

Insecticide Sprays, Surface. Treat surfaces where insects crawl with a spray having 2 percent of chlordane, 3 to 5 percent of malathion or ronnel, or 1/2 percent of lindane or diazinon. Read and follow the directions on the container.

You may buy these insecticides in ready-to-use pressurized containers that deliver a coarse spray, or you may buy a liquid insecticide and apply it with a household hand sprayer that delivers a continuous coarse spray. When the spray dries, it leaves a deposit (thin layer of insecticide) which kills insects that crawl over it.

Surfaces to spray are as follows: along the edges of wall-to-wall carpeting; behind radiators; along baseboards and moldings; in corners, cracks, and other hard-to-clean places. In spraying closets, take clothing out of the closets and apply the spray to corners; to cracks in the floor, walls, and ceiling; along baseboards; around shelves; and at the ends of clothes rods.

Mosquito Repellent. Cleaning window and door screens with kerosene is a doubly good idea, because it not only removes dust from the screen, but keeps mosquitoes from settling on them.

Moth-Preventive Storage. You can protect woolen articles by placing paradichlorobenzene crystals or naphthalene flakes or balls (popularly known as moth crystals, flakes, or balls) in the container or closet in which the articles are stored.

As these chemicals evaporate they produce a vapor that, in sufficent concentration, kills both clothes moths and carpet beetles. The mere odor of the chemicals does not repel the insects and is no indication that the concentration of vapor is sufficient to kill them.

In order to gain full efficiency, hang moth preventives high in the closet. The fumes filter downward.

To be effective in holding the vapor, the container (which may be a trunk, chest, box, or garment bag) must be airtight. If you store woolens in a closet without first placing them in containers, see that the closet is tightly sealed. If there are cracks around the door, seal them with tape or fit the door with gaskets. If there are cracks in the closet walls, floor, or ceiling, fill them with putty or plastic wood. Protection is lost if the closet door is opened frequently.

In a trunk or closet, use 1 pound of the crystals, flakes, or balls for each 100 cubic feet of space. Because the vapors are heavier than air, the chemicals should be placed in a shallow container on a shelf, or suspended from a clothes rod or hook in a thin cloth bag or perforated container.

You also can protect woolen articles by wrapping them in paper or sealing them in a cardboard box. Before wrapping or sealing, be sure the articles are not infested. In making a paper bundle, carefully fold back and seal all edges of the paper with paper tape.

Cedar chests are good pestproof containers primarily because of their tight construction. Before placing woolen articles in a cedar chest, see that they are free of larvae. After cedar chests are 2 years old, scatter moth crystals, flakes, or balls among the woolens stored in them.

Mothproofing.

1. *Clothing and Blankets.* One of the best ways to protect clothing and blankets against clothes moths and carpet beetles is to spray them with an oil-solution insecticide containing methoxychlor.

You may buy these insecticides in ready-to-use pressurized containers that deliver a coarse spray, or you may buy a liquid insecticide and apply it with a household hand sprayer that delivers a continuous coarse spray.

To apply the insecticide, hang the clothing and blankets on a clothesline and spray them lightly and uniformly until their surfaces are moist. Do not soak or saturate them. Excessive spray may cause a white deposit after the fabric dries. A slight excess deposit can be removed by brushing. A heavy deposit will require drycleaning, which will remove the insecticide and leave the article unprotected.

Let sprayed articles dry before you wear or store them.

2. *Furs.* Furs can be protected from insect damage during summer by placing them in commercial storage where they will receive professional care and can be insured against damage.

If you store furs at home in summer, place them in a tight container with moth crystals, flakes, or balls for protection

3. *Household Furnishings.* Spray furniture upholstery and drapes containing wool or mohair with any of the chemicals recommended. When sprayed on mattresses, pillows, or upholstered furniture, the chemicals help prevent infestation; they do not kill pests already inside the stuffing.

Felts and hammers in pianos often become infested and so badly damaged by clothes moths and carpet beetles that the tone and action of the piano are severely affected. Chemicals recommended will protect the felts and hammers, but they may damage other parts of the piano if applied incorrectly. To prevent damage, it is advisable to have a piano technician do the job.

4. *Rugs and Carpets.* If you have woolen rugs or carpeting that need protective treatments, seek professional advice and treatment.

Pesticides used improperly can be injurious to man, animals, and plants. Follow the directions and heed all precautions on the labels.

Store pesticides in original containers—out of reach of children and pets—and away from foodstuff.

Apply pesticides selectively and carefully. Avoid prolonged inhalation of a pesticide spray or dust. When applying a pesticide it is advisable that you be fully clothed.

Keep children and pets away from sprayed surfaces that have not dried.

After handling a pesticide, do not eat, drink, or smoke until you have washed. In case a pesticide is swallowed or gets in the eyes, follow the first aid treatment given on the label, and get prompt medical attention. If a pesticide is spilled on your skin or clothing, remove clothing immediately and wash skin thoroughly.

Dispose of empty pesticide containers by wrapping them in several layers of newspaper and placing them in your trash can.

Apply insecticide to infants' sweaters, blankets, or other woolen articles only if they are to be stored. Launder or dryclean them before returning them to use.

Do not use chlordane, malathion, ronnel, lindane or diazinon on clothing or furniture; on rugs and carpets, use only for surface spraying. Do not use these insecticides for overall spraying of rooms.

Do not spray oil-solution insecticides near open flames, sparks, or electrical circuits; or on silk, rayon, or other fabrics that stain easily.

Do not spray them on asphalt-tile floors, because they will dissolve the asphalt. They will also soften and discolor some linoleums and certain plastic materials; if in doubt about spraying such a surface, test the spray on a small inconspicuous place.

If you apply an oil-solution insecticide to the cracks in a parquet floor, apply it lightly; an excessive amount will dissolve the underlying black cement, and the dissolved cement will stain the floor.

Do not put any weight or pressure on sprayed rugs, carpets, or upholstered furniture (as by walking, sitting, or pressing with your hand) until the spray has dried. Doing so gives the damp pile a mashed-down appearance, which lasts for several days.

Roach Extermination.

1. One tip for preventing or getting rid of roaches involves the use of chrysanthemums, which

are rich in the pyrethrum that is deadly poison to roaches. Save the blooms and let them dry. Shred them slightly and scatter them in storage places, garages, behind stationary appliances, and in other favorite haunts of roaches.

2. An area frequented by cockroaches can be painted with a mixture of lime, water, and a small quantity of salt, and the insects will be gone in a short time.

Silverfish feed chiefly on substances containing starch, such as starched fabrics, book-bindings, and wallpaper paste. An effective remedy is pyrethrum powder, obtainable where insecticides are sold. Apply with a powder puff or wad of absorbent cotton, wherever the silverfish may be seeking their food — on bookshelves, at the baseboards where wallpaper is used, and so on.

A little cinnamon spice in the corners of drawers, cupboards, or other areas will also discourage silverfish.

Inside Flat Paint, see PAINTS.

Instant coffee can be made in a percolator. Just add instant coffee and water without adding the coffee basket or stem. You can then keep your coffee at the correct drinking temperature, even though it is instant coffee.

Insulation. Most ordinary building materials do not provide enough protection against extreme heat and cold. In order to keep the well-built house tight and prevent heat loss, you should add insulation wherever practicable. Special insulation materials are manufactured to be used as barriers against temperature changes. They will add greatly to the year-round comfort of your home—and save money in heating bills.

Because heated air flows to the top of a room, most of the heat loss from a house is through the ceiling and the roof. It is here that you must take the most care to insulate. In a two-story house, the space between ceiling and floor is usually insulated by fill, and the roof itself is insulated not only under the roof sheathing, but above the ceiling surface too.

Heat leaks through walls and through windows and through doors by conduction. If there are cracks, crevices, leaks, or gaps anywhere in the walls or in the ceiling, the heat will rush out by convection, and the warm air inside will be replaced immediately by cold air.

The more tightly built your house is, the less heat will be lost by conduction or convection. And the less heat lost, the less a heating plant has to work to heat the inside air. That means there will be a similar reduction in the amount of fuel consumed. Consequently, the smaller your heating bill will be. For comfort and for thrift, it pays to keep your house well-insulated and your heating plant in perfect working order.

Attic. More than one-quarter of your heat loss is through the roof. Because of this fact, you should insulate your attic before you insulate anywhere else.

Whether your attic is insulated or not, it must have ample ventilation. Otherwise, you may get excess dampness and mildew damage to stored materials, along with the possibility of spontaneous combustion from lack of proper ventilation.

Boiler. A hot-water boiler should be well-insulated to prevent any escape of heat. You should be able to touch the outside of the boiler when the water inside is very hot. If the insulation has become worn or if it has fallen off, you can buy a type of rock wool insulation kit that can be applied to the boiler. The rock wool comes in the form of blocks about 1½ inches thick.

You cover the boiler with high temperature cement, composed of rock wool asbestos, then place the blocks in this layer of cement, secure it by a winding of wire, and finish it off with muslin. A thoroughly good job of boiler and pipe insulation will save you its cost in a year by the reduction in fuel consumption.

Floor. If you have no basement, or if you have a room built over a porch, you should insulate the underside of the floor. You may be able to have insulation blown into such a floor space. If you do, you'll have to remove the underside surface, and nail insulation batts to the joists.

Materials. Commercial insulating materials come in four forms: blankets or batts; loose fill; rigid boards; and metal reflective sheets.

Blanket or batt insulation. Strips or rolls of material 1-inch to 3-5/8-inches thick and 16 inches to 24 inches wide come in rolls up to 100 feet long. Batts are 2 to 4 feet long. You can get both of these

INTERIOR PAINTING

types with vapor barrier on one side and protective paper on the other. Some brands have paper flanges on the sides to facilitate nailing or stapling to studs, joists, or rafters.

Loose fill insulation. You can get loose fill in bags in 2 consistencies: a fine white material that is blown into walls; or a coarser brown material that you place by hand.

Board insulation. These tiles and panels come 1/2 inch and 3/4 inches thick, from 12 by 12 inches to 12 by 16 inches. You can use board insulation as sheathing on walls, or the decorated types for interior finishing. Boards have less insulating value per square inch than batts, however.

Reflective insulation. This is usually in the form of metal foil or sheets of aluminum or stainless steel. Generally this type of insulation is used where its heat-reflecting quality helps keep out summer heat. But you can use it in combination with batt or blanket insulation in colder areas. Reflective foils and sheets also serve as a vapor barrier by keeping moisture from seeping through.

The best insulating materials should be fire-resistant, moisture-resistant, and insect- and fungus-resistant. Make sure it is by questioning the dealer who sells it to you.

Pipes and Ducts. Any pipes or ducts that are exposed to cold air, as in an unheated attic or basement, should be surrounded with insulating coverings.

(See also PLUMBING.)

Walls. You should be protected by insulation in all outside walls and in walls next to unheated areas. In existing walls, you can use only two types of insulation: loose fill, installed by professionals; or insulating wallboards attached to the surface. If you can take off the wall surface, then you can insulate inside any way you please.

Interior Painting, see PAINTING, INTERIOR.

Iodine Stain, see STAIN REMOVAL.

Iron, Corrugated. Painting the edges and ends on each side of a sheet of corrugated iron before fixing it in position on a roof will pay dividends.

On the edges paint a strip about three corrugations wide and at the ends a strip about 6-in. to 9-in. wide.

Ironing

Buttons. Have you ever melted plastic buttons with your iron? This can be avoided by taking an old spoon and holding the bowl portion over the button while ironing around it.

Cord Tip. One little tip which helps effectively in preventing the housewife from constantly tangling herself in her ironing cord is an electrical outlet installed directly on the ironing board. Of course, a box underneath the board is a little easier to install, since it requires no hole — but the first suggestion is more handy.

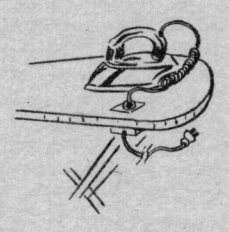

Sticking Iron. A sticky iron can be made to operate smoothly again if it is run back and forth while hot over a paper on which salt has been sprinkled.

Tip. Ironing can be made much easier if a sheet of aluminum foil is used under the ironing board cover. The foil will retain the heat, and make it possible to iron both sides at once.

Iron, Soldering, see SOLDERING.

Iron, Steam, see STEAM IRON.

Ivory Care. Wipe with denatured alcohol and polish with chamois.

To whiten, keep wet with alcohol and dry in sunlight. Or apply salt and then rub with lemon.

Ivory objects, all in one piece, can be cleaned safely with soap and water, however if several pieces are glued together, better take a piece of raw lemon, dip it into salt, and rub this over the surface. Let the juice dry on the ivory before wiping it off with a damp cloth.

Ivy, see GARDENING.

J

Jamb, see DOOR REPAIR, DOORS.

Jar Lids.
1. To insure the easy removal of fruit jar lids, lubricate the threads of the lids with some wax. A few drops of wax from a candle on the inside of the lid will do the trick, and will not interfere with screwing the lid on the jar. This will also prevent the formation of corrosion between the lid and the jar.

2. A stubbornly tight fitting screw top on a large-diameter jar can be removed if you'll wrap a damp cloth around the jar, twisting the ends around together to form a handle. This will enable you to grip the jar securely while you unscrew the top.

3. Screw-top lids or corks on jars or cans containing glue, shellac, or other adhesives often stick and resist removal. A way to prevent this the first time the lid is removed is to rub a small amount of petroleum jelly over the inside of the threads on the lid, or on the cork. Future removals will then be easy.

Jar Wrench. You can improvise a very powerful, yet flexible, wrench for removing tight screw lids by using a stick of wood and a short leather strap. Merely wrap the strap around the lid or cap and grip the stick and strap ends as illustrated. The cap will open with the greatest of ease.

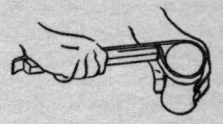

Jewelry.
 Bead Repairing. If you have broken the clasp on a string of beads and do not have another on hand, you can replace it with a hook and eye. Use the loop-type eye and press the prongs together. Be sure to lace the thread through both sides of the hook and eye so that they will lie flat against the neck.

 Bead Restringing. When restringing beads, especially tiny ones through which a needle will not pass, dip the end of the string into clear nailpolish and let dry. The thread will then pass easily through the smallest beads.

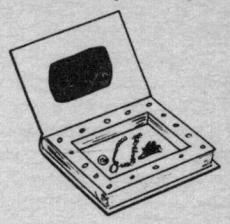

 Box. Here's a novel and very attractive jewelry box which can be fashioned from a book you may not care to read again. First, nail the pages together one-half inch from the edges, leaving the front cover free. Use 3/4-inch brads for this purpose and nail from both sides. Then, with a sharp knife and metal-edge ruler, cut out the central portion of the pages, leaving a 3/4-inch margin. Glue the bottom cover to the back page of the book. Finally, give the finished product several thin lacquer coatings.

Care. Jewelry can be cleaned nicely in warm water and soap. If very dirty, you can use a soft brush on which you've rubbed a little soap. Another excellent cleanser is a teaspoonful of ammonia in a teacup of warm water. After any of these cleanings, be sure to rinse the article in clear cold water.

Diamond Cleaning. If your diamond is to sparkle, it must be kept scrupulously clean so that the light striking at every facet breaks down into rainbow colors. If the diamond is dirty and gummed up with soap, you might as well be wearing glass. A diamond that is worn every day needs special cleaning at least once a month.

For cleaning diamond rings, any good dentifrice used with a small brush, will cut off all the grease and dirt from behind the stones and leave them sparkling clean again.

Earring Easing. If you have a pair of clip-type earrings that are painful to your ear lobes, try cutting off a tiny piece of moleskin corn plaster and sticking this to the underneath flap of the earring.

Gem Resetting. When gems keep falling out of earrings or other costume jewelry, try resetting them with some clear nail polish. Brush the colorless stuff into the setting, then press in your jewel, and allow to dry thoroughly. If the "stickum" pushes up around or over the stone, clean up the overflow with a piece of cleansing tissue barely dampened with nailpolish remover.

Gold Cleaning. Cleaning and polishing your gold jewelry can be accomplished with some toothpaste and an old toothbrush.

Painting Tip. When painting jewelry or other small articles which are difficult to hold securely, try sticking them onto masking tape. This will hold them in place while you use your small paintbrush on them, and they can be left on the tape while drying.

Scatter Pin Idea. Old or discarded earrings can be converted into attractive scatter pins for some of your outfits if the screw back is snipped off and a small safety pin soldered on in its place.

Tarnish Prevention. An effective tarnish preventive for costume jewelry is a thin coating of colorless nail polish. This will not harm the jewelry's finish, and will also protect it from minor scratches.
(See also SILVER CARE.)

Tight Ring. When a ring is too tight on a finger, it is seldom that you can't remove it after the hand has been held in ice-cold soapsuds for a minute or so.

Watch Crystal, Scratched. Scratches on an unbreakable plastic watch crystal can be polished off with nail-polish remover or acetone. Use the liquid sparingly, applying it with a small wad of soft cloth.

Watch, Water Removal. To get water out of a watch case before it does serious damage, strap the watch around a light bulb, and leave the bulb on until the water is warm to the touch, or about two minutes, then cool the watch crystal with a cool, damp cloth. Any water in the watch will form a vapor in the inside of the crystal. Open the watch and wipe the droplets from the inside of the crystal, using a clean dry cloth. If considerable water was in the watch, it may be necessary to repeat this operation two or three times.

Joints

Board. If you wish to nail two boards together at true right angles, first draw a guide line on the inside of the overlapping boards and clamp a block of wood even with that line. Then place the upright against the block and nail into place. When nailing long boards together, set them on edge and square at the corners of a box for nailing.

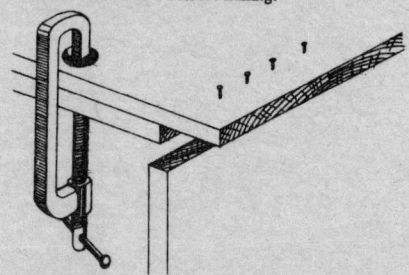

Bridle. This joint is similar to the corner bridle joint. Measure and mark. Remove waste wood by sawing and chiseling. Let the entering piece project

JOINTS

1/16-inch for final cleaning. This joint is used in stands or frames.

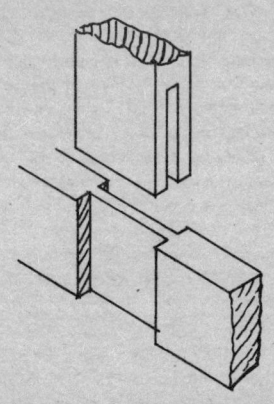

Butt. If you want to effect a butt joint for gluing together and don't have a jointer to produce matching edges, try this little gimmick: Place the two pieces edge-to-edge and lightly nail a strip of scrap wood over the joint. Invert the pieces and saw ALONG THE JOINT LINE. The saw kerf will remove material from both meeting edges, and any variation on one edge will be compensated for on the other. After the scrap has been removed and the two pieces glued together, the joint will be perfectly fitted.

Corner Bridle. Both members are usually the same thickness, in which case the "entering" piece is one-third the thickness of the wood.

It should be marked out with a mortise gauge, both ends of the joint being allowed to project 1/16-inch to be cleaned off.

Remove central waste portion by sawing down waste sides of lines and chiseling inwards from each direction, and also into the end grain. Suitable joint for tray frame, greenhouse staging, etc.

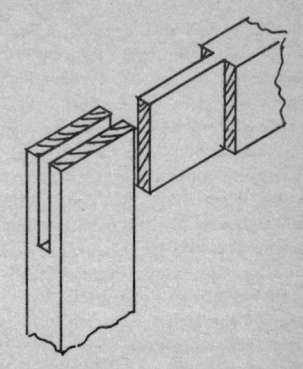

Halved. The strength, rigidity, and appearance of any wood-working project depends mainly upon the way the various parts have been joined together.

A halved joint as shown offers a simple means of jointing a framework like a cupboard door or the side of a cabinet.

It is a quick substitute for the mortise and tenon joint, and for many purposes it is just as good.

The use of good quality woodworking glue adds to its strength and reliability.

The ends of the wood must first be marked and cut square.

They are then marked with a line across the end equal to the width of the wood, using a try-square.

One piece of wood is marked on the face and the other on the opposite side.

These marks should be made with a chisel or marking knife rather than with a pencil.

This provides a clean shoulder before using the saw.

A marking gauge is then set to exactly half the thickness of the wood and used to mark the depth of the joint along the edge of each piece.

In each case the gauge must be used from the face side.

The cuts are made with a fine tenon saw, kept slightly to the waste side of the gauge line.

So that both faces can be kept in view when ripping down the length of the joint, it is best held at an angle in the bench vice.

After sawing down to the squared line on the edge in this way, the wood is gripped upright and the cut finished in this position.

The shoulder cut across the wood is then made down to the gauge line.

JOINTS

The two halves of the joint, left rough from the saw, are brushed with wood-working glue, brought together, and squeezed up with a thumbscrew or clamp.

If no clamp is available, the joint must be held together while setting by driving in a few panel pins.

These may be safely withdrawn after about 12 hours.

Once the glue has completely set it forms the strongest part of the joint.

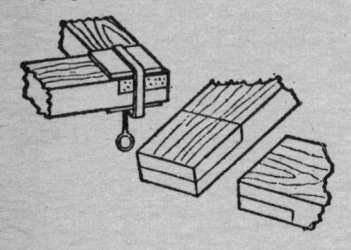

Mitered. To have mitered corners square up when the two angle-cut surfaces are united, simply overlap the two pieces at right angles to each other, tacking them temporarily to a flat surface, and sawing both at the same time. You will then have a perfectly mitered joint. This procedure is especially good when you are cutting moldings, screen and picture frames.

Perfect fitting joints can be cut at the corners of window-screen molding without using a miter box.

Tack the molding in place on the screen, but do not fasten the last six or seven inches at each end.

Slip a piece of hardboard or thin plywood under the molding where it intersects at the corners.

Cut through both pieces with a coping saw or panel saw to form a 45-degree miter. See illustration.

The cut ends will match exactly, and can be pressed tightly together and tacked into place.

Mortise and Tenon. The mortise and tenon joint when cut and fitted properly, then glued and wedged, is perhaps the strongest woodworking joint of all.

Cutting of a tenon by hand is not a difficult job, but there are certain definite rules to observe.

As a guide, the thickness of a tenon is about one-third the thickness of the wood being used. For example, have the wood 3/8-inch thick for stock up to 1-1/4-inch thick.

Tenons are marked out with a two-pin mortise gauge.

Marking in all cases is done from the face side of the wood.

The square lines across the face of the wood on each side to mark the position for cutting the shoulders are best made with a sharp marking knife rather than a pencil.

This gives a much sharper shoulder line and results in a tighter joint when the parts are cramped.

The main precaution, however, is to see that the saw is used correctly when cutting down the length of the tenon. The sketches explain this point clearly.

At (A) the tenon has been marked out and is in vice ready for ripping.

This is being done correctly at (B) with saw-cut on waste side of lines, leaving the tenon full-size.

The other two sketches show common tenon-cutting faults.

At (C) the saw-cut is on line and, worse still, at (D) completely inside, so making the tenon too small.

These long rip cuts are made first, then the two cross-cuts to form the shoulders of tenon.

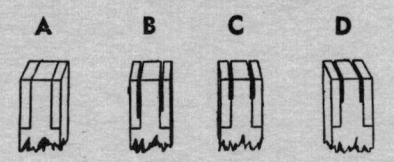

Open-housing joint is a simple effective corner joint for small boxes or cabinets where no great strength is needed.

The receiving member should project 1/16-inch to be cleaned off after gluing and nailing.

Used in all kinds of small boxes and small cabinets up to 6 inches or 7 inches wide.

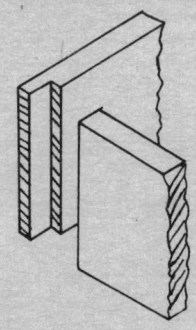

Pipe, see PLUMBING.

Woodwork joints in window frames and furniture will last longer and be more serviceable if they are reinforced at the first sign of weakness.

Of the many types of joints used in woodworking the simpler ones shown here may be used either in new construction or in repairing loose joints.

A quick and sturdy repair for corners when pieces are simply butted together is to use two dowels.

Drill two holes through the outer member and well into the adjacent member and drive in glue-coated dowels (A).

These should be flattened slightly on one or more sides to allow air and excess glue trapped at the bottom of the holes to escape.

Trim the dowels flush and refinish.

For an extra strong joint use three dowels.

For picture frames and other articles having mitered joints where inconspicuous bracing is required, use a thin piece of plywood.

Saw a slot across the joint to take a thin plywood block snugly (B).

Apply a thin coat of glue to both sides of the block, insert it and clamp until dry.

The block should be trimmed to fit flush and a matching finish applied on the exposed edge.

Another method of strengthening a mitered joint is to drill both pieces at right angles to the joint and drive in a glue-coated dowel.

Where members are of sufficient width, reinforce the joint with two dowels.

Trim and finish dowel ends when the glue is dry.

To save time when reinforcing a mitered corner, use metal angle brackets on screen doors, windows and other places where appearance is not too important.

Brackets can be painted over to make them less noticeable.

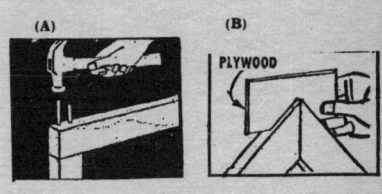

Joint Sealer. If water seeps into the joint between the bathroom wall and the tub, no matter what kind of compound you use, try running a strip of waterproof surgical tape across the joint.

Joints, Loose, see FURNITURE REPAIR.

K

Kegs, Carrying. Every man knows that carrying a couple of kegs is a real awkward task. You can make it much easier just by fitting your kegs with some large-sized C-clamps, as illustrated, tightening the clamps securely so they won't slip off. A keg can then be picked up in each hand, using the clamps as handles.

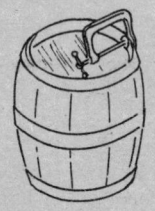

Keyhole Saw, see TOOLS.

Keys.

Broken. If your key should break off in your car lock, here is a little trick which might help you. Smear the broken end of the key with some adhesive obtainable at the hardware store for mounting sanding disks. Push the smeared end of the key gently into the lock and then withdraw it. The tip of the key inside the lock will often adhere to the adhesive and come out with it.

Identification.

1. Do you have many keys on a chain together? Try using the nailpolish trick on the ones most often used. Not only can it readily be seen in the light, but it can be felt in the dark.

2. You can eliminate the usual fumbling for the right key for a particular lock and getting it right side up, if you'll just file some identifying notches on the top edge.

Permanent. In many cases, doors that are fitted with the old-type removable key are, in practice, locked only from one side. This key can be prevented from accidentally falling out or being removed by a child or thoughtless adult if you will equip the lock with a permanent key, as illustrated. Cut a strip of tin to fit under the escutcheon plate of the lock, and clip out a long slot to the width of the key shank. Insert the tin strip under the escutcheon so that it blocks the key opening. This device has a safety factor, too — making it impossible for the door to be opened with a skeleton key from the opposite side.

Kilowatt Hours, see ELECTRICITY, THEORY OF.

Kindling, see FIRE OPEN.

Kitchen Fixtures, see LIGHTING FIXTURES.

Kitchen Floor Coverings, see LINOLEUM; NON-RESILIENT TILE FLOORS; RESILIENT TILE FLOORS.

Kitchen Knives, see KNIVES.

Kitchen Painting, see PAINTING, INTERIOR.

Kitchen Odors, see COOKING ODORS.

Kitchen Planning.
  Dual-Purpose Centers. In some kitchens it is not possible to arrange counters which serve only one work center. Each dual-use counter should be 12 inches wider than the largest recommended work center. For example, if the mix center (36 inches) is combined with the right side of the sink center (30 or 36 inches), the dual counter should be 36 inches plus 12 inches (or 48 inches).
  Location. Today's best kitchens are planned to fit into modern family life. Although the kitchen may be a separate room, many are "open" to major living areas, and almost all include space for serving food. The choice of arrangement depends on the amount and kind of space provided, and the family habits.

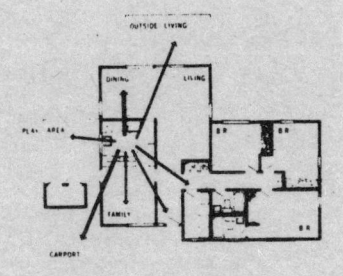

KITCHEN PLANNING

L-shaped. Two doors, one at or near the end and the other farther away on an adjacent wall, permit an L-shaped plan. Other arrangements and more doors than these create broken centers.

Mixing Center. The mixing center is the area in which all of the mixing of doughs and batters, the preparation of casseroles, puddings, meats for oven cookery, frozen desserts, and salads is done. Leftovers are returned to this area to be prepared for storage in the refrigerator or freezer. Because of their related activities, the refrigerator should be near, if not adjacent to, the mix counter. Storage cabinets should also be available holding all the cooking needs and utensils needed for food preparation.

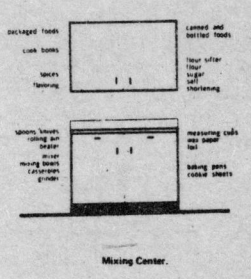

Mixing Center.

One-wall kitchens are used where only one wall is available for arrangement of equipment. Often such an arrangement is provided in small apartments and may be closed off by doors.

Range-Oven-Serve Center. If an undivided range is used, all methods of cooking are performed in this center. If separate surface units and oven are used, the cookery appropriate to each is divided. Surface cookery includes pan frying, deep fat frying, stewing, boiling, and steaming. Oven cookery includes baking, broiling, barbecuing, and roasting.

  A separate oven may be placed near the surface units, but it should never be placed in a run of counters where it might break the continuity of a work process. A surface unit or portable heating appliance, such as an electric saucepan or skillet, could well be located at the mix center for making sauces or custards, frying breaded meats, or other purposes. It is important to supply the storage space for supplies and utensils needed in this work center.

185

KITCHEN PLANNING

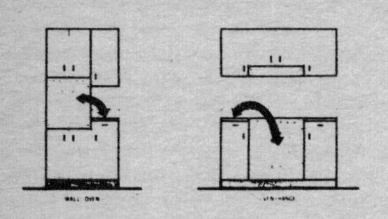

OVEN CENTER

A counter 2 feet wide is a sufficient serving area when placed to one side of the range. Provide storage space for trays, trivets, serving dishes, along with foods that are served without cooking, such as crackers, pickles, and olives.

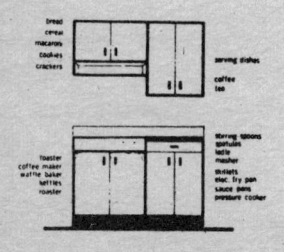

RANGE-SERVE CENTER

Rectangular. A rectangular kitchen usually provides more perimeter and thus more wall space for placing the needed built-in cabinets and equipment than a square room with a similar amount of floor space.

Two-door openings on opposite ends of a rectangular kitchen require the arrangement of equipment in a two-wall or corridor shape. The triangle can be relatively small in this kitchen, but it is difficult to prevent traffic through the triangle.

Sink Center. Much of the food preparation involving water is done at the sink center. In addition, dishes and cooking utensils must be prepared and washed, both during food preparation and after use. Water is drawn for drinking, ice cubes, making hot beverages. Garbage is collected in and removed from this area, or is ground in the garbage disposal. Because this is such a busy work center, storage for many items necessary for convenient use includes foods, cleaning utensils and linens.

If a dishwasher is provided, it is best placed at the left of the sink which has in that case, usually a single rather than a double bowl. A front-loading dishwasher provides adequate counter space over it for stacking clean dishes. If a portable dishwasher is used, operating space in front of the sink is important, but the dishwasher may be stored elsewhere.

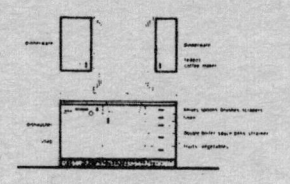

SINK CENTER

U-shaped. One door, or two doors adjacent to one corner, leaves the greatest amount of free wall space. These arrangements and two doors on opposite walls near one end block off through traffic and permit a U-shaped arrangement. The work triangle or work square in a U-shaped kitchen is usually small, making for compactness and efficiency.

Work Centers. The areas around the three basic pieces of kitchen equipment - the refrigerator, the range, and the sink - are usually designated as centers. These centers divide the kitchen into areas where tasks that require similar ingredients, utensils, or processing can be handled.

The centers can be arranged in any logical way dictated by the space available and the importance attached to any particular center. The arrangement should enable foods in preparation to move production-line fashion from center to center. There should be enough storage space at each center to hold the supplies and utensils used there, with each article in reach where it first comes into use.

Thus, it should be unnecessary to transport either equipment or supplies from one center to another. Preparation of a meal does involve inevitable backtracking, and the paths connecting range, sink, and refrigerator best form a triangle bounding the work area.

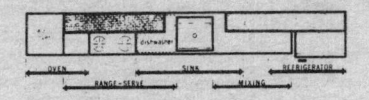

WORK CENTER

Work Triangle. In general, a work triangle should be no longer than 22 feet, with 20 feet being best. However, a distance of less than 12 feet provides insufficient storage or counter space. Ideally, there should be from 8 feet 6 inches to 13 feet 6 inches of base cabinets, including those under the sink and range. Over the base cabinets there should be a similar number of feet of wall cabinets. The counters should be no less than 8 feet 6 inches long, including spaces as follows:

15 to 18 inches next to the latch side of refrigerator; 24 to 36 inches at right side of sink for stacking soiled dishes (for righthanded people); 18 to 36 inches at other side of sink for draining and drying washed dishes (if there is no dishwasher); 24 inches at one side of range or 12 to 24 inches on both sides for serving food; 36 inches or more for mixing and preparing food.

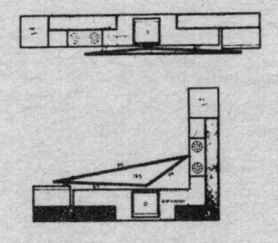

WORK TRIANGLE

Kitchen Sink, Stained, see STAIN REMOVAL.

KNIVES

Kneepads.

1. When household duties bring you to your knees, relieve the pressure with a kneepad made by folding a heavy turkish towel and putting it in a heavy paper bag. The towel stays clean and the paper bag can be discarded when you are finished.

2. If you are the type of homemaker who likes to get down and scrub your floors — but your knees don't enjoy it — try a pair of basketball players' knee pads. If you do not have a son with such equipment, it might be worth your while to go to a sporting goods store and purchase a pair. They move right along with you — you finish the job in less time, and in comfort.

Knife Safety. Safety with knives is essential. Do not use knives larger than can be safely handled. Use knives only for the purpose for which they were designed. Always cut away from your body. Do not carry open knives in your pocket or leave them where they may come into contact with or cause injury to others. Put knives away carefully after use to protect sharp cutting edges from contacting other hard objects.

Knife, Stained, see STAIN REMOVAL.

Knits, see CLOTHES CARE.

Knitting Needle Reshaping. To reshape the broken edge of a plastic knitting needle, sand it to a new point, then pass it through the steam from a boiling teakettle. The steam will soften and blend the tiny scratches on the tip into a smooth surface.

Knitting Tip. Stitches often slip off knitting needles when knitting is put aside. You can avoid this if you'll take an ordinary cork from any bottle top and place it on the ends of your knitting needles.

Knives,
See also TOOLS, HAND.

KNOBS

Cleaning. You'll minimize the chances of cutting your fingers, when scouring the blades of sharp-edged knives, if you'll substitute a large cork for the usual cloth. Then, too, the dampened cork allows you to apply a firm pressure over a fairly large area, thus making a quicker and better job of cleaning then when using a cloth.

Kitchen. A hacksaw blade can be fashioned into a useful kitchen knife that has both a keen cutting edge for vegetables or meat and a sharp saw-tooth edge for bone and gristle. Fit this blade with a handle of one-fourth-inch tempered hardboard. A piece of the board is cut to fit each side of the saw blade and registering holes are drilled through both pieces to permit riveting them together. The ends of the rivets are ground flush with the rounded handle. Then fill in the crack between the handle sections with some plastic wood, and finally give a coat of shellac to the finished handle.

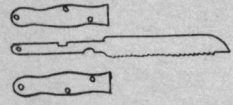

Polishing. The next time your knives are to be polished, try dipping them into boiling water, drying them, and then applying your polish at once while the metal is still warm.

Rust Removal. To remove rust from a knife blade, plunge the blade into an onion and leave it there for an hour or so. Then, before you remove it, work the blade back and forth in the onion a few times. Finish off by washing and polishing it as usual.

Storage.

1. Your paring knives will keep sharp for a much longer time if they are kept in a holder, especially if the holder is filled with sand. The sand tends to sharpen the cutting edges and keep the blades separated. Such a holder can be easily made by slitting the top of a baking-powder can for insertion of the knives. Then you can decorate this container with some attractive decals.

2. The kitchen knives will stay sharper for a much longer time if they are prevented from rubbing and banging against each other in the knife box or drawer. Provide the box or drawer with a one-inch dowel fitted with slanted saw kerfs, as illustrated, and this will keep the blades of your knives separated and upright.

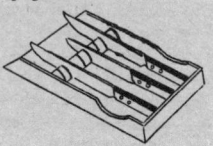

Knobs.

Constructing. Plastic screw caps from toothpaste and similar tubes can be converted into very usable knobs for small items. Simply cut off the lead neck of the tube, attach this to the article with a wood screw, then screw on the cap.

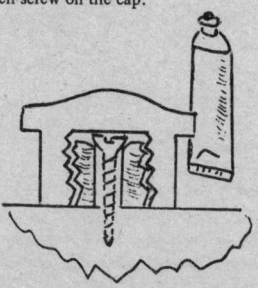

Decorating. You can add a handwrought appearance to plain wooden drawer or cabinet knobs by denting the knob faces with a ball-peen hammer. This can best be accomplished first by drilling a hole in a block of wood to accommodate the shank of the knob, and then tapping the face of the knob lightly with the ball part of your hammer to dent the wood fibers. Paint the knob a dull "iron" black, or apply some stain for an antique finish.

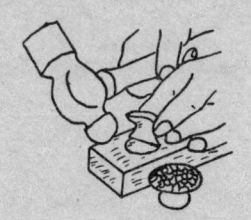

Loose.

1. If a drawer-knob screw refuses to hold, try bending a piece of soft wire into the hole. It acts as a shim for the screw and will last for a long time. Another way to correct loose knobs on drawers is by cutting a small washer of sandpaper, threading this onto the screw with the rough side of the paper against the drawer, then tightening the screw.

2. Very irritating are those wooden drawer knobs which persist in working themselves loose. You can make them stay tight if you'll sand the back face of the knob to a slight bevel. In this way, the knob will twist slightly on the threaded bolt when you tighten it, and will thus grip the drawer front more securely.

Painting, see PAINTING TIPS.
Repairing, see DOOR REPAIR.
Replacing. A pot lid without its knob? Don't discard it. A sharp-pointed screw thrust up through the hole and into a cork will put the lid back into the knob class. The cork is heat-proof, too.

Knotting Tips.

1. The knot in the end of a rope will stay tied and you will eliminate the unraveling of any rope strands if you'll dip the knotted end of the rope into shellac. This is an especially good idea when the rope is to be in an inaccessible place, such as a sash-weight cord inside a window casing.

2. You can assure yourself of slip-proof knots when tying packages for mailing if you'll just pull the string through a dampened cellulose sponge so as to wet it thoroughly. As the wet string dries, it will shrink slightly and thus tighten your knots.

LADDER

2. It's always a tricky, and sometimes hazardous, job using a stepladder on stairways for painting or washing the ceilings and walls. However, a couple of extensions, secured with two bolts each to the front legs of your ladder as illustrated, will provide you both safety and adaptability for this kind of work. Just by moving such a ladder up or down two steps at a time usually permits you to reach all surfaces.

3. If your ladder isn't already fitted with safety "feet," a pair of old rubber heels, attached to the lower ends of your ladder rails, will prevent the ladder from slipping when it is used on a smooth or slippery surface. You can use either nails or screws with fairly large heads, so the rubber heels are firmly held — but be sure to countersink the heads to prevent their contacting good floor surfaces.

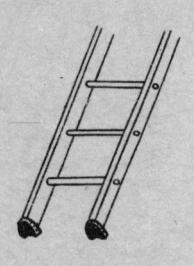

4. If the ground on which you place your ladder is soft, you can prevent the feet of the ladder from sinking into the ground by inserting them into a couple of empty coffee cans. The cans will act as snowshoes, distributing the weight of the ladder over a greater area, and they also help to prevent the ladder from slipping away from the structure against which it is leaning.

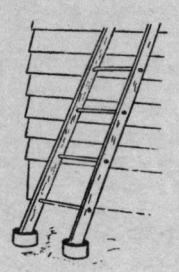

5. By replacing the top rung in your ladder with a rubber-covered chain, you will be able to use the ladder against round posts and trees with much less danger of its slipping. The chain should be long enough to hang in a slight arc, and rubber hosing is used to cover it. The end links of the chain are passed through the rung holes in the ladder sides and held in place by slipping 1/4-inch steel pins through the links. The ends of the pins are flattened and drilled to receive wood screws, which hold the pins on the ladder sides.

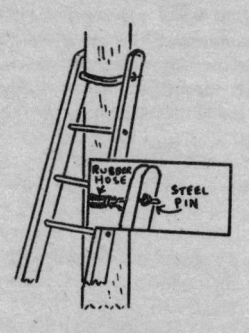

Storage.

1. The problem of storing a long extension ladder is solved easily by suspending it from joists underneath a house with fairly high foundations, or from the garage ceiling joists.

All you need are four L-shaped hooks pivoted to the joists by means of heavy screws passing through an eye in the end of each hook.

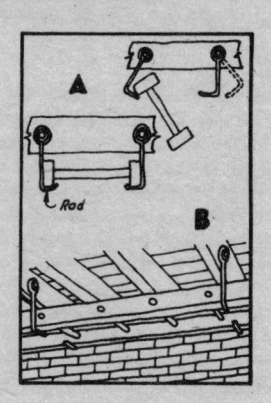

LANTERN, CAMP

The hooks are bent from 1/4-inch steel rod.

In use they are swung outward and one rail of the ladder placed upon two of them, after which the opposite rail of the ladder is raised upward and the other hooks swung under it as suggested in (A).

Detail (B) shows the ladder in place.

Note (B) that the outer ends of the hooks are bent to form a shallow U-shape so that there is no possibility of the ladder slipping off them.

2. You can support a stepladder flush against the wall of your garage or utility room by means of an ordinary wire coat hanger, as illustrated. In this way, the ladder will consume the least possible amount of space when not in use. Merely set your ladder flush against the wall, measure and drive in an L-hook so that it centers about three inches above the top of the ladder to grasp the hook of the hanger.

Tray. You can make a convenient and handy tray for holding tools on the top of your stepladder. Construct this from 1/4-inch plywood, with a 3/4-inch strip of wood inserted as a spacer between the tray itself and the projecting piece underneath. In this way, the tray can be slipped over the top step of your ladder and will remain securely in place while you are performing your chore.

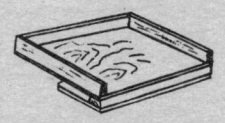

Window Adapter. Working around a window from an ordinary ladder is usually a tricky job, due to the fact that your ladder must be placed either at one side of the window or with its top below the window — and from either of these positions you have a problem reaching all parts of the window. One efficient way to solve this little problem is by making a "window adapter" for your ladder — a crossbar cut from 1-1/2 by 3-inch stock and fitted with two strap iron hooks, as shown in the illustration. By hanging this bar on the top rung, you will be able to place the top of your ladder directly over and out from the window.

Lamps, see LIGHTING, PORTABLE

Lamp Shade Cleaning, see LIGHTING PORTABLE.

Lamp Shade Decorating, see LIGHTING, PORTABLE.

Lantern, Camp. You can fashion a very efficient, windproof camp lantern just by cutting an opening in the side of a baking powder can and inserting some screen wire to cover the opening. A candle is attached to the cover, and holes are punched in the top of the inverted can to permit the heat and smoke to escape. The screening will break the force of an average wind to prevent its extinguishing the candle flame.

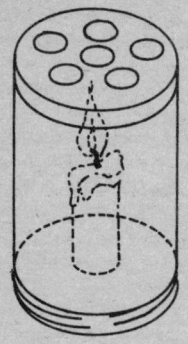

LATCH REPAIR

Assemble as in the accompanying illustration. Before filling the drum with concrete mix, cut holes in the center of the bottom and lid of the drum, insert your pipe in the bottom hole, and after filling the drum with concrete, push the lid into place — which will assure you of accurately centering the pipe for even rolling.

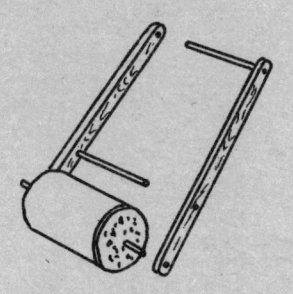

Latch Repair, see DOOR REPAIR.

Latex Paint, see PAINTS.

Laundering
    Bathroom Rugs. Place in bucket of soapy water and agitate with plumber's plunger.
    Clothes, see CLOTHES CARE.
    Guest Towels. If, after your guests have departed, you notice that one or two of your fancy guest towels have been just slightly used, wash them out quickly in the bathroom wash basin, then stretch them flat against the tile wall or on the bathtub to dry. In the morning, fold them by hand, hang them up, and you are ready for your next party.
    White Braid. To clean white braid, wet an old toothbrush, rub it across a cake of mild soap, and scrub the braid with this. The lather can be removed with a damp cloth.

Sprinkler. Here is a lawn sprinkler that will water large areas of your lawn with just a few settings. It can be made by attaching wheels to a drilled length of 1/2-inch galvanized water pipe. The wheels are mounted to a 6-inch length of 2-by-3 inch lumber with 2-inch lag screws. Then secure the wheel assembly to the capped end of the pipe, as illustrated. To space the sprinkler holes evenly, scribe three lines 1/4-inch apart along the length of the pipe. Then, using a No. 60 bit, drill alternate holes 3 inches apart as shown.

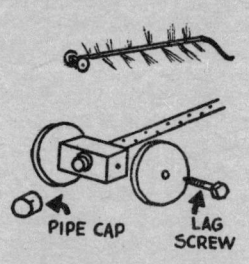

    Laundry Tub Repair. A crack in a laundry tub can be repaired by getting a waterproof paste or glue and completely coating a piece of cotton cord with it. Pack this cotton cord tightly into the crack with a knife, and the crack will be sealed.

Lawn.
    Chair, see CHAIR MAKING.
    Roller. You can make your own lawn roller quite easily. What you need is a discarded five-gallon can or drum, a piece of 3/4-inch pipe six to eight inches longer than the drum, an old broom handle, four two-inch No. 12 screws, two four-foot lengths of two-by-four, and enough concrete to fill the drum.

Tamper. You can make your own lawn or sod tamper out of a discarded one-gallon oil or cleaning fluid can. First, cut a hole in the center of one side of the can to take a five-foot length of one-inch pipe. Screw a "T" joint to the pipe on the inside of the can, then fill the can with concrete mix and, when dry, you'll have your tamper.

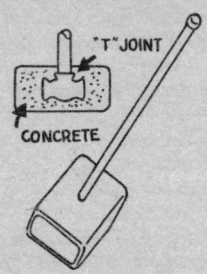

(See also GARDENING.)

Leaking Pipes, see PLUMBING.

Leather, Attaching to Wood. If you wish to cover a wooden surface, apply a coat of liquid cement to the leather and to the wood surface. The wood must be clean and free of wax (wipe off with turpentine). Allow to dry. Then apply a second coat of cement and press the leather to the wood. The welding takes place during the drying process, and better adhesion results with two coats.

Leather Book Bindings, see BOOK CARE.

Leather Care.

1. Neat's-foot oil does not clean leather, as some people suppose. It protects it from deterioration due to drying. So use saddle soap or mild soap and water first on the leather, then rub the oil in with your fingertips or with a cloth. Neat's-foot oil is not suitable for articles on which a glossy shine is desired. It leaves a dull finish, difficult to polish.

2. The usually messy job of applying neats-foot oil or other liquid compounds to leather garments is a much cleaner task if the oil is applied with a household sprayer, preferably the continuous-spray type. Mildew spots that are not too deep can be removed by spraying heavily, letting the oil soak in, then rubbing the spots lightly with a soft cloth.

3. An excellent leather conditioner is castor oil, especially for types of leather that are to be polished afterward. Clean the leather first, apply a small amount of the oil, rub in well, then remove the excess oil carefully with a clean soft cloth.

4. You can darken light tan leather just by rubbing over it with a cloth dipped in ammonia ... produces a deep brown finish. Be sure, however, to apply uniformly, so as to avoid any spottiness in your finished job.

5. To remove mildew from leather, wipe it with a cloth wrung out of a solution of denatured alcohol and water, equal parts. Dry in the open air. If this fails, wash it with a thick suds of mild neutral soap, rinse with a damp cloth, and dry in an airy place. Polish shoes and other articles afterwards with a good wax dressing.

6. Leather covered furniture can be kept from cracking by polishing it regularly with a cream made of one part vinegar and two parts linseed oil.

7. If a small hole has been burned into a leather covered table top perhaps by a carelessly placed cigarette — it can often be camouflaged quite successfully by melting some candlewax of a matching color, then smoothing this into the hole while it is still soft.

8. To keep leather upholstery soft and prevent its cracking, brush it with skim milk several times a year and polish with a soft cloth.

9. For leather that has become water-stiffened, rub a damp cloth in some saddle soap and give the leather a vigorous massaging with this. Rinse with a water-dampened cloth, and let dry without any exposure to heat. Finally, apply some polish.

Kerosene will soften leather hardened by water.

10. To waterproof leather, use this mixture: Melt one cup of tallow and 1/4-cup of beeswax over a low flame, then blend in 1/2-cup of castor oil. That done, add 1/2-ounce of jet black, let cool, and apply.

Leather, Chamois, see CHAMOIS.

Leather Craft.

1. An old fork is a handy tool for crafting of leather. It is especially good for scoring lines on heavy belt leather. Place the leather on a wooden block with a perfectly straight edge. Bend up an outer tine of the fork, and draw this tine over the leather. The adjacent tines act as a guide, keeping your line straight.

2. When punching holes through heavy leather, such as cowhide, it is sometimes difficult to remove the tool without an extra twist and push. Paraffin

LEATHER GLOVES

applied to the punch will act as a lubricant and make the hole-punching job easier and faster. The paraffin may be rubbed on the leather at the center line of the holes, or you can apply it to the punch tube. In either case, the tube will pierce the leather and come out easily.

Leather Gloves, see CLOTHES CARE.

Leather Stain, see STAIN REMOVAL.

Leather Upholstery
Cleaning. Dry-dust leather upholstery with an untreated cloth and clean, as required, with saddle soap or with a thick suds of mild, pure soap. Use as little water as possible. If using saddle soap, follow the directions on the container. Wipe off soap traces with a clean, damp cloth, and when thoroughly dry, polish briskly with a soft cloth.
Preserving. To keep leather upholstery soft and prevent its cracking, brush it with skim milk several times a year and polish with a soft cloth.
Shining. One effective method of shining up leather upholstery is by using a soft piece of cotton dipped in vinegar. Squeeze the cotton almost dry, then polish.
Stain Removal, see STAIN REMOVAL.

Leftovers, see FOODS.

Lemonade, Lemons, see FOODS.

Letter Holder. The variable condensers of an old-fashioned, discarded radio can be converted into a very usable and attractive letter holder for a desk. After polishing the flat plates, mount them on a wooden base, or a metal or plastic base, as in the illustration. The outer plates can be enameled, painted, or otherwise decorated as you wish.

Letter Opener. You can fashion a colorful letter opener from a discarded toothbrush. Cut off the bristle end of the brush, and file the handle to a point. Then sand-file the section to an oval shape to produce cutting edges on each side of the oval.

Lettuce, see FOODS.

Level, see TOOLS, MEASURING.

Light Bulbs, Incandescent. General household bulbs, the most commonly used type, range from 15 to 300 watts. They are available in three finishes—inside frost, inside white (silica-coated), and clear.

Inside frost is the older bulb finish still in general use. Use bulbs of this type in well-shielded fixtures.

Bulbs with *inside white* finish (a milky-white coating) are preferred for many home uses. They produce diffused, soft light and help reduce bright spots in thin shielding materials.

Decoratively shaped *clear* bulbs add sparkle to chandeliers or dimmer-controlled simulated candles.

Three-way bulbs have two filaments and require three-way sockets. Each filament can be operated separately or in combination. Make sure that a three-way bulb is tightened in the socket so both contacts in the screw-in base are touching firmly.

The three lighting levels offered by these bulbs are particularly nice in portable lamps and pull-down fixtures. You can turn the lamp high for reading and sewing, on medium for televiewing, conversation, or entertaining, and on low for a night light or a soft subdued atmosphere.

Selection Guide.

Activity	Minimum recommended wattage[1]
Reading, writing, sewing:	
Occasional periods	150.
Prolonged periods	200 or 300.
Grooming:	
Bathroom mirror:	
1 fixture each side of mirror	1–75 or 2–40's.
1 cup-type fixture over mirror	100.
1 fixture over mirror	150.
Bathroom ceiling fixture	150.
Vanity table lamps, in pairs	
(person seated)	100 each.
Dresser lamps, in pairs	
(person standing)	150 each.
Kitchen work:	
Ceiling fixture (2 or more in a	
large area)	150 or 200.
Fixture over sink	150.

LIGHT DIFFUSERS AND SHIELDS

	Minimum Recommended wattage[1]
Fixture for eating area (separate from workspace)	150.
Shopwork: Fixture for workbench (2 or more for long bench)	150.

[1] White bulbs preferred.

Sizes and Uses for Three-Way Bulbs

Socket and wattage	Description	Where to use
Medium: 30/70/100—	Inside frost or white	Dressing table or dresser lamps, decorative lamps, small pin up lamps.
50/100/150—	Inside frost or white.	End table or small floor and swing-arm lamps.
50/100/150—	White or indirect bulb with "built-in" diffusing bowl (R-40).	End table lamps and floor lamps with large, wide harps.
50/200/250—	White or frosted bulb.	End table or small floor and swing-arm lamps, study lamps with diffusing bowls.
Mogul (large): 50/100/150—	Inside frost—	Small floor and swing-arm lamps and torcheres.
100/200/300–	White or frosted bulb	Table and floor lamps, torcheres.

Light Bulb Storage.

You can always keep a close check on your supply of light bulbs if you make this quick and easy storage panel. The panel is made of a 12-inch square of hardboard, into which you drill 16 evenly-spaced one-inch holes to receive the bulb bases. Cut two empty thread spools in half and use the halves as spacers under the four corners of the panel when you screw it onto the wall.

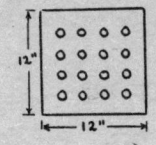

Light and Color. Light affects color. A lovely room by day can be even lovelier by night. Before you choose wall and fabric colors, try them under the same combination of lighting you will be using at home. Remember, too, that dimming of incandescent bulbs changes the color of their light—makes it yellower.

The light from some fluorescent tubes appears blue-white when combined with the yellowish light from incandescent lamp bulbs. To minimize color distortion, get deluxe fluorescent tubes in warm or cool white for both wall and ceiling lighting units.

You'll find that light from deluxe warm white tubes (marked **WWX**) blends well with light from incandescent bulbs and enhances complexions, foods, fabrics, and paints. Deluxe cool white tubes (marked **CWX**) create a cool atmosphere and are effective in rooms with blue or green color schemes.

Light Diffusers and Shields. Diffusers are bowl- or disc-shaped devices that surround the lamp bulb under the shade. They scatter and re-direct light, soften shadows, and reduce reflected glare.

Effective diffusion materials in order of preference include: blown milky glass, enameled glass, flashed opal, and plastics.

Undershade diffusers are now being offered by manufacturers for use in study and reading lamps. One is a highly reflective, inverted metal cone. Other new diffusers are bowl-shaped, prismatic reflectors.

Shields are also used to prevent glare.

Perforated metal shields or plastic louvered shields, placed above the bulb, keep direct glare from reaching the eyes of the passerby. The mushroom-shaped (R-40 type) 150 watt bulb made of white diffusing glass needs no diffuser or shield. It serves well for casual reading.

LIGHT DIFFUSERS

Shielded fluorescent fixtures provide the right lighting for grooming at a bathroom mirror. In a small bathroom, the overhead fixture, as mounted here, also gives general lighting. If a bathroom has a ceiling fixture, the overhead tube can be mounted directly above the mirror.

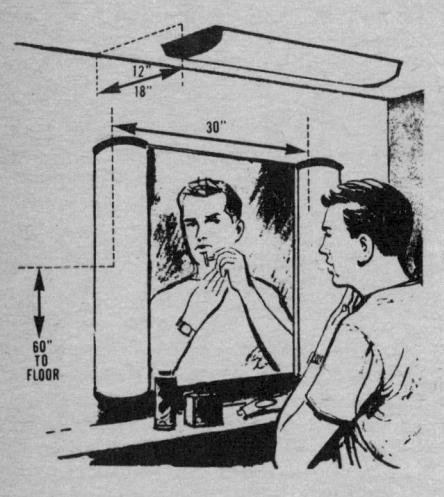

Types of Diffusers.
Upper left: Molded prismatic diffuser has a louvered top shield that diffuses light and prevents direct glare from the bulb. Study lamps with such diffusers give an exceptionally good spread of light over desk areas. *Upper center:* Prismatic refractor at base of bulb helps distribute light and reduce direct and reflected glare. Top diffusing shield also restricts glare. *Upper right:* CLM (Certified Lamp Makers) glass diffuser shields bulb from top viewing and gives an effecient spread of light below. *Lower left:* White glass bowl-shaped diffuser reduces direct glare from bulb and provides both up an down light. *Lower center:* Large size and whiteness of R-40 white indirect bulb in wide harp helps diffuse light. *Lower right:* Plastic or white glass diffusing disc at the bottom spreads light and reduces glare from the bulbs. Perforated disc at top shields the bulb from top viewing and re-directs light downward.

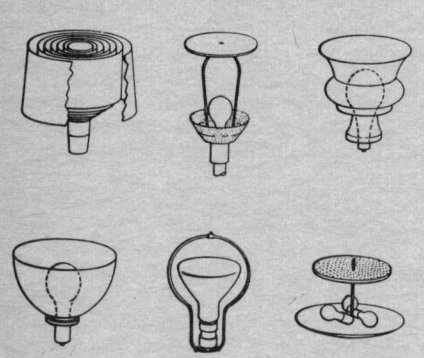

Light Dimmers. Add convenience, safety, and flexibility to your home lighting by using dimmer controls on fixtures in bedrooms, bathrooms, halls, and living rooms. Gradations of light—from full bright to very dim—are possible simply by turning a knob.

A low level of lighting is helpful in the care of small children, sick persons, and others who need assistance during the night. House guests who are unfamiliar with their surroundings, appreciate night lights.

You can make dramatic changes in the mood of a room by softening lights with a dimmer switch. Lights can be lowered when listening to music or enjoying a fire on the hearth.

Dimmers for incandescent bulbs are simple, compact, and can be mounted in walls in much the same way as off-on switches. Be sure that the wattage capacity of the dimmer control is equal to or more than the total wattage to be controlled.

Dimmer-controlled fluorescent fixtures must be preplanned with your power supplier or electric contractor before installation. They are considerably more expensive than incandescent dimmer units. The control combines with a special built-in ballast, and can operate one or more specially designed fluorescent fixtures as a unit.

Lighting fixtures usually provide the general lighting in a home. When they are well chosen, they also add decorative tone and a pleasant atmosphere.

The basic principles of lighting—quantity, quality, color, and reflectance of light—should be considered in selecting fixtures. You will find that individual fixtures may be combined with structural lighting for pleasing effects.

The manufacturers' wattage rating and the size of the fixture must be large enough to accommodate the largest wattage bulb needed to light the area.

LIGHTING FIXTURES

Often, you need more than one fixture. For example, a large rectangular kitchen may need two 48-inch tow-tube fixtures placed end to end.

Fixtures shown below have design features that function well in areas indicated. They are many other types of fixtures.

Points to Check. Check fixtures carefully before buying them. Here are some points to keep in mind—

Incandescent bulbs should be no closer than one-fourth inch to enclosing globes of diffusing shields.

Top or side ventilation is desirable in a fixture to keep temperatures low and to extend bulb life.

Inside surfaces of shades should be of polished material or finished with white enamel.

Shape and dimension of a fixture should help direct light efficiently and uniformly over the area to be lighted.

Plain or textured glass or plastic is preferred for enclosures and shades.

Bathroom Fixtures.

Side and Overhead Fluorescent Fixtures. Pair of 24-inch long fixtures are spaced 30 or more inches apart at mirror sides. Use fixture above mirror if no ceiling light in room.

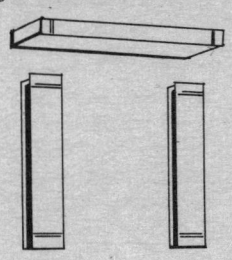

Side and Overhead Incandescent Units. One- or two-socket fixtures at mirror sides are centered 60 inches above floor. Note overhead fixture. Bulbs are well shielded to reduce glare.

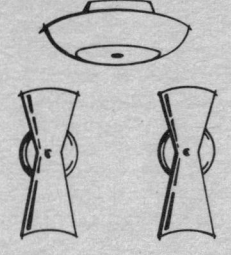

Vapor-proof Ceiling Fixture. A good type for a shower stall. Use a 60-watt bulb. Make sure that the switch is located outside of the shower.

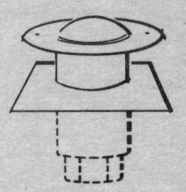

Bedroom Fixtures.

Ceiling Fixture. Twelve or 14-inch width. Surface-mounted, with plain or textured glass or plastic diffuser.

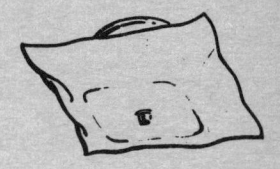

Surface Mounted Ceiling Fixture. Twelve-inch minimum diameter, single socket or three sockets. Shallow-wide diffuser is desirable.

Ventilated Ceiling Fixture. One or two sockets, diffusing shade to extend below trim to give side lighting. Unit is surface-mounted on ceiling.

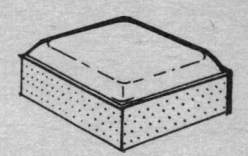

LIGHTING FIXTURES

Dining Room Fixtures.

Lantern-style Pulldown. Unit has a three-way socket, takes a 50/100/150-watt bulb, and a diffusing globe.

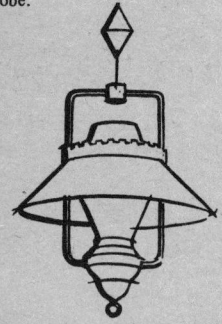

Pulldown Fixture. Ventilated unit has three-way single socket or three sockets, and white glass diffuser.

Ventilated Ceiling Fixture. Bent glass diffuser, 14-inch minimum diameter. Interior reflecting surfaces should be white or polished.

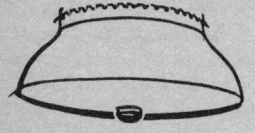

Hall Fixtures.

Closed Globe Fixture. Unit is mounted on ceiling. Choose a white glass globe for diffusion of light.

Hanging Bowl Fixture. Eight-inch diameter. A good choice for lighting a high-ceilinged hall or stairway.

Wall Bracket Fixture. May be used to supplement general lighting. Can be mounted on wall near a mirror.

Kitchen Fixtures.

Closed Globe Unit. Minimum diameter of bowl is 14 inches. White glass gives good diffusion of light.

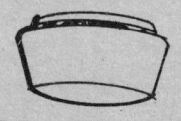

Fluorescent Fixture with Diffusing Shield. Two or four tubes as needed in a 48-inch unit. For a large kitchen, two 2-tube fixtures can be placed end to end.

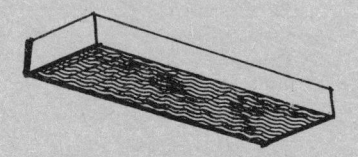

Shielded Fixture. Three of four sockets, 14 to 17-inch diameter. Shallow-wide bowl is desirable.

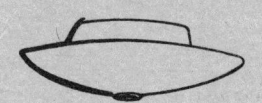

LIGHTING, FLUORESCENT

Utility Room Fixtures.
Reflector and Reflector Bowl Bulb Unit. Twelve- or 14-inch minimum diameter. Use to reduce glare and to spread light.

Surface-mounted Ceiling Fixture. Minimum diameter of 12 inches is desirable. Unit may have one or two sockets.

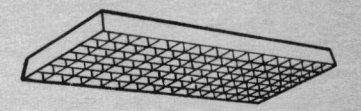

Shielded Fluorescent Fixture. Two- or four-tube fixture can be centered in ceiling or mounted over work area.

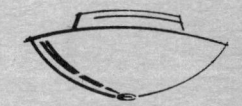

Lighting, Fluorescent.

Selection Guide for Fluorescent Tubes
[All are T12 (1½ inch diameter) tubes]

Use	Wattage and color[1]
Reading, writing, sewing:	
Occasional	1 40w or 2 20w, WWX or CWX.
Prolonged	2 40w or 2 30w, WWX or CWX.
Wall lighting (valances, brackets, cornices):	
Small living area (8-foot minimum)	2 40w, WWX or CWX.
Large living area (16-foot minimum)	4 40w, WWX or CWX.
Grooming:	
Bathroom mirror:	
One fixture each side of mirror	2 20w or 2 30w, WWX
One fixture over mirror	1 40w, WWX or CWX.
Bathroom ceiling fixture	1 40w, WWX.
Luminous ceiling	For 2-foot squares, 4 20w, WWX or CWX
	3-foot squares, 4 30x, WWX or CWX
	4-foot squares, 4 40w, WWX or CWX
	6-foot squares, 6 to 8 40w, WWX or CWX
Kitchen work:	
Ceiling fixture	2 40w or 2 30w, WWX.
Over sink	2 40w or 2 30w, WWX or CWX.
Counter top lighting	20w or 40w to fill length, WWX.
Dining area (separate from kitchen)	15 or 20 watts for each 30 inches of longest dimension of room area, WWX.
Home workshop	2 40w, CW, CWX, or WWX.

[1] WWX=warm white deluxe; CWX=cool white deluxe; CW=cool white.

LIGHTING, FLUORESCENT

Lighting, Fluorescent. Most households use fluorescent lighting in some form. Although know-how is needed to select and use this light source correctly, it does offer advantages in home lighting. For guidance in selecting fluorescent tubes and fixtures, see the table on page 201.

Fluorescent tubes must be used in fixtures that contain the necessary electrical accessories. The basic structure of a fluorescent fixture is shown below.

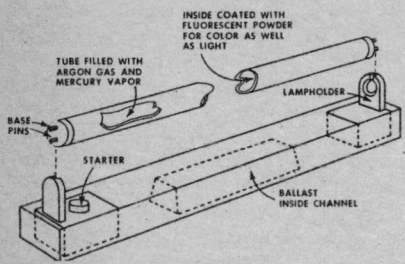

The fluorescent phosphor coating on the inside of the tube is activated by electric energy passing through the tube; light is given off. The starter in standard starter-type fixtures permits preheating of the electrodes in the ends of the tube to make it easier to start. The ballast limits the current to keep the tube functioning properly. The channel holds ballast and wiring and spaces the lampholders.

White fluorescent tubes are labeled "standard" and "deluxe." The whiteness of a standard tube is indicated by letters, WW for warm white; CW for cool white. The addition of an "X" to these letters indicates a deluxe tube.

A deluxe warm white (WWX) tube gives a flat-tering light, can be used with incandescent light, and does not distort colors any more than incandescent light does. A deluxe cool white (CWX) tube simulates daylight and goes nicely with cool color schemes of blue and green. Deluxe tubes are the only fluorescent tubes recommended for home use. They are worth waiting for if your dealer has to order them for you.

Lighting, Improvements on Existing. When you redecorate, finish walls in light pastel colors and ceilings in white or near white or a pale tint. Flat or low-gloss paint on walls and ceilings helps diffuse light and makes lighting more comfortable. Use sheer curtains or draperies in light or pastel tints.

Add portable lamps for better balance of room lighting.

Install structural lighting (valance and cornice) in living areas where there is only one ceiling light or none. Eight to 20 feet of wall lighting will add a feeling of spaciousness to an average-sized room and make the lighting more flexible.

Replace present bulbs with those of higher wattage, but do not exceed the rated wattage of the fixture. A minimum of 150 watts is needed in many single-socket lamps. For better control of lighting, use three-way bulbs or dimmer switches. If you want a higher-wattage fluorescent unit, the fixture must be changed.

For efficiency, use one large bulb rather than several small ones. A 100-watt bulb gives as much light as six 25-watt bulbs, but only uses about two-thirds as much current.

Replace outmoded bare-bulb fixtures with well-shielded ones. You'll enjoy the difference.

Cover all bare bulbs or tubes in a ceiling fixture with a shade or diffuser. Some of these diffusers clip to the bulb. Others hang from small chains attached to the husk of the fixture. Large diffusers, sometimes called adaptors, may have supporting frames that are screwed on the sockets of single-bulb fixtures. An inexpensive way to avoid the glare of bare bulbs in a ceiling fixture is to replace these bulbs with silver bowl bulbs or decorative mushroom shaped bulbs.

Keep all light sources operating efficiently by replacing blackened bulbs and tubes promptly.

Put in additional convenience outlets if needed for correct lamp placement. Added outlets prevent

Type of Tube For Ballast Used

[Fluorescent tube wattages vary with length of tube and are not interchangeable]

Length of tube (inches)	Wattage	Diameter of tube	Ballast marking[1]
	Watts	Inches	
15....	14	1½ (T12) ..	Preheat start.
18....	15	1 (T8)	Trigger start or preheat.
		1½ (T12) ..	Trigger start or preheat.
24....	20	1½ (T12) ..	Preheat or rapid start.
36....	30	1 (T8)	Rapid start.
		1½ (T12) ..	Rapid start or dimming.
48....	40	1½ (T12) ..	Rapid start or dimming.

[1] Only preheat ballasts require starters and use standard-type tubes.

LIGHTING MAINTENANCE

the use of dangerous "cube" plugs and extension cords. Surface wiring strips may be attached along baseboards or counter tops. These strips may be more economical than adding built-in convenience outlets. Be sure any surface wiring system you choose is of the correct size and carries the Underwriters' Laboratories seal of approval.

Ask your electric power supplier or electrical contractor for the correct size.

Lift the lampshade on a portable lamp with a riser if the bulb is too high. When a bulb is too high it restricts the downward circle of light and shines into the eyes of persons standing near. Risers come in multiples of one-half inch and can be screwed to the top of the harp to lift the shade the amount needed.

Replace the lampshade with a deeper shade if bulb is too low in lamp and bulb shows beneath lower edge of shade. Or, if you prefer, use a shorter harp or a different diffusing bowl.

If a lamp base is too short, set the base on wood, marble, ceramic, or metal blocks to raise lamp to proper height. For ease in handling, cement the block to the base.

Get replacement shades for table lamps if present shades do not meet specifications. Choose shades made of translucent materials with white linings and open tops.

Invert and rewire the socket of old-style bridge lamps. Then add 6-inch diffusing bowls and larger, wider shades that give soft, better lighting.

Lighting for Machine Sewing. For machine sewing, mount a wall lamp 14 inches above the working surface, 12 inches to the left of the needle, and 7 inches from the wall. The bottom of the shade should be at eye level.

Lighting Maintenance. Home lighting equipment needs regular care and cleaning to keep it operating efficiently. A collection of dirt and dust on bulbs, tubes, diffusion bowls, lampshades, and fixtures can cause a substantial loss in light output.

It's a good idea to clean all lighting equipment at least four to six times a year—bowl-type portable lamps should be cleaned monthly.

Here are some suggestions for taking care of lamps:

1. Wash glass and plastic diffusers and shields in a detergent solution, rinse in clear warm water, and dry.

2. Wipe bulbs and tubes with a damp, soapy cloth, and dry well.

3. Dust wood and metal lamp bases with a soft cloth and apply a thin coat of wax. Glass, pottery, marble, chrome, and onyx bases can be washed with a damp soapy cloth, dried, and waxed.

4. Lampshades may be cleaned by a vacuum cleaner with a soft brush attachment, or dry-cleaned. Silk or rayon shades that are hand sewn to the frame, with no glued trimmings, may be washed in mild, lukewarm suds, and rinsed in clear water. Dry shades quickly to prevent rusting of frames.

5. Wipe parchment shades with a dry cloth.

6. Remove plastic wrappings from lampshades before using. Wrappings create glare and may warp the frame and wrinkle the shade fabric. Some are fire hazards.

7. Replace all darkened bulbs. A darkened bulb can reduce light output 25 to 50 percent, but uses almost the same amount of current as a new bulb operating at correct wattage. Darkened bulbs may be used in closets or hallways where less light is needed.

8. Replace fluorescent tubes that flicker and any tubes that have darkened ends. A long delay in starting indicates a new starter is probably needed. If a humming sound develops in a fluorescent fixture, the ballast may need to be remounted or replaced.

Lamp Repair. When a lamp flickers, something is wrong with it. Unplug it from the electrical outlet first, then unscrew the bulb and try it in a properly working lamp. If it flickers there too, throw it away. If it does not flicker, go back to the lamp in question, and remove the bulb socket by loosening the screws that attach it to the frame. Pull the socket

LIGHTING NEEDS

free and examine the connections, making sure no loose wires are causing a short circuit. Now examine the length of wire inside the fixture for frayed cord. Tape up all bare spots. Trace the wire to the plug for loose connections. Then reassemble all the parts of the lamp.

Tips.

1. Broken Bulb Removal. Often the stub of a shattered light bulb is difficult to extract from the socket without danger of cutting the fingers. One way to deal with this is to press a cake of soap over the broken ends, and this will give you a safe grip for twisting the light bulb out. A wad of putty or modeling clay can be used in the same fashion.

2. Fixture Cleaning. To remove fly specks from lighting fixtures, sponge with alcohol. Rinse with soapsuds and polish with a flannel cloth moistened in sewing-maching oil. Rub bronze chandeliers with a cloth that has been spread with a little petroleum jelly.

3. Pull Chain Repair. If the pull chains on a lamp or light socket persist in snapping up and tangling, use solder to stiffen a couple of inches of the chain next to the socket.

Lighting for Needlework. A double swing-arm lamp concentrates light on hand sewing and needlework. Sewing requires twice as much light as casual reading. To position lamp, measure 15 inches to the left of center of sewing, and place center of shade 12 inches back from this point.

Lighting Needs.

Checklist. Using checklist below, note the number of family members that participate in activities in the various rooms in the house.

Living Areas (living room, dining room, family or recreation room):
  Reading or studying (prolonged).
  Reading (casual, intermittent).
  Viewing television.
  Visiting and conversation.
  Playing games (adult, children).
  Reading music.
  Setting table.
  Dining.

Work Areas (kitchen, laundry, workroom, home office):
  Reading recipes and measuring ingredients.
  Reading labels and following directions.
  Inspecting and sorting foods.
  Reading dials, and checking foods as they cook.
  Washing dishes and cleaning equipment.
  Sorting and pretreating laundry.
  Ironing or pressing.
  Sewing (reading directions, cutting, fitting, machine and hand stitching).
  Repairing small appliances.
  Working on hobbies (artwork, collections, model building, photography).
  Housekeeping (dusting, vacuuming, waxing, washing walls, woodwork, and other surfaces).
  Deskwork (recordkeeping, studying, typing, reading telephone directory).

Private Areas (bedrooms, bathrooms):
  Personal grooming (bathing, shaving, manicuring, shampooing and arranging hair, applying cosmetics).
  Assembling clothes from closet or storage unit.
  Dressing.
  Caring for infants, small children, or the sick.
  Reading medicine labels or taking temperatures.
  Reading in bed or at bedside.

Halls, Stairways, Entrances:
  Moving between rooms.
  Using steps and stairs.
  Reading house numbers.
  Identifying callers.
  Safe access to house or garage.

Check present lighting for each task using a light meter, and compare with suggested Minimum Levels of Illumination, page 205.

Minimum Levels of Illumination.
[Recommended by Illuminating Engineering Society]

Specific visual task — Amount of light on task[1] (foot-candles)[2]

Reading and writing:
- Handwriting, indistinct print, or poor copies .. 70
- Books, magazines, newspapers 30
- Music scores, advanced 70
- Music scores, simple 30
- Studying at desk 70

Recreation:
- Playing cards, table games, billiards 30
- Table tennis 20

Grooming:
- Shaving, combing hair, applying makeup 50

Kitchen work:
- At sink 70
- At range 50
- At work counters 50

Laundering jobs:
- At washer 50
- At ironing board 50
- At ironer 50

Sewing:
- Dark fabrics (fine detail, low contrast) 200
- Prolonged periods (light-to-medium fabrics) .. 100
- Occasional (light-colored fabrics) 50
- Occasional (coarse thread, large stitches, high contrast of thread to fabric) 30

Handicraft:
- Close work (reading diagrams and blueprints, fine finishing) 100
- Cabinetmaking, planing, sanding, glueing 50
- Measuring, sawing, assembling repairing 50

General lighting — Average light throughout area[3] (foot-candles)[2]

- Any area involving a visual task 30
- For safety in passage areas 10
- Areas used mostly for relaxation, recreation, and conversation 10

[1] Average of light measured over the task area.
[2] A foot-candle is the amount of light falling on a surface 1 foot away from a standard candle (ordinary 1½-inch diameter candle).
[3] Average of light measured on a horizontal plane 30 inches above the floor.

LIGHTING, PORTABLE

Lighting for Piano Playing. To read music and play the piano, center the shade of a swing-arm floor lamp 22 inches to the right or left of the middle of the keyboard, and 13 inches in front of the lower edge of music rack.

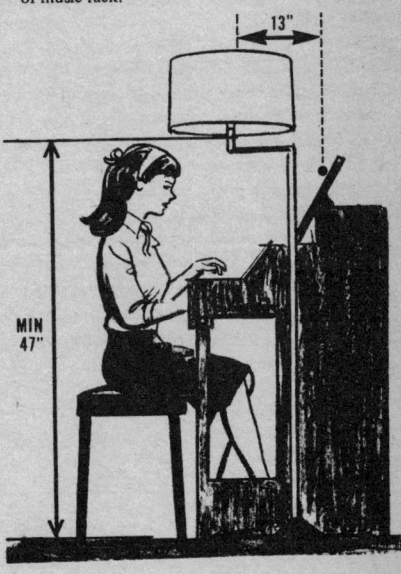

Lighting, Portable. Most living rooms need at least five portable lamps, most bedrooms, three. So sooner or later, you'll be lamp shopping.

Well-designed floor and table lamps may be difficult to find, but keep looking. Look for lamps that combine function and beauty—pay close attention to what's under the shade! Choose lamps that make seeing comfortable and, at the same time, harmonize with your furnishings, color schemes, and with other lamps and accessories.

Generally speaking, the *design* of a lamp should be akin to the style and decoration of the room; its *scale* in accord with the furniture it appears on or over; and the *amount of light* it radiates suitable for the purpose intended.

Dimmer-switch controlled lamps give greater flexibility than three-way lamps that use three-way sockets and require three-way bulbs.

The small *high-intensity lamps* now on the market are not designed for study, reading, or general work. They can, however, provide a concentrated area of high-level light for special tasks, such as sewing, crafts, or fine-detail work. They should always be used in combination with good general lighting.

If you select a lamp for style or color alone, do not expect to use it for close work. It is a *decorative* lamp. Use it to—

Give limited general lighting.
Brighten a corner, foyer, or hallway.
Display an object of art or an accessory.

Any portable lamp, regardless of size, should be sturdily built. See that the power cord is well protected from sharp edges where it enters the lamp base and the vertical pipe.

Bedside Lamps. Reading in bed is relaxing when there is an adequate spread of light. Place lamp as indicated. Bottom of shade of table lamp should be at eye level, and approximately 20 inches above the top of mattress. The general recommendation for wall lamps and wall brackets mounted behind a bed is 30 inches above top of mattress.

Desk and Study Lamps. A well-lighted desk or study center makes it easy to concentrate. Good-quality light falls on the task at hand. Eyestrain and physical tension are reduced to a minimum because the worker has enough light and little or no glare.

For continued study or deskwork, be sure your lighting arrangement gives an average of 70 footcandles over the work area. A lamp—correctly placed and fitted with a 200-watt bulb—will give this amount of light. If you do not have a diffuser on the lamp, using a white bulb helps to reduce glare.

To serve the growing student population in this country, several lamp manufacturers are now making and selling specially designed, higher-wattage study lamps. Tags attached to the lamps state, "This is a Better Light Better Sight Bureau Study Lamp." They also give nearly twice as much light as other study lamps and spread light over a wider area. For these lamps, 200-watt bulbs are recommended.

When a study lamp is placed properly, it gives excellent lighting for intensive and prolonged deskwork. For a right-handed person the center of the lampshade should be about 15 inches to the left of the work center, and the lamp about 12 inches back of the front edge of table. Place the lamp to the right for a left-handed person.

A swing arm on a floor lamp makes it possible to place light in good position for study or deskwork. Such a floor lamp should measure 47 to 49 inches from the floor to the bottom of the shade. It is usually fitted with a white glass diffusion bowl and a mogul socket for a 100/200/300-watt three-way bulb or a medium socket for a 50/100/150 or 50/200/250 three-way bulb or a single 150-watt bulb.

If you plan to study under a wall bracket or "pin-up" type lamp, choose a bracket with a swing arm so you can move the center of the shade forward. Then you can position the light to your best advantage.

Here are other suggestions to improve light in a study center:

Choose a desk with a light-colored, nonglossy finish.
Use a light-colored blotter or desk pad.
Paint walls in neutral or light colors or select a plain wallpaper or one with a small, quiet design.
Make sure that the desk does not face a window

Dressing Table Lamps. Shades on dressing table lamps should be translucent to let the light through. Choose lamps tall enough so the center of shade is 15 inches above the table, approximately at eye level. Use high-wattage bulbs.

Floor Lamps. In choosing a floor lamp, keep in mind exactly where it is to be located in your home. Floor lamps should harmonize with furnishings, and be carefully sealed to space. Choose lamps sized and constructed for proper placement without interfering with house traffic.

Small floor lamps—standard, swing-arm, or bridge

LIGHTING, PORTABLE

type—may be 43 to 47 inches from the floor to the bottom of the shade. Large lamps—standard or swing-arm—measure 47 to 49 inches from the floor to the bottom of the shade.

For reading, a floor lamp with a fixed or swing-arm is correctly placed when the light comes from behind the shoulder of the reader, near the rear of the chair—either at the right or the left—but never from directly behind the chair.

If a floor lamp is used for prolonged reading or sewing, it should have a bulb wattage of 200 or 300 watts; the minimum bulb wattage that may be used for reading is 150 watts.

Lamp Bases. The base of a portable lamp needs to be heavy enough to support the lamp firmly and keep it from upsetting easily. The design of the base should be appropriate to its function—it should please, but not distract. Grotesquely shaped bases are seldom in good taste.

Materials in lamp bases often relate to certain furniture styles or periods. Some popular furniture styles and appropriate base materials include: *Early American*—pewter, brass, stoneware, copper, wrought iron, pottery, wood; *18th Century or Traditional*—silver, porcelain, china, cloisonne, crystal, marble; *Contemporary*—metals, glass, wood, cork, ceramics.

Lamp Making.

1. *Hurricane.* You can fashion this very attractive and quaint little hurricane lamp out of scrap material. The base is made from a tin can, and the chimney from a catsup bottle. Cut away the bottom and part of the neck of the bottle by scoring around the outside with a glass cutter, then tapping the inside with a bent rod. Smooth the jagged edges of the glass with a file wet with turpentine, and with abrasive cloth. To make the base, hammer a 6-3/4 inch tinplate disk over a wooden form — or spin it on a lathe — or convert an inexpensive tin skillet into a ready-made base by shortening the handle and bending it into the finger loop. The handle, candle cup, and bottle-holding ring are made from strips of tinplate bent and soldered. Be sure to punch two rows of holes near the bottom of the ring to provide draft for your candle.

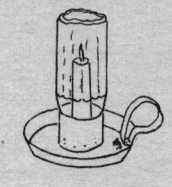

2. *Juice Can.* You can make a very attractive lamp, and very reasonably, just by using two tall juice cans. Bore holes into the cans to accommodate a 1/2-inch threaded pipe and elbow, as in the illustration. The pipe should extend 1/2-inch above the top of your juice-can base. Then thread your wire through the pipe and fittings, and assemble the pipe and cans — the holes which were originally punched for the juice being joined in the center of the base. Tape the cans together at the joint with

LIGHTING, PORTABLE

waterproof tape and fill them with plaster of Paris. Cover the entire base by gluing some leatherette to it, holding the seams with some masking tape until they dry. If the juice cans are grooved, you can obtain a pretty effect by tying string tightly around in these grooves, allowing it to remain for a couple of days, then removing — and you will have a tooled appearance on your lamp base. Finally, install the electric socket and fixtures, and an appropriate lampshade.

3. Marine. Here is a real fine lamp, with a nautical touch, suitable for a sportsman's den. You need a piece of three-by-three inch hardwood seven inches long, a threaded electric rod of the same length, two boat cleats, an electric socket, some wire, a plug, and a suitable lampshade. Drill your center hole into the hardwood from both ends, if your bit happens to be too short, and countersink the bottom hole. Screw the boat cleats on opposite sides of the base. Then drill a hole through another side of the base near the bottom for bringing out your lamp cord. Insert rod and cord into center hole, screw the rod firmly into the socket at the top, and tighten the entire assembly by screwing a nut on the bottom end of the rod. Sand, stain, and polish the base.

4. Rolling Pin. You can fashion a really attractive lamp with a rolling pin. Cut both handles off the rolling pin, and then mark off a spiral around the pin by wrapping a strip of one-half inch tape around it. Use a fine-toothed saw and cut a groove along each edge of the tape one-fourth inch deep. Remove the tape and cut out the wood between the saw cuts with a narrow wood chisel. Drill a hole through the center of the rolling pin with a sharp auger to accommodate a length of one-eighth inch electrical pipe. Use three disks to make your lamp base, 3-1/2, 4, and 4-1/2 inches in diameter, respectively. The smallest disk is bored out to receive the lower end of the rolling pin. You can purchase your light sockets and lamp harps at your local appliance or hardware store.

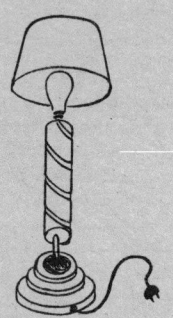

5. Vase. Here's a quick and easy way to convert a narrow-necked vase into a lamp. At the same time, you'll always be able to restore the vase to its original function. You do this by means of a wooden dowel insert. Make the insert by turning a length of dowel to a diameter slightly smaller than the inner diameter of the vase neck. Cross-drill it near the top for the lamp wire. Then fill the vase to within a few inches of the top with some clean, dry sand, and insert the dowel into the vase gently until it touches the bottom of the vase.

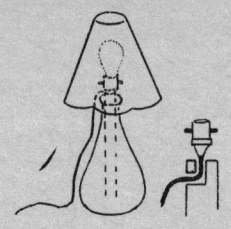

Lamp Shade Cleaning. Washable. Wash in a solution of mild soap and water. A bathtub is a good place to do this.

Pasted or Pleated. Clean with cheesecloth dipped in dry soap suds.

Nonwashable. Clean with cheesecloth dipped in cleaning fluid.

LIGHTING, PORTABLE

Parchment. Clean by rubbing with a fresh piece of white bread, or with an art-gum eraser, or with a cloth dipped in milk.

Lamp Shade Decorating. Decorate some lampshades with maps from an old atlas. This is particularly good in a boy's room. Glue the map down tightly to the shade and allow to dry, then lacquer the entire shade. Or, leftover pieces of wallpaper can be used instead of maps.

Lamp Shades. Shades made of translucent materials are usually chosen for portable lamps.

Desk lamps use slightly translucent shades to avoid uncomfortable brightness in the eyes of the person using the lamp. Shades for dressing table or dresser lamps should be highly translucent because light reaching the face must come through the shade. Shade materials suitable for vanity lamps are too translucent for reading, study, and decorative lamps.

For effective light reflectance, the inside of the shade needs to be white or near-white. Good color choices for the outside of the lampshade are: neutral or pale tints, off-white, beige, and light gray. Try to avoid excessive contrast between the color of the shade and adjacent walls.

The shape of a lampshade also affects lighting. Straight or nearly straight lines are preferable to extreme curves. Look for a shade that gives a wide spread of downward light as well as some upward light.

Table Lamps. Before you shop for table lamps, jot down the heights of tables on which lamps will be placed, and the height of any chair or sofa seat on which a person using the lamp will be seated. Take these figures with you as you shop. You may also want to consider the eye level height of persons using a lamp, particularly if an individual is unusually tall or short.

As you shop, keep this rule in mind: *Table height plus lamp base height (to the lower edge of shade) should equal the eye height of the person using the lamp.*

Eye height, of course, depends on the height of the chair or sofa seat and the eye level of the person seated. Generally eye height is 40 to 42 inches above the floor. For comfortable seeing, the bottom of the lampshade should also be 40 to 42 inches above the floor.

Here are other points to consider in selecting and using table lamps:

Shade dimensions. Shade on lamps for reading, sewing, or studying—16 inches wide or more at the bottom; 9 inches wide at the top; and at least 10 inches deep.

Minimum bulb wattages. Single-socket lamps for reading, sewing, or studying—150 watts; multiple-socket lamps—at least three 60-watt bulbs.

Sockets. Center of the light source (bulb) always located in the lower third of the shade.

Diffusers. They soften and spread light.

TYPICAL HEIGHTS OF LAMPS AND TABLES FOR SHADE AT EYE LEVEL

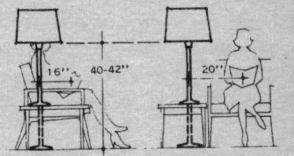

PLACEMENT DIMENSIONS FOR SHADE AT EYE LEVEL

TYPICAL HEIGHTS OF LAMPS AND TABLES FOR SHADE ABOVE EYE LEVEL

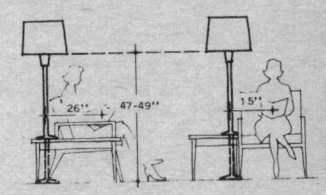

PLACEMENT DIMENSIONS FOR SHADE ABOVE EYE LEVEL

LIGHTING, STRUCTURAL

Lighting, Structural.

Bracket. A lighted bracket is similar to a lighted valance except that it is located on a wall instead of over windows. A bracket can provide both general and local lighting. Brackets can be mounted at suitable levels for lighting work counters, snack bars, pictures and wall hangings, and for reading in bed. For reading in bed, place bottom edge of bracket faceboard 30 inches above the top of mattress. For general lighting, the bottom edge of bracket should be at least 65 inches from the floor; for local lighting, bottom edge of bracket should be about 55 inches from the floor.

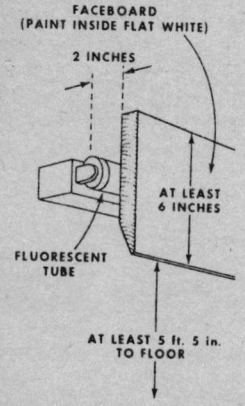

Cornice lighting, generally mounted at junction of wall and ceiling, is closed at top and extends full length of wall. A lighted cornice may be used without draperies, or with draperies. Cornices direct light downward to enliven wall textures, murals, scenic wallpaper, picture arrangements, art objects, or draperies. Lighted cornices are effective in low-ceilinged rooms where they give an illusion of height. Exteriors of faceboards may be painted, wallpapered, or covered with fabric. Since lighted cornices do not supply upward light, it is well to use open-top lamps in the same room.

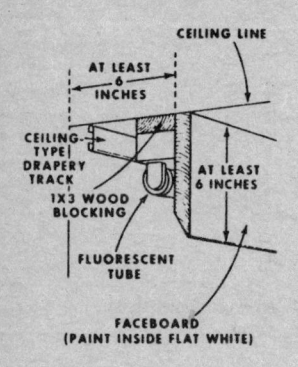

Soffit. Two 30-watt or 40-watt fluorescent tubes (deluxe warm white) may be recessed in soffit above kitchen sink. The fixture may be shielded with frosted glass or plastic to make it similar to a recessed unit. The entire interior of soffit should be painted flat white to reflect the light downward.

Such an installation gives comfortable, diffused down light for easy seeing at sinks or along dressing counters in bathrooms. You can also use incandescent lighting in a soffit. Two 75-watt inside frosted bulbs, spaced 15 inches apart, can be mounted on ceiling or front edge of soffit behind a faceboard.

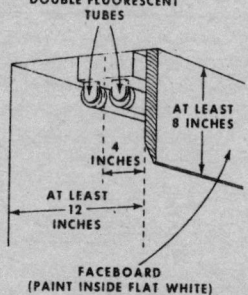

Valance. A lighted valance makes a room appear more spacious and dramatizes colors and textures.

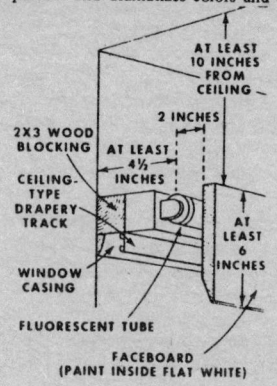

Valance boards are open at top and bottom, and are usually mounted above draperies. They provide up light that spreads across ceiling for generally lighting and down light that accents draperies. Allow from 10 to 12 inches between the ceiling and top edge of the valance. For efficient structural lighting, follow dimensions exactly. Valance lighting fixtures can be wired for entrance switching, and dimmer-controlled fixtures may be installed to increase or decrease the level of the lighting.

Lighting for Televiewing. Viewing television in a darkened room is extremely tiring to the eyes because of the sharp contrast between the bright screen and unlighted surroundings. To avoid eyestrain and fatigue, provide a low to moderate level of lighting throughout the viewing area.

Wall lighting from valances and brackets creates a delightful background for watching television. When you use these types of lighting, position your TV set to the side or in front of the lighted walls.

Another way to offset the brightness of the screen and make viewing comfortable is to place one or two portable lamps behind or at the sides of the set. This helps prevent reflections on the TV screen. If the lamps have three-way controls, turn them on the low settings.

Lighting Test. Test the lighting layout in your home by answering the questions below (the more "yes" answers, the better).

CAN YOU

1. Light your way as you go from room to room?
2. Switch lights from each doorway in rooms with two or more doorways?
3. Turn on stairway lighting before you start up or down steps?
4. Light front hall and living room as you enter?
5. Control garage or carport lighting from the house?
6. Control outdoor floodlights from inside the house?
7. Dim lights in bedrooms for the convenience of sick persons and small children?
8. Dim living area lighting for change of mood and atmosphere?

Light Reflectances. When planning the lighting of any interior, consider color and finish of walls, ceilings, wood floors or floor coverings, and large drapery areas. These large surfaces reflect and redistribute light within a room. Their lightness or darkness greatly affects the mood of a room.

White surfaces, of course, reflect the greatest amount of available light. Light tints of colors reflect light next best. Somber color tones absorb much of the light that falls upon them and reflect little light. See **Reflectance Table**, below.

If a large room gets plenty of daylight, you probably can use fairly strong color. Light tints on walls make a small room seem larger.

Whatever the room size, try to keep colors within the 35 to 60 percent reflectance range. Ceilings should have reflectance values of 60 to 90 percent; floors at least 15 to 35 percent. Matte finishes (flat or low-gloss surfaces) on walls and ceilings diffuse light and reduce reflections of light sources. Glossy, highly polished or glazed surfaces produce reflected glare.

Reflectance Table.

Color	Approximate percent reflection
Whites:	
Dull or flat white	75–90
Light tints:	
Cream or eggshell	79
Ivory	75
Pale pink and pale yellow	75–80
Light green, light blue, light orchid	70–75
Soft pink and light peach	69
Light beige or pale gray	70
Medium tones:	
Apricot	56–62
Pink	64
Tan, yellow-gold	55
Light grays	35–50
Medium turquoise	44
Medium light blue	42
Yellow-green	45
Old gold and pumpkin	34
Rose	29
Deep tones:	
Cocoa brown and mauve	24
Medium green and medium blue	21
Medium gray	20

LIGHT REFLECTORS

Unsuitably dark colors:
Dark brown and dark gray	10–15
Olive green	12
Dark blue, blue-green	5–10
Forest green	7

Natural wood tones:
Birch and beech	35–50
Light maple	25–35
Light oak	25–35
Dark oak and cherry	10–15
Black walnut and mahogany	5–15

Light Reflectors.

Christmas Lights. Start saving your aluminum foil pie tins for use as reflectors for outdoor lighting at Christmastime. Small bulbs appear larger — and reflected in this manner they can be seen as far away as a mile, if space permits.

Rejuvenating. If the reflector on your floodlight or photo-flash gun has become so dulled that it is no longer efficient, you can try this method of rejuvenating it. Buy some aluminum paint and a small quantity of reflective glass beads, obtainable at most art-supply stores. These beads are of the type used to make reflective signs for highways and advertising signs. Brush a coat of the aluminum paint over the reflector surface, allowing it to set until it has become tacky, then flowing the beads over the surface. These will stick to the paint, making a smooth, even coating. In most cases, this new surface will possess as much, or even more, reflective quality as the original product.

Light Sources. Incandescent bulbs and fluorescent tubes—in portable and wall lamps, in ceiling and wall fixtures, and in built-in lighting units— are the usual sources of electric light in homes.

But bulbs and tubes do not insure good lighting by themselves! You must select the right bulb or tube for the purpose you have in mind. Then the bulb or tube has to be placed in an appropriately designed lamp or fixture. And finally, the lamp or fixture must be correctly placed in the room.

Dimmer switches are now available on some lamps. They make it possible to light from very low to the maximum output of the bulb.

Tinted bulbs create decorative effects indoors and outdoors. Silica coatings inside these bulbs produce delicate tints of colored light—pink, aqua, yellow, blue, and green. Home uses of these bulbs are best limited to lighting plantings, flowers, or art objects. You'll need to buy tinted bulbs of higher wattage because they give less light then white bulbs.

Silver-bowl bulbs are standard household bulbs with a silver coating applied to the outside of the rounded end. They are used base up, and direct light upward onto the ceiling or into a reflector. You can get them in 60-, 100-, 150-, and 200-watt sizes. They are generally used with reflectors in basements, garages, or other work areas. Fixtures for silver-bowl bulbs are widely available.

Reflector bulbs are available with silver coatings either on the inside or outside of the bulbs. The *spotlight bulbs* direct light in a narrow beam and generally accent objects. The *floodlight bulbs* spread light over a larger area, and are suitable for flood-lighting horizontal or vertical surfaces. Typical floodlight sizes include 30, 50, 75, and 150 watts.

Heat-resistant bulbs, called PAR bulbs because of their parabolic shape, are used outdoors. They are resistant to rain and snow. Common sizes are 75 watts, 150 watts, and up.

Bulbs in decorative shapes are designed to replace bare bulbs in older fixtures and sockets. Some shapes and sizes are made for traditional fixtures (chandeliers and wall sconces); others combine contemporary styling and function. Bulb shapes include globe, flame, cone, mushroom, and tubular.

Some of these bulbs are made of diffusing type glass and are tinted to produce colored lighting effects. Clear bulbs may be needed to produce sparkle in crystal chandeliers. When selected to harmonize with fixtures and room decor, these decorative bulbs may offer a pleasing, low-cost solution to a lighting problem.

Colored floodlight bulbs are available for indoor or outdoor use. The tints—particularly pink and blue-white—create nice effects on planters or flowers and are acceptable for lighting people and furnishings. Strong colors—blue, green, and red—are best reserved for holiday and party decorations.

Comparison.

Incandescent Bulbs	Fluorescent Tubes
Can be concentrated over a limited area or spread over a wide area.	Provide more diffused lighting—a line of light, not a spot.
Initial cost less than fluorescent tubes.	Higher initial cost, but greater light efficiency—three to four times as much light per watt of electricity.
Designed to operate at high temperature.	Cool operating temperature. Generally about one-fifth as hot as incandescent bulbs.
Have average life of 750 to 1,000 hours.	Operate seven to ten times longer than incandescent bulbs.
Wattages range from 15 to 300 watts.	Wattages for home use range from 14 watts (15 inches long) to 40 watts (48 inches long).
Amount of light can be increased or decreased by changing to bulbs of different wattage because most bulbs have same size base.	Cannot be replaced by higher or lower wattage tubes.
Require no ballast or starter.	Require ballasts, and in some cases, starters.
Do not interfere with radio reception.	May cause noise interference with radio reception within 10 feet of the tube location.
Suitable for use in less expensive fixtures.	Adaptable to and commonly used in custom-designed installations and in surface-mounted and recessed fixtures.
Available in colors to enliven decor and accessories. Colored bulbs are 25 to 50 percent less efficient than white bulbs.	Available in many colors (plus deluxe cool white, CWX, and deluxe warm white), WWX, at much higher light output than colored incandescents.
Gain flexibility by use of three-way bulbs and multiple-switch controls for dimmer controls designed for incandescent bulbs.	Gain flexibility by use of dimming ballasts combined with dimmer controls designed for fluorescent tubes.

Lima Beans, see FOODS.

Limed Oak Finish, see FURNITURE REFINISHING.

Linen, see FIBERS, NATURAL.

Linens, Scented. A variation on the Colonial custom of spicing bed linens can be achieved if you will buy quantities of toilet soap in advance of your needs and store these unwrapped among your linens.

Linoleum is a mixture of linseed oil, resins, and ground cork pressed upon a burlap backing, *or* a mixture of wood fibers, linseed oil, and resins attached to a felt backing.

It has excellent resistance to grease and makes

good recovery from indentation. Needs protection from continued dampness because backing may mold or rot. Not recommended for use on floors either below or on grade.

Linoleum Care. Both the backing and the adhesive that binds the linoleum to the subfloor are susceptible to *water* damage. Water seeps around the edges or through the cracks and attacks the backing, loosening the linoleum from the floor. This results in curling of edges and eventual destruction of the floor surface. Therefore, keep the use of water on linoleum to an *absolute minimum.* Flooding the surface with water is *positively prohibited.* When using water, wash a small area at a time, so that the water can be picked up quickly, thereby reducing the possibility of damage.

Linoleum is also highly susceptible to *alkali* damage. Alkali will remove the linseed oil binder, drying out the floor, causing it to become brittle and crack.

Cleaning. Add luster to your linoleum—without actually waxing it — by adding a little sour milk to the rinse water when you wash the floor.

Grease Removal. If you have inadvertently spilled grease on your kitchen linoleum, pour ice water over the area immediately. This will make the grease harden before it has a chance to soak into the linoleum, and then you can scrape it off with a dull knife.

Mark Removal. To remove stubborn marks on linoleum, such as those caused by table and chair legs and rubber heels and rust spots, make a jelly out of mild soap and rub it carefully over the spots with a dry piece of fine steel wool. Then wipe up the soap and rewax the spot. Or, first try wiping heel marks away with liquid floor wax.

Polishing. An effective homemade linoleum polish consists of a mixture of equal parts of thick, boiled starch and soapsuds. This has a way of preserving the finish of your linoleum and making it resistant to soil.

Linoleum, Inlaid. The main precaution with genuine inlaid linoleum is not to use too much water for washing it, and to avoid scrubbing the surface.

This material is really a cork mat, and dampness will cause particles of cork to fret away to form holes.

An occasional wipe over with a cloth wrung out in mild suds should maintain a clean surface.

A good furniture cream rubbed thoroughly into the surface and polished should give the desired shine.

Several plastic polishes on the market also protect the surface.

Linoleum Installation.
Step-by-step:

1. Remove old linoleum, wash the floor and let it dry.

2. Remove the remaining adhesive from the floor by scrubbing with a strong, hot solution of sal soda concentrate — about a pound of the sal to a gallon of water. Let the solution work on the adhesive for about an hour, then scrub again with a brush, or scrape up with a wide-headed putty knife.

3. If the floor is in bad shape, cover the surface with a layer of plywood for a smooth base.

4. Remove the baseboards.

5. If the linoleum is not felt-backed, lay a felt base and cement it to the floor.

6. Unroll the linoleum and let it lie overnight in place. You can prevent any danger of its cracking if you'll warm it up a bit before unrolling it. One easy way to do this is to place an electric heater at one end of the roll and a fan at the other end directed away from the linoleum. The fan will thus suck the heat from the heater through the roll of linoleum, making it more pliable and easily handled.

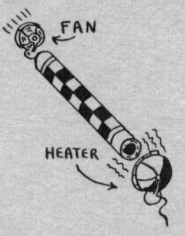

7. With a linoleum knife, cut the linoleum to fit walls, door jambs and other obstacles.

LINOLEUM REPAIR

8. Apply cement with a spreader to the floor or felt base.

9. Press the linoleum firmly down, correct for air bubbles, and when linoleum is laid, roll it with a heavy roller. Place bricks or other weights on all seams.

10. Replace baseboards, leaving room for the linoleum to expand and shrink.

Installation tips.

1. When laying new linoleum, your two most important rules are first to follow closely the directions on the can of cement you are using, and second to make sure you have a good, sharp cutting instrument. Ordinary kitchen knives or penknives aren't very handy for this job. If you can't buy or borrow a regular linoleum knife, you can make out second best with a razor blade cutter.

2. Amateurs can fit linoleum better around projections or odd-shaped objects if a template is first bent to shape from stiff wire, such as a wire hanger. Then trace around this on the linoleum.

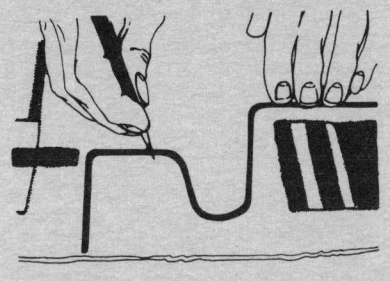

3. A large suction cup, such as a drain plunger can be used for lifting and fitting the corners. For a tighter grip, rub some soap on the edges of the plunger.

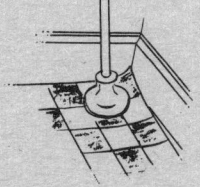

Linoleum Renewal. Here is one way to give your worn linoleum a new look. First, scrub the linoleum clean, then give it several coats of deck paint — any color you wish. After this has dried, scrub it again, then stipple it with some enamel of a contrasting color. To perform this last job, pour a small amount of enamel into the lid of a coffee can, lightly dab a dry sponge into it, and tap this briskly on the surface of the linoleum. Be sure not to drag the sponge, but merely slap it down with a wrist motion. After allowing this to dry, repeat the stippling job with another color of enamel, and you will thus give your linoleum a three-colored finish and a new, attractive look. Finish off the whole job with some wax, shellac, or varnish.

Linoleum Repair.

Bulges. If the linoleum on your floor has bulged in one spot, use a very sharp knife to make a cut across the high part of the bulge. Then with the knife or other tool, force the slit open slightly, and into it work a quantity of linoleum cement. Wipe off the surface and place a thin sheet of paper over it. Then place a weight on the bulge to hold it down flat. On the following day, remove the weight and scrape off any paper that is sticking to the joint, or remove it with a damp rag.

You can eliminate a bulge in a linoleum floor if it is by a seam by lifting the edge and applying linoleum cement to the floor. Then lay weights on the area.

Gouges. If your linoleum floor has become accidentally gouged, here is a suggestion for its repair. Scrape the surface of a matching scrap of linoleum, and when you have sufficient powder, mix it with some shellac to make a paste. Fill the damaged spot with this, and when it has dried, wax and polish.

Holes, gouges or cuts in linoleum can often be

LINT REMOVAL

repaired nicely by melting crayons of the same color and pouring this into the holes. This makes a surprisingly long-lasting repair job.

You can also mend small holes in linoleum with a thick paste composed of finely chopped cork and shellac. After this has hardened, sandpaper the surface smooth, then touch it up with matching paint.

Fill the holes in linoleum with a mixture of finely chopped cork and liquid glue. When this mixture hardens, smooth down by rubbing with emery paper. Paint with matching paint.

Patching. You can patch damaged linoleum by using a new piece of the same pattern. Cut the new piece and lay it directly over the damaged spot. Trace along the edge of the new piece with a razor or linoleum knife, remove the old piece, and apply the new one to the hole with linoleum cement.

Lint Removal, see CLOTHES CARE.

Lipstick, Recycling, see CANDLES.

Lipstick Stain, see STAIN REMOVAL.

Lock Maintenance. For smoother working locks, a shot of graphite powder into them at least once a year will keep them in prime working order. Pencil point shavings will also do the same thing.

Locks, Frozen, see DOOR REPAIR.

Locks, Lubricating. One quick and easy method of lubricating a lock is to put your key into some light sewing machine oil, insert it into the lock, then work the key back and forth several times.

Log Storage Rack. If you are bothered with rodents or other animals nesting in the fireplace wood you have stacked on the ground near your house, exterminate the animals, and then build a rack for the wood, as in the illustration. The rack can be made as tall and as long as desired, depending upon the amount of wood to be accommodated at one time.

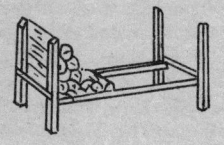

This will work out very well if constructed of 2 x 4's, with perhaps the corner posts of 4 x 4's, sunk into the ground after first being treated with some sort of wood preservative such as creosote.

Loose Casters, see CASTER REPAIR.

Loose Fill Insulation, see INSULATION.

Louvered Windows, see WINDOWS.

Lubricants.
  Glycerin. A little glycerin applied with an eye-dropper to the moving parts of your kitchen gadgets makes an ideal lubricant. And you don't have to worry if any of the glycerin accidentally gets into your food...it's harmless.
  Kitchen, see COOKING TIPS.
  Paraffin. A block of ordinary paraffin makes a handy, all-purpose lubricant to have on hand. Gives an effective treatment to sticky window sashes, sawblades, and threads of screws.
  Substitutes. Don't postpone a lubrication job just because you don't have the proper oil. When light grease is needed, petroleum jelly works just fine. Mineral oil makes a good lubricant for fans, lawn mowers, and the like. Drip it in with a broom straw. For dry lubrication, rub with paraffin or with the graphite shavings from the lead of a lead pencil.
  Waxed coated cartons from dairy products cut into flat pieces can be used to lubricate all kinds of flat surfaces — saws, lawnmower blades, and assorted tools.

Luggage.
  Cleaning. To clean luggage, such as the popular cotton-canvas carryalls, use thick suds to shampoo the surface. Work quickly with overlapping strokes, and rinse as the job progresses.
  Storage. It's a good idea, when putting away a little-used overnight bag or suitcase, to put a cake of unwrapped soap into it. This prevents any chance of a stale, musty ordor in the luggage.

Lumber. See also, WOOD, WORKABILITY OF.
  Buying. Lumber is described—and purchased—by numbers designating its thickness, width, and length—in that order. Width and thickness are usually stated in inches, length in feet. A 2 x 4 is

2-inches thick and 4-inches wide when it is first cut from the log. A 1 x 8 is 1-inch thick and 8-inches wide. Actually, when you get the 2 x 4 finished piece of wood, it is 1-5/8 inches by 3-5/8 inches; in milling, 3/8 inch has been shaved off. A finished 1 by 8 is really 25/32 inch thick and 7½ inches wide. If the lumber is tongued and grooved, scratch another 3/8 inch. You must take these differences into consideration when figuring the amount of wood to order for a particular area of wall or floor. The only thing that comes out the way you order it is the length.

Board foot. When you buy wood, you are billed by the board foot. A "board foot" of wood is a piece of rough, green, unfinished wood 1 inch thick, 1 foot wide, and 1 foot long, or an equivalent volume. In other words, a 1 by 6 strip of wood 2 feet long is a "board foot" of lumber. Likewise, a 2 by 4, 3 feet long is also a "board foot."

You can figure board feet this way: multiply the thickness in inches by the width in feet by the length in feet. A 2 by 4 that is 6 feet long would be calculated 2 x 1/3 x 6—or 4 board feet. Remember that the width is always divided by 12 to convert it to feet.

COMPUTATION OF BOARD FEET

Multiply the number of pieces times the thickness in inches times the width in inches times the length in feet and divide by 12.

Example No. 1: Find the number of board feet in a piece of lumber 2 inches thick, 10 inches wide and 6 feet long.
$$\frac{1 \times 2'' \times 10'' \times 6'}{12} = 10 \text{ bd. ft.}$$

Example No. 2: Find the number of board feet in 10 pieces of lumber, 2 inches thick, 10 inches wide, 6 feet long.
$$\frac{10 \times 2'' \times 10'' \times 6'}{12} = 100 \text{ bd. ft.}$$

Example No. 3: Find the number of board feet in a piece of lumber 2 inches thick, 10 inches wide, 18 inches long (all in inches).
$$\frac{1 \times 2'' \times 10'' \times 18''}{144} = 2\text{-}1/2 \text{ bd. ft.}$$

Running foot. You can buy lumber by the "running foot," which means exactly what it says. You buy 10 feet of 1 by 8 at so much a foot. That means a 10-foot length of 1 by 8 at 18 cents a running foot would cost $1.60.

Ordering. In ordering wood you should specify actual length of each given board. Suppose you wanted 14 pieces of 1 by 12 No. 2 white pine, each 10 feet long. The shipping ticket would read:

14/10 1x12 com pine 140 feet 250M $35.00

140 is the number of board feet obtained by multiplying 1 x 1 x 10 x 14. 250 is the price in dollars per M (thousand board feet), from which the charge amount of $35 is obtained by multiplying 140/1000 x $250.

Sizes. There are many types of lumber, some prepared for industrial uses, but the boards you will be working with are called "yard" lumber. Terms like "boards," "timbers," and so on each refer to a specific size, and are defined as follows:

"Strips" are pieces of wood 1 inch thick but less than 6 inches wide; "boards" are pieces less than 2 inches thick and 6 or more inches wide, including fencing, sheathing, sub-flooring, roofing, concrete forms, and box materials; "dimensions" are pieces from 2 inches to 5 inches thick, and 2 or more inches wide, including framing, joists, planks, rafters, studs, and small timbers; and "timbers" are pieces 3 or more inches in the least dimension, including beams, stringers, posts, caps, sills, and girders.

Cuts. The way wood is sawed at the mill gives it special characteristics. It can be cut from a log at right angles to the growth rings, or tangent to the growth rings. Right-angle cuts are called "edge-grain" or "vertical grain" in softwoods, and "quarter-sawed" in hardwoods. Tangent cuts are called "flat-grain" in softwoods and "plain-sawed" in the hardwoods.

Right-angle cuts keep shrinkage or swelling to a minimum. For paneling, however, tangent cuts are preferable, particularly if you are looking for a striking pattern in the wood.

Defects. The most obvious defects are: "knots," the cross-sections of branches; "decay," disintegration of wood fiber caused by fungus growth; "dote" and "doze" are other words for decay; "stain," or discoloration, usually brown or blue; "pitch pockets," or hunks of pitch embedded in the wood; "wane," bark left on the edge of a board after trimming; "bark pockets," or bits of bark enclosed in the

TRUE LUMBER SIZES

Nominal Size	After Dressing	Nominal Size	After Dressing
1 x 3	25/32 x 2-5/8	3 x 8	2-5/8 x 7-1/2
1 x 4	25/32 x 3-5/8	3 x 10	2-5/8 x 9-1/2
1 x 6	25/32 x 5-5/8	3 x 12	2-5/8 x 11-1/2
1 x 8	25/32 x 7-1/2	4 x 12	3-5/8 x 11-1/2
1 x 10	25/32 x 9-1/2	4 x 16	3-5/8 x 15-1/2
1 x 12	25/32 x 11-1/2	6 x 12	5-1/2 x 11-1/2
2 x 4	1-5/8 x 3-5/8	6 x 16	5-1/2 x 15-1/2
2 x 6	1-5/8 x 5-5/8	6 x 18	5-1/2 x 17-1/2
2 x 8	1-5/8 x 7-1/2	8 x 16	7-1/2 x 15-1/2
2 x 10	1-5/8 x 9-1/2	8 x 20	7-1/2 x 19-1/2
2 x 12	1-5/8 x 11-1/2	8 x 24	7-1/2 x 23-1/2

wood; and "skips," or rough, undressed areas caused when the plane misses a portion of the surface.

In many cases you can buy lumber very cheaply if it contains such defects. That can be a big saving to you, particularly if the use you put it to doesn't expose any of the marks.

Dressed. The fact that wood is "dressed" does not mean that it can be finished without further treatment. Machine-dressed wood straight from the lumber yard always has very fine surface "ripples" left by the rotary blades of the planer. Such wood should always be slightly dampened on the surface before final cleaning up for staining and polishing or varnishing. The dampening has the effect of raising the grain so that this can be smoothed down thoroughly before the stain goes on.

Grading. Quality grading of all woods is done according to rules written to cover individual characteristics of species in performances and appearance.

Select grades of softwood are best. Wood graded "select" is used for finishing purposes, and is broken down into 4 sub-grades usually designated by letter. The two highest subgrades of select, A and B, are combined and sold as B and Better Select. The high select grade is usually a clear, or practically clear, wood. B and Better Select (B & btr) is stamped on the highest quality of interior and exterior finish, trim, moldings, paneling, flooring, ceiling, partition, beveled siding, and drop siding. C and D Select grades can be used where saving is considered more important than perfect appearance. All select grades, including C and D, take natural finishes well.

Common grades. Next step down are the "common" grades. These woods are used for utility and construction purposes. Common grades are subgraded 1 to 5, or 1 to 3. You can use No. 2 "common" pine or No. 2 "common" cedar if you are interested in letting the knots show for informal effect in a paneled wall. A good common grade of some species of softwood will give you a very satisfactory surface for paint.

As a matter of fact, the best thing to do is use the lowest possible grade for the job you have in mind. Many times you can get twice as much lumber for the price. Your local retail lumber dealer can give you the best practical advice. Just tell him what you are going to use the wood for, whether it is to be painted or not, what tools you have, and your own special preferences.

Dimension timber is graded by natural characteristics which affect its strength, stiffness, and general suitability. Usually dimension is subgraded 1, 2, 3 and sometimes 4, representing the range of qualities for joists, studding, and bracing. The top grade carries more load, but all grades are suitable for most light construction projects in which you might be interested.

In industrial grades of hardwood, "dimension" includes interior trim and molding, hardwood stair treads and risers, and solid hardwood wall paneling. Hardwoods are used in flooring, cabinet work, millwork, and in making containers. When working with hardwood, you should pre-bore your holes if you think there is any danger of splitting the wood.

Kinds. There are two kinds of wood—softwood and hardwood. Softwood comes from needle-bearing trees like pine and fir. Hardwood comes from broad-leaved trees like oak and ash. Some so-called soft woods are actually harder than certain hardwood, and vice versa. Because of the nature of the wood and of the uses to which each specific species is to be put, softwoods and hardwoods are cut and graded differently.

Your work in home repair will deal mostly with softwoods: Douglas fir, pine, spruce, cedar, and so on. Maple and oak are hardwoods; they are used for floors and stair treads.

Seasoning. After lumber is cut green, it must be seasoned, or "dried out," so that its moisture content of 25 to 70 percent at felling is reduced to from 6 to 20 percent for working. The way lumber is seasoned can cause defects, and defects are keys to the grading, and pricing of wood.

If it is seasoned too slowly, wood may develop stain spots. If it is seasoned too quickly, it may warp. Warped boards are hard to work with, and may split when they are nailed up or even later.

Luminous Marks. You can simplify the job of locating flashlights, tools, and other such items when the lights suddenly go out during a power failure if you'll take the time now to paint dabs of luminous paint or stick on strips of luminous tape on these items. These will glow in the dark, and make your repair efforts much easier.

M

Magazine Racks.

Wire. You can fashion some bookends to keep your favorite magazines in place with ordinary wire clothes hangers. Use hangers made of heavy-gauge wire, cut off the top hooks, and bend to shape as illustrated, making the height about three inches.

Wood. An attractive door or wall magazine rack, which can be used in a small den or playroom, can be fashioned of two sloping sides of 3/4-inch stock nailed to a 3/4-inch by three-inch by twelve-inch bottom piece and a back of 1/2-inch plywood. The front is made of perforated sheet metal which is held in place by a three-sided rabbeted-and-mitered frame. This rack can be screwed to the back of a door or to a wall, as you wish.

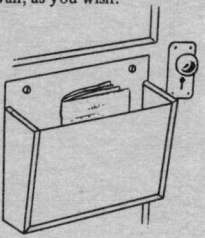

Mailbox Identification. Have you ever thought of using strips of reflective tape for printing your name on your roadside mailbox? At night the name is clearly visible at some distance in the beams of an auto headlight, providing easy identification for you rural dwellers. The reflective tape also lessens the chance of your mailbox being struck by a careless motorist.

Mailbox Rural. A very novel and attractive, yet simple, support for the rural type of mailbox can be fashioned with an old-fashioned wagon wheel, which can be painted any color that suits your fancy or general scheme. The bottom of the wheel can be fastened securely with some large boulders and concrete mix.

Mailing Tips.

1. You can cut down on the danger of damage to photographs you are mailing if you place them in an envelope that is taped in the center of a larger piece of cardboard. The extension of the cardboard beyond the edges of your photographs acts as a cushion against the possibility of wrinkles and dog-ears on your pictures.

2. One easy way to mail newspapers or magazines is to address an envelope and slit the sides open. Wrap the envelope around the middle of the paper so that the gummed flap is at the top—then seal.

3. Tighter packages for mailing will be insured if, before tying them up, you moisten your string. Then when the string dries, it will shrink and tighten up your knots.

Manicuring, see HAND CARE.

Marble.

Care.

1. Usually coffee stains on a marble tabletop come away with a mixture of four parts water and one part glycerin. First, rinse the surface well with clear water, then saturate a cloth with the aforementioned mixture, and weight it down over the stain and leave until dry. Follow this with a light coating of wax.

2. When washing the sleek surface of marble, be sparing with the soap, since it will work its way into the marble's somewhat porous surface and eventually cause it to yellow. Normally, clear water is enough to keep the surface clean. For any superficial stains, use detergent.

3. Marble table tops are very susceptible to staining by spilled liquids. Therefore, it's a good idea to protect the marble by coating it periodically with some hard, automobile-type paste wax, then buffing it to a high shine. Be sure also to wipe up any spilled liquids as quickly as possible.

Waxing of white marble is not recommended since continuous use leaves a yellowish tinge on the marble.

Repair.

1. To mend broken marble, make a thick paste of Portland cement with water. After cleaning the broken area edges, apply the cement, press the pieces together tightly, and tie firmly in place until the cement has set.

2. Marble is inclined, through use, to lose some of its lustrous polish and sometimes even becomes a little scratched. If the scratches are quite fine, they can often be buffed away and the entire surface repolished with putty powder applied with a damp cloth. You can perform this polishing either by hand or with an electric polisher. This takes some persistent elbow grease, however, and a degree of patience. Waxing is never necessary for marble, but if you really must, use a colorless, light paste wax.

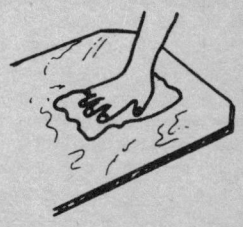

Marine Lamp, see LIGHTING, PORTABLE.

Marking Gage, see TOOLS, MEASURING.

Masonry. In every home there is some kind of masonry work—concrete, plaster, brick, stone, concrete blocks or combinations of each—so that some knowledge of it is necessary to you as a homeowner. The cost of masonry is astronomical. (See BRICKS, CONCRETE, CONCRETE BLOCKS, STONE WALLS.)

Cutting. You can cut masonry with a cold chisel and hammer, or with a special blade designed for use with an electric power'saw. Generally, bricks and tiles can be cut accurately enough with a hammer and cold chisel.

Drilling. Masonry can give you some problems in cutting and drilling. Some types, such as brick and cinder block, are soft and easy to drill, as is sandstone in the rock division. Granite, however, is hard. So is poured concrete. Mortar joints are easier to drill and cut than solid masonry sections, so try to locate the hole in mortar rather than in the masonry. (See also TOOLS.)

Nails, see NAILS.

Paint, see PAINTS.

Massager. If you own an orbital, portable electric sander, you can equip this with a lambswool pad

MATCHES

and use it as a massaging machine. It's great for stimulating circulation and relaxing those aching muscles.

Matches.
Extra-Length. When necessary to light tall, hard-to-reach candles, or a deep fire in the fireplace, ordinary short matches make it necessary to stretch needlessly, and also bring one's hand dangerously close to the fire. To simplify this job, use an ordinary paper drinking straw. Light the end of this first, then use it as a colorful taper for lighting the candles or the fire.

Waterproof Matches.
1. Hunters or fishermen who want to take a supply of waterproof matches with them on trips can quickly make them just by dipping ordinary wooden kitchen matches into clear nail polish. And not only does this treatment waterproof the matches, but it causes them to burn better and stay lit even in quite a strong breeze. When dipping, allow the nail polish to cover about half of the matchstick.

2. Merely dipping match heads into melted paraffin does not provide full protection against moisture, as the water can still soak the wood or paper stems and travel up to the heads. For real thorough protection, dip the ENTIRE match into the melted paraffin. Paper matches treated this way are not affected by perspiration in a workman's pocket, and similarly treated wooden matches are ideal for the outdoor man.

Meal Planning, see FOODS.

Measuring Tips.
1. When you need something to measure with, it might help to remember that a dollar bill is just about one-eighth of an inch more than six inches long.

2. Sometimes when using a ruler on a sheet of glass, the job can be annoying because of the slippage of the ruler about on the glass. You can avoid this if you will rub the underside of the ruler with a cake of laundry soap.

3. When attempting a "solo" job of measuring floors or material with a tape measure, you can make the job easier by sticking the other end of the tape measure down with adhesive tape.

Measurements, see TOOLS, MEASURING WITH.

Measurements, Foods, see COOKING TIPS.

Meats, see FOODS.

Medicine. Nasty tasting medicines will not taste quite so nasty if you'll hold an ice cube on your tongue for a minute or two beforehand. The ice has a way of "desensitizing" your taste buds.

Medicine Cabinet. It's a good idea to line the shelves of medicine cabinets with strips of blotting paper—ideal for absorbing any possible spills and also to help prevent your bottles from sliding off the shelves.

Melons, see FOODS.

Membrane Vapor Barriers, see VAPOR BARRIERS.

Mercurochrome Stain, see STAIN REMOVAL.

Mercury Switches, see ELECTRIC SWITCHES.

Metal Chisel, see TOOLS, HAND.

Metallic Fiber, see FIBERS, MAN-MADE.

Metals. See individual metals: ALUMINUM, BRASS, BRONZE, CAST IRON, COPPER, NICKEL, PEWTER, SILVER, STAINLESS STEEL, TIN, WROUGHT IRON, ZINC.

Chrome, see AUTOMOBILE.
Copper Roofs, see ROOF SURFACES.
Cutting. One good emergency method of cutting circular openings or other holes in light sheet metal is with a stubby knife blade tapped with a hammer. After penciling the outline of the hole you want, drive your blade through the metal, then guide it along the line while tapping the blade with a hammer.

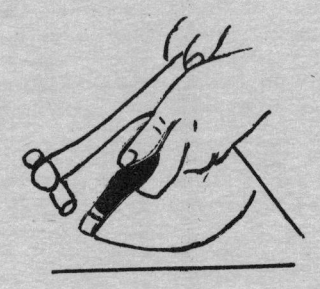

Furniture Painting, see FURNITURE, PAINTING TIPS.
Gluing, see ADHESIVES, USE OF.
Gold and Silver Cleanser. Cigar or cigarette ashes provide a very effective, lightly-abrasive cleanser for gold or silver. Just take a pinch of the ashes, add a little water to make a paste, and rub this gently over the metal. Then wipe off and shine. It's that easy.
Painting, see PAINTING TIPS.
Polishing.

1. A stick of ordinary blackboard chalk makes a very capable substitute for regular metal polish. Just rub a little soft-grade chalk onto a dry or damp cloth and apply to the metal surface that needs polishing. There is just enough abrasiveness in the chalk to remove dirt and grease without scratching, and it leaves a nice, glossy finish on the metal, too.

2. You can make your own very good metal polish just by mixing a half-cup of cigar ashes with one tablespoon of bicarbonate of soda. Make a smooth paste with water, then rub on with a soft cloth. (See also POLISH.)
Preserving Shine. Any metalwork, such as brass and copper fixtures, can be kept lustrous the same as silver bric-a-brac if, after polishing it thoroughly, you coat it with some colorless nail polish.
Rust-Proofing. A good grade of clean synthetic resin mixed with lamp black, or any colored pigment, provides an excellent rust-proofing coating for metal. Apply two heavy coats to the metal that is exposed to the weather or to metal equipment in your workshop.

Mildew.
Odor. If humid weather has left some of your closets with the odor of mildew, hang the clothes out to air and spray the interior of the closet with a strong solution of one cup baking soda per bucket of hot water.
Prevention.

1. You can protect bamboo blinds from mildew with a thin coat of clear shellac.

2. Prevent any inroads of mildew on your refrigerator gaskets, and also the inside, by wiping over them with vinegar. The acid destroys mildew fungus.

3. Mildew is a fungus that discolors paint. In warm, humid weather it will form on interior and exterior walls.

One fundamental precaution is to improve the circulation of air so that dampness, necessary for its growth, is eliminated.

When painting or repainting, select a mildew-resistant paint. Those based on zinc oxide counter it better than others. In addition, you can buy anti-mildew preparations.

Before painting an affected surface, clean the area with a detergent or a solution of trisodium phosphate.

Rinse thoroughly, and make sure the surface is dry before starting to paint. If a thorough cleaning job is not done, mildew will eventually re-appear on the surface of new work.
Stain Removal.

1. *from Books.* Mildew stains on books, which have been stored away for some time, can be removed

(and prevented in the future) by sponging the stains with some denatured alcohol and placing the books in the sunlight.

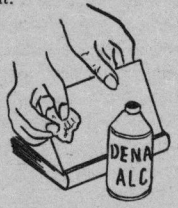

2. *from Exterior Walls,* see PAINTING, EXTERIOR.
3. *from Floors,* see WOOD FLOOR CARE.
4. *from Leather.* To remove mildew from leather, wipe it with a cloth wrung out of a solution of denatured alcohol and water, equal parts. Dry in the open air. If this fails, wash it with a thick suds of mild, neutral soap, rinse with a damp cloth, and dry in an airy place.
5. *from Linen.* To renovate mildewed linen, soak for a few minutes in sour milk or lemon juice, following with a hot sun bath. This usually removes the stain, but if not, repeat the routine.
6. *from Paper.* Mildew, in many cases, can be removed from valuable papers and book pages if you dust them with cornstarch and allow the powder to remain on for several days before brushing it off.
7. *from Shower Curtains.* Use some baking soda to remove a small area of mildew from your shower curtains. For more extensive mildew stains, wash the curtains in hot suds, then rub the stains with a lemon. Allow to dry in the sun.
8. *from White Fabrics.* To remove mildew stains from white fabrics, moisten with a mixture of lemon juice and salt, then spread in the sun to bleach.
9. *from Woodwork.* Wipe mildew from floors and woodwork with a cloth dipped in water containing a little kerosene, or wash it with warm water and soap. Let dry thoroughly. Standard paint cleaners are usually effective in removing such stains from painted surfaces.

Milk, see FOODS.

Mirrors.
  Homemade. Here's a novel, easy-to-make wall mirror that can add an attractive touch to one of your walls. All you need is a mirror of about six inches diameter, a piece of 1/2-inch plywood sawed to the same diameter, and a square foot of craft aluminum sheet, and some glue. Cut your aluminum into a circular piece to whatever diameter you wish. Then fold this circular piece of aluminum in half along its diameter, creasing the fold with your finger. Then unfold, and repeat this process for as many folds as you wish. Next, press your mirror into the center, flattening the area. Make a scalloped effect around the outer edge of the aluminum with your scissors, cutting down the line of each fold about 1/2-inch, then cutting on a straight line to the point of the next fold. Glue your mirror to the round plywood piece and glue the plywood into the center of the aluminum. Finally, edge the mirror and plywood with a strip of the aluminum, screw an eye into the back of the plywood, and hang.

Polishing. Clean and polish a mirror at the same time by adding some starch to your water. Or, rub a little alcohol or spirits of camphor over the mirror to brighten it.
Repairing. One way to mend scratches on the back of a mirror is to smooth a piece of aluminum foil the size of the scratch over the mirror back, then coat this with one or two coatings of shellac, and allow to dry.

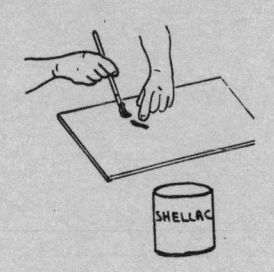

Miter Block, see CARPENTRY.

Miter Box, see CARPENTRY.

Mitered Joints, see JOINTS.

Mixing Paint, see PAINTING TIPS.

Mobile Desk. To make the desk and shelves use a sheet of ¾ in. plywood plus 8 ft. x 4 ft. plus a piece 26 in. x 7 in., for CII. Draw the plan on the board with pencil and cut carefully along the lines. Section CI and CII can be cut in one extra piece, 25 in. x 26 in.

Sandpaper and paint the shelves. Fit them to the wall by one of the many types of shelf brackets available.

For the desk, glue and nail sections B to supports C and D, using simple butt joints. Sandpaper the unit, fit castors and paint it. A simple drawer can be fitted below the desk top. This can be a plastic or aluminum vegetable or meat keeper, available from most kitchenward departments. Fit into place with aluminium drawer tracking.

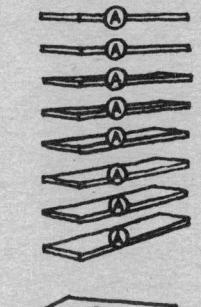

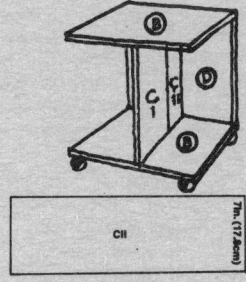

Modacrylic, see FIBERS, MAN-MADE.

Model Airplane Dope. If you use balsa wood for model making, you know it tends to swell and shrink excessively with changes in humidity, and ordinary painted finishes will crack every time. For this reason, model airplane dope (available in all colors at hobby shops) should be used as a finish, because of its flexibility. A drop of castor oil per ounce of dope will give even more flexibility to the finish.

Model Glue Stain, see STAIN REMOVAL.

Modeling Clay. It's a good idea to keep your children's modeling clay wrapped in aluminum foil. This will keep it moist and pliable indefinitely.

Modeling Clay, Emergency. An emergency clay to amuse your children on a rainy day can be made by adding a cup of water to a cup of flour and a cup of salt. Stir this over a low flame until the mixture thickens to the consistency of clay.

Moldings. If you take a look around your room, you'll see that there are strips of wood running along the joint where the wall and the ceiling meet. And you will also frequently find such a strip running vertically at the point where two walls intersect. At the floor you will find a larger strip of wood running along the base of the wall where it meets the floor. Around each window and each door you will see other strips of wood.

Called molding at the ceiling, baseboard at the floor, casing around doors and windows, and collectively trim, this running strip is not a decorative device at all, but a cover-up to conceal the holes where the ceiling and the wall do not exactly meet.

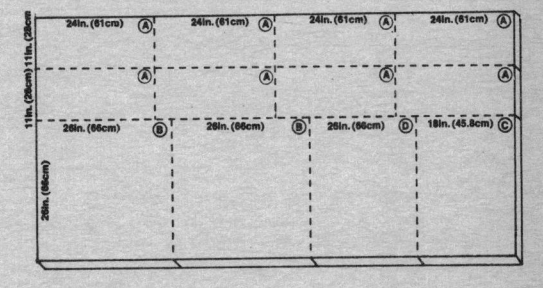

225

Around doors and windows, casing serves the same purpose, to hide the faulty fitting between window sash and frame, and perhaps to keep out cold air leaks. And there is a special strip of molding on every door that serves an unusual purpose: it's the "stop," and it keeps the door from passing on through its shut position.

Molding sometimes rots away, especially if it is in place near a leak. If it has deteriorated to the point where it will no longer take paint, you must remove the entire strip and replace it with new stock from your lumber dealer. Molding comes in all kinds of designs; you can usually find a duplicate of the one you already have. Carpenters attach molding with long finish nails driven in at a diagonal angle; remember that when you try to remove the stripping from its position.

Quadrant. It is quite common practice to use quarter-round molding—called quadrant—to seal the joint between linoleum, or other floor covering and the skirting board attached to the wall.

If you plane the bottom edge of the molding, as indicated in the sketch when the quadrant is nailed into place against the skirting, the front edge embeds itself into the linoleum to make a snug fit.

This should be done only on linoleum that has been laid for some time.

Linoleum laid loosely usually expands, and if held tightly at the edges is likely to buckle.

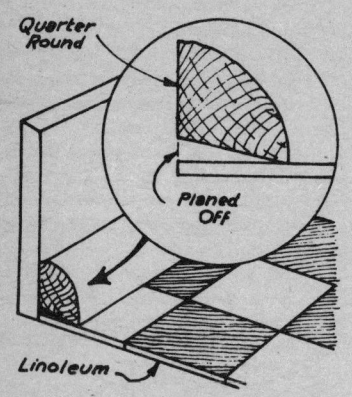

Repairing Ornamental. Chipped ornamental moldings on picture frames, furniture, and other woodwork can be easily repaired by rebuilding the missing sections with wood putty. This is sold in powder form and, when mixed with water, dries into a hard, woodlike material which can be carved, sanded, or sawed.

Sanding, see ABRASIVES.

Mortar, see ADHESIVES.

Mortar Joints, see CONCRETE BLOCKS.

Mortise and Tenon, see JOINTS.

Mosquito Repellent, see INSECTS.

Mothball Container. A baking-powder can, perforated and fastened to the underside of a closet shelf, provides an excellent container for mothballs. The lid of the can is screwed to the underside of the shelf.

Mother-of-Pearl, see PEARL HANDLES.

Mothproofing, see INSECTS.

Moths, see INSECTS.

Mousetrap Bait. If you have no cheese around the house, try baiting your mousetraps with peanut butter. Mice love it. Or, bait the trap with some absorbent cotton. The mice will attempt to use this cotton as a lining for their nests.

Movie Screen, see HOME MOVIE SCREEN.

Moving Heavy Items. When it's necessary to slide heavy crates or furniture along cellar floors, garage floors, or driveways, try using corrugated metal caps from empty soda bottles as "glides." Put one cap upside down under each corner and tap with a hammer so that the metal edge of the cap digs in. The corrugations will hold the cap in place, and the smooth top will permit easy sliding of the article.

Mustard Stain, see STAIN REMOVAL.

Musty Furniture, see FURNITURE, MUSTY.

N

Nail File, see EMERY BOARD.

Nail Polish.
Bottles.
  1. When you open a new bottle of fingernail polish, try applying a bit of cold cream along the outside rim of the bottle. Then, when you re-open the bottle the next time, the top will come off easily—and will never stick.
  2. When the cap on your fingernail polish bottle resists your efforts to twist it off, the problem can usually be dealt with by running hot water over the cap.
  3. When the top of your nail polish bottle stubbornly refuses to loosen, turn the bottle upside down and put a drop or two of polish remover around the edge of the cap. Let it stand a few seconds, then turn the bottle rightside up and try it—the cap will usually yield quite readily.

Spills. If someone spills nail polish on your waxed wood floor or tile, let it solidify before attempting removal. When the polish is barely solid and pliable, it can be peeled right off. Smears are left when the polish is wiped up before it has dried or by using a solvent on completely hardened polish.

Stain, see STAIN REMOVAL.

Thinner. If your fingernail polish has aged to a thickness and gumminess that makes it impossible to use, you can thin it out to the proper consistency with some fingernail polish remover.

Nails. The chart on page 228 shows actual length of the nail according to penny size, the diameter of the head of a common nail in inches, the shank diameter in gauge, and the number of nails to the pound.

Box nails are flat-headed with the same kind of points as common nails. Box nails have less diameter than common nails, but measure the same to the penny size.

Brads are simply miniature finishing nails, and are used mostly in cabinet work, in picture frames, or in small work where a very tiny entrance hole is needed.

They are also used for fixing linoleum and holding glass in a sash frame before applying putty.

Cement-coated nails come in common, finishing, or box types. The surface is coated with resin that melts as the nail is driven into the wood, forming a tough bond. Cement-coated nails are used in flooring, where nails must be firmly planted and—hopefully—immovably.

Coated nails have great holding power. You can of course buy these nails already coated with cement, or rosin—but you can also coat your own by dipping them into a strong syrupy solution before using them.

NAILS

SIZE	LENGTH AND GAGE		APPROXIMATE NUMBER TO POUND
	INCHES	NUMBER	
A 60d	6	2	11
B 50d	5½	3	14
C 40d	5	4	18
D 30d	4½	5	24
E 20d	4	6	31
F 16d	3½	7	49
G 12d	3¼	8	63
H 10d	3	9	69
I 9d	2¾	10¼	96
J 8d	2½	10¼	106
K 7d	2¼	11½	161
L 6d	2	11½	181
M 5d	1¾	12½	271
N 4d	1½	12½	316
O 3d	1¼	14	568
P 2d	1	15	876

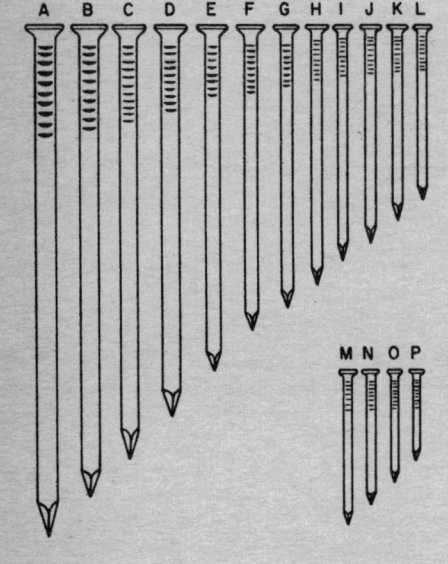

Common nails are generally used for rough work such as framing—that is, fastening the two-by-fours and timbers inside the walls of your home, or anything else that is not visible to the eye. Because its head is large, the common nail gives greater support and strength to the joint.

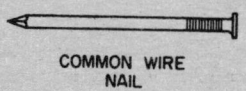

COMMON WIRE NAIL

Cut nails are a type used in attaching flooring to joists. They are not round like common nails, but are thin, flat and rectangular. They have blunt heads and their points are flat. The blunt point will tear through the fibers of wood rather than slide in the way a sharpened point does; this bluntness prevents the flooring timber from splitting.

Drywall nails are nails with big heads and small spirals.

Escutcheon pins have numerous other uses apart from fixing the cover plate around a keyhole. These decorative brass or chrome-plated pins are made in several lengths.

Finishing. The *finishing nail* has what is known as a "brad" head. A brad, actually, is simply a very small finishing nail. The brad's head is not much larger than the diameter of the nail itself. The purpose of the finishing nail is to attach material that will be visible. The head itself, because of its small size, can be driven down below the surface of the material with a nailset, and then puttied over, or covered with colored wax, or left flush with the surface.

Finishing nails come in the same penny sizes as common nails, but the diameter of an 8 penny finishing nail is smaller than that of an 8 penny common nail, although the length is the same. See also **Brads**, above.

MOLDING OR FINISHING NAIL

Common. The *common nail* has a broad flat head plainly visible after the nail is driven into the material. Its point is pyramidal in shape, so that it slides into the material it is to hold. These nails are always graded in size by the English penny system, and because the English monetary sign for the penny is a "d", we identify nail sizes in this fashion: 8d, for an 8 penny nail. The "penny" price is the cost of a hundred such nails—many, many years ago. An 8 penny nail is 2½ inches long.

Flooring nails are nails with threads like a screw.

Lubricating.

1. If you're finding it tough going driving some nails into hardwood, try dipping your nails beforehand into linseed oil. This will lubricate the nails and make your job much easier with less danger of the nails' bending.

2. Nails can be driven into hard wood with a minimum of difficulty if the nails are dipped into oil or grease beforehand. This also works with screws.

Masonry nails are nails with fins used for fixing battens or other woodwork directly to brickwork or other masonry.

They are made of toughened metal and driven with a hammer in the same way as ordinary nails.

Panel pins are very fine-gauge nails with a flat head, suitable for fixing hardboard or plywood panels. They range in length from ½-in. to 1½-in.

Roofing nails are nails with spiral threads.

ROOFING NAIL

Rusty. Is the outside of your house defaced by rust spots and bleeding nails? This often happens if the putty shrinks and cracks appear. You can remove the stains with some steel wool dampened with detergent, and then prevent any future such trouble by brushing the nails with some spar varnish.

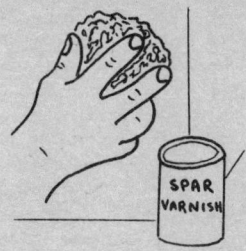

Scaffold nails have a double head, which allows them to be used for assembling concrete formwork or other temporary structures, and at the same time permits easy withdrawal for dismantling.

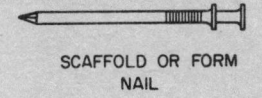

SCAFFOLD OR FORM NAIL

Tacks are big-headed, short-bodied nails used mainly for attaching carpets or rugs to wooden floors. They have a rapidly expanding body in order to secure quick purchase in a very short distance. The wide head keeps the carpet fibers from tearing apart and pulling out.

Cut tacks are perhaps the most useful item to have when doing upholstery repairs.

They hold the webbing and hessian in place and are also useful for hanging notices or decorations.

Wire nails are simply a type of brad that resemble miniature common nails.

Nail Set, see TOOLS, HAND.

Name Plaque. Here's a rustic-looking and very attractive name plaque you can easily construct for the entrance to your walk or driveway. The plaque itself can be cut from any piece of solid board or plywood of suitable size, and suspended from a crosspiece driven into an undersize hole bored into an upright planted in the ground. The upright and crosspiece can be of locust or birch, and to insure durability, coat the part of the upright that is to be buried in the ground with some creosote. Suspend the plaque from the crosspiece with cross links of an old tire chain, spreading these apart and then closing them into eyebolts in the crosspiece and screw eyes in the plaque. Brace the crosspiece with some wire.

Name Plate. You can fashion very nice frames for personal names or for directions out of short sections of flat curtain rod. Merely cut the ends of these sections round with some tin snips, file smooth, and punch holes in both ends for nailing or screwing to doors or walls.

Neckties, see CLOTHES CARE.

Netting Staples, see STAPLES.

NEWSPAPER LOG

Newspaper log can be made by tightly rolling up the Sunday paper or several daily papers to the size of an average fireplace log. Tie the ends securely. These "logs" will burn slowly and can be used in the fireplace instead of wood.

Newspaper Uses.

1. Newspapers can be put to very good use, even after the family has read them. They are fine for packing clothes out of season, or for rolling inside rugs to be stored away, or several thicknesses of newspapers makes good under-carpet padding. The newsprint is high on moths' "hate parade". Also, a well-crumpled newspaper is very handy for wiping windows dry, since it leaves no linty coating on the glass.

2. For many mop-up jobs, from wiping off an oilstone-honed blade to cleaning up paint remover—a piece of newspaper can be the handiest item in the home workshop. You can keep an easily-available supply on tap, if you'll pile up some old newspapers to an inch or so thick, then cut the papers into quarters with a sharp knife. Then drill a hole in one corner with your electric drill, and hang the papers on a conveniently located nail with a wire.

Nickel. Clean nickelware by washing with soap and water, rinsing, then polishing with a soft cloth. If this treatment is not sufficient, use whiting, or a fine polish. Nickel has a way of darkening if it is not cleaned frequently enough.

Nicotine Stain, see STAIN REMOVAL.

Non-resilient tile floors include terrazzo, made of marble chips or rock chips set in cement and buffed flat, and ceramic tile, composed of clay mixed with water and fired in a kiln.

Non-Washable Fabrics, Stain, see STAIN REMOVAL.

Nuts, see FOODS.

Nuts.

and Bolts, see BOLTS.

Kinds. Square and hexagonal nuts are standard. Jam nut is used with the standard nuts to lock it in position. Castellated nuts are used with safety wire. Wing nuts are used where the desired degree of tightness can be obtained by the fingers. Cap nuts are used where appearance is important. Thumb nuts are also turned by hand. Elastic stop nuts are used where it is imperative that nuts do not come loose.

SQUARE   HEXAGONAL   JAM   CASTELLATED

WING   CAP   THUMB   STOP

Securing. If you happen to be without lock washers and are putting on a nut that may eventually work itself loose, you can prevent this with a center punch. After tightening the nut into position, put the center punch in the middle of the bolt end and give it a sharp rap with your hammer. This will spread the bolt slightly and prevent the nut from working off without being forced.

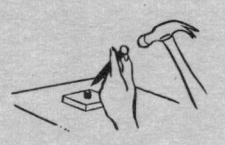

Storage. A board makes an ideal means of storing nuts and washers. Attach the board to the wall of your workshop, drive some long nails into it, then place all the nuts of one size and type on each nail, and you'll have a handy reference file the next time

NYLON CORD

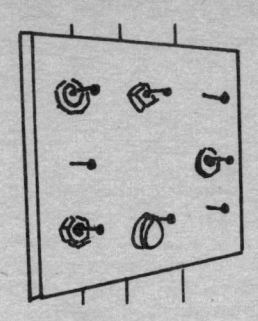

you are in need of a particular kind of nut or washer for a particular job.
Washers, see WASHER.

Nylon, see FIBERS, MAN-MADE.

Nylon Care, see CLOTHES CARE.

Nylon Cord, see CORD, NON-FRAY.

O

Oarlocks. One effective method of muffling squeaks in your oarlocks that may be scaring away the fish is to fit the pin of each oarlock with a steel washer, and under this another washer cut from felt and soaked with gun oil or petroleum jelly.

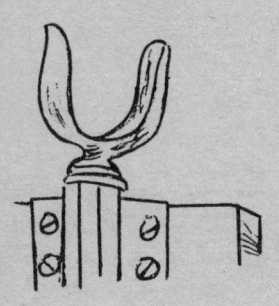

Oar Storage. Here's a convenient gimmick for storing those oars out of the way while you are fishing—and thus avoid your stumbling over them and also getting water all over the rear seat of your boat. Take some heavy-gauge wire coat hangers, cut the hooks off them, and bend as illustrated to hook over the sides of your boat—two on each side. These make convenient resting places for those idle oars.

Odor Removal, see DEODORIZING.

Oil, Oil Burners, see HEATING.

Oil Can Tips.

1. Sometimes an oil can delivers too much oil for single applications on small motors or appliances. If you are experiencing that difficulty, clean the end of the spout and cover the opening with a drop of fingernail polish. Then when the polish is dry, make a small hole in it with a pin. The oil will then come out a drop at a time.

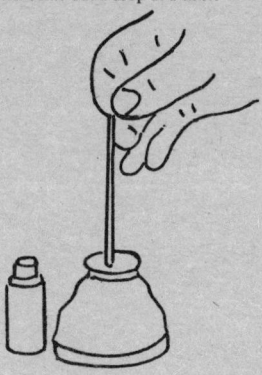

2. When you find it necessary to lubricate some hard-to-reach spots, your job will be made much easier if you fit an extension to the spout of your oil-can. You can do this with a plastic drinking

straw. If the straw does not go on over the end of the spout easily, warm the end of the straw and expand it with an ice pick or center punch.

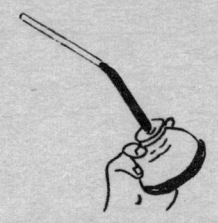

Oil Finish, Furniture, see FURNITURE REFINISHING.

Oiling Tip. When oil must be placed in spots which are hard to reach, even with a small oilcan, take an ordinary drinking straw and use it as a funnel.

Oil Mop. To clean an oil mop, use hot water, ammonia, and a small amount of washing powder.

Oil Paint, see PAINTS.

Oil Paintings, Cleaning.
 1. Oil paintings, if they are of any considerable value, need professional cleaning and treatment from time to time. If, however, you would like to try cleaning them yourself, you can do so by washing a small area at a time with lukewarm mild suds, drying immediately. After the entire surface has been cleaned, go over it lightly with a flannel moistened with linseed oil.
 2. Rub the surface of the painting with the juicy side of a cut onion, then allow the painting to dry out in the air.
 3. Oil paintings can often be cleaned nicely by washing them gently with warm milk and water. Dry them with a soft cloth, but do not rinse.

Oils, Cooking, see FOODS.

Oil Stain, see STAIN REMOVAL.

Oilstone, see TOOLS, HAND.

Olefin, see FIBERS, MAN-MADE.

Olive Oil, see FOODS.

Omelet, see FOODS.

Onions, see FOODS.

Open-End Wrench, see TOOLS, HAND.

Opener. A very effective wrench for opening tight-fitting caps on small-mouthed bottles or cans is an ordinary squeeze-type nutcracker. Apply only a moderate pressure—just enough to prevent slipping—and on cans be careful not to squeeze so hard that the top is bent out of shape.

Open-Housing Joint, see JOINTS.

Oranges, see FOODS.

Outdoor Fireplace, see BARBECUE.

Outdoor Furniture, see FURNITURE CARE, FURNITURE PAINTING TIPS.

Outdoor Statuary. Scrub with scouring powder or washing soda, then rinse with warm water.

Orbital Sander, see TOOLS, POWER.

Outlets, Electrical, see ELECTRICAL OUTLETS.

Oven Cleaning, see COOKING TIPS.

P

Pail Handle, see BUCKET HANDLE.

Paint Brushes. It is always advisable to buy good quality brushes although these cost considerably more than poor quality products.

Good brushes not only give a much better finish, but last much longer because of the extra length and better quality of the bristles.

Brushes with the bristles set in rubber are the type in general use, and these should never be soaked before use. Soaking of such brushes probably will ruin them.

Paint brushes can be ruined in two ways, first by allowing paint to harden in the bristles, and second, by misuse.

Dry your brush before putting it away. If the bristles are allowed to remain damp, mildew will set in.

To clean a brush first dissolve out the material with a suitable solvent, cleaning right up to the ferrule.

Next wash away the solvent with weak soap and water, then thoroughly rinse and hang up to dry in the open.

Bristle Shedding. Increase the usefulness of old paint brushes with lacquer. By applying the lacquer to the base of the brushes, you prevent shedding of bristles.

Cleaning Agents. One of the most important parts of any paint job is the cleaning of your brushes after you have finished painting. A properly-cared-for brush will last a long time, and it is well worth the few minutes' work of cleaning it thoroughly. Here are the cleaning ingredients for the various kinds of paints: After using an oil paint, clean with turpentine, then soap and water. After enamel, clean with turpentine, then soap and warm water. After varnish, use benzine or turpentine. After stain, clean with denatured alcohol. After shellac, use denatured alcohol, or diluted ammonia rinsed with water. After cold-water paint, warm water. After whitewash, warm water. After lacquer, use lacquer thinner. Finally, after having cleaned your brush, hang it up to dry with the bristles down, and when dry, wrap in waxed paper or aluminum foil to keep it fresh and free of dust.

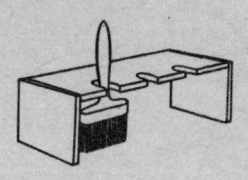

Cleaning Tip. Try using a plastic bag for a quick and efficient cleaning of your paintbrushes. Put your

PAINT BRUSHES

brush and solvent into the bag, tie the top of the bag tightly around the handle of the brush, and then knead the solvent into and through the bristles of the brush. After this treatment, you can wash the brush in the same bag, substituting soap and water for the solvent. This system of cleaning does a wonderful job, and it keeps your hands out of the mess, too.

Correct Usage. Shown in the sketches are three examples of the right and wrong methods of using a paint brush.

Fig 1 illustrates clearly that using a wide flat brush edgewise will cause the bristles to twist and "finger" and ruin it in a very short time.

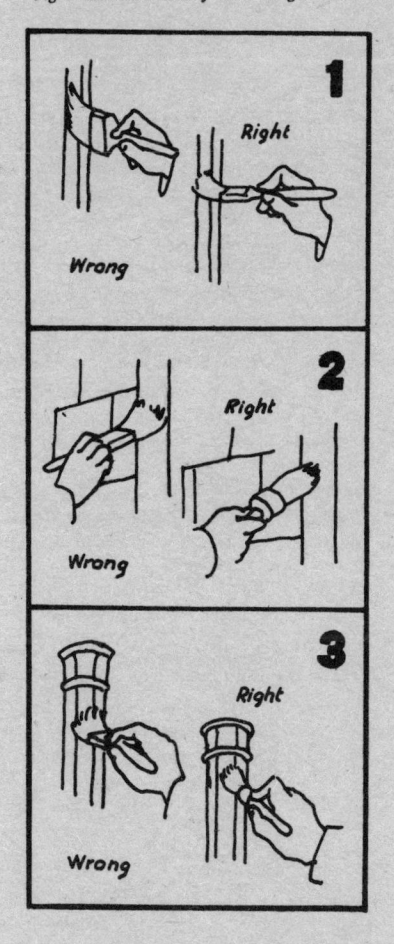

Painting pipes and railings with a flat brush wears down the center.

In a short time the brush will be useless for normal work.

Use a round or oval brush (Fig 2) to get best results.

Finally, using a wide brush on downpipes and similar shaped or molded surfaces will mean irregular wear on the bristles, so spoiling it for normal flat surface work.

Use a narrow brush in such cases.

One ranging in width from 1-inch to 1½-inches is usually satisfactory (Fig 3).

Holder. A large-headed nail or tack driven into the wooden handle of a paintbrush near the ferrule, as shown in the illustration, provides a convenient means of hanging the brush over the inside edge of the container ... serving as a brush rest between strokes and while the container is being moved.

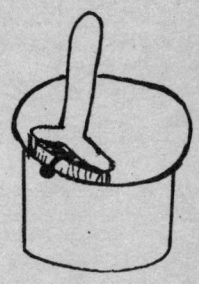

New. A good preparation for the new paint brush, before using it, is to soak its bristles for a short time in linseed oil. The bristles of the brush will then remain flexible and easy to clean after each use, the linseed oil preventing hardening of paint on them.

Reconditioning.
1. Not too much sympathy should be wasted on

PAINT BRUSHES

the painter who neglects to clean his brushes. But, at least, here's a tip on how to recondition those paint-hardened brushes: Fill up an old tin can with vinegar, stick the brushes into it, and put the can on the stove until it boils for ten or fifteen minutes. This may cause falling bristles in inferior-quality brushes, but it will soften them up considerably, and a good washing in warm soap and water should complete the rejuvenating process.

2. Old, stiff and dry paintbrushes can be softened if they are boiled in vinegar, then cleaned with hot soapy water. Or, clean the paint brushes with a mixture of two tablespoons of salt, one-half cup kerosene, and one quart of warm water. Soak the brushes for about two hours in this, then wipe with a clean cloth.

3. You can often salvage paint-hardened brushes by soaking them in banana oil (amyl acetate), and then rinsing in some turpentine or mineral spirits. The banana oil loosens the paint, and the turpentine or mineral spirits cleans out both the oil and the paint. BE SURE—as with all solvents—to work either out-of-doors or in a well-ventilated room away from any heat or flames!

Reshaping.

1. You can often renovate a worn or misshapen paintbrush just by trimming it back into shape. By holding a razor blade against a pocket comb, as shown in the illustration, and gently pushing the comb through the bristles of the brush, you can remove the stray hairs and perform a very neat job of trimming.

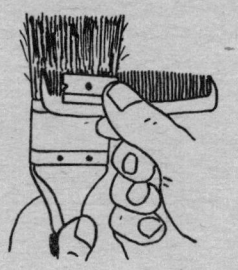

2. You can reshape your old paintbrushes simply by soaking the bristles in a water-soluble glue, shaping and allowing to dry thoroughly. Then rub the bristle tips over some coarse sandpaper to the form desired. You can then remove the glue by setting the brush in hot water.

Sizes. The paint brush you will find most convenient for use on exterior siding and interior wall surfaces is one about 3½ inches wide to 4 inches wide. A 3½-inch brush is easiest for someone not familiar with painting.

For applying trim, use a flat brush, 2 inches wide with bristles 3 inches long. For smaller trims, use a flat or oval sash brush, 1½ inches wide with 2-inch bristles.

Storage. If you have been using a paintbrush and wish to set it aside for a few hours or overnight, it is not necessary to clean it. All that is necessary is to protect the bristles from the air, and you can do this by wrapping them tightly in some wax paper or aluminum foil, twisting and taping the ends of the sheet around the brush handle. This will prevent the paint in the bristles from hardening.

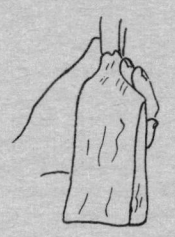

Support. Do you ever wonder just where to lay down that paint brush you've been using? It's an easy matter to make your brush self-supporting, if you'll just drive a couple of small nails into the ferrule of the brush, as illustrated. The nails serve as legs to support the bristles, and the brush can be laid on any surface without smearing the paint.

Paint Components. Paint is made up of four components: pigment, binder or vehicle thinner or solvent, and drier.

Binder is the liquid medium in which the pigment floats, binds the pigment together to give it spreadability. Oil, resin, varnish, or resin emulsion are all vehicles. Oil, usually linseed oil, is used in an oil-based paint; varnish is used in an enamel; resin emulsion and water are used in a water-based paint.

Drier is a specially compounded chemical that hastens the drying of paint.

Pigment gives a paint its ability to cover. An opaque pigment will hide the surface below completely. A pigment without opacity is called an inert, a filler, or an extender.

Solvent, see **Thinner,** below.

Thinner works on the binder and pigment in order to give the paint a good flowing quality, making it easier to apply. Gum turpentine, wood-distilled turpentine, and mineral spirits (a petroleum solvent) are used for thinning.

Vehicle, see **Binder,** above

Painting, Exterior. Your house should be painted about every 5 years, according to most experts. Costs these days are extremely varied in different parts of the country, but you can safely estimate that a paint job on your house will run into several hundred dollars. It's a tough job to do, but if you have the determination and enough skill, you can do it and beat the high cost of the paint pro.

Exterior paint coverings, by the very nature of the work, are difficult to do. You have to be a little more adept at brush work outside than inside, and there are added perils like heights, weather conditions, and fatigue to face. However, with ordinary conditions, prevailing, you can do an exterior job yourself.

Application. When painting an outside wall, start at the top and move down. Cover one stretch of surface, and then move across to another. Brush out the paint to a thin even coating. Stroke up and down as well as across. After the entire surface within arm's reach has been covered, draw the empty brush lightly and smoothly across the entire length, from the edge of the unpainted surface toward the painted portion. Use a long stroke with the grain of the wood.

Exterior paint may be applied by brush, roller, or spray. Most home-owners use a brush.

Paint the windows, trim, and doors before you paint the body of the house. Paint wood porches and steps last.

Read the paint-can label carefully before you start to paint. It will contain specific directions for applying the paint.

Blistering and Peeling. Excessive moisture in the wood behind the paint will cause blistering. Outside water may be coming in, inside water may be working out, or it may be cold weather condensation. (Water vapor inside the house passes through the interior walls, condenses, and soaks into the outer walls.) Blisters appear first; cracking and peeling follow.

Prevention. Correct possible sources of moisture before you paint. Repair leaks in roofs and sidewalls. Ventilate a damp basement or crawl space. Get rid of moisture originating in the house by means of vents and fans. For instance, vent clothes driers to the outside. Repair leaky plumbing.

Correction. Correct the cause of the moisture before you repaint.

Remove all loose paint. Apply a water-repellent preservative to joints that show damage from rain or dew; allow it to dry 2 days (or as directed on the label). Prime bare surfaces and repaint. Consider using blister-resistant paint.

Chalking may occur where poor quality paint was used, the paint was improperly applied, or the paint was thinned excessively.

Prevention. Use non-chalking paint.

Correction. Remove the chalk by brushing the surface or washing it with mineral spirits. Apply two coats of good quality paint. Allow 3 days drying time between coats.

PAINTING EXTERIOR

Cross-grain cracking may be caused by too-frequent repainting. The thick paint coating built up by many paintings becomes too hard to stand the constant expansion and contraction of the wood and eventually cracks.

Prevention. Repaint only when necessary.

Correction. Remove all of the paint, down to the bare wood. Prime the bare wood properly and repaint.

Intercoat Peeling. Peeling usually is caused by lack of adhesion between the top and under coats. The primer and top coat were incompatible, the surface was too smooth or glossy, or oil or grease was not removed.

Prevention. Use primer and top coats of the same brand. Remove gloss with a strong detergent, steel wool, or sandpaper. Remove oil or grease with mineral spirits.

Correction. Remove all loose paint, sand the edges, properly prime the bare surfaces, and repaint.

Mildew may occur where continuous warm and damp conditions prevail.

Prevention. Use mildew-resistant paint or add a mildew resistant compound to the paint.

Correction. To remove mildew, wash the surface one or more times with a solution of—

2/3 cup of trisodium phosphate
1/3 cup of detergent
1 quart of household bleach
Enough water to make 1 gallon

Caution. Wear rubber gloves when applying mildew-resistant paint or when using the trisodium-phosphate solution.

Natural Wood Finish. For a natural wood finish on a ranch-type or Western house, use a transparent sealer or an exterior varnish. You can get special clear coating for redwood and cedar. For wooden shingles or shakes, use either regular house paint, or stain them with tinted preservatives.

Number of Coats. Three coats of paint are recommended for new wood surfaces—one primer and two finish coats. (Two-coat systems are sometimes used and give long service when properly designed and properly applied.)

On old surfaces in good condition, one top coat may be sufficient. But if the paint is very thin, apply two top coats.

On bare surfaces or surfaces with very little paint left on them, apply a primer and two top coats. Do the same on very chalky surfaces.

On metal surfaces, prime both new metal and old metal from which the paint has been removed.

After the primer has dried sufficently, apply one or two finish coats of paint.

Paint Selection. There are a number of different types of paint. Selection need not be too much of a problem however.

First consider the type of surface. Are you painting wood, metal, or masonry? Some paints can be used on all three; others on two. Condition of the surface may be important also. Old chalky surfaces, for example, are not generally a sound base for latex or water-base paints.

Next consider any special requirements. For example, nonchalking paint may be advisable where chalk rundown would discolor adjacent brick or stone surfaces. Or mildew may be a problem in your area; mildew-resistant paint is available. Lead-free paints may be used in areas where sulfur fumes cause staining of paints containing lead pigments.

Color is a third consideration, but it is mostly a matter of personal preference. Some colors are more durable than others, and some color combinations are more attractive than others. Your paint dealer can help you on color durability and combinations. (See also PAINTS.)

Porch floor a tough, wear-resistant porch-and-deck enamel designed to withstand weather and leather. You can get deck enamel in solvent-thinned or water-thinned latex formulations.

Preparation. To prepare an already painted surface for repainting, scrape off all the peeling paint with a wire brush. Smooth the surface with sandpaper and remove loose or crumbly putty or filler from the windows. Prime the sash and apply new putty.

Renail all loose boards and prime all nail heads with anti-corrosive primer. Rub varnished or enameled surfaces with fine sandpaper or steel wool. Use a varnish remover on all marred surfaces, then smooth the surface with steel wool or sandpaper. Wash off the dirt with warm water and soap, and grease with a thinner. Spot-prime any brown stains caused by moisture in the wood with two coats of primer. Wash off all mildewed surfaces.

If mildew and fungus growths are a problem, mix a solution of sodium hypochlorite by adding 1½ cups of full-strength household bleach to a gallon of water. Apply this solution to the mildew and allow it to remain about 5 minutes. Rinse the surface with clean water, scrub with a bristle brush, and then paint over the surface with a paint with mildewcide mixed in it.

Rust Prevention. Before painting the exterior of your house, it's a good idea to paint the iron nails and the area immediately surrounding them with a coat of plastic aluminum. Thin this plastic with some lacquer thinner to the consistency of house paint and apply it with a small brush. Nails treated in this manner will not rust and cause streaks later on your house siding.

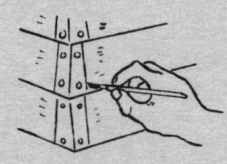

Rust Streaks. Rust stains on exterior painted house siding are frequently caused by exposed nail heads that may be corroding beneath the surface of the paint. To remedy the situation, sand off the nail head and spot-prime it with a little shellac or metal primer. Then counter-sink the nail head and fill the hole with putty before repainting.

Siding. Clapboard or vertical siding will take a linseed oil paint, alkyd-based paint, or oil-modified alkyd paint. You can even get water-thinned latex house paint, but when you use this, put it on only over the primer specified by the manufacturer.

Wood siding preferably should not contain knots or sappy streaks. But if new siding does, clean the knots and streaks with turpentine and seal with a good knot sealer. The knot sealer will seal in oily extractives and prevent staining and cracking of the paint in the knot area.

Tips. Take time to do a good job when you paint:

 1. Use good quality paint. It will give longer and better protection.

 2. Prepare the surface properly for painting. Even the best paint won't last on a poorly prepared surface.

 3. Apply the paint correctly. Improper application can be as damaging as a poorly prepared surface.

 4. Too-frequent repainting builds up an excessively thick film that is more sensitive to the deteriorating effects of the weather. Ordinarily, every 4 years will be often enough to repaint a house.

Sheltered areas, such as eaves and porch ceilings, may not need repainting every time the body of the house is repainted; every other time may be sufficient.

Weather. The ideal weather for painting is a clear dry day with the temperature 50 degrees or above. Don't paint if it is 90 in the direct sun. Spring and fall are the best seasons. If the temperature falls below 50 while you're working, stop in the afternoon and allow the paint to set before the night comes on.

Wood trim on the outside of the house will do best with a bright exterior enamel or a "trim-and-trellis" paint. You can use regular house paints on these surfaces, but they do not have the toughness and the brightness of exterior enamels.

Painting, Furniture, see FURNITURE PAINTING TIPS.

Painting, Interior. You will save the most money on paint inside your house by using a flat paint with an alkyd or latex base.

Bathrooms and Kitchens. For bathroom and kitchen, use a semi-gloss enamel; it has greater washability and is resistant to steam, moisture, and grease. If you use a alkyd paint, prime any bad patches first. A latex paint will prime itself.

Ceilings. Use a flat paint for your ceiling. A long-handled roller is probably the easiest way you can paint a ceiling. Roll the paint on with the first stroke going away from you, and paint in that fashion across the width of the room. Then start a new stroke in a dry area, painting toward a wet one. Finish up by making right-angle criss-cross strokes to cover all the surface.

To protect the walls when you're painting the ceiling, paint a narrow band all around the perimeter of the ceiling, protecting the walls with a metal strip or a makeshift guard of shirt cardboard.

Ceilings, New. If you are painting a new ceiling, follow this procedure to prevent peeling in the future.

 1. Wipe over the ceiling with a damp cloth (this removes all dust).

PAINTING, INTERIOR

2. After leaving to dry, apply a good sealer.
3. Apply two coats of enamel-based paint.

Walls. Before you start to paint an interior wall, remove all wax and polish from its surface. Scrape away any peeling paint and sand down all the rough spots. Fill any cracks with plaster and patching compound. Dust off the walls. Remove the wall switch covers and the electric outlet covers and all ceiling fixtures. Cover the furniture and the floor with drop cloths or newspapers.

Let's assume that you are using a latex paint and have followed the directions on the can carefully in mixing it and preparing it for application. You can put on latex paint either with a roller or with a brush.

Brush Application. Dip the brush one-third the length of the bristles into the can, and tap off the extra paint. Use rhythmical strokes back and forth, always painting from a dry area into a wet one. Start at the upper right-hand corner and work down toward the floor. Cover an area only as wide as you can comfortably and safely reach from a ladder.

Roller Application. Pour the paint into the paint tray, covering about two-thirds of the bottom. Roll the applicator in the paint, coating it evenly. Brush a narrow strip on the wall next to the ceiling, rolling the paint upwards from a dry surface into a wet one. To protect the ceiling from fresh paint, use a guard made of a shirt cardboard held over the ceiling, a paint guard, or a special roller painter for the wall edges.

After you have coated an area about 2 feet by 3 feet with up-and-down strokes, cover it with back-and-forth strokes. Don't spin the roller at the end of the pass. When you reach the baseboard or woodwork, protect the surface with cardboard or paper, exactly as you did above.

Warning. Never paint in a room without adequate ventilation.

Windows. Paint the windows in the order shown in the drawing: (1) Mullions, (2) Horizontal of sash, (3) Verticals of sash, (4) Verticals of frame, (5) Horizontal frame and sill. Windows are easier to paint and to clean afterward if the glass is masked. Both masking tape and liquid masking are available at hardware and paint stores. A simple way to protect the glass is to cover it with a piece of wet newspaper. The moisture will paste the newspaper to the glass and also prevent paint from soaking into the absorbent paper. When you strip the paper from the glass after painting, the paint will come with it.

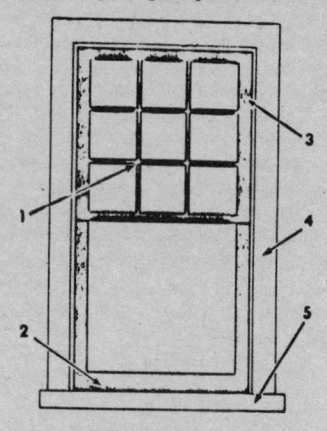

Paint windows in this order: (1) Mullions, (2) horizontal of sash, (3) verticals of sash, (4) verticals of frame, (5) horizontal frame and sill.

Wood Floors. To paint a wooden floor, first remove the old wax with mineral spirits and wipe up the dissolved wax. Use steel wool on any thick spots and sand the wood smooth with an electric sander.

There are five steps necessary to give your floor a new finish. You must stain it, apply a filler, apply a sealer, buff it, and apply the finishing coat.

1. Stain is the first step in preparing a floor for painting. Select the color you want, and test it on a scrap of flooring that matches the wood you intend to stain. Apply the stain to the floor with a 3- to 4-inch varnish brush, or with a rag. Brush in 30-inch widths starting at one corner. Apply the stain evenly, and remove the excess with a clean soft cloth. Let any stain you apply dry overnight.

2. Filler is necessary if you are preparing an oak floor for painting. Oak pores dry out and the filler fills up the pores to give your paint a good surface.

3. Sealer can be applied with a long-handled lamb's wool or nylon applicator. Apply the sealer across the grain, and then with the grain. Wipe off all surplus with a rag. Be sure to burn the rags when you are finished, or they may catch fire. For the best job with a sealer, use two coats.

4. Buffing follows the application of the sealer,

after the sealer has dried. To buff, use steel wool, and remove all particles of sealer from the surface.

5. Finish can be a varnish application. This kind of paint forms a surface coating resistant to spots and stains. You'll probably need two coats of varnish for uniform gloss, particularly if you haven't used a sealer. If you have used a sealer, you can get away with one coat of varnish.

To apply varnish, flow it on liberally from a well-loaded varnish brush, working with the grain. Remove any bubbles by brushing back into the area with light feathering strokes. Allow the varnish to dry for 8 hours and then apply a second coat.

If your finish is varnish and if it isn't in too bad shape, you can apply fresh varnish directly onto the old surface.

Floor enamel can be used in place of varnish, if you prefer it. The directions on the container will give you all the instructions you need.

Shellac is another possible finish coat for a wooden floor. Such a surface should not get too much wear, for shellac scratches easily.

Apply shellac in long, even strokes with a wide brush. Let it dry 15 to 20 minutes, and then rub it lightly with steel wool or fine sandpaper. Sweep the surface clean. Apply a second coat and allow it to dry for 2 or 3 hours. Then rub and sweep it again. Don't use the floor for 24 hours.

Lacquer is a good wooden floor finish. Just follow the instructions on the paint can.

Woodwork. For moldings, baseboards, and trim, use a semi-gloss enamel the same color as the walls. In kitchen and bathroom, use a full gloss. If you're painting new moldings, or bare wood of any kind, use an enamel undercoater in addition to the top coat.

Painting Safety Tips. Never paint in a completely closed room, and use caution when painting in a room where there is an open flame or fire. Some paints give off fumes that are flammable or dangerous to breathe or both. Avoid prolonged exposure to paint fumes for a day or two after painting. Such fumes can be especially harmful to canaries, other pet birds and plants.

Use a sturdy stepladder or other support when painting high places. Be sure that ladder is positioned firmly, with the legs fully opened and locked in position. Face the ladder when climbing up or down, holding on with at least one hand. Lean toward the ladder when painting. Do not overreach. Move the ladder frequently rather than risk a fall. And, to avoid spilling the paint, take the few seconds required to remove the paint can from the ladder before you move it.

When you finish painting, dispose of the used rags by putting them in a covered metal can. If left lying around, the oily rags could catch fire by spontaneous combustion.

Store paint in a safe, but well-ventilated place where children and pets cannot get to it. A locked cabinet is ideal if well-ventilated. Unless needed for retouching, small quantities of paint may not be worth saving.

Painting, Spray. Spraying is a fast, efficient method of getting paint where you want it. The result is usually smoother than most people can brush, with less paint used. Hold the business end of your sprayer six to eight inches from the surface so that the spray strikes at right angles. On each stroke, begin your sweep from a point at one side of the surface to be covered, pressing the trigger at the starting point, and releasing at the end without halting the gun. Lap the top fourth of each new stroke over the lower fourth of the preceding stroke, since the center half of each sprayed strip gets the thickest coat. Don't change your pace, since halting or hesitating results in a buildup of paint.

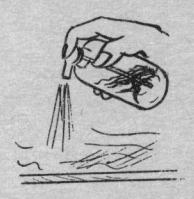

To avoid overspray and multi-colored fingers when painting a small item with a paint bomb suspend the part from a nail pushed through one side of a cardboard box. Use the nail to rotate the part as it is being sprayed. Tape up one flap of the box as a shield to prevent the overspray from reaching the hand holding the nail.

Painting Tips.
Baseboards. When painting baseboards, first cut in the wall edge, then the floor edge, then fill in be-

PAINTING TIPS

tween. Since dropcloths would be in the way, work with a rag close at hand. To wipe up drips on the floor or wall, use a rag folded over a putty knife.

Bubble-Free Paint. When applying varnish or enamel, assure a bubble-free finish by never wiping your freshly-loaded brush over the rim of the can to remove the excess. This usually causes a foamy bubbling on the surface that is almost impossible to brush out smoothly. Instead, pat the sides of the bristles lightly against the side of the can above the surface of the paint to remove the surplus. Then flow your varnish or enamel on liberally, using a moderate pressure and cross-stroking lightly with an almost dry brush.

Can Anchors.

1. A paint can resting on top of a stepladder is always a precarious proposition. You can prevent its overturning with a very simply device. Equip the top of your stepladder with a turn button, as illustrated. With this in its vertical position, you can place the paint can against it and hold it securely in place with a large rubber band.

2. When you are painting from a stepladder, there's always the danger of accidentally knocking over your can of paint. You can avoid this if you'll screw a 1 x 2 x 10-inch strip of wood to the edge of the top shelf of your ladder, as in the illustration. If you'll use just one screw, it will enable you to swing the strip down out of the way when it is not needed. To make use of this gadget, all you have to do is drop the pail handle of your paint can over the wood strip, and this will keep your container in place.

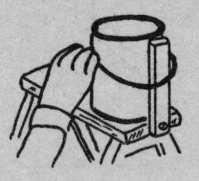

Can Carrier. If you have to paint up on a ladder and the paint can you are using has no handle, place it in a child's sand bucket. This will make it much easier to carry up the ladder.

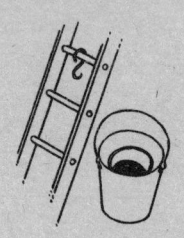

Can Handle. A good non-slip handle can be made for your small paint cans with a band of sheet metal and the handle from a discarded coffee-maker. Cut the band to grasp the sides of the can firmly and fasten both ends of the band to the sides of the handle with some small bolts and nuts.

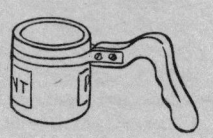

PAINTING TIPS

Can Hanger.

1. You can make yourself a very handy hook for supporting a bucket of paint on the rung of your ladder from an ordinary steel coat hanger, as in the illustration. This is in fact more efficient and steady than a hook bent from a single wire. First, straighten your wire hanger to form a long loop, then bend the loop into a hook.

2. A hook by which a paint can may be hung on the rung of a ladder can be fashioned very easily from a short length of plumber's perforated metal strap. Loop a short section of the strap around the top of the can and bind it tightly with a bolt and nut. Then bend the other end of the strap into a simple hook.

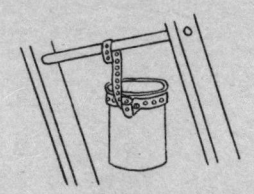

Ceilings. An old India-rubber ball cut in half and pressed firmly on to the handle of the paint brush will catch drips which run down the brush on to the hands and arms when you are painting ceilings and wall sections well above your head.

Color Test. The shade of paint on a color chart or in its container seldom looks quite the same after it has been applied to a wall. To ascertain how your paint will look when dry on the wall, try brushing some of it on a clean white blotter.

Dipper. For the handling of gummy or sticky paints and oils, you can fashion a very serviceable dipper from an ordinary tin can with a pair of tin snips. Cut the top of the tin can off at an angle and fasten it with two nails to a broomstick handle about twelve inches long, as illustrated. Such a dipper is very convenient to use, since it saves soiling the fingers and avoids wasting material.

Doors. The sketch shows in numbered sequence the way a paneled door should be painted, so that the direction of final brush marks will be generally the same as that of the actual wood itself. This principle should be applied to all panels of a similar nature. The dotted lines show where the wood grain end butts into the long grain. The arrows indicate direction of grain. Paint all areas marked #1 first, then areas marked #2, and so forth with the brush strokes going in the direction of the arrows.

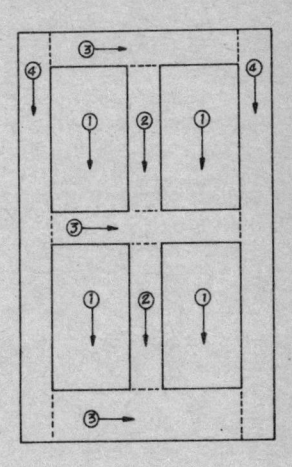

PAINTING TIPS

Drop Clothes. Old shower curtains make fine drop cloths for home painters.

Filtering. You can drain sediment out of paint solvents or other thin liquids by pouring out of a bottle corked with steel wool.

Frames. When you are painting a window or picture frame, if you will rub some soap around the edge of the glass beforehand, any paint that edges onto the glass will be easily removable with a soft cloth.

When painting frames of screens or windows, hold a piece of metal slat from a discarded Venetian blind over the adjacent area of screen or glass to protect it from your paint brush and thus make your job easier.

Germ Killer. There are, of course, a good many practical reasons for repainting the interior walls and ceilings—but one very good and beneficial reason often overlooked is its healthfulness. Painting kills germs.

Hardware. Here's one method to ease the usually tedious job of painting around the hinges and other hardware on doors and woodwork. Coat these metal items lightly beforehand with some petroleum jelly. Then any paint that does happen to get on them will wipe off readily with the jelly after the rest of the paint has dried.

Hiding Laps. Paint laps that sometimes show on a ceiling after it has been painted are caused by the edge of the paint starting to dry on one section before the next is started. To avoid this, paint as rapidly as possible, and keep the sections to a size that will permit your starting the next section before the first has begun to dry.

Jewelry, see JEWELRY

Knobs. The knobs that have been removed from drawers are too often a ticklish job to paint without messing up your fingers. You can make this chore much easier if you'll stick the knobs on the tines of an iron garden rake while you dab your paint on them.

Ladder Accessary. The next time you do some painting on a stepladder, try tacking lightly to the folding shelf or platform of the ladder a paper picnic plate. This will provide a good catch-all for the sticky drippings from your paint can and also a place for you to lay down your paintbrush whenever you take time-out from your job.

Ladder Safety. Empty cans can be put under the feet of a ladder used outside to act like snowshoes and to prevent the ladder from sinking into soft soil.

Level. Before storing that partly used can of paint, paint a thin line on the outside of it, at the level of the leftover paint. You can then tell at a glance how much and what color paint is in the can without having to pry up the lid.

Lumpy Paint. If you have some old, lumpy paint you'd like to use, and you don't want to go to the bother of straining it, try this easy remedy: After mixing thoroughly, lumps and all, cut a piece of wire screening the size of your paint can, put this screen into the can, and it will sink to the bottom, carrying all the lumps with it.

Mixer. You can make your own paint mixer, which will not dig into the bottom or sides of the paint can, won't splash or throw the paint, and yet it will raise the pigment from the bottom of the can and do a first-class job of mixing in a short time. You

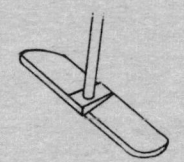

PAINTING TIPS

fashion this mixer into a propeller blade by shaping an iron bar one-eight inch by one-half inch. Grind one side of the bar to form opposite bevels, leaving the underside of the bar flat. Rivet or solder the propeller to a one-fourth inch steel rod, which can be chucked into your electric or hand drill. File the tips of the mixer blades round to prevent any danger of their damaging the paint can.

Mixing. Paint mixing will be easier if, for a few days prior to your paint job, you keep the paint can inverted. It will then mix well with less stirring.

A can of paint should be stirred for 15 minutes with a flat piece of wood for all the pigment to be distributed evenly. If the paint is not stirred correctly the painted surface will be streaky or uneven.

Good painters always box their paint as well as stir it—that is, they pour it from one container to another and back again—which speeds up the mixing process and makes it more thorough.

Never mix oil paints and synthetic paints.

They are composed of entirely different ingredients, and their inter-mixture is likely to cause faults.

Mixing Small Amounts. If you need only small amounts of enamel for painting, mix a few drops of varnish with color from tubes of oil paint in can tops until the paint is of the right consistency and luster. This makes very good enamel. Use the very pale, almost transparent, varish called copal varnish, as it does not darken pastel tints of paint.

New Metal Surfaces. When painting new, bare metal surfaces, first wash off the usual oily film with mineral spirits, then etch the new metal to assure a good bond for your paint. Metal other than aluminum can be etched by washing with a solution of one-half pound copper sulphate to a gallon of water, following with a clear water rinse. New aluminum is etched by roughing it up with steel wool.

New Wooden Surfaces. A new wooden surface should be rubbed lightly with sandpaper and dusted down. Then a coat of primer should be applied and allowed to dry 24 hrs. Only after the surface has dried should any nails be punched or holes filled and this should not be done before the primer is applied. Holes should be filled with a linseed oil putty. Other putties crack and ruin the finished surface. This should be followed by a white undercoat and allowed to dry overnight. Two coats of a gloss finish can then be applied and each coat allowed to dry overnight.

Paint Saver. A strong rubber band wrapped vertically across the mouth of your paint can catches excess paint from your brush and keeps the sides and rim of the can paintless.

Patch Painting. When painting door jambs, baseboards, and other often-abused surfaces around the home, it is a very good and practical idea to save a bit of the paint in an old fingernail-polish bottle. This will provide you a color-matched, touch-up kit that comes in very handy for covering up marks and scratches which might accumulate later.

Peeling. When paint peels from steel windows a few months after application, it is a pretty good indication that the metal was not entirely free from rust, or possibly oil and grease, when originally painted.

It is probable, also, that a metal primer was not used.

To get over the trouble, remove the old paint, clean the bare metal with fine steel wool, and wipe clean with a cloth dipped in turpentine.

Then apply a metal primer and allow plenty of time to dry.

Finish with one or two coats of exterior grade paint.

Plasterboard. Painting the porous surface of plasterboard before papering would be advantageous. First apply a pigmented cement sealer followed by a fairly thin coat of flat undercoat.

Thin this undercoat in the proportions of one part white spirit to three parts of the paint.

When, at a later date, you have to remove the old paper, it should come away cleanly after thorough soaking, but be careful not to dig the stripping knife into the board surface.

Plaster Sizing. You can do a finished job of painting over patched plaster surfaces if you will first sandpaper over the patched areas, when they have completely dried, and then apply a coat of shellac to them. The shellac will size the porous plaster and

245

PAINTING TIPS

prevent its bleeding through or absorbing the fresh paint.

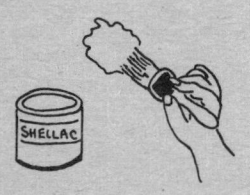

Plaster Sizing Substitute. If you have no commercial sizing on hand, plastered walls that are to be painted with oil paints may be sized with carpenter's glue diluted with a large quantity of water.

Plastered Walls. Before painting a plastered wall surface the first time, you'll probably save an extra painting coat if you'll size the surface first. A good preparation for sizing can be purchased from a paint dealer, or a coat of first-class interior varnish, thinned with turpentine and colored with a little wall paint, will serve the same purpose.

Over Plastic Paint. To repaint a wooden surface previously painted with a plaster paint, it should be sanded down—preferably with a sander, dusted down, then a coat of white undercoat applied. Then the final two coats can be applied in whatever finish is desired. Drying time will differ with type of paint used.

Pouring Tips.

1. When paint must be poured from a large container into a small jar or can, a handy disposable funnel can be improvised from an inexpensive cone-shaped paper drinking cup. Snip off the bottom end with a pair of scissors, and use the remainder as your funnel. The cup can be thrown away when the job is done, thus eliminating another clean-up.

2. Pouring a small amount of paint from a large can into a small one will not be messy and wasteful if you'll hold a length of wire across the center of the large can. Leave a short length projecting below the side of the can. When the paint touches the wire, it will follow the projecting end and fall into the smaller container placed beneath the wire.

Preserver. If the lid of a paint container has been inadvertently thrown away or lost, and there is a little unused paint left, pour some hot paraffin over the paint, and this will keep it in usable condition.

Putty requires two coats of paint over the top of it to give a satisfactory finish.

The first coat should be applied immediately after the application of the stopping putty to any holes or cracks.

By doing this, any surplus putty around the hole or crack will be brushed off and the area smoothed down flush.

Raw Wood. Knots and sap streaks in raw wood should never be painted over unless they are first sealed, otherwise they will bleed through your paint in short order and leave an unsightly brown stain that will show up even after several additional coats of paint. Prevent this by touching up all knots or sap streaks with shellac.

Reconditioning Paint. If oil-base paint has become dry and apparently useless, try renovating it by pouring an inch of turpentine or mineral spirits on top of it, letting it remain for a few days, then stir well with a stick until it is soft and ready for practical use.

Repairing Enamel Scratches. The best way to repair a scratch in an enameled surface is with some of the original enamel, dripped in with a toothpick. After the enamel dries, rub it down with some rottenstone. Another treatment is to fill the mar with a wax crayon matching the enamel color, following this with a wax polish.

Saving Paint. You can avoid having the rim of your paint can clog up with paint if you'll punch ten or twelve holes into the bottom of the lid groove with

PAINTING TIPS

a nail, as illustrated. These holes will then drip the paint back into the can. Also, the holes won't affect the tightness of the seal when you replace the lid, nor will any paint spatter when you hammer on the cover.

Scaffolding. When working with a scaffold and planks on exterior housepainting work, always mount the scaffolding on the inside of the plank, between the wall and the scaffold.

This safety measure will minimize the risk of accident.

Sealing Paint Can. When replacing the cover on a partly used can of paint, spread a rag over the lid before hammering it shut or before stepping on it to seal it. Excess paint that has accumulated in the rim will be caught by the rag instead of being spattered onto you, or instead of oozing down over the sides of the can.

Shoe Protection. When embarking on an interior painting job in your home, pull an old pair of socks on over your shoes to keep them clean, and you can also use your feet to wipe up drippings from the floor.

Slick Finishes. When painting over enamel or varnish, first either wash the surface down with special binding solution or roughen it with sandpaper or steel wool. Otherwise, your paint will not adhere properly to the slick finish. Another method, often effective, is to add a little cornstarch to your enamel.

Solvent Dispenser. A very handy dispenser for adding solvent to paint is a syrup pitcher of the type illustrated. The glass permits you to see exactly how much is in the container, and the snap top lets you measure it to the drop.

Spattered Paint. Paint spatters can be removed from linoleum and hardwood floors very easily with fine steel wool, even after the paint has partially hardened. Use a light pressure and short strokes, just long enough to cover the affected spot without dulling the finish of the surrounding area more than

necessary. Then wax and polish the spot. This method is usually more effective than the use of solvents.

Starch Coating. The freshly-painted or washed walls and ceilings will keep looking new for months if you give them a starch coating. This is transparent and does not alter the color values of your paint—it can be used on any oil-painted surface in good condition, but does not work too well over most water-mix paints. New paint must be completely dry and hard before starching. To mix the solution, dissolve one cup of laundry starch (the lump variety) in one cup of cold water. Then stir in two quarts of boiling water, and boil and stir until the milky look is almost gone. While boiling, add two tablespoons of vinegar to prevent "creeping" when solution is applied. Apply this solution either with a large brush or a roller. Apply it in yard-square areas, and then each area is stippled with a fine-grained sponge or a large, clean brush, before it dries. The stippling obscures pattern effects and brush marks.

Stirrers.

1. You can make an efficient paint stirrer by grasping the two ends of a coat-hanger and bending until they meet. The two rounded ends will break up the pigment much better than a wooden paddle, and they can be bent to fit any can.

2. An old dinner fork does a faster and more thorough job sometimes in the stirring of small cans of paint than the traditional wooden paddle.

PAINTING TIPS

Stoppers and Fillers. These are materials and terms which often cause confusion.

Originally, stoppers were materials for the stopping-up of nail and screw holes, while fillers are materials applied over large areas by knife, brush, cloth or spray.

The arrival of water-mixed, plaster-type cellulose fillers has lessened the distinction.

But generally, a stiff paste (for instance, putty) is used as a stopper and a thinner paste as a filler.

Stopping-up refers to the operation of filling nail, screw and other holes.

Filling means building-up or hiding the grain of wood over a large area, even if the same materials are used.

Storm Windows and screens. You can make a much easier job of painting your screens or storm windows if you'll convert your stepladder into an easel, or painting stand, with the fittings illustrated. Suction cups on the upper fittings will hold the windows for painting. The upper block is reversed for screens, which are hung on the finishing nails protruding from the ends of the blocks. On the lower blocks, pointed finishing nails keep the lower edges of the windows or screens from contacting any surface.

Straining Tips.

1. One very easy and simple way to strain sediment out of paint solvent and other such liquids is to pour them out of a bottle which is "corked" with some loosely-packed steel wool. You can then discard the steel wool after it has served its purpose.

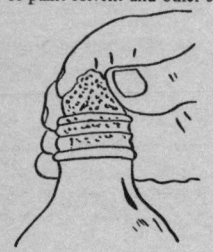

2. A discarded nylon stocking and an embroidery hoop make an efficient strainer for paint, and is easy to hold spread out to receive the paint stream without suddenly slurping into the paint. Simply slip the top of the stocking into the hoop, and cut off and knot the other end to make a shallow bag.

3. If a can of paint contains hardened particles and other foreign matter, it is a simple matter to restore it to a usable condition if you'll just strain the paint through a piece of cheesecloth. Hold the cheesecloth tightly over half of the open can, and pour the paint through it into another container. You may find it necessary to fold the cloth double to insure removing all the small particles from the paint.

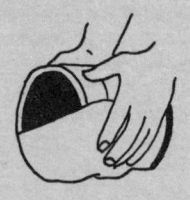

Substitute. If only a small amount of paint is needed for a touchup job on your walls, try using ordinary wax crayon. Scrape or shave off the desired color into a small container, add turpentine a drop at a time, and stir until the shavings are dissolved. Apply with an artist's brush. If it's too light in tone, darken by applying a second, and perhaps a third, coat. When dry, apply a thin coat of white shellac to prevent bleeding or wearing off.

Surface Preparation. Remember always that paint, varnish, and other such finishes will not dry properly when applied over surfaces that have been previously waxed. Always clean thoroughly beforehand, using turpentine, mineral spirits, or a special surface preparation sold for this express purpose by almost all paint stores.

Switch Plates. It's a very simple matter to tint plastic switch and wall plates so that they will harmonize with the other furnishings of a particular room. Merely wipe some liquid food colorings on the plastic with a soft cloth or cleaning tissue. Then,

PAINTING TIPS

if later you wish to change or renew your colors, all you have to do is to remove the plate and wash it off with cold water.

Tarnish Prevention. All metalic gold paints eventually tarnish, since they are made of bronze powders rather than of real gold. To a great extent, this tarnishing can be prevented or postponed for a considerable length of time if you give the surface a coat of clear fresh shellac.

Techniques. Some of the generally-accepted rules governing the proper use of a paintbrush include the following: Dip half the length of the bristles into the paint. Tap the brush gently against the side of the can, but do not wipe it across the lip. Hold the brush comfortably near the handle base, applying light pressure with your fingertips. The bristles should flex slightly toward the tip as you begin a stroke, but you should not bear down on the brush.

Thinning Oil Paints. Never use kerosene for thinning oil paints. Even though the initial combination may be obtained, the durability of the mixtures will be affected.

Tile. Go over the surface of the tiles with fine sandpaper working out the joints just enough to give a roughness or "tooth" to the surface and go ahead and paint after dusting well to remove sanding fluff. However, painted tiles will never equal new ones in appearance although they may be better looking than the situation you are trying to remedy.

Tin. Paint will adhere to tinware much more readily if you'll rub the tin beforehand with rough pumice stone or coarse sandpaper, and then apply a thin coating of shellac.

Touch-Up Tips.

1. When small chips or scratches on painted walls or woodwork need touching up and no leftover paint is on hand, you can usually mix the necessary color with some poster paints. Intermixing the primary shades will give almost any tint desired, and easily mixed paint can then be dabbed on with a pointed brush. This won't be a washable job, but it will serve nicely as a temporary repair until the next full-scale painting job. It can be made washable by coating it with some thin shellac or varnish.

2. When you are painting the interior walls of your home, it's a good idea to fill some well-washed shoe polish bottles with some of each color of paint, and label them. Then later when a scratch or nick appears on a wall, you're all set for a quick touchup.

Varnish. Do not shake or stir glossy varnish before using. Agitation will only whip up small air bubbles into the varnish and make it harder to brush out. These bubbles often remain in the varnish film and thus thwart your achievement of a truly smooth finish.

Wall Finish. You can impart an attractive, striated finish to walls of plain plywood or hardboard by coating them, one panel at a time, with a heavy consistency of plastic or texture paint, then creating the striations by drawing the serrated edge of a trowel which is used for spreading linoleum mastic or adhesive through the paint from top to bottom. Use a straight wood board on one side of your

PAINT REMOVING

trowel and ride your trowel down against this to form straight striations.

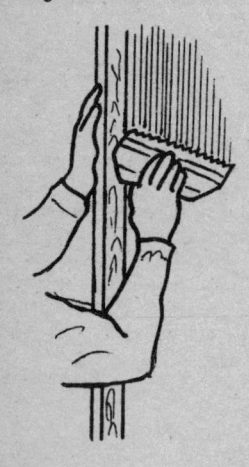

Wax Removal. Paint, varnish and other substances will not dry properly if they have been applied over surfaces that have been previously waxed. Remember, therefore, always to clean the surfaces thoroughly beforehand, using turpentine, mineral spirits or a special surface preparer for this express purpose, sold in almost all paint stores.

White Enamel. Add one teaspoon of black enamel to each quart of white enamel to insure that it will not yellow later.

White Paint. Add a few drops of black paint to a can of white paint, and it will make the white paint whiter.

Wire Netting. A paint roller is a much more effective tool for painting wire netting than a brush. With a roller you can cover a much greater area more quickly.

Wood Grain. Rubbing down paint work on wood surfaces should be carried out in the direction of the grain.

This will prevent cross scratches that will spoil the appearance of the finished paint surface.

Paint Removing.

from Bricks. To remove fresh paint from bricks, use paint remover, and follow with a water wash. In the case of old paint, scrape as much off as possible with a putty knife and steel wool, and then if necessary use paint remover.

from Carved Wood. For the quick removal of paint or varnish from carvings and curved surfaces moisten it with some paint remover, then wrap some steel wool around a pencil or small steel rod and work it off.

from Hinges. Old paint on hinges and other metal objects will loosen if soaked in household ammonia for an hour or two.

Scrapers. Try tacking a rectangular piece of ordinary window screening to a block of wood, and you'll have a scraper that is as good as, or even better than, a wire brush for removing blistered, checked, or alligatored paint prior to a repaint job. The rough, open mesh of the screening does an excellent job of breaking up the old paint, and also feathers the edges of the blistered area so that they won't show through the new coat of paint. This is a fine gadget, too, for removing loosened pigment, dust, and grime from paint that is solidly bonded to wood, but which needs a good cleaning before the new paint is applied.

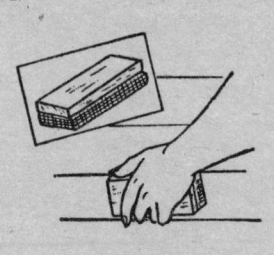

The strain on your hand will be considerably reduced and you'll provide yourself much better control of your paint scraper with a drawer knob on the top of the utensil, as shown in the illustration. By using both hands, you can apply extra pressure on the scraper when it is needed. The short screw which holds the scraper plate to the handle can be replaced by a longer one which can be screwed through the tool and into the knob.

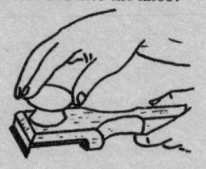

Strippers. For removing old paint and varnish from interior woodwork, it is best to use a liquid or paste stripper.

The majority of paint strippers are supplied in the form of a viscous liquid.

They consist essentially of a blend of powerful active solvents which act as the penetrating medium and which are normally, mobile and extremely volatile liquids.

This means that if they were applied in their natural form they would evaporate rapidly and have not the slightest effect on the paintwork.

Manufacturers get over this by incorporating evaporation retarders in the strippers.

These act by causing a thin skin to appear over the surface of the solvents as they start to volatize, and this skin acts as an effective seal to prevent further evaporation of the solvent.

In a way, the term solvent as applied to paint strippers should not be interpreted too literally. In actual fact, the old paint does not dissolve, but merely softens, wrinkles, and blisters as the stripper penetrates the various coatings.

It is this penetrating and loosening action which is the chief advantage, and it is a mistake to attempt removal before the old paint film has been thoroughly conditioned.

Stripping solutions are best applied with an old paintbrush and the coating allowed to remain in contact with the old paint until the entire surface wrinkles.

A broad-bladed scraper used with an upward movement is then used to remove the softened paint.

When there has been a build-up of successive coats of paint, it may be necessary for a second application, and the procedure is repeated as before.

Tips.

1. To remove paint, mix two parts of ammonia and one part of turpentine. Apply this with a brush, leave on for a few minutes, then wipe off the paint and varnish easily with a cloth.

2. Don't attempt to paint over chipped or cracked paint or marred varnish. Your new finish will only accent the defects. Instead, strip the old finish off down to the bare wood with some chemical paint-and-varnish remover. Apply the remover with a clean old brush, leaving a heavy coat. Don't brush back over an area. Give the remover time to work through to the wood.

3. The use of paint remover on chair or table legs often results in excessive waste, because the remover runs rapidly down the leg if too much is applied. One good way to avoid this waste is to stand each leg in an old coffee can. Your surplus remover will then run down into the can, and it can be salvaged by pouring it back into its original container after the job is done.

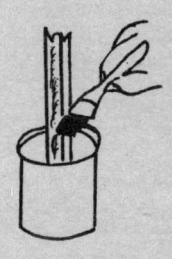

from **Wood Surfaces.** To soften and remove old paint and varnish from wood surfaces, apply a mixture of two parts spirits of ammonia and one of turpentine or mineral spirits, either with a cloth or stiff-bristled brush. And don't forget the sandpaper when removing paint or varnish.

Paint Rollers. A good general purpose home maintenance roller is a 9-inch roller. Good mohair will give you the smoothest surface finish with all kinds

PAINTS

of paint. Top quality mohair must be used with enamels and varnishes.

Cleaning. To clean a roller, roll out all the excess paint on an old newspaper. Wash the roller in solvent, then rinse, and roll out again on additional layers of clean newsprint. The porous paper will suck out the excess paint so that a final rub with a clean rag will leave the roller soft and fluffy and almost as good as new.

Tips.

1. If you are planning on painting some of your walls via the popular roller method, try this little trick: Line the roller-pan with some hardware cloth or sand screen, and this will permit you to load your roller much more evenly to improve the finished paint job and to prevent splattering.

2. When using a paint roller to apply a number of different colors of paint, there is always the messy job of cleaning out the tray.

In this way, too, a lot of paint is wasted.

However with several sheets of aluminium foil we can get over this problem and speed up the job considerably by eliminating the need for cleaning the tray.

Press a sheet of aluminium foil into the tray and smooth it over the edges.

When ready to change colors, simply lift the foil and pour the surplus paint back into the container.

Paints are extremely important preservatives that will keep your house in good shape against weather conditions, wear and tear, and even old age. Not only that, a good paint job will add value to your home—whether you've got it on the market for sale or not.

There is a great variety of different types of painting mixtures: oil paint, alkyd resin paint, emulsion (latex) paint, water-thinned paint, casein paint, calcimine, enamel, varnish, shellac, lacquer, and paints made to cover specific surfaces.

Alkyd Resin. An alkyd resin paint contains a synthetic resin replacing part or all of the oil as the vehicle; alkyds and acrylics give it tougher coating properties. Alkyds are usually used with enamel or wall paint; acrylics or alkyds are used with exterior paint.

Calcimine is powdered chalk or whiting mixed with glue and pigment, used for ceilings or on plaster.

Casein. A casein paint is made of skim milk and whiting, plus pigments, water, and protein binders. It dries with a dull finish.

Dripless. A dripless paint contains pigment particles that have been homogenized and suspended so that the paint flows on without dripping. It's great to use for ceilings.

Enamel is varnish carrying a pigment, in flat eggshell and semigloss finish. Some enamels employ alkyd resin for the vehicle. *Interior enamel* comes in high gloss, semigloss, and flat; *exterior enamel* is used for trim, window frames, door frames, porch railings. *Enamel undercoat* is used to seal a surface at reduced cost. *Screening enamel* clings to galvanized iron, brass, or copper screening without clogging the openings.

To prepare enamel, do not shake the can. Pour the paint into another pail and stir thoroughly. Then pour the mixed material from bucket to can several times. Add thinner if the paint does not flow easily.

Epoxy resin is a waterproof compound that bonds to any type of surface and holds back water even under great pressure.

Exterior trim (or trim-and-trellis) paint is the favorite finish. It is an oil-alkyd-resin base enamel. Its properties include rapid drying, high gloss, good color and gloss retention, and good durability. House paint may be used, but it does not retain its gloss as long. Also, any chalking may discolor adjacent surfaces.

Finger, see FINGER PAINTS.

Hobby Enamel. If you need small amounts of enamel for painting models or gift pieces, mix a few drops of varnish with color from tubes of oil paint in can tops, until the paint is of the right consistency and luster. This makes a very good enamel.

Use the very pale, almost transparent varnish called copal varnish, as it does not darken pastel shades of paint.

House paint contains lead, zinc, or titanium pigment. Its vehicle is linseed oil; it has a drying agent, and a solvent like turpentine or mineral spirits. It dries with a gloss, is resistant to water, and resists temperature changes.

Inside flat paint contains zinc and/or titanium. Its vehicle is turpentine and it has mineral spirits on a "flatting" oil that dries without a gloss.

Lacquer is composed of nitrocellulose—cotton fibers

EXTERIOR PAINT SELECTION CHART

	Aluminum Paint	Cement Base Paint	Exterior Clear Finish	House Paint	Metal Roof Paint	Porch-and-Deck Paint	Primer or Undercoater	Rubber Base Paint	Spar Varnish	Transparent Sealer	Trim-and-Trellis Paint	Wood Stain	Metal Primer
Wood													
Natural finish			X						X			X	
Porch floor						X							
Shingle roof												X	
Shutters and trim				X●			X				X●		
Siding	X			X●			X						
Windows	X			X●			X				X●		
Masonry													
Asbestos cement				X●			X	X					
Brick	X	X		X●			X	X			X		
Cement and cinder block	X	X		X●			X	X			X		
Cement porch floor						X		X					
Stucco	X	X		X●			X	X			X		
Metal													
Copper									X				
Galvanized	X●			X●			X	X			X●		X
Iron	X●			X●							X●		X
Roofing					X●								X
Siding	X●			X●							X●		X
Windows, aluminum	X			X●							X●		X
Windows, steel	X●			X●							X●		X

Black dot (X●) indicates that a primer or sealer may be necessary before the finishing coat or coats (unless the surface has been previously finished).

PAINT STAINS

treated with nitric and sulphuric acids—mixed with solvents, gums, and pigments. It is a resin varnish, good for furniture finishing; sanded it gives a hard glossy surface.

Latex. A latex paint is actually an emulsion paint; the emulsion looks like rubber latex. Oils, resins, or mixtures are emulsified so that they can be thinned with water. Emulsion paint is quick-drying and odorless and is easy to work with. You can clean brushes, rollers, and equipment with soap and warm water. It will act as a primer on uncured plaster. You can apply it to wood, plaster, metal, or wallpaper. It has good hiding power, especially when applied with a roller. You can recoat emulsion paint in a half hour.

Other emulsion paints are *polyvinyl-acetate (vinyl) paint, acrylic paint, butadiene styrene paint, alkyd paint,* and others

Masonry. Exterior latex masonry paint is a standard paint for masonry. Cement-base paint may be used on nonglazed brick, stucco, cement, and cinder block. Rubber-base paint and aluminum paint with the proper vehicle may also be used.

Metal. Ordinary house or trim paints may be used for the finish coats on gutters, downspouts, and hardware or grilles. A specially recommended primer must be used on copper or galvanized steel. Use house paint, aluminum paint, or exterior enamel on steel or aluminum windows. Paint window screens with a special screen enamel.

Oil. An oil paint contains a natural oil, like linseed, soybean, china wood, or fish. Exterior house paints, wall paints, floor paints, primers and so on, are oil paints, although some of them may be considered alkyds.

To prepare oil paint for application, shake the can, open it, and pour the paint into another pail. Stir thoroughly and then pour the mixed material from bucket to can several times. Add thinner if the paint does not flow easily.

Primer is used to seal wood. It covers previous coats and will save you money by giving you a thick first paint layer at less cost.

Rubber paint is made for outside masonry and interior concrete floors.

Sealer is a varnish, made of resinous materials which bond with the fibers of hardwood to make a tough, abrasion-resistant surface impervious to wear.

Shellac is a spirit varnish, used on floors, best as an undercoat or sealer for raw wood. Clear shellac is quite a versatile product, with many uses for indoor painting and wood finishing. But, it should never be used outdoors as a primer under varnish or other clear finish or as a finish by itself. It turns white quickly when it comes into contact with even the least amount of moisture.

You can color shellac to any shade by adding spirit soluble aniline dyes dissolved in alcohol, then strained.

Be sure to remove all stains from a wood surface before shellacking, otherwise your polished surface will show the stains up even plainer than originally.

Texture paint is applied as a thick paste, textured or troweled on, giving a plastered effect.

Undercoat, see **Primer,** above.

Varnish. A varnish is made of gum or resin, usually carried in a linseed or tung oil vehicle, and is thinned with turpentine or other solvents. Varnish provides a tough film when dried, through which wood grains show up nicely. Varnish gives a wooden floor great resistance to wear and tear.

Waterproofing sealer containing silicones, synthetic resin or varnish, penetrates masonry to help it shed water.

Water-Thinned. A water-thinned paint is simply a paint that can be thinned with water instead of with turpentine or mineral spirits.

To prepare a water-thinned paint, simply follow the directions printed on the container. Each brand has its own idiosyncracies.

Whitewash is slaked lime and water, used on temporary structures.

Paint Stains, see STAIN REMOVAL.

Paint Vapor Barriers, see VAPOR BARRIERS.

Pancakes, see FOODS.

Panel Doors, see DOORS.

Paneling. A surface very popular these days is prefinished plywood paneling. This wall surfacing requires absolutely no upkeep, except a bit of polishing now and then. You need never paint it, or refinish it in any way, and for this reason alone it is almost worth the amount of money it costs. Actually you save money in the long haul because of the avoidance of repainting.

You may find this kind of paneling in the house you live in, or if you do not you can always install it yourself, directly over whatever wall surface you have. Prefinished paneling can be attached to plaster walls, drywall, or cement block or brick surface using either nails or adhesive. You'll save a lot of interior decorating money if you put up one of these wall surfaces over your old wall.

Outdoor. When the home handyman is making outdoor cabinets, storage boxes, or other projects calling for plywood or hardboard, he should make certain he buys only those grades designed for weather exposure. Hardboard comes with a special tempered variety for outdoor use, and plywood is obtainable in an exterior grade made with special waterproof glues.

Pine. One excellent method of cleaning pine paneling is by use of a small amount of vinegar and a large amount of water. Wring out a cloth as dry as you can in this solution, then wipe off each panel with it. It's a wonderful dirt remover, and it also leaves a shine.

Wood. Wood-paneled walls, if waxed, require little other attention than dusting. If they become soiled or begin to look dry, clean them with liquid wax, apply a fresh coating, and rub to a soft polish. Varnished or shellacked wood paneling that is not waxed can be cleaned with a polish made by mixing a half-cup of turpentine with a cup of boiled linseed oil and about a tablespoon of vinegar. Apply sparingly, let stand for 15 minutes, then rub until no smudge is left by a clean dry finger.

Panel Pins, see NAILS.

Pans.

Dented. The most efficient way to hammer out dents in pots, pans, or other such items made of sheet metal is first to lay the dented article over a sack of sand. Then hammer from the inside with a rubber mallet, or use a hammer with a rubber crutch tip slipped over its head. The sand affords a solid support so that no new dents are created, yet it permits the metal to give under the blows of your hammer.

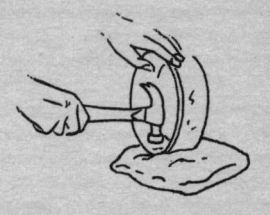

Leaking. If there is a small leak in a pan or bucket, turn the container upside down, cover the leak with a little powdered sulphur, heat an old knife blade until it is very hot, and spread the sulphur around the leak with this for a good seal.
(See also ALUMINUMWARE.)

Pants Hanger, see CLOSET ACCESSORIES.

Paper.

Flattening Rolled Paper. Before removing a rolled calendar or something similar from the tube in which it has been mailed, hold the open end of the tube over the steam from a teakettle to moisten the paper. This will cause the article to lie flat.

Mildewed, see MILDEW.

Removing from Polished Surface. During hot, humid weather paper will often stick to a polished surface.

Care should be taken when removing this paper, otherwise it may damage the polish.

One simple method of removal is to apply olive oil.

If the oil is allowed time to soak in thoroughly after application, the paper should peel off easily.

Repairing Notebook Paper. If you have torn the ring holes on notebook paper or ledger paper, and have no gummed stickers on hand with which to repair the sheets, cut the gummed flap of an envelope and paste this over the hole. Then recut the hole and your sheets will be reinforced.

Thumbing Through. When you have to thumb through many thicknesses of paper, as in leafing through magazines, or doing work where paper shuffling is concerned, moisten your thumb and forefinger with a drop of two of glycerin and rub it into the skin. This will enable you to separate many thicknesses of paper, sheet by sheet, in a very short time.

Serrating Edges. Serrated paper edges as attractive decorations for the edges of paper stock you are using to make individual greeting cards, stationery, and the like, are easy to make if you tear your paper along the teeth of a hacksaw. Crosscut saws make a finer deckling or serrations than do ripsaws. And, if you need curved or circular edges, try the same technique with a circular saw blade.

Paper Bag Holder. A neat way to store paper bags is to install on the inside of any convenient kitchen cabinet door or cupboard door, an ordinary screen-door spring, horizontally, fastened at either end with 1/2-inch screws, so spaced as to be under light tension. This will hold the bags securely against the door.

Paraffin, see LUBRICANTS.

Paraffin Wax to most people is something used to seal off the tops for bottled jam, but it has many other useful applications.

Many woodworkers rub nails and screws on a bar of soap for easier driving.

Paraffin wax does it better. Soap tends to rust the nail or screw in place, making it almost impossible to remove later.

Just rub the screw or nail over the flat surface of the paraffin wax cake a few times, or thrust into some of the wax which has been melted and poured into a hole in the hammer handle.

Paraffin wax is useful when curtain rings and drapery hooks refuse to slide on the metal rods or poles.

Take down the rod and rub the inner and top surfaces with a cake of paraffin until a thin film is evident.

Place the hooks back on the rod and restore it to service.

Paraffin wax will also help a tight drawer to run freely.

Remove a drawer which has a tendency to stick, turn it over, and rub a cake of paraffin up and down the edges and also the sides, especially on those spots that appear rough from rubbing against the drawer frame.

Garden markers of the flat, white wooden stick variety have an irritating way of becoming illegible.

A dip in a pan of hot melted paraffin wax after the desired details have been printed with pen or pencil will preserve the writing for a considerable time.

Wooden porch and window boxes decay rapidly from within unless they are protected with a metal lining of some kind.

The life of a less expensive box may be prolonged many times if the box is treated with paraffin wax when it is new.

Paraffin should be melted in a convenient pan or can and brushed over the dry inner surfaces of the boxes before they are used.

Particle Board. Gouges in particle board can be filled with plastic wood and sanded smooth when dry. And, if the particle board happens to be stained a certain hue, some matching stain should be mixed with the plastic wood before being applied.

Pasta, see FOODS.

Paste, see ADHESIVES.

Patent Leather Care, see CLOTHES CARE.

Patent Leather Shoes, see SHOE CARE.

Patio Construction. One of the easiest terraces for the "do-it-yourself" man to build is one constructed simply of loose bricks and sand. First, prepare your base by breaking the ground to a depth of three or four inches, then cover it with sand three inches deep, Level off the surface of the sand and tamp it down very thoroughly. This leveling-off process can be done with a board fastened to the end of your rake. Then edge the area, either with strips of 3/4-inch redwood or bricks planted on edge in a trench. Lay your terrace bricks on the surface of the sand in the pattern you like best, tamp these firmly down, and finally spread loose sand over the entire surface and sweep it into the cracks between the bricks. In time these bricks will become almost as solidly implanted as if set in concrete.

Patio, Rustic. You can do things with old, discarded railroad ties to add a very attractive, rustic touch to your yard or garden. For example, as shown in the accompanying illustration, you can fabricate these ties into a retaining wall at the end of a terrace. They can also be made into garden steps, benches, and wooden walks.

Patio Table, see TABLES.

Peaches, see FOODS.

Peaked Roof, see ROOF STRUCTURE, ROOF SURFACES.

Pearl Handles are made of mother-of-pearl, the nacre that lines the shells. They need only soap and water...no ammonia. Do not let the pearl handles soak in water, since this treatment could loosen the cement that holds them in place.

Pears, see FOODS.

Peas, see FOODS.

PENCIL SHARPENER

Pegboard is actually a kind of informal wall-storage space. It is hardboard either 1/8- or 1/4-inch thick that is dotted with small holes at 1-inch intervals. Mounted on a wall surface like that of a garage, the board becomes a perfect spot for hanging all kinds of things on specially designed hooks, brackets, tool holders, small shelves, ties and so on. You can slip these holders into the board or out of them at will. Each hook can hold considerable weight. A large board can hold hundreds of pounds of tools, utensils, and so on.

Pegboard comes in panels up to 4 by 8 feet. You have to mount it out 1/2-inch from the wall so the hooks can be inserted. Half-inch furring strips will keep the board far enough away from the wall to accommodate the hooks.

In places where moisture may be a problem, you can get tempered hardboard which will serve the same purpose. (See also BULLETIN BOARD.)

Pencil Holder. One good tip for the "do-it-yourselfer" who is forever losing his pencil is to drill a hole behind the blade in the top of the saw handle. This hole should be drilled for a snug fit, so the pencil won't drop out—and it will always be at hand for those important measurements.

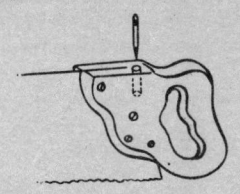

Pencil Sharpener. You can maintain a good, sharp point on your workshop pencil just by pulling it at an angle against the blade of your wood plane, turning the pencil after each shaving.

Pencil Sharpener, Mechanical. In using a mechanical pencil sharpener, handle your pencils gently. Pressing the point in too firmly can waste twice as much wood as necessary to get a sharp point.

PENCIL STAIN

Pencil Stain, see STAIN REMOVAL.

Pens, see BALLPOINT PENS.

Perfume Stain, see STAIN REMOVAL.

Perfume Use, see CLOTHES CARE.

Perspiration Stain, see STAIN REMOVAL.

Pesticides, Insecticides, see INSECTS.

Pet Care, see CAT CARE, DOG CARE.

Pewter may be cleaned successfully by applying a paste made with equal parts of flour, vinegar, and salt. Let the paste remain on for about an hour, then rub off, and wash the metal with warm water. (See also COPPER CLEANING.)

According to most collectors and dealers, pewter should never be polished unless you want to decrease its market value. If, however, you do polish it, stay away from any gritty polishes, and do the job this way: Drop a small lump of potash into a quart of water and soak the pewter in this for at least twenty-four hours, then take it out, and rub all over with a cork dipped in olive oil or mineral oil. Follow with a brisk dry-chamois rubdown.

Phillips Screwdriver, see TOOLS, HAND.

Phonograph Records, see RECORDS.

Photographs, Cleaning. When an uncolored photograph (not glossy) needs cleaning, wipe it with a damp cloth, then place it face-down on a smooth, dry cloth until it is dry.

Photograph Stain, see STAIN REMOVAL.

Piano Key Care. The white keys on your piano will stay white if you'll keep the keyboard always exposed to the light. Ivory has a way of turning yellow if continually kept in the dark.

Piano Keys, Cleaning. An ordinary pencil eraser makes an ideal tool for removing fingermarks from piano keys. It fits easily between the black keys and gets into all the corners. For real difficult spots, requir-

ing cleaning fluid, just wrap the eraser with a cloth soaked in the fluid. The eraser will make the application of the fluid easier in hard-to-get-at places.

Many people use milk successfully for cleaning piano keys. Yogurt works even better.

Three methods for cleaning piano keys are: a cloth moistened with lemon juice and dipped in whiting; a cloth moistened with vinegar; a cloth moistened with alcohol.

Picnic Basket Tip. If you want to keep the food in your picnic basket cool and tasty during the warmest weather, try standing an ice-filled fruit jar in the center of your hamper and packing the food around this. After your basket is packed, cover it with a towel or folded tablecloth tucked in tightly at the sides. If you wish, you can pour some concentrated fruit juice or double-strength tea over the ice, keeping in mind, of course, that the melting ice will dilute the beverage.

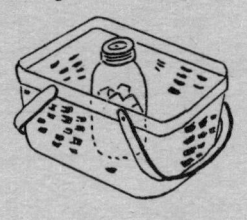

Picnic Tablecloth Tip. Avoid the common annoyance of having the tablecloth on your picnic table constantly blowing and flopping about by weighting it down with dowel rods inserted in the hems of the tablecloth.

Picnic Table Cover. If your backyard picnic table is not in a shady spot, you can help to make your mid-day cookouts a little more bearable by erecting an awning cover over your table. Set a post firmly into the ground at either end of your table, and attached to the table. On these posts, build a framework of light wood, sloping down from the center and extending beyond the outer edges of the table. You can procure awning material in any number of attractive colors or designs, and can easily cut and fit it to your frame. This not only produces more shady comfort, but also adds a nice decorative touch to your picnic area.

Pictures, Curled. Here's a handy little tip for the amateur photographer whose prints are inclined to curl up after drying. These can be straightened by rolling them into a roll of shelf paper. Place the prints face down, as illustrated, so that the curl is reversed. For small photos, two hours in the roll should do the trick, while larger prints may require an overnight treatment in the roll.

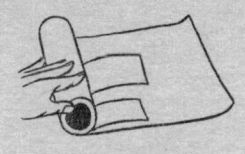

Picture Frames, see FRAMES.

Picture Hanging. (See STUDS, LOCATING.)

Using screw eyes, place them about three-quarters of the way up the picture then attach wire, a galvanized steel type being the most reliable. Give the wire about 2-inch leeway. Remember, the looser the wire, the more the tilt of the painting.

The most commonly used hook for hanging is an angle drive pin, but for anything over eight pounds the wall should be drilled and plugged with a rawl plug. A 1- to 1½-inch screw should then be screwed into the plug. A heavy or large painting should have two hanging hooks about 1-foot or more apart.

Paste-on hangers are only reliable with very light weights.

Tips.

1. It's not a good idea to hang pictures in a room whose walls are covered with a scenic-type wallpaper. Pictures with this kind of background add a cluttered, overdone effect.

2. Here's one efficient way of hanging a picture exactly where you want it on a wall. Cut a cardboard the size of your picture frame, and punch a hole through it at the point where the hook will fall when the wire is extended. Place the cardboard on the wall where you want your picture to hang, then mark the wall for the nail hole.

3. It's a good idea, when hanging pictures, to place a thumbtack in each of the corners behind the frames, and this will permit the air to circulate behind the pictures and prevent dust from settling and creating that familiar and disfiguring dark line on the wall across the bottom of the picture.

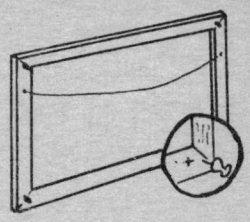

4. The plaster under picture hangers is oftentimes marred or cracked when you drive in or remove a hanger. You can avoid much of this simply by applying a small strip of cellulose tape over the area into which the nail is to be driven.

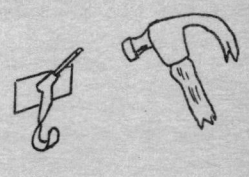

5. When hanging small pictures in light weight frames, you can improvise a good picture hanger from a paper clip. Use a long strip of adhesive tape to attach the clip to the top and back of your picture, then hang the clip on a small brad or nail.

6. One effective way to prevent your pictures from slipping and hanging at unattractive angles on the wall is to make use of a couple of lead-shot

fishline sinkers, pressing these over the picture wire on either side of the hook that holds the picture on the wall.

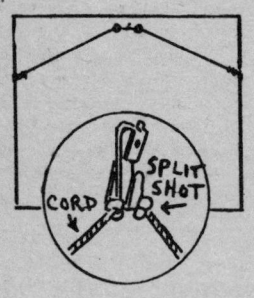

7. Your pictures on the wall won't slip and hang crookedly if you'll wrap a little adhesive tape around the center of the picture wire.

8. If the nail supporting one of your pictures should come loose in the plaster, try this little remedy: Wrap a narrow strip of cloth spirally around the shank of the nail and dip this into some glue. Replace the nail in the hole and allow the glue to dry for a day or so before rehanging the picture.

9. If you want to provide a firm hold for a mirror or picture on a plaster wall where there is no stud into which you can drive a nail—and if the object to be hung isn't too heavy—drill a hole into the plaster with a twist drill and fill the hole with plastic wood, obtainable at your hardware store. After this has hardened overnight, drive your nail into the plastic wood.

Pie, see FOODS.

Pigment, see PAINT COMPONENTS.

Pineapple, see FOODS.

Ping Pong Balls, see TABLE TENNIS BALLS.

Pipe Cutting. When cutting short lengths of small threaded pipe—for example in assembling electrical fixtures—slip the pipe over a piece of steel rod clamped in the vice.

The rod supports the pipe without damage to the threads.

Small-diameter tubing that would be crushed or damaged if clamped in a vice for cutting can be supported by using the same method.

Pipe Joint Repair, see PLUMBING.

Pipe Measuring, see TOOLS, MEASURING WITH.

Pipe Racks.

1. Here is a simply-made, but attractive, pipe rack you should be able to complete in one evening. The material is of 1-7/8-inch stock, and a suggested height for the sides is 4-3/4-inches. The length of the rack can be varied, depending upon the number of pipes you wish to accommodate. And, if you wish, small partitions can be fitted onto the base between the bowls of your pipes.

2. A handy pipe rack for the workshop or garage can be very quickly constructed from a wire coat hanger. Just bend in the two bottom corners to provide the necessary slack for forming the loops to accommodate your pipes. Then attach the rack to a convenient wall.

3. The ordinary kind of rubber door stop provides a very usable pipe rack, as shown in the illustration. This stop can be used alone as a pipe rest, or it can be combined with an ashtray and the two screwed to a wooden base to form a smoking set.

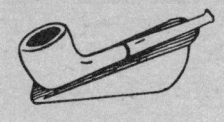

Pipe Repair, see PLUMBING.

Pipe Stem. When the push-pull stem on a man's smoking pipe breaks off, more often than not it breaks off flush with the wooden shank of the pipe, making its removal a tough problem. In a case like this, try removing the broken stub by inserting a screweye into it, then working the whole thing out.

Pitched Roof, see ROOF STRUCTURE, ROOF SURFACES.

Pivot Door, see CLOSET DOORS.

Plane, Planing, see TOOLS, HAND.

Planters.
  Mobile. Housekeeping chores can be made much easier if your large plants are mobilized. Mount those heavy plant containers on small platforms with casters underneath, and it will be a simple matter to move them about when cleaning a room. Make the platform of thick plywood, cutting the piece slightly larger in diameter than the base of the flowerpot. Then drill the underside of the circular-shaped platform to receive three casters. You can paint the platform in a harmonizing color. 
  Watertight. You can make a wooden planter watertight by brushing three coats of liquid rubber on its interior. Reinforce the corners of large boxes with screening laminated between two coats of your paint.

Plants, House.
  Beautifying. To beautify house plants from ivy to rubber plants, put some baby oil on their leaves.
  Care.
    1. Rub a little castor oil or mineral oil lightly over the leaves of your house-plants to keep them looking green and healthy, and to stimulate their growth by cleaning the pores with which the plants breathe.
    2. Green plants will have a brighter color if their leaves are washed with a little beer once a week.
  from Carrots. Cut about an inch off the large end of a carrot, place it in a shallow container in some water and watch it grow. Makes a lovely fern.
  from Citrus Fruit Seeds. Try planting eight to ten orange, lemon or grapefruit seeds about one-half inch down in the soil of a four-inch flowerpot. They will produce a lovely seven-inch citrus bush within a year.
  from Lemon Seeds. Try planting some lemon seeds and treating them as you would any houseplant. They'll grow into attractive plants, and their leaves can be used for delicate flavoring of some of your cookery.
  from Peach Pit. If you plant a peach pit one-inch deep in a pot of soil, it will grow with long, thin, willow-like leaves, tropical in appearance.
  from Pineapple. Another lovely houseplant will result from placing the top of a fresh pineapple in a pot of water.
  Nourishment. Put the shells from your breakfast eggs into a quart of water, let stand overnight, then water your house plants with this mixture. This gives the plants "something extra" in the matter of nourishment.

PLANT STAKES

Watering. Water your house plants regularly, but do not let the soil get soggy. Aerate the soil from time to time with a fork.

Stale club soda is good for watering plants. The chemicals which remain add vigor and color to the greenery.

Plant Stakes, see GARDENING.

Plant Stand. Here is an attractive and easily-made plant stand which will add both beauty and utility to your porch. It is assembled throughout with finishing nails. You will need one-by-twelve-inch lumber and some one-inch dowel. The back of the stand is 28 inches high by 12 inches wide. The top shelf is 12 by 12 inches, the middle shelf is 15 by 12 inches, and the bottom shelf is 18 by 12 inches. There are 12 inches between the center-edges of the shelves, and the center-edge of the bottom shelf sits three inches from the floor.

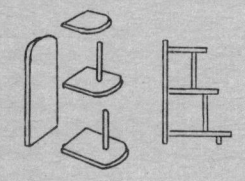

Plant Support, see GARDENING.

Plaster, Plastering.

Cracks at Joints. If you have a large crack where the wall joins the ceiling, where one wall joins another, or where the wall joins the floor, do not bother to fill the crack at all, but cover the entire joint with molding. If you have old molding there, but it is not wide enough to cover the hole, remove it and replace it with new molding of a greater thickness.

Cracks, Hairline. If you have a hairline crack, cut into it to widen it so that it will receive the spackling compound. Undercut the cracks; that is, make it wider beneath the surface in order to hold in the wet patching compound until it dries.

Mix the spackle or patching plaster in an old dish or pan following the directions on the package. Wet down the crack with a wet paint brush so that the old plaster in the crack is moist.

Force the spackle into the crack with a putty knife or with your finger.

Allow it to dry. Now sandpaper off the rough spots, blending in the edges with a circular motion.

If the crack is not sealed, repeat the job until it is. Spackling and patching compounds frequently shrink as they dry, drawing away from the old plaster. The resulting gap must be filled again.

Cracks, Wide. If the crack is too wide to take spackling compound, you may have to use what is called drywall joint cement. This is a type of plaster that has more body than spackling compound. Follow the directions on the package.

Holes or Bulges. Large holes or bulges in plaster can be fixed by using painter's patching plaster, also called plaster of Paris. If you use this, follow the directions on the package.

If the hole is larger than 16 inches, patch it up by putting in a piece of new drywall and covering the join with spackling compound.

Marking Holes in. Anyone who has drilled holes into plaster walls for wall plugs into the base brickwork knows how the plaster shatters away around the hole and makes the precise hole position difficult to determine.

This problem can be overcome by using the procedure shown.

Just mark the position of the hole before drilling with a cross and circle it with a penciled ring which will mark the approximate circumference of the plug. The center of course, will be the point where the two lines intersect (A).

At detail (B) is the ragged area in the plaster after the plugging operation, but after this has been adjusted with a little patching plaster the lines can be re-drawn to mark the precise position of the center of the plug.

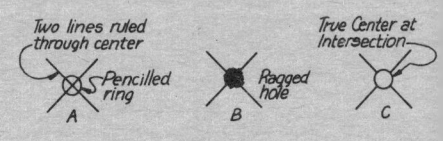

Mixing Tips.

1. When getting ready to plaster some cracks or holes in a plastered wall, if you'll add your plaster to your water, instead of the water to the plaster, your mixture will have no lumps.

2. For mixing small amounts of patching plaster or spackling compound, cut a large rubber ball in

half. Each section will make an excellent mixing container, which can be easily cleaned by squeezing flat or by turning inside out if necessary.

3. When you are using lime in plaster, mix it in mortar boxes prior to the time of plastering, so that it will be thoroughly slaked and cool when it is used. "Hot" mortar has a tendency to continue to "work" after it has been applied, and this could well result in popping and blistering.

Patching Tips.

1. When using spackling compound for patching large holes in walls and ceilings before painting, always apply the material so that it is a bit higher than the surrounding surface. This allows for the slight amount of shrinkage that often occurs and will enable you to sand it flush after it has thoroughly dried.

2. When you are patching cracks or small holes in walls, your plaster compound sometimes has a way of hardening so quickly that you haven't time to work on it with your trowel. You can slow down the hardening by adding a little vinegar to your mix.

3. For a glass-smooth finish when patching plaster walls, allow your patch to set until the plaster begins to stiffen. Then dip a putty knife or trowel into water, and drag the wet tool over the surface of the partially hardened plaster. This will leave it with a smooth, glazed surface which will need little or no sanding.

4. Thin cracks in plaster walls or ceilings can be repaired quite easily. First score them lightly with the V-point of a beer can opener. Then dust them clean and dampen with a sponge. Finally, apply a thin mixture of spackle.

5. To fill nail holes in a plastered wall, rub a cake of wet soap over these holes until they are filled. Then, when dry, paint the wall.

6. You can often do a good job of patching small nail or screw holes in a white wall simply by filling them with baking soda moistened with water.

7. Nail holes in plastered walls, small and deep, can be filled by mixing up a little talcum powder or cornstarch with a few drops of water forcing this into the holes, then smoothing it off with your fingers around the edges.

Powdering. If the plaster on one of your walls is beginning to turn to powder, the usual cause lies in its having been first applied in a dry, hot room so that it dried out before it could set. A remedy for the situation is a gentle spraying with water.

Sizing, see PAINTING TIPS.

Wall surfaces of plaster are excellent for taking paint and wallpaper. Horizontal laths—narrow strips of wood just over an inch wide and a quarter of an inch thick—are attached horizontally to wall studs with a quarter inch or so between. Wet plaster (hence the term "wetwall" as opposed to "drywall" is applied to the laths; as it pushes into the space between the laths and hardens, the plaster holds to the surface. The plaster face is smoothed over and allowed to dry. After that, paint is applied, or wallpaper is affixed.

Plasterboard, see DRYWALL.

Plasterer's Small Tool, see TOOLS, HAND.

Plaster-of-Paris.
Cleaning.

1. To clean plaster-of-Paris figurines, use mild soapsuds and a shaving brush. Rinse well. Dip the items into a strong solution of alum water to give them the appearance of alabaster.

2. Plaster busts or ornaments can be cleaned by applying a coat of heavy starch, then, after this has dried thoroughly, removing it with a brush.

Hardening. To harden the surface of plaster-of-Paris, include in the wet mixture a small quantity of gum arabic. It is also possible to harden the surface of a casting by immersing it in a solution of alum.

Mixing. If you are mixing plaster-of-Paris and want to delay hardening, use glycerin or vinegar instead of water and your mixture will not harden for twenty or thirty minutes. Use more or less of the liquid, according to the time required to complete the use of the mixture.

Plaster Stain, see STAIN REMOVAL.

Plastic Tile, see TILE, PLASTIC.

Plastic Bag Sealer. One good way to seal a plastic bag is to fold aluminum foil along the top edges of the bag, then run a hot iron over the aluminum. The plastic bag edges will seal effectively and the foil will prevent the plastic from melting on your iron. Let the bag cool before removing the foil.

PLASTIC CEMENT

Plastic Cement, see ADHESIVES.

Plastic Materials.

1. Sprinkle talcum powder on plastic materials to prevent their sticking when folded and stored away.

2. Most plastic material, when wrinkled, apparently cannot be ironed. In that case, try this: Pass your iron over your ironing board cover until the cover is quite warm, then spread the plastic over it, smoothing it over with your hand. This often has a surprising way of smoothing out those wrinkles.

Plastic, Stains on, see STAIN REMOVAL.

Plastic Toy Repair. Plastic toys with cracks and small tears in inflatable plastic items can be quickly and easily repaired by pressing plastic electrical tape over the damaged parts. This tape will stay in place indefinitely.

Plastic Wood. This literally covers a multitude of mistakes in amateur woodworking. Just remember to allow for considerable shrinkage when it hardens, and keep on hand a supply of various colors to match different surfaces.

Playing Card Tray, see CARD TRAY.

Pliers, see TOOLS, HAND.

Plumb Bob, see TOOLS, MEASURING.

Plumbing. It is in the general area of plumbing around the home that your may experience your most tricky repair problems. There are some things that you should absolutely not try to do, and there are other simple things that you should do. Knowledge of what is difficult and what is easy is essential if you are to save money in plumbing repairs.

Plumbing involves the bringing in of water from outside and the taking away of waste water used in the house. Pipes are the medium of conveyance, and controls like faucets and taps are placed for your convenience for instant supply of water throughout the house. There are also a number of automatic controls in automatic washers, in heating appliances, and in air conditioners. At any one of these spots you may develop trouble.

Let's trace the water in its passage through your house. It comes from a main supply system in the street. At a point of entry in your house there is a valve controlled by a turn-on wheel. From here the water goes to your kitchen, bathroom, and heating plant. At each of these three junctures the water can be diverted for use. Once it is used it is sent out again in a separate system of drainage. All water going out gathers eventually in a main drainage pipe and from there empties into a sewer, septic tank, or cesspool.

Basin Drain, Clogged, see Drainpipes, Clogged, below.

Bathtub Drain, Clogged. First try to move the waste material by chemical solvents. If these fail, try using a plunger. But, before using the plunger, remove the attachment in the tub that turns on the shower extension. Stick a wet cloth or wash rag into the hole so that no air leaks through. Fill the tub with enough water to cover the suction cup of the plunger. Then place the plunger over the drain and agitate it vigorously up and down. This should dislodge whatever is clogging the pipe. If it doesn't, use a snake.

Cesspool. A cesspool is a brick-lined or stonelined underground well where liquid sewage can seep through the walls and be absorbed in the earth. Most cesspools can be used for years, unless they become clogged up and overflow. An overflow may be caused by the stopping up of the openings in the masonry itself by such things as grease from the kitchen sink or other matter. Since grease is lighter than water, it is drawn into the masonry openings by the force of the water and closes them up.

Sometimes pumping out a cesspool will help the problem, but frequently it will not. You may have to resort to chemical cesspool cleaners that will break up the grease coating and permit the water to flow through into the earth.

If nothing works to clean an overflowing cesspool, you may have to build another one next to the original to receive the overflow. Place a grease trap in the waste pipe from the kitchen sink; this is made of earthenware and looks like a length of sewer pipe. The grease will catch on its surface and you can skim it off as often as necessary.

Drain Care.

1. Keep the drains in your kitchen sink, as well as in your laundry tubs, clean and free of grease

accummulations and disagreeable odors by rinsing some strong hot salt water through them at least once a week.

2. Before shampooing your hair in your washbowl or shower, it's a good idea to place a piece of steel wool in the drain opening. Loose hairs will cling to the steel wool as the water runs out, and these can be removed to prevent clogging of the drain.

Draining Water Systems. Where extensive plumbing repairs are necessary, the main water supply should be cut off and the entire water system drained. If a house is to be vacated and there is to be no heat during cold weather it is also advisable to drain the heating system. This is a job for a reliable plumber who will also do whatever is necessary to protect fixtures and pipes against freezing and damage.

To drain the pipes, first shut off the main supply of water. Then, starting at the top floor, open all faucets, working down to the basement. When water ceases to run from the faucets, the small cock in the main pipe valve may be opened to allow the remaining water to drain off into a bucket or tub.

Traps under sinks, toilets, tubs, etc., should be drained by opening and draining, or using a plunger or suction. After emptying, the trap may be filled with ½ cup of anti-freeze.

The toilet tanks should be emptied by flushing after the water has been turned off, and any surplus water removed from the bowl with a sponge.

If a house is to be left vacant, the hot-water tank should be drained by opening the valve at the bottom. All hot-water faucets should be open while the tank is being drained.

In a house heated by hot water or steam that is to be left vacant during winter months, the heating system should be drained unless an automatic oil or gas burner is going to be used to maintain above-freezing temperatures. To drain the system, the fire should be out and the main water supply shut off. The water from the boiler is drawn off by opening the draw-off valve in the lowest part of the system. The water-supply valve to the boiler should be open so that no water is trapped above it. Then, in hot-water systems, beginning at the hightest radiator, the air valves should be opened as fast as the water lowers. In a one-pipe system, every radiator valve should be opened. After a heating system has been drained, it must be properly refilled before a fire can be started.

Drainpipes, Clogged. Any drainage pipe in the house may become clogged. You can try three different methods to unstick it, in this order:

1. Use a plunger—a rubber suction cap screwed onto the end of a long wooden pole—to try to suck out the refuse. Hold the cup over the drain, cover it with 3 or 4 inches of water, and pump the handle up and down, agitating it briskly.

2. If the plunger doesn't work, use a plumbing solvent. There are many different brands available. Use your own favorite, and follow the directions carefully, observing all precautions.

3. If both plunger and solvents fail, examine the fixture for a trap below (it's a loop in the pipe). Place a bucket below the trap, and then remove the connections holding the trap with a pipe wrench, clean the trap with a wire or auger, and scour it with hot soapy water. Then replace the trap.

Drainpipes, Frozen. If you are thawing out waste or drain pipes, start heating them from the end away from the fixtures. You may be able to thaw drainpipes sometimes by pouring boiling water into the fixture.

In any case, you're better off letting a plumber take care of this specialized work.

Drainpipes, Leaking. Leaks in drainpipes can be effectively sealed for quite a long time with a homemade poultice. Wrap layers of cloth and wet plaster around the leaky sections of the pipe, using some strong cord to tie the "bandage" in place. Let this dry hard before using.

Drainpipes, Obstructed. Obstructions in drainpipes other than in traps may be cleared by the following methods.

1. Cleanout augers—long, flexible, steel cables commonly called "snakes"—may be run down drainpipes to break up obstruction or to hook onto and pull out objects. Augers are made in various lengths and diameters and are available at hardware and plumbing supply stores. (In some cases, you may have to call a plumber who will probably have a power driven auger.) Small obstructions can sometimes be forced down or drawn up by use of an ordinary rubber plunger.

2. Grease and soap clinging to a pipe can sometimes be removed by flushing with hot water. Lye or lye mixed with a small amount of aluminum shavings may also be used. When water is added to the mixture, the violent gas-forming reaction and production of heat that takes place loosens the

grease and soap so that they can be flushed away. Use cold water only. Chemical cleansers should not be used in pipes that are completely stopped up, because they must be brought into direct contact with the stoppage to be effective. Handle the material with extreme care and follow directions on the container. If lye spills on hands or clothing, wash with cold water immediately. If any gets into the eyes, flush with cold water and call a doctor.

3. Sand, dirt or clothing lint sometimes clogs floor drains. Remove the strainer and ladle out as much of the sediment as possible. You may have to carefully chip away the concrete around the strainer to free it. Flush the drain with clean water. If pressure is needed, use a garden hose. Wrap cloths around the hose where it enters the drain to form a plug to prevent the backflow of water. You may have to stand on this plug to keep it in place when the water is turned on.

Drains, Outside. Roots growing through cracks or defective joints sometimes clog outside drains or sewers. You can clear the stoppage temporarily by using a root-cutting tool. However to prevent future trouble you should replace the defective portion of the line, using sound pipe and making sure that all joints are watertight.

If possible, sewer lines should be laid out of the reach of roots. But if this is impossible or impracticable, consider using impregnated fiber pipe which tends to repel roots.

When sewer pipe is being laid, if bare copper wire is wound around each joint, as illustrated, this will prevent danger of small roots entering the pipes and eventually clogging the tile, since the roots that come into contact with the copper will be killed. And even if the sewer line should sometime settle so that the joints are no longer sealed, the copper wiring will still act as a protective.

Faucet Polishing. To polish old faucets or other plumbing fixtures that appear hopelessly corroded and pitted, try using automobile rubbing compound scrubbed on vigorously with a damp rag. A heavy string coated with the abrasive compound can be drawn back and forth around narrow curves or in tight corners.

Faucets and globe valves, the type commonly used in home water systems, are very similar in construction. By turning a handle, you screw a valve stem down into a valve opening called a seat in the pipe, thus closing the valve opening, and preventing the water from moving through.

In order to keep this closing watertight, there is a valve washer at the bottom of the valve stem attached with a set screw. This washer fits snugly against the seat when the faucet is closed. If the washer is old and worn, water may leak through the pipe. If the seat itself is pitted or worn, water may likewise spill through.

At the top of the valve stem there is another protective device called a packing nut, covered by washers. This check keeps water from traveling up the stem and spilling out of the handle.

These three crucial spots are points of potential trouble: valve washer, seat, and packing nut.

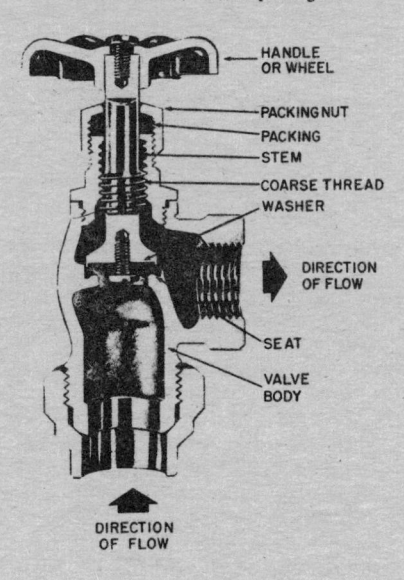

Faucets, Frostproof, see **Hydrants, Frostproof** below.

Faucets, Leaking. There are a number of reasons for faucet leaks. The most common one is a worn washer. Second most common is the deterioration of the packing around the faucet stem. Third most common is the pitting or scoring of the "seat" against which the valve washer closes, thus allowing water to travel through rather than halt. Sometimes faucet parts become loose and need to be tightened or replaced.

1. Washer. Follow these steps to replace a washer.

Shut off the main supply valve that brings water into the house.

Locate the hexagonal packing nut to which the faucet handle is attached and unscrew it from the faucet with a pipe wrench.

Turn the faucet handle toward the "turn-on" direction and keep turning until you can lift out the handle, packing nut, and valve stem from the body of the faucet. The valve stem is smooth at the top with strong wide threads at the bottom.

Unscrew the set screw at the bottom of the threaded stem and remove the valve washer. If the groove of the screw head has corroded over, make a new groove with a file or hacksaw, or replace it with a new set screw.

Pry off the old washer and screw in a new one.

Replace stem, packing nut, and handle in the faucet, and screw it back toward the "turn-off" direction.

Turn the packing nut back into the faucet body, and tighten with a wrench.

Turn on the main shut-off valve.

2. Packing. To replace deteriorated packing, first turn off the water supply at the shut-off valve. Remove the faucet handle, the packing nut, and the stem from the faucet as instructed in the section of washer replacement. You'll find a kind of twine pushed into the packing nut. Dig this old packing out from the nut. Wind new packing twine or candlewicking around the stem in the same direction the handle turns when screwed into the faucet. Now screw the packing nut over the stem to hold the packing in place. Be sure you haven't got too much packing in the nut. If you have, remove it until it is right. Now reassemble the faucet.

3. Seat. It is a bit more complicated to redress or score a pitted seat. First of all, turn off the water supply at the shut-off valve. Remove the faucet handle, the packing nut, and the faucet stem as instructed in the section on washer replacement. Then insert a faucet seat dresser into the body of the faucet. The dresser is a device that shaves off all irregularities in the surface of the seat. You simply turn the handle of the dresser three or four times. Remove the tool and inspect the seat to see if it is sufficiently smooth and shiny, without any grooves or scoring. If it is still irregular, use the dresser again until it is smooth. Then flush out the shaved metal particles from the seat and reassemble the faucet.

Faucets, Noisy. If a faucet has developed a howl or chatter anytime it is turned on, it can frequently be silenced simply by replacement of its washer. To play safe, replace the brass screw that holds the washer in place, too—then tighten it securely.

Floor Drain Trap. The floor drain in your basement, no doubt, has a trap which holds a water seal to prevent sewer gas from escaping. This water may evaporate, however, if the drain is used only occasionally. To preserve the seal in a seldom-used drain outlet, flush it regularly with water.

Hydrants, Frostproof. Frostproof hydrants are basically faucets, although they may differ somewhat in design from ordinary faucets.

Two important features of a frostproof hydrant are: (1) The valve is installed under ground—below the frostline—to prevent freezing, and (2) the valve is designed to drain the water from the hydrant when the valve is closed.

The illustration shows one type of frostproof hydrant. It works as follows: When the handle is raised, the piston rises, opening the valve. Water flows from the supply pipe into the cylinder, up through the riser, and out the spout. When the handle is pushed down, the piston goes down, closing the valve and stopping the flow of water. Water left in the hydrant flows out the drain tube into a small gravel-filled dry well or drain pit.

As with ordinary faucets, leakage will probably be the most common trouble encountered with frostproof hydrants. Worn packing, gaskets, and washers can cause leakage. Disassemble the hydrant as necessary to replace or repair these and other parts.

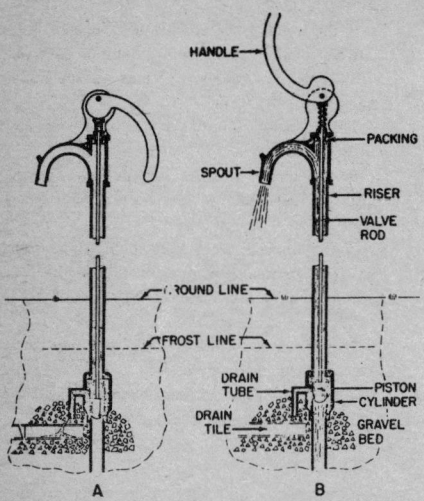

PLUMBING

Frostproof hydrant; A. Closed; B, opened. As soon as the hydrant is closed, water left in the riser drains out the drain tube as shown in A. This prevents water from freezing in the hydrant in cold weather.

Frostproof yard hydrants having buried drains can be health hazards. The vacuum created by water flowing from the hydrant may draw in contaminated water standing above the hydrant drain level. Such hydrants should be used only where positive drainage can be provided.

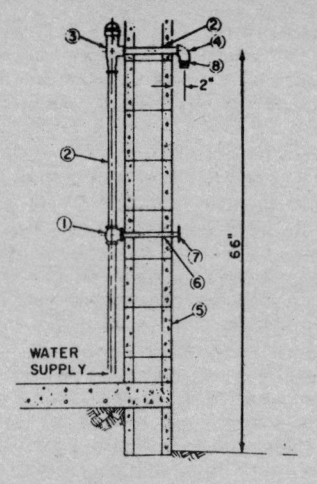

① 3/4" BALL OR GATE VALVE
② 3/4" PIPE, GALV.
③ 3/4" VACUUM BREAKER
④ 3/4" ELL. M.I. GALV.
⑤ EXTERIOR BUILDING WALL
⑥ 1" SLEEVE
⑦ VALVE HANDLE
⑧ HOSE ADAPTER

Protected wall hydrant suitable for filling agricultural sprayers.

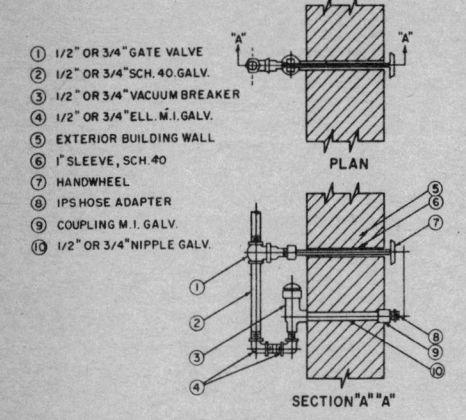

① 1/2" OR 3/4" GATE VALVE
② 1/2" OR 3/4" SCH. 40. GALV.
③ 1/2" OR 3/4" VACUUM BREAKER
④ 1/2" OR 3/4" ELL. M.I. GALV.
⑤ EXTERIOR BUILDING WALL
⑥ 1" SLEEVE, SCH. 40
⑦ HANDWHEEL
⑧ IPS HOSE ADAPTER
⑨ COUPLING M.I. GALV.
⑩ 1/2" OR 3/4" NIPPLE GALV.

Vacuum breaker arrangement for outside hose hydrant.

Frostproof wall hydrants are the preferred type. For servicing sprayers using hazardous chemicals, hydrants having backflow protection should be used.

Pipe Insulation. To avoid frozen pipes and to save money on heating costs, you can insulate all exposed plumbing and piping. In a hot-water heating system, you should insulate both supply and return pipes.

Insulation you can use might be asbestos, magnesium mineral, or rock wool. Molded mineral and rock wool are the simplest to apply. Before putting on the insulation, clean the pipe of all rust, dirt and loose scale. Check for leaks, naturally, and make all the necessary repairs.

Cut the sections of the insulation to size and hold them in place with a canvas covering.

PLUMBING

Pipe Joint Repair.

1. Threaded pipe joints that have become frozen tight by heavy accumulations of rust can usually be loosened with normal wrench pressure if a few drops of household ammonia are first applied around the joint. Give the ammonia a few minutes to work and help it to penetrate by tapping lightly with a hammer to set up a slight vibration.

2. Leaking water pipe joints can often be repaired, without taking the pipe apart, by smearing the joint with pipe cement, which costs very little and is procurable at hardware stores.

Pipe Patching. It isn't necessary to own a pipe threader to replace a short length of leaking water pipe at a distance from a union. Cut out the defective section with a hacksaw and make a coupling from radiator hose, as shown in the illustration. Such hose comes in sizes to fit most home water pipes, and if slightly oversize, it can be drawn tight with hose clamps. A hose coupling such as this is also very handy on horizontal drain pipes that have to be parted periodically for cleaning.

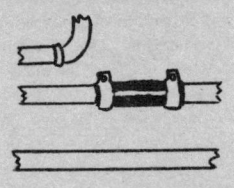

Pipes, Corroded. Occasionally waters are encountered that corrode metal pipe and tubing. (Some acid soils also corrode metal pipe and tubing.) The corrosion usually occurs, in varying degrees, along the entire length of pipe rather than some particular point. An exception would be where dissimilar metals, such as copper and steel, are joined.

Treatment of the water may solve the problem of corrosion. Otherwise, you may have to replace the piping with a type made of material that will be less subject to the corrosive action of water.

It is a good practice to get a chemical analysis of the water before selecting materials for a plumbing system. Your state college or university may be equipped to make an analysis. If not, you can have it done by a private laboratory.

Pipes, Cracked. The following is a suggestion for mending cracked water pipes.

If the water is not under much pressure, force stiff bituminous roofing compound into the crack.

Then wrap several layers of adhesive tape around the pipe over the repair.

This should hold until you can get a permanent repair made.

If the water is under considerable pressure, brighten the metal round the crack with emery cloth.

Then wrap a piece of clean copper wire around the pipe over the crack, smear with soldering flux, and flow solder over the wire so that it adheres to the pipe.

This repair should last a long time if properly done.

Cold solder, sold in tins by hardware shops, can also be used for repairing water pipes.

You should turn off the water before doing repairs.

Pipes, Frozen. If you are unlucky enough to find that one of your pipes has frozen up and you cannot call in a professional plumber in time to check it, open up all the faucets connected to the pipe after turning off the main supply valve. Then apply heat in some form to the pipe at the end nearest the fixture.

There are various electrical appliances such as small portable heaters, and even heating pads you can use for this purpose. The use of a blow torch is dangerous and should be avoided unless absolutely necessary.

One of the best household gadgets for use in thawing a frozen water pipe is your electric iron, because of its concentrated heat. Then move it along the pipe away from the faucet as the thawing progresses. If you have copper or brass pipes, the heat from the iron will be effective as far as ten feet from the point of contact. Just exercise a little patience—and be sure not to allow the hot iron to come into contact with any of your woodwork.

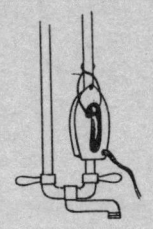

Electric heating cables up to 100 feet may be purchased in hardware stores. Wrap the cable around the frozen pipe and plug it into an electrical outlet. Heating cables with thermostat controls are available and can be connected throughout the winter months.

If you cannot use any of these electrical aids, wrap the frozen pipe with cloths and pour boiling water over the cloths. This sometimes works.

Pipes, Hammering. If you hear a hammering in your water pipes whenever you turn off one of your faucets too quickly, you may have to put in an air cushion. The hammering is caused by the abrupt halting of the water as it courses through the pipes. The banging is the water bouncing against the sides of the pipe as it stops.

To cure this disturbance, install as near the water meter as possible a 3-foot length of pipe capped at the end and screwed into the main pipe. When the water supply is arrested at the faucet, the water that is stopped will force itself up into the air pocket in the air cushion and will slow down gradually against the compressed air without knocking in the pipe.

Hammering of a pipe may also be due to improper support at some point along its length. Check the pipe wherever it is exposed in the basement to see that all mounting straps are tight. The pipe should be solidly anchored at frequent intervals along its length. Look for places where the pipe has given or sagged out of line so that vibrations are set up when water rushes rapidly through it.

Pipes, Leaking. Nothing can be quite so disconcerting in the home as a sudden spurt of water from a broken pipe. Such a leak, if unchecked, can cause you all sorts of costly damage—to furniture, woodwork, floors, and to the heating system. Take these immediate steps to stop the flow of water:

Turn off the main supply valve that lets the water into your house. You should find out where this shut-off valve is when you first take possession of your home.

Trace back to the source of the leak. If you can see the pipe and the site of the leak—it may be at a connection point—tape the joint up with aluminum-coated or waterproof pressure-sensitive tape, or with friction tape. If you do not have tape and simply want temporary relief, you can always push chewing gum into the hole.

A leak at a threaded connection can often be stopped by unscrewing the fitting and applying a pipe joint compound that will seal the joint when the fitting is screwed back together.

Replace the faulty connection yourself, or call in a plumber. In the case of pipes, it is usually best to call in a plumber; you have already saved the cost of his call by cutting off the main water supply at the shut-off valve.

Small leaks in a pipe can often be repaired with a rubber patch and metal clamp or sleeve. This must be considered as an emergency repair job and should be followed by permanent repair as soon as practicable. Large leaks in a pipe may require cutting out the damaged section and installing a new piece of pipe. At least one union will be required unless the leak is near the end of the pipe. You can make temporary repair with plastic or rubber tubing. The tubing must be strong enough to withstand the normal water pressure in the pipe. It should be slipped over the open ends of the piping and fastened with pipe clamps or several turns of wire. Vibration sometimes breaks solder joints in copper tubing, causing leaks. If the joint is accessible, clean and resolder it. The tubing must be dry before it can be heated to soldering temperature. Leaks in places not readily accessible usually require the services of a plumber, and sometimes of both a plumber and a carpenter.

Pipes, Sweating. To solve the problem of sweating pipes, wipe the pipes dry, then use some of the special insulating strips sold in plumbing establish-

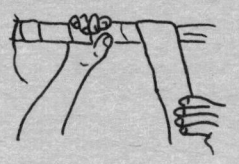

PLUMBING

ments. Cut strips to cover four or five feet of pipe at a time, and use a cord to hold the wrapping on the pipe while you are applying the outer wrapper.

Pipes, Temporary Repair. Clamps may be used for temporary repair of leaking pipes. They should be used only with a rubber security guard. A rubber sheet or an old inner tube is suitable. Put the clamp directly over the leak. Sleeve clamps are preferable. Hose clamps will also do the job. A C-2 clamp may be used. Three layers of plastic electrical tape will stop small leaks. On dry pipes and where clamps cannot be used, epoxy putty makes a good repair.

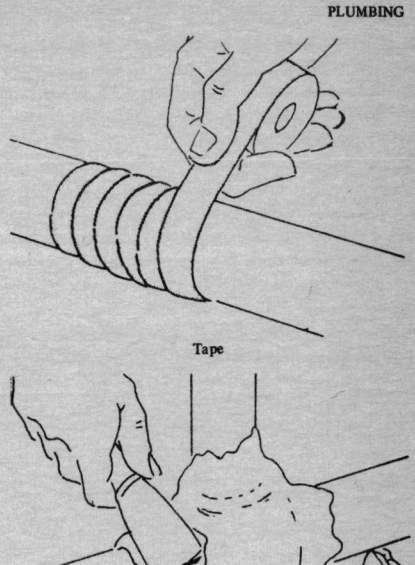

Tape

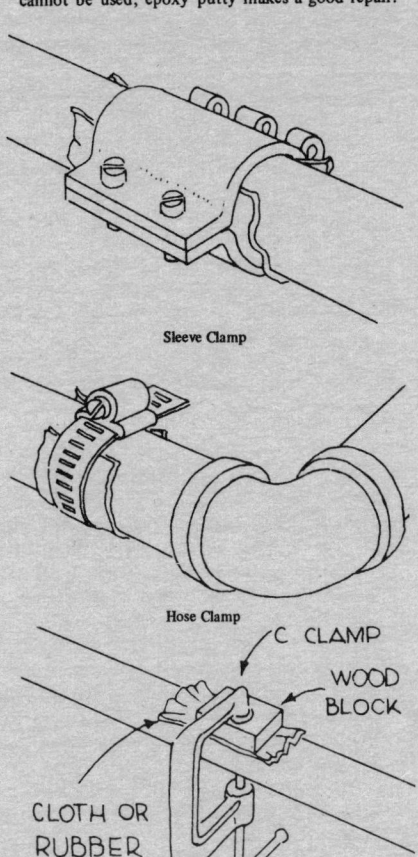

Sleeve Clamp

Epoxy Putty

Hose Clamp

Water pipes can be plugged temporarily, if you do not have any pipe caps on hand. Just press a wooden plug into the end of the pipe, wrapping it with cloth, if necessary, for a tight fit. Then use a C-clamp to hold the plug firmly in place.

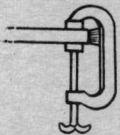

C-2 Clamp

You can effect a good temporary repair on a leaky water pipe if you'll simply cover the leak with a split piece of rubber garden hose, holding this in place with an ordinary hose clamp. For a more permanent repair, of course, drain the pipe and patch it with iron cement.

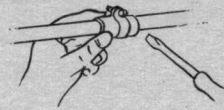

271

Small leaks in water pipes can also be stopped temporarily by wrapping an old leather belt around the pipe. Wrap a wire around this and tighten it with pliers. Then, be sure to call a professional plumber as soon as possible.

Precautions. Polluted water or sewage may carry such diseases as typhoid fever and amoebic dysentery. If you do your own plumbing work, be sure that—

There are no leaks in drainpipes through which sewage or sewage gases can escape.

There are no cross connections between piping carrying water from different sources unless there can be reasonable certainty that all sources are safe and will remain safe.

There can be no back siphonage of water from plumbing fixtures or other containers into the water-supply system.

Once a pipe has become polluted, it may be difficult to free it of the pollution. For this reason, building codes do not permit the use of second-hand pipe. All initial piping and parts and subsequent replacements should be new.

Since a plumbing system will require service from time to time, shutoff valves should be installed at strategic locations so that an affected portion can be isolated (water flow to it cut off) with minimum disturbance to service in the rest of the system. Shutoff valves are usually provided on the water closet supply line, on the hot- and cold-water supply line to each sink, tub, and lavatory, and on the water heater supply line. Drain valves are usually installed for water-supply piping systems and for hot-water storage tanks.

A pressure-relief valve should be installed for the water heater storage tank to relieve pressure buildup in case of overheating.

Septic Tank. A septic tank differs from a cesspool only in design and construction. Its purpose is to decompose solids and treat sewage by bacterial action before it seeps out into the earth. Solids are separated from liquid in the tank and the solids sink to the bottom. Bacterial action then works on this matter to decompose it. The liquid overflows into a series of disposal lines buried in the soil to form a drainage field carrying the water away from the tank.

Septic tanks must be cleaned periodically—work done by professionals.

If you have either a cesspool or a septic tank, you should not pour fats or oil into the drains. Store grease in cans and throw it out with the garbage. Some grease may sneak through, and you should dissolve this at intervals by using a prepared household drain cleaner.

Do not flush heavy paper, rags, coffee grounds or other foreign matter down the drain. Do not connect roof gutters, storm drain, or other large-volume water wastes to the septic tank or cesspool; you should build separate dry wells for them.

Incidentally, detergents are frequently fatal to the bacteria in a septic tank. If the bacteria are killed, the solids cannot be digested and the waste will clog the tank. Do not use detergents if the sink is connected to the septic tank. Connect your sink drain to a cesspool, which can easily take detergents. Drain cleaners also may be fatal to bacteria in the septic tank.

In order to start bacterial action once again in a septic tank if it has been stopped by detergents, run a quantity of water into any of the plumbing fixtures, dissolve yeast in tepid water, and let the mixture drain out into the tank. This should start the action once again.

Shower Head, Clogged. If your shower head is clogged with lime and mineral deposits, try boiling it in one-half cup of vinegar and one quart of water for about fifteen minutes. This will usually make it work like new.

Shower Head, Dripping. If a shower head drips, the supply valve has not been fully closed, or the valve needs repair.

Shutting Off Water. For many plumbing repairs and for emergency purposes, it is neccessary to shut off the water supply to the house or to certain areas in the house. Water pipes are supplied with cock or valves which serve to shut off the flow of water.

Water may be cut off outside the home, and this should be done during the winter months when the house is going to be vacant. This will prevent the freezing of pipes between the cellar wall and the main shut off valve in the cellar.

The main supply of water can be cut off as it enters the house through the main pipe in the basement.

Many houses have shut-off cocks for specific plumbing fixtures or for areas of water supply, such as a bathroom or kitchen. Cut-off valves inside the house control the flow of water to faucets outside the house.

It is important that all members of the family know where the major cut-off valves are located, and it is a good idea to label the valves according to outlet location.

Sink Drain, Clogged, see **Drainpipes, Clogged,** above.

Toilet Bowl Removal. An obstruction in the toilet trap or leakage around the bottom of the toilet bowl may require removal of the bowl. Follow this procedure:

1. Shut off the water.
2. Empty the tank and bowl by siphoning or sponging out the water.
3. Disconnect the water pipes to the tank.
4. Disconnect the tank from the bowl if the toilet is a two-piece unit. Set the tank where it cannot be damaged. Handle tank and bowl carefully; they are made of vitreous china or porcelain and are easily chipped or broken.
5. Remove the seat and cover from the bowl.
6. Carefully pry loose the bolt covers and remove the bolts holding the bowl to the floor flange.
7. Jar the bowl enough to break the seal at the bottom. Set the bowl upside down on something that will not chip or break it.
8. Remove the obstruction from the discharge opening.
9. Piece a new wax seal around the bowl horn and press it into place. A wax seal or gasket may be obtained from hardware or plumbing supply stores.

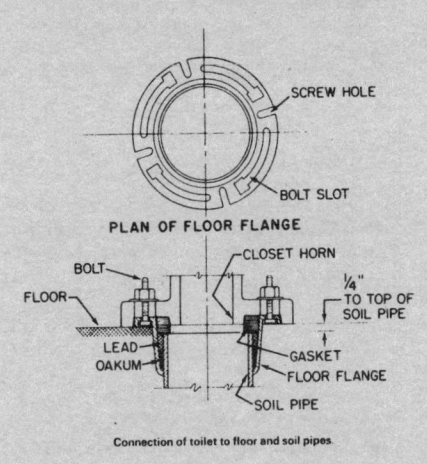

10. Set the bowl in place and press it down firmly. Install the bolts that hold it to the floor flange. Draw the bolts up snugly, but not too tight because the bowl may break. The bowl must be level. Keep a carpenter's level on it while drawing up the bolts. If the house has settled, leaving the floor sloping, it may be necessary to use shims to make the bowl set level. Replace the bolt covers.

11. Install the tank and connect the water pipes to it. It is advisable to replace all gaskets, after first cleaning the surfaces thoroughly.
12. Test for leaks by flushing a few times.
13. Install the seat cover.

Toilet Float Ball Repair. The float ball may develop a leak and fail to rise to the proper position. (Correct water level is about 1 inch below the top of the overflow tube or enough to give a good flush.) If the ball fails to rise, the intake valve will remain open and water will continue to flow. Brass float balls can sometimes be drained and the leak soldered. Other types must be replaced. When working on the float ball, be careful to keep the rod aligned so that the ball will float freely and close the valve properly.

Toilet Flushing Mechanism. Toilets vary in general design and in the design of the flushing mechanism. But they are enough alike that general repair instructions can suffice for all designs.

In areas of corrosive water, the usual copper flushing mechanism may deteriorate in a comparatively short time. In such cases, it may be advisable to replace the corroded part with plastic parts. You can even buy plastic float balls.

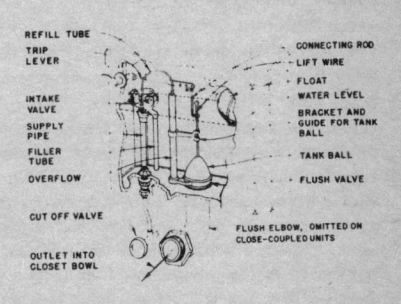

Connection of toilet to floor and soil pipes.

Common type of flushing mechanism. Parts that usually require repair are the flush valve, the intake (float) valve and the float ball.

PLUMBING

Most plumbing codes require a cut off valve in the supply line to the flush tank, which makes it unnecessary to close down the whole system. If this valve was not installed, you can stop the flow of water by propping up the float with a piece of wood. Be careful not to bend the float rod out of alignment.

Toilet Intake Valve Repair. A worn plunger washer in the supply valve will cause the valve to leak. To replace the washer:

1. Shut off the water and drain the tank.

2. Unscrew the two thumbscrews that hold the levers and push out the levers.

3. Lift out the plunger, unscrew the cup on the bottom and insert a new washer. The washer is made of material such as rubber or leather.

4. Examine the washer seat. If nicked or rough, it may need refacing.

If the float valve assembly is badly corroded, replace it.

Toilet, Non-Flushing. A toilet that does not flush is an annoyance that must be cared for immediately, if not for aesthetic reasons at least for hygienic ones.

Remove the top of the tank. Note the floating metal ball that operates the valve filling the tank with water. If the hollow ball has a leak, it will not rise when water flows in and will fail to operate the cut-off mechanism. Replace a leaky ball.

Check the valve washer for wear and replace a worn one.

The flush valve is operated by a rubber ball that drops into a hole in the tank bottom when the water has flowed out; it seals the hole until the tank fills again. This ball may be rotten. If so, replace it with a new one.

Sometimes the wires and arms that hold the float and operate the turn-off mechanism become bent or stuck. Twist them straight, or free them.

Toilet Tank Sweating. When cold water enters a toilet tank, it may chill the tank enough to cause "sweating" (condensation of atmospheric moisture on the outer surface of the tank). This can be prevented by insulating the tank to keep the temperature of the outer surface above the dew point temperature of the surrounding air. Insulating the jackets or liners that fit inside toilet tanks and serve to keep the outer surface warm are available from plumbing supply dealers.

Toilet Trap, Clogged. If the toilet bowl becomes clogged, you'll need to use a closet auger—a large snake-like tool with a hook on the far end that can be turned by a handle at the near end. Insert the hooked end of the auger into the bowl opening at its base, and rotate the handle until the end reaches the trap. Now agitate the auger until you dislodge the obstruction or catch it on the hook of the auger. Remove the obstruction. Empty a pail of water into the bowl. Do not flush it. If the water rushes through, the trap is free.

If the trap is free and the water still backs up, you had better call in a plumber. There is some kind of obstruction farther on in the plumbing and it is unlikely that you can get it out yourself.

Tools, see TOOLS, PLUMBING.

Water Tank, Leaking. Leaks in tanks are usually caused by corrosion. Sometimes a safety valve may fail to open and the pressure developed will spring a leak.

While a leak may occur at only one place in the tank wall, the wall may also be corroded thin in other places. Therefore, any repair should be considered as temporary, and the tank should be replaced as soon as possible.

You must first ascertain the thickness of the metal in the leaky tank before you can start to repair it. If the metal is thick enough for you to cut a minimum of four inner threads with a pipe tap, simply drill an enlarged hole, cut threads in the hole with the pipe tap, and screw in a standard-size pipe plug into the enlarged hole.

If the tank is made of thinner metal, enlarge the hole with a tapered steel punch. Hold the punch at a 90-degree angle, and drive it in with a hammer to

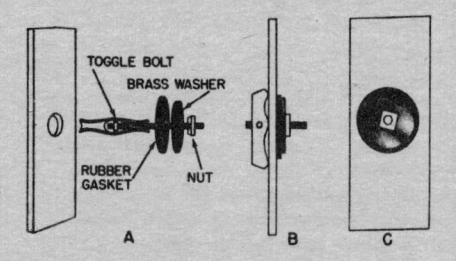

Closing a hole in a tank: A, The link of the toggle bolt is passed through the hole in the tank (hole is enlarged if necessary). B, Side view of tank edge (nut is drawn up tightly to compress washer and gasket against tank). C, Outside view of completed repair.

form a recess deep enough to permit the cutting of four threads. Thread the hole with a pipe plug as above.

If you do not have a pipe tap, you can get special repair kits with the necessary plugs, bolts, gaskets, and other parts you will need. The advantage of these kits is that they eliminate the necessity of threading the enlarged hole. You simply drill a hole in the tank until it is large enough to permit the turned head of a toggle bolt to be slipped through; then you place the head of the bolt at right angles to the threaded bolt, which receives and holds a gasket, a washer, and a nut. Complete instructions come with the kit.

Water Tank Noise. Rumbling noise in a hot water tank is a sign of possible overheating which could lead to the development of explosive pressure. (Another indication of overheating is hot water backing up in the cold-water supply pipe.) Cut off the burner immediately. Be sure that the pressure-relief valve is operative. Then check (with a thermometer) the temperature of the water at the nearest outlet. If above that for which the gage is set, check the thermostat that controls burner cutoff. If you cannot correct the trouble, call a plumber.

Plunger, see TOOLS, PLUMBING.

Plywood. For the home repairman trying to do the job as simply as possible at the least cost plywood is a life-saver. It is tough, easy to work, and available everywhere. In most cases, it will serve your purposes better than regular lumber. Here is why.

Makeup. Plywood is wood made up of an odd number of veneer sheets glued together, the layers at right angles to one another. Because of its crossply lamination, it has strength across the grain as well as lengthwise. With half the wood grain in one direction, and the other half at right angles, plywood shrinks or swells less in the direction at right angles to the grain of the face ply. The impact of a blow is dissipated over the whole surface of the panel. Nails and screws can be placed with less chance of splitting the wood. Plywood can be worked easily because of its freedom from chipping and breaking. It has excellent insulating qualities and can be bent for special uses.

Types. Plywood comes in two basic types: exterior and interior. The difference lies in the durability of the adhesives employed. You should never use exterior inside, or interior outside.

Classes. Plywood comes in hardwood and softwood classes. The outer layer, called the "face veneer" determines the class.

Softwood. For softwood plywood, there are six grades of quality. H, A, B, C, C (plugged), and D. All panels are stamped for grading and type (EXT or INT.) A panel marked A-A has the highest standard quality veneer on both face and back panels. A-B means there is A appearance on the face panel, B on the back. For average use in home repair, where only one side will be seen, you should use A-C or A-D paneling.

Hardwood. Hardwood ply is generally used for desks, wall covering, cabinets, and other fine work. Hardwood face veneers are frequently cut to accentuate their natural beauty. You've probably seen a great deal of hardwood face veneers in newly built homes and in offices. It's the easiest kind of surface to maintain in the home. You can buy prefinished hardwood paneling in plywood and nail it in place or fix it with adhesive to your existing wall surface. You can get a great variety of finishes.

Generally speaking, you should shop for plywood with the following in mind: For a paint finish, "Sound" or B-grade plywood is adequate. However, if you want a natural-wood effect, you must get "good" or A-grade face. In both cases, use "utility" grade for backs and concealed areas. You can save a bundle of money by knowing exactly what to shop for.

Sawing. Before sawing plywood, it's a good idea to score both sides of the sheet along the line to be cut

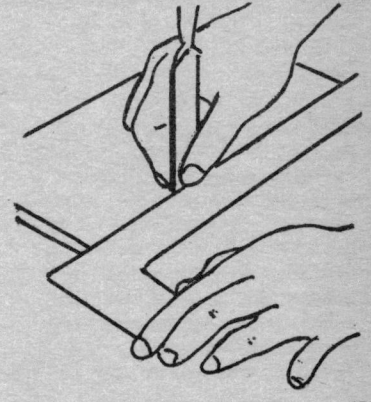

PLYWOOD

with a sharp chisel or knife. This scoring should be deep enough to separate the top layer of veneer. This helps avoid splintering and splitting of the wood. Another way to prevent splitting is to press a layer of cellophane tape along the cutting line on the bottom side of the panel. A fine-toothed saw is best for cutting plywood.

The sawing of plywood always presents the problem of controlling the splintering of the wood on the bottom side. One easy way to prevent this is to apply a strip of cellophane tape along the underside of the cut you are planning. Then, after sawing through this, you can strip the tape from the wood, and you will have a nice, smooth cut.

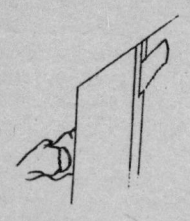

To prevent kerf splintering when sawing a plywood panel, try putting a thin scrap of lumber under the plywood panel and cutting it along with the plywood. Hold your saw at a low angle, and if you have trouble with it binding in the plywood, hold the kerf open with a screwdriver blade as you saw.

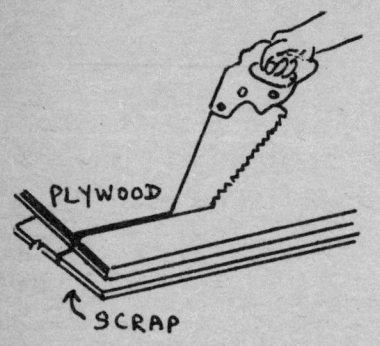

When you are cutting a large sheet of plywood or hardboard with a handsaw, the severed pieces will not bind your saw if the material is placed on a two-by-four braced against a wall, as illustrated. This support will prevent the plywood or hardboard from bending, and thus insure you a better and easier job.

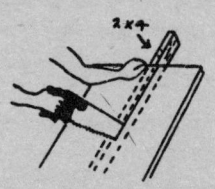

If you've ever had a beautifully veneered panel of plywood spoiled because the saw splintered the veneer on the underside of the cut, here are a couple of hints that will help you on future jobs. Square the line across the panel where it is to be cut, and over this apply a length of cellophane tape, as in Figure 1 of the illustration. This tape will hold just enough to keep the veneer from splintering. Another good way to avoid splintering is shown in Figure 2. The veneer is heavily scored with a sharp knife along the line. When sawing, it is important to saw just to the line. The scored side of the panel should be down. If the panel is being sawed by hand, the scored side will still be down, and another line squared across the upper side of the panel to guide the saw.

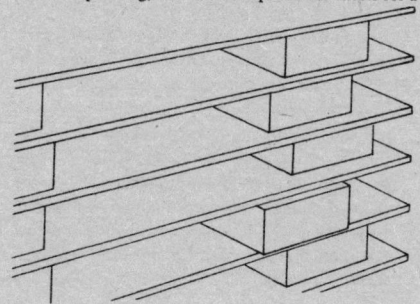

Stacking Plywood Panels. When you receive your wood paneling, it is wise to separate the sheets for a few days by putting furring strips between them. Before you start your installation, make a final check to see that the corners are square and that everything is plumb.

Plywood Edges, see CARPENTRY.

Plywood Wall Construction, see BASEMENT FINISHING.

Pocketbook Care, see CLOTHES CARE.

Pocket Knife, see TOOLS, HAND.

Pocket Reinforcement, see CLOTHES CARE.

Poison Ivy, see GARDENING.

Polish.
  Applicators.
    1. *Felt.* An economical and useful polisher can be made by tacking a piece of felt around an old broom.
    If the felt is too fluffy to be effective, cover it with an old piece of silk or linen and the floor may be polished quickly and easily without stooping.
    2. *Lambswool.* A new lambswool shoe-polishing brush makes a fine buffer for your tablestops after you have waxed them.
    3. *Newspaper.* You can keep glass coffee table tops and mirrors gleaming with a minimum amount of work by wiping them with a dampened newspaper, then polishing with a dry one. This leaves no lint.
    4. *Powder Puffs.* Old powder puffs, which have been laundered well, make excellent applicators for shoe polish, paste-wax, and other such commodities.
    5. *Velvet.* Save old velvet garments and tear them into pieces to use as polishing cloths. This is especially good for polishing highly finished furniture, because they do not leave lint on the surface.
  Emergency Silver. If you happen to be out of silver polish, and your forks and spoons are tarnished from egg, use some toothpaste or powder.
  Excess. In the event that too much oil polish has collected on furniture, mix 1/4-cup of vinegar with 1/2-cup of water, dip a soft cloth into this, and rub the furniture with it. Dry immediately with a soft cloth.

Furniture. Before embarking on the job of polishing furniture, place the bottle of polish in a pan of hot water for a while. Warm polish has a way of penetrating the wood pores faster, and will perform a faster, better job.
Homemade Furniture. Mix your own furniture polish by adding two tablespoons of olive oil and one tablespoon of vinegar to a quart of warm water. Keep this solution warm while using. It will wash off dirt and dust, and leave a light oil treatment on the wood. Rub dry with a clean, soft cloth.
Metal. A stick of ordinary blackboard chalk proves a very capable substitute for regular metal polish. Just rub a little soft-grade chalk onto a dry or damp cloth and apply to the metal surface that needs polishing. There is just enough abrasive quality to the chalk to remove dirt and grease without scratching, and it leaves a nice gloss finish on the metal.

Polish, Furniture, see FURNITURE, CLEANING AND POLISHING.

Polished Cotton, see CLOTHES CARE.

Polyester, see FIBERS, MAN-MADE.

Pool Chair, see CHAIR MAKING.

Pool Repair, see CONCRETE REPAIR.

Pool Table Repair. If the cloth on the cushions of your pool table has become worn, it can be repaired with adhesive tape so that the latter does not show. First cut the tape to size, then work it under the tear in the cloth with the adhesive side towards the cloth. Next, carefully pull the torn edges of the cloth together and press firmly against the tape.

Popcorn, see FOODS.

PORCELAIN ENAMEL REPAIR

Porcelain Enamel Repair. Several prepared porcelain repair kits can be bought from paint and hardware stores. The epoxy resin type consisting of two tubes is the most durable. All these repair materials have detailed instructions for use and it is essential to follow these closely. It's especially important that the entire area to be patched be thoroughly cleaned of all grease and soap residues. Allow to dry thoroughly before applying the patching material.

If there are some chipped spots on the enamel surface of your stove or refrigerator, you can improve the situation considerably by dabbing the chipped spots with clear nail polish and finely-ground zinc white, procurable at a hardware store.

One usually satisfactory and simple method of repairing a chipped spot on the refrigerator is to lay a small piece of matching-color wax crayon on the spot, cover with cellophane, then press gently over this with a iron set at rayon heat. When cool, remove the cellophane.

Porcelain Enamel, Stains on, see STAIN REMOVAL.

Porch Painting, see PAINTING EXTERIOR.

Portable Circular Saw, see TOOLS, POWER.

Portable Cooker. You can make your outdoor and camp cooking a much easier job with the construction of this simple device: Procure at your hardware store four steel strips about 40 inches long and an inch or so wide. Bend these in your vise as illustrated, to form legs, the two longest of which are about eight inches long. Bend the top, or longest, strip first—the other three correspondingly shorter so as to fit inside each other. Then drill a hole in the top center of each, fasten in a bolt, and you will have a cooking rack that is easy to carry and adjusts to fit any size pan.

Postage, Return. The best way to send a stamp in a letter for return postage is to attach it by a small spot in its center, leaving the glue around the edges untouched.

Postal Scale. Oftentimes at home, one is very much in doubt as to whether a second postage stamp is required for a heavier-than-usual letter. At such times, it is possible to improvise a surprisingly accurate postage scales, just by balancing a one-foot rule across a hexagonal pencil. Place this "scale" on a flat surface and use two half-dollar coins or four quarters as weights, centering them over the two-inch mark on the rule—the letter over the 10-inch mark. For 1/2-ounce air mail to overseas destinations, use one half-dollar or two quarters.

Potatoes, see FOODS.

Pots, see ALUMINUMWARE, ENAMELWARE CARE, PANS.

Pottery.
  Chipped. As soon as a small chip is noticed in that white pottery lamp, vase, or statue, coat the roughtened surface with some clear nailpolish. Sealed in this way, the exposed porous clay won't absorb dust and stains which would make the chip very conspicuous in a short time.
  Waterproof. If the inside glaze of a pottery flower bowl is imperfect and moisture forms on the outside, warm the pottery with hot water, and wipe. Then pour into it a few spoonfuls of melted paraffin and turn and tip the vessel until the whole interior is coated.

Potting Plants, see GARDENING.

Poultry, see FOODS.

Pouring Technique. When there is no funnel at hand, here's an oldtime trick that's still good for pouring of liquids into small openings—especially such liquids as cleaning fluid, gasoline, and alcohol. Just take an ordinary wooden matchstick, and lay it across the opening in the can or bottle from which you are pouring. Clamp down on the match with your forefinger and pour slowly. Hold the receptacle directly under the end of the match, and the fluid will run right down the match in a thin stream. This is particularly good for filling cigarette lighters.

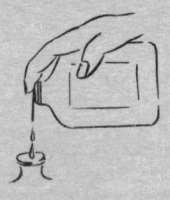

A string, a large nail or a pointed pencil held across the opening before pouring will achieve the same effect.

When pouring liquids, such as turpentine or shellac, from a square can which has an opening in one corner, it's best to hold the can so that the opening or spout is at the top while the can is in pouring position. This enables air to enter freely above the liquid, giving a steady, easy-to-control stream which will not gurgle or splash.

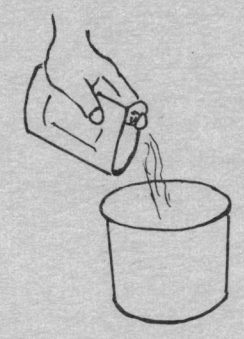

Make two holes in a can of liquid to acquire speed in pouring. One hole is for the liquid to pour out and the other to allow air in as the liquid comes out.

Powdered Pumice, see ABRASIVES.

Power Tools, see TOOLS, POWER.

Prefabricated Closets, see CLOSETS.

Primer, see PAINTS.

Pruning, see GARDENING.

Pumice Applicator. An inexpensive blackboard eraser makes a very efficient pad, when rubbing down a finish with pumice. It will do the job faster and more easily than a felt pad usually used for this type of work. Its still back provides a more comfortable grip and prevents the curling commonly experienced when using the ordinary felt pads.

Pumpkin Pie, see FOODS.

Pushbroom Repair. To reinforce the handle of a pushbroom at the point where it's traditionally the weakest and to hold the handle in despite worn threads, a couple of angle irons do a good job. Use wood screws in the brush head, and drill the handle for a bolt and wing nut.

To prevent the handle of a pushbroom from working loose, place an ordinary hose washer on the threaded end before screwing it into the head.

Putty.

Application. When spreading putty around a newly-installed pane of window glass, the job can be speeded up if you'll first roll the putty into long strips about as big around as a pencil, then press

PUTTY KNIFE

each one into position against the glass with the fingers, and smooth off with a putty knife.

Coloring. To avoid the tiresome task of touching up putty after it has dried, or possibly forgetting it altogether, mix with it a little paint of the same color as that of the windowframes.

Handling. Fresh putty sometimes has an annoying tendency to stick to the hands when using for filling nail holes in exterior woodwork or for replacing broken window glass. You can prevent this by rubbing a little flour on your hands before starting.

Preservation. Putty often hardens when the previously uncapped and used tube has been stored too long. The next time you uncap one of these tubes you can guard against its hardening later by storing the partially used tube inside a screw-top jar. This double-sealing of the tubes usually keeps their contents in soft and usable condition.

Removal.

1. *Lacquer Thinner.* Old, dry, and hardened putty sometimes proves very difficult to strip off and remove. You can make the job much easier if you'll coat the old putty with some lacquer thinner. Use a small brush for this job, and apply enough thinner to soak the putty. Then, after a few minutes for the thinner to penetrate the putty, you'll be able to lift it off easily with a sharp chisel or putty knife.

2. *Rubber Cement.* When installing new window glass, remove the old putty by spreading a thin film of rubber cement over it, then touch a match to it, and when the flame dies down the softened putty will peel off readily.

Softening. You can soften up dry or hardened putty to usable consistency by mixing well with a few drops of linseed oil.

Storing. When storing leftover putty, work in some linseed oil, place the putty in a plastic bag, close out as much of the air as you can, then seal tightly.

Substitutes.

1. A satisfactory substitute for putty, when only a small amount is needed to finish a job, can be provided by a mixture of talcum powder and linseed oil. Mix these two ingredients to a putty-like consistency, and apply in the usual way. A stick of chalk, ground to powder, can be used instead of talcum, if you don't have any of the latter.

2. If you don't have any putty on hand to fill in the nail holes in a wall you are about to paint, just rub a cake of wet soap over the holes until they are filled. Let this dry, then paint the wall for beautiful results.

Putty Knife, see TOOLS, HAND.

Putty, Painting, see PAINTING TIPS.

Q

Quadrant Molding, see MOLDING.

R

Radiant Heating, see HEATING.

Radiation, see HEAT THEORY.

Radiators, see HEATING.

Radio, see APPLIANCES.

Radishes, see FOODS.

Rafters, see ROOF STRUCTURE.

Rag Rugs, see RUGS.

Rails, Crossrails, see DOOR REPAIR, DOORS.

Rain Bonnet. To keep your head dry in snowy or rainy weather, iron your scarves between two sheets of waxed paper. This waterproofs the scarves and prevents the water from soaking into and through them.

Rake, see GARDEN TOOLS.

Rattail File, see TOOLS, HAND.

Rattan Furniture, see FURNITURE CARE.

Rayon, see FIBERS, MAN-MADE.

Rayon Brightening, see CLOTHES CARE.

Razor Blade.
  Cork Handle. Make a handle for a razor blade to use in ripping by slipping a large slotted cork over one edge of the blade. The cork provides a convenient handle and affords adequate protection to your fingers.
  Sharpening. You can give a new lease on life to some of the razor blades you would otherwise be discarding. As soon as they become dull and begin pulling on your whiskers, lay them one at a time on the inside edge of a glass tumbler, and rub back and forth a few times. This works very well for rehoning the edges of the blades to shaving sharpness.

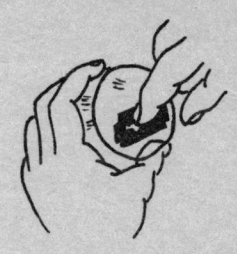

  Storage.
    1. A single-edged razor blade is an invaluable cutting tool for many odd jobs around the home and workbench, but when it is not in use it can be a real hazard — unless that sharp edge is covered. Slip the blade into a squeeze-type paper clip, as in the

illustration, and hang it up on a convenient hook or nail until the next time you need it.

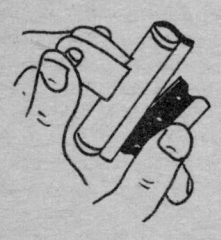

2. A single-edged razor is a very handy tool around the workshop but it does present a problem sometimes so far as storage is concerned. You can solve this by cutting a deep V-notch in a large cork and gluing this to the wall or other convenient spot near your workbench. Your blade is then always handy — and safe.

Recipe File. When you snip recipes from newspapers or magazines, paste them on three by five index cards and file in categories. A shoe box makes a good filing cabinet for these cards.

Record Cabinet. Here is a very attractive and usable record cabinet you can construct yourself — one that should keep that precious record collection of yours in very good order. The cabinet illustrated has an over-all height of 34 inches, a width of 20 inches, and a depth of 15 inches. The top and middle shelves are 13 inches apart, and the divided-section at the bottom is 17-1/2 inches high. For added attractiveness, there is a two-inch recessed pedestal base.

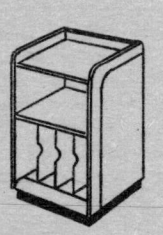

Do some of your precious record albums have the annoying habit of toppling over whenever some of them are removed from the shelf? You can prevent this simply by gluing a sheet of corrugated cardboard inside the back of your cabinet. The ridges in the cardboard will hold the albums erect.

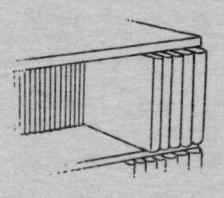

Records.

Cleaning. Remove fingerprints, grease and dirt from phonograph records by wiping with some cotton that has been moistened in a weak solution of soap and water. Finally, wipe the surface with plain water.

Identification. When your records are to be mixed with others at a big party, you can make their identification easier this way. Dip a thin brush sparingly into quick-drying enamel, and brush a double stripe down the edge of your stacked-up records, taking care that no paint seeps in between the records. Then each record will have two identifying dots on its edge.

Warped.

1. Warped phonograph records can be flattened out under the even heat of an infrared lamp. Place

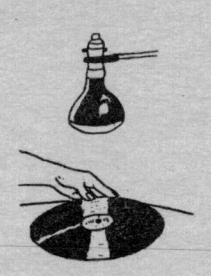

the disk either on a turntable or on a felt-covered surface, and let the beam from the lamp play over it for about five minutes. The record, when warm, will usually straighten out itself, but you may help the leveling-out process with a little gentle pressure. Be sure to guard against uneven or excessive heating, which could damage your records!

2. To straighten out a warped phonograph record, place it between two pieces of glass and set it where the sun will shine on it for an hour or two.

Reed Furniture, see FURNITURE CARE.

Refinishing Furniture, see FURNITURE REFINISHING.

Reflection, see LIGHT REFLECTANCES.

Reflective Insulation, see INSULATION.

Reflectors, see LIGHT REFLECTORS.

Refrigerators, see APPLIANCES.

Refrigerator Storage Guide, see FOODS.

Resilient tile floors can be composed of asphalt tile, rubber tile, vinyl and vinyl asbestos tile, and of linoleum. All these types are bonded to the floor with mastic, either directly or over a layer of felt.

Asphalt Tile Floor. Asphalt tile is a mixture of asbestos fibers, lime rock, inert fillers, and colored pigments with an asphalt or resin binder. The tile is very brittle and, like linoleum, is bonded to the floor with mastic either directly or over a layer of felt. Sometimes a plywood subflooring is used to provide a smooth surface.

It has poor resistance to grease but excellent resistance to surface alkali; fair recovery from indentation. Can be used anywhere. Some change in color with wear; dark colors change more than light.

Asphalt Tile Floor Cleaning. Most soaps contain materials that form an emulsion when they come in contact with the component parts of the asphalt tile which weakens the tile. That is why a synthetic liquid detergent which does not contain soap is used. Water seeping between seams can loosen the binding between the tiles and subfloor. Use water sparingly and remove immediately during cleaning operations.

Solvents and oils also attack asphalt tile, causing it to break down. NEVER use solvent-type liquid waxes and cleaners or solvent paste wax. Use a water emulsion resin finish.

Alcohol dropped on an asphalt tile floor causes little white patches. They can be removed by rubbing in a little baby oil or olive oil.

Asphalt Tile Removal. To remove damaged asphalt tiles from a finished floor without damaging those tiles adjacent to it, use an ordinary electric iron. Lay a sheet of paper over the damaged tiles to protect the iron, heat thoroughly until the tile becomes soft and pliable. It can then be pried up easily with a wide putty knife after one corner has been cut away with a sharp knife.

Installation. A good way to save money if you find that your floor surface needs replacing is to lay a new one, either over the present floor, if it is truly a flat surface, or over an underlayment of plywood. The easiest way to do this, and the cheapest, is to replace the old floor with a resilient-tile floor. The tiles come in 9-inch or 12-inch squares, and are simply attached, one by one, to the surface with mastic supplied by the tile manufacturer.

The surface to be used as the base of a resilient tile floor must be smooth and flat. If you plan to lay the tile on concrete, wash it first to remove all grease or oil stains. If you plan to lay it on a wooden subfloor, be sure the surface is flat and smooth by planing and sanding all irregularities. If the old floor is unsatisfactory, lay a plywood underlayment over it.

Some tiles come with felt bottoms, but others need felt paper cemented to the surface below. Follow the instructions the manufacturer gives.

Remove all baseboards before starting to lay tile. When floor is completely laid, replace the baseboards.

Step-by-step installation procedure:

1. Determine the middle of both ends of room and strike a line through these points which will give you center line AA. Find the center of line AA, which gives point B. Measure 4' from point B along line AA, which is point C. 3' from point B at a 90-degree angle to line AA, swing an arc at D. Swing a 5' arc from point C through arc D. Snap a chalk line through the intersection of the two arcs at point D, through point B, which is line EE.

RESILIENT TILE FLOORS

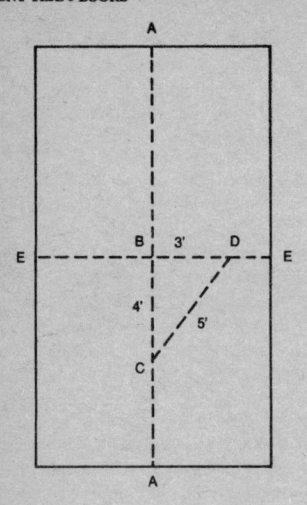

2. To determine the width of a border, lay a row of loose tiles across the room from wall to wall. The space between the last tile and the baseboard will constitute the border width for the room. **Dividing this distance in half will result in the exact width of the border on either side of the room.** Should this width be too narrow, deduct one tile from the layout and add the dimension of the tile to the double border width before dividing. Repeat this operation in the other direction of the room.

3. Spread cement over lines AA and EE approximately 1' wide, leaving portions of the lines at intersection and ends open. Allow set-up time for adhesive and resnap chalk lines over cemented surface.

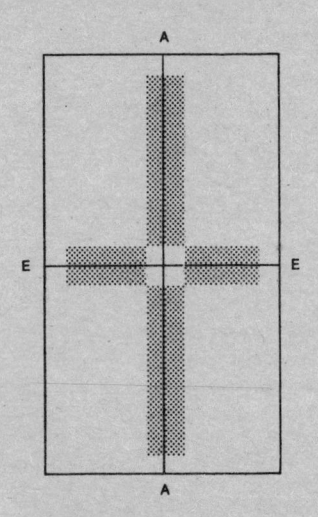

Spreading Cement on Center Lines

4. Spread cement over one-half of area and allow set-up time before starting installation of tile. Count the tiles in each row. If there is an even number of tiles, the two tiles in the center of each row, (tiles 1 and 2 and tiles 2 and 3) should meet exactly in center lines. If there is an odd number of tiles, the edges of the middle tile should fall at equal distances from the center lines. Install the tile in somewhat of a semi-circle around the first tile. It is important to remember the center lines are guide lines and must be followed or else the "field" will not square. After the entire field has been laid, then lay border tile.

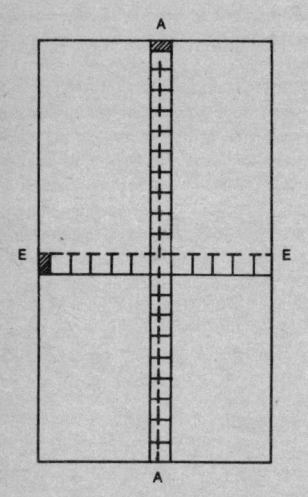

Arranging Tiles on Center Lines

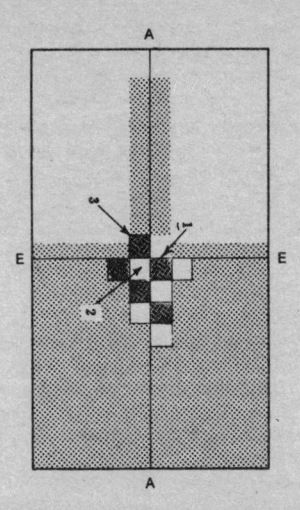

Spreading Cement and Installing Tile

5. To fit tile for border, place a loose tile X in exact position over tile adjacent to border. Place tile Y on top of tile X. Butt tile Y against wall or cabinet. Draw line on tile X. Cut the X to size required.

Follow same procedure in fitting each piece of border tile. Since tile Y will get dirty, use it over and over.

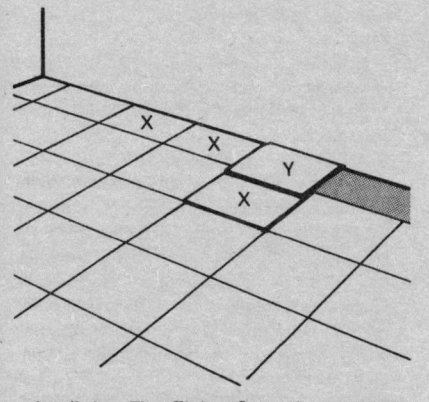

Installation Tip. Fitting floor tiles individually around pipes, door casings, and other obstructions can be a messy job when the floor has been coated with mastic. One tip worth remembering is to first lay a piece of wax paper over the sticky mastic, and this will permit you to cut and try your tiles for good fits without getting it smeared with cement. Since the mastic will not cling to the wax paper, it can be removed easily.

Linoleum, see LINOLEUM FLOORS.

Rubber Tile Floor. Rubber tile, sometime containing asbestos fibers, is colored by mineral pigments. Rubber tile is seriously affected by *oils* and *solvents*, strong soaps, and *alkalies*. It has good resistance to grease; good resistance to surface alkali; excellent recovery from indentation; quiet.

Rubber Tile Removal. Old rubber tile that is embedded in water-proof cement can be removed by laying a damp cloth over it and heating with a warm electric iron for a minute or two. Then free the tile with a spatula. Remove the remaining cement with sandpaper on a rubber pad in a portable drill. Use a chisel and hammer near any remaining tiles to avoid scoring.

Vinyl Tile Floor. Vinyl and vinyl asbestos tile floors are resistant to water, acids, alkalies, grease, and oil. They can be *damaged* by seepage of water between the tiles which loosens them from the subflooring.

Waxing. When waxing resilient floors — such as linoleum, vinyl, cork, rubber, or asphalt — thin coats of wax are best. Spread the wax so thin you'll wonder how it can protect the surface at all. Two or three thin coats are recommended for best wear results. When a wax coating is applied too thickly, the top of the film hardens but the wax under the surface remains soft. Such a deposit of wax catches the dirt, but gives very little protection to the floor.

Rice, see FOODS.

Rings, see JEWELRY.

Rip Saw, see TOOLS, HAND.

RIVET REMOVAL

Rivet Removal. The old way of removing rivets with a hammer and cold chisel is not nearly so easy as using an electric drill. Center-punch the head of the rivet and select a drill the same size as the rivet. Drill just through the head, the rivet can then be punched out without damaging the hole, which generally happens when the head is cut off.

Rivets are one-headed nails that become two-headed after securing two pieces of material together. A rivet gun enables you to rivet light goods together like leather and wood, or leather and leather. You insert the rivet from the back of the material, with the head pulled tight; you then activate the trigger of the rivet gun and the gun forms a new head on the headless end of the rivet as it releases it.

Roach Extermination, see INSECTS.

Rock Cornish Game Hens, see FOODS.

Rockwall, see DRYWALL.

Roller Skate Cleaning. If the action of your roller skates is sluggish, remove the wheels and soak them in kerosene to remove dust, dirt, and gummy grease in the bearings. Then fill the bearing sleeve with some petroleum jelly and replace the wheels.

Rollers, Paint, see PAINT ROLLERS.

Rolls, see FOODS.

Roof Flashing. One of the most vulnerable portions of any roof is the flashing, the metal stripping used to protect joints where two roof surfaces join, where roof and dormer join, where roof and chimney join, or where roof and vent pipes join.

Flashing is made out of some type of rust-proof metal—copper or aluminum usually—or sometimes galvanized iron. However, rust-proof or not, the flashing may rust through. If you are troubled by leaks near the flashing, check the metal for rust, and then look around the flashing where it fits under the roofing paper, shingles, or shakes. Flashing attached to a roof and a chimney may be intact; the leak may be in the masonry of the chimney.

If the flashing has pulled away from the surface of the roofing, brush on a heavy layer of roof cement or roof coating after you clean the surface of dust and grit. Cover the patch with a piece of heavy roofing paper. Spread a second layer of roof coating over this.

If the flashing must be replaced, pry up the shingles or the roofing paper from 6 to 8 inches from the edge and insert the flashing in under it. Coat the bottom edge with asphalt-roofing cement or tar, and then nail the shingles through the flashing and into the sheathing beneath.

Roof, Flat. Generally a flat roof is covered with roll roofing paper; this type of surface is called a built-up roof. It consists of several layers of heavy roofing felt cemented to a solid roof sheathing with tar, asphalt, or a similar material. The top surface is covered with a crushed mineral-like gravel to take wear and tear and to protect the roofing from the direct rays of the sun.

Leaks. The leaks you are liable to find in a built-up roof are generally caused by blisters and cracks in the paper. Blisters can be caused by nails that have worked loose at the seams, or they may be caused by roofing material that has begun to dry out too much.

You can locate leaks in a flat roof by searching out loose nails, blistered sections of roofing, and dried out and cracked areas. Check for openings where seams overlap or where the roof meets flashing around vents, pipes, or corners.

Repair.

1. Blisters. Slit a blister with an X cut. Remove all sediment and force roofing cement into the hole. Press the paper down flat and keep weights on it while it dries out.

2. Large Blisters. If the blister to be patched is an extremely large one, cut out a section of roofing paper around it all the way down to the sheathing. Cut out a patch of brand new paper that will fit the square you have removed, and cement this down, then nail it tightly. Add more layers, cementing and nailing each until you get up to the surface of the roof around the patch. Cut out a large patch, cover it with roofing compound, and nail it on top. Apply a final layer of cement over all nails and over all edges.

3. Loose Nails. Hammer down all loose nails. Do not hit so hard that the hammer cuts into the surface of the roofing material. After the nail is

pounded in, cover the head with a liberal application of roofing cement, otherwise the nail will rust and disintegrate.

Roofing Nails, see NAILS.

Roof Inspection. A pair of binoculars is a useful item to have when you wish to inspect roofs for defective gutterings, chimneys, loose slates or tiles, etc. Your inspection can be carried out from the ground.

Roof, Laying, see ROOF SURFACES.

Roof, Leaking. A hole in a roof can be costly, for many items of furniture and clothing may be ruined by the water. You must try to locate the leak immediately. The best way is to trace the water back along the ceiling or wall where it first appears, and then poke a thin wire through the hole when you find it.

On the roof outside, find the wire, and lift up the shingles, or roofing paper, apply a new strip of roofing paper over the damaged section, slip roofing cement under the paper, and press it in tightly. You can repair leaky asphalt roofs by applying roofing tar under the edges of the shingles and pressing them in place.

Even if you decide not to risk the repair yourself, it is essential that you trace the leak to find out where it is immediately. If the rain stops, make an artificial storm yourself with a garden hose, and watch the ceiling for moisture.

Roof Repair, see ROOF SURFACES.

Roof Safety. When making repairs to a roof, you must pay attention to several important safety factors.

Always wear tennis shoes or shoes with soft rubber soles when you are roof walking. You not only protect yourself from slipping, but you protect the surface of the roof as well.

If possible, never walk erect, for a sudden gust of wind or rain may bowl you over. Keep your center of gravity as close to the roof as possible at all times.

Fashion a temporary catwalk along a steep slope by laying a section of ladder flat on the roof from the peak on down. Tie a rope to the top rung, throw the rope over the peak, and anchor it to a tree or something solid on the far side.

Roof Structure. It's a good idea to know a little about the fundamentals of roof structure before you begin to try roof repairs on your house. Such knowledge can help you avoid possible costly mistakes.

There are two kinds of roofs: flat roofs and pitched or peaked roofs. Flat roofs appear in more temperate climes and are usually covered with built-up roofing or metal. Peaked roofs, also called shed roofs, are surfaced with shingles of all kinds and sometimes roll roofing paper and metal. Usually they appear in more northerly climes.

No matter what kind of roof you have—flat or peaked—the outer surfacing is held up from the ceiling inside the house by framing timbers called rafters, usually 2 by 6 pieces or better. In a flat roof, the rafter runs from the top plate of one wall to the top plate of the opposite wall. In a peak roof the two slopes, or sheds, are held up by common rafters. Each of the common rafters runs from the top plate of the wall to the peak, or ridge rafter. Attached to the rafters are strips of roof sheathing, or plywood sheathing, to which the finish surface is applied.

In a flat-roofed house the rafter that holds the roof surface may also hold the ceiling surface below. In a peak-roofed house the rafters form the peak of a triangle, and the base of the triangle supports the ceiling.

Depending on the span of the roof, the weight of the roof material, the expected snow and wind loads, and so on, the rafters may be 2 by 6, 2 by 8, or more. Most roof rafters, like wall studs, are placed 16 inches on center, or 16 inches apart.

Sheathing may be ship-lap lumber, tongue-and-groove lumber, or plywood. Between the roofing surface and the sheathing a thickness of felt building paper may be placed for added insurance against leakage.

Roof Surfaces.
Asbestos Shingles, see Cement-Asbestos Shingles, below.
Asphalt-prepared roll roofing is used for both pitched roofs and for flat roofs. It comes in 36-inch rolls and is rolled on in strips which overlap 4 inches. Overlaps are blind-nailed and cemented.

ROOF SURFACES

Asphalt shingles come in strip-shingle form, or in individual shingle form. Asphalt shingle strips are constructed so that when laid on, each gives the appearance of being three separate smaller shingles. You insert the nails so that each of the three shingles is held by two nails.

1. *Laying.* To lay a roof of asphalt shingles, start at the eaves, laying one strip parallel to them, working from left to right nailing the first strip with 6 nails just above the bottom border of the second overlapping row. Leave 3/4 of an inch between strips.

Continue the course along the eave. Cut the last strip at the right end to fit. Lay the second course so that the shingles overlap in the middle, that is, so that the spaces separating the three shingles are staggered from row to row. Embed the shingle strip over any flashing in quick-setting asphalt cement. Do not nail through the flashing. Continue the courses to the ridge.

2. *Rejuvenation.* To rejuvenate asphalt shingles and roll roofing surfaces, brush in a special compound that keeps the shingles from drying out and becoming brittle. You can get this compound at your hardward dealers or building supply house.

3. *Repair.* To repair a damaged asphalt strip, lift the shingle in the second course above the damaged shingle. Pull out all the nails in the first course above the damaged shingle. Lift the shingles in the first course above, and withdraw all the nails in the damaged strip and remove it completely. Insert a new strip of shingle the same size and style as the old. Paint the edges of the new shingle with asphalt cement to keep it secure from the wind. Nail the new shingle strip down. Renail the two overlapping strips.

To secure loose asphalt shingles, squeeze roofing cement in under the free ends. Weight the shingles down with bricks or stones while they are drying.

If you have no replacement for a damaged asphalt shingle, slide a sheet of aluminum, copper, or galvanized iron under the torn shingle. The piece should be wider than the ruined shingle. Tap it upward until it extends under the next course of shingles above the damaged one. The metal will protect all the other shingles around it.

Built-up roofing is used on relatively flat slopes of less than 2 inches per foot, or on flat roofs.

Cement-asbestos shingles are much stiffer than asphalt shingles, and are considered to be rigid roofing. They usually come in 12-inch by 24-inch rectangles and are laid individually.

Repair. Are some of the asbestos shingles on your roof broken at the corners? You can make them look as good as new by gluing the broken pieces back into place with white or matching calking compound.

Flat tiles can be used on pitched roofs in parts of the country not subject to snow or ice.

Galvanized iron sheets, usually in corrugated form, can be used for roof surfaces, too, although the effect is not particularly an esthetic one.

Sheet copper roofs are made of 16-ounce copper. The sections of copper have to be soldered together and must be arranged in such a fashion that there is room for expansion and contraction.

Slate shingles are nailed to the sheathing of pitched roofs and are the most permanent type of rigid roofing material.

Spanish tiles can be used on pitched roofs in parts of the country not subject to snow or ice.

Wood shingles are usually made of cedar and are sometimes called shakes. They should be stained or treated with creosote. They are nailed to the sheathing.

1. *Laying New Roof.* If there are too many broken shingles in the roof, you may find it advisable to put on a whole new roof. There are two possible alternatives. You can either tear off all the shingles in the original roof, and put on a whole new set of shingles, or you can build a whole new roof over the original ones.

Let's assume that you decide to remove all the old shingles and put up a new roof. Take off the shingles, leaving the sheathing there. If the building paper is torn, replace it. Then apply the new shingles in the same manner as the old ones were applied. Start at the bottom of the slope, and move upward row by row. Fasten the new shingles with the same lapping distance as the old ones had.

If you want to apply a new shingle roof over the old one, simply lay new shingles over the old, and use nails that will pass through the new shingles and the old shingles, and anchor into the sheathing beneath. Use cut nails rather than wire nails—aluminum copper or hot-dipped zinc-coated—preferably size 5d, or nails 1¾ inches long.

2. *Preservation.* After the new shingles are in-

stalled, treat them with a preservative that penetrates the wood and prevents them from rotting. Roof shingles may be finished, too, but not with paint. Paint closes the pores and retards drying, causing rotting. For roof shingles, you should use stain or oil only.

3. *Rejuvenation.* If you simply want to rejuvenate an old worn-out wood shingled roof, brush the shingles with linseed oil or brush in a thin commercial compound of asphalt and asbestos fibers to fill the holes and the splits.

4. *Repair.* If you have a roof covered with wooden shingles, you should periodically replace each missing shingle, each curled shingle flattened by splitting, and nail down each loose shingle. Use galvanized, aluminum, or copper shingle nails for this job. All other nails will rust, disintegrate, and stain the shingles. If shingle nails rust, they will split the shingles and let in wind and rain and possibly tear the building paper beneath and cause a leak.

Room Air Conditioner, see COOLING.

Room Deodorizing, see DEODORIZING.

Room Divider. At some time or other even the best-furnished rooms need a divider, perhaps to hide an ugly feature, prevent draughts, or create an intimate area in a large room. Permanent dividers tend to be expensive and don't allow for a change of heart! One of the best and oldest forms of divider is a movable screen. Here are simple directions for making an inexpensive screen of pineboard. Alter the size to your particular needs.

Materials: Pineboard; wallpaper, felt or fabric; 2 in. wide canvas tape or metal hinges; nails; glue that can be wiped off with a damp cloth if necessary.

This screen is 6 ft. high by 8 ft. long, and of four sections to suit the size of the design on the fabric used. Two large sheets of pineboard, 4 ft. wide by 6 ft. long were cut into four equal sections, each 2 ft. wide by 6 ft.

Directions. Paste fabric or wallpaper on to one side of each board, over-lapping the edges for at least one inch on each side. Carefully smooth out all wrinkles to obtain a flawless surface. Apply covering to the other side of each board either folding under to give a neat clean edge or cutting a straight edge. If it is wallpaper or felt, cut square with the edge of the board so that material from one side of the board overlaps the edges while the other only covers the flat surface.

Once the four sections are covered on each side, attach metal hinges or cut three lengths of canvas tape 6 ft long. Place two boards together and run tape down the two edges. Nail and glue this on, keeping edges together as tightly as possible. Repeat this until all sections are joined together as a screen.

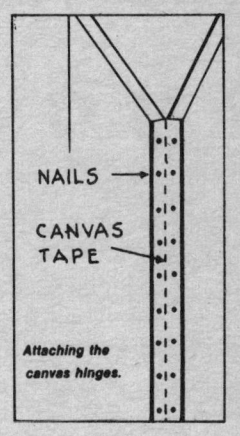

Attaching the canvas hinges.

If you wish, the edges can have a contrasting or matching tape glued along them. We used black half-inch bias binding. To protect the finished screen from dust and dirt it can be sprayed lightly with a coat of stain repellent.

Room Fans, see COOLING.

Root Vegetables, see FOODS.

Rope Hanger. A very useful wall hanger for a coil of rope or line can be made out of a short length of automobile radiator hose. Just slit the hose lengthwise and round off the corners at the ends of the cut to permit the easy insertion and removal of your rope. Punch two holes into the hose and screw it to the wall, being sure to use washers under the screwheads.

Rose Cuttings, see GARDENING.

Rottenstone, see ABRASIVES.

Rouge Stain, see STAIN REMOVAL.

Round File, see TOOLS, HAND.

Rubber, see FIBERS, MAN-MADE.

Rubber Articles. Clean with mild soap and warm water, followed by a dusting of cornstarch or powder. Keep away from heat, radiators, grease or oil.

Use adhesive tape for emergency repair; use tire patch for permanent repair.

Soft rubber articles can be preserved if they are suspended several inches above a dish in which a small quantity of kerosene has been placed. The vapor arising will prevent cracking without harming the rubber.

Rubber Cement Stain, see STAIN REMOVAL.

Rubber Gloves. Your rubber gloves will slip on easily if you keep a salt shaker full of cornstarch handy and sprinkle a little of this on your hands before donning your gloves. Cornstarch will not cake, as talcum powder sometimes does.

If your rubber gloves make your hands perspire uncomfortably, try wearing a pair of old fiber gloves under them.

Rubber Paint, see PAINTS.

Rubber Stamp. If one of your rubber stamps isn't printing as clearly as it used to, run some hot water over it for a few minutes, then scrub it with an old toothbrush. The stamp will usually print like new.

Rug Care, see CARPET CARE.

Rugs.

Cleaning Fiber. Fiber and sisal rugs should be vacuum-cleaned or brushed on both sides with a stiff brush, and wiped occasionally with a damp cloth. Roll them up frequently, too, so as to clean the floor underneath, since dirt does sift readily through this type of rug. When very soiled, send to a professional cleaner. To freshen up faded rugs of this type, canvas dye paints can be used — being sure, of course, to put plenty of newspapers underneath the rug to protect your floor.

Curl Prevention.

1. If you'll rinse your rag rugs in some thin starch water, they will not be so likely to curl on the floor.

2. You can insure your scatter rugs lying flat on the floor if you will give their undersides a sizing of laundry starch. First, seal the underside of the rug with a coat of shellac, then apply a thin solution of starch, and allow to dry before using.

Recoloring, Fiber.

1. An old fiber rug can be made to look like new again. Lay the rug on a plastic dropsheet in your basement or the garage. Then brush on the type of color stain that is meant for shingle siding. The fiber of the rug will absorb the stain beautifully. Despite hard use and vacuuming, the stain will not chip or flake off. If the rug previously contained faded spots or animal accident stains — these too will be obliterated.

2. To add new life to a faded fiber rug, use your favorite color of paint, thin with turpentine (one

part turpentine to three parts paint). For best results work this thoroughly into the fibers with a stiff brush.

3. For recoloring a fiber rug, one may use any dye such as used on cotton material. Dissolve it in boiling water and apply on the rug by means of a brush.

Skid Prevention.

1. Scatter rugs that have the annoying and dangerous habit of sliding and slipping about on polished floors can be made to stay in their places better if an old rubber bath mat or dish-drain mat is placed under each rug.

2. One way to take the throw out of throw rugs is by winding three preserving jar rubber rings together with thread, then sewing them to the corners of the rug. The rings form suction cups that eliminate skidding and serious accidents.

3. Small throw rugs that persist in slipping and sliding all over the place can often be immobilized simply by shellacking their undersides.

Washing.

1. Try washing your throw rugs in your bathtub, using a broom as your scrubber. This simple operation is usually very effective.

2. To wash bathroom rugs and other such heavy things without too much trouble, drop them into a bucket of soapy water, or your laundry tub, then swash them up and down with an ordinary long-handled plumber's force pump. This suction-type of washing does a fine job on these small rugs.

Rule Measuring, see TOOLS, MEASURING WITH.

Rules, see TOOLS, MEASURING.

Running Foot, see LUMBER.

Rustic Furniture, see FURNITURE CARE

Rust Prevention.

Metal. One excellent rust-proofing coating for metal is a good grade of clean synthetic resin mixed with lamp black, or any colored pigment. Apply two heavy coats to the metal that is exposed to the elements or to metal equipment in your workshop. Also, black asphaltum varnish does a good job of rust-proofing.

Nuts and Bolts.

1. To prevent nuts from freezing on bolts through rusting, dip the threads of the bolt beforehand in shellac. They will then always come apart.

2. You can check rusting of bolts and threads by coating the bolt with a mixture of zinc filing and grease. This has a galvanizing action which helps to prevent rusting.

Tinware. To keep new tinware from rusting, rub the surface with lard and thoroughly heat it in the oven before using. It will not rust no matter how much it is placed in water.

Rust Remover. To remove small patches of rust from polished metals and tools, try rubbing with a hard typewriter eraser. The fine grit of these erasers usually works fine for polishing out the rust, without scratching the finish.

Rust Stain, see STAIN REMOVAL.

Rusty Knives, see KNIVES.

Rusty Nails, see NAILS.

S

Saber Saw, see TOOLS, POWER.

Sachet. One formula for making a good sachet powder for bureau drawers and linen closets consists of a half-ounce of lavender flowers and a half-teaspoon of powdered cloves.

Safety Box. A box made from 1/4-inch thick marine ply can be waterproof and fireproof, yet lightweight.

Tack and glue together and reinforce with corner blocks.

Afterwards line the inside with thin sheet asbestos. The alternative is to make the box from sheet aluminium.

Safety, Knife, see TOOLS, HAND.

Safety, Power Tools, see TOOLS, POWER.

Safety, Vise, see TOOLS, HAND.

Salad Bowls, Wooden. Wooden salad bowls develop a mellow odor with age, and the flavor of garlic is preserved if the bowls are not washed. Drain the bowl each time after use, dry with absorbent paper, and polish with oiled paper. Keep in a cheesecloth bag when not in use.

Wooden bowls that have no shellac or varnish finish will often become discolored through washing. So, use a dry method of cleaning. Scrub the inside of the bowl with fine, dry sand, using a circular motion in the direction of the grain so you won't roughen the wood fibers on the surface. Follow with a quick – very quick – rinse under the cold water faucet, and use a towel to dry.

Cracks can be repaired with shellac.

Salad Dressings, see FOODS.

Salad Dressing Stain, see STAIN REMOVAL.

Salad Making Tips, see FOODS.

Salmon, see FOODS.

Salting Foods, see FOODS.

Salt Shaker. If you have a shaker that delivers salt too fast and abundantly, it is a simple matter to plug some of the holes. First, wash the shaker to remove the salt and dry thoroughly. Then merely stop up the desired number of holes with fingernail polish.

Sanders, Electric, see TOOLS, POWER.

Sanding, see ABRASIVES.

Saran, see FIBERS, MAN-MADE.

Sawdust Use. It's a smart idea, when you are doing some heavy sanding on a cabinet or other woodworking project, to save all your sawdust. Mixed with glue, this makes excellent crack filler.

Sawhorse.

Collapsible. Here's a way to make a folding sawhorse that you can easily store away and protect from the weather when not in use. Use two-by-fours for the crosses, pivoting them with 3/8-inch carriage bolts. The feet of the two-by-fours are tied together with 3/4-inch by 4-inch boards screwed into place. It's best to determine the distance between each cross by the length of the logs you're likely to be cutting. Two long hooks fashioned from 3/8-inch iron bars are placed across the ends to keep the horse rigid while in use.

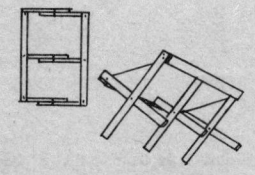

Padded.

1. Many of the jobs the home craftsman has to do call for some kind of padding over the top rails of the sawhorses to prevent damage to such items as doors, hardboard panels, and other materials.

Shown in Fig. 1 is a quick way of padding sawhorses with a piece of old innertube.

The rubber provides a non-slipping surface and can readily be wiped free of dust and grit.

Also, the grit cannot work into the rubber as it can with some types of cloth padding.

Cut the inner tube about 3 inches longer than the top of the horse, then make a cut-out as shown in Fig. 2.

The length of this cut-out section should be about 2 inches less than the distance between the outside edges of the legs, so that the tube must be stretched over the top of the horse.

This holds the tube in place.

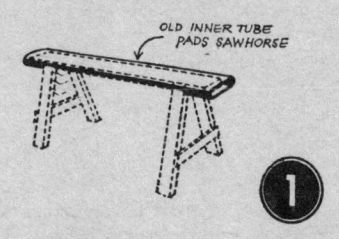

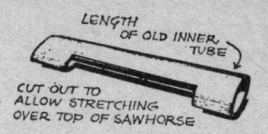

2. You can protect doors or panels from scratches and marring when resting them on sawhorses for sawing or sanding. Cut up an old automobile tire casing into pads, as illustrated. These can be clamped easily over the horizontal parts of your sawhorses and, when not in use, they take up little storage space in your tool chest.

for Planing. Fitting the top of a wooden sawhorse with four stops will permit it to be used to hold work on edge for planing. The stops are made simply by driving wooden dowels into holes drilled into the top of the sawhorse, the dowels being placed about one inch apart.

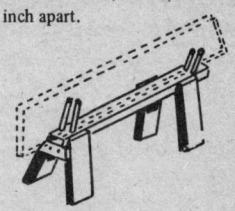

Saws, see TOOLS, HAND.

Scaffold Nails, see NAILS.

Scatter Pins, see JEWELRY.

Scatter Rugs, see RUGS.

Scissor sharpening. Dull scissors can be easily sharpened by cutting them up and down on the rim of an ordinary water glass. Even if you have a nick in the blades from cutting into pins, this will smooth out the rough edges. It also works for pinking shears.

SCORCH REMOVAL

An old, tried and true, easy method of sharpening a pair of scissors is by snipping a piece of sandpaper.

Scorch Removal, see STAIN REMOVAL.

Scrapers. Try using peach stones as pot and pan scrapers. They really work. Put a couple of these stones in the vacuum bottle and fill with soapy water. Then shake vigorously, and the inside of the bottle will be as clean as the proverbial whistle.

Scrapers, Paint, see PAINT REMOVING.

Scratch Pads. You can make some very handy and useful scratch pads out of discarded letterheads and other printed matter. First, purchase a little padding cement from a printer, this being the adhesive used for binding the edges of such pads and books. After cutting your paper to the desired size, stand all the original edges together and place the stack between some heavy weights, such as a couple of bricks. This will keep the edges aligned while you coat them with the padding cement, as in the illustration.

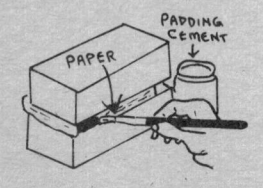

Scratch Prevention, see FURNITURE, SCRATCH PREVENTION.

Scratch Repair, see FURNITURE, SCRATCH REPAIR.

Screen Care.
Galvanized. A good protective coating for galvanized screens is a mixture of two parts of boiled linseed oil and one part of turpentine. Apply this to the screen with a pad you have made by tacking a piece of carpeting to a wooden block.
One-Way. To fix window or door screens so that you see out without passersby seeing in, use white paint thinned with turpentine.
Washing. Your window screens can be kept off the ground while you are washing them with a hose, if you'll place each screen on a saw horse, as in the illustration. When one side is finished, the screen is simply leaned against the opposite legs and doused from the other side. This not only eliminates extra handling, but also simplifies inspection of the screen as it is being washed.

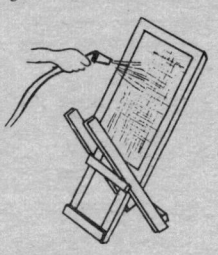

Weatherproofing. Wood-frame screens, which are exposed to the weather, often collect water and moisture behind their moldings, which rusts the screening and rots the wood frames. This can be forestalled if you'll use some calking compound on the edges of the screen where they are tacked to the frame. The molding is then tacked over the screen, forcing the calking through the screen and filling any irregularities in the wood. Scrape away the excess calking, and then paint your screens.

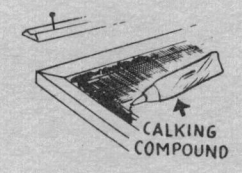

Window. A coat of colorless lacquer will keep metal work shiny.

Screen, Outdoor. Fences and screens for an area should be chosen with their visual "weight" in mind. For example, massive posts and rough cut boards would suit an expansive, wooded garden, but would be overpowering in the pocket garden of a city home.

The following slotted pattern will give a lightweight look.

The vertical posts are 2 in. x 3 in. set 18 in. apart with a facing of alternating slots of 1 in. x 3 in. and 1 in. x 1 in. spaced 1 in. apart. Where the screen turns the corner, the pattern changes. Here the cross

SCREEN REPAIR

pieces are 1 in. x 1 in. slats only, extended at the corner to act as spacers for the main face of the screen. This ladder of 1 in. x 1 in. slats can serve as a support for climbing plants.

Be sure to use a weather-proof wood such as Western Red Cedar. All nails and hinges should be non-corrosive.

If using wooden posts, soak ends in a good preservative.

SLATTED SCREEN

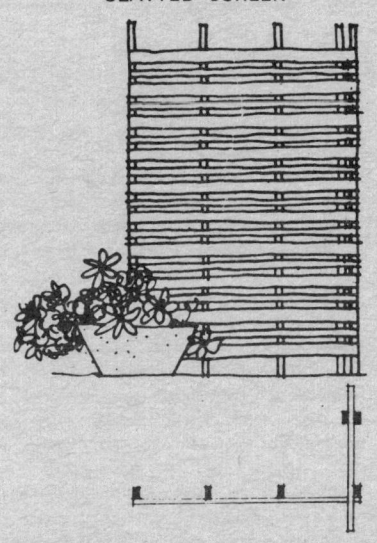

Screen Repair.

Emergency. Here is a good emergency repair for your window screens. When holes appear in the screens, and you don't have any extra screen wire to mend them, try covering the holes with some mosquito netting and applying two or more coats of shellac over this to cement it in place. When dry, these patches will effectively bar the way to all insects until such a time as you can give the holes a permanent kind of repair.

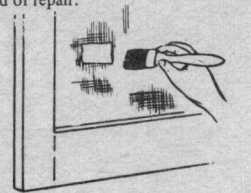

Rips. When a window or door screen pulls away from its frame, replace it quickly before it tears out any farther. First detach the outer molding that covers the site where the screen is attached to the frame. There is a tight groove in the frame into which the end of the screening fits. Pull hard on the screen and tuck the end of it back in the groove. Press a staple gun against the screen and fire staples into. When the screen is as tight as it can be, replace the molding.

Small Holes.

1. For holes less than a half-inch across in screen wire, you can avoid the usually tiresome wearing and unsightly wire patches. Try instead dabbing some clear fingernail polish on in successive layers until the hole is covered. Since the polish dries very quickly, several applications can be put on in rapid succession.

2. Clear nail polish will plug up small holes in window screens. Dab on enough to create a film of the nail polish across the opening.

3. To repair a very small hole in the middle of a screen, fill in the gap with model airplane cement or a similar kind of adhesive.

4. You can patch small holes in window and door screens by cutting rectangular pieces of scrap screen wire to proper size, fraying the edges back a quarter-inch or so, and bending these wires over at right angles. These frayed edges are worked through the spaces in your screen and bent over by tapping with a hammer against a wooden block, to hold the patch in place.

SCREWDRIVERS

Screwdrivers, see **TOOLS, HAND.**

Screws. (See also **BOLTS.**)
Anchor, for.

1. When it is necessary for you to drive some screws into the end grain of a piece of wood, you can provide a firmer anchor for them if you will first plug the wood with a dowel to provide a tight fit, and coat the dowel with some glue before driving it in.

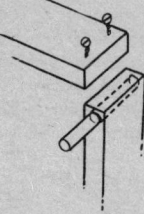

2. Aluminum foil can be used to make a very secure fixing anchor for screws in brick or masonry walls.

First punch a hole in the wall surface to a depth of at least 2-in. Then roll up some aluminum foil to fit the hole firmly and make a small hole down the center with a scriber or drill.

This provides a starting hole for the screw.

As the screw is driven in the outside of the roll tightens securely into the wall, and the screw cuts its own thread into the comparatively soft metal foil.

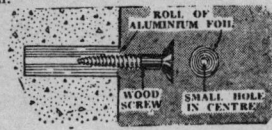

3. An ordinary wooden clothespin, inserted into a hole in cement or concrete as illustrated, makes a fine and firm anchor for a lag screw. To save the work of drilling a deeper hole into the concrete, saw off the head of the clothespin.

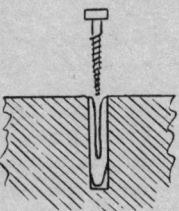

4. When you have to locate wood screws in a plastered wall, ordinary hexagonal lead pencils serve very well in a pinch as expansion plugs. Simply cut a pencil into 3/4-inch sections and push the lead out of these sections. Drill holes into the plaster to make a snug fit for these pencil lengths. Then drive in your screws, which will split and expand the wood for firm settings.

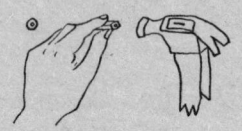

Brass. In the long run, heavy brass screws are best for attaching gate or garage-door hinges, or hinges on any other outside job.

Steel screws will rust and may become irremovable.

But brass ones can be turned out easily, specially if they are lubricated with soap or grease when driven in.

Make certain, however, that the pilot holes, particularly those in hardwood, are the correct size.
Broken.

1. If the shank of a screw is broken off in wood, if the wood is thick enough and a new screw must be reset in the same place, drive the screw shank deep into the wood with a nail-set. If this is impossible, punch a small hole in the top of the screw shank with a steel punch, then drill out the shank with an electric drill.

2. When a wood screw breaks off below the surface of the wood, it is usually almost impossible to remove without damage to the wood. Better in this case to drive the screw deeper with a nail set, then fill in the hole with plastic wood, and start with a new screw.

Caution. Don't run your thumb or finger over a screw head. Small, almost invisible burrs may stick into your hand or cause bad cuts.

Damaged. If you have otherwise good screws on hand with heads so badly mangled that you cannot fit a screwdriver into them, you can usually salvage these screws by making new slots in their heads with a hacksaw.

Flat-Head, see **Wood,** below.

Loosening. If you are having difficulty loosening a tight screw, try putting a few drops of peroxide on

SCREWS

it and allowing this to soak in for a few minutes. Or, try heating the business end of your screw driver.

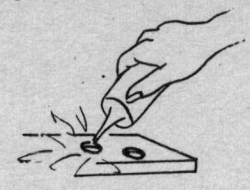

Machine. The term "machine screw" is the general term used to designate the small screws that are used in tapped holes for the assembly of metal parts. Machine screws may also be used with nuts, but usually, they are screwed into holes that have been tapped with matching threads.

Measuring, see TOOLS, MEASURING WITH.

Oval-Head, see **Wood,** below.

Phillips. A Phillips screw is a flat-head screw that has two grooves crossed at right angles on its head. Do not use a regular screw driver in a Phillips head, because you are liable to strip the grooves. (See TOOLS, HAND.)

PHILLIPS HEAD

Pulley. When a small set-screw in a pulley allows it to slip on the shaft, and the screw cannot be tightened to hold it, cut a thin slice from the end of a piece of wire solder and drop this in the set-screw hole.

When the screw is tightened against the solder it is squeezed down into all irregularities on the shaft surface.

Also the solder covers more contact surface and so increases the holding power of the set screw.

Round-Head, see **Wood,** below.

Rust-Proof. Screws used in outdoor woodwork are prone to rust unless made of brass or aluminum. You can, however, rust-proof the ordinary kind by dipping into a thick paste made by stirring powdered graphite in linseed oil. Mix only enough for immediate use, since it thickens like paint when exposed to the air.

Rusty. Stubborn, rusty screws will usually yield if you'll first apply a red-hot iron to their heads for a short time, then twisting the screws out with your screwdriver while they're still hot.

Shortening. It is often necessary to shorten machine screws and small bolts for use in locks, catches.

To prevent damage to the thread by gripping in a vice, try the method illustrated.

First drill a hole or holes slightly smaller than the diameter of the screws in the end of a block of close-grained wood.

Thread the screws in to the desired depth, then grip the block in a vice for cutting the screws with a hacksaw.

This method allows a number of screws of exactly the same length to be cut at one time.

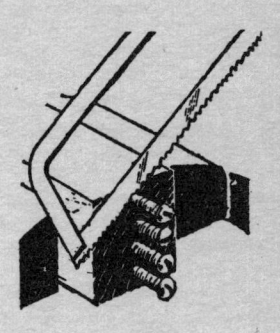

Size. Screws come in sizes from 1/4-inch long to 5-inches long, and in body diameters from .060 inches to .372 inches. Gauge numbers indicate the body diameter of the shank at the point where it intersects with the head. The length of a flat-head screw is measured from the point to the flat top; the length of an oval-head screw is measured from the point to the widest part of the head; and the length of a round-head screw is measured from the point to the intersection of the shank and the head.

You buy wood screws by gauge number and length. For instance, a No. 4 screw is actually .112 inches in diameter; it comes possibly in 1/2-inch, 3/4-inch, and 1-inch lengths. You specify a No. 4, 3/4-inch screw, for instance.

The gauges range from No. 0 (1/16-inch diameter) to No. 24 (3/8-inch diameter). Commonly used sizes include 3/4-inch-No. 7 for hinges, 1-1/4-inch-No. 9 for fastening two 3/4-inch boards together, and 2-inch-No. 14 for heavy work.

SCREWS

A glance at the chart below will give you some figures for comparison:

Screw Number	Body Diameter	Diameter Round Head	Diameter Flat Head
0	.060	.106	.112
1	.073	.130	.138
2	.086	.154	.164
3	.099	.178	.190
4	.112	.202	.216
5	.125	.228	.242
6	.138	.250	.268
8	.164	.299	.320
10	.190	.347	.372
12	.216	.394	.424
16	.268	.490	.528
20	.320	.587	.630

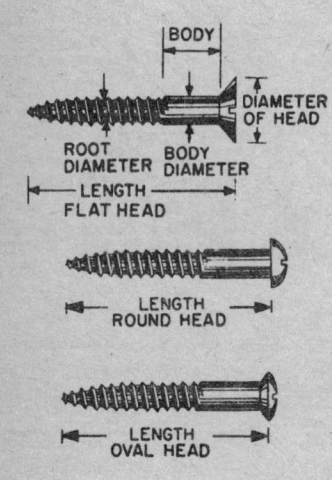

Stronger. The holding power of screws driven into the end grain of a board is much less than when the screws are driven into the side grain of the board. When extra strength is needed, the holding power of screws in end grains can be increased by first drilling through the board at right angles to the direction of the screws and directly through the path the screws will take. Then fit a short piece of dowel into this hole, positioning it so that the screws will pass through it when inserted. This will insure a strong bite or grip for the screws.

Tightening.

1. When screws develop that tendency to work loose, lock them securely back in place by turning the screw down tightly and then nicking the edge of the head on opposite sides with a center punch.

The nicks lock the screw in its place indefinitely.

2. with Aluminum Foil. When a screw hole in wood has become worn, one way to make the screw hold firmly is to wrap a piece of aluminum foil around the shank of the screw, then drive it back in.

3. with Glue. If screws work loose, remove them and dip them into glue, then replace. They will hold tight. Or, wind a few strands of steel wool around the threads of the screw.

4. Hinge. When a hinge screw has become loosened because of the hole being enlarged, remove the screw entirely and press in a small wad of steel wool. When the screw is replaced, the steel wool will take up the slack, and the screw will once again grip firmly.

5. with Putty. When a screw hole in wood has become worn, one way to make the screw hold firmly is first to remove it and drill the hole a little larger. Then fill the hole with wood putty, turn the screw about halfway into the hole while the putty is still soft, then remove it. Allow the putty to harden, then drive the screw all the way in.

6. with Solid Wire Solder. To tighten screws that have worked loose, fill the enlarged screw hole with solid wire solder — then reset your screw. You should find this method much easier than whittling a wooden plug to fit into the hole.

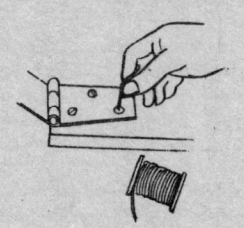

7. **with Staples.** When a certain wood screw persists continually in working loose, especially in soft wood, one effective and simple method of locking it into place is to drive a staple across the screwhead so that it rests in the screw slot. This will prevent the screw from turning and working loose.

Wood. Screws have several advantages over nails. They may be easily withdrawn at any time without injury to the material. They also hold the wood more securely, can be easily tightened and, generally, are neater in appearance.

As a general rule, the length of a screw for holding two pieces of wood together should be such that the body extends through the piece being screwed down so the threaded portion will then enter the other piece. The wood screw simply passes through the hole in the top piece and the threads take hold in the bottom piece.

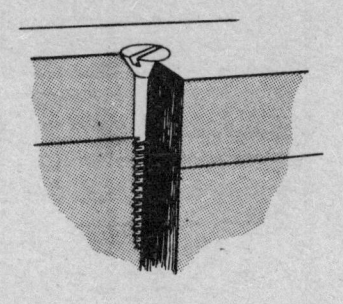

There are three kinds of wood screws: flat-head screws; oval-head screws; and round-head screws. The flat-head screw must be countersunk into the material it penetrates, otherwise the head will stick above the surface. To countersink a hole for a wood screw, you first start the screw hole with an awl, and then ream out an appropriate cone-shaped depression in the wood; then you drive in the screw until it fits snugly, its top flush with the surface of the wood.

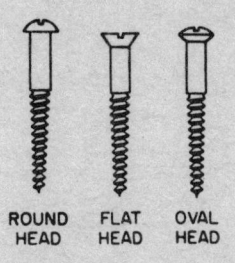

The *oval-head screw* is almost the same as a flat-head screw; it simply has a rounded top rather than a flat top. The top also tapers in to the shank, and you must countersink the hole for an oval-head exactly as you do for a flat-head.

The *round-head screw* is not countersunk. The head rests on the surface of the material into which it is driven.

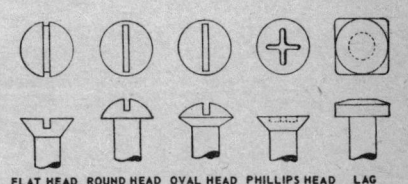

FLAT HEAD   ROUND HEAD   OVAL HEAD   PHILLIPS HEAD   LAG

Scribing. Where the outline of a wall is irregular and you wish to fit a board snugly into it, you can transfer the rough outline to the board by scribing. An art compass is the best tool for this. The point of the compass follows the outline of the wall and the pencil transfers the outline to the board. Be certain the board is in an exact vertical position.

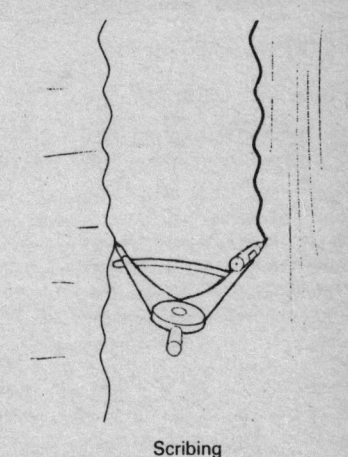

ROUND HEAD   FLAT HEAD   OVAL HEAD

Scribing

Scrubbing Aid. When you are doing an extra-heavy job of scrubbing a floor where your fingers and arms tire because of the heavy downward pressure, you

SCRUB BRUSH

can ease the strain considerably by placing an ordinary brick over the sponge, brush, or steel wool you are using. The weight of this brick will take care of much of the pressure needed, and you'll do the job faster and easier.

Scrub Brush. You can make an efficient scrub brush by cementing a piece of rubber stair tread to a wooden block. The corrugated rubber tread is excellent for cleaning linoleum and painted surfaces, and also acts as a squeegee to remove excess water.

Sealer, see FURNITURE REFINISHING, PAINTS.

Sealing Wax. If you wish to apply a seal to very important letters — or if you simply want to achieve an attractive effect — a dab of thick fingernail polish makes a fine substitute sealing wax. It doesn't need warming in a flame, is quite flexible when it dries, and it sticks just as well as wax.

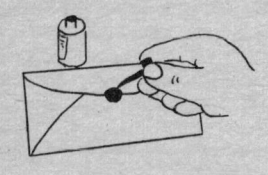

Seedling Protector, see GARDENING.

Seersucker, see CLOTHES CARE.

Septic Tank, see PLUMBING.

Sewing Cupboard. This is an easy-to-build multi-purpose storage unit. Use it as a sewing cupboard, for instance, or a kitchen breakfast bar and cupboard. You'll need:- 2 sheets of 1/2-in. x 8-ft. x 4-ft. plywood; 3-ft. of 1/2-in. dowel rod; 7 small 1-1/2-in hinges; 1-in. panel pins; 11-ft. 10-3/4-in. x 2-in. x 1-in. dressed lumber; 2 pieces of masonite or pegboard 48-in. x 37-in. and 23-3/4-in x 17-1/2-in; an easy-to-fit colorful 37-in. wide holland blind 8-ft. long; piece of elastic 36-in. long, to be doubled and nailed to the ironing board hinge beam.

When building a unit such as this, make all the markings on the plywood first, with pencil. Take careful note of the sizes and the manner the joints are put together. After all sizes and measurements have been checked, cut out panels slowly along pencil lines. Then cut the 2-in. x 1-in. wood to size. These pieces are important as supports.

When assembling, first glue and nail 3-ft. x 2-in. x 1-in. pieces of wood A and B to the 8-ft. x 1-ft. sides C and D (see diagram). Then at the top glue and nail the top panel 3-ft. x 11-1/2-in. x 1/2-in. plywood. Now fit in between the two base supports a piece of plywood 3-ft. x 10-in. x ½-in. This gives you the outer frame complete.

Now fit pegboard on back of top half.

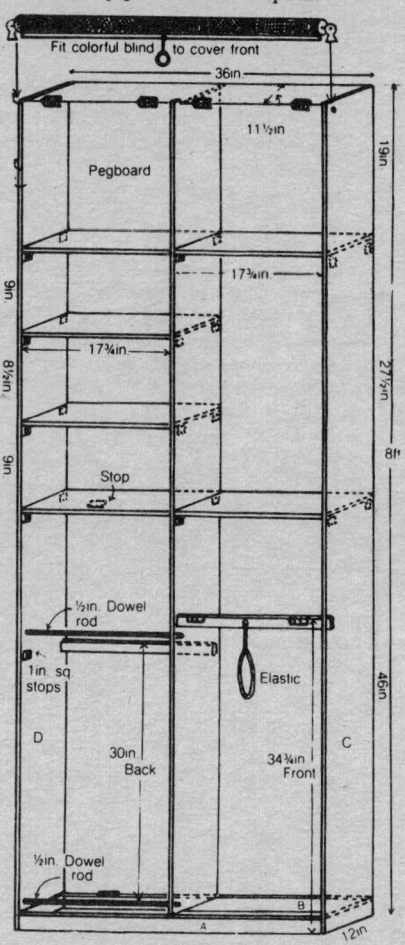

SEWING CUPBOARD

The next stage is to fit the inner pieces. Start with the center panel 1-ft. x 7-ft. 10-in. x 1/2-in. This panel has a piece taken out of the top 1/2-in. x 11-1/2 in. This makes all three panels level and allows the top tilt doors to fit flush. Now fit all stops or shelf supports except for the large tilt drawer stop (marked X). Leave this until the bottom tilt drawer is fitted. Fit all the 17-3/4-in. x 11-1/2-in. x 1/2-in. shelves. These can be fitted in to rest on stops, then nailed and glued in place. Next fit the rear small cross support 17-3/4-in. x 2-in. x 1-in. to be 2-ft. 6-in. from the floor, and the front cross support which measures 17-3/4-in. x 2-in. x 1-in. to be 2-ft. 10-3/4-in. from the floor.

Now, as shown in diagram 1, drill 1/2-in. holes for dowel rods. The top rod is fitted 17-in. down from the last shelves in the center of the unit. The bottom rod is fitted 3-in. from the floor.

Top tilt drawer. First cut out the front panel 17-1/2-in. wide by 18-in. high. To this panel fit sides, base and back as shown in the diagram. Check measurements and see that all butt joints are cut to fit into the area allowed. Cut out oblong holes in front panels for hand-in opening.

Note: Side panels are fitted to the front panel, and therefore should be 11-1/2-in. wide. The rear panel fits in between the rear of the side panels. The base is fitted in last and should be 16-1/2-in x 11-in.

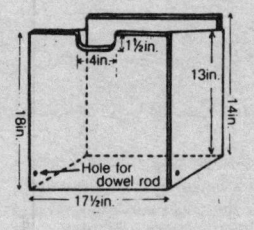

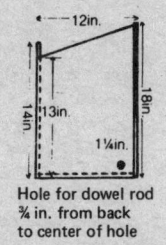

Bottom tilt drawer. Again first cut the front panel 27-in x 17-1/2-in. x 1/2-in. and fit sides, base and masonite back as shown in the diagram. Check measurements.

Note: Side panels are fitted to the front panel and should be 11-1/2-in. wide. Now fit base 16-1/2-in. x 11-1/2-in. in level with the sides and front. Then fit masonite back 23-3/4-in. x 17-1/2-in. To allow tilt drawers to work, a gap of 1/2-in. must be left be-

tween the top drawer and the bottom drawer. Also between the bottom drawer and base, a piece of plywood about 3-in. long and 1/2-in. thick should be fixed to the rear of the base to allow the bottom drawer to stay flush in front.

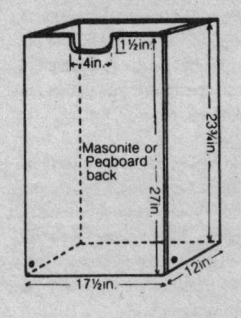

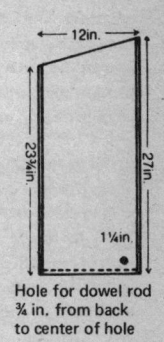

The ironing board is cut out as shown in the diagram and the single leg support fitted.

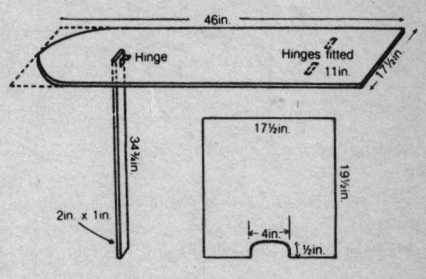

To finish the unit, cut two doors for top of unit 17-1/2-in. x 19-1/2-in. and fit with hinges at the top to make swing doors. When the glue has dried, give the unit two coats of undercoat and enamel. When the paint dries the final touch is added — the bright colored blind at the top.

Roller Blind. To give the cupboard a bright finishing touch make up a colorful roller blind with fabric to match the room. Inexpensive kits of roller, brackets, narrow wooden rod for the base of the blind, pull cord and iron-on blind backing are available from most hardware stores. We chose a heavy cotton so we decided not to use a backing, and just bought separate components which came to less than one dollar.

SEWING MACHINE OIL STAIN

Attach blind brackets to sides of cupboard facing the top (or sides if space demands). If you are using a very thick fabric it may be necessary to raise the brackets to allow more clearance.

Cut fabric the length of the cupboard plus about 8-in. to allow for hem and roller. Turn up a 1-1/2-in. hem (this is for the wooden base rod) at one end. If you are using backing, cut it to the width of the cupboard and iron on the fabric, carefully smooth out all wrinkles and overlap edges. If you decide not to use backing, hem the side edges of the fabric to the width of the cupboard.

Attach the pull cord to the base of the blind by drilling a hole in the center of the board and threading the cord through with a knot to hold it in place. Thread the board through the hem and close off ends of hem with hand sewing. Then bring the cord out through an eyelet in the back of the blind or just through an opening in the hem.

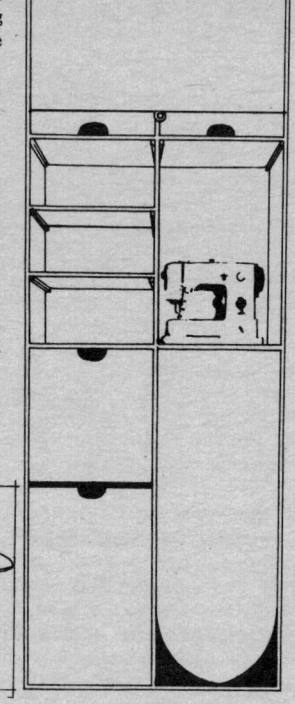

Glue fabric to roller with fabric glue, attaching a full roll. Make sure the ends of roller are facing in the right direction for the brackets. Clip roller into brackets with fabric coming over the top of the blind.

Sewing Machine Oil Stain, see STAIN REMOVAL.

Sewing Tips.

Cutting Fur. When you find it necessary to cut some furs for the remodeling or altering of a coat or other garment, don't use scissors. Much better for cutting the skin at the back of the fur is a very sharp knife or razor blade.

Heavy Thread. Dental floss makes a fine thread for attaching buttons to men's work clothes and children's play garments. It's ever so much stronger than the run-of-the-mill thread, and withstands the roughest of wear.

Hemstitching. Threads can be easily drawn in hemstitching if you will scrub them with a wet brush which has been rubbed over a bar of soap.

Hose Darner. A burnt-out electric light bulb makes an ideal hose darner.

Patching Trousers. When patching a trouser leg, slip a large rolled magazine up inside the leg, under the hole, and then let the magazine unroll inside. This will hold the cloth smooth while you sew the patch in place.

Pincushions. The shavings from a pencil sharpener make an ideal filling for a small pincushion to keep in your sewing basket. The graphite in the shavings will keep your pins and needles sharp and rust-free.

If you'll fill your pincushions with steel wool, you'll avoid dull or rusty needles and pins in the future.

Positioning Buttons. To check the position of a button before sewing it on a garment, use a very fine hairpin to hold it to the garment. Pass the end of the hairpin through the holes in the button and through the fabric. Then bend the ends. They are easily adjusted.

Pressing Seams. To give your sewing a professional look, dampen the seams with a medicine dropper and press with a dry cloth. There will be no shine or print of the seam on the right side of the material.

Preventing Puckering. To prevent puckering while sewing thin silk on the sewing machine, put white paper underneath it ... this paper being easily removable when the job is done.

Removing Buttons. When snipping buttons from a piece of clothing, slide a thin comb between the button and the fabric. The teeth of the comb will protect the material from accidental damage, while you cut the threads with a razor blade.

Ripping Seams. When necessary to rip long seams, you'll have an easier ripping time if you hold the material under the presser foot of your sewing machine, making the presser foot serve as a third hand.

Shrinking Thread. It is sometimes necessary to shrink thread if it is to be used for drawn work. This can be done by placing the spool of thread in a pan of boiling water for about an hour. It will not destroy the gloss.

Stiff Fabric. You can make the sewing of stiff fabrics an easier chore if you'll occasionally stick your needle into a bar of soap. This will lubricate the needle and make the going much easier.

Stitching Heavy Fabrics. If stitching seams in heavy materials — such as denim, canvas, or draperies - rub the seams with hard soap and your needle will go through much easier.

Strengthening Buttons. When sewing buttons on garments where there is a good deal of strain, try sewing a smaller companion button on the other side of the material. This makes for greater strength, and also prevents tearing of the material.

Tape Measure Aid. When measuring clothes or material, make the job easier by holding down the end of the tape measure with adhesive tape.

Tape Measure Holder. A handy holder for your tape measure can be provided by an empty adhesive tape spool. Use the spool cover to keep your tape measure free of dirt and dust.

Thimble Substitute. For a real flexible thimble, put several coats of nailpolish on your fingertips to avoid pricked fingers while sewing.

Tightening Buttons. If you have a very loose button on a jacket and haven't the time to stitch it at once, wrap a narrow strip of cellophane tape around the remaining thread. This will hold it safely until it can be repaired.

Shades, Window, see WINDOW SHADES.

Sharpening Stones, see TOOLS, HAND.

Sheathing, Roof, see ROOF STRUCTURE.

Sheetrock, see DRYWALL.

Sheets, Contour. If one of your contour sheets is giving you a hard time fitting it over a particular mattress, try fixing into place the diagonally opposite corners first, and your job will be much easier.

Shellac, see FURNITURE REFINISHING, PAINTS.

Shelves. There are fixed shelves that are attached to the wall, to the floor, or to a base. There are adjustable up-and-down shelves. There are slanted shelves. There are drop shelves that fold down out of the way when not in use. There are revolving shelves like lazy-Susan kitchen cabinets. There are sliding shelves like in a refrigerator. There are lift-up shelves, like typewriter shelves used by secretaries.

There are also shelves that are built into other storage units. There are shelves recessed into walls and shelves cantilevered from walls and posts. There are shelves suspended between facing walls, boards, or pairs of posts. There are shelves suspended between single posts and shelves hung in wire or wood brackets.

There are shelves made of wood, sheet metal, heavy wire, plate glass, slabs of stone, reinforced-concrete slabs, and chipboard covered with laminated plastic.

Adjustable. A sturdy method of making adjustable shelves is illustrated. Here a series of notches are cut into the inside edges of light strips of wood which are screwed to the uprights.

Naturally these supporting strips must be cut in pairs, and the notches should not be too deep.

Another point to note is that the bottom edges of the notches are square, with the upper edges sloping at an angle of about 45 degrees.

SHELVES

Supporting strips for the shelves (A), are cut with an angle at each end to suit the notch size, and they should be a firm but not tight fit between the notched strips when pushed into place.

Arrange the spacing and number of notches so that there is a range of alternate shelf openings which can be adjusted as needed to suit books or other articles stored on the shelves.

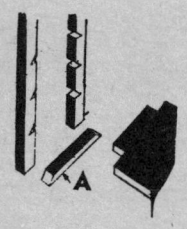

Board and Brick. If you're in a real hurry, you can build those much-needed shelves in your garage or basement. Boards, supported by loose stacks of clean bricks, afford shelves that can hold a lot of things. If you happen to like this easy sort of construction, but don't like the crude appearance of building bricks, you can use glass bricks for the supports. Your shelves can be as long as eight feet with a minimum of sagging.

Corner shelves are always something of a problem to fit and support, but the method shown is very practical.

Use fairly light soft-wood — say, dressed 2-in by 1-in. pine — for the uprights and rails.

The rails are joined with a halved joint at the corner as shown in the detail, then screwed to the uprights.

For the shelves, use nothing less than 1/2-inch thick plywood.

Each shelf is notched at the three corners to fit around the uprights.

If this cutting is done accurately they should rest on the rails without nailing.

Entrance-hall. You can turn out a very attractive entrance-hall shelf that appears to have a machine-molded edge by using just some of your hand tools. The dimensions of the shelf can vary to suit a particular location, although one measuring 8 inches long by 5 inches wide should fit most requirements. Make the top of the shelf from two pieces, glued together, the lower piece being about 3/8-inch smaller than the top. Round the edge of the top piece and leave the edge of the lower piece square to provide the molded-edge effect of the finished shelf. The brace consists of two pieces, a straight length that rests flat against the wall and a curved piece that supports the shelf. You can jigsaw this latter piece from a single piece of wood.

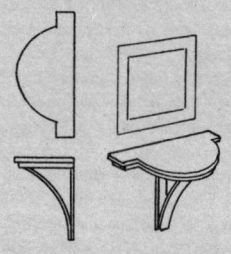

Finishes for. Shelves are great grease catchers and may be stained or damaged by the objects placed on them. You need some kind of finish to protect them.

You can usually stain or paint the wood with hard finishes.

One of the most durable shelf-coverings is a thin rubber sheeting you can place in standard kitchen cabinets. It is completely washable, and cushions what is placed on it. Because it is rubber, it lies flat and does not rumple up.

Contact paper, a colorful vinyl fabric with an adhesive backing, is a good covering, too.

You can use washable vinyl wall covering in the same way. Stick this down with wallpaper paste.

Linoleum or vinyl flooring, glued down with linoleum cement, makes a permanent covering.

If you must have a shelf that is decorative as well as completely washable and stainproof use plate glass or laminated plaster bonded to chipboard. Glass permits you to look up and see what is stored on a high shelf, and it lets light in to dark corners of shelf cabinets.

Glass. Here's one way to guard against the danger of breaking or chipping the edges of glass shelves . . . also to prevent articles from sliding off their slick surfaces. Just slit some small gauge hose lengthwise along one side and press this over the edges of your glass shelves.

Installation. In installing a shelf, there are three points you should consider as critical.

The upright or uprights that support the shelf must be strong and steady.

The shelf hangers must be secure.

The shelf itself must be strong enough to bear the weight of the objects you expect to put on it.

If a shelf is to be suspended between 2 solid facing surfaces—as in a bookcase—you can nail the ends to wooden cleats fastened into the end supports. Or you can set them on adjustable L-shaped metal hangers that plunge into holes drilled in the end supports.

The easiest way, however is to nail two long, slotted, vertical metal brackets to the surface of each end support, and hang the shelves between these on V-shaped clips that snap into slots cut at any desired height.

You can cantilever shelves from walls on a variety of plain or ornamental hanger brackets screwed to the walls in fixed positions.

The most useful hanger is a long, slotted metal standard into which one or more slender metal hanger brackets can be hooked. You must be sure to fasten these standards securely into the wall, usually with long screws.

You can suspend shelves from the ceiling joists—usually in the basement—resting them in U-shaped cradles of heavy wire or wood.

You can even install sliding shelves with the same kind of slides used for drawers. Or slide them in grooves cut in supports on either side, or in rails nailed to the support.

Rough. One quick and easy way to build some rough shelving is to support the ends of each shelf on corrugated fasteners, procured at any hardware store and driven part way into the vertical framework. After your shelves have rested on these fasteners for some time, the fasteners will become embedded in the shelves and prevent their slipping off.

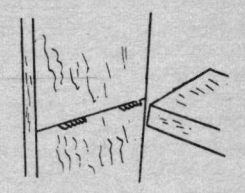

Sink Cabinet. If the shelves under your sink cabinet are hard to work out of because they are dark, try lining these areas with some aluminum foil. The foil reflects the light . . . also cleans in a jiffy.

Storage. You can easily install a very handy storage shelf for infrequently used items over the inside top of a closet door frame. Cut, square, and sand a suitable length of board. Then saw off a strip of wood to the width of the board, minus the width of the door frame, and use the door frame and the wood strip to support one side and one end of your shelf.

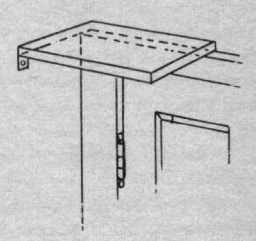

SHINGLES, ROOF

Utility. Just one, ordinary, wooden coat hanger can be used to fashion the brackets for a very attractive and usable little kitchen shelf. The top of the shelf is a piece of one-quarter inch plywood. Drill holes for the necessary screws, and for the dowel, and finish the shelf with enamel.

Wall. Think twice before discarding that old wooden Venetian blind. The slats can be used for making many useful and attractive items, such as planter baskets, wastepaper baskets, magazine racks, and the like. One very decorative item is a wall shelf, as illustrated. Before fashioning the contoured ends of the slats for this shelf, space them evenly with the ends flush and at an angle. Draw angled lines on both sides to indicate position of the shelves. Attach the shelves. Then scribe the cutting lines at both ends of the slats in a curved pattern, as shown, and scroll-saw to shape. You can paint the slats Chinese red and the shelves black for an attractive combination — or any other colors which may suit your fancy.

Whatnot. Here is a simple plywood-and-dowel assembly for making some very attractive whatnot shelves for room corners. Two, three, or more plywood shelves are cut at the same time to insure identical size and shape. Drill the aligning holes while the shelves are clamped together, and when assembling, glue and brad each shelf to the dowels as illustrated. Ordinarily, one-fourth inch plywood and dowels can be used if the shelves are to hold small bric-a-brac, but for larger objects, use correspondingly heavier stock.

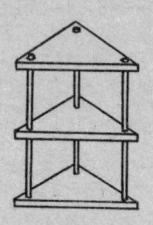

Shingles, Roof, see ROOF SURFACES.

Shingles, Siding.

Asbestos-cement siding shingles cannot become rotten or split, and are highly resistant to disintegration. However, they do need repair if they are cracked or broken because of heavy impact or because of extreme shifting of the wall. Break the ailing shingle into pieces with a hammer and cold chisel, taking care not to smash any good shingles. Cut off the nails with a hacksaw. Insert the new shingle under the row above and nail into place.

Wooden. If a wooden shingle has split or warped, nail it down carefully with copper, aluminum, or galvanized rust-proof nails. If the shingle has split into separate pieces, remove all the pieces and replace them with a new shingle of the same material. If the shingle is on the weather side of the house, cut a piece of building paper about the same size as the shingle and slip it underneath before you nail it.

Shoe Care.

Black suede shoes take a new lease on life when they are sponged with black coffee.

Boots. Salt rings can be removed easily from snow boots and galoshes just by brushing them with a solution of vinegar and cold water.

Buckskin. A good renewing job can be done on buckskin shoes simply by giving them a going-over with a medium grade of sandpaper.

Color Change. To make brown shoes black, rub them with a small piece of sandpaper to remove all the dirt, then rub with a flannel wet with liquid ammonia. Next apply some black India ink with a brush, let dry, then polish as usual.

Damp. If a little sweet oil is rubbed on shoes while they are damp, it will prevent the leather drying and cracking when dry.

Laces. You can easily make replacement tips for your shoe laces with some cellulose tape and a little fingernail polish. All you have to do is wind several turns of the tape around the end of the lace, then seal this in place with an application of nail polish. The resultant tip will last almost as long as the regular tip.

Patent leather is apt to crack sometimes, due to changes in temperature. Warm new patent leather shoes before wearing by rubbing with a cloth. Then bend the feet to limber the shoes while they are warm. If the shoes are warmed each time before putting them on, by rubbing with the palm of the hand, they will not crack so readily. Use sparingly patent leather cream or oil polish that contains no turpentine. Store them wrapped in a cloth or cotton wadding.

When patent leather has become badly scuffed, blacken it with black shoe polish, then cover with clear fingernail polish, The leather should shine like new.

Restoring Leather. To rehabilitate leather shoes that have been out of service for some time, or are dried after a thorough wetting, rub the leather with the cut side of half a raw potato — then polish the shoes.

Scuffed. When leather shoes have become scuffed, trim off the scuffed flaps of leather with a scissors or razor blade, rub the rest of the scuffed area with the palm of your hand, brush on some liquid stain polish, and buff. Then apply paste polish.

When your young fry's leather shoes have begun to scuff, rub them with a white of egg. This pastes down the broken places and removes those untidy scuff abrasions.

Slip-Proof. Sometimes the soles of overshoes or boots wear smooth, which makes them dangerous for walking on smooth, wet surfaces, or on snow or ice. It's a very easy matter to retread these soles and give them slip-proof traction. Using a hot soldering iron, burn some shallow diagonal grooves in a criss-cross pattern, as in the accompanying illustration.

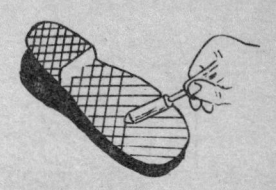

Softening Leather.

1. *with Glycerin*. If a pair of leather shoes becomes stiff after being in the rain or snow, soften them by washing them with warm water, then rubbing either glycerin or castor oil thoroughly into the leather.

2. *with Kerosene*. Kerosene will soften leather boots and shoes that have been hardened by water.

3. *with Saddle Soap*. You can prevent wet leather shoes from stiffening by applying saddle soap to them generously while they are still wet. Let the shoes dry with the soap on them, and they will be soft and wearable.

Tight Heels. If the heel of a shoe is too tight for comfort, try moistening the inside of the back of it where the binding is sewn. Then heat the handle of an old metal knife on the stove, and when this is hot, pick it up with a good, thick potholder and put the hot handle back and forth over the moistened part of the heel. This usually smooths out any roughness there and also slightly stretches this area of the heel.

Too Tight. If an otherwise good pair of shoes are too tight for comfort around the toes, try crushing newspaper into a ball, thoroughly wetting this, then stuffing several balls of it into the toes of the tight shoes, and let them stay there for several days. This treatment usually stretches the shoes into more comfortable wearing.

Waterproofing. You can waterproof your hunting boots and give them longer life, too, if you will soak them in a mixture consisting of five parts mutton tallow, four parts beeswax, and two parts rosin. Heat and blend these ingredients in a shallow pan large enough to accommodate the boots and immerse the soles in it while the mixture is warm. Soak the leather until it is thoroughly impregnated.

See also LEATHER CARE; SHOE POLISH, POLISHING.

Shoe Polish, Polishing.
Applicator. When that shoe polish dauber becomes caked with dry polish, you don't have to throw it away. Soak it overnight in a cupful of paint solvent. Then clean out the brush with a rag and it will be like new.
Banana Skin. For an emergency shine, rub leather shoes with the inner side of a banana skin. Wipe clean and polish with a woolen cloth.
Cloth. When discarding old trousers, cut out their pockets. When these are slipped over the hands, they make handy mitts for applying shoe polish or for buffing your shoes to a high gloss.
Damp Shoes may be given a high polish by adding one or two drops of paraffin oil to the polish. This also prevents the leather from cracking.
Lemon Juice. You can produce an elegant finish on black or smooth-tan leather shoes by spreading a few drops of lemon juice on them, then massaging briskly with a soft cloth.
Lighter Fluid. The shine on your shoes will be greatly improved if you give a few squirts of lighter fluid to the tin of shoe polish whenever you take some of the polish up with your brush. The fluid will make the polish spread more easily and it will penetrate the leather of your shoes. Only a little buffing is needed for a good shine. In addition, after a few of these treatments, the shoes tend to become waterproof and dirt-resistant.
Orange Peel. Try rubbing the leather of shoes with the inside of a freshly-cut orange peel, then polishing with a soft cloth and see how this improves their appearance.
Petroleum Jelly. Leather shoes that are rubbed over with a soft cloth and smeared with petroleum jelly every other day or so will wear much longer, and will not require polishing so frequently.
Softening. Should a tin of your shoe polish become too dry and hardened for easy and practical use, try pouring a few drops of turpentine or mineral spirits into it. This will soften it to usable consistency.

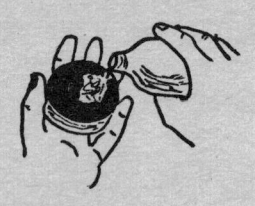

You can rejuvenate it simply by heating it very slowly. The broken pieces will melt down to a soft fresh cake. It is probably better to do this heating over an electric plate, because some polish is flammable.

Water. Shoes can be shined quickly, if they are shined with a dry cloth, a few drops of water are added to the shoe, and they are then buffed to a high gloss.

Shoe Polish Stain, see STAIN REMOVAL.

Shoe Rack, see CLOSET ACCESSORIES.

Shoe Scrapers.
1. A shoe cleaner, installed just outside your rear door, will go a long way towards saving your floors

and carpets during muddy weather. Just one ordinary scrubbing brush, nailed upside down on a block of wood, will serve nicely. But if you'd like even greater efficiency, attach TWO brushes, face to face, about five inches apart, on the wooden block (as we've shown in the illustration). Then, by running your shoes back and forth between these two brushes, you'll accomplish a good cleaning job.

2. Here's a really efficient, and easily made, scraper for removing mud from the shoes before entering the house. Just nail a number of discarded bottle caps, as illustrated, to a board about one by two feet in measurement. Use a ball-peen hammer for this, the rounded end coming in handy for the final hammering to avoid flattening the edges of the bottle caps. You can keep this mud-scraper outside your rear door during muddy weather.

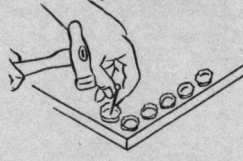

3. A shoe scraper on the back porch or near the back door saves considerable tracking of mud into the home, but many parents object to the fastened-down type, because of children constantly stumbling over it. Here is a safety scraper, cut from a length of pine board, six inches wide and fitted with a metal scraping blade across the lower opening. The upper end is slotted for a convenient hand-hold, which also serves to hang the scraper on a hook on the side of the porch near where it's usually needed.

4. You can improvise a very efficient shoe cleaner or scraper from a discarded broom and a short length of pipe. Drive the pipe into the ground close to your back steps. Then cut the bristles of your broom square and insert the handle into the pipe.

Shower Head Repair, see PLUMBING.

Shop Knife, see TOOLS, HAND.

Short Circuit, see ELECTRICAL FUSES; ELECTRICITY, THEORY OF.

Shower Door, Cleaning. You can get soap and water marks off glass shower doors by rubbing lightly with a sponge dampened with undiluted vinegar.

Shuffleboard. Ever rapidly growing in popularity is the game of shuffleboard. And it isn't too difficult to lay out your own court, either on a smooth cement or tile surface. The accompanying illustration will show you the approved dimensions of a shuffleboard court. The over-all length, as you can see, is 52 feet. The width of the lines you paint on the court should be no more than 1-1/2 inch, nor less than 3/4-inch.

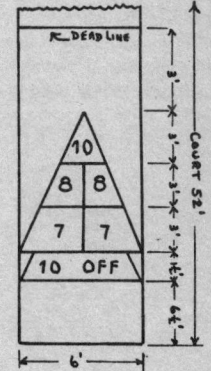

Shutting Off Water, see PLUMBING.

Sidewalk Repair, see CONCRETE REPAIR.

Siding. There are a number of types of siding, among them vertical siding and horizontal. Horizontal sidings include shiplap, beveled, rustic, drop, clapboard.

To repair a piece of siding that has rotted out or has become water-soaked or weathered until it will no longer take paint, remove all the nails visible and pry off the entire length of siding. Most horizontal siding is lapped under the next layer up. Take care when pulling it out that you do not split the good strip. It is sometimes best to remove the lowest row of nails from the upper strip to facilitate removal.

Check carefully to see that the building paper underneath is in perfect condition. It may be that a rip in the paper has allowed moisture to condense and then freeze there, in turn rotting the wood outside it. If the paper is at fault, patch it with building paper cement, or nail a new piece over the bad spot.

Replace the rotted siding with a similar type and size by inserting it under the neighboring strip above and nailing it securely to the sheathing. Set the nails with a nail set. Then prepare the surface for painting and paint.

Siding Shingles, see SHINGLES, SIDING.

Sign Making. When you wish to jigsaw some letters for the manufacture of name plates or other signs, the big, black headlines of your newspapers make excellent patterns. Simply cut out the letters you need, then paste them on the wooden board you are going to jigsaw, and saw around their outlines. Then, after proper smoothing off of these letters with some sandpaper, glue them in place on the board or other surface that will be your name plate or sign.

Silk, see FIBERS, NATURAL.

Silk Ironing, see CLOTHES CARE.

Silver Care.
Cleaning.

1. Your silverware will emerge bright and shining when washed in very hot, soapy water, and then dried as though you were polishing it. It's the drying process that makes for sparkling silver.

2. One excellent agent for cleaning silverware is common lump starch. Rub it on with a damp cloth, allow to stand for a few minutes, then rub off with cheesecloth.

3. Dry baking soda is an excellent cleaner of silver. Try it on jewelry, tableware, candlestick holders, trays, etc.

4. One easy, but effective, method of cleaning tarnished silverware is by rubbing with a soft cloth dipped in toothpaste, then washing the silver in warm soapsuds, rinsing, and wiping dry.

Homemade Polish. Here's a recipe for a good, homemade silver polish: get a little loose prepared chalk from your druggist and make a paste by mixing with ammonia in a small jar. Rub the paste on the silver with a soft cloth, rinse the silver in piping hot water, dry it well and the job is done. Keep the jar of polish tightly covered when not in use . . . and if it dries up, just add more ammonia.

Preventing Tarnish. The simplest way to retard tarnish in your silverware is to rinse it thoroughly after washing it. Even the slightest bit of soapy residue will hasten tarnishing.

Removing Scratches. Remove scratches from silverware by mixing enough putty powder with a little olive oil to make a paste, then rub this over the silver with a soft cloth, following with a chamois polishing.

Removing Tarnish. If your silverware is somewhat tarnished looking, place it in some potato water for a while, and you'll usually find it much better looking when dried.

Silverfish, see INSECTS.

Silver Nitrate Stain, see STAIN REMOVAL.

Silver Plate Refinishing. If you happen to have some old candlesticks, or other silver-plated items, which have become too badly worn for further polishing, you can give these articles a new and very attractive appearance by painting them with refrigerator enamel. The resultant hard, bright gloss looks much like a porcelain finish, and is very easy to keep clean.

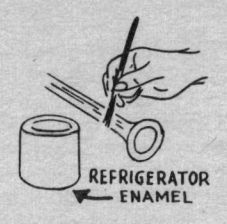

Sink Drain Repair, see PLUMBING.

Sisal Rugs, see RUGS.

Skewers, Cleaning. Shishkebab skewers that have been charred are difficult things to clean. Try pushing them through soap-filled pads, and they'll usually come clean . . . then wash as usual.

Skidding Furniture, see FURNITURE SKID PREVENTION.

Slate Roof, see ROOF SURFACES.

Sleeve Board.
   Any knot-free softwood 3/4-in. thick can be used for the construction of this sleeve board, and the drawing gives the necessary dimensions.
   The base measures 2-ft. long, 8-in. wide and housing joints are cut in this to a depth of 3/8-in. to take the two uprights which support the top.
   The first upright is positioned 2-1/2-in. from the end, and this piece is tapered from 8-in. at the bottom to 6-in. at the top.
   The second upright is placed 5-in. from the first as shown, and in this case the housing joint is stopped 1-in. from each edge.
   Housing joints are cut in the top also to receive the uprights.
   The top board is 6-in. wide and 30-in. long. It is planed on a taper, the end being rounded off.
   To assemble, glue and screw the uprights to the base, driving the screws from the underside.
   The top is fitted in a similar manner. To the square end, an asbestos mat is tacked.
   The remainder of the top is covered with a double thickness of blanket, this being turned over and tacked to the underside.

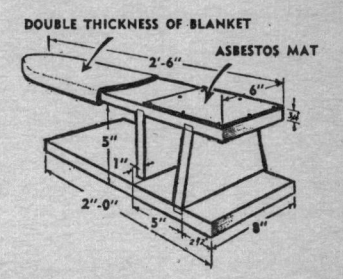

Slicing Board. If your kitchen slicing board is continually slipping and sliding all over the place, try sticking four or five rubber-headed tacks into the underside of the board, and this should anchor it.

Sliding Board. If the outdoor slide in your children's play area has become rusty and no longer gives a fast, slippery ride, give each of the children a large piece of waxed paper on which to go down the slide. The oftener they slide and the more the waxed paper is used, the slicker the slide becomes.

Sliding Door, see CLOSET DOORS.

Smoke Stain, see STAIN REMOVAL.

Snow Shovel. That usually arduous job of shoveling snow can be made quite a bit easier if you'll give your snow shovel two thick coats of automobile wax. This will prevent the wet snow from sticking to your shovel.

Soap.
   Dish. If you have trouble with your plastic soap dish harboring water, making the soap mushy and soft,

SOFFIT LIGHTING

pierce several holes in the bottom with an ice pick or a metal knitting needle that has been heated over a flame. The water will then drain off and leave the soap hard and dry.

Dispenser. With a popular type of beer can, you can fashion a very handy and efficent soap dispenser for your workshop. Cut away the bottom of the can, as in the illustration, drop a marble into the funnel neck, and nail the can to the wall in a convenient spot. Fill the can with some granulated soap, and then when you are ready to wash those work-grimed hands, push up on the marble to permit your soap to sift out.

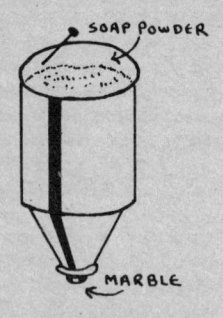

Jelly. Soap jelly, which has a number of uses around the home, can be made easily by dissolving about three tablespoons of white soap flakes in one cup of boiling water. This basic formula can be varied as desired. To increase its cleaning ability add a teaspoon of ammonia or two teaspoons of borax. To give it mild scouring properties, add 1/4-cup of whiting. This variation is good for flat paints.

Leftover. Don't throw away a cake of soap when it has worn thin. Instead, soften one side of a new cake with hot water, press the leftover sliver to it, and they'll stick together so you can use them as one cake. Or, you can drop leftover slivers of soap into a cold-cream jar, add boiling water to form a jelly, and keep this jelly in the bathroom for light laundry work there, such as washing out those dainties at bedtime.

Recipe. One excellent recipe for a homemade abrasive soap that will work wonders for the cleaning of very grimy hands is the following: Mix equal quantities of powdered pumice and borax. Then grate part of a bar of laundry soap into a pot, and melt it over a low fire with just enough water to cover the soap. After it's completely melted, give it a little time to set, and then add enough of the borax-and-pumice mixture to make a substantial paste. Use this as you would sand-soap.

Soffit Lighting, see LIGHTING, STRUCTURAL.

Soldering is a metal-joining process in which a lower melting-point metal (called solder) is heated to the point where it melts and wets the joint surface and then is allowed to solidify in place. To enable the solder to wet the surfaces readily and be drawn into fine cracks, the surfaces and the solder must be clean and free of oxide film. When necessary, the cleaning is done with chemicals or abrasives. One cleaning substance frequently used is called flux. Copper, tin, lead, and brass are examples of readily solderable metals. Galvanized iron, stainless steel, and aluminum are difficult to solder and require the use of special techniques which are beyond the scope of this manual.

Soldering is a practical method of forming reliable electrical connections where bare wires are twisted together or are wound on terminals. Soldering is also used to make tight joints, such as lap seams of sheet metal, and to hold parts together physically. Soldered joints, however, do not support loads for long periods of time as well as welded joints do.

Electrical Connections, see ELECTRIC WIRE.

Fluxes are agents which clean solderable metals by removing the oxide film normally present on the metals and also prevent further oxidation. Fluxes are classified as noncorrosive, mildly corrosive, or corrosive, ranging from mild substances such as rosin to chemically active salts such as zinc chloride. Rosin is an effective and nearly harmless flux used for electrical connections that must be reliable, tight, and corrosion free. Rosin flux is available in paste, or powder form for direct application to joints before soldering, or incorporated as the core of wire solders. Unless washed off thoroughly after soldering, salt type fluxes leave residues that tend to corrode metals. Because of their corrosive effects, so-called acid core solders (which incorporate salt-type fluxes) must NOT be used in soldering electrical connections.

Gun. The soldering gun operates from any standard 115-volt outlet and is rated in size by the number of

SOLDERING

watts it consumes. All good quality soldering guns operate in a temperature range of 500° to 600° F. The important difference in gun sizes is not the temperature, but the capacity of the gun to generate and maintain a satisfactory soldering temperature while giving up heat to the joint soldered. The tip heats only when the trigger is depressed, and then very rapidly. These guns afford easy access to cramped quarters, because of their small tip. Most soldering guns have a small light that is focused on the tip working area.

The tip of a soldering gun should be removed occasionally to permit cleaning away the oxide scale which forms between the tip and metal housing. Removal of this oxide increases the heating efficiency of the gun. If for any reason the tip does become damaged, replaceable tips are available.

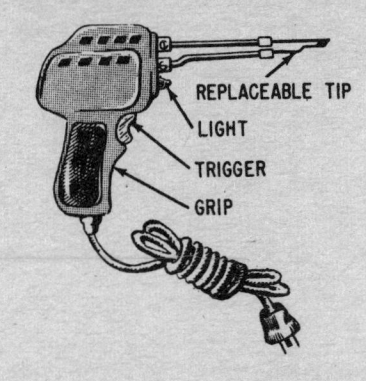

Holes. When you are soldering small holes in a bucket or other such receptacle, turn the vessel upside down over a lighted electric bulb, and the light will show through the holes making it easier for you to determine where to place your solder.

When a small hole needs to be filled up, and it is not convenient to fit a patch, difficulties are usually experienced in getting solder to run into the hole. It has a habit, as a rule, of floating round it instead.

If a cloth is held hard up at the back, and the solder dripped on, the job can be done with ease.

Acid flux used for soldering is corrosive, so always wash the finished joint thoroughly, preferably with warm water in which a small piece of soda has been dissolved.

Iron Dressing. By "dressing" is meant filing the copper to remove hammer marks resulting from the forging process and to round off the sharp corners slightly. Hold the iron in a vise and file it with a well-chalked file.

Iron Maintenance. To perform satisfactorily, this tool must have a well-formed, well-cleaned, and well-tinned point.

1. File all old solder and scale from point end. This is important. If neglected, solder and scale will prevent proper tinning of point.

2. Heat soldering copper to a dull red. Do not direct heat at point because of danger of burning it. Use gas flame, blowtorch, or charcoal fire.

3. File point to proper shape. Point should taper back to efficient working angle, depending on size of copper. Point should be slightly rounded.

4. Plunge red-hot soldering copper into cold water. This anneals copper, making it softer for filing, easier to tin, and more efficient at giving off heat.

5. File all rough spots from point end of copper, finishing with a fine file to a flat, smooth surface. This polishing makes tinning last longer.

6. Heat copper so it will just melt solder. Wipe copper on wet rag to clean surfaces. Place a few drops of solder on block of ammonium chloride (sal ammoniac). Rub copper on ammonium chloride and in melted solder until copper acquires a bright tinned surface.

7. Clean tinned point each time it is removed from heater. When pits form on copper back of tinned area, heat copper and dip in water to remove scale, or insert it while hot in a wad of steel wool and twist it.

Irons. There are two general types of soldering irons, one is electrically heated and the other non-electrically heated. The essential parts of both types are the tip and the handle. The tip is made of copper. Nonelectric irons have permanent tips and must be heated over an ordinary flame, or with a blowtorch.

The electric soldering iron transmits heat to the copper tip after the heat is produced by electric current which flows through a self-contained coil of resistance wire, called the heating element. Electric soldering irons are rated according to the number of watts they consume when operated at the voltage stamped on the iron. There are two types of tips on

313

SOLDERING

electric irons: plug tips which slip into the heater-head and, which are held in place by a setscrew, and screw tips which are threaded, and which screw into or on the heater head.

Electric iron tips must be securely fastened in the heater unit. The tips must be clean and free of copper oxide. Sometimes the shaft oxidizes and causes the tip to stick in place. Remove the tip occasionally and scrape off the scale. If the shaft is clean, the tip will not only receive more heat from the heater-element, but it will facilitate removal when the time comes to replace the tip.

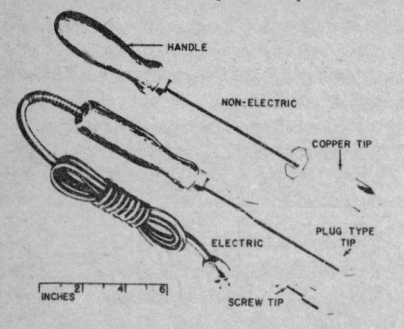

Iron Storage. You can provide a very efficient storing rack for your soldering iron with an ordinary tin can. If you have one of these cans mounted on the wall over your workbench, you can store your iron without waiting for it to cool. As an extra precaution — and if the can is mounted on wood — you can insert a piece of asbestos between the can and the wall.

Iron Tinning. If a soldering iron is new or has just been forced, it will need to be tinned (coated with solder). Heat the copper tip hot enough so that it will readily melt solder. Try melting solder with the copper frequently as it is being heated, and as soon as it will melt solder, it is ready for tinning.

To tin the copper, first quickly dip it into rosin or apply rosin core solder to the tip of the iron. The coating of solder is bright and shiny and very thin. It aids in the rapid transfer of heat from the iron to the work.

Materials. By definition, solders are joining materials or alloys that melt below 800° F. They are available in various forms—wire, bar, ingot, paste and powder. Solders used for electrical connections are alloys of tin and lead whose melting points range between 360° F and 465° F (both endpoints are approximate).

A tin-lead solder alloy is usually identified by two numbers indicating the percentages of tin and lead in the alloy. The first number is the percentage of tin. For example, a 30/70 alloy is made of 30% tin and 70% lead. Likewise, a 15/85 alloy is made of 15% tin and 85% lead. In general, the higher the percentage of tin in a solder alloy, the lower the melting point.

Precautions. Electric soldering irons must not remain connected longer than necessary and must be kept away from flammable material.

In order to avoid burns, always assume that a soldering iron is hot.

Never rest a heated iron anywhere but on a metal surface or rack provided for this purpose. Faulty action on your part could result in fire, and serious injuries.

Never swing an iron to remove solder because the bits of solder that come off may cause serious skin or eye burns or ignite combustible materials in the work area.

When cleaning an iron, use a cleaning cloth or damp sponge, but DO NOT hold the cleaning cloth or damp sponge in your hand. Always place the cloth or damp sponge on a suitable surface and wipe the iron across it to prevent burning your hand.

Hold small soldering jobs with your pliers or a suitable clamping device. Never hold the work in your hand.

After completing the task requiring the use of a soldering iron, disconnect the power cord from the receptacle and, when the iron has cooled off, put it away. Do not throw irons into a toolbox. When storing irons for long periods of time, coat the shaft and all metal parts with rust-preventive compound and store in a dry place.

Preparations. The parts to be soldered must be

absolutely clean (free from oxide, corrosion and grease). During the cleaning process, when removing insulation from wire, care must be taken to avoid producing cuts or nicks which greatly reduce the mechanical strength of the wire, especially under conditions of vibration.

The joint should be prepared just prior to soldering since the prepared surfaces will corrode or become dirty if it remains exposed to the air.

The parts to be joined must be securely joined mechanically before any soldering is done.

Tips. So often a small soldering job needs to be done — and you only have a large soldering iron. For doing fine work, simply get a short length of 12 gauge copper wire and coil it around the tip of the iron, leaving a little tail.

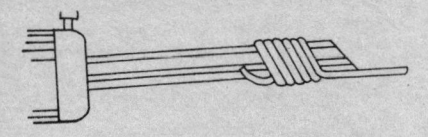

If electricity is not available in some out-of-way place, the copper tip of an electric soldering iron can be transferred to a small gasoline or alcohol blowtorch. Attach the tip to the jet tube with some stiff, heavy wire in such a way that the flame will enter the tip. Adjust the amount of flame to the size of your work so as to keep the tip of the soldering iron at continuous soldering temperature, taking care not to turn the copper.

Warning. Never use a soldering gun when working on solid state equipment. Serious damage to diodes, transistors, and other solid state components can result from the strong electromagnetic field surrounding the tip of the soldering gun.

Wire. Instead of hunting around for extra lengths of wire solder during the course of a soldering job, try this idea.

SPONGE FRESHENER

Wind a good length of the wire solder into a neat coil that is easy to find, and in use, just pull a length from the coil as needed.

To do this, wind the solder in a loose spiral around a short length of dowel, allowing one end of the solder to stick straight out from the coil for a few inches.

Squeeze the loops together to form a compact coil and slip it off the dowel.

Then pull the straight length of solder through the coil so that it extends a short distance from the other end.

The coil itself provides a convenient handle for holding the solder when working, and the straight end is simply pulled through the coil as the solder is needed.

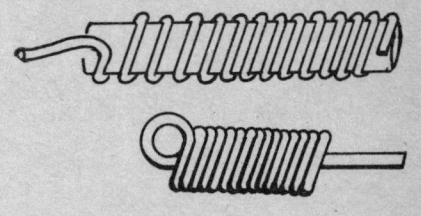

Softwood, see LUMBER; WOOD, WORKABILITY OF.

Solvent, See PAINT COMPONENTS.

Soup, see FOODS.

Spackle, see PLASTER, PLASTERING.

Spandex, see FIBERS, MAN-MADE.

Spanish Tile, see ROOF SURFACES.

Special Purpose Outlets, see ELECTRICAL OUTLETS.

Splinter Removal. Oftentimes tiny splinters can become so deeply embedded in one's fingers and hands that they are difficult to see and remove. You can make these slivers easier to locate if you apply a drop of iodine to the spot. This will stain the wood dark enough for you to see and work on it.

Sponge Freshener. Keep your household sponges fresh and clean by soaking them in cold salt water from time to time.

SPRAY PAINTING

Spray Painting, see PAINTING, SPRAY.

Squares, see TOOLS, MEASURING.

Squeaking Furniture, see FURNITURE REPAIR.

Squeegee. A rubber dish scraper makes a very effective squeegee for washing small window panes. It fits between the frames that are too narrow for the ordinary wiper, and does a very thorough job in all the corners of the panes.

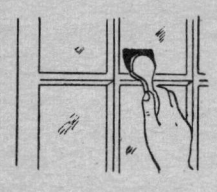

Stain, Furniture, see FURNITURE REFINISHING.

Staining Furniture, see FURNITURE REFINISHING.

Staining Wood, see WOOD STAINING.

Stainless Steel Care.
  Cleaning.
    1. Stainless steel usually requires only hot suds for cleaning. It never rusts and is damaged only by long contact with foods containing salt and acids. Pit marks, when they occur, are practically impossible to scour off, although you can try steel wool and scouring powder.
    2. Renew the appearance of your stainless steel toaster, coffeemaker, pots, pans and the bottom of your iron by rubbing off with a damp sponge sprinkled with dry baking soda. Rinse with a fresh, damp sponge, and wipe dry.
    3. For quick results in the cleaning of stainless steel kitchen utensils, add baking soda, sodium perborate, borax, soda ash, trisodium phosphate, or any non-abrasive commercial cleanser to your wash water. Or, wash the utensils, then scour them with lemon juice and water.
  Removing Scratches. Scratches on stainless steel can be minimized almost to invisibility by rubbing over them with some baby oil.
  Stained, see STAIN REMOVAL.

Stain Removal, See also STAIN REMOVING CHEMICALS.
    1. Determine whether fabric is washable or not.
    2. Try to remove stains as soon as possible. Stains are more difficult to remove if allowed to stand.
    3. Test fabric for colorfastness before applying chemicals.
    4. Do not smoke when using chemicals. Many are inflammable.
    5. Apply chemicals sparingly with light strokes. Do not rub.
    6. Be sure cloths used are lint free.
  Acid.
  from Non-washable Fabrics.
    1. Sponge immediately with water. Add a few drops of ammonia or white vinegar to restore color if fabric is colorfast.
    2. Apply baking soda to both sides of fabric, allow to stand and sponge off.
  Adhesive Tape. Use cleaning fluid for both washable and non-washable fabric.
  Airplane Glue. If your young hobbyist has inadvertently spilled or spattered some airplane cement on your furniture, it can usually be removed with ordinary cold cream.
  Albumen. Sponge with cold water.
  Alcohol.
    1. *from Asphalt Tile.* When alcohol is dropped on an asphalt tile floor, you eventually notice white patches appearing. These patches can be removed by rubbing a little baby oil or olive oil into them.
    2. *from Non-washable Fabrics.* Sponge with denatured alcohol.
    3. *from Washable Fabrics.* Soak for half hour in strong ammonia solution, then wash.
  from Aluminumware. If one of your aluminum cleaning vessels has turned black inside, try boiling grapefruit or lemon rinds in the pot with cold water for at least a half hour . . . or until the black is gone. Then empty the vessel, and all that is needed is a light scouring with soap-filled steel wool pad.
    Boiling some apple parings will also brighten the interiors of aluminum pans. Boiled rhubarb is another effectived cleaner.
  Ammonia may bleed dyes or cause color changes in materials and these color changes can be corrected by applying white vinegar and water to the affected areas.

STAIN REMOVAL

Animal stains on carpets should be dealt with as quickly as possible by sponging with a salt solution, half a cup to a quart of water, and then with a solution of one-part ammonia to twenty parts water. This is about the only home method you can use, and it isn't always completely successful.

Argyrol. Sponge with warm water. Sprinkle with pepsin powder and work into fabric. Allow to stand half an hour. Sponge again.

from Ashtrays. Those stubborn and unsightly stains on copper or brass ashtrays will vanish easily if, after a good washing, you brush over them with some denatured alcohol.

Banana. To remove banana stains from fabrics, cover the cloth with a liberal paste of fuller's earth and water, let dry thoroughly, then brush off.

from Bathroom Tile. When the joints between bathroom tiles become extremely dirty and stained so that no amount of scrubbing seems to get them clean, use either a common laundry bleach or a little ordinary kerosene, scrubbing this on vigorously with an old toothbrush. Allow the bleach (if that's what you're using) to soak on the surface for several minutes, then rinse off thoroughly and repeat if necessary.

from Bathtub. A drippy faucet discoloration left in the washbowl or bathtub will vanish when a paste of cream of tartar and peroxide is applied with a stiff brush. Plain vinegar sometimes works fine, too.

Beer stains are usually as easy to get rid of as they are to acquire, because beer is water soluble. So, ordinary laundering will do the trick for washable fabrics, and sponging with a cloth dipped in soapy water can be used for unwashables. If the stain is old, add a little ammonia to the wash water.

Blood.

1. *from Carpets.* For bloodstains on carpets, sponge with cold water. If a spot still remains use a small amount of detergent and water, then follow with clear water.

2. *from Hard to Clean Objects.* To remove blood stains from a cushion or other hard-to-clean object, cover the spot immediately with a paste of cornstarch and water. Rub it on, and put the cushion in the sun to dry. The sun will draw the blood out into the cornstarch. Brush off when dry and, if the spot is not completely gone, repeat the process.

3. *from Mattresses.* Bloodstains on mattresses can be removed if you'll cover them with a starch paste, then remove this paste when it has dried ... and keep repeating the routine until the stains have vanished.

4. *from Non-washable Fabrics.* Soften with a castor oil solution, then sponge with warm water. If stain persists add a few drops of ammonia to solution.

5. *from Washable Fabrics.* To remove bloodstains from materials, soak in cold water overnight, if possible, then wash in warm water and soap. If the stains prove obstinate, soak in a mixture of cold water and salt, then wash.

Blueberry, same as **Fruit,** below.
Bluing, same as **Rust,** below.
from Bricks, see BRICKS.
Butter, same as **Grease, Food,** below.

Candle Wax. Gently scrape off wax. Cover with blotter and press on reverse side with iron. If stain persists, treat with carbon tetrachloride.

Candy. Almost all candy stains on fabrics, except chocolate, are removable with hot water. Cleaning fluid is a better bet for chocolate. Or, peroxide if the fabric is white.

from Canvas. Smudges on canvas fabrics — such as a convertible top, tent, windbreak, or camp cot — can often be erased by aid of a soft art-gum eraser.

Carbon Paper stains on washable fabrics can be laundered in heavy suds. On unwashables, sponge with denatured alcohol diluted with two parts of water. Rinse by sponging with clear water.

from Carpets. Many stains on carpets can be eradicated with this simple method. Make a paste of starch and buttermilk, spread over each stain, let dry, then rub off.

Catsup stains, if set by heat or age, can be tough to remove. On washable articles, sponge with cool water and let stand for thirty minutes, after which work a detergent into the stain, and rinse as usual.

Cheese. Treat with cold water.

Chocolate.

1. *from Non-washable Fabrics.* Treat with carbon tetrachloride and then sponge with warm water. If stain persists, use pepsin powder, allow to stand 30 minutes. Sponge with warm water.

2. *from Washable Fabrics.* Chocolate stains on fabrics can usually be dealt with by wetting the item, then rubbing borax soap powder into the spot. Roll the garment up, lay it aside for fifteen minutes, then scrub with a brush.

Or, rub in glycerin thoroughly, then wash out in clear water. In some cases it may be necessary to repeat this routine several times.

Cigarette, same as **Nicotine**, below.

Cocoa, same as **Chocolate**, above.

Cod Liver Oil. Treat with carbon tetrachloride.

Coffee.

1. *from China.* Old pieces of chinaware are often spoiled in appearance by coffee stains in the hairline cracks of the glaze. To remove these blemishes, make a paste of baking soda and water and apply to the stained areas. After letting stand for about an hour, wash the pieces with soap and water.

2. *from Coffee Pots.* To get rid of the brown stains inside a glass coffee maker, fill it with water, add a spoonful of baking soda and a spoonful of soap powder, bring to a boil, let simmer for about ten minutes, then rinse out.

3. *from Cups.* Cups, which are discolored with tea or coffee, can be cleaned by wetting in vinegar, then dipping a damp cloth in salt, and rubbing the stains away.

4. *from Washable Fabrics.* Stretch fabric over bowl and pour boiling water from height of two feet.

If necessary, repeat after spot has been covered with glycerin.

from Concrete, same as **Grease, Automobile**, below. (See also CONCRETE FLOOR CARE.)

from Cork Floors. If some stains on your cork floor don't yield to soap-and-water washing, try sanding them out with No. 1/2 sandpaper.

Crayon.

1. *from Linoleum.* Crayon marks on enamel surfaces or on linoleum can be removed with a little silver polish, applied with a damp cloth.

Silver polish will remove crayon marks from linoleum or tile floors.

2. *from Painted Walls.* Crayon marks on painted walls will come off easily if they are rubbed with lighter fluid. Or, you can remove crayon writings from any painted surface by rubbing them briskly with a dry turkish towel, turning the towel surface frequently. This takes a while, but it works!

Or, coat with toothpaste, letting this set for about fifteen minutes, then wipe off with a damp cloth.

3. *from Wallpaper.* Crayon marks on wallpaper will usually vanish when lightly rubbed with very fine steel wool . . . without damage to the wallpaper.

4. *from Wood.* An effective remover of crayon marks on woodwork is kerosene. For crayon marks on furniture, paste wax is a good removing agent. Still another way is to remove these marks from woodwork is with a plain old piece of cotton fabric, rubbed gently over the stains. This works nicely on plastic tabletops, linoleum and glass.

Cream, same as **Grease, Food**, below.

Cream Soup. Sponge with warm water, followed by carbon tetrachloride or benzine.

Drawing Ink.

1. *from Non-washable Fabric.* Treat with denatured alcohol or cleaning fluid.

2. *from Washable Fabric.* Wash with small amount of ammonia and lots of soap suds.

Dye. Soak in warm water for 15 minutes. Wash in soapy water and dry in sun.

Egg.

1. Treat with cold water. If persistent, sponge with cleaning fluid. Warm water will set the stain.

2. *from Silver.* Egg-stained silverware can be cleaned very easily by rubbing with some common table salt.

Fruit (except Peach).

1. If warm water does not remove stain, sponge with cold water and a few drops of glycerin. Let stand for three hours, then sponge with vinegar an oxalic acid followed by water rinse.

2. *from Tablecloths.* Remove fruit stains from tablecloths at once by stretching the stained part over a bowl or sink and pouring boiling water through from a height of eight to ten inches.

from Furniture, see FURNITURE MARK AND STAIN REMOVAL.

Glue.

1. *from Non-washable Fabrics.* Dampen, sponge with vinegar, rinse.

2. *from Washable Fabrics.* Soak item in warm water.

Grass stains are among the toughest. A solvent that usually works well on cotton and on most colorfast materials is ordinary rubbing alcohol. But, for safety's sake, test first on a corner of the garment, and if this works out all right, rub the alcohol into the grass stain until it disappears, then wash as usual. Or dip fabric in Javelle water and wash as usual.

STAIN REMOVAL

Gravy. Sponge with carbon tetrachloride, followed by lukewarm water. Or, use cornstarch. (See STAIN REMOVING CHEMICALS.)
Grease.
  1. *from Carpets.* For the removal of grease spots from rugs, try mixing a paste of dry cleaning fluid and powdered starch, spreading this over the grease spot, letting dry completely, then carefully scraping and vacuuming up the dry dust. Stubborn spots may require several repeats.

Baking soda or cornmeal does a good job of removing grease spots from your rugs. Just pour a generous amount over the spots and lightly brush the powder into the carpeting. Leave overnight, then vacuum off the next day.

  2. *from Linoleum.* Grease spots on linoleum or wood floors should not be washed with hot water, as this sets the grease. Wash with cold water and soap powder until the spots are removed.
  3. *from Marble.* Grease spots are sometimes difficult to remove from marble. Apply a paste made of crude potash and whiting mixed with water, or mix quicklime to the consistency of cream with strong lye. Apply with a brush. For either method, let remain for 24 hours and wash off with soap and water. Polish the surface and your marble should look like new.
  4. *from Non-washable Fabrics.* To remove grease spots from woolens or silks, use talcum powder. Rub this over the stains, then brush off with a stiff brush after the powder has stood for a day or two.
  5. *from Suede.* Remove grease from suede by sponging it with cloth dipped in vinegar, when dry, restore nap by brushing.
(See also CLOTHES CARE.)
  6. *from Upholstery.* Grease spots on upholstered furniture can often be dealt with successfully in this easy way: Add enough water to a quantity of baking soda to make a paste, and rub liberal amounts of this into the spotted areas. Allow this paste to dry, then remove it with a brush, a vacuum cleaner, or carpet sweeper. If the stain proves a little stubborn you can repeat this operation several times.

  7. *from Wallpaper.* One method of removing grease stains from wallpaper is to take a clean powder puff and sprinkle it with white talcum or baby powder. Rub the powder puff over the spots, repeating the process until the grease disappears. If the puff gets greasy, turn it over and use the other side. Be sure to keep the puff well covered with powder so that it works into the grease. See also **Wallpaper,** below.
  8. *from Work Clothes.* Greasy or oily work clothes or overalls will get cleaner if soaked for about fifteen minutes in hot water containing a half-cup of household ammonia.

For removal of grease stains from work clothes, soak the grease-spotted areas with kerosene for about fifteen minutes prior to laundering.
Grease, Automobile.
  1. *from Concrete.* To remove spilled oil or grease from unpainted concrete floor, cover with a one-half inch thick layer of dry, powdered Portland cement. Let stand for twenty-four hours or more, then sweep it up. Scrub any remaining stains with a piece of burlap dipped in mineral spirits or turpentine. In stubborn cases, apply a second coat of cement powder, saturate with mineral spirits, and let stand overnight before sweeping up.
  2. *from Washable Fabrics.* Automobile grease stains can be removed from dress fabrics by applying a little butter, then washing and rinsing.

Grease, Food.
  1. *from Non-washable Fabrics.* Sponge with carbon tetrachloride, holding gauze or blotter under stain to absorb excess fluid.
  2. *from Washable Fabrics.* Rub soap into stain and soak in warm water.

Grease, Machine. *from Non-washable Fabrics.* Rub with lard and carbon tetrachloride.
Heat and Water *from Furniture,* see FURNITURE MARK AND STAIN REMOVAL.
Indelible Pencil, same as **Grease, Machine,** above.
Ink.
  1. The juice of a ripe tomato is an excellent agent for removing fresh ink stains.
  2. *from Carpets.* For ink stains on carpets, apply a paste of milk and cornmeal to the stain and allow to stand a few hours before brushing off. Or, cover the stain with table salt for a minute, then wash with vinegar.

For ink stains on rugs, take three tablespoons of

baking soda to one quart of lukewarm water. Saturate the spot well with this mixture, and use several clean cloths to blot it up. You usually find that no trace of ink will remain, no matter how old the spot is.

3. *from Plaster.* As plaster is so absorbent there is little that can be done about removing the stain unless you remove some of the plaster. It should be possible to gouge a little from the surface, then repair damage with a patching plaster.

4. *from Wallpaper.* Ink stains on wallpaper will usually yield to a solution of equal parts of ammonia and hydrogen peroxide.

5. *from Woodwork.* To remove ink stains from varnished woodwork, rub them well with a soft cloth that has been dipped into a mixture of equal parts of vinegar and linseed oil.

VINEGAR & LINSEED OIL

Iodine.

1. *from Non-washable Fabrics.* If still wet, apply soap and water; if not, use ammonia solution. Or apply a cornstarch paste.

2. *from Washable Fabrics.* Hold item over steam.
from Kitchen Knives. Stains on kitchen knives are more readily removed if a large cork is used for rubbing instead of a cloth. Wet the cork, dab it in a little cleanser, then rub it back and forth on your paring and carving knives and other steel equipment.
from Kitchen Sink. Stains in your kitchen sink, general or unidentified, can be removed usually if you will close the drain and fill the sink at bedtime with a mixture of vinegar and laundry bleach. Then, in the morning, open the drain and chances are excellent that the stains will gurgle away with the liquid.

If your kitchen sink has become very greasy, pour a little household ammonia into it, and rub with a cloth. This will remove all dirt and grease, and will serve as a deodorant, too.
Leather. Stains caused by the rubbing of leather against a textile are among the tough ones. If the fabric is washable, try soap-and-water, using plenty of soap and rubbing well. If glycerin is worked into the stain at first and left on for a half hour or more, the stain will yield more easily. On unwashables, try glycerin, working this into the stain well by rubbing lightly between the hands. Let remain for a half hour, then rinse by sponging with water.
from Leather Upholstery. Old stains may be removed from leather upholstery by coating it with a mixture of powdered pipe clay and water, mixed to a paste, allowed to remain on for several hours before brushing off. Repeat the process if necessary.
Lipstick.

1. *from Non-washable Fabrics.* Rub with lard, then sponge with carbon tetrachloride. Or sponge with a mixture of hydrogen peroxide and sodium perborate.

2. *from Washable Fabrics.* Try rubbing stains off washable clothes with some petroleum jelly before laundering them in hot suds. Or try rubbing a slice of bread over the area. Then, when you brush away the bread crumbs, you should also brush away the lipstick.
Mercurochrome.

1. *from Non-washable Fabrics.* Sponge with sodium perborate.

2. *from Washable Fabrics.* Sponge with a half and half solution of alcohol and water. If stain persists, apply glycerin, wash in soapy water; rinse in ammonia and water.
Milk, same as **Grease, Food,** above.
Mildew, see MILDEW.
Model Glue. If some model glue has been spilled or spattered on your furniture, it will usually yield to a rubbing over with some cold cream.
Mustard.

1. *from Non-washable Fabrics.* Apply warm glycerin and sponge with water. If this fails, use diluted denatured alcohol.

2. *from Washable Fabrics.* Apply glycerin before washing with soap and water.
Nail Polish. Use alcohol or lacquer thinner.
Nicotine. If someone leaves a burning cigarette on one of your china dishes, you can remove the nicotine stain by dipping a cork into moist salt, rubbing the spot with this cork, the nicotine will come off.
from Non-washable Fabrics, see individual stains.
Oil.

1. *from Concrete.* If oil, dropped on concrete, is

mopped up immediately and covered with fuller's earth, hydrated lime, whiting, or dry Portland cement, there should be no stain. If a light stain does remain, scrub with gasoline or benzine. If the stain has soaked deep into the concrete, saturate some white flannel with a mixture of equal parts of acetone and amyl acetate, place this over the stain, then cover with a slab of concrete or glass. Re-saturate the cloth until the stain disappears.

WHITE FLANNEL

2. *from Driveway.* If car oil has leaked on your driveway, you can cope with the spot by sprinkling sand over it, leaving it for half an hour or so, then sweeping it away. The sand has a way of absorbing the oil.

3. *from Garage Floor.* One way of coping with the problem of oil spilled on your garage floor is to spread several thicknesses of newspaper over the area. Saturate the newspaper with water and press firmly against the floor. Allow to dry thoroughly, remove, and usually the oil spots will have disappeared.

Paint.

1. *from Tile.* One of the easiest and simplest ways to remove paint spatters from tile is with fingernail-polish remover.

2. *from Washable Fabric.* Immerse in turpentine.

Peach. Bleach with oxalic acid and ammonia.

Pencil.

1. *from Non-washable Fabrics.* Sponge with clear water. If stain persists, dip into chloroform.

2. *from Washable Fabrics.* Try an eraser. If persistent, rub soap solution into stain.

Perfume. Most perfume stains can be removed from linen dresser scarves by the application of peroxide of hydrogen, followed by laundering.

Perfume stains on fabrics are among the toughest to deal with, but here is one often effective treatment: Wet the spot with water, then work on it with glycerin, and a piece of cheesecloth, and rinse out under water. Traces may still remain, and if so, use a twenty per cent solution of vinegar, and flush it out with water.

Perspiration. For fresh perspiration stains on fabrics, flush the area with detergent water, and ammonia in solution. For old stains, use a solution of water, detergent, and vinegar. Sometimes color changes occur from either acids or alkalies in perspiration, and acid or alkali will restore the color, depending on which agent originally caused the color change.

Table salt is still an effective way to remove perspiration stains, especially from dark fabrics. Dissolve a cup of salt in hot water and sponge the fabric until the ring disappears.

from Photographs. To remove spots from photographs, paintings, or prints, add a few drops of ammonia to a cupful of warm water, apply carefully with a soft cloth which has been wrung out quite dry in this solution.

Plaster. When plaster drops onto painted surfaces during a patching job, the stain can be removed easily by first scraping lightly with steel wool, then sponging the area with a little lemon juice diluted with three parts of water, and rinsing with a damp cloth immediately afterward.

from Plastic.

1. *Cups.* As plastic cups get older, the stains sometimes penetrate and are very difficult to remove. Procure some silicone carbide paper (this is like fine black sandpaper). Wet this paper, and rub the stains right off your plastic cups. This treatment will not mar the finish, but will in fact make it as smooth as glass.

If tea or coffee has stained the insides of your plastic cups, you can clean them out very nicely by scouring out with a paste made of baking soda and water. And, if you remember to rinse out these cups well after each use, you won't be bothered by such stains.

2. *Dishes.* If conventional detergents and soaps fail to remove stains from plastic dishes, soak them for about twenty minutes or so in a gallon of warm water to which a cup of bleach has been added. Then wipe with a dishcloth and wash in the usual manner.

3. *Utensils.* You can often do a very good job of cleaning stains and scuff marks off hard plastic utensils by rubbing gently with a bit of toothpaste on a soft cloth, then washing and drying as usual.

from Porcelain Enamel.

1. To remove stains from porcelain, rub with a damp cloth dipped in baking soda. The soda will not scratch the porcelain. This treatment is also excellent for removing coffee stains from dishes.

2. A stubborn rust spot on porcelain from a leaky faucet will come off if you saturate a paper towel with some household bleach and leave it on the stain for a few hours.

3. For stains in the bathtub or kitchen sink (usually yellow), Javelle water (better known as chlorine) will usually do the trick. Or, use three tablespoons of cream of tartar and one tablespoon of hydrogen peroxide, making a thin paste, and wipe on with a cloth. Kerosene is also an excellent cleaning agent for bathtubs and sinks.

4. To remove surface discolorations from a bathtub or sink, use a mixture of baking powder and peroxide. Make a paste of these two ingredients and apply it to the discolored areas with a cloth. Then, after this has dried, wash it away, and the original luster will be restored. This solution is also very good for brightening the finish on your refrigerator.

Printer's Ink, same as **Grease, Machine**, above.

Rouge. To remove rouge stains from a fabric, apply undiluted detergent to the stained area, working this in well until the outline of the stain is gone. Then rinse and allow to dry. Repeat this routine if necessary.

Rubber Cement. For rubber cement stains on fabrics, rub off as much as possible with your finger or with a dry ball of rubber cement, then sponge with rubber cement thinner.

Rust.

1. *from Chrome.* Rust on chrome will usually yield readily to a rubbing over with aluminum foil dampened with water. Wipe dry with a soft cloth.

2. *from Clothing.* One old but good way to remove rust stains from clothing is to squeeze some lemon juice on the spots, pat salt on this, then hang the garment in the sun. Or use an oxalic acid solution.

3. *from Kitchen Sink.* Try using vinegar for the removal of those yellow rust stains in your kitchen sink, caused by persistently leaking faucets.

4. *from Linen.* For iron rust stains on linens, try a mixture of lemon juice and salt.

5. *from Siding.* Rust stains on exterior painted house siding are frequently caused by exposed nail heads which may be corroding beneath the surface of paint. To correct this, sand off the nail heads and spot-prime with a little shellac or metal primer. Then countersink the nail head and fill the hole with putty before repainting.

6. *from Steelware.* Rub rusty steelware thoroughly with sweet oil, allowing the oil to remain on for some time before beginning your rubbing.

Salad Dressing, same as **Gravy**, above.

Scorch.

1. *from Cotton.* To remedy scorch spots on cottons (provided they aren't too deeply burned in), wet the stains with water, and cover with a thick paste of laundry starch. After this has dried, sponge it off with peroxide, iron the article, and put into the sun for a few hours.

2. *from Wool.* For scorch stains on wool fabrics, apply hydrogen peroxide, then place the garment so that the stained area faces the sun. Watch from time to time until the stain is gone. If necessary, apply more hydrogen peroxide as it dries out. If the dye begins to lighten, stop the procedure and rinse the peroxide from the fabric.

Sewing Machine Oil. Should oil from your sewing machine spot the fabric on which you are sewing, immediately apply a liberal coating of talcum powder. Let this stand for fifteen to twenty minutes, then brush off. Repeat, if necessary.

Shellac, same as **Varnish**, below.

Shoe Polish. Rubbing alcohol usually serves nicely for the removal of shoe polish stains from clothing. Or, use carbon tetrachloride.

Silver Nitrate. *from Non-washable Fabrics.* Apply ammonia solution.

Smoke.

1. *from Fabrics.* Sponge with cleaning fluid or

gasoline; then apply, absorbent powder. See STAIN REMOVING CHEMICALS.

2. *from Wood.* Grease and smoke stains on woodwork can be dealt with by painting over the woodwork a solution of starch and water. After this has dried, rub it off with a soft brush or clean cloth. This also removes stains. Woodwork treated in this manner doesn't harm the paint and it stays good looking for a longer time.

from Stainless Steel. If your stainless steel kitchen utensils have become somewhat discolored from heat, you can clean them nicely with a little steel wool moistened in lemon juice.

Cream of tartar is effective for removing stains from stainless steel. Pour some boiling water into a pan and add cream of tartar. Also, put some into your dishwasher to clear away stains.

To remove water stains from stainless steel sinks and chromium faucets, use a cloth that has been sprinkled with a few drops of vinegar. Vinegar also removes the lime deposits which are apt to collect around the faucets.

Starch. Spot fabric with cold water.

Sugar, same as **Blood,** above.

Tar. Use lard to soften; sponge with cleaning fluid.

Tea, same as **Coffee,** above.

Tobacco. Treat with cold water followed by an application of glycerine and cold water.

Tomato juice stains in fabrics should be sponged thoroughly with cold water to dissolve any solid particles, then work some glycerine into the stain, and wash or sponge with soap and water. Finish with a good rinsing.

from Upholstery. One easy method of cleaning soiled furniture upholstery is merely to sprinkle some dry cornstarch on the stains, rubbing it in with the fingers, letting stay overnight, then vacuuming it off. Greasy spots will clean especially well with this method.

Urine. Wash in a solution of warm, soapy, ammonia water.

Varnish stains on fabrics can often be dealt with by saturating them with turpentine or mineral spirits, rubbing between the hands, then sponging with alcohol.

Verdigris stains on copper utensils or ornaments can be removed quickly by the following method:

Mix a tablespoon of bicarbonate of soda with an equal quantity of kerosene. Scour the copper with the mixture, then rinse and dry.

from Wallpaper. When youngsters have soiled wallpaper, dampen these areas with cold water, then dust on a little fuller's earth, and after this has dried, brush off with a soft cloth or brush.

If tackled promptly, many grease stains can be removed from wallpaper with a sheet of clean white blotting paper and an ordinary electric iron. Lay the blotting paper over the stain and press for a few minutes with an iron set at medium heat. Most fresh grease stains will be liquified by the heat and absorbed by the blotting paper. If necessary, repeat several times, using a clean section of the blotting paper for each operation. (See also WALLPAPER CLEANING.)

from Walls. For inkstains, blood stains, and the like, on wallpaper or plastered walls, wet the spots with water, rub with white magnesia, and then after the chalk dries to a loose powder brush it off.

from Washable Fabrics. First try soaking. If stains persist follow procedure suggested for removal of same stain from non-washable fabrics. Be sure to check safety of chemical for fibers involved.

Watercolor Paint. Treat with turpentine, and then apply benzol to remove turpentine. Or, treat with glycerine and lukewarm water.

Water.

1. *from Ceilings.* If the roof has leaked and stained the ceiling, cover the stains with block magnesia, rubbing the block over the stains until they are covered, then smooth over with the fingertips. Usually does a fine job.

2. *from Fabrics.* Water rings on fabrics usually vanish when they are rubbed gently with a silver spoon or coin.

3. *from Wood Floors.* For stains on oak floors, caused by standing water, rub the area with No. 00 steel wool, and rewax. If this fails, sand lightly with fine sandpaper. Clean the spot and surrounding area using No. 1 steel wool and mineral spirits. Let the floor dry. Apply matching finish on floor, feathering out into the surrounding area. Wax after the finish dries thoroughly.

To remove water spots on finished wood floors, rub gently with a cloth dampened in alcohol, and wipe with an oily cloth.

Wine. When wine is spilled on a white linen tablecloth, cover the stains immediately with salt, then

STAIN REMOVING CHEMICALS

proceed with your meal. Your laundering job will be much easier.

Stretch wine stains on washable fabrics over a bowl and secure with a rubber band. Then sprinkle salt over the area and pour some boiling water on it from a height of two or three feet — being careful, of course, not to splash any on yourself. For fresh wine stains on unwashable fabrics, try an absorbent, such as fuller's earth or cornstarch. Apply the moistened absorbent, let remain for a while, then brush off.

from Wooden Counters. When a wooden cutting board or counter top becomes stained and discolored, first scrub it well with scouring powder, then use household bleach to remove any stubborn stains. The natural wood finish can be restored by rubbing in several coats of boiled linseed oil, applied 24 hours apart. Swab each coat on liberally, then wipe off the excess after about 15 minutes.

from Woodwork. Kitchen woodwork that has become stained from smoke and grease can be cleaned by painting with a solution of starch and water. After the solution has dried on the woodwork, rub it off with a soft brush or clean cloth, which removes the stains. This will not harm the paint and any finished surface treated with starch will remain in good condition for several years.

Stain-Removing Chemicals.
Acetic Acid. Used to restore color.
Acetone, see **Denatured Alcohol.**
Ammonia, see **Acetic Acid.**
Banana Oil, see **Petroleum Jelly.**
Carbon Tetrachloride. General cleaning fluid, especially good for removing grease, etc.
Chloroform, see **Denatured Alcohol.**
Cornmeal, see **Cornstarch.**
Cornstarch. Used to absorb grease, oil and other stains. A dry-cleaning method, it is applied as a paste and brushed off when dry.
Denatured Alcohol. Good for removing gum and grease. Saturate fabric, absorbing excess by placing blotter on wrong side. Inflammable.
Ether, see **Denatured Alcohol.**
French Chalk, see **Cornstarch.**
Fuller's Earth, see **Cornstarch.**
Gasoline, see **Petroleum Jelly.**
Hydrogen Peroxide, POISONOUS, see **Javelle Water.**
Javelle Water. 1/2 lb. washing soda in 1-quart cold water and 1/4 lb. chloride and lime. A bleach used to remove persistant stains. Use with caution and remove immediately after using. POISONOUS.
Kerosene, see **Petroleum Jelly.**
Lard, see **Petroleum Jelly.**
Nail Polish Remover, see **Denatured Alcohol.**
Oxalic Acid. A teaspoon of oxalic acid crystals to 3 cups water. See **Javelle Water.**
Pepsin. Used to remove albumin stains. Mix a solution of 1 teaspoon to 1 pint lukewarm water.
Petroleum Jelly. Loosens dirt and softens oil stains, e.g. lipstick, pitch. It is usually rubbed into the fabric and followed by other cleaning methods.
Potassium Permanganate. 1/2 teaspoon of purple crystals to 1 pint water. POISONOUS. See **Javelle Water.**
Salt. Used to absorb fresh stains, e.g. juice.
Sodium Perborate, POISONOUS, see **Javelle Water.**
Talcum Powder, white, see **Cornstarch.**
Turpentine, see **Petroleum Jelly.**
Water. First choice and usually most effective stain remover. Test non-washable fabrics for color fastness and water marks.
Vinegar, see **Acetic Acid.**

Stair Safety. The bottom step of cellar stairways is where many accidents occur. It is a good idea to paint that bottom step — and only the bottom step — white.

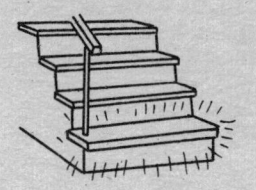

Stairs, Creaking. Each step of a stair is made up of a horizontal board called a tread and a vertical board at the back called a riser. The inner ends of treads and risers rest on two notched timbers running diagonally from the first floor to the next floor above. The treads and risers are secured by wedges glued into the grooves. As the stairs age with use, the wedges loosen and the treads spring away from the risers. As you walk along the treads, you force them down onto the risers and the ends move in the grooves, causing creaking and groaning.

The way to cure a creaking step is to secure the tread to the riser that supports it. Get someone to stand on the offending tread, forcing it down onto the riser. Drive 2-inch finishing nails—cement-coated preferable—solidly through the tread into the riser. Drive these nails in pairs at opposite angles, toe-nailing them, then sink the heads below the surface with a nail set and press in plastic wood.

Stamp Moisteners. When your glue bottle is empty, remove the rubber dispenser on top, wash out the bottle, fill it with water, replace the rubber dispenser — and you'll have a handy and effective moistener for stamps and envelope flaps.

A cut potato surface is just moist enough to use for dampening stamps or envelopes if you haven't a sponge handy. Just slice a small potato in two, snip off a bit of the potato on the bottom so it will remain upright, and then slide your stamps or envelopes over the cut surface.

Stamp pad ink can be made by grinding up about an inch of lead from an indelible pencil, and mixing with a teaspoonful of glycerine and a teaspoonful of water. Let it settle for 8 to 10 hours, and it's ready for use.

Stamps, Postage.

Removing. You might have a much easier time removing an uncancelled stamp from an envelope if you'll just reverse the usual method of attempting this. Instead of trying to pull the stamp from the envelope, place the envelope on a flat surface and bend it back sharply just at the edge of the stamp. Then hold the edge of the stamp down and gradually work the envelope loose.

Unsticking. Attempting to soak stamps apart spoils the mucilage.

Instead, lay a thin paper over them, and run a moderately hot iron over the paper.

They should then come apart easily and the mucilage can still be used.

Another method is to place the stamps in the freezer for a few hours and then slide a knife under the stamps.

Staple Gun, see TOOLS, HAND.

Staple Remover. An ideal tool for removing wire staples from walls and bulletin boards is a discarded fingernail clipper.

Staples.

Netting. For fixing wire netting on fences or cages, use netting staples, while insulated staples are ideal for anchoring bell wires and extension speaker leads to picture rails or skirting boards.

Square carpet staple is used for fixing thin carpets and similar coverings. They are easier to remove than tacks.

Starch Stain, see STAIN REMOVAL.

Star Drill, see TOOLS, HAND.

Static Electricity. You can remove static electricity from sweaters and slips by going over them lightly with a damp sponge or cloth. This can be done even while you are wearing them, since the sponge needs only to be slightly damp.

Try running a wire coat hanger between your dress and nylon slip. This will draw out the electricity and eliminate some of the clinging which is so annoying.

Steam Iron.

Cleaning Soleplates.

1. If the bottom of your iron has become stained with starch, wipe it with a cloth wrung out of hot soapsuds. If necessary, a mild abrasive, such as whiting, may be used to clean the soleplate of the iron — but be cautious, as the chromium plating is damaged easily. Rubbing with whiting will remove even melted nylon. Rinse afterwards with a cloth wrung out of clear water and dry the iron carefully before putting it away.

STENCIL

2. To clean the holes in the bottom of a steam iron, use a pipe cleaner dipped in a solution of detergent and water.

3. The bottom or soleplate of an old iron can be renewed to a glistening, glasslike finish if you'll rub it with slightly dampened salt and a crumpled piece of newspaper. This treatment not only smooths scratches, but removes corrosion and starch from the bottom of the iron.

4. When trying to get the underside of an electric iron clean, use some fine steel wool, powdered whiting or pumice. These will polish and smooth the surface without scratching or scoring it. Do not use harsh abrasives for cleaning that iron!

Removing Starch. If some starch has accumulated on the bottom of your iron, remove this, after the iron has partially cooled, by sprinkling baking soda on a damp cloth, then rubbing the soleplate of the iron with this. Wipe off with a clean, damp cloth, then run the iron over waxed paper.

If some starch has burned on the bottom of your electric iron, disconnect the iron, allow it to cool, then apply some paste silver polish to the starch. Then wipe the iron with a slightly damp cloth, and follow with a dry one.

Scratched. The bottom or soleplate of an old iron can be renewed to a glistening, glasslike finish if you'll rub it with slightly dampened salt and a crumpled piece of paper. This treatment not only smooths scratches, but removes corrosion and starch.

Tap Water. Ordinary tap water may be used in your steam iron if you'll add a tablespoon of ammonia to each cup of water. This softens the water and prevents accumulation of hard particles or sediment in the reservoir of water. Ammoniated water also seems to make for smoother ironing.

Stencil. A unique decorative touch can be added to a small box, plaque, or other such item by making use of an ordinary double-edge safety-razor blade as a stencil. The various blades on the market have differently-shaped openings, which allows you a choice of designs, and the blade affords you a flexible, easily-cleaned stencil. For safety's sake, stick a piece of adhesive tape to one edge of the blade, and use a stiff-bristled brush with a minimum amount of paint or ink.

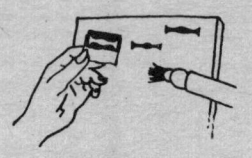

Stepladder, see LADDER.

Step-Stool. Do you need a lavatory step-up so your small child will find it easier to wash his hands at the washbowl? Just replace the empty beverage cans, washed out of course, in their six-pack carton, cover the whole thing with foil or plastic, and your child can stand on this while performing at the bowl.

Stiles, see DOOR REPAIR, DOORS.

Stillson Wrench, see TOOLS, HAND.

Stocking Care, see CLOTHES CARE.

Stone walls are somewhat similar to block concrete and brick walls, since they too are put together with mortar. When a stone wall leaks, the fault is almost always in the mortar. Remove it and replace it. If a single stone has cracked, seal the crack with a clear waterproofing compound.

A stone wall should be at least 16 inches thick, twice as thick as a brick wall. You lay it up the same way you do a concrete block or brick wall with equivalent mortar.

Stopper, Glass. If a glass stopper gets stuck in a bottle, put a few drops of glycerin around the stopper and let stand for several hours. The glycerin usually works down and loosens the stopper.

Storage, Document.

1. You can preserve valuable documents that

you are storing away by rubbing them all over with a gutta-percha solution, obtainable at most drugstores.

2. Before storing away those diplomas, certificates, marriage licenses and other documents you wish to save, roll them and insert them into the tubes that come inside paper towels. You will not only avoid the creases that are usually inevitable when these documents are folded, but they will stay clean and dry.

3. When storing away important documents, you can prevent their yellowing with age if you'll wrap them in blue tissue paper, or in a cloth dyed with bluing.

Storage, Foods, see FOODS.

Storage, Hobby. Help your children to keep their rock and shell collections neatly stored by providing them with empty egg cartons. The compartments in these cartons are ideal for storing your small fry's precious items.

Storage Space.
  Balustrade. On second floor, secure a large flat chest to the railings and finish it like antique furniture.
  under Basement Stairs. A rack built under the basement stairs is another good place for storing window and door screens.
  under Eaves. Build a triangular storage unit with shelves that roll all the way out from the closet on casters.
  Front Hall. If the doorways into the living room, and dining room are wide, put in smaller doors and fill the rest of the space with shelves and cabinets.
  Hallway. Build cabinets below the ceiling at the end of the hall, from ceiling to top of door.
  Living Room. If the fireplace sticks out into the room, make floor-to-ceiling shelves and cabinets on both sides.
  Radiators. Enclose them behind grills and build storage cabinets and shelves against walls on both sides.
  Refrigerator Alcove. Use extra space up by putting in roll-out shelf unit for canned goods.
  Stairwell. Replace the useless closet space with 2 or 3 storage units that roll out endways.
  under Steps. Closets are frequently located under stairways, but quite often the space directly under the steps is unused. You can easily install shelves in these recesses, each shelf no wider than the stair tread, and each shelf held in place with 2-inch metal brackets screwed to the back of the riser, as in the illustration. These shelves prove very handy for holding the overflow of small articles which clutter the larger shelves or get pushed into a corner of the closet.

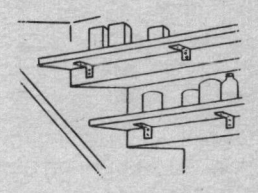

Storage, Workshop, see WORKSHOP.

Stove Cleaning. To clean the cast iron grids of the stove the easy, no-scrub way, submerge them in a non-aluminum pan full of water spiked with three tablespoons of sal soda concentrate, and let simmer for a few minutes on the stove. Then wash as you would your dishes.

Stoves, see HEATING.

Straws, see DRINKING STRAWS.

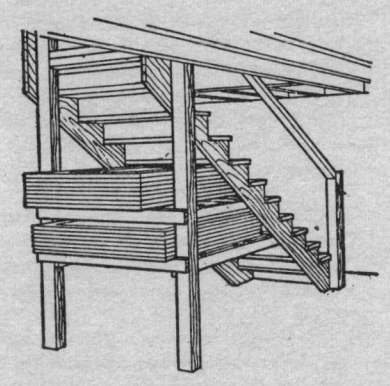

Bedroom. Build low book shelves above headboard and flank bed with cabinets and chests of drawers.
Dining Room. Remodel an ordinary window into a bar window, and build a chest or cabinet under it.

STRING DISPENSER

String Dispenser. You can improvise a very handy and workable string or cord dispenser just by suspending a small funnel from a convenient place on the kitchen or closet wall by means of the small ring usually attached to the funnel. Place the ball of string inside the funnel so that one end of the string can be run out through the funnel end.

Stringed Instrument Repair. When the key slots in a stringed musical instrument become so enlarged from wear that they do not hold the string securely, glue some small pieces of sandpaper in the slots. These will provide a non-slip surface that will hold the string securely. If the slots should then be too narrow, first enlarge them slightly with a file or razor blade. After the sandpaper is glued in the slit, trim off the excess paper with a razor blade.

Structural Lighting, see LIGHTING, STRUCTURAL.

Stucco. Usually applied in three coats—a scratch coat, a brown coat, and a finish coat—stucco may crack from the settling of a house, from improper mixing or application, or from movement of its base. In the average house, stucco is usually applied to a metal lath base, although it goes directly on poured concrete, concrete blocks, brick, or hardburned clay tile.

You must repair a crack in stucco to prevent the nails and metal lath underneath from rusting out and letting water inside that may freeze and break the stucco. To repair, cut out the crack and pack it with patching mix, which should match the original stucco in color.

If the stucco is cracked very badly all over but is still firm to the metal lath, clean the old surface thoroughly, remove all broken pieces, and apply a new stucco layer.

If the stucco wall leaks and there are no visible spiderweb cracks, try waterproofing it with a waterproof compound. Or you might try one of the stucco paints developed to take care of waterproofing and color at the same time.

Studio Beds. To anchor a studio bed to the wall so that it won't keep sliding forward, attach two curtain rings low on the baseboard, then slip the back legs of the bed into these rings.

Studio Couch. Make your own smart and modern studio couch by first removing the headboard and footboard from an old single bed. Cover the bed with a bright felt bedspread. And you can make throw pillows for this from old bathtowels. Fold these to the size and thickness you wish, then cover with some of the felt.

Studs, Locating. A very heavy picture should be hung only where the nail holding it goes directly into a stud. A plaster wall or a drywall simply won't give enough support. Locating the position of a stud in a wall can be trying, but with a little guesswork, a bit of savvy, and a lot of luck, you can do it.

As has been said, studs are located 16 inches on center; that is, the center of adjoining studs will be 16 inches apart. Sometimes you can locate the position of the stud in the wall by finding the nails holding the drywall on; vertically, along the stud, you will find drywall nails at regular intervals.

You can also locate the stud by measuring 16 inches in from the corner of the wall. This method might bring you within an inch of the stud, or it might miss by up to 16 inches. The problem is this: the wall may not be a multiple of 16 inches, and the first stud off one corner may **not** be 16 inches from the corner.

All right, if you don't have any luck with the 16-inch theory, try this. Tap the wall gently with a hammer. You can hear the difference in the sound when you approach the stud. Between studs, the wall sounds hollow; on the stud it sounds solid. If you think you have located the stud, drive in a small nail. If you have hit the stud, measure from that one in both directions 16 inches for the next.

If that approach doesn't work (usually because the drywall has bulged away from the stud and doesn't touch it) try a small child's compass. Run it up and down the wall surface. Where the magnetized arrow twitches and points, there's a nail head, and that's a sign of a stud. Drive in a test nail and see.

Suppose you've located the stud and put up the picture and it's off center and destroys the aesthetic qualities of the room. The stud is out.

But there is a way. For hanging all manner of things onto drywall surfaces, you can get a toggle bolt, a type of screw with a winged anchor on the end. You drill a hole through the drywall, insert the bolt **and** winged anchor through the hole, and tighten the bolt to make the wings fold back against the other side of the dry wall. Then you screw the bolt into the anchored nut.

To hang a picture on a brick wall, use a masonry expansion screw. It's a thick plug of lead with a screw provided. Drill a hole in the masonry big enough to take the plug. Insert the plug and then drive the screw into the plug. The lead expands for a tight fit.

For the locations of studs in walls when you haven't a stud-finder, an ordinary pocket compass will sometimes serve very well. Hold the compass level with the floor and at a right angle to the wall, moving it slowly along the surface of the wall. Movement of compass needle will tell you of the presence of nails and thus locate the stud for you.

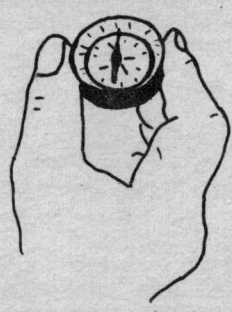

Stylus. If you wish to do some lettering or drawing on a mimeograph stencil, you can improvise a very efficient stylus for the job by making use of a discarded ballpoint pen, one that has gone dry. This will not dig into and tear the stencil as sometimes the real thing is wont to do.

Subflooring, see FLOOR SUPPORT.

Suction Cup. Oftentimes certain brackets fitted with rubber suction cups fail to grip a smooth, slick wall properly, and are continually falling off. Try rubbing the rims of the cups with glycerin before you press them back into place. This usually provides a better, more air tight fit than does water.

Also, suction cups will adhere better to a flat surface if the inside rims are rubbed with wet soap.

Suede Care, see CLOTHES CARE.

Sump Pump. Where gravity drainage is impossible or impracticable, or where a serious water problem arises after the completion of the house, a sump pump or cellar drainer may be used to raise the water to a level where it can be carried off through a drain line.

Sump pumps are small, simple, compact units and are installed in a sump, or pit, at the low corner or other wet spot in the basement. To prevent caving in of the sides, line the sump, or pit, with a length of large draintile or with concrete or metal. Inlets, or holes, should be provided in the lining material to admit ground water. Manufacturers of sump pumps specify the size of sump, or pit, required for a particular pump.

Sump pumps are designed for automatic operation. If correctly installed and not abused, a pump requires very little attention. Dirt, lint, trash, and other waste can clog the strainer and should be kept out of the pit.

Sweater Care, see CLOTHES CARE.

Sweeping Compound. During the summer months, freshly-cut grass clippings make an excellent sweeping compound for dusty concrete floors in the basement or garage. Sprinkle the clippings liberally over the floor, and they will effectively hold down the dust as you make a clean sweep of things.

Sweet Corn, see FOODS.

Sweet Potatoes, see FOODS.

Swimming Pool Repair, see CONCRETE REPAIR.

Switch, Automatic, see ELECTRIC SWITCHES.

Switch, Light, see ELECTRIC SWITCHES.

Switch Plate, Loose. The small screws on switch plates can be kept from working loose with a dab of glue.

After driving the screws until the heads are about 1/8-in. in from the plate surface, dip a toothpick in the glue and wipe off the surplus.

Then dab a little glue under the head of each screw before tightening it.

Although the glue will keep the screws from working loose, it will not interfere with removing the plate when necessary.

T

Table Lamps, see LIGHTING, PORTABLE.

Table Tennis Balls. Instead of discarding dented table tennis balls as worthless, it's worth at least a try at renovating them. Pour some boiling water over them, and often the heat of the water will expand the air inside the balls and cause the dents to pop right out.

Tabletops.

Heatproof. You can produce your own heatproof tabletop. First, remove the old finish. Then mix one-third turpentine and two-thirds linseed oil, shake well, and rub this into the wood, using an old, soft, clean cloth. After thorough application, rub the surface dry. Hot dishes will not leave marks on this surface.

Plastic. If a plastic tabletop seems to have lost some of its luster, rub in some toothpaste to make it shine again like new. There will be no greasy oil finish either. Or, cover with paste wax and buff.

Plateglass. When plateglass is used to protect polished woodwork, the formation of moisture can be prevented by fitting very small washers or tabs of cork or felt at the corners of the table under the glass. These have the effect of raising the glass just a fraction so that air can circulate underneath.

Warp Prevention. In replacing a tabletop that requires wide panels, it is best, in order to prevent warping, to make the panels by gluing three or more boards together. If a 21-inch panel is needed, glue up three 7-inch pieces to make the 21 inches. Wide pieces, such as are shown in Figure 1 of the illustration, should be cut to narrow widths, then the pieces rearranged for gluing as shown in Figure 2. By inverting the center piece to change the growth-ring direction, the warping of the outer pieces is counteracted by the direction of warping of the center piece.

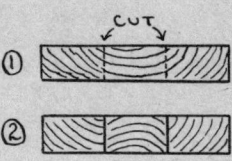

Tables.

Card, see CARD TABLES.

Drop Leaf. The annoyance of having the drop leaf of a table rattle against the legs, and probably mar them, can be avoided simply by sticking a small adhesive bandage to the underside of the drop leaf at each point of contact. You can color the "bumpers" to match the tone of the wood.

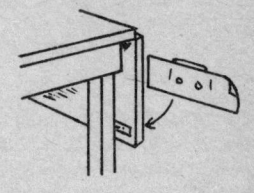

Mats for. You can make your own heatproof table mats by mounting some colorful lengths of linoleum on pieces of thin plywood, cementing the linoleum

TACKS

to the wood, then painting the edges of the wood a gay color.

Patio. Here is an easily-constructed—but attractive and efficient—table for use on your porch or patio. All you have to do is screw a deep-lipped round metal tray to a two-foot length of three-inch-diameter stock (or square stock, if you wish), and then set this firmly into a ten-inch square box of cement. You can then finish the tray and stand with enamel.

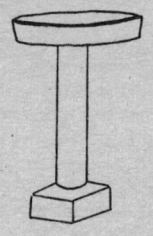

Portable. A very useful, portable, outdoor table can be fashioned from one section of broomstick or dowel, and a cakepan or serving tray. Sharpen one end of your "leg," and fasten the pan to the other end with a wood screw. When setting up this table, all you have to do is thrust the pointed end firmly into the ground beside your chair. A whole set of these tables are ideal for serving snacks to outdoor guests.

Stilts for. Sometimes for eating or working purposes, you wish that your card table were a little higher. You can give it a boost to the height of your dining table simply by making these easy leg extensions: Drill holes two inches deep and of a circumference to match those of the legs into four blocks of wood four by four by six inches. These blocks will provide solid extensions to raise your table to the desired height.

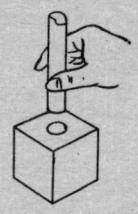

Storage of Leaves. You can provide a good, safe rack for storing those extra table leaves in a closet or other out-of-way place by use of an ordinary towel bar. Stand one leaf on end against the wall and mark its height. Then screw the towel bar to the wall at an angle, the high end just above the mark. This permits the leaves to be placed under the bar from the side.

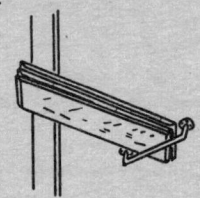

Tacks, see NAILS.

Tack Starter. If you don't have a magnetic hammer, here's a very simple and easy way to hold your tacks while you hammer them. Just tear a slit in a small piece of cardboard, and use this for starting your tacks.

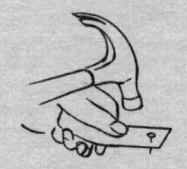

Taffeta Care, see CLOTHES CARE.

Tailpipe, see AUTOMOBILE.

Tape Holder. It's always a problem, when measuring with a steel tape, to keep the other end of it in the proper place. You can hold the starting tip of your steel tape firmly in position by using a rubber suction cup. First stick the cup to the surface, then insert the hook in the end of your rule into the cup and make your measurement.

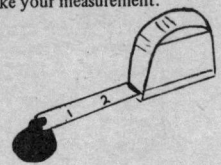

Tape Measure. You can revitalize a limp and lifeless tape measure by placing it between two sheets of waxed paper, then pressing with a slightly hot iron.

Tape Measure, Magnetic. You can increase the usefulness of a cloth tape measure by cementing a bar magnet at one end of it.

The magnet will hold the end of the tape against any steel object, freeing one hand. Also, it will weight the tape of vertical measurements, even when there's no metal to anchor it to.

Tapes, see TOOLS, MEASURING.

Tarnish Prevention, see JEWELRY.

Tar Removal, see AUTOMOBILE.

Tar Stain, see STAIN REMOVAL.

Tea, see FOODS.

Tea Stain, see STAIN REMOVAL.

Teakettle. Scale or lime formations inside your teakettle can be prevented simply by keeping an oyster shell in the kettle, replacing this whenever it accumulates all the scale it can hold.

When you are finished with your teakettle, empty any water that may be left. Then, before filling it again, rinse it out with some cold, clear water. This prevents the formation of sediment in the kettle.

Telephone.
Amplifying Ring. You'll be able to hear your phone ring when you are in the basement if you place a metal pan on the floor and the phone on top of it.
Cleaning. Clean the dust and grime from under the dial of your telephone with an ordinary cotton-tipped swab stick.
Dialing. When dialing a number on your phone, don't use a pencil. Its action is too harsh, and constant use will loosen mechanism and damage the dial.

Finger dialing is the safest and cleanest way.

Television Stand. You can add a touch of modern decor with this attractive and "different" stand for your table-model television set. This stand is made entirely of brick. You can use any type of brick, but colored face brick and the modern, long, thinner brick will probably look better than the common type. No mortar is used, the bricks being stacked squarely on one another and held in place by their own weight. Select your bricks carefully to see that only those with undamaged edges and corners are used, both because of appearance and stability. You can also project some of your bricks, if you wish, for use as shelves to hold flowers, ashtrays, or other knicknacks.

Tennis Court Broom. A stiff brush is good for dragging over a tennis court before wetting and rolling, since it distributes the loose clay evenly over the court. A wide brush can be made by joining three push brooms with a strip of wood screwed across their tops, and this will cut down the work considerably. The handle of the center broom is extracted from its socket and fastened across the outer handles as a crossbar.

TEXTURE PAINT

Texture Paint, see PAINTS.

Thermometer. If the mercury in one of your thermometers has separated, first try to shake it together. Or, dip it into very cold water for a few minutes. If both of these methods fail, the condition is usually hopeless and a new thermometer is in order.

Thermostats, see HEATING.

Thinner, see PAINT COMPONENTS.

Throw Rugs, see RUGS.

Tie Rack, see CLOSET ACCESSORIES.

Tile, Acoustical.
  Cleaning.
    1. Discolored acoustical tile can often be cleaned very nicely by sponging with a mild soap solution, using care not to get the tile surface too wet, and rubbing only lightly. These tiles can also be repainted with any interior latex paint. Just apply your paint evenly, and avoid filling in any of the holes in the tile.
    2. For weekly cleaning, use the brush attachment of your vacuum cleaner to clean acoustical tile on your ceiling or wall. Stubborn smudges can be removed with wallpaper cleaner or a cloth slightly moistened with soapy water.
  Repairing. If the acoustical tiles in your ceiling have become loose or bulging, if they are applied to wood furring strips, nail them back to the strips with flat-headed nails. If they are applied on plaster, use cement-coated nails, countersinking the nailheads, and covering with spackle.

Tile, Asphalt, see also RESILIENT TILE FLOORS.
  Cleaning. Marks on asphalt tile, which refuse to yield to ordinary scrubbing, can be removed by rubbing the surface lightly with some No. 00 steel wool, using a concentrated solution of neutral soap or cleaner in some warm water.

Cutting. The job of cutting and fitting rubber or asphalt tile can be made much easier if you'll just heat the tile squares first. In the case of rubber tile, just about one minute under an infra-red lamp makes them easy to trim with either a knife or scissors. With asphalt tile, a little longer time under the lamp will make it pliable and easy to cut.

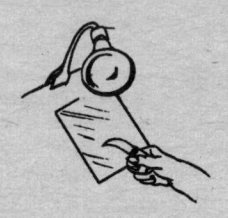

Tile, Bathroom, see BATHROOM WALLS.

Tile, Ceiling.
  Installation. As a general rule in laying out ceilings, first establish center lines. Run a line between the midpoint of each of the two short end walls. Next locate the midpoint of the center line. At this point establish an intersecting line at right angles to the first center line. If the ceiling figures so that an even number of tiles are to be used, the joint will occur

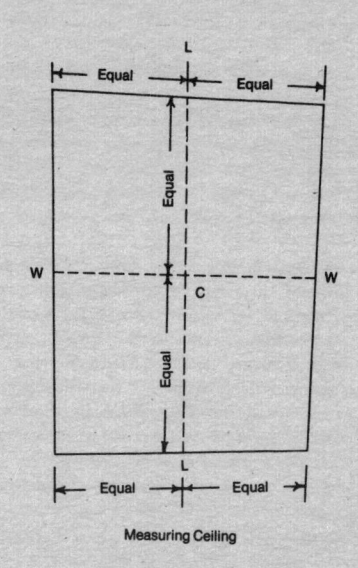

Measuring Ceiling

334

on the center line. If you have to use an odd number of tiles, the center line of the room will fall on the center line of the tile. After spots of adhesive have been put on tile or plank, it should be placed in the approximate position that it will occupy. Then, slide it back and forth pressing with the hands at the same time to work the adhesive into place to get a good bond. Be sure the tiles are level and even. If you prefer to nail or staple, read the manufacturers' instructions carefully.

Repair. You can do a very effective job of patching a dig or scratch in ceiling tile with some dry plaster or talcum powder. After dampening the damaged area with a wet sponge or cloth, tamp the powder in with your thumb, brushing away the excess with a soft brush or whisk broom. Repeat the process if necessary, so as to level the patched spot with the surrounding area. This patch will dry without a sheen, and will match the finish of the rest of your tile perfectly.

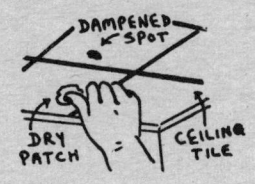

Tile, Ceramic. This widely used and popular finish for bathroom floors comes glazed or unglazed—with a bright or dull finish—and in multiple colors and shapes. Most ceramic tile sold today is factory assembled on paper or mesh. The traditional method of setting ceramic tile is in cement mortar. However, organic adhesives are extensively used today.

Ceramic tile floors are easy to keep clean. Washing with mild soap, powdered cleanser, or a synthetic detergent solution is usually sufficient. In areas where the water is hard, soap is less satisfactory than synthetic detergent or cleaning powder because of the insoluble film that forms from the reaction of the soap with salts in the water. If necessary, scouring powder can be used on heavily soiled areas. Ceramic floors should not be waxed.

Cleaning. You can give glazed wall tiles the sparkle of newness by wiping with a sponge dipped in ammonia and water.

Polishing. Try covering your freshly-washed ceramic tile with a thin coat of laundry starch, then after this is dry, polishing with a dry cloth. You'll like the rich gloss this produces on your tile.

Rust Removal. Remove rust spots on a ceramic-tile floor with a washing compound of one part sodium citrate dissolved in six parts of commercial glycerin. Add water to thin this mixture, then mix with sufficient whiting to form a paste. Spread this over the spots in thick coatings.

Tile Floors, Resilient, see RESILIENT TILE FLOORS.

Tile, Paint Stains on, see STAIN REMOVAL.

Tile, Plastic. Stick-on plastics—in flexible sheets or tiles—are today's high-speed method of decorating.

You peel off the protective paper backing, press the sheet or tile into position and there it stays.

These plastic materials are unaffected by stains, splashes, grease and dirt.

They can be repeatedly washed and make pretty and practical coverings for wall and furniture surfaces liable to specially hard wear.

Three practical ways of using them are:

The wall area around the sink can be an awkward place to fit a conventional splashback, but flexible plastic sheeting can be cut with scissors to fit any wall space.

The wall behind the hall table is another area liable to wear and tear, particularly if you have decorated the hall with delicate wallpaper.

If cigarette burns, stains and scratches have left their mark on your favorite coffee table, give it a face lift with a new top of gleaming plastic tiles.

Cleaning. Plastic wall tile will sparkle like a mirror when it is cleaned with a vinegar-and-water solution, then dried and polished with a bath towel.

Cutting. For cutting plastic wall tile, a coping saw with a fine blade having thirty-two teeth per inch is just the thing, especially where you have to make short-radius cuts in fitting the tile around bathroom fixtures or pipes that come through the wall. Beeswax or paraffin rubbed on the sides of your blade will prevent its binding in these short-radius cuts.

Refastening. If one of the plastic wall tiles in your bathroom becomes loosened, one effective way to refasten it is with chewing gum. Just stick a small wad of gum near each corner of the tile, and press it into place with a warm iron.

Tile Repair. You can make a quick and effective repair on a loose tile in the hearth or floor, just by lifting it out, pouring in some hot paraffin, then quickly replacing the tile. It will stay in place indefinitely.

Tile, Roofing, see ROOF SURFACES.

Tin Can Disposal. Here's one neat and novel way to dispose of those tin cans and prevent their cluttering up your kitchen rubbish container. If you have a kitchen closet, cut a six-inch hole in the floor and use a stovepipe to lead the cans into a cellar basket or container.

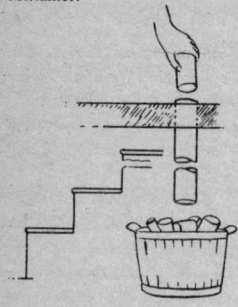

Tin, Polishing. Tin can be polished by rubbing with a freshly sliced onion, then with a dry, clean cloth.

Tires, see AUTOMOBILE.

Tissue Paper. Don't throw away any tissue paper, even if it is too crumpled for wrapping purposes. It's great for shining washed windows or mirrors.

Toaster, see APPLIANCES.

Tobacco Freshener. Cigars and pipe tobacco can be kept fresh and moist if a few fresh apple peelings are kept in their containers. Replace these peelings when they wither.

Tobacco Stain, see STAIN REMOVAL.

Toilet Repair, see PLUMBING.

Toilet seats are finished with plastic coverings, paint, or enamel. If the finish on a painted or enameled seat and cover is marred, it may be renewed by taking off the finish with paint remover and recoating with quick-drying (4-hour) enamel. If plastic coatings have become unsightly or the seat itself is cracked and the joints have become loosened, the seat and cover should be replaced.

Tomatoes, see FOODS.

Tongue Depressor. Keep a supply of wooden tongue depressors (as used by doctors) on hand in your home workshop. They make convenient, disposable applicators for all types of glue, mastic, and adhesive, and are also fine for mixing small quantities of paint. These tongue depressors are obtainable at most drug stores.

Tongue and Groove Boards, see CARPENTRY.

Tool Care.
  Oiling. An oil can, is a must, not only for use with the oilstone in sharpening tools, but for use with your saw blades and for all your tools to keep them from rusting. Oil keeps hinges from squeaking, too.
  Preservative. You can make an excellent varnish for your tools by combining two ounces of tallow with one ounce of resin, melting these two ingredients together and straining while hot to remove any spots that might be in the resin. Apply a light coating of this to your tools, and it will serve as a long-lasting resistant to rust.

  Rust Prevention. If you keep some of your tools in the basement, the garage, the tool shed, or any place where there is a tendency to dampness, you can safeguard them from rust by storing them in a box

TOOL HOLDERS

of oil-soaked sand. Use a large enough box to accomodate the tools you are storing; fill it with clean sand; then saturate the sand with motor oil.

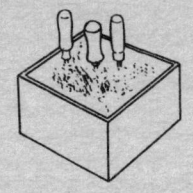

Rust Removal. You can remove rust spots from your metal tools by rubbing over them with some steel wool soaked with lubricating oil. For stubborn spots, repeat the process, using rust solvent. It's a good idea, too, to leave a light film of oil on your tools for permanent protection.

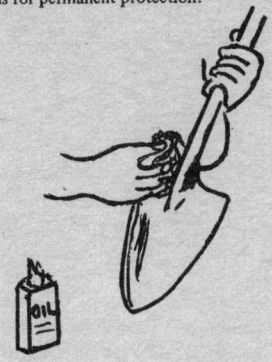

Sharpening. First place the blade on the stone at the correct angle or bevel and maintain this position while sharpening.

There is always a tendency to let the blade rise and fall in a rocking motion, and this will produce a rounded bevel on the cutting edge, so keep it steady.

The oblique oval movement can be used to advantage when sharpening wide plane irons on a narrow oil stone.

It allows the full width of the cutting edge to be in contact with the oil stone surface all the time.

In any case, when sharpening chisels and other narrow tools always move from side to side of the stone.

A great advantage when sharpening chisel and plane irons is to use a special honing guide which holds the blade at correct angle and insures that the bevel edge of the blade is not rounded over.

It is a hone made by attaching a strip of emery cloth to a block of wood with thumbtacks.

It is a good idea to make two such hones — or whetstones — one with coarse grit emery cloth and the other faced with a fine grade.

With the tool blade at a right angle to the abrasive, move the cutting edge sideways the length of the strip, first on the coarse strip, then on the fine grade.

Finish with a few strokes on a leather strap for a razor-sharp edge.

When you have no honing stone handy to sharpen the blade of your plane, chisel, or other cutting tool, you can do the job very nicely with a piece of emery cloth laid out on a flat, smooth surface. Be sure to vary the pressure on the tool, bearing down hard at first in order to wear the edge down, then gradually decreasing your pressure so as to produce a keen cutting edge.

Tool Carrier. You can make a very handy and efficient tool-holder to carry on your belt, from an old, discarded leather glove. This will accommodate such small tools as a screwdriver, file, nail set, pliers, or punch. Simply remove the front half of the cuff, fold the back of the glove, and stitch so that it can be slipped onto your belt. You can remove the thumb of the glove, or leave it on for short tools, as you wish.

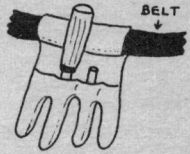

Tool Holders. A handy, portable container for your tools and other small parts while you are performing ladder jobs can be made from a large juice can with

337

TOOL KIT

its lid partly cut off, trimmed, and bent over the rung of the ladder.

It's always annoying when your screwdriver or other tools persist in rolling off the top tread of your step ladder while you're working at a high altitude. You can easily prevent this just by boring some holes large enough to accommodate the blades or handles of these tools. Of course, if you make use of the top tread of your ladder quite often, you can drill these holes through the extension tray of the ladder. If the holes are drilled to a size to take the tools snugly, the ladder can be tipped for carrying without their falling out.

Excellent tool holders can be provided by the simple variety of drawer handles, attached inside a tool cabinet or over your workbench. They're very quickly installed, and several of your smaller tools can be kept in each holder.

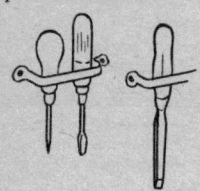

Tool Kit, Basic Tools.
- 1 utility knife
- 1 hand crosscut saw, 10 point, 24-inch
- 1 hand rip saw, 5 point, 24-inch
- 1 each, chisels—1/4-inch, 3/8-inch, 1/2-inch, 3/4-inch, 1 inch, 1-1/2 inch
- 1 junior jack plane, 11-1/2 inch
- 1 pocket "Surform," 5-1/2 inch
- 1 ratchet brace, 8-inch sweep
- 1 set auger bits, 1/4-inch to 1 inch
- 1 hand drill, 1/4-inch
- 1 combination square, 12 inch
- 1 marking gauge

- 1 folding rule, 8 feet
- 1 claw hammer, 13 ounces
- 1 each, screwdriver, 4-inch blade, 6-inch small blade, 4-inch Phillips blade
- 1 each, nail set, 2/32-inch and 4/32-inch tips
- 1 brad awl, 1-1/2-inch blade
- 1 combination oilstone, fine and coarse, 8 inch x 2 inch x 1 inch.
- 1 oiler
- 1 pair combination pliers, 6 inch
- 1 adjustable wrench (crescent type) 5 inch
- 1 staple gun

Tool Rack. If you have some wooden shelves over your workbench, a series of small holes bored into the edge of the shelving on a slightly downward angle will prove ideal for holding punches, nail sets, and various small, round tools. It is then very easy to make your selection of the desired tool without delay.

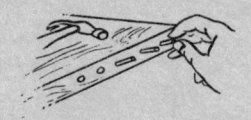

Tools, Gardening, see GARDEN TOOLS.

Tools, Hand.

Awl. The proper way to start a hole for a wood screw is to use a brad awl, driving in the blade at the correct angle to lead the screw into the material. An awl will also start a good hole for a brace and bit. One with a 1-1/2 inch blade should be part of your tool survival kit.

Bench Plane, see **Plane,** below.

Bench Vises, see **Vises, Bench,** below.

Box Wrench, see **Wrench, Box,** below.

Brace and Bit. A drill is simply a cutting edge mounted spirally around a spindle. Drill cutting edges are called bits, or auger bits.

To control and turn the bit, you fit it into a brace, manipulated by turning a handle in a clockwise direction to drive the auger bit into the wood. There is a chuck, or grip, at the end of the brace where different-sized bits can be fitted in at will.

A cutting bit is usually identified by the diameter of the hole it will drill. You should have a set of auger bits running from 1/4-inch in diameter to

TOOLS, HAND

1-inch in diameter. Braces come in various sizes. For the home workshop, a brace with either an 8- or 10-inch sweep—the diameter of the circle described by the handle in one turn—should be large enough.

For drilling smaller holes—1/4-inch or less—you should use a hand drill, similar in appearance to an egg-beater, with bits instead of beaters. The handle of the drill turns in a vertical plane rather than in a horizontal one, and the bits which fit into the chuck are smaller than those in a brace. A set of 1/4-inch and smaller usually comes with each hand drill. (See also **Drill, Drilling**, below.)

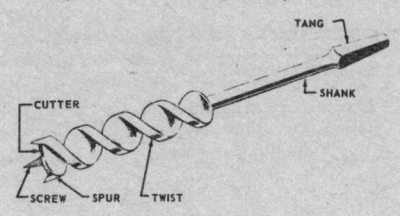

Nomenclature of an auger bit.

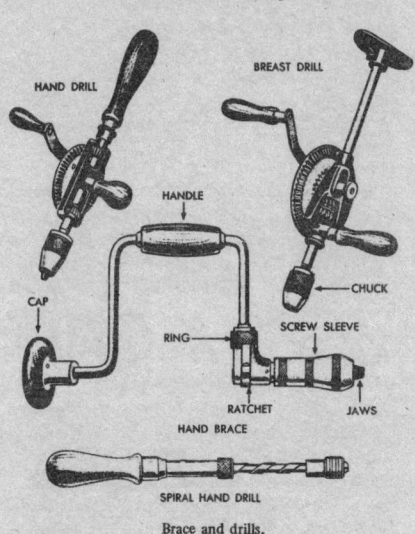

Brace and drills.

Chisel Holder. Bruised hands are a common hazard when using a cold chisel. You can prevent this if you'll make a holder, as illustrated, from two lengths of one-inch stock and a heavy rubber band. Each length of wood is beveled on the inside surface near the end and a notch is cut three inches from the end to receive the chisel. Another shallow notch on the outside of each strip will hold the rubber band in place.

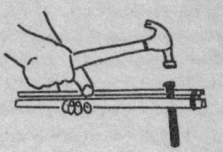

Chiseling Brickwork. Whenever a mirror, cupboard, or any other type of frame has to be secured to a wall, it is usually necessary to plug the brickwork so that the attachment screws or bolts can get a firm hold.

Where the brickwork has been plastered over, or the wall is of concrete or stone, a round drill with either a diamond or starshaped point is used to make the holes for the plugs.

On open brick work, however, we can do the job much more efficiently by using the flat plugging chisel shown.

A hammer is used to drive the flat blade of the chisel into the mortar joints between the bricks and make a cavity at least 2-in. deep and 1-1/2-in. wide.

Flat wooden plugs are cut to drive tightly between the bricks, then cut off flush with the surface.

The best wood for the plugs is dry cedar or any other dry, close-grained timber.

Chiseling Corners. To chamfer (bevel) with a chisel, you flatten the sharp corner between two right-angled surfaces. The ends of a chamfer may be flat or curved. You may produce a round corner with a

TOOLS, HAND

chisel, doing rough work with the bevel side of the chisel held toward the wood, and finishing with the bevel held up.

Chiseling Wood. To drive a chisel into wood, use light blows of a wood mallet rather than a steel hammer. Hold your chisel at a diagonal when cutting, and keep both hands behind the cutting edge. Always work with the grain of the wood. Do not hurry.

Wood carving is chiseling which may be brought to a fine art, and, of course, a wood carver has special tools.

Chisel Shield. One of the common hazards of using a chisel on stone, concrete or cement is the flying of the chips and pieces. As a safety-first measure to your eyes and face, you can improvise a guard for your chisel with a piece of ordinary screen wire. Punch a hole through this screening, slip it over your chisel, and anchor it in place with a couple of tight-fitting rubber washers which you can cut from an old automobile inner tube.

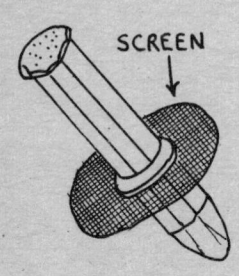

Chisels, Metal. Chisels are tools that can be used for chipping or cutting metal. They will cut any metal that is softer than the materials of which they are made. Chisels are made from a good grade tool steel and have a hardened cutting edge and beveled head. Cold chisels are classified according to the shape of their points, and the width of the cutting edge denotes their size. The most common shapes of chisels are flat (cold chisel), cape, round nose, and diamond point.

The type chisel most commonly used is the flat cold chisel, which serves to cut rivets, split nuts, chip castings, and cut thin metal sheets. The cape chisel is used for special jobs like cutting keyways, narrow grooves and square corners. Round-nose chisels make circular grooves and chip inside corners with a fillet. Finally, the diamond-point is used for cutting V-grooves and sharp corners.

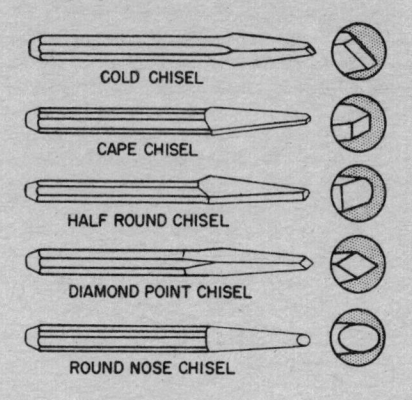

Types of points on metal cutting chisel.

Chisels, Wood. A wood chisel is a steel tool fitted with a wooden or plastic handle. It has a single beveled cutting edge on the end of the steel part, or blade. According to their construction, chisels may be divided into two general classes: TANG chisels, in which part of the chisel enters the handle, and SOCKET chisels, in which the handle enters into a part of the chisel.

A socket chisel is designed for striking with a wooden mallet (never a steel hammer), while a tang chisel is designed for hand manipulation only.

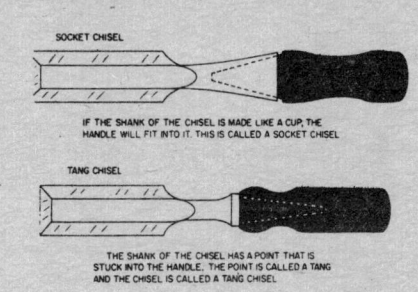

SOCKET CHISEL

IF THE SHANK OF THE CHISEL IS MADE LIKE A CUP, THE HANDLE WILL FIT INTO IT. THIS IS CALLED A SOCKET CHISEL

TANG CHISEL

THE SHANK OF THE CHISEL HAS A POINT THAT IS STUCK INTO THE HANDLE. THE POINT IS CALLED A TANG AND THE CHISEL IS CALLED A TANG CHISEL

Wood chisels are also divided into types, depending upon their weights and thicknesses, the shape or design of the blade, and the work they are intended to do.

TOOLS, HAND

The shapes of the more common types of wood chisels are shown below. The FIRMER chisel has a strong, rectangular-cross-section blade, designed for both heavy and light work. The blade of the PARING chisel is relatively thin, and is beveled along the sides for the fine paring work. The BUTT chisel has a short blade, designed for work in hard-to-get-at places.

The butt chisel is commonly used for chiseling the GAINS (rectangular depressions) for the BUTT hinges on doors; hence the name. The MORTISING chisel is similar to a socket firmer but has a narrow blade, designed for chiseling out the deep, narrow MORTISES for mortise-and-tenon joints. This work requires a good deal of levering out of chips; consequently, the mortising chisel is made extra thick in the shaft to prevent breaking.

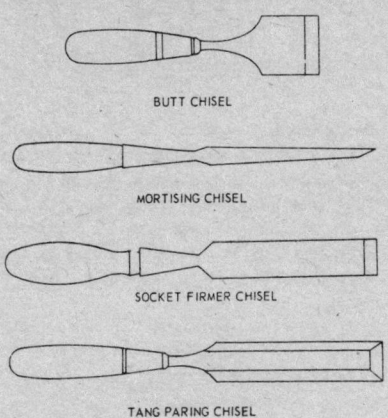

BUTT CHISEL

MORTISING CHISEL

SOCKET FIRMER CHISEL

TANG PARING CHISEL

Clamps are used for holding work which cannot be satisfactorily held in a vise because of its shape and size, or when a vise is not available. Clamps are generally used for light work.

A C-clamp is shaped like the letter C. It consists of a steel frame threaded to receive an operating screw with a swivel head. It is made for light, medium, and heavy service in a variety of sizes.

A hand screw clamp consists of two hard maple jaws connected with two operating screws. Each jaw has two metal inserts into which the screws are threaded. The hand screw clamp is also issued from supply in a variety of sizes.

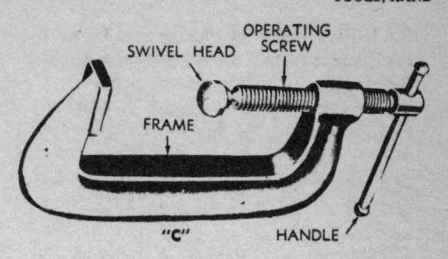

"C" — SWIVEL HEAD, OPERATING SCREW, FRAME, HANDLE

HAND SCREW — OPERATING SCREW, OPERATING SCREW, JAWS

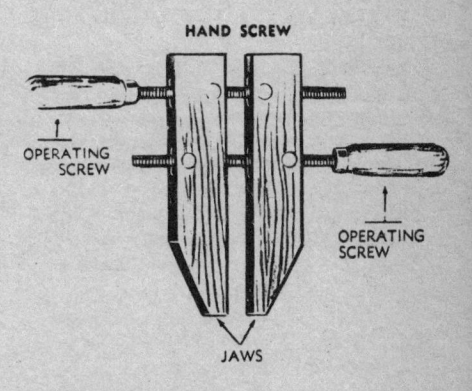

Compass Saw, see **Saw,** below.
Coping Saw, see **Saw,** below.
Crescent Wrench, see **Wrench, Adjustable,** below.
Crosscut Saw, see **Handsaw,** below.
Drill, Automatic. A very handy drill is the automatic drill, often called a push drill. This drill can be used to drill either horizontal or vertical holes when the accuracy of the right angle with the work is not critical.

The drill point used in push drills is a straight flute drill. Sharpen its point on the grinder and provide only a slight clearance behind the cutting edge. It will drill holes in wood and other soft materials.

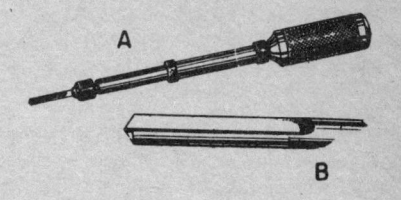

Push drill and drill point.

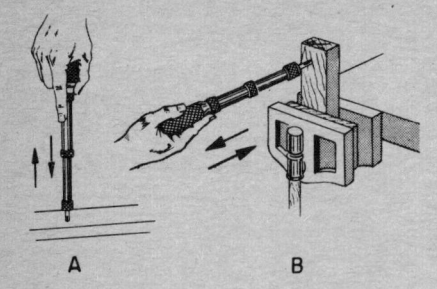

TOOLS, HAND

Drilling horizontal and vertical holes with a push drill.

Drilling Aid. You can waste a lot of time blowing away the chips and dust that accumulate while you are drilling several holes close together in a single piece of work. This annoyance can be eliminated if you'll wire or tape a few bristles from an old floor or paint brush around your drill, as illustrated. In this way, the waste will be whisked away as you drill.

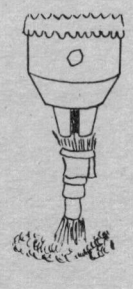

Drilling Glass. When drilling holes in bottles, jars, or other items made of glass, try using a short piece of an old triangular file as your drill bit. Build a dam of putty around the spot where the hole is to be drilled, and fill this with turpentine. Sharpen the end of your file on a grinding wheel into a point, then use this in your drill chuck to bore a hole in the middle of the pool of turpentine.

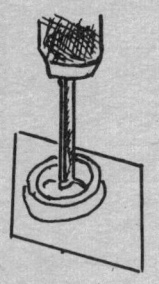

Copper or brass tubing, with notches filed into one end, and chucked into your drill press, is very effective for drilling holes in glass. Use a rubber cushion under the glass and build a clay dam around the drilling area to retain turpentine and grains of carborundum or emery. Start your drilling with easy pressure and, when half through, drill from the other side to finish.

Drilling Holes. When you are drilling holes into a finished surface, you can protect the surface by slipping a rubber washer over the drill bit. Then, should the bit unexpectedly break through, the washer will prevent the chuck jaws from marring the finish. The washer can be the kind used in faucets, or it may be cut from an old automobile inner tube or stair thread.

Drilling Larger Holes. When it becomes necessary to bore a larger hole over a smaller hole, sometimes it's very difficult to center your bit accurately. Here's one good way to insure accurate drilling. Drive a wood plug or dowel through the small hole, and this new wood will guide your bit screw through.

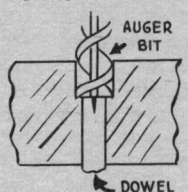

Drilling Masonry. When using a star drill to cut a hole in tough masonry or rock, you require not only the star drill and a hammer, but a lot of patience. Hold the drill loosely in one hand with the point against the hard surface, then tap it sharply with your hammer. A tiny chip will break loose. Give the drill a quarter-turn and tap it again. Proceed in this manner until the hole is finished.

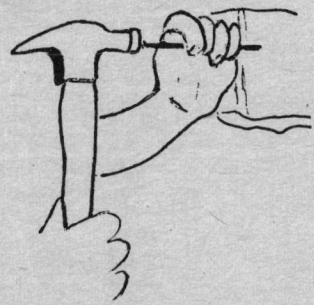

Drilling Metal. If you are going to drill a hole through metal, you can prevent your drill from slipping by affixing a small piece of masking tape to the spot.

Drilling Overhead. Whenever you are drilling some spot overhead, there's always the danger of plaster bits or wood dust falling into your eyes. You can prevent this, and still see what you are doing, if you'll place the clear plastic top of a cheese container over the area you wish to drill, then drill through the plastic.

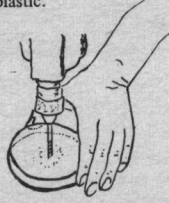

Drilling Pilot Holes. If you are lacking a twist drill of the proper size, try chucking a finishing nail into your portable electric drill and using this for drilling pilot holes for screws.

Drilling Plaster. The drilling of small holes in plaster walls usually dulls ordinary bits quickly. Improvise a disposable bit by cutting the head off an ordinary nail and chucking this into your drill. This "throwaway" bit will drill the holes you need very nicely.

Drilling Techniques. Drilling and boring are operations which are constantly called for in the workshop.

In some cases you need to work with the utmost accuracy, such as in doweling; in others, speed is more important.

In any case, knowing the basic operating principles of both power and hand tools and what each type of bit can do will save considerable time and work and produce more satisfactory results.

It is essential that any piece of wood be held securely while it is being drilled or bored.

Any movement will undoubtedly cause the hole to be crooked and will produce rough sides and edges.

It is also very likely that the bit will be snapped off.

The sketches show several ways in which work may be held for drilling or boring.

The standard workshop G clamp is the handiest standby and at "A" the wood being bored is clamped to the bench or table.

Note the block placed under the bit near the chuck.

This serves as both a support and distance piece to ensure that the bit is level.

If you need to hold the work vertically in a vice, always keep the section in which the hole or holes are being bored well down near the vice jaws to avoid any possibility of spring and movement.

Don't clamp it in the vice in one position and try to drill several holes.

Move it after each drilling to conform with the approximate position suggested in detail "B".

In detail "C" a pair of clamps are being used to permit a series of holes to be drilled horizontally.

This procedure calls for protective strips on each side to prevent possible splitting of thin wood.

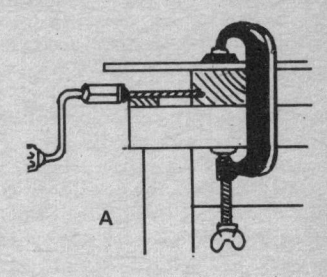

TOOLS, HAND

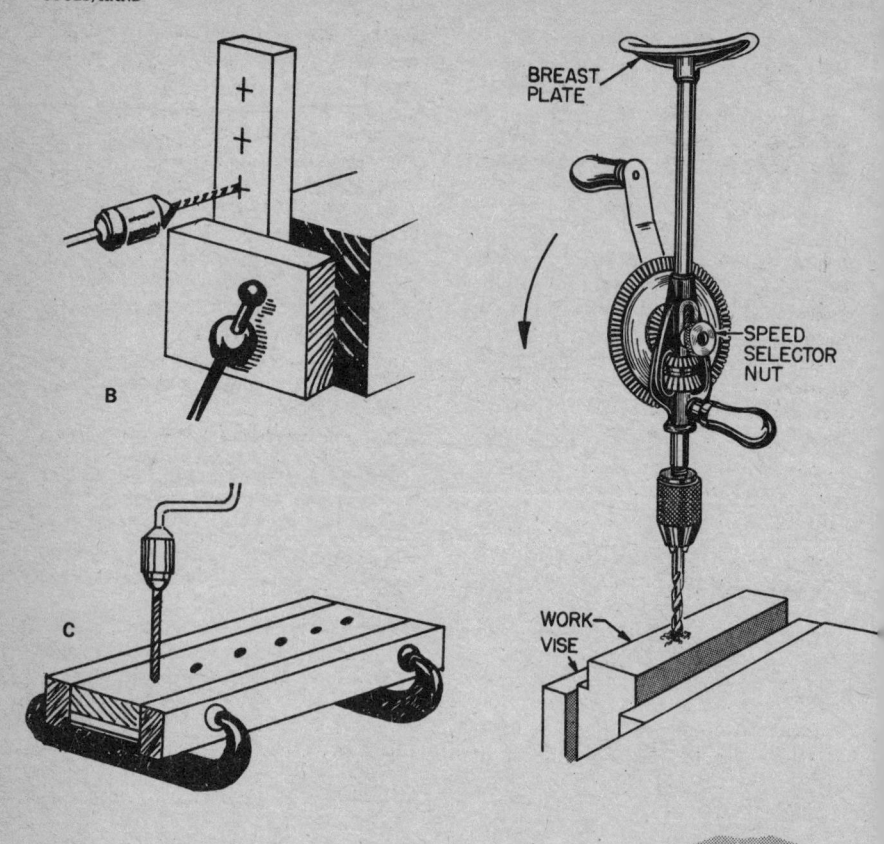

Drilling with Breast Drill. Turn the crank handle with one hand as you hold the side handle with the other hand. This will steady the breast drill while feed pressure is applied by resting your chest on the breast plate. Notice, too, that the breast drill has a high or a low speed available, according to the setting of the speed selector nut. When drilling a horizontal hole, apply feed pressure by resting your body against the breast plate.

Drilling with Hand Drill. In drilling a horizontal hole with the hand drill, operate the crank with the right hand and with the left hand guide the drill by holding the handle which is opposite the chuck end of the drill.

Drilling without Splintering. To bore a horizontal hole in the stock held in the bench vise, hold the head of the brace with one hand, steadying it against your body, while turning the handle with the other hand. Scrap stock behind the job will prevent splintering.

TOOLS, HAND

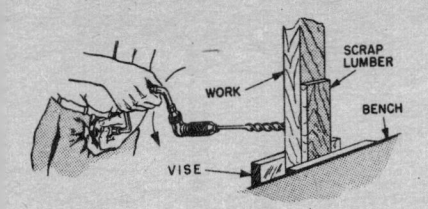

Drill Maintenance. The frequent breaking of very fine or small drills can be reduced if they are chucked short, as in the illustration. If your particular chuck doesn't permit this, try running a 1/8-inch drill up into the chuck body, thus providing clearance for drill shanks. Very high spindle speed and good cutting oil are also big aids in cutting down excessive breakage of small drills.

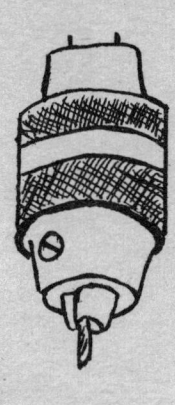

Drill, Masonry. For most electric hand drills you can buy carbide-tipped masonry drills. The common ¼-inch electric drill will handle a ¼-inch carbide-tipped drill, but be careful not to let the drill get too hot, or it will burn out. Use the power drill only to make holes for anchor bolts, not to drill completely through solid masonry. If you must penetrate through masonry, use a ½-inch electric drill.

Drill, Push, see **Drill, Automatic,** above.

Drill Sanding Disk. The sanding disk on your electric drill often becomes clogged and here is an effective way to restore the cutting surface.

Get a wire brush and tap the disk face with it as the disk rotates.

Drill, Star. This is a steel rod with a star-shaped point. You hold the drill in one hand with its point against the masonry. Then you strike the drill end a sharp blow with a mallet, and after each blow rotate the drill a quarter turn. Wear goggles and heavy gloves when you work with a star drill.

File, Improvised. A round, or "rattail" file, is a very handy tool, but when you do not have one on hand, improvise your own with a length of dowel spiral wound with a strip of emery cloth, or other such abrasive sheet, glued in place.

File Maintenance. Much can be done to add to the life of a file by the way you use it.

In filing remove the pressure during the backward stroke so as to bring the file lightly across the surface of the work.

If pressure is maintained on both strokes, there is much more chance of breaking the teeth.

Another mistake is to use a coarse file on hard steel.

A file of medium roughness is best for this work.

Files, Grading of. Files are graded according to the degree of fineness, and according to whether they have single- or double-cut teeth.

Single-cut files have rows of teeth cut parallel to each other. These teeth are set at an angle of about 65 degrees with the centerline. You will use single-cut files for sharpening tools, finish filing, and drawfiling. They are also the best tools for smoothing the edges of sheet metal.

Files with crisscrossed rows of teeth are double-cut files. The double cut forms teeth that are diamond-shaped and fast cutting. You will use double-cut files for quick removal of metal, and for rough work.

Files are also graded according to the spacing and size of their teeth, or their coarseness and fineness.

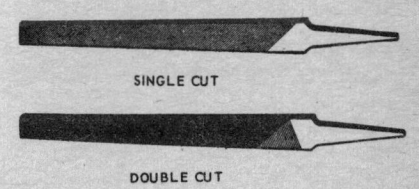

SINGLE CUT

DOUBLE CUT

File Shapes. Flat files are general-purpose files and may be either single- or double-cut. They are tapered in width and thickness. Hard files, not

345

TOOLS, HAND

shown, are somewhat thicker than flat files. They taper slightly but their edges are parallel.

The half round file is a general-purpose tool. The rounded side is used for curved surfaces and the flat face on flat surfaces. When you file an inside curve, use a round or half-round file whose curve most nearly matches the curve of the work.

Mill files are tapered in both width and thickness. One edge has no teeth and is known as a safe edge. Mill files are used for smoothing lathe work, draw-filing, and other fine, precision work. Mill files are always single-cut.

Square files are tapered on all four sides and are used to enlarge rectangular-shaped holes and slots. Round files serve the same purpose for round openings. Small round files are often called "rattail" files.

Triangular files are tapered (longitudinally) on all three sides. They are used to file acute internal angles, and to clear out square corners. Special triangular files are used to file saw teeth.

CROSS-SECTIONAL SHAPES OF FILES

Hacksaw. Hacksaws are used to saw metals. There are two parts to a hacksaw—the frame and the blade. Common hand hacksaws have either adjustable or solid frames.

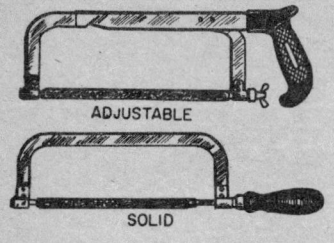

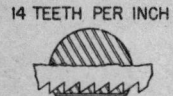

24 TEETH PER INCH
FOR ANGLE IRON, HEAVY PIPE, BRASS, COPPER

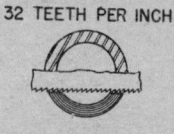

32 TEETH PER INCH
FOR THIN TUBING

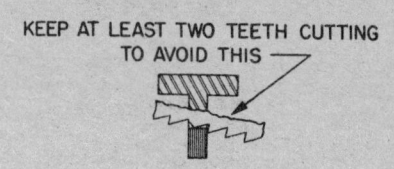

KEEP AT LEAST TWO TEETH CUTTING TO AVOID THIS

Selecting the proper hacksaw blade.

Hacksaw Frames. Most hacksaws are now made with an adjustable frame. Hacksaw blades of various types are inserted in these adjustable frames for different kinds of work. Adjustable frames can be changed to hold blades from 8 to 16 inches long. Solid frames, although more rigid, will take only the length blade for which they are made. This length is the distance between the two pins which hold the blade in place.

The better frames are made with a pistol-grip handle. Recently, several manufacturers have produced frames with the handle in an inverted position. The idea is that the force applied on the forward stroke of the saw is delivered in direct line with the blade.

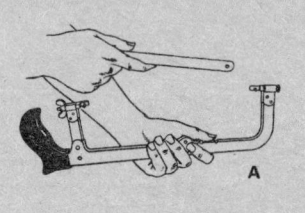

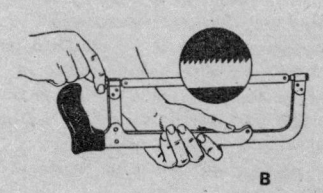

14 TEETH PER INCH
FOR LARGE SECTIONS OF MILD MATERIAL

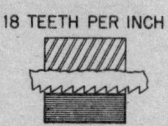

18 TEETH PER INCH
FOR LARGE SECTIONS OF TOUGH STEEL

TOOLS, HAND

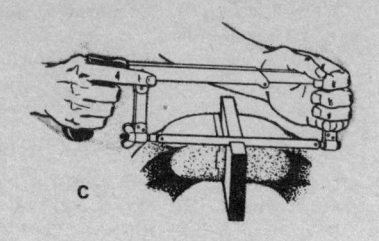

A and B Installing a hack saw blade.
C Proper way to hold a hack saw.

Hacksaw Innovation. When it is necessary to cut metal in an awkward place where there is no room for a standard hacksaw, the blade alone may be used, if reinforced.

Remove a metal rib from an old umbrella, slip it over the back of a good hacksaw blade, then pound down the edges of the rib gently with a hammer until they grip the blade tightly.

Wind a few turns of friction tape around each end of the stiffened blade to form hand grips, and your tight corner hacksaw is complete.

Hacksaw Use.

1. Sawing Metal Sheet. When sawing a thin piece of metal with your hacksaw, put the metal between blocks of wood, clamp in a vise, and saw through both wood and metal. The wood will hold the metal firm, keeping the edges from bending with the strokes of your saw.

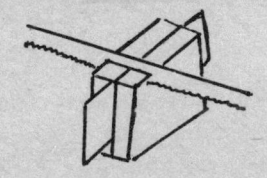

2. Sawing Tubing. Most of the difficulty encountered when cutting thin-wall tubing with a hacksaw can be eliminated by using two blades in the saw frame.

The teeth of one blade should face opposite the teeth in the other. When cutting to an accurate measure, allow for the wider kerf resulting from the double blade.

Hammer, Ball-Peen. The ball-peen hammer, as its name implies, has a ball which is smaller in diameter than the face. It is therefore useful for striking areas that are too small for the face to enter.

Ball-peen hammers are made in different weights, usually 4, 6, 8, and 12 ounces and 1, 1 1/2, and 2 pounds.

Simple as the hammer is, there is a right and wrong way of using it. The most common fault is holding the handle too close to the head. This is known as choking the hammer, and reduces the force of the blow. It also makes it harder to hold the head in an upright position. Except for light blows, hold the handle close to the end to increase the lever arm and produce a more effective blow. Hold the handle with the fingers underneath and the thumb along side or on top of the handle. The thumb should rest on the handle and never overlap the fingers. Try to hit the object with the full force of the hammer. Hold the hammer at such an angle that the face of the hammer and the surface of the object being hit will be parallel. This distributes the force of the blow over the full face and prevents damage to both the surface being struck and the face of the hammer.

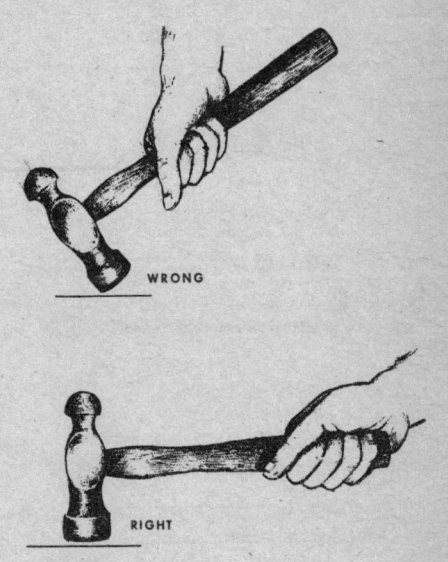

WRONG

RIGHT

TOOLS, HAND

Hammer, Claw. There are two kinds of hammers, one for carpentry work and the other for machine-shop usage. You should have a claw hammer for jobs around the house, with a head for driving nails, and a claw for extracting them. A 13-ounce claw hammer is the best you can get for around-the-house work; it will fulfill just about all your requirements.

Hammer Handle. If the handle of your hammer is loose, tighten it by soaking in engine oil for a few hours. This swells the wood.

Hammer Holder. Bent from a section of a wire hanger and hooked over your belt, this holder provides a handy means of carrying a hammer when doing repair work.

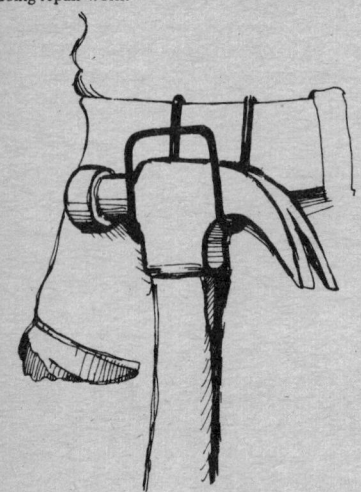

Hammering Techniques. The proper way to handle a hammer is by gripping the handle near its end (not the center of the handle as some are prone to do). Swing it with a full stroke and strike the nail squarely with the center of the hammer's face, keeping the pivot point at the handle's end level with the nailhead.

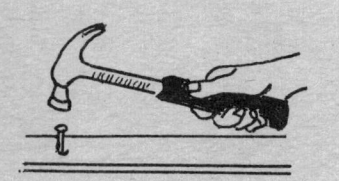

To avoid hitting your thumb, watch what you are hitting—not the hammer.

Do not use the side of the hammer for hitting anything. This part is deliberately made soft to absorb shock from blows on the face and use of it could break the shaft.

To ensure that the hammer does not slip off the nail and damage the timber surface, check that the hammer face is clean and free from grease.

Never use a hammer which has a chipped face and to avoid this damage do not hit the hammer against anything harder than or as hard as itself.

When pulling a long nail out with the claw of a hammer, slip a piece of scrap timber of suitable thickness under the hammer head to increase leverage and also protect the timber surface.

Hammering Tips.

1. Do not use your nail hammer to work metal, or pound cold chisels, or to drive rivets. Use it only to drive nails and brads.

2. Countersinking. Here is one sure and simple way of protecting wallboard from a slip of the hammer when you are countersinking the nails used to attach it. Place the ball of a ball-peen hammer against the head of the partly-driven nail. Then hit the flat face of that hammer with another hammer, and your nail is set. The little dimple made by the ball of the hammer makes it easier later to fill in the nail holes with plaster.

3. Cramped Nailings. If you must drive a nail in close quarters where there isn't enough handle space to swing your hammer, here's one usually effective solution. Take a bolt or machine screw as long as needed with a diameter slightly larger than the head of your nail. Thread a nut one turn onto this. Then fill the remaining space in the nut with some putty to hold the nail while you hammer on the bolt head to drive the nail in.

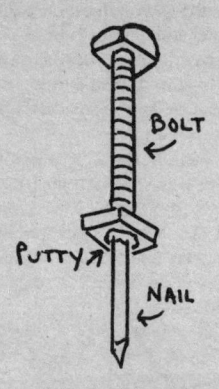

4. into Difficult Places. When attempting to nail in a hard-to-get-at place, a piece of cellophane tape will hold the head of the nail in place on your hammer to help get it started. After the nail is firmly in the wood, just tear the hammer away and drive the nail home.

When you find it difficult to start a nail in a place that is too high to reach with both hands, try this little trick. Press your nail through a small square of aluminum foil, then wrap the foil around the business end of your hammerhead, with the point of the nail pointed in the hammering direction. This will enable you to start your nail with just one hand.

5. Hiding Nailheads. One simple and effective way to camouflage those nailheads in furniture construction is to cover each nail with a wood chip lifted from the surface with a wide-sweep gouge. Don't cut the chip loose. Just drive the nail into the recess under the chip, using a nail-set to drive it in, so as to avoid breaking the chip. After the nail is set, coat the chip with glue and press it into place, holding it flat with a weight. Then, when the glue has hardened sufficiently, sand the surface smooth.

6. Increasing Accuracy. Here's a tip on the use of a hammer that will increase accuracy. When driving a nail, first rest the hammer on the head of the nail, then lift the hammer, and give the nail a light tap to start it. Resting the hammer on the nailhead first tends to increase your accuracy.

7. into Mortar. Have you ever bent a half-dozen or so nails attempting to drive one nail for a picture into the mortar in a brick wall? Heat the nail first for an easier job.

8. One-Armed Nailing. Doubtless you've had trouble on occasion in driving a nail into a spot where you could get only one hand. You can solve this little problem much more easily the next time if you'll first push the point of your nail into a wad of adhesive weatherstrip putty, and then stick the nail into place. After you have started the nail, remove the putty, and then proceed with your hammering.

9. into Plaster. The driving of nails into plastered walls is more often than not a disastrous operation. However, the danger of cracking the plaster can be considerably reduced if you dip your nail into piping hot water for a minute or two before driving it into the wall. Or, you can stick a small piece of adhesive tape on the spot where you want the nail to go, drive your nail through this, and then remove the tape with scarcely any trouble at all.

When picture nails come loose in a plastered wall, all you need to put them firmly back in place is a strip of cloth and some glue. Wrap the narrow strip of cloth around the shank of the nail, dip into the glue, then replace it in the hole in the plaster. Allow the glue time to dry for about twenty-four hours, then replace the picture.

10. **Preventing Disfiguring.** Never strike a finished wood surface or any semi-finished work with a hammer. Instead, use a block of hardwood between the hammer head and the work, to prevent disfiguring dents.

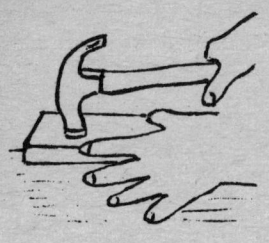

11. **Preventing Splitting.** You can minimize the danger of splitting when driving a nail into wood if the point of the nail is first blunted. To blunt the point, place the nail head down on a solid surface and tap the point with a hammer.

12. **Protruding Nails.** When nailing two boards together, face to face, you sometimes find that your nails are so long that they protrude slightly on the other side. One solution to this little problem is to drive your nails at a sharp angle—which not only lengthens the distance through which the nails must go, but also makes for a stronger grip.

13. **Removing Bent Nails.** If you inadvertently bend a nail you are attempting to drive, it's always a good idea to make use of a wood block as a fulcrum to pull the nail out. This not only makes for much easier removal of the bent nail, but also saves the wood you're working on from being marred by your hammer.

14. **Removing Nails.** Extracting a nail is a simple job, but there are two ways of doing it.

The hard way (below in A) needs a lot of effort because the nail has to bend as it comes out. You may also bruise the wood, due to heavy leverage on the pincers.

The easy way is B. The pincers swivel on the nail as it is levered out, a little at a time, and it comes out straight and fit to reuse.

Put a flat piece of metal under the opposite corners of the pincers' jaws so they do not dig into the timber.

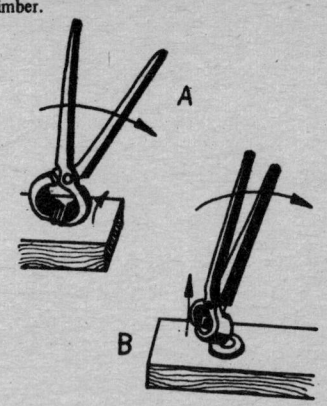

15. **Removing Nails from Corrugated Roofing.** With a large pair of pincers nip off the nail heads and remove the sheet, then pull the nail stubs with the pincers. Another way is to lay a short scrap piece of pipe in the groove next to the nail and use this as a fulcrum for the hammer. You can generally press down on the ridge next to the nail and get enough slack to grasp the nail in the hammer claws.

16. **at Right Angles.** If you wish to nail two boards together at true right angles, first draw a guide line on the inside of the overlapping board and clamp a block of wood even with that line. Then place the upright against the block and nail into place. When nailing long boards together, set them on edge and square at the corners of a box for nailing.

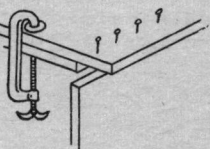

17. **Saving Fingers.** Avoid bruised fingers when hammering small nails by using an old comb to hold them in place.

18. **Starting Small Nails.** One of those long rubber erasers with the beveled ends, such as is found in any stationery store, comes in very handy as a starter for small nails and brads (and as a preventive to any smashed fingers). Merely notch one of the beveled ends and use this notch to hold your nail, tack, or brad while you hammer it into place.

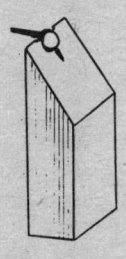

19. **Tight Nailing.** Nails always hold much better when they are clinched over. Bend the nail (that protrudes at least 1-1/2 inches) by striking its tip at an angle and forcing it down to the wood with light taps of your hammer. Sink the point of the nail below the surface of the wood with a sharp rap on the end of the nail's point—and always clinch with the grain of the wood.

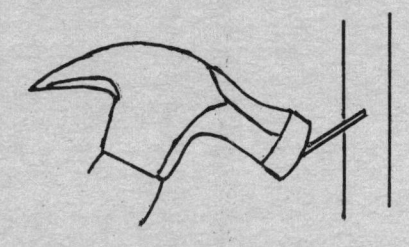

20. **into Unseasoned Wood.** Oftentimes unseasoned wood will split when you attempt to drive nails into it. If, however, you would blunt the points of your nails beforehand, it will help prevent injury to the wood.

21. **Upholstery.** If you're planning to do some upholstering, buy a rubber crutch or chair tip to fit over the head of your hammer... then pound away. This will save the beauty of your upholstery tacks, also the woodwork if you happen to miss the mark with your hammer.

Hammer, Magnetic. Here's one way to improvise your own "magnetic" hammer for driving carpet tacks: Just rub the striking face of your hammer over a cake of soap, and your tacks will cling to it as they do to the regular magnetic hammers.

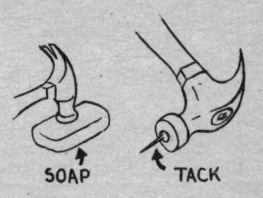

Hammer Repair. A wedge to hold that hammerhead or hatchet head on its handle can be made by driving an ordinary wood screw into the top of the handle. Flatten the screw first so that it has a triangular shape. The teeth which are formed by the flattened threads serve to hold the wedge securely in place.

Handsaw. There are two different kinds of handsaws, each designed for cutting lumber a certain way. A crosscut saw cuts across the grain of the wood and a ripsaw cuts with the grain. The teeth in a crosscut are formed like small chisel points, tilted at opposite angles so that they chop through the wood against the grain and gouge out everything in their path. The teeth in a rip saw are formed like small knife blades that slice through the wood with the grain.

A crosscut saw has more teeth per inch than a rip saw. The average crosscut has about 8 to 10 points (teeth) per inch; the average ripsaw, 5. When sawing with a crosscut saw, hold the saw at a 45-degree angle to the board. In using a ripsaw, hold it at a 60-degree angle to the surface.

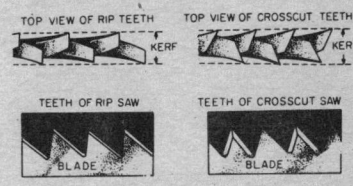

Comparing rip and crosscut-saw teeth.

TOOLS, HAND

You should have at least one crosscut and one rip-saw in your tool box. A good average crosscut is the 10 point, 24-inch size. For a rip, get a 5 point, 24-inch size.

Parts of a handsaw.

Handsaw Care.
1. When work is complete hang up the saw.

2. Do not pile tools on top of the bench so as to distort the blade.

3. Look carefully over repair or alteration work to see that all nails are removed to avoid cutting into metal.

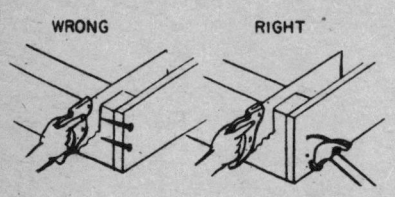

4. Strips of waste should not be twisted off with the blade, but should be broken off with the hand or a mallet.

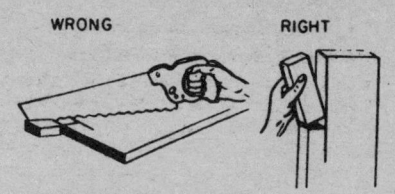

5. Supporting the waste side of the work will prevent splitting off.

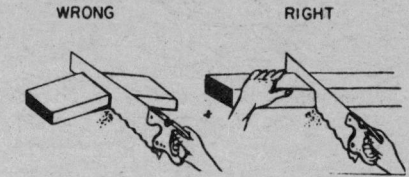

6. Raise the work to a height sufficient to keep the blade from striking the floor. If the work cannot be raised, limit the stroke.

Handsaw Maintenance. Your saws will keep their set and sharpness much longer if you protect the teeth with a simply made sheath as shown.

Select a piece of wood about ½-inch x ¾-inch in section and slightly longer than the saw blade.

Make a kerf wood with the saw selected.

Work the blade in the kerf until it is a loose fit.

Tack a piece of tape to the uncut edge of the wood and, with the saw in the kerf, tie the tape over the back of the saw.

Make quite sure that the tack holding the tape does not enter the kerf.

To protect the keen edge on your favorite saw while it is not in use, a discarded section of old garden hose is ideal. Use a piece of hose the length of your saw blade, slit its entire length with a linoleum knife, then slip it over the cutting edge of your saw.

Handsaw Sharpening. Keep your saw razor sharp by filing with a hand file, or grinding it on a whet-stone or grindstone, or take it to a professional. This is important, for even an expert could not do good work with a dull saw.

Here's a little tip which should make the job of filing the teeth of your saw a little easier for you. Pass a lighted candle, as shown in the illustration, back and forth under the teeth of the saw. This will leave a smudge on the teeth. Then, when you file the teeth, the smudge is cleaned away and shows you readily the ones that have been filed. This eliminates the all-too-common mistake of filing a tooth over again.

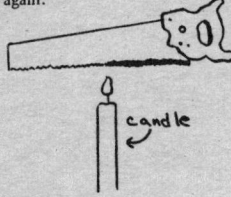

Handsaw Storage. Here is a convenient method for storing handsaws in the workshop so they are ready for use.

At the same time it will protect them from dulling contact with other tools.

Three discs of fairly hard wood or thick plywood are attached to a baseboard, one in the center being stationary, and the other two pivoted off-center.

These discs could be about 2-inch diameter, and in use the saws are slipped between them from below.

The weight of the saw tends to pull the pivoted disc tight, thus gripping the blade.

The grip of the discs can be improved further by covering the edges with friction tape or thin rubber.

The short dowel stops are merely to prevent the off-center disc swinging too far.

Handsaw Tips.

1. Binding. If your handsaw binds, try rubbing soap on both sides of the blade, and this should facilitate your sawing.

2. Knuckle Guide. Start your handsaw by using the knuckle of your thumb as a guide for the blade. Pull the saw toward you, cutting a slot for the next downward stroke. Keep the knuckle against the blade for the next few strokes—until the saw is started. Your saw stroke should rock slightly, following a normal arc as your arm swings from the shoulder. Let the weight of your saw do the cutting for you.

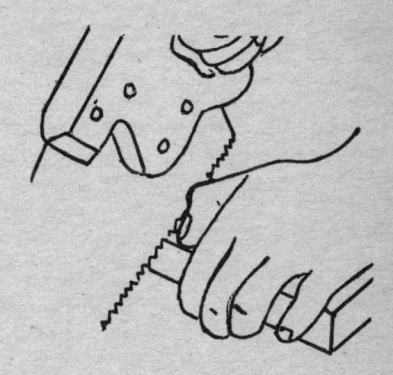

3. Smooth Edges. One good way to avoid that usual ragged edge left by your saw when cutting siding board is to score the board first before sawing

with a sharp knife or awl. This scoring breaks the outer grain of the wood, giving a smooth, even cut after the sawing.

4. **Straight Edges.** Have trouble sawing a straight edge with a handsaw? Here are helpful tips: First, be sure the line you mark is sharp and straight, because lines made with a blunt pencil are often too wide and cause crooked cuts. Second, when starting your cut, guide the saw against the line with your left thumb until the groove is formed. Third, don't bear down on the saw; use long, easy strokes and let the saw's own weight carry it through; also, keep the index finger of the right hand straight along the top edge of the handle. Fourth, never twist or bend the saw.

5. **Thin Slice.** You know from experience, of course, that whenever you attempt to saw less than a quarter-inch from a piece of wood, you are likely to run into trouble. You can make this job much easier, though, if you'll just clamp the work to a piece of waste stock protruding an inch or so beyond the piece to be trimmed. By cutting both pieces at once, you can take off as thin a slice as you wish.

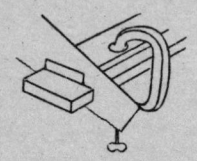

6. **Unseasoned Wood.** How often have you run into trouble while attempting to make a long cut with your saw, especially in damp or green wood? You can eliminate the binding of your saw and keep your piece of mind if you'll just use a table knife, as illustrated, to keep the cut in your wood open.

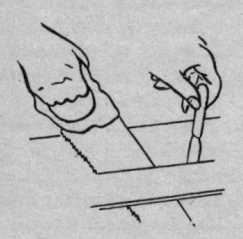

Another way to make this job much easier is to use the discarded ends of a candle or a piece of beeswax or paraffin, and rub this on both sides of your sawblade.

If ever you have had to do any sawing through heavy stock, or wet or green lumber, you've no doubt experienced the annoyance of a stuck and binding saw. You can alleviate this condition by pushing a nail into the saw kerf. Then, as the cut progresses, either drive in more nails closer to the saw, or drive a larger-sized nail into the end of the cut.

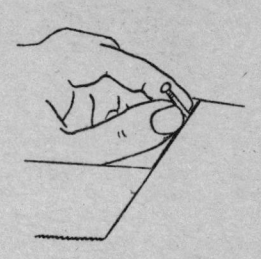

7. **Wedge.** When ripping a long board with a handsaw, you usually need a wedge of some sort to hold the saw cut open and prevent the binding of your saw. A wedge for this purpose can be improvised by driving a large nail through a block of wood, then inserting the pointed end of the nail into the saw cut while grasping the block of wood to move it along the board as your saw cut progresses.

Handsaw Use. To saw across the grain of the stock, use the crosscut saw, and to saw with the grain, use a ripsaw. Study the teeth in both kinds of saws so you can readily identify the saw that you need.

Place the board on a saw horse, or some other suitable object. Hold the saw in the right hand and extend the first finger along the handle as shown in the figure. Grasp the board as shown and take a position so that an imaginary line passing lengthwise of the right forearm will be at an angle of approximately 45 degrees with the face of the board. Be sure the side of the saw is plumb or at right angles with the face of the board. Place the heel of the saw on the mark. Keep the saw in line with the forearm and pull it toward you to start the cut.

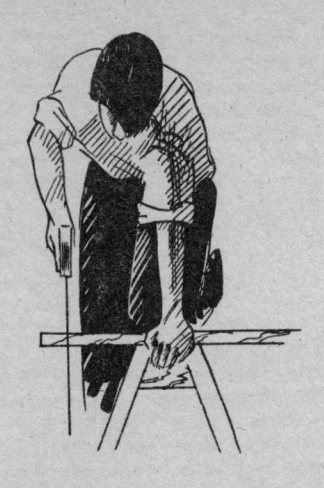

To begin with, take short, light strokes, gradually increasing the strokes to the full length of the saw. Do not force or jerk the saw. Such procedure will only make sawing more difficult. The arm that does the sawing should swing clear of your body so that the handle of the saw operates at your side rather than in front of you.

Use one hand to operate the saw. You may be tempted to use both hands at times, but if your saw is sharp, one hand will serve you better. The weight of the saw is sufficient to make it cut.

A hand saw will stay sharp longer and will cut with less effort if your pressure is applied only on the cutting, or forward, stroke. Bear down firmly while pushing the blade forward, but lift up slightly when drawing it back. This avoids wearing down the cutting teeth needlessly.

Jointer, see **Plane**, below.

Knife, Pocket. Pocket knives are used for light cutting, sharpening pencils, cutting strings, etc. They are unsuited for heavy work. Multi-purpose knives have an assortment of blades designed for forcing holes, driving screws and opening cans, as well as cutting. The blades are hinged and should be contained within the case when not in use.

Knife, Putty. A putty knife is used for applying putty to window sash when setting in panes of glass. The blade has a wide square point available in different lengths and widths.

It's always risky business using a hammer for driving glazier's points next to a newly-placed window pane. You can make a safe and effective driver for these glazier's points by cutting a 1/2-inch nut with a hacksaw through to the threads and then slipping this over a putty knife, as illustrated.

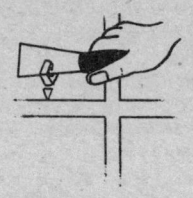

When you are using putty, it's a good idea to dip your putty knife into a solution of soap or detergent suds. The putty will then stick where you want it to, rather than to the blade of your knife.

Knife, Shop. The shop knife can be used to cut cardboard, linoleum, and paper. It has an aluminum handle and is furnished with interchangeable blades stored in the 5-inch handle.

Nailset. If you do any inside work at all, you'll need a nailset. This tool sinks finish nails to or below the surface of the material. In order to keep hammer marks off the wood, use the nailset, driving the nail in below the surface. Two nailsets, one 2/32-inch and one 4/32-inch should be enough.

Nailset Use. Use a nailset for countersinking finishing nails below the surface of wood. Place the tip of your nailset squarely on the nailhead, then drive it 1/16 to 1/8-inch into the stock with a series of taps. Then fill the holes with putty.

TOOLS, HAND

Oilstones, see **Sharpening Stones**, below.

Plane. The plane is simply a wide chisel blade set in a block to regulate the depth of cut you want to make. The blade has a cap iron screwed to it to deflect the shavings from the wood as they come up through a slot. A lever cap locks the blade in place. You adjust the angle of the blade by a straight lever and fix the blade at its correct depth by turning an adjusting screw.

The smallest planes run from about 5½ inches to 10 inches long: these are smoothing planes. A junior jack plane is about 11½ inches long, and a regular jack plane is from 14 to 15 inches. For bigger work, a fore plane is 18 inches. A jointer is one of the largest, 22 to 24 inches.

For the average home workshop, you'll do well if you have a junior jack plane 11½ inches long. However, if you use a plane more than the average man, you may want to get a regular jack plane which runs about 14 inches. If you have smaller work to do occasionally, get yourself a 6-inch block plane, convenient for such jobs.

The back iron, or cap, as on smoothing planes, should be set back a bare 1-16th inch from the edge of the cutting iron to break shavings effectively and produce a smooth surface.

Make sure the cutting edge projects evenly across the width of the mouth of the plane. On most planes a lateral adjusting level at the back of the iron will correct any deviation.

In use, press down the knob at the beginning of the stroke and the handle at the end of the stroke.

An oilstone is necessary for sharpening plane irons. A combination stone, with a rough side and smooth side, is best, and the stone should be kept in a protective wooden case.

Plane, Block. In a block plane, the plane iron does not have a plane iron cap, and unlike the iron in a bench plane, the iron in a block plane goes in bevel-up. The block plane which is usually held at an angle to the work, is used chiefly for crossgrain squaring or end stock.

JACK

SMOOTHING

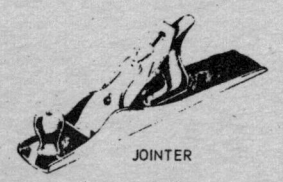

JOINTER

Plane, Bench. The correct angle for the cutting edge of a bench plane is 30 degrees, honing guide used with the oilstone will help to maintain this angle.

Don't plane right across end grain as it will splinter the edges. Plane half way, turn round and work from the other side.

BLOCK

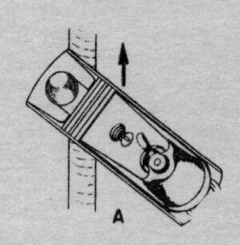

A

PLANE IRON — LEVER CAP — FINGER REST
LEVER
ADJUSTMENT SCREW — PLANE IRON BEVEL UP

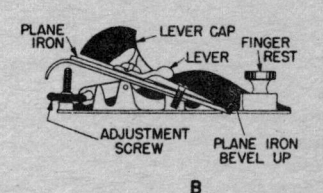

B

Block plane showing direction of work (A) and parts (B).

Planing Aid. The planing of the edges of doors, storm windows, and screens always presents quite a problem. You can simplify the job of holding them upright by making a steel fork, as illustrated. Shape the fork from steel rod, grinding the bottom ends to points. When used, the fork is driven into the ground and the door, window or screen fitted inside. If you want to provide even greater support and allow yourself to plane in either direction, make two forks—one for each end.

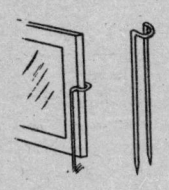

Planing Technique. As direction of grain plays such an important part in woodwork, it is worthwhile giving some attention to the best method of using a plane in relation to the grain.

In a coarse-grained wood it is only too easy to tear the wood deeply with one stroke of a plane in the wrong direction, and if the wood has little thickness to spare, you might have to make it thinner than you intended to plane out these blemishes.

Fig. 1 shows a piece of timber which is to be planed on surface (A). Study the grain on the side (B).

The grain indicates that planing should be in the direction of the arrow—that is, the direction in which the grain runs uphill.

Enlarged detail of the grain (Fig. 2) shows how the cutter forces up the individual wood fibers if you choose the wrong direction.

The grain may, in fact, be likened to the hair on an animal's back.

If stroked the right way, the hair feels smooth and tends to lie flat. If stroked the wrong way, it becomes roughened.

Sometimes the grain is interlocked, and, although sloping one way on surface (B) at the end, it may slope the opposite way in the middle of the piece.

This is known as "cranky" grained wood. With wavy grain, also the slope will often alternate throughout the length.

Where these conditions occur, the only method of finding the best direction is that of trial and error in planing.

Of course, don't forget to have the plane sharp and set finely.

Even then, you might tear out a certain amount of grain, but these patches can be eliminated by using a steel wood scraper after planing.

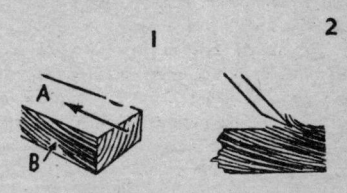

Planing Tips. A wood plane will cut smoother and easier when it is held at a slight angle to the cutting line as it is moved forward over the surface of the work. This slight angle gives the cutting edge a slicing or shearing action that is much easier to control than when the plane is pushed straight forward with its cutting edge at right angles to the grain. Be sure to maintain a steady downward pressure at the same time.

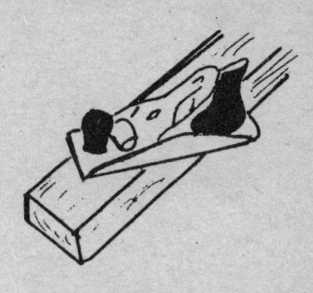

Planing Tip. When planing the end grain of a board, there is always the danger of splitting off the corners as the blade travels past the edge. On wide boards, you can prevent this by planing from either edge in toward the center, going no more than halfway across with each stroke. But on narrow boards where only one-way planing is feasible, try clamping a piece of scrap wood tightly against one edge, then running your plane from the good piece onto the scrap piece. In this way, any damage done by the blade will be to the far edge of the waste lumber rather than to the good lumber.

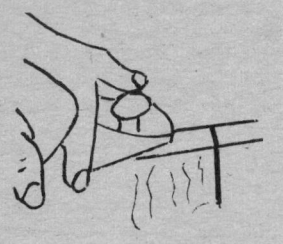

Plasterer's. A plasterer's small tool is used for all types of plaster-repair work, and could be classed as an essential item in the tool kit.

With such a tool it is very important to buy the best quality, as the pointed trowel end and flat spatula must be flexible and strong, and only high-grade steel will provide this.

For home use, buy a small tool that is at least 10 inches long. When it is not in use, or likely to be used for some time, smear with a little petroleum jelly to protect the metal against rust.

In addition to applying patching plaster, a small tool is ideal for repointing brickwork, applying roofing compound to holes or cracks in a gutter or around faulty flashing and for all types of jobs where plaster, cement, or other plastic materials are used.

Pliers are used for cutting purposes as well as holding and gripping small articles in situations where it may be inconvenient or impossible to use hands.

The combination pliers are handy for holding or bending flat or round stock. The long-nosed pliers are less rugged, and break easily if you use them on heavy jobs. Long-nosed pliers commonly called needle-nose pliers are especially useful for holding small objects in tight places and for making delicate adjustments. The round-nosed kind are handy when you need to crimp sheet metal or form a loop in a wire. The diagonal cutting pliers, commonly called "diagonals" or "dikes," are designed for cutting wire and cotter pins close to a flat surface and are especially useful in the electronic and electrical fields. The duckbill pliers are used extensively in aviation areas.

Here are two important rules for using pliers:

1. Do not make pliers work beyond their capacity. The long-nosed kind are especially delicate. It is easy to spring or break them, or nick their edges. After that, they are practically useless.

2. Do not use pliers to turn nuts. In just a few seconds, a pair of pliers can damage a nut. Pliers must not be substituted for wrenches.

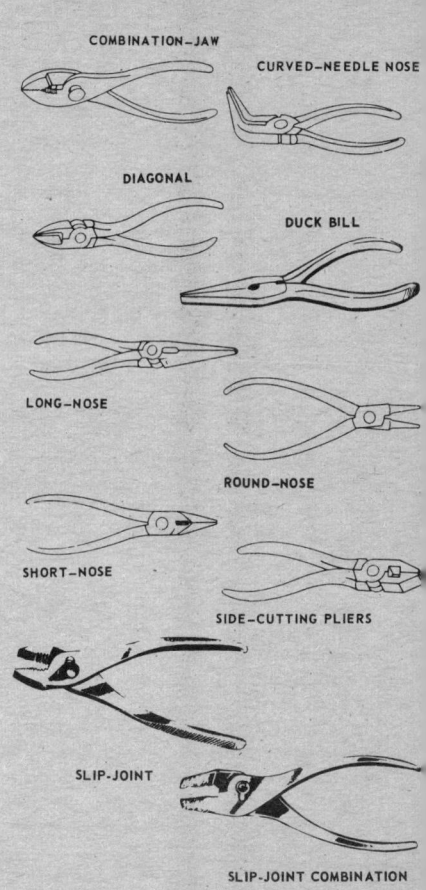

COMBINATION-JAW
CURVED-NEEDLE NOSE
DIAGONAL
DUCK BILL
LONG-NOSE
ROUND-NOSE
SHORT-NOSE
SIDE-CUTTING PLIERS
SLIP-JOINT
SLIP-JOINT COMBINATION

TOOLS, HAND

Punch, Improvised. When you break a taper-shank drill don't throw it away. Ground to a point, it makes a center-punch and if ground flat it makes a nail-punch.

Ripsaw, see **Handsaw,** above.

Saw, Compass. When the rather large frame of a coping saw makes it impossible to use on a job, a compass saw is useful. Usually you drill a hole with brace and bit where you wish to start, then insert the pointed tip of the blade of your compass saw, and go ahead at a curve or angle.

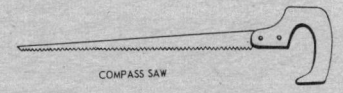

COMPASS SAW

Saw, Coping. A coping saw can do fine work and allows the craftsman to cut wood a different angles and curves. This type of saw has removable blades which are thin and fragile. They should be changed frequently.

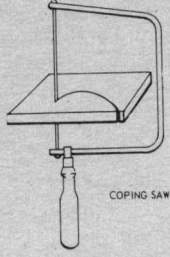

COPING SAW

Saw, Keyhole. A keyhole saw resembles a compass saw, but is smaller, and is used mainly for curves on delicate, small pieces.

Screwdriver. A screwdriver is one of the most basic of basic handtools. It is also the most frequently abused of all handtools. It is designed for one function only—to drive and remove screws. A screwdriver should not be used as a pry bar, a scraper, a chisel, or a punch.

When using a screwdriver it is important to select the proper size so that the blade fits the screw slot properly. This prevents burring the slot and reduces the force required to hold the driver in the slot. Keep the shank perpendicular to the screw head.

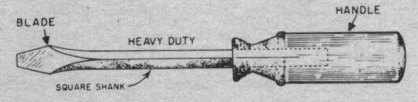

BLADE   HANDLE
HEAVY DUTY
SQUARE SHANK

Screwdriver Guide. How many times has your screwdriver slipped off the screwhead and scratched or gouged your piece of work? This can be avoided in the future if you will make yourself a simple, little guide block. All you have to do is drill some holes of graduated sizes through the wood block, to accommodate screwdrivers of various sizes. And then, when using, the block is held with one hand while you handle the screwdriver with the other. Its confinement in the hole prevents the screwdriver from slipping beyond the screwhead.

Screwdriver Handle Repair. Instead of discarding an old screwdriver with a broken handle, you can give it new life by fashioning a handle from an old rubber bicycle pedal. Force the pedal tread over the shank and drill two holes through both the rubber and shank. Fit steel pins into the holes to prevent the handle from turning. The pins should be short enough to permit the rubber to close over them, insuring a shockproof handle.

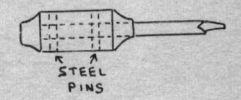

STEEL PINS

Screwdriver, Lighting. To help you locate spots for screws in dark corners, try taping a small pen flashlight to the shank of your screwdriver.

Screwdriver, Magnetic. If you don't have a magnetic screwdriver, here's one way you can improvise one. Rub your screwdriver over a wet cake of soap a couple of times, then place your screw on it, and it will hold like magic to enable you to get the screw started.

TOOLS, HAND

Screwdriver Maintenance. For top efficiency, your screwdriver must be kept properly shaped. Usually an ordinary file can be used to reshape it easily and smoothly. If you're doing the job with a power grinder, use the finest wheel and take precautions not to overheat the tip of your screwdiver.

SQUARE END

Screwdriver, Phillips. The head of a Phillips-type screw has a four-way slot into which the screwdriver fits. This prevents the screwdriver from slipping. Three standard sized Phillips screwdrivers handle a wide range of screw sizes. Their ability to hold helps to prevent damaging the slots or the work surrounding the screw. It is a poor practice to try to use a standard screwdriver on a Phillips screw because both the tool and screw slot will be damaged.

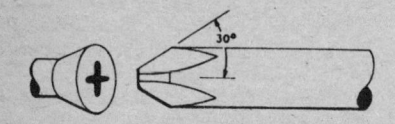

If you have no tool for a Phillips screw, adapt any screwdriver by grinding off the corners of the blade. Or, try using a large, new nail. It will often do the job if the screw isn't too tight.

Screwdriving Tips.

1. One of the annoying little exigencies in the life of every handyman is a screwdriver whose tip persists in slipping out of a screw's slot. One easy way to remedy this situation is to tape the screw and screwdriver together with a small piece of masking tape, then remove the tape after the screw has achieved a good start into the wood.

2. The matter of lubrication also enters into the job of driving a screw.

If you place a little grease or petroleum jelly on the point of the screw, it not only makes driving it in much easier, but also simplifies the task of removing it later if that should become necessary.

3. One usually effective way to cope with a stubborn screw is first to heat it with the tip of a soldering iron, then after allowing the screw to cool, remove it with your screwdriver.

4. For easier removal of paint-covered screws, a piece of hacksaw blade clamped in a dowel is an efficient tool. Use the pointed end of the blade to get a start for your screwdriver, then clean the slot completely.

5. When space is limited and it is impossible to hold a screw in place while starting it, start it as shown in the illustration. Set the screwdriver in the screw slot and tape them together with some cellophane tape. Wood screws should have a pilot hole, but it is possible to start them in soft wood without a pilot hole if done carefully.

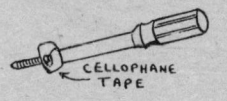

6. When driving screws, use a long-shanked screwdriver. It enables you to get more torque or turning force on the screw.

Shaper. Using a wood file in combination with sandpaper is the accepted way to obtain a smooth finish on a surface of wood. For average household situations, you can use a combination file and plane, a tool that cuts, shapes, and smooths woods, plastics, and some softer metals. The simplest and handiest is a 5½ inch block-plane tool that is held in the palm of the hand.

Sharpening stones are divided into two groups, natural and artificial. Some of the natural stones are oil treated during and after the manufacturing processes. The stones that are oil treated are sometimes called oilstones. Artificial stones are normally made of silicone carbide or aluminum oxide. Natural stones have very fine grains are excellent for putting razorlike edges on fine cutting tools. Most sharpening stones have one coarse and one fine face. Some of these stones are mounted, and the working face of some of the sharpening stones is a combination of coarse and fine grains. Stones are available in a variety of shapes.

Staple Gun. A good fastening tool which you should have around the house is the staple gun. You can use it for repairing screening which has pulled out of the frame, for tacking on upholstering which has fallen away, and for doing a number of jobs for which nails and screws are unsatisfactory. The staple gun has a rubber-coated handgrip. You simply squeeze the grip and a powerful spring shoots the staple into the material with a quick, penetrating thrust.

Stillson Wrench, see **Wrench, Stillson,** below.

Tweezers. A pair of tweezers can often prove a very handy tool in the home workshop. You can make yourself a real, rugged pair of tweezers by grinding out two pieces of old hacksaw blade, riveting them together at one end, and springing them apart.

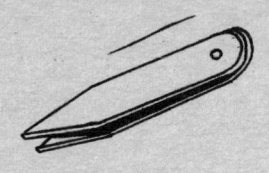

Vise Care. Keep vises clean at all times. They should be cleaned and wiped with light oil after using. Never strike a vise with a heavy object and never hold large work in a small vise, since these practices will cause the jaws to become sprung or otherwise damage the vise. Keep jaws in good condition and oil the screws and the slide frequently. Never oil the swivel base of swivel jaw joint; its holding power will be impaired. When the vise is not in use, bring the jaws lightly together or leave a very small gap. (The movable jaw of a tightly closed vise may break due to the expansion of the metal in heat.) Leave the handle in a vertical position.

When clamping a piece of work into a bench vise that might be marred by the vise jaws, get a pair of discarded rubber shoe heels and use as auxiliary jaws. The heels can be coated on the back with a little rubber cement that will hold them in position. This is also good to hold a saw when filing it, for the rubber heels will muffle the nerve-shattering screech made as the file crosses over the teeth.

Vise, Clamp Base. For apartment use, the clamp base vise is very handy. It usually has a smaller holding capacity than the machinist's or the bench and pipe vises. It clamps to the edge of a bench with a thumbscrew. This kind of vise can be obtained with a maximum holding capacity varying between 1-1/2" to 3". It does not normally have pipe-holding jaws.

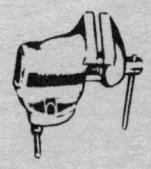

Vises are used for holding work when it is being planed, sawed, drilled, shaped, sharpened, or riveted, or when wood is being glued.

Vise Safety. When closing the jaw of a vise or clamp, avoid getting any portion of your hands or body between the jaws or between one jaw and the work.

When holding heavy work in a vise, place a block of wood under the work as a prop to prevent it from sliding down and falling on your foot.

Do not open the jaws of a vise beyond their capacity, as the movable jaw will drop off, causing personal injury and possible damage to the jaw.

Vises, Bench. A machinist's bench vise is a large steel vise with rough jaws that prevent the work from slipping. Most of these vises have a swivel base

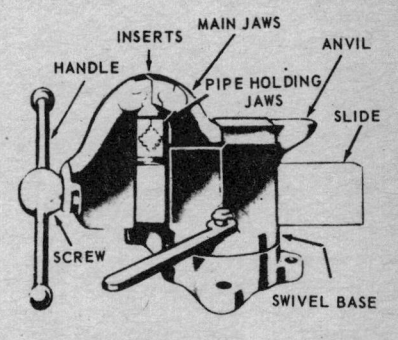

BENCH AND PIPE

with jaws that can be rotated, while others cannot be rotated. A similar light duty model is equipped with a cutoff. These vises are usually bolt-mounted onto a bench.

The bench and pipe vise has integral pipe jaws for holding pipe from 3/4 inch to 3 inches in diameter. The maximum working main jaw opening is usually 5 inches, with a jaw width of 4 to 5 inches. The base can be swiveled to any position and locked. These vises are equipped with an anvil and are also bolted onto a workbench.

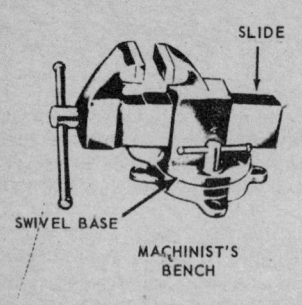

Vise, Soft Jaws. Soft jaws, inserts made of brass, copper, or other soft metal, are mounted on the jaws of the vise when the surface of your work must be protected. If soft jaws are not available you can easily make a pair out of scrap metal.

Vise Tip. The illustration shows a method of holding irregularly shaped pieces of wood or other material in a bench vise.

All that is needed is a short length of half-round molding. It is slipped into the vise jaws with the piece which is to be worked. The flat surface of the molding bears against the work which is to be held, and the semi-circular side adjusts itself to the face of the vise jaw.

A refinement of this idea is to cover the flat face of the segment with a thin strip of self-adhesive foam plastic draft-excluder material.

This prevents any chance of the work slipping and at the same time protects the surface of the work.

Vise, Use. If you have to pound against metal parts held in the vise be sure you pound against the back jaw—it's heavier than the front jaw and strong enough to absorb the shock of the blows. Always tighten and loosen a vise by holding the handle with your hands and applying the weight of your body to secure turning pressure. A good workman never hammers on his vise handle because he knows it may break the sliding jaw or spring the clamping screw.

Wrench. Wrenches are indispensable to turn screws and bolts and other heavy work. Try not to overstrain your household wrench by expecting the impossible.

The most frequently used wrench has 12 points or notches arranged in a circle in the head, and can be used with a minimum swing of 30 degrees. For heavy duty use 6 and 8 point wrenches are used, for medium duty 12 point and for light duty only 16 point.

Wrench, Adjustable. An adjustable wrench, also called a crescent wrench, can be used for loosening or tightening square or hexagonal head lug bolts, stove bolts, and even long wood screws. The wrench has a fixed jaw and a movable jaw, operated by an adjusting nut. The jaws are shaped like crescents, which gives the tool its distinctive name. This is the smallest and most handy of all adjustable wrenches, and is the most commonly used. Get the regular 5 inch size.

The monkey wrench is another adjustable wrench.

There are also bigger wrenches for work with pipes. Many of these have special kinds of grips and adjustable parts. If you're going in for a lot of plumbing work you'll want to look into a set of these.

Adjustable wrenches are shaped somewhat similarly to open-end wrenches. The big difference is that one jaw is adjustable. The angle of the opening to the handle on an adjustable wrench is 22½ degrees. It has a spiral screw-worm adjustment in the handle. The width of the jaws may be varied from 0 to ½ inch or more. This tool has smooth jaws, and is designed as an open-end wrench. It is an especially good emergency tool, since one adjustable wrench can be made to serve for several open-end wrenches.

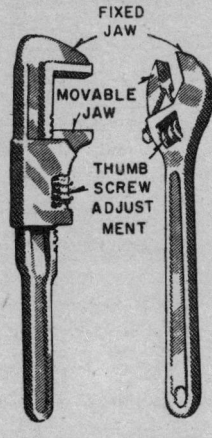

MONKEY   CRESCENT

Wrench, Box. Box wrenches are safer than open-end wrenches since there is less likelihood that they will slip off the work. They completely surround or 'box' a nut or bolt head.

One advantage of the 12 point construction is the thin wall. It is more suitable for turning nuts which are hard to get at with an open-end wrench. Another advantage is that the wrench will operate between obstructions where the space for handle swing is limited. A very short swing of the handle will turn the nut far enough to allow the wrench to be lifted and the next set of points fitted to the corners of the nut.

One disadvantage of the box-end wrench is the loss of time which occurs whenever a craftsman has to lift the wrench off and place it back on the nut in another position in case there is insufficient clearance to spin the wrench in a full circle.

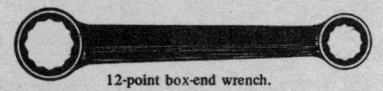

12-point box-end wrench.

Wrench, Combination. After a tight nut is broken loose, it can be unscrewed much more quickly with an open-end wrench than with a box-wrench. This is where a combination box-open end wrench comes in handy. You can use the box-end for breaking nuts loose or for snugging them down, and the open-end for faster turning.

The box-end portion of the wrench can be designed with an offset in the handle. The 15-degree offset allows clearance over nearby parts.

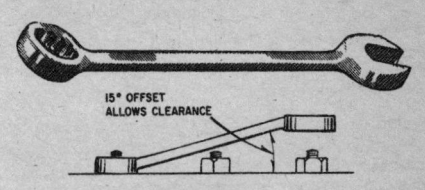

Wrench, Homemade. There really is no need for your rummaging through your toolbox when you have to drive or tighten screw-eyes, cuphooks, and the like. A wooden clothespin, used as in the illustration, makes a very efficient wrench for the job.

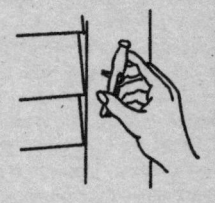

Wrench, Improvised. In an emergency, you can improvise a very efficient adjustable wrench from a heavy bolt and two nuts. The adjustable jaws of your "wrench" are provided by the two nuts, threaded onto the bolt at the proper distance apart. Of course, the shallow throat of such a wrench sometimes necessitates your pressing down with one hand to prevent its slipping off. The longer the bolt you use, too, the greater your leverage.

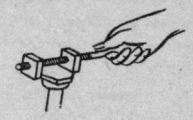

Wrench, Open-End. Solid, nonadjustable wrenches with openings in each end are called open-end wrenches. In an average set there are about 10 wrenches with openings that range from 5/16 to 1 inch in width.

TOOLS, MEASURING

Wrench, Stillson. For the kitchen and bathroom plumbing crises that inevitably arise, and for automobile repairs, a wrench is one of the tool kit's essential items. A Stillson wrench has grooved jaws that allow you to get a firm grip on a smooth round pipe, and they are adjustable. This tool must be used with discretion, as the jaws are serrated and always make marks on the work unless adequate precautions are observed.

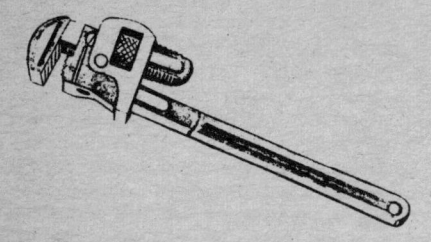

Wrench Use. The correct use of open-end and box-end wrenches, can be summed up in a few simple rules, most important of which is to be sure that the wrench properly fits the nut or bolt head.

When you have to pull hard on the wrench, as in loosening a tight nut, make sure the wrench is seated squarely on the flats of the nut.

PULL on the wrench—DO NOT PUSH. Pushing a wrench is a good way to skin your knuckles if the wrench slips or the nut breaks loose unexpectedly. If it is impossible to pull the wrench, and you must push, do it with the palm of your hand and hold your palm open.

Tools, Measuring.

Graduations on rules, squares and other marking tools are often difficult to read.

A simple way to remedy this is first to clean any grime out of the markings and then use a knife to spread patching plaster over the entire surface. Wipe off the surplus and allow to dry. Rub the whole surface with fine emery cloth and the markings will stand out clearly.

Level. When it is important to have a piece of work either horizontal or vertical, it may be checked with a level. This is a block with a glass tube in the center with a floating bubble of air that comes to rest in the center of the tube when a level surface is achieved. It is useful in hanging pictures, placing shelves or checking a table.

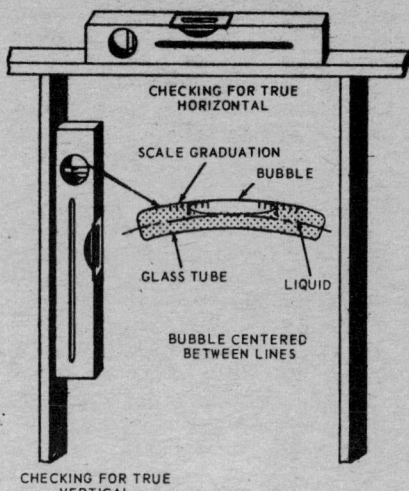

CHECKING FOR TRUE HORIZONTAL
SCALE GRADUATION
BUBBLE
GLASS TUBE
LIQUID
BUBBLE CENTERED BETWEEN LINES

CHECKING FOR TRUE VERTICAL

Level, Improvised. If you don't have a carpenter's level at hand, you can improvise one from a steel square, a piece of string, and a plumb bob. Place the square on the edge of the surface being tested, then suspend the plumb bob (or other weight) at the end of the string, as shown in the illustration. The surface is exactly level when the string is parallel to the upright leg of the square.

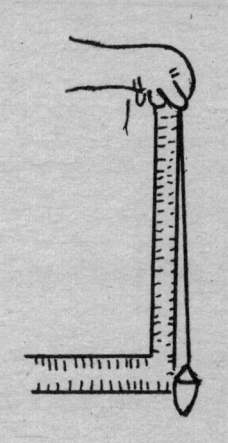

TOOLS, MEASURING

When in need of a temporary surface level to ascertain whether a piece of furniture or large appliance is standing level, you can improvise one with an ordinary glass measuring cup which has markings on both sides. If this cup is filled with water to any one of the markings, it will show that the surface is level when the water contacts the marks on all sides of the cup.

Marking Gage. In conjunction with the combination square, you need a marking gage, which is a two-piece adjustable tool for drawing a line parallel to a straight edge. A marking gage consists of a square stake of wood with a right-angle adjustable gage. As you slide the gage along the edge of a length of wood, a metal point draws a straight line on it.

When using a marking gage or bevel it is a good thing to mark all the required pieces at one setting to avoid errors in attempting to reset at the same dimension. (See also CARPENTRY.)

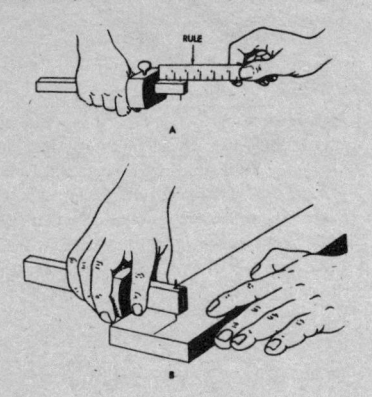

Plumb Bob. A plumb bob is a pointed, tapered brass or bronze weight which is suspended from a cord for determining the vertical or plumb line to or from a point on the ground. Common weights for plumb bobs are 6, 8, 10, 12, 14, 16, 18, and 24 oz.

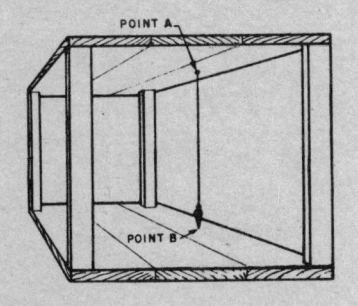

The plumb bob is used in carpentry to determine true verticality when erecting vertical uprights and corner posts of framework. Surveyors use it for transferring and lining up points.

Rule and Tape Care. Rules and tapes should be handled carefully and kept lightly oiled to prevent rust. Never allow the edges of measuring devices to become nicked by striking them with hard objects. They should preferably be kept in a wooden box when not in use.

To avoid kinking tapes, pull them straight out from their cases—do not bend them backward. With the windup type, always turn the crank clockwise—turning it backward will kink or break the tape. With the spring-wind type, guide the tape by hand. If it is allowed to snap back, it may be kinked, twisted, or otherwise damaged. Do not use the hook as a stop. Slow down as you reach the end.

Rules and Tapes. Of all measuring tools, the simplest and most common is the steel rule. This rule is usually 6 or 12 inches in length, although other lengths are available. Steel rules may be flexible or non-flexible, but the thinner the rule, the easier it is to measure accurately because the division marks are closer to the work.

TAPE RULE   STEEL OR FIBERGLASS RULE   HOOK RULE
STEEL RULE WITH HOLDER   STEEL OR FIBERGLASS TAPE   FOLDING RULE

Some common types of rules.

Generally a rule has four sets of graduations, one on each edge of each side. The longest lines represent the inch marks. On one edge, each inch is divided into 8 equal spaces; so each space represents 1/8 in. The other edge of this side is divided into sixteenths. The 1/4-in. and 1/2-in. marks are commonly made longer than the smaller division marks to facilitate counting, but the graduations are not, as a rule, numbered individually, as they are sufficiently far apart to be counted without difficulty. The opposite side is similarly divided into 32 and 64 spaces per inch, and it is common practice to number every fourth division for easier reading.

There are many variations of the common rule. Sometimes the graduations are on one side only, sometimes a set of graduations is added across one end for measuring in narrow spaces, and sometimes only the first inch is divided into 64ths, with the remaining inches divided into 32nds and 16ths.

Rule, Folding. A metal or wood folding rule may be used for measuring purposes. These folding rules are usually 2 to 6 feet long. The folding rules cannot be relied on for extremely accurate measurements because a certain amount of play develops at the joints after they have been used for a while.

Square, Carpenter's. The size of a carpenter's steel square is usually 12 inches x 8 inches, 24 inches x 16 inches, or 24 inches x 18 inches. The flat sides of the blade and the tongue are graduated in inches and fractions of an inch. (The square also contains information that helps to simplify or eliminate the need for computations in many woodworking tasks.) The most common uses for this square are laying out and squaring up large patterns, and for testing the flatness and squareness of large surfaces. Squaring is accomplished by placing the square at right angles to adjacent surfaces and observing if light shows between the work and the square.

Square, Combination. A combination square is equipped with movable heads called a square head, protractor head, and a center head. These combine the functions of several tools, and serve a wide variety of purposes. Normally, only one head is used at a time.

The square head may be used for squaring lines, laying out angles, drawing parallel lines. The center head is useful in locating the exact center of round stock. The protractor head can be attached to the scale adjusted to any position on it, and turned and locked at any desired angle.

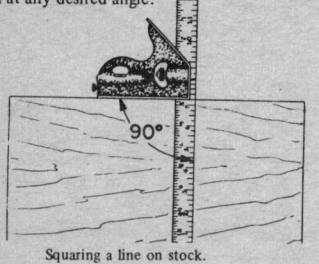

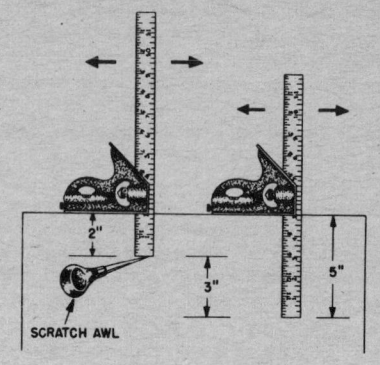

Drawing parallel lines.

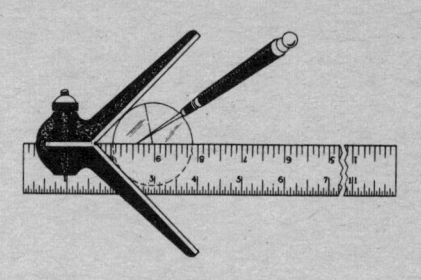

Locating a shaft center.

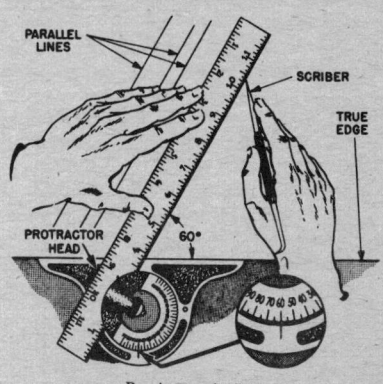

Squaring a line on stock.

Drawing angular lines.

TOOLS, MEASURING WITH

Squares are primarily used for testing and checking trueness of an angle or for laying out lines on materials. Most squares have a rule marked on their edge. As a result they may also be used for measuring.

Square, Try. The try square consists of two parts at right angles to each other; a thick wood or iron stock and a thin, steel blade. Most try squares are made with the blades graduated in inches and fractions of an inch. The blade length varies from 2 inches to 12 inches. This square is used for setting or checking lines or surfaces which have to be at right angles to each other.

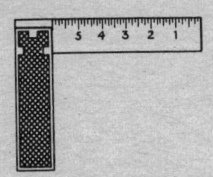

Tape, Steel. Steel tapes are made from 6 to about 300 ft. in length. The shorter lengths are frequently made with a curved cross section so that they are flexible enough to roll up, but remain rigid when extended. Long, flat tapes require support over their full length when measuring, or the natural sag will cause an error in reading.

The flexible-rigid tapes are usually contained in metal cases into which they wind themselves when a button is pressed, or into which they can be easily pushed. A hook is provided at one end to hook over the object being measured so one man can handle it without assistance. On some models, the outside of the case can be used as one end of the tape when measuring inside dimensions.

Tools, Measuring With.

Bolt or Screw Measurement. The length of bolts or screws is best measured by holding them up against a rigid rule or tape. Hold both the bolt or screw to be measured and the rule up to your eye level so that your line of sight will not be in error in reading the measurement. The bolts or screws with countersink type heads are measured from the top of the head to the opposite end, while those with other type heads are measured from the bottom of the head.

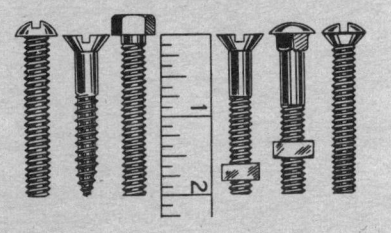

Common Rule Measurement. To take a measurement with a common rule, hold the rule with its edge on the surface of the object being measured. This will eliminate parallax and other errors which might result due to the thickness of the rule. Read the measurement at the graduation which coincides with the distance to be measured, and state it as being so many inches and fractions of an inch. Always reduce fractions to their lowest terms, for example, 6/8 inch would be called 3/4 inch. A hook or eye at the end of a tape or rule is normally part of the first measured inch.

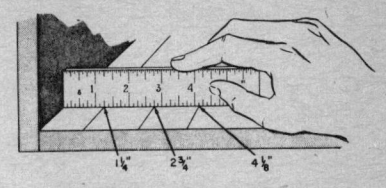

Inside Dimension Measurements.

1. **Folding Rule.** To take an inside measurement, such as the inside of a box, a folding rule that incorporates a 6— or 7-inch sliding extension is one of the best measuring tools for this job. To take the inside measurement, first unfold the folding rule to the approximate dimension. Then extend the end of the rule and read the length that it extends, adding the length of the extension to the length on the

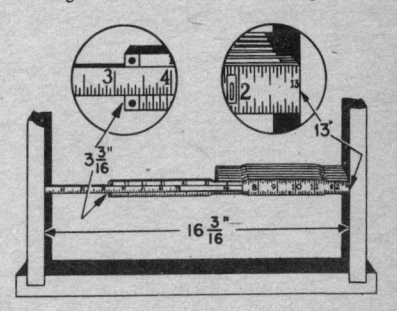

main body of the rule. In this illustration the length of the main body of the rule is 13 inches and the extension is pulled out 3 3/16 inches. In this case the total inside dimension being measured is 16 3/16 inches.

2. Tape Rule. The circled insert below, shows that the hook at the end of the particular rule is attached to the rule so that it is free to move slightly. When an outside dimension is taken by hooking the end of the rule over an edge, the hook will locate the end of the rule even with the surface from which the measurement is being taken. By being free to move, the hook will retract away from the end of the rule when an inside dimension is taken. To measure an inside dimension using a tape rule, extend the rule between the surfaces as shown, take a reading at the point on the scale where the rule enters the case, and add 2 inches. The 2 inches are the width of the case. The total is the inside dimension being taken.

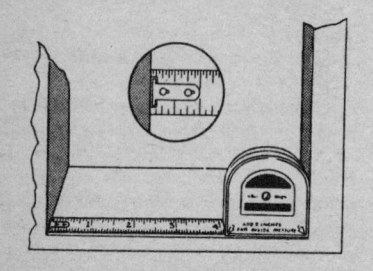

Outside Dimension Measurement. To measure an outside dimension using a tape rule, hook the rule over the edge of the stock. Pull the tape out until it projects far enough from the case to permit measuring the required distance. The hook at the end of the rule is designed so that it will locate the end of the rule at the surface from which the measurement is being taken. When taking a measurement of length, the tape is held parallel to the lengthwise edge. For measuring widths, the tape should be at right angles to the lengthwise edge. Read the dimension of the rule exactly at the edge of the piece being measured.

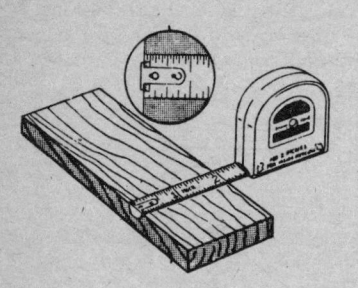

It may not always be possible to hook the end of the tape over the edge of stock being measured. In this case it may be necessary to butt the end of the tape against another surface or to hold the rule at a starting point from which a measurement is to be taken.

Pipe Circumference Measurement. To measure the circumference of a pipe, a flexible type rule that will conform to the cylindrical shape of the pipe must be used. A tape rule or a steel tape is adaptable for this job. When measuring pipe, make sure the tape has been wrapped squarely around the axis of the pipe (i.e., measurement should be taken in a plane perpendicular to the axis) to ensure that the reading will not be more than the actual circumference of the pipe. This is extremely important when measuring large diameter pipe.

Hold the rule or tape as shown. Take the reading, using the 2-inch graduation, for example, as the reference point. In this case the correct reading is found by subtracting 2 inches from the actual reading. In this way the first 2 inches of the tape, serving as a handle, will enable you to hold the tape securely in place.

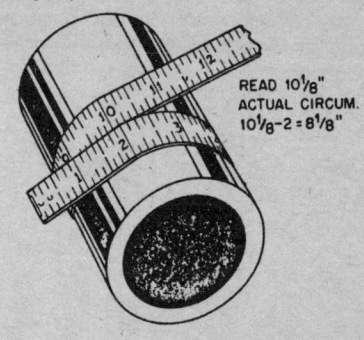

Pipe Diameter Measurement.
1. Inside Diameter. To measure the inside diameter of a pipe with a rule, hold the rule so that one corner of the rule just rests on the inside of one side

of the pipe. Then, with one end thus held in place, swing the rule through an arc and read the diameter across the maximum inside distance. This method is satisfactory for an approximate inside measurement.

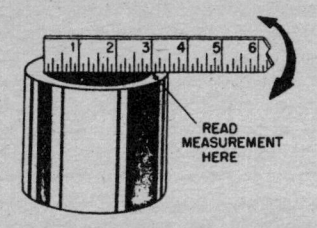

2. Outside Diameter. To measure the outside diameter of a pipe, it is best to use some kind of rigid rule. A folding wooden rule or a steel rule is satisfactory for this purpose. As shown, line up the end of the rule with one side of the pipe, using your thumb as a stop. Then with the one end hold in place with your thumb, swing the rule through an arc and take the maximum reading at the other side of the pipe. For most practical purposes, the measurement obtained by using this method is satisfactory. It is necessary that you know how to take this measurement as the outside diameter of pipe is sometimes the only dimension given on pipe specifications.

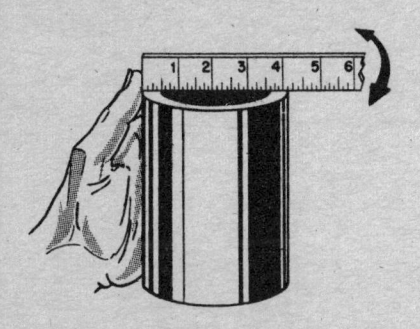

Tools, Plumbing. (See also PLUMBING.)

Basic tools that you should have on hand to make simple plumbing repairs include:

wrenches—including pipe wrenches in a range of sizes to fit the pipe, fittings, equipment and appliances in the system,

screwdrivers—in a range of sizes to fit the faucets, valves and other parts of the system,

ball-peen hammer—or a 12 or 16 oz. claw hammer,

rubber force cup (plunger or plumber's friend),

cold chisel and center punch,

clean out auger (snake),

friction tape,

adjustable pliers,

faucet washers and packing,

a few feet of pipe strap.

Additional tools required for more extensive plumbing repairs may be rented if needed. These include:

set of pipe threading dies and stocks,

hack saw and blades—blades should have 32 teeth per inch,

pipe cutter—roller type,

tapered reamer or half-round file,

carpenter's brace,

set of wood bits,

gasoline blowtorch,

copper tube cutter with reamer (if you have copper tubing).

Force Pump. When using a plumber's force pump or "plunger" for unclogging a drain pipe, remember that the clearing action occurs on the upstroke, rather than the downstroke. So, after pressing downward, pull up vigorously for maximum suction action. The cup works by drawing the obstruction back up into the pipe so that it can be broken up by the down rushing water. Forcing it downward may only pack the debris in more tightly and thus make it harder to break up.

Force Pump Handle. One of the provoking things about handling a plumber's force pump is the tendency of the handle to pull loose from the suction cup. You can anchor the handle securely with an ordinary bottle cap. Just remove the handle from the rubber cup, screw the bottle cap to the end, as illustrated, and then force the handle back into place.

TOOLS, POWER

Tips. Always use the proper size wrench or screwdriver. Do not use pipe wrenches on nuts with flat surfaces, use an adjustable or open-end wrench. Do not use pipe wrenches on polished-surface tubings or fittings such as found on plumbing fixtures, use a strap wrench. Tight nuts or fittings can sometimes be loosened by tapping lightly with a hammer or mallet.

Tools, Power.

Belt Sander. The belt sander is commonly used for surfacing lumber used for interior trim, furniture, or cabinets. Wood floors are almost always made ready for final finishing by using a belt sander. Whereas these types of sanding operations were once laborious and time-consuming, it is now possible to perform the operations quickly and accurately with less effort.

The portable belt sanders use endless sanding belts that can be obtained in many different grades (grits). The belts are usually 2, 3, or 4 inches wide and can be easily changed when they become worn or when you want to use a different grade of sanding paper.

The first thing to do when preparing to use the sander is to be sure that the object to be sanded is firmly secured. Then, after the motor has been started verify that the belt is tracking on center. Any adjustment to make it track centrally is usually made by aligning screws.

The moving belt is then placed on the surface of the object to be sanded with the rear part of the belt touching first. The machine is then leveled as it is moved forward. When you use the sander, don't press down or "ride" it, because the weight of the machine exerts enough pressure for proper cutting. (Excessive pressure also causes the abrasive belt to clog and the motor to overheat). Adjust the machine over the surface with overlapping strokes, always in a direction parallel to the grain.

By working over a fairly wide area, and avoiding any machine tilting or pausing in any one spot, an even surface will result. Upon completion of the sanding process, lift the machine off the work and then stop the motor.

Some types of sanders are provided with a bag that takes up the dust that is produced. Use it if available.

Bench Grinder. The electric bench grinder is designed for hand grinding operations, such as sharpening chisels or screw drivers, grinding drills, removing excess metal from work, and smoothing metal surfaces. It is usually fitted with both a medium grain and fine grain abrasive wheel; the medium wheel is satisfactory for rough grinding where a considerable quantity of metal has to be removed, or where a smooth finish is not important. For sharpening tools or grinding to close limits of size, the fine wheel should be used as it removes metal slower, gives the work a smooth finish and does not generate enough heat to anneal the cutting edges.

When sharpening tools on a power-driven grinding wheel, the angle at which the tool is held against the surface of the wheel is extremely important for getting an accurate, smooth edge. You can assure a solid rest of exactly the right angle for a particular tool by cutting a wooden block with a bevel at the top, shaping this bevel to hold the blade of your tool at the correct angle.

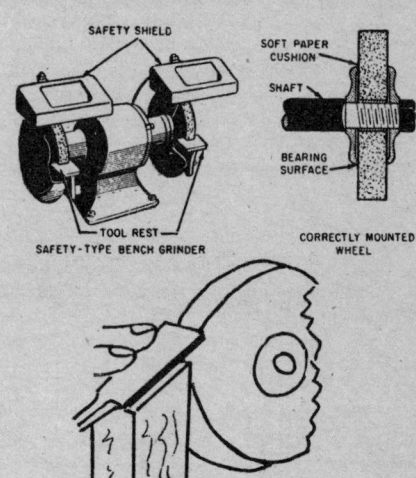

Circular Saw, Portable. The portable circular saw is becoming more and more popular as a woodworking tool because of the time and labor it saves, the precision with which it works, and its ease of handling and maneuverability.

The sizes of portable electric saws range from one-sixth horsepower with a 4-inch blade to one-and-one half horsepower with a 14-inch blade. They are so constructed that they may be used as a carpenter's handsaw, both at the job site or on a bench in the woodworking shop.

Most saws may be adjusted for cross-cutting or for ripping.

Circular Saw Safety. The portable electric saw is one of the most dangerous power tools in existence when it is not properly used. Make sure the board you are sawing is properly secured so it will not slip or turn. After making a cut be sure the saw blade has come to a standstill before laying the saw down.

When using an electric saw remember that all the blade you can normally see is covered; the portion of the blade that projects under the board being cut is not covered. The exposed teeth under the work are dangerous and can cause serious injury if any part of your body should come into contact with them.

Make sure the blade of a portable circular saw is kept sharp at all times. The saw blade will function most efficiently when the rate of feed matches the blade's capacity to cut. You will not have to figure this out—you will be able to feel it. With a little practice you will know when the cut is smooth and you will know when you are forcing it. Let the blade do its own cutting. The tool will last longer and you will work easier because it is less fatiguing.

Disk Sander. Electric disk sanders are especially useful on work where a large amount of material is to be removed quickly such as scaling surfaces in preparation for painting. This machine, however, must not be used where a mirror smooth finish is required.

The disk should be moved smoothly and lightly over the surface. Never allow the disk to stay in one place too long because it will cut into the metal and leave a large depression.

Drill, Portable. The portable electric drill is probably the most frequently used power tool. Although it is especially designed for drilling holes, by adding various accessories you can adapt it for different jobs. Sanding, sawing, buffing, polishing, screwdriving, wire brushing, and paint mixing are examples of possible uses.

Drill Press. The drill press is an electrically operated power machine that was originally designed as a metal-working tool. Available accessories, plus jigs and special techniques, now make it a versatile wood-working tool as well.

There are two basic types of drill presses, the bench-type and the upright-type. These are basically the same, the difference being in the mounting. As the names suggest, the bench-type drill press is mounted on a work bench and the upright-type drill press is mounted on a pedestal on the floor.

When operating a drill press make sure the drill is properly secured in the chuck and that the work you are drilling is properly secured in position. Do not remove the work from the tilting table or mounting device until the drill press has stopped.

Before operating any drill press, visually inspect the drill press to determine if all parts are in the proper place, secure, and in good operating condition. Check all assemblies, such as the motor, head, pulleys, and bench for loose mountings.

While the drill is operating, be alert for any sounds that may be signs of trouble, such as squeaks or unusual noise.

After operating a drill press, wipe off all dirt, oil, and metal particles. Inspect the V-belt to make sure no metal chips are imbedded in the driving surfaces.

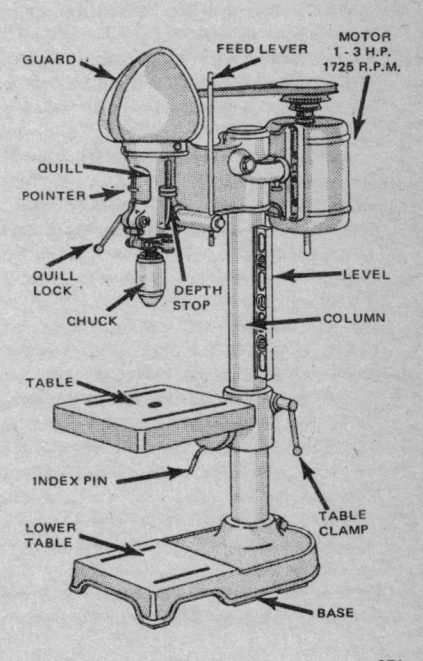

Maintenance. A power tool must be looked after if it is to work efficiently. It should be kept clean and free from sawdust clog. If sawdust collects inside the tool it causes over-heating and eventual failure. From time to time use a vacuum cleaner or the air hose at your local garage and blow out the sawdust from inside your power tool.

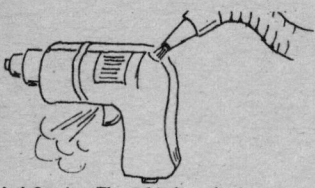

Orbital Sander. The orbital sander is so named because of the action of the sanding pad. The pad moves in a tiny orbit, with a motion that is hardly discernible, so that it actually sands in all directions. This motion is so small and so fast that, with fine paper mounted on the pad, it is nearly impossible to see any scratches on the finished surface.

The pad, around with the abrasive sheet is wrapped, usually extends beyond the frame of the machine so it is possible to work in tight corners and against vertical surfaces.

Some models of the orbital sanders have a bag attached to catch all dust that is made from the sanding operation. Orbital sanders (pad sanders) do not remove as much material as fast as the belt sander or disk sander but do a better job on smoothing a surface for finishing.

Saber Saw. The saber saw is a power driven jigsaw that will let you cut smooth and decorative curves in wood and light metal. Most saber saws are light duty machines and are not designed for extremely fast cutting.

There are several different blades designed to operate in the saber saw and they are easily interchangeable. For fast cutting of wood, a blade with coarse teeth may be used. A blade with fine teeth is designed for cutting metal.

The best way to learn how to handle this type of tool is to use it. Before trying to do a finished job with the saber saw, clamp down a piece of scrap plywood and draw some curved as well as straight lines to follow. You will develop your own way of gripping the tool, and this will be affected somewhat by the particular tool you are using. On some tools, for example, you will find guiding easier if you apply some downward pressure on the tool as you move it forward. If you are not firm with your grip, the tool will tend to vibrate excessively and this will roughen the cut. Do not force the cutting faster than the design of the blade allows or you will break the blade.

Safety. Safe practices in the use of power tools cannot be overemphasized. There are several general safety measures to observe in operating or maintaining power equipment.

1. Never operate power equipment unless you are thoroughly familiar with its controls and operating procedures.

2. All portable tools should be inspected before use to see that they are clean and in a proper state of repair.

3. Have ample illumination. If extension lights are required, ensure that a light guard is provided.

4. Before a power tool is connected to a source of power be sure that the switch on the tool is in the OFF position.

5. When operating a power tool, give it your full and undivided attention.

6. Keep all safety guards in position and use safety shields or goggles when necessary.

7. Fasten all loose sleeves and aprons.

8. Do not distract or in any way disturb anyone who is operating a power tool.

9. Never try to clear jammed machinery unless you remove the source of power first.

10. After using a power tool, turn off the power, remove the power source, wait for all rotation of the tool to stop, and then clean the tool. Remove all waste and scraps from the work area and stow the tool in its assigned location.

11. Never plug the power cord of a portable electric tool into an electrical power source before ensuring that the source has the voltage and type of current (alternating or direct) called for on the nameplate of the tool.

12. If an extension cord is required, always connect the cord of a portable electric power tool into the extension cord before the extension cord is inserted into a convenience outlet. Always unplug the extension cord from the receptacle before the cord of the portable power tool is unplugged from the extension cord.

13. Be sure to use a grounded plug and a 3-conductor cord.

Tools, Soldering, see **SOLDERING.**

Tool Use.

If you plan to do—	Minimum equipment	Desirable equipment	Supplementary equipment
Household or kitchen activities:			
open crates and boxes	crate opener or pry bar or 8" screwdriver. jar and can openers.	12 or 13 oz. claw hammer. combination opener.	
open jars, can, etc	scissors and paring knife.	utility knife.	
cut cardboard	high-grade oil suitable for small appliances.	powdered graphite. graphite in oil.	
lubricate appliances, locks, hinges, etc.	ruler or yardstick or good-quality measuring tape. paste-on tabs for light items.	6' – 10' steel tape or folding rule.	25' or 50' tape.
measure and space items			
attach items to walls	hangers with nails or screws for heavier items: 12 or 13 oz. curved claw hammer. hand drill and bits. screwdrivers.	hollow-wall screw anchors and toggle bolts: hand or electric drill and twist drills ¼" and up. stud locator.	For masonry or concrete: screw anchors and screws. proper size star drill or electric drill and tungsten carbide masonry drill
level items	pan of water to level appliances. string with attached weight.	level as part of combination square.	9" – 12" level.
Small repair jobs:			
tighten or loosen screws	4" and 6" screwdrivers. Nos. 1 and 2 Phillips screwdrivers.	hex wrenches. special screwdrivers and wrenches. locking-type wrench pliers.	ratchet screwdriver. open-end and box-end wrenches.
tighten nuts or hold small items	6" – 7" slip joint pliers. adjustable wrench.	needle-nose pliers.	
drive or pull nails, etc	12 or 13 oz. curved claw hammer. 6" screwdriver.	hand stapler. pry bar.	staple gun. tack puller.
repair plastic items	plastic mending tape.	liquid mender for type of plastic.	plastic repair kit with strips and adhesive.
seal openings and joints	special sealants and tapes.	calking gun.	
replace ordinary faucet washers.	adjustable wrench. screwdrivers.	tape or cloth to place between wrench and polished fitting.	
open drains and pipes	force cup.		flexible drain auger.
other minor jobs	packaging material and string. polishes and waxes. cleaning supplies and equipment. step stool.	small wire. putty knife. vacuum cleaner. stepladder.	glass cutter. fabric mending and fastening kits.
Small jobs with wood:			
measure and mark	sharp pointed No. 2½ or 3 common pencil.	8" by 12" utility, steel combination, or try square.	dividers. rafter or framing square.
(Note.–Operations are listed in their usual sequence.)	ruler or yardstick. tablet back or drawing triangle may serve as a square. pencil compass.	6' to 10' steel tape or folding rule.	
cut wood	coping saw. friction vise or bench hook to hold wood.	20" 22", 10–11 point hand saw. two 4" C-clamps.	hand ripsaw. miter box. electric hand and sabre saws.
smoothen wood (may be repeated after assembly).	fine, medium, and coarse sandpaper. sandpaper block.	block, plane, or multiblade wood smoothing tool. rasps and scraper.	jack or smoothing plane. electric sander.
assemble pieces into unit	assorted sizes of wire nails and brads. 12 to 13 oz. curved claw hammer. 1/16" nail set. 6d nails. white glue (not moisture resistant).	wood screws. countersink. 4" and 6" screwdrivers. hand drill with drills and bit brace with bits or light duty electric drill with bits. nails with heads cut off may be used as small drills. urea or plastic resin glue (moisture resistant).	gluing clamps. 8" or stub screwdriver. assorted sizes of common, finish, and special nails. set of combination drill and countersink bits for use with screws. resorcinol glue (waterproof).
fill holes in wood:			
nail holes	colored putty.	spackling compound for surfaces to be painted.	
larger holes	wood dough, plastic wood, or surfacing putty.		
finish wood	see other chapters.		
Work with metals:			
measure and mark	see measure and mark wood.	see measure and mark wood.	metal scribe.
cut	utility saw or keyhole-type hacksaw.	tin snips. 3/8" cold chisel. vise. hacksaw with set of blades.	power grinder and safety goggles.
drill holes	hand drill with twist drills.	light-duty electric drill with a set of twist drills.	high-speed drill bits desirable for frequent heavy use.
smoothen or sharpen	8" mill file. sharpening stone.	8" half round file. 8" round file.	emery cloth. grinder and safety goggles.
assemble	4" and 6" screwdrivers. Nos. 1 and 2 Phillips screwdrivers. 6" – 7" slip-joint pliers.	locking-type wrench pliers. adjustable wrench.	small sets of open-end and box-end wrenches.
polishing		emery and crocus cloths.	
repairing	epoxy resin.	epoxy resin and fiber glass.	soldering equipment.

TOOLS, YARD

Tools, Yard, see GARDEN TOOLS.

Toothbrushes. Save your old toothbrushes! They make handy gadgets for intricate cleaning chores. The bristles penetrate hard-to-clean spots on numerous household appliances, such as the gear-type of can opener, the egg beater, the food chopper, the grater, and so on.

Children's size toothbrushes can be used as bottle brushes or to remove dust from odd corners of your sewing machine or typewriter.

When the bristles are too worn for further use, put the old handles into water and boil for a few minutes.

Pull out the bristles and bend the handles to form a colored chain for baby to play with.

Torch, Homemade. You can make a practical torch for burning the nests or webs of tree spiders or caterpillars if you'll nail a scrap of insulation board to the end of a pole, saturate the board with some kerosene or fuel oil, and then when this is ignited, your "torch" will burn for quite a length of time — until you've finished the job at hand.

Tortoise Shell. Clean with denatured alcohol then polish with chamois dipped in borax.

Towel Rack Repair. You can repair that bathroom towel rack which has loosened by removing the screws, wrapping cotton around them, dipping into glue, and replacing the screws in their original holes. Wait until the glue is completely dry before using the rack.

Trading Stamps. Here's one idea for pasting trading stamps in the books without the arduous chore of licking them. Place a double page at a time upside down on your ironing board and use a spray to dampen them. A little practice will show you just how many squirts you need to make them stick.

Trailer Laundry. For tourists with trailers or mobile homes, here is an easy and effective way of handling the family laundry. Fill a small plastic trash can one-third full of water and add detergent and your soiled clothes. Clamp on the lid, and tie the can securely with a rope and suspend it from the center beam of the clothes closet. The motion of the trailer as it is pulled along the highway will make for a clean wash, ready for a quick rinse at day's end.

Trap Repair, see PLUMBING.

Trash Can Lid. You can secure the lid on your trash or garbage can, and prevent the annoyance of having it tipped over by stray dogs and the contents spilled all over the place. Just take a screen-door spring, fasten a hook to each end, engage each handle of the can with these, and up and over the lid. The hooks are easily detachable for removing the cover.

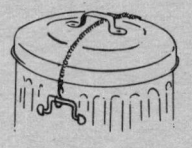

Trash Can Repair. If the bottom of your trash can has rusted out, you can prolong the life of the container by use of a wood or hardboard disk. If the can has tapered sides, cut the disk slightly oversize so that it will fit tightly against the sides just above the original bottom. You'll have to use angle brackets if the can has straight sides. Paint the disk and inside of the can with some roofing cement to make a still better job of renovating.

TWINE HOLDERS

Tree Bench. The old-fashioned tree bench still provides an attractive touch to almost any yard. If you have a shade tree in your yard with a trunk large enough to provide a comfortable back rest, here's a good way to construct a circular bench around it: Measure the diameter of the tree and build the bench in two halves to fit snugly around it. Fasten the boards of the bench together with solid strips across them underneath. To these strips fasten sturdy triangular wood brackets — three or four to each bench half. These brackets should be placed so that one leg of the triangle rests against the tree and the other leg supports the bench. When everything has been assembled around the tree, level the bench and nail the bottom parts of the brackets firmly to the trunk of the tree.

Tree Measuring. To estimate the height of a tree, you can use the shadow method of setting a short pole in the earth near the tree. Measure the height of the pole and the length of the shadow it casts, and the length of the shadow being cast by the tree at the same time. Multiply the length of the tree's shadow by the height of the pole, then divide this product by the length of the pole's shadow, and you'll have the height of your tree.

Tree Preservation. The best way to preserve shade trees that have started to decay is to cut out all the dead and decayed matter, making the cavities absolutely clean — then fill with concrete mix. If the cavity is extra-large, your concrete filler can be reinforced by driving 20-penny nails into the wood and tying on one-fourth-inch reinforcing bars, which will help hold the concrete in place and prevent its cracking up.

Trellis, see GARDENING.

Triacetate, see FIBERS, MAN-MADE.

Trouser Hanger, see CLOSET ACCESSORIES.

Try Square, see TOOLS, MEASURING.

Tub Drain Repair, see PLUMBING.

Tube Sealer. Those collapsible tubes that hold cement, glue, or wood putty can be effectively sealed after use with small cup hooks, as shown in the illustration. These hooks also come in handy for hanging the tubes on a wall.

Tubing, Copper.
1. Here's an easy and effective way to straighten out that soft copper tubing. Nail two long boards on top of another board, with just enough space between the two top boards to accommodate your tubing. Then all you have to do is place one end of the tubing in the channel provided by the boards and walk over the tubing while pushing it through the channel. The thickness of your boards will prevent your crushing the tubing, while the sides of the boards will straighten it out as you pull it through.

2. Green discoloration which often appears on copper tubing, etc, can be removed by rubbing it with a paste made of soap and ammonia.

Turkeys, see FOODS.

Tweezer, see TOOLS, HAND.

Twine Holders.
1. A very handy and workable twine holder can be improvised just by suspending a small funnel

TWISTS

from a convenient place on the kitchen or closet wall by means of the small ring usually attached to the funnel. Place the ball of string inside the funnel so that one end of the string can be run out through the funnel end.

2. Here is a simple little homemade device which will keep that ever-disappearing ball of twine in a handy place for you. Simply bore a 1/4-inch hole through a shelf support or cupboard wall and attach the jar top, as illustrated, with two screws.

Twists. Never throw away those little twists that come on some plastic-wrapped foods. They have many uses. For instance, when you want to drip-dry a dress outside, but are afraid the hanger might blow off the line, use one of these twists to fasten the hanger hook to the line.

Typing. When you are using your typewriter, some words can be emphasized if you'll slip a strip of plain paper in front of the ribbon, holding it there while you type the desired words with one hand.

Typewriter.
   Cleaning.
   1. A pipe cleaner, bent into the proper shape, makes a dandy gimmick for cleaning the hard-to-get-at places inside a typewriter.
   2. For cleaning typewriter keys, cigarette lighter fluid is a good agent. Use it sparingly with a type cleaning brush, or with an old toothbrush.
   3. You can clean clogged letters on typewriter keys by pressing on a strip of adhesive tape and then lifting it off.

Noise Reduction. If the other members of your family are sometimes annoyed by the clatter of your typewriter working far into the night, here is one way to put a "muffler" on the racket. Because the table on which your typewriter sits often provides an active sounding board you should try to insulate it as much as possible. You can do this with a layer of sponge rubber, a piece of acoustical tile on this, and the typewriter placed on top of these. These two "sound barriers" will help considerably.

Platen Repair. If the platen on your typewriter has become rather worn and indented with rows of type impressions, you can compensate temporarily for this by inserting extra sheets of paper behind your master sheet. A still better way, however, is to cut a piece of plastic material of the type with an adhesive backing to the size of a sheet of typing paper. The comparative stiffness of this backing gives a clear imprint.

To renew the surface of a rubber typewriter roller which has been dented by the continual pounding of the keys, remove the roller from the machine, sand it with fine sandpaper, then wipe clean with a cloth dampened with cleaning solvent.

Ribbon Renewal.
1. The life of a worn typewriter ribbon can be extended by soaking it in hot water. Drop the spool of ribbon into a jar of water, seal it, and let it stand for a few days. Then remove the ribbon and permit it to drain dry before reinstalling it into your typewriter.

2. When your typewriter ribbon has become quite faded, and you don't have a new one at hand, you can try heating your old ribbon to redistribute the ink. One good way to do this is to lay the spool on the bottom of an electric iron set for the lowest heat and cover it with a paper napkin. Warm the ribbon for five or ten minutes (no longer), and then you should be able to get some more "mileage" out of it.

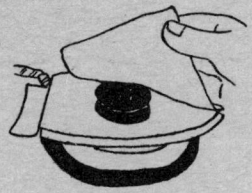

3. If your typewriter ribbon is beginning to make faint impressions, you can often give it a new lease on life as follows: fill a small oil can with olive oil and sprinkle the ribbon with this as you run it from one spool to the other. Allow to stand for a day, and you will be surprised at the nice, clear, black letters produced the next day.

4. Typewriter ribbons that are beginning to fade can often be revived by applying stamp-pad ink sparingly to the top of the ribbon as you wind it from one spool to the other. Or, dip a toothpick into ordinary mineral oil and dab bits of it over the entire length of the ribbon at intervals of about an inch. A few hours later, the ribbon will usually be ready to make a good impression on what ever confronts it.

u

Umbrella

Repair. If the handle on your umbrella is very loose, remove the handle and coat the hole in it with some epoxy glue. Replace on the shaft, and let the glue dry for at least 24 hours.

Stand.

1. A very convenient and neat umbrella rack can be made just by nailing a length of board to the baseboard of a front hall or closet. The board can be sawed out in the pattern illustrated, and then drilled between the scallops to accommodate the umbrella tips. The bottom of the rack can be shaped to fit over the shoe mold, or the latter can be cut away so that the rack will fit flush against the flooring.

2. You can easily make your own umbrella holder by punching four holes in a metal wastebasket, and inserting separation rods which are bent from coat-hanger wire, as illustrated. You can then paint or decorate the container to your taste.

Unpainted Furniture, see FURNITURE PAINTING TIPS.

Upholstery Cleaning. Hard-finish upholstery can be cleaned if, after a thorough brushing and vacuuming you'll mix up some pure castile soapsuds and lukewarm water and scrub the upholstery with a brush. Take one workable area at a time, and remove the suds with a rough cloth dipped in clear water to which a little powdered alum has been added.

To shampoo soiled upholstery, first vacuum it thoroughly to remove all loose dirt, paying special attention to the crevices. Then whip a thick dry suds, using an eggbeater, a little water, and lots of good, mild, synthetic detergent. Brush the dry suds onto the upholstery a small area at a time, remembering to use ONLY the suds, no water to soak the fabric. Wipe the soiled suds off right away with a damp cloth.

Upholstery, Leather, see LEATHER UPHOLSTERY.

Upholstery Repair.

1. One often-satisfactory way to repair cigarette burns in upholstered furniture consists of darning the hole in close stitches with a color-matching yarn, then placing a damp cloth over the spot and ironing the area.

2. Rips in upholstery can usually be invisibly mended by applying adhesive tape a little longer than the the tear underneath the fabric, sticky side up. Press the torn edges together closely and firmly with the raveled threads underneath.

Upholstery, Stained, see STAIN REMOVAL.

Upholstery Tacks. To complete the driving of brass-headed upholstery tacks without crushing them, use a short dowel in one end of which a shallow hole has been drilled—setting this drilled end on the tack and tapping the other end of the dowel with your hammer.

Urine Stain, see STAIN REMOVAL.

Utility Room Fixtures, see LIGHTING FIXTURES.

V

Vacuum Bottle, Cleaning. A method of getting the inside of a vacuum bottle thoroughly clean is to fill it with warm water to which a heaping teaspoon of baking soda has been added, and let stand overnight. Do this at least once a week with bottles that are used regularly.

Vacuum Cleaner. Empty your vacuum cleaner over dampened newspaper to prevent scattering dust.
Joints. Sometimes the vacuum cleaner's hose attachments prove a little stubborn when you are attempting to fit them together or pull them apart. You can avoid this annoyance if you'll occasionally lubricate the joints of these tubes with some waxed paper. Just rub the paper well over these areas, and it will deposit enough lubricant to make for much easier action.

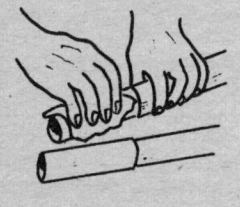

Repair. If your vacuum cleaner is not picking up enough dirt, check the nozzle: it may be too close or too far from the surface that you are cleaning. Turn the screw until a quarter will slide between the nozzle and the floor. For cleaners with revolving brushes, use a half-dollar.

Inspect the belt to see that it is firmly set around both brush and motor shaft. Clean all string, hair, and other dirt away from the belt. If the belt still doesn't work, replace it.

As to oiling a vacuum cleaner, do not touch it with oil unless specific instructions tell you to do so. If so, follow the instructions carefully.

If the vacuum cleaner vibrates excessively, examine the blower itself. If one of the blower blades is broken, remove the blower from the motor. You can see if the blower is broken or not when it becomes visible. If it is, replace it. If it is too difficult to remove, you'll have to take the cleaner to a repair shop.

Valance Lighting, see LIGHTING, STRUCTURAL.

Valves, see PLUMBING.

Vapor Barriers. In northern parts of the country, storm doors are used to prevent moisture from condensing on the insides of windows and doors. Moisture will also collect on the insides of walls, and between the inner and outer layers of the walls and roof of a house. The only way you can prevent this is by using a vapor barrier.

Many insulating materials have vapor barriers fastened to one side. Others can be built in separately.

Paint vapor barriers seal the pores in plaster wood or wallpaper, and prevent moisture in rooms from getting into the wall structure. A paint vapor barrier is aluminum paint with a spar varnish base.

You apply it to wall areas as a prime coat and then paint over it, or put wallpaper over it.

Membrane vapor barriers come in three types: shiny-surfaced, asphalt-treated kraft paper; polyethylene sheets; or reflective metal foil sheets. You apply these over the inner faces of the studs, with the shiny surface always facing the room. You get the best results by fastening the sheet laps firmly together with plastic cement.

Varnish, see FURNITURE REFINISHING, PAINTS.

Varnish Stains, see STAIN REMOVAL.

Vase Lamp, see LIGHTING, PORTABLE.

Vases.
1. If you're finding it difficult to insert a cleaning cloth into a deep vase, try using a double sheet of newspaper rolled into a compact cylinder. Clip and fray one end of this to provide a brush for scouring the bottom and sides of the vase with a cleaning solution.
2. Fragile ornamental vases will be more likely to survive weekly dusting if you pour enough sand into them to give them more weight and balance.

Vegetables, see FOODS.

Vehicle, see PAINT COMPONENTS.

Velvet Care, see CLOTHES CARE.

Veneer Repair, see FURNITURE REPAIR.

Venetian Blinds.
Cleaning. One easy and speedy way to clean those usually hard-to-do venetian blinds is to make yourself a pair of special mitts out of old turkish towels. To make these, outline your hand on a sheet of paper, then use this as a template to cut the toweling about an inch larger all the way around. Sew together, then turn inside out. With one of these, both sides of each slat can be wiped at the same time.

Smudges are easily removed with art gum.

Cord Installation. Best and easiest way to install a new venetian blind cord is before the old, frayed one breaks. Let the blind down, cut one side of the knot on the old cord at the bottom of the blind and tie, sew, or tape the new cord to it. Then, with the blind still hanging down, pull the other end of the old cord and this will draw your new cord easily into the blind.

Cord Repair. If venetian blind cords begin to slip and slide, it means that the metal gears that control the slats are worn and no longer grip the tapes that move the slats. Replace the pulleys and gears with new ones. Read the instructions on the replacements.

You'll need no more than a screwdriver to put them in.

Installation. Built-in venetian blinds are generally hung on special fixtures built in a window frame, or from hinges installed outside the frame. You can install a venetian blind over your window with a valance-type hanger. Instructions come with all blinds and valances. Just follow them carefully. Usually two mountings are fastened to the top border of the window frame, and the hanger is slipped into two slotted boxes.

Scratch Prevention. If your window casings are becoming scarred from the constant raising and lowering of your venetian blinds, glue small pieces of felt to the bottom crosspieces of the blinds. The felt will absorb future blows.

Slat Replacement. If the slats become worn, warped or bent, replace them with new ones. Loosen the cords running through the center of the tapes at the bottom of the blind and remove it from the bottom bar. Repeat for the other side. Slip out the ailing slat and replace it with a new one. Run the cords back through the slats and refasten them to the bottom bar. You can leave the blind hanging to replace one or two slats.

Tape Cleaning. Venetian blind tapes can be cleaned easily without taking down the blinds. For white tapes, try ordinary white shoe cleaner just as you would on shoes. Cleaning fluid works well on colored tapes. These tapes can be shampooed, if you wish, with upholstery-type washes (if the tapes are color-fast, of course). Let the tapes hang down full-length until dry to avoid any possibility of shrinkage.

Tape Repair. If you replace defective tapes, remove the cord, and then take out all the slats one at a time. Replace your old tapes with new ones. Slip the slats back in place and replace the cord.

VENTILATION

Ventilation. Fresh air, even during a driving rain storm, can be provided in your home by closing a window on an old wooden shutter. cut to fit in horizontally. Be sure to put the shutter in with the slats sloping against the direction of the wind.

Verdigris Stain, see STAIN REMOVAL.

Vine Supports. If the vine growing up your concrete wall needs some supports, and you don't feel up to the job of drilling into the concrete, here is a quick and simple answer to your little problem: Press some dabs of plastic wood at intervals on the concrete wall. It is weatherproof and waterproof, and will adhere firmly to stone, brick or stucco. When the plastic wood has hardened, staples can be driven into it for holding your guide wires or string.

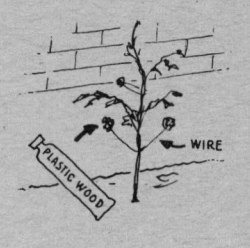

Vinyl Tile, see RESILIENT TILE FLOORS.

Vinyon, see FIBERS, MAN-MADE.

Vises, see TOOLS, HAND.

Vise Safety, see TOOLS, HAND.

Voltage, see ELECTRICITY, THEORY OF.

W

Wading Pool. Here is an easily-assembled home wading pool which will give fun and relaxation to both children and adults. The uprights and frame are cut from two-by-four stock, with the corner braces being one-by-four stock. The illustration shows one corner of the pool, and the entire assembly may be of any size you wish. The uprights are driven into the ground, the horizontal members are bolted to them, and the corner braces are nailed in place. Then, a waterproof tarpaulin is tied to the frame and filled with water, being sure that the bottom of the tarpaulin rests squarely on the ground to prevent damage to it. In emptying the pool, you can simply lower one corner of the tarpaulin — or you can use a garden hose to siphon most of the water into a sewer.

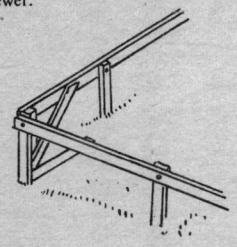

Waffle Iron, see APPLIANCES.

Walk Repair, see CONCRETE REPAIR.

Wallboard, see DRYWALL.

Wall Brackets, see BRACKETS, WALL.

Wall Construction, see BASEMENT FINISHING, DRYWALL.

Wall Insulation, see INSULATION.

Wall Painting, see PAINTING, INTERIOR.

Wallpaper.
  Air Bubbles.
  1. If you are doing some of your own wallpapering, and if some of those familiar bubbles should pop up on the surface of the paper, clamp down on them with tissue paper and a warm iron.
  2. A paint roller of the type used for enamel makes a fine tool for smoothing out air bubbles under the freshly-applied paper.
  Bleeding. If you are applying some new wallpaper over old, and there are any grease spots present on the old paper, there's danger of these "bleeding" through and spoiling the appearance of your newly papered walls. You can avoid this possibility of "bleeding" if you'll first coat the grease spots with some clear shellac.

Brush Rest. Where to rest the brush while pasting wallpaper is solved by inserting a length of stiff wire through the bail eyes of the pail. Wire from a wire hanger serves nicely. When you want to stir the paste, merely withdraw the wire.

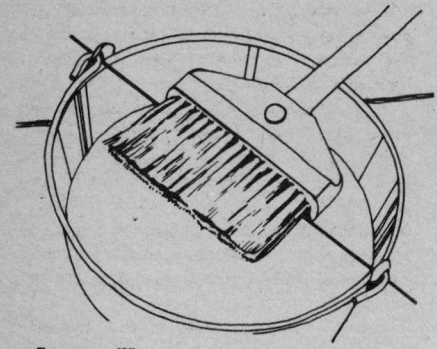

Economy. When cutting wallpaper around the windows or doors, don't discard those scrap pieces simply because they're damp with paste. You may need only a fragment later, but to get it you may be forced to cut into a whole strip. The pasted pieces can be smoothed out and hung over a chair back or ladder, and be used for fragment coverage at the end of the job.

Edges. One of the familiar problems with wallpapered rooms is peeling around window and door edges. You can solve this by shooting staples through the wallpaper around these loose edges.

Hanging. To start with, you'll need a smoothing brush, a roller trimmer, a seam roller, paste brush, plumb bob, wallpaper paste, ladder, pail, and rags.

Prepare your walls by removing any other wallpaper, by patching up holes in drywall or plaster construction, and by cleaning the surface thoroughly and allowing to dry.

Holding the paper up next to the wall, cut it in strips, allowing an extra 8 to 16 inches for the pattern, since you will have to shift each strip up and down to meet its neighbor. Cut holes for windows, door edges, and so on.

Mix the adhesive according to the instructions.

Place a cut strip of wallpaper pattern down on a long table. Brush paste on 2/3 of the strip with the paste brush. Fold the pasted part onto itself, and continue brushing paste on the final third, leaving a one-inch strip at the end for holding.

Grasping the pasted strip at the top, place it against the wall, checking its vertical hang with a plumb bob held from the ceiling. Slide the paper strip into proper position. Flatten the paper against the wall with the smooth brush, and work out air bubbles from the middle of the strip.

Now run the roller cutter where the paper meets the top of the baseboard to trim it. Do the same at the ceiling molding. Use a trimmer around the window molding. Make all ends meet the trim tightly. Now use the seam roller to flatten the seams where the strips join.

Wipe off the excess paste with a rag.

Loose. If your wallpaper has loosened on the wall, mix a thin paste of flour and water which can be picked up in a medicine dropper. If the bulge in the paper is at a seam, lift the edge of the paper with a knife and squirt paste under it. If the bulge is in the middle of a sheet of paper, puncture the paper at the top of the bulge so that the tip of the dropper can be inserted. Rub with a damp sponge or cloth to smooth the paper and remove the excess paste.

Mildewed wallpaper should be dried thoroughly, if damp, and if necessary, dry also the plaster wall behind the paper. To do this, heat the room well for several hours beforehand, or even for several days. Then wipe the paper with a cloth wrung out of thick, mild soapsuds... and be careful not to get it too wet or to rub too vigorously. Rinse with a cloth wrung out of clear water. Finally, pat with a dry cloth.

Nail Holes. Tack and nail holes in light colored wallpaper can be covered up nicely with a little dry cornstarch. Press a bit of it into the hole, then rub your fingers lightly over the surface to smooth it. The holes will not be noticeable.

Paste. To mix wallpaper paste, add a tablespoon of powdered alum to a quart of water. Sift flour into the water, stirring continuously, until it has acquired the consistency of dough. Then pour in boiling water until the paste turns, and dilute to the proper consistency.

Patching. Most wallpapers fade in strong light, so if it becomes necessary to patch them, it's a good idea to put the patch pieces in the sun until they fade to the same shade as the paper on the wall. After this treatment, they will not be noticeable.

Prepasted. If you are working with prepasted wallpaper, you can avoid dry spots if you will insert a metal rod in the roller before you submerge it in the water box.

Quantity. In order to estimate how many rolls of wallpaper you'll need for a room, measure the distance around the room in feet, multiply that by the height of the room, and divide by 30. The answer will tell you how many **single** rolls of paper to get. Subtract from that number 1 roll for any 2 openings such as a door or window. Then when you have the total number of single rolls, add 1 for wastage. ("Single," is specified because many rolls are sold as "double" rolls. Two of your "single" rolls equal one "double" roll.)

Repairing. If your wallpaper is torn, repair it by using ordinary library paste; or, if the wallpaper bulges out from the surface beneath, cut a slit with a sharp knife along the edge of the design, push in paste with a small brush, and then press the paper in place, holding a blotter against it until the paper sticks.

If the paper is ripped off completely, get a matching piece of the same design, cut out the ripped section to form a perfect rectangle using a square and a razor blade, and replace the old with a new piece. You can avoid errors by cutting through both new and old section with the same stroke of the razor.

Touch-up Color. Often wallpaper is damaged when moving furniture and one has no paper with which to match and patch it. If this is the case, touch up the vacant spots in the paper with watercolors to harmonize with the pattern, and if you do this deftly, your repair job will hardly be noticeable.

Wallpaper Cleaning.

1. One quick and effective way to clean soiled wallpaper is to dip a cloth into powdered borax, then rub this over the soiled areas.

2. **Fabric Cover.** If you have a fabric cover, consider it a washable wallpaper, but try out a small practice section first.

3. **Finger marks** on wallpaper can be dampened with a little cold water, then dusted with some fuller's earth. After a few minutes, when the absorbent has dried, brush it off.

4. **Grass Cloth.** Do not wash grass cloth or rice paper; clean them with regular wallpaper cleaner.

5. **Grease, Oil, or Crayon Stains.** To get rid of grease, oil, or crayon stains on wallpaper, cover the dirty surface with a quarter-inch layer of paste made from powdered chalk, or regular flour mixed with carbon tetrachloride or clear liquid spot remover. Let the paste dry, and then remove it with a small brush.

6. **Ink Stains.** You can remove ink stains from paper by using a commercial ink remover, or with a weak solution of chloride bleach, immediately followed by cold water.

7. **Non-Washable.** If you have non-washable paper, clean it with a special putty-like cleaner. Rework the cleaner frequently so that you get a fresh surface next to the paper. Or, use any of the following: Art gum, the inside of a loaf of stale bread (preferably rye bread), wheat bran sewed in a bag, or pipe clay. Overlap your strokes, and proceed with the utmost of care so as to avoid streakiness on your paper.

8. **Plastic-Surfaced.** If you have plastic-surfaced paper, use ordinary soap and water on it. Keep the cloth or sponge as dry as possible, and do only a small area at a time, washing from the bottom up.

Wallpaper Removal.

1. **with a Chemical Compound.** You can try chemical compounds sold for the purpose of removing wallpaper. The idea is to smear the chemical remover on the wallpaper; the chemical passes through the paper and works on the adhesive underneath. You just pull the loosened paper off.

2. **with a Commercial Steamer.** For the removal of wallpaper that has had one or more coats of paint applied over it, steaming with one of the special machines available at tool-rental agencies is still the best method. However, there is some extra elbow-grease involved. You must first sand with a very coarse grade of sandpaper through the paint down to the paper underneath in enough places to enable the steam to penetrate through and under the paper . . . which will permit you to peel it off in sizable sections.

The steamer works rather like a steam iron except that the bottom is hollow. You press the bottom against the paper, section after section. The steam enters the paper and the heat and moisture break down the adhesive that holds the wallpaper on. It will peel off easily with a scraper.

3. **with a Flour Mixture.** Mix up a quart of flour paste and add it to a pail of piping hot water. Swash

WALL PLUGS

the mixture all over the wall and let it soak in. Being thick, it won't dry very quickly, and you'll have plenty of time to scrape or peel off the old paper.

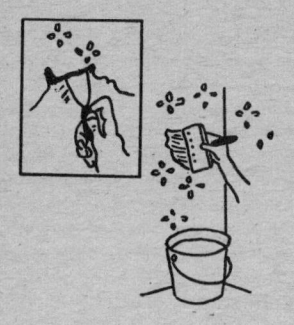

4. with a Paint Roller. A method of removing old wallpaper from a wall is to use a paint roller, immersed in warm, sudsy water, to soak the old wallpaper. Then pull the paper off with the aid of a painter's broad knife.

5. with a Saltpeter Solution. To remove wallpaper, mix a solution of four ounces of pulverized saltpeter to a gallon of water, and swab the walls with it. The solution will soak through and loosen the paper in a hurry, so you can strip it off. However, with this mixture you must work fast, because once the saltpeter solution dries, you'll probably have to apply it again to get results.

6. with a Steam Iron. You can avoid the bother and expense of renting a wallpaper steamer for the removal of a small amount of wallpaper, by using a steam iron as you would a commercial steamer. This usually does a good job of loosening the paper so that you can peel or scrape it right off.

7. with a Teakettle. The very easiest and quickest way to remove old wallpaper is by steaming. You can do this nicely by holding the spout of a steaming teakettle near the paper and, after the paper has darkened with the steamed-in moisture, peel it off either with a wide-bladed putty knife or razor blade.

Wall Plugs. Below are various methods of securely fixing articles to a wall surface where it is not possible to screw directly into the wall material.

1. For most fixing jobs, the fiber plug is most suitable. In solid brick, stone or cement, it proves an extremely strong fixing and needs only a small hole drilled in the wall.

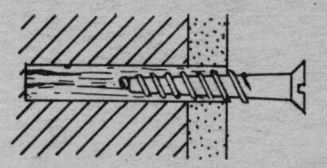

2. Where the hole has become enlarged or the brickwork has cracked, use asbestos filling compound. A tool is sold with the compound for pressing it well into the hole, and piercing a start for the screw.

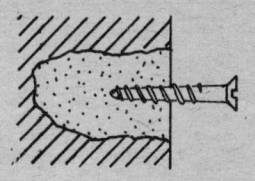

3. All-metal wallplugs resemble fiber plugs, but obviate the necessity to center the screw on to the plug, as both are inserted as one unit.

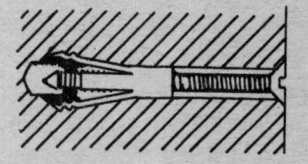

4. Where a hole drilled for a fiber plug or filling compound breaks through into a cavity, use U clips. They prevent the compound from being pushed through the hole.

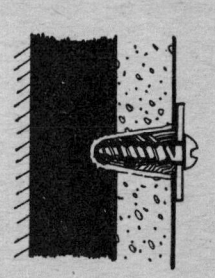

5. Ideal for lath and plaster walls is the spring toggle. A spring opens the "wings" inside the wall, and they provide a large bearing surface.

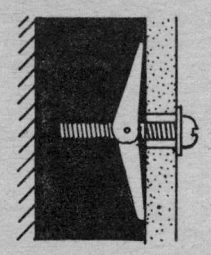

6. The bolt with rubber sleeve is an adaptable method of fixing to partition walls, wallboards, plaster boards, etc. It is sound-resistant, vibration — and water-proof.

7. Rawlanchors are another type of fixing for artificial boards, cavity walls etc. The action of screwing in the bolt bends the arms of the rawl-anchor behind the wall which hold the nut permanently in position.

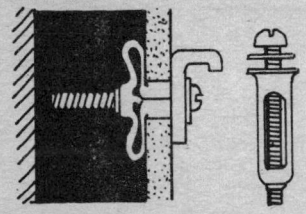

8. For pictures, mirrors and other light fixtures use an angle-drive. Held by either one or two steel pins they are strong and neat.

Walls, Exterior. Although there are infinite numbers of outer coverings for houses, they generally fall into two categories: masonry or wood. All manner of variations on these two types, as well as metal coverings (usually aluminum or steel siding) are available too, as well as asbestos-cement shingles and related products. (See MASONRY; PAINTING, EXTERIOR.)

Leaking. A wall can leak not only water but cold air as well. Quite often you'll find that the place where the water or air enters the inside of the house does not correspond to the actual point of entry outside. A great many leaks in walls occur around window frames and door frames, especially in masonry walls. Also, it is wise to remember that a good proportion of leaks begin at the top of the wall where it meets the roof. Walls can also leak from loosened flashing around chimney or in roof valleys: the water runs down inside the roof to the wall, where it eventually comes out inside as a wall leak.

You may even get a leak in the face of a wall, as in a brick veneer, with the water coming in through the mortar itself. In this special case, you need not repair the brick wall or the mortar. Simply let the water come through the brick, run down in the air space between veneer and wall, and make sure that there is an exit for the water just above the flashing shelf on which the brick wall is laid. Drill a quarter-inch upward-slanting hole in through the mortar joint as near the bottom of the wall as possible to act as a drain.

Stucco veneer may crack, letting water through where sheathing is rotted out or faulty. A stucco leak is extremely difficult to spot.

Leaks in a wooden wall are usually easier to isolate, unless, of course, the hole is in the joint between the wall siding and the window or door frame. You can use a calking gun to get at this kind of hole.

To waterproof a brick wall, paint it with a sealing coat of spar varnish, red-lead paint, and turpentine. Repaint all crumbling mortar joints, and calk all cracks, breaks and holes. Apply the sealing coat liberally on the brick surface.

To tighten cracks in mortar joints, rake the mortar from the outside joints a half-inch deep and fill with a mixture of 1 part Portland cement, 1 part hydrated lime, and 5 parts sand. Or buy prepared mortar at a building supply store and follow direc-

WALLS, INTERIOR

tions. To close up hairline mortar cracks, use a prepared waterproof compound.

A masonry wall tends to crack as it settles, but it is senseless to repair it until the settling stops. You can always fill a crack with plastic roofing cement.

A leak may appear in your wall at the point where the sill meets the foundation—the sill is the timber that lies embedded in the foundation concrete and supports the framework of the house. Usually the foundation has split, letting in water. Close this leak by mortar of 1 part Portland cement and 3 parts sand. Slope the new surface so that it will shed rainwater.

You may find a leak caused by the metal sheeting placed between sill and foundation as a termite barrier; this strip may be sloped toward the sill rather than away from it, trapping the water there. Bend it outward to shed the water away.

A chimney may cause a leak in an inner wall, too. Examine the bricks on the chimney cap for a break. The joint between masonry and house may be open. Pack tow or fiber mixed with plastic roofing cement into the joint and finish it off with calking compound.

Structure. The strength of an exterior wall comes from vertical two-by-fours set 16 inches on center along a sole plate and attached to a top plate. To these studs a wooden sheathing of either plywood or stripping is attached.

In a wooden wall, the horizontal siding, shingles, or beveled wood is applied directly to the sheathing with building paper between unless the sheathing is plywood.

In a plaster wall, building paper is applied to the sheathing, then metal lath, and the plaster or stucco is applied to the metal lath.

In a brick wall, building paper is applied to the sheathing, then the brick or masonry wall is laid with an appropriate air space between it and the building paper.

Insulation, if it is used, is placed inside the wall space between the studs. In repairs of all kinds to siding it is important to know the various layers of the wall as you are called on to replace bad sections.

Walls, Interior. There are three kinds of interior wall surfaces in common use today: plaster, drywall, and paneling. Actually, there are many more than that, including natural brick, stucco, concrete, non-plywood paneling, redwood, and so on. (See DRYWALL, PANELING, PLASTER.)

Painting, see PAINTING, INTERIOR.

Plaster Repair, See PLASTER, PLASTERING.

Structure. You can make all minor repairs to your inside wall surfaces yourself. First, however, you should understand how an interior wall is put together, and what is inside it.

Vertical two-by-fours, called "studs," run from floor to ceiling, attached at the bottom to another horizontal two-by-four called a "sole plate" and at the top to another called a "top plate." It is to these studs that the material that makes up the wall surface is fastened.

Inside the wall flexible BX electric cables run through the studs bringing power lines to wall outlets and switches. Water and heating pipes may also run through the studs, particularly through the wall separating bathroom and kitchen.

Washing.

1. When washing walls and wood trim, work from the bottom upward — and not from the top downward, as some people are prone to do. When water drips down on a soiled wall surface, it leaves streaks that are extremely difficult or impossible to remove. This will not stain a wall that has already been moistened and cleaned. Use a soft sponge, rather than a cloth, because good sponges are more absorbent. Two pails should be used, one for suds and one for rinse water. And remember to change your water frequently, because it is impossible to cleanse anything thoroughly with dirty water.

It's always exasperating when you try to cope with that continuous stream of water that trickles down your arm while you're washing the walls and ceiling of one of your rooms. You can eliminate this annoyance just by wrapping a washcloth around your wrist and securing this with a thick rubber band, as illustrated.

WASHERS

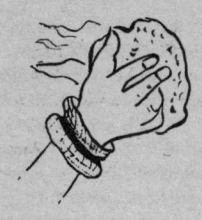

WASHER CHART

OO $\frac{15}{32}$ or $\frac{1}{2}$ O.D.	"O" 1" or $\frac{17}{32}$ O.D.	¼" S $\frac{17}{32}$ O.D.	¼" $\frac{9}{16}$ O.D.
¼" L $\frac{19}{32}$ O.D.	⅜" $\frac{5}{8}$ O.D.	⅜" M $\frac{21}{32}$ O.D.	⅜" L $\frac{11}{16}$ O.D.
½" $\frac{3}{4}$ O.D.	½" L $\frac{25}{32}$ O.D.	⅝" $\frac{13}{16}$ O.D.	
⅝" L (Beveled) $\frac{27}{32}$ O.D.	¾" (Beveled) $\frac{7}{8}$ O.D.	¾" (Flat) $\frac{15}{16}$ or 1" O.D.	
1" (Flat) $1\frac{9}{64}$ O.D.	1" (Beveled) $1\frac{1}{8}$ O.D.		

2. *with Borax and Ammonia.* One good solution you can easily whip up for cleaning some of your painted walls is a mixture of two ounces of borax, one teaspoon of ammonia, and two quarts of water. You will need no soap. Apply with a soft cloth or sponge.

3. *with Burlap.* Washing down walls and ceilings to remove old water paint or grime, use a piece of burlap or some old curtain material. The material's rough texture cuts below the surface of the old finish.

4. *with Turpentine Mixture.* To make a good cleaning compound for painted walls, dissolve one ounce of soap flakes in sixteen ounces of water, and add about three ounces of turpentine. Stir this mixture rapidly, and apply with a brush or sponge.

Wall Switch. The spaces on the walls around light switches see a lot of traffic and, therefore, are apt to smudge up frequently. After cleaning off this space, a thin coat or two of fresh white shellac will make the area around the switch much easier to clean. An occasional quick dab with a damp cloth will do the trick.

Wall Studs, see STUDS, LOCATING.

Warped Doors, see DOOR REPAIR.

Warped Wood, see WOOD CARE TIPS.

Washable Fabrics, Stains on, see STAIN REMOVAL

Wash-and-Wear, see FIBERS, MAN-MADE.

Washers.
  Faucet. When replacing washers get the exact size and type as the one removed. Faucet washers are standardized. (See also PLUMBING.)

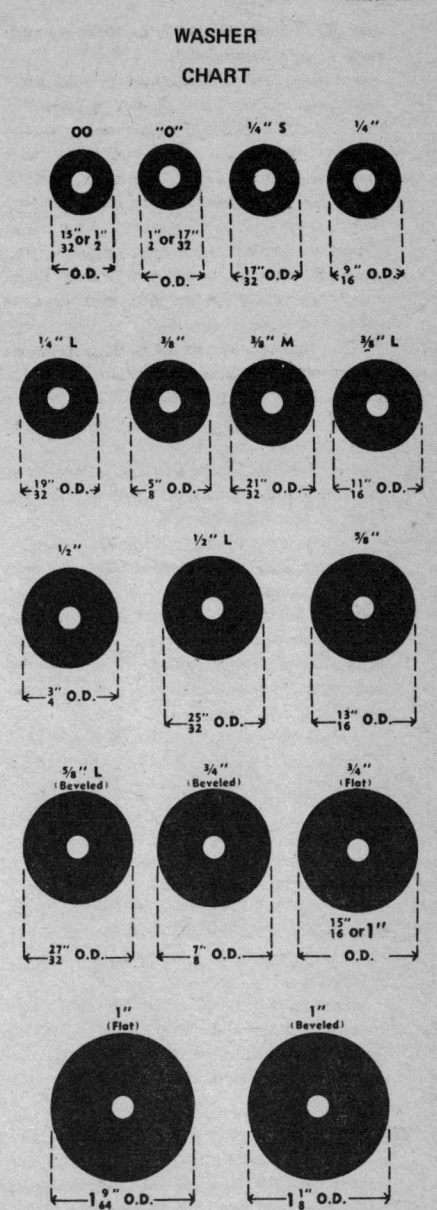

Flat washers are used to back up bolt heads and nuts, and to provide larger bearing surfaces. They prevent damage to the surfaces of the metal parts.

FLAT WASHER

Lock, Substitute. If you are completely out of regular lock washers, you can improvise one with an ordinary flat metal washer. Just bend this flat washer slightly across its middle, and when it is drawn up tight, the arc provides tension that will hold the nut in place and prevent it from turning.

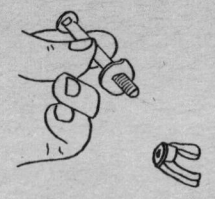

Split lock washers are used under nuts to prevent loosening by vibration. The ends of these spring-hardened washers dig into both the nut and the work to prevent slippage.

SPLIT LOCK WASHER

Shakeproof lock washers have teeth or lugs that grip both the work and the nut. Several patented designs, shapes, and sizes are obtainable.

SHAKE PROOF WASHER

Washboard, Miniature. The coarse side of a haircomb makes an ideal miniature scrub board for removing small stains. Use soap and water, and rub the material across the teeth of the comb.

Wastebaskets.
Early American. If you go in for Early American decor, you can make a lovely wastebasket from an old nail keg purchased from your local junk dealer or nearby lumber yard. Spray it with high-gloss black enamel and apply a gold eagle decal in the middle of one side.

from Paneling. You can fashion a wastebasket that will match the paneling of your room, from leftover pieces of prefinished hardboard. Cut four tapered sides and a square piece for the bottom of the basket. Then drill these pieces with matching edge holes and thread them together with some plastic or leather laces.

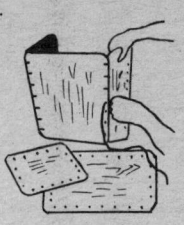

from Venetian Blinds. A very attractive and usable wastebasket can be fashioned from the wooden slats of a discarded Venetian blind. These slats are very nice to work with, and you can use a coping saw for cutting the curved tops of your basket. For the bottom, cut a square from three-quarter-inch stock, and a suggested length for the slats is 12 inches, with a square framework located inside about nine inches from the bottom. For uniform spacing of the slats and a pleasing effect, it's best to lay the slats on a flat surface, spacing them as desired. Then measure across them and cut the bottom and frame accordingly.

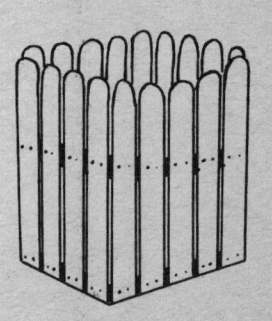

Watches, see JEWELRY.

Water Carrier. By use of a discarded automobile inner tube, you can make a very handy emergency water carrier, which can be taken in the car and will use up little storage space. All you have to do is cut the tube, as illustrated, then cut two oval handholes for carrying. This "bucket" can prove itself very useful on a fishing or camping trip.

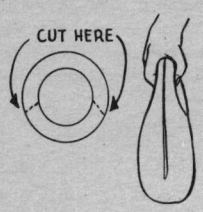

Watercolor Paint Stain, see STAIN REMOVAL.

Water-Evaporative Cooling, see COOLING.

Watermelons, see FOODS.

Water Mixer. If you have no commercial mixer to provide you with water of the temperature you desire, you can make your own by slipping a short section of rubber tubing over the hot and cold water faucets, then making a 90-degree-cut opening in the bottom-middle of the tubing, as in the illustration.

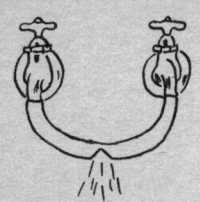

Water Pipe Repair, see PLUMBING.

Waterproof Cement, see ADHESIVES.

Waterproofing Basements, see BASEMENTS, DAMP or WET.

Waterproofing Foundation, see FOUNDATION WATERPROOFING.

Waterproofing Furniture, see FURNITURE CARE.

Waterproofing Sealer, see PAINTS.

Water Softener. Washing soda is one of the best, most economical, and effective water softeners.

Water Stain, see FURNITURE MARK and STAIN REMOVAL, STAIN REMOVAL.

Water System, see PLUMBING.

Water Tank Repair, see PLUMBING.

Water-Thinned Paint, see PAINTS.

Wattage Chart, see APPLIANCE WATTAGE CHART.

Wattage, Watts, see ELECTRICITY, THEORY OF.

Wax, Paraffin, see PARAFFIN WAX.

Weatherproofing Wood, see WOOD CARE TIPS.

Weatherstripping. Doors and windows not only leak around the outside of the frames, but many times they leak where sash or door meets the frame. You can eliminate this leakage in an inexpensive way by using weatherstripping.

Weatherstrippings are made of metal, rubber, felt, and plastic. Metal weatherstripping is permanent and the most efficient. You can get it in zinc, bronze, or aluminum. Strips for the threshold of a door are usually made of brass. Door strips frequently come in two parts. You attach one to the frame and the other to the door. When you close the door, the strips interlock and keep out all stray air.

For windows you can use rubber stripping with the contact edge of foam rubber, and the outer edge of metal and fabric woven together. Felt weatherstripping is made so that either edge can be used as the contact edge.

All kinds of weatherstrippings are easy to apply. Metal strips come with nails or small screws. You simply cut them to size with scissors, put them in place, and nail them tight. Rubber or felt strips come with rust-resistant nails which you drive in 2 inches apart. Full instructions come with any kind of weatherstripping. You can save a great deal of money in heating bills if you use your weatherstripping properly.

Weeding, see GARDENING.

White Glue, see ADHESIVES.

Whitewash, see PAINTS.

Wicker Basket. Give your new wicker clothes basket a going-over with a spray-can of enamel. Your enameled basket will then be easily washable with hot suds, and there will be no danger of black marks on your clothes from a mildewed unfinished basket that absorbs moisture.

Wicker Furniture, see FURNITURE CARE.

Wicker hampers can be kept in first-class condition if they are coated regularly with shellac. This is best applied by spraying, but may be brushed on in a fairly uniform coating if thinned with alcohol to a watery consistency. Use only fresh, white shellac.

Window Cleaning Tips. Never clean while the sun is shining on the window, as this way it is practically impossible to get the glass bright and clear.

When washing windows, use an up-and-down stroke on the outside of the pane and a side-to-side stroke on the inside. Then, if a mark is left, you can quickly tell which side needs additional polishing.

An ordinary blackboard eraser makes an ideal polisher.
Ammonia. Housewives frequently complain that their window cleaning appears dull, where window cleaning can achieve a much better shine.

The trick is to add two tablespoonsful of liquid ammonia to the water before the glass is cleaned.

After the solution has been well stirred, it can be used on the glass with a soft cloth and another clean dry cloth used for the final even polish.
Cornstarch. Old fashioned cornstarch is great for washing windows. Put a half gallon of warm water in a container and stir one-fourth cup cornstarch into it. Then wash away, wiping off the windows with a squeegee or crumpled newspapers. This mixture not only cuts the dirt quickly, but causes the windows to glisten . . . and they seem to stay clean longer, too.

Kerosene.

1. First rub over the glass with a flannel duster to remove all the surface dirt; then add a teaspoonful of kerosene to a quart of water, and rub this over the glass.

Finally, polish with a piece of newspaper or a chamois leather cloth.

2. Kitchen windows usually present a tough cleaning chore, because of the thin layer of grease and oil they are prone to pick up. If you are having trouble on this score, add a spoonful of kerosene to your wash water to help cut the grease. This works well, too, for cutting the putty oil on newly installed windowpanes.

Laundry Starch. The addition of a little laundry starch to your water when washing windows and mirrors will give the glass a sparkling cleanliness.
Methyl Alcohol. Ordinary water is not sufficient to clean frosty windows.

A chamois moistened with methylated spirit should be used here.
Pumice Polishing Cloth. Some windows accumulate a lot of dust from passing vehicles, and here again a lot of work can be saved by using a pumice polishing cloth.

This can be made from five 6-in. squares of muslin sprinkled with a little finely ground pumice powder.

Each layer should then be piled on top of each other, and the edges stitched to prevent the powder falling out.

It is then ready for use, and should last a long time.
Vinegar. Windows will also wash better with 1/2-cup of white vinegar in warm water. Or, for a really sparkling job, wash them with a cloth soaked in vinegar, then polish. Discarded nylon stockings, used as cleaning rags, give windows and mirrors a bright, lint-free shine.

Vinegar, Turpentine, Ammonia. Sometimes window glass becomes discolored and stained, and the best method of cleaning in most cases is to rub with a solution made by mixing together a tablespoon of vinegar and a quarter cup each of turpentine and ammonia.

The stains soon disappear if the glass is rubbed briskly with this solution, and the polish obtained will prove high and enduring.

Window Fans, see COOLING.

Window Painting, see PAINTING, INTERIOR.

Window Repair. Broken glass around the house is not only dangerous as a cause of accidents, but also as a source of damage by rain water, snow, or cold air. A window pane must be immediately replaced to prevent costly injuries to your furniture and possessions. You can save good money by knowing how to replace a window.

A pane of glass is held in the window frame on one side by a wooden recess called a rabbet and on the other by an application of putty. First remove all the putty from the front of the glass.

Tiny metal wedges called glazier's points hold the glass firmly to the wood. Remove them. The glass can now be removed completely from the rabbet. Scrape the rabbet clean of putty and paint.

Measure the exact area of the rabbet where the pane of glass will fit, deducting 1/16 inch to allow for wood expansion. Buy a piece of glass cut to that size. You can cut the glass yourself, but it's hardly worth the effort in the long run.

Paint the rabbet with linseed oil. Soften a mound of putty with linseed oil and spread a bed of putty 1/16 inch thick on the rabbet for the glass to fit against.

Sight along the glass pane. You'll see that it curves. Press the pane against the putty seat, concave side in. Insert glaziers' points with a screwdriver, holding the glass firmly against the putty.

Roll putty to the thickness of a pencil, and lay the roll along the outside of the glass pane. Slide a putty knife along the edge of the glass and wood sash, smoothing the putty.

When the putty is smooth, let it dry, and then paint it.

Cracked Pane. A cracked pane of glass in your window can be temporarily held together with a coat of fresh, white shellac on the inside. Your vision won't be obscured by the shellac, and breezes and rain will be kept out until the pane is replaced.

Leaking. Unless the glass itself is broken, most windows that leak air or water have holes around the joints or in the frame. You can find the spot by placing your hand in various positions around the edge during a high wind. With a calking gun, seal up the loose space, attacking the area under the sill or around the frame.

Loose Frame. Jamming may be caused by a loose frame. This can be remedied by screwing into place an "L" shaped bracket firming up the frame (see diagram).

Loose Pane. If the pane in the window is loose, you can remove the putty, reset the glaziers points, and reputty. Pry out the old putty with a knife and remove the glaziers points: these are small steel holders that slip into the rail and stile to press the pane against the rabbet. Remove the glass. Scrape the wood clean. Paint the rabbet (the L-shaped seat where the glass pane sits) with linseed oil. Soften a mound of putty with linseed oil. Spread a putty base 1/16-inch thick on the rabbet. Insert the glass, concave side to, and press firmly in. With a screwdriver insert the glaziers points so the glass won't move. Roll putty into a pencil-size and press it against the glass. Move a putty knife along it to press it against the glass. Let the putty dry and then paint.

Puttying, see PUTTY.

Rattling. Inspect the window first to determine what makes it rattle. You may find the trouble to be a loose pane of glass or a loose sash in the frame. If either of these is the case, you can always get temporary relief by sticking a piece of folded up cardboard, rubber or wood in the sash to arrest the movement.

WINDOWS

Double-hung windows that persist in rattling even when locked can usually be silenced just by driving two or three large rubber-headed tacks or rubber bumpers against the bottom edge of the lower sash. Then when the window is closed, these will absorb the vibration and will take up the slack when the sash lock is closed so that adequate pressure will be maintained to prevent looseness.

Reglazing Tips.

1. When you are installing a new pane of glass in a window, if you'll mix your putty with a little house paint of the appropriate color, it will make subsequent painting of that putty strip unnecessary.

2. Sometimes when you replace glass in an old, wood window frame, the sash is too weathered and porous to get the glazing compound to stick. In this case, apply some gasket shellac instead of paint or linseed oil as a primer on the wood. You will find that putty applied over the gasket shellac will stick in any kind of weather. Of course, the glazing compound should be painted as usual to finish your job.

3. It's usually a risky business using a hammer for driving glaziers' points next to newly-installed window panes. However, you can make a safe and efficient driver for these glaziers' points by cutting a 1/2-inch nut with a hacksaw through to the threads and then slipping this over a putty knife, as in the illustration.

Removing Sash.

1. *From a Casement Window.* Unscrew the hinges from the sash of the frame. Do not let the sash drop when you lift it out. Have someone help you: you loosen the hinges while he holds the sash.

2. *From a Sliding Window.* Pry out the inside window stop on one side and the bottom. Simply lift the sash out.

Sticking. There are four main reasons why a window sash may stick tightly in its frame. It may be frozen there by drying paint; it may bind because of swelling due to weather; the stop may be too close to the sash; or the sash itself may be too big for the frame.

1. To free a paint-frozen sash, run the point of a sharp knife all around between the sash and the stop, scraping away all extra paint. If this action does not free the sash, remove the stop, clean it with a file or sandpaper, and replace it.

2. If the sash has become moisture-swollen, locate the point where it binds and force wax in between sash and stop. If the sash still sticks, remove it and plane it down where it sticks.

3. If the stop is located too close to the sash, remove it and renail it 1/8 to 1/4 inch farther away from the sash. To prevent loss of weather tightness, do not move the stop at the bottom of the window more than 1/8 inch from the sash.

4. If the sash is too wide for the frame, remove it and plane down the edge that binds. Coat the sash with linseed oil, wax it completely when dry, and replace it.

Windows. All windows are composed of two major units: the frame and the sash. The frame is built into the wall to hold the window; the sash is the framework that holds the glass panes together.

The principle parts of the rough framing that forms the window space in a wall are the *sill*, the bottom piece; the *jambs*, the side pieces; and the *lintel*, the upper piece.

Like a door, the parts of a window sash are called *rails* (horizontal borders) and *stiles* (vertical borders). The center rail that splits a window into two panes is called the *muntin*.

The purpose of a window is to supply light and ventilation, and to bar bad weather from the interior. The glass area of a window should be equal to 10 percent of the floor area of the room. Ventilating areas should equal from 4 percent to 8 percent of the floor area.

Awning. Wood awning windows have the sash hung from the top and are hinged by brackets attached to the jamb. The bottom rail of one window or tier

WINDOWS

interlocks with the top rail of the window below. Opening and closing of awning windows is done by a worm gear drive usually at the right hand side of the opening. Each tier operates independently. Multiple window openings are made possible by use of muntins. Awning windows permit wide latitude as to illumination and ventilation. The tilted sash deflect air currents upward and help keep the air at the ceiling moving.

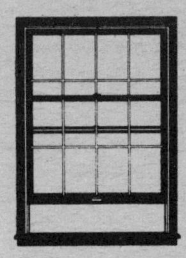

Fixed windows which have no ventilation function and may be combined with operating windows in a wide variety of arrangements. Alone, they are sometimes called picture windows.

Casement. A window widely used in homes today is the casement window. Casement sash are side-hinged and usually of the outswinging type. Screens and storm sash are fitted on the interior.

Hopper windows are bottom-pivoted and open inward from the top.

Insulating-glass. Factory-built transparent insulating glass units, as shown in the cut-away view, are composed of two or more lights of glass separated by dehydrated air space, and hermetically sealed around the edges at the factory, with a metal-to-glass bond. They may be made up of two or three panes of glass.

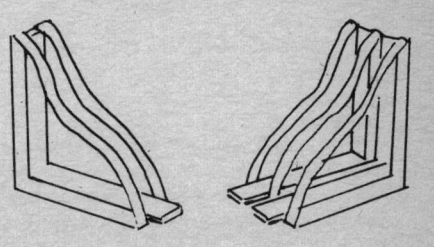

Double-hung. The double-hung window of modern design is one of the two kinds of windows most commonly used in homes today. There are many variations of double-hung windows. In one kind the friction pressure between sash and weatherstripping holds the sash open at the desired point. The sash may be removed by depressing it against one spring-activated side of weather-stringing. In another kind the sashes are counterbalanced by weights. The cut-away view shows the construction of this unit with its system of weights and pulleys.

WINDOWS, FROSTED

These factory-fabricated units, which cannot be altered without damaging them, come in different types of glass and in many sizes. Manufacturers also furnish them in special sizes to meet unusual conditions. Insulating glass units serve several purposes. The warm side surface temperature is appreciably higher than that of a single glazing. It has been the usual practice to locate sources of heat near glass areas in buildings to offset both the conducted loss of heat from the room and the radiant loss from bodies of persons near such cold glass areas. The high glass surface temperature of insulating glass units reduces the amount of heat that must be supplied near such areas, permitting flexibility in room design.

A second important aspect of the warmer inside surface temperature is that insulating glass can be designed to reduce condensation otherwise resulting during cold weather, from interior humidification. The reduction of condensation on the warm side is important where visibility is desirable, and to prevent deterioration of sill, wall and floor by water drippage.

Louvered windows, also called jalousies, are like awning windows, but have more glass sections.

Sliding. Also available are gliding (sliding) windows which open sidewise. The horizontal sliding action permits large sizes of ventilating windows.

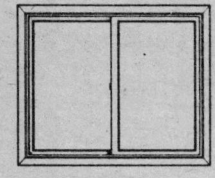

Weatherstripping, see WEATHERSTRIPPING.

Windows, Frosted. Frost on your windows during the wintry days can be prevented from gathering if you rub some alcohol or salt water on the outside of the glass, then polish over this with some newspaper or dry cloths.

Windows, Frosting.

1. If you're looking for a little more privacy in one of your rooms, in which the window isn't frosted, here's one method of frosting that window. Soften some putty with a few drops of linseed oil and dab this all over the outside of the window glass. This will dry into a nice frosting in a day or two, whereupon another coating may be applied. This frosting is more or less permanent and weatherproof, and can be safely washed with soap and water. But it is possible, too, to "defrost" the glass at any time, if you wish, with some concentrated ammonia.

2. Another easy way to frost a window pane to insure privacy, but still permit light to enter, is to apply a coat of linseed oil paint to the glass and stipple this with a cheesecloth pad while it is still wet.

3. If you'd like to insure a little more privacy in one of your rooms by frosting the window, one excellent solution for the job consists of a tablespoon of epsom salts dissolved in a small quantity of beer. Just paint this with a brush over the inside of the windowpane.

4. Not enough privacy in one of the rooms in your house? You can make a good frosting for the windows by dissolving three teaspoonfuls of epsom salts in a glass of water. Add a teaspoonful of liquid glue, stir the mixture thoroughly, then apply to the glass with a brush.

5. To make windows like ground glass, make a hot solution of sal ammoniac, and brush this over the glass. The moisture will evaporate in an instant and leave a beautifully radiated deposit.

Window Safety. The danger of small children falling from a second-story window can be eliminated by the installation of some protective bars across the window. Cut some lengths of one-half-inch pipe to the width of the window and set these into holes drilled into wooden spacers attached inside the upper sash track.

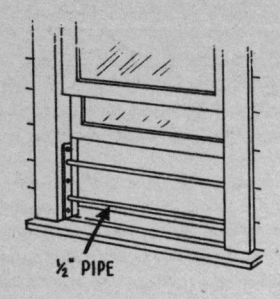

Window Shade Roller. A window shade roller that just falls short of the distance between its supporting brackets can be "stretched" if you'll first remove the pin from the roller and carefully pry off the metal cap. Then slip a washer into the cap, push the cap back onto the roller, and replace the end pin. Return the roller to its brackets, and presto... you're in business again.

Window Shades.
 Cleaning. Dirty window shades can be cleaned quickly and easily with a rough flannel cloth dipped into flour.
 Painting. Cracked and soiled window shades can often be renewed by painting them with rubber-base paint.
 Rewinding.
  1. If the spring tension of a window shade isn't what it should be, and ideal winding key for the spring is an ordinary table fork. Just slip the flat shaft at one end of the shade roller between the tines of the fork, and turn the fork. Works easier than pliers or a wrench.

  2. One of the easiest and most effective methods of rewinding the spring in the roller of a window shade is by inserting the flattened end in the lower part of a keyhole, then turning.

Windowsills, Discolored. When your wooden windowsills have become spotted from rain or discolored, put a little weakened alcohol on a soft cloth and rub over the entire sills. They will then usually look as if freshly painted.

Windows, Steamy. One way to prevent steam from gathering on your windows is, after they're perfectly clean, to rub them with a thin film of glycerine. You can repeat this process at any time when the effect seems to be wearing off.

Windshield, see AUTOMOBILE.

Wine, Chilling. A bottle of wine can be chilled quickly if you wrap it in a piece of flannel that has been dipped in cold water and not wrung out. This will usually bring the wine below room temperature in fast time.

WINE STAIN

Wine Stain, see STAIN REMOVAL.

Wire, Copper, see ELECTRIC CORD, ELECTRIC WIRE.

Wire, Electric, see ELECTRIC WIRE.

Wires, High-Resistance, see ELECTRICITY, THEORY OF.

Wire Straightening.
1. Wire that's kinked and bent can often be quickly restored to its original straightness, and in a very simple manner, too. Fasten one end of the wire in a vise and pull the wire taut. Then run a hardwood dowel or a plastic-handled screwdriver firmly down its length, or, if easier, draw the wire between thumb and screwdriver handle with a motion similar to combing long hair. After a few passes like these, the kinks will disappear and the smoothed-out wire will take on a long, uniform curve, making it easy to roll into coils for storage or immediate use.

2. Kinks and bends in a stiff electrical wire can be straightened out by placing the wire on a board or other hard flat surface, then going over it with a cold iron, using just enough pressure to make the wire roll.

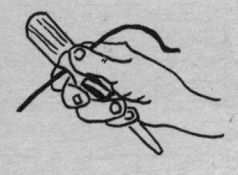

Wire Nails, see NAILS.

Wire Netting, Painting, see PAINTING TIPS:

Wiring, Extension. A much better idea than carrying electric wiring for extension outlets over the top of a doorway is to remove the sill and replace it with some electric conduit of the two-piece molding type illustrated.

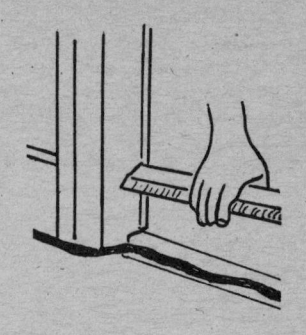

Wood Care Tips.
Crack Repair. You can make your own filler for cracks in wood by mixing some flour with enough brown shellac to make a paste. Rub this filler on the wood, and after it has dried completely, sandpaper the surface and rub with a soft cloth that has been dampened with a little oil and thin shellac.
Dented.
1. Sometimes when you use a nail puller, you create dents in the wood. Remove these dents by laying small pieces of wet cotton in each dent, then applying an iron hot enough to cause steam. This will usually cause the wood fibers to swell and the dents to disappear.

2. When you have inadvertently marred the finished surface of a piece of woodwork with a hammer, sometimes it is possible to raise the grain of the wood back into place. Try covering the area with several sheets of damp wrapping paper, then pressing over this with a hot iron. The heat expands the wood.

Gluing. When gluing pieces of wood together, it's a good idea to press a few shreds of steel wool between them. This prevents slipping and makes a better bond.
Hardening. For you woodcarving hobbyists, one good way to harden the wood that has been cut out

or sculptured into its desired shape, is to boil the pieces in pure olive oil for eight to ten minutes.

Hole Repair. Thumbtack holes in a drawing board, or brad marks in salvaged lumber, and other tiny holes in wood can be effectively plugged with the smooth, round variety of toothpick. Simply dip the end of the toothpick into the glue, force it into the hole, and trim it flush with a razor blade. Then sand the area smooth.

Inlaid. For inlaid wood an occasional application of olive oil is good, this preventing the inlay and veneer from chipping off. The oil should be rubbed in with warm linen rags, wiped off with clean cloths after an hour or so, and the piece then polished.

Straightening. If you have a solid wooden panel that is warped, here is one way in which you can straighten it out. First, make several cuts with your saw about halfway through the panel on the convex side at right angles to the warp. Then press the panel down on a flat surface and drive some corrugated fasteners into the panel across the grooves. Your fasteners should be of a size that will drive about one-third of the way through the panel.

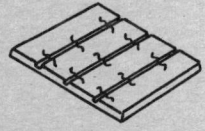

Waxing. One thing to remember when waxing painted woodwork is that this wax will have to be removed completely before the trim can be repainted. For this reason, it's smart to use the liquid self-polishing kind of wax, which is easily removable when necessary with warm, soapy water and will not require the use of strong solvents.

WOOD FLOOR CARE

Weatherproofing. To make wood durable and weatherproof, cover it with several coats of hot linseed oil varnish.

Wood, Chisel, Chiseling, see TOOLS, HAND.

Wooden Counters, Stain on, see STAIN REMOVAL.

Wooden Salad Bowls, see SALAD BOWLS, WOODEN.

Wood Floor Care.
Caster Marks. If you'll add a cover of adhesive tape to rubber or composition casters that are mounted on furniture, this will prevent them from making unsightly marks on your polished floors. Wrap the tape around the caster wheels two full turns to prevent it from unraveling. The tape will also muffle some of the noise when you are rolling the furniture across the floor.

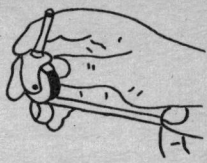

Chair Marks. Your chairs and rockers will not mar the finish on a freshly waxed floor if you'll wax the feet on the rocker and chairs at the same time that you do the floor.
Faded Spots. You can renew floors which have become faded in spots by mixing some brown shoe polish with your floor wax and apply this to the spots. This will give your floor an antique look.
Grease. Don't use hot water for washing grease off linoleum or wooden flooring, since this will tend to set the grease. Instead, wash with soap powder and cold water until the grease comes off.
Ground-in Dirt. If dirt is ground into a waxed floor, rub the spots with a cloth moistened with turpentine or mineral spirits until the wax coating is removed. Then wash the floor with alcohol and wax it to restore the polish. If the varnish is removed, apply white shellac before waxing again.
Heel Marks. Rubber heel marks can be erased from hardwood floors with a light rubdown of steel wool.
Mildew. Floors that have been attacked by mildew show little white spots. Wash these areas with water containing a little kerosene, or with soap and water.

WOOD FLOOR PAINTING

Polish. Equal parts of melted candlewax and turpentine makes a good floor polish.

Scratches. By slipping some leather pads over the ends of the feet of metal chairs, as shown in the illustration, you'll go a long way towards preventing your floors from becoming marred and scratched. These pads are cut from old belting or other heavy leather.

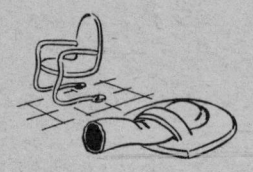

Streaks. Dark streaks on a bare floor where furniture used to stand can be removed with a soapy cloth dipped in paraffin.

Washing. When washing wood floors and woodwork, you can add a good gloss by adding three tablespoons of turpentine or mineral spirits to your wash water, then wiping the woodwork with a clean, dry cloth when you finish. Another method is to add a teaspoon of baking soda to your wash water.

Wood Floor, Painting, see PAINTING, INTERIOR.

Wood Floor Repair.

Cracks between floor boards, shrunken because of proximity to heat, can be filled with a paste made of fine sawdust and shellac, with whiting and color added.

Filling Holes. Fill holes in a wooden floor with plastic wood or with wood putty, stained to match. If you mix the wood putty or plastic wood with household cement, you'll get a harder patch.

Relaying Floor Section. The best way to get rid of damaged and worn floorboards is simply to relay a section of the flooring. With a brace and bit bore a hole in one of the boards as near to the edge of a joist as possible, but still clear of it. Using a keyhole saw, cut across the worn board. Measure to the next joist and drill and saw the board to clear the second joist *inside* it. Remove the board. Measure a new board to fit the gap. Square the ends so they match the ends of the original flooring. Nail a 2 by 4 cleat against the edge of the joist to support the end of the new board; repeat at the other end. You will have to remove the bottom half of the groove side of the new board in order to slide it in place. Fitting the tongue end into the flooring groove already there, push the new board in for a tight fit. Nail it to the cleats. Sand down the joints.

Replacing Single Board. When a single board must be removed from the center of a floor which is covered with tongue-and-groove flooring and then replaced with a new one, use a sharp chisel and hammer or a power saw to remove the defective board, splitting it out in sections and working carefully so as not to damage any adjoining boards. Cut a new length of board for a snug fit, then trim off one-half of the grooved side on the bottom, as shown in the illustration. The piece can then be dropped into place from above, sliding it in at an angle so that the tongued edge meshes first, then tapping the grooved side down with a block of wood and a hammer.

Sagging floors are caused by serious warping of the floor joists. They can also be caused by sinking of the house foundations. You must pay immediate attention to a warped floor before it tears away from the foundation or actually caves in of its own weight.

If you have a basement below the sagging floor, you can use a screw jack and a piece of 4 by 4 timber to hold the floor up from underneath. You work the jack in the same way you elevate a car to repair a flat tire. Set the jack on the floor of the basement, place a 4 by 4 timber running at right angles to the joists, and elevate the jack until it supports the timber. By turning the handle a little bit each day, you can slowly lift the floor back to its original position.

You must not operate the jack more than one or two turns a day. When you have lifted the joists back to their original height, measure the distance between the floor and the 4 by 4 supporting the joists. Cut a new 4 by 4 to that same length and stand it vertically on the floor under the horizontal 4 by 4, so that it props the floor up. Remove the screw jack.

If you have no basement under a sagging floor, or if the floor is inaccessible for one reason or another, remove the finish flooring over the sag as described above until the underlayment or subflooring is exposed. Using a straight edge, sight across the gap and estimate exactly the level where the subfloor should be. Cut narrow strips of wood called "filler strips" and lay them in the sag until they bring the level of the subfloor up to the proper point. As soon as you are certain the level is correct, push filler compound, a semi-plastic material, in around the strips with a putty knife. This compound will harden and keep the filler strips rigid. Now nail back the finish flooring.

Squeaking floors can be due to their having loosened from the joists underneath. If you can't get at the bottom side of the floor in the basement, you'll have to work from above. First locate the joists, which are spaced 16 inches apart at right angles to the floor boards. Using a small wood block as a buffer, tap on this with a hammer against the floor. A higher, more solid sound will indicate a joist below. Then drive pairs of eightpenning flooring nails into the joists at the squeaky spots, first drilling pilot holes slightly smaller than the nails, then driving the nails in X-form, as shown in the illustration. For any squeaks between joists, drive nails in the same X-form to tie the top and sub-floor together.

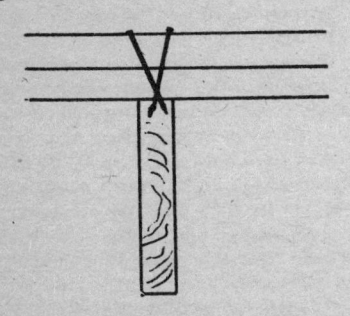

You can use a cement-coated finishing nail to fasten the loose strip of flooring to the subflooring. It is coated with a resinous material on the outside that melts from the friction of being driven in and bonds the nail to the wood fibers.

Squeaking can often be silenced indefinitely merely by pouring some liquid soap into the cracks between the boards causing the trouble. The soap acts as a lubricant where the boards rub together, and should be applied hot to assure penetration into the wood fibers.

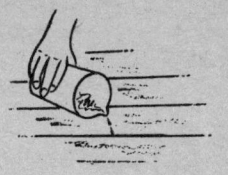

One often-successful cure for squeaking floors is to squirt graphite into the cracks between the noisy boards. This is the type of graphite commonly sold in hardware stores for lubricating locks.

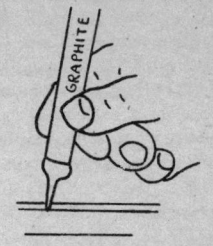

Wood Floor, Relaying. You may be forced sometime to relay a wooden floor. Your first piece of business is to inspect the subfloor after tearing up the old floor. Remove all protruding nails and replace all warped boards in the subflooring. If there are any high ridges at the joints, sand them down until the surface is smooth and flat.

Clean the floor by removing all dust, dirt and lint. In all first-floor situations, building paper under the finish floor is essential. The paper will keep moisture away from the bottom of the finish floor, preventing warping and expansion. Also, this paper will help deaden the sound of heavy tread on the floor. The best building paper to use is 15-pound asphalt-saturated felt. Lay the paper, rolling it from wall to wall, lapping each strip about 4 inches. When you have laid the paper, begin with the floor.

Start laying the flooring strips square with one wall of the room. Lay the strips as you face the direction of greatest dimension. The first strip you lay will have the tongue edge out, with the groove edge butted tightly against the wall. The first nail you drive will be at the groove end of the first board, in a position where it will be hidden by the addition of the baseboard. Then face-nail finish nails all along the wall into the subfloor.

Now secure the tongue edge of the strip by driving an 8d steel-cut flooring nail in through the top of the tongue at an angle of 50 degrees. Be sure the nail enters the subfloor. Driving a nail like this is called blind-nailing; it means the next groove will cover the nail head. Spacing nails at 10-inch intervals, blind-nail the entire strip. With a nail set, countersink each nail before adding the second strip.

Fit the groove edge of the next strip against the tongue of the first. Place a short length of square-edge hardwood against the tongue of the second strip and drive it up snugly so the second strip fits tightly to the first. At 10-inch intervals blind-nail the tongue all along the strip.

Proceed in this fashion all the way to the end of the room. You may have to rip the last strip down the middle to fit it in. When you have it placed snugly to the tongue of the next to last strip, face-nail finish nails in the end of the strip where the finish nails will be covered by the baseboard.

Wood Floors. Hardwood floors are usually oak and maple, with beech and birch sometimes used. Softwood floors are usually Southern pine, Douglas fir, Western hemlock, redwood, Ponderosa pine, and Eastern white pine.

Wood Floor, Sanding. Not only can you prepare a brand new wood floor for a finish coat after laying it, but you can also renovate an old wood floor at practically no cost simply by sanding it yourself.

Start out by renting a power sander from a power-tool supply house. Do not rent the sander until the day you intend to use it. Be sure you have nailed down all loose boards, have moved all the furniture out of the room, and have cleaned everything thoroughly before you start.

Rent an edger with the sander. The edger lets you sand close in to the walls, to the stairs, and to other places the larger machine won't reach.

Be sure to tell your dealer what kind of floor and finish you have. He will then be able to recommend the kind of abrasive to use and whether you'll need two, three, or more sandings to complete the job.

Generally speaking, there are several rules of thumb you should remember. When sanding, for instance, at the end of each pass raise the sander from the floor before the machine comes to a standstill. Never let the drum touch the floor when the sander is not in use. Also, any sander cuts equally well backward and forward.

When you have finished your sanding job, look up the section on painting, for details on finishing a new floor.

Wood Joints, see JOINTS.

Wood Paneling, see PANELING.

Wood Shingle Roof, see ROOF SURFACES.

Wood staining, is an uncomplicated method of obtaining a high quality finish.

Stains enhance the grain and give even common woods a distinctive appearance. Stains should always be applied by hand in a circular motion with a soft cloth. Before you start the job, test the stain on a piece of the timber to be used or part of the job which cannot be seen — in case the stain has to be lightened to the desired shade. This can be done by thinning with mineral turpentine or a special stain reducer — depending on the type of stain used.

The stain should be applied liberally — completing only one section at a time. The stain should not be rubbed out too thinly as this can cause a streaky appearance. When the surface has been completely stained, it should be wiped lightly along the grain with a clean, soft cloth to even out the stain and remove excess. A clear finish, stain finish or a Scandinavian matte or oil finish can then be applied for protection and an extra touch of beauty.

Oil or Water. One efficient way to apply oil stains or water stains on raw wood is to use a cellulose sponge, rather than a brush. The sponge will require less frequent dipping, and will make it easier to regulate the amount being applied.

Shoe Polish. Ordinary shoe polish does a good job of staining wood, and you can mix two or more different colors of shoe polish proportionately in empty containers to obtain some distinctive color tones for use in staining and waxing your finished wood projects. Simply apply your mixture with a dry cloth, rubbing it well into the wood to achieve a mellow patina.

Wood, Workability of. Every different kind of wood has its own individual reaction to cutting tools. One of the roughest decisions you must make in regard to wood is the proper kind of lumber to use for a specific job. Don't assume that "softwood" means it's wood for a "soft job," or that "hardwood" means it's for a "hard job." A lot of softwoods are murder to work; and a lot of hardwoods are a dream.

Hardwoods.
Easy to work. Maple is light reddish brown, and is used for flooring and other planing mill products, interior finish, furniture, handles, vehicle parts, and athletic equipment.

Fair to work. Gum ranges from light gray to reddish brown and is moderately heavy, fine and uniform-textured. It is used for furniture, interior finish, millwork, shipping containers, and novelties.

Walnut ranges from light to dark chocolate brown, is heavy and moderately hard, and develops beautiful finishes. It is used in cabinet work, interior finish, paneling, furniture, flooring, gun stocks, and caskets.

Tough to work. Beech ranges from whitish to reddish brown, and is heavy, hard, and strong. It is used in furniture, flooring, interior finish, handles woodenware, and containers.

Oak ranges from brownish to reddish brown, and is heavy, hard, and strong, with pronounced flecks of wood rays visible on vertical grain lumber. It is used for flooring, interior finish, furniture, cabinet work, planing mill products, vehicle parts, timbers, handles, and agriculture implements.

See also LUMBER.

Softwoods.
Easy to work. Cedar is a red wood with a broad grain, is soft, and is resistant to decay. It is used for siding, shingles, light construction, paneling, poles, posts, boxes and crates. A type of cedar called "incense cedar" is used for siding, finish, framing, boards, panel work, pencils, posts, cedar chests, and closet linings.

Lodge pole pine, Norway pine, Ponderosa pines, and white pine (including Idaho, northern white, and sugar pine) all range from white to yellow, are all soft, and are all easy to work. Lodgepole ranges from yellow to brown, and is used in siding, framing, boards, paneling, ties, poles, and mining timbers. Norway ranges from light red to reddish brown. It is moderately heavy and moderately soft, and is used for light construction, poles, boxes, and crates. Ponderosa ranges from creamy white to reddish brown, is soft and strong, and is used for millwork, light building construction, boxes, crates, and paneling. White ranges from creamy white to light brown, is soft, light, easily worked, and stable under moisture changes. It is used for millwork, patterns, sheathing, subflooring, boxes and crates. Ponderosa and white are the easiest to work with, incidentally.

White fir is oyster white, lightweight, soft, and straight-grained. It is used for framing and sheathing, millwork, and boxes. It will take paint and finish well, and is non-reinous.

Fair to work. Cypress ranges from yellowish brown to dark reddish brown, and is a moderately light, strong, and decay-resistant wood. It is used for siding, millwork, finish, greenhouse construction, tanks, boxes, and boat work.

Rangewood ranges from creamy white to dark brown, is moderately light and strong, and is resistant to rot and decay. It is used for general construction and building purposes, millwork, shingles, and outdoor furniture.

Spruce ranges from yellow to brown and is moderately light, strong, stiff and tough. It is used in millwork, siding, light framing and some cabinet work.

Rough to work. Douglas fir ranges from yellow to reddish, and is heavy and strong, used for all types of building and general construction, siding, flooring, millwork, doors, plywood, boxes and crates.

Southern pine ranges from yellow to reddish brown, is moderately dense, strong, and stiff, but splits and warps. It is used for all types of building and construction, siding, flooring, planing products, millwork, doors, boxes and crates.

WOODWORK CLEANING

Woodwork Cleaning.

Enameled. For cleaning enameled woodwork, mix up a cup of kerosene, a cup of vinegar, and a half-cup of water in a bottle. Shake this up thoroughly, apply to the woodwork with a soft cloth, and follow that with a dry clean cloth. If you prefer using soap and water, you can achieve a higher gloss on your woodwork by adding three tablespoons of turpentine to the wash water. Wipe the wood with a clean dry cloth when you have finished, and it should shine.

Fingermarks on. For fingermarks on painted woodwork, rub with a cloth that has been dipped in kerosene. On varnished woodwork, remove fingermarks with sweet oil. On oil furniture, rub with kerosene.

Smoke and Grease on. To remove smoke and grease stains from woodwork, paint it with a solution of starch and water. After the solution has dried, rub with a soft brush or clean cloth.

Stain on, see STAIN REMOVAL.

Varnished woodwork or floors can be given a beautiful luster if they are cleaned with cold tea.

White woodwork can be cleaned nicely with some baking soda dampened with water, then rubbed on with a soft cloth.

Woodwork Joints, see JOINTS.

Woodwork, Painting, see PAINTING, INTERIOR; PAINTING TIPS.

Woodwork Repair.

1. Woodwork nailholes can be filled in by using sawdust from the same wood, mixed with liquid glue, smoothed into the holes. Then, after applying a coat of shellac or varnish, the nailholes will blend in nicely.

2. To repair deeply scratched woodwork, fill the scratches with a mixture of fine sawdust and spar varnish. After this filler has hardened completely, smooth it down with fine sandpaper.

3. For gouges in stained or painted woodwork, or for a gapping joint, mix some wood putty with the appropriate color stain or paint, and fill in with this, smoothing off neatly.

Wool, see FIBERS, NATURAL.

Wool Care, see CLOTHES CARE.

Workbench.

Aid. When you are marking wood on your workbench against a pattern or template, you can do the job much easier and faster if you'll fit the end of your bench with a turning piece of wood against which you can butt your pattern and work simultaneously. This little piece of wood can be turned out of the way when not in use. For even greater convenience, fit a yardstick to the end of your bench, as illustrated, to use in conjunction with this other gadget.

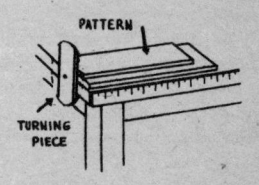

Construction. This unit is built from 3/4-in. thick plywood. Use two 8-ft. x 4-ft. boards and cut them as shown in the diagram. The height of the unit is 26-in. First build the shelf units, then add the tops A, with E attached underneath for strength and support. Use simple butt joints — and before nailing make sure all parts fit together.

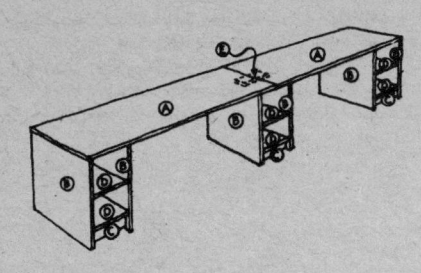

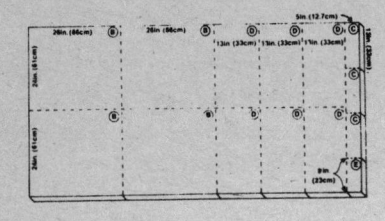

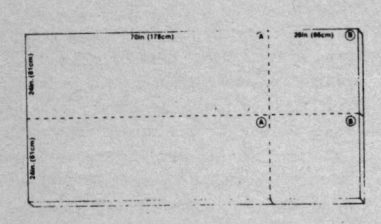

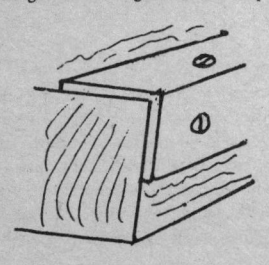

Sliding Tray. One of the simplest improvements to the workbench in the homeworkshop is a sliding tray attached to the underside of the bench top.

This attachment (A) can be put to many uses.

It affords a convenient place where small parts or tools may be laid during construction or assembly.

For persons doing any amount of wood carving or model work, a well-type tray provides a secure place for the tools when needed.

In addition to keeping the working surface of the bench free of tools, the tray removes the danger of having a carving tool pushed off the bench top and falling to the floor.

The tray sides and ends are made of lumber 3/4-in. wide and 1/2-in thick.

It is cut and assembled as suggested in the sketch (B).

Fine-gauge nails, or countersunk head screws could be used to assemble the parts.

Note that there is a fair amount of overhang at the back of the frame to allow it to be withdrawn for effective use without tilting.

The tray bottom can be made of 1/4-in. thick plywood or hardboard, and is attached to the frame with glue and brads.

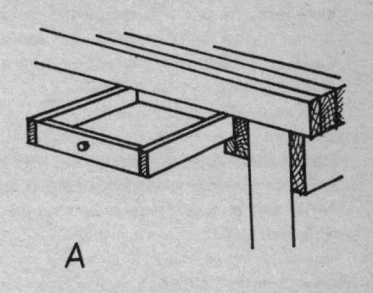

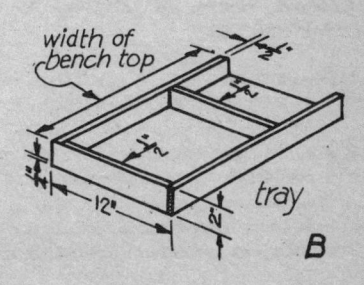

Iron Edge. One way to increase the versatility of your home workbench is to screw a length of angle iron to the front edge. This will serve three purposes: (1) It protects the front edge of the bench from chipping. (2) It serves as a lip or raised edge to prevent small parts from rolling or slipping off the bench. (3) It provides a handy anvil for bending or hammering when working on small metal parts.

WORKSHOP

Runners to carry the tray can be made up of two pieces of hardwood nailed together.

They are attached to the underside of the bench top with 2-in. countersunk head screws set in holes drilled in the runners.

When fitting the runners, make sure that the tray runs freely without binding.

The tray has a secondary use.

Whenever a flat working or writing surface is required the tray is simply inverted in its runners and drawn out the required distance.

Made purposely shallow so that they won't be used as storage drawers, the trays offer extra convenience to every woodworker.

Storage. Muffin tins make ideal containers for small items in your workshop. Attach cleats to the underside of your bench or of a shelf to serve as runners for the flanges of the muffin tin. The separate compartments will hold such items as nails, screws, bolts, nuts, washers, cotter pins, and the like.

Tools, see TOOLS, HAND; TOOLS, MEASURING; TOOLS, POWER.

Workshop.

Storage. For either the amateur handyman or the expert, here's a very good idea for the efficient and easy storage of nails, screws, and other small parts. Merely secure with nails or screws the tops of screw-lid jars to the underside of your workbench or a shelf. Then turn the jars containing your items into their tops, and the contents will be readily visible and easily accessible.

Towel Rack. A roll of paper towels is a very handy item for any home workshop. You can easily make a dispenser for one of these rolls from two long "L" screws and a 3/4-inch dowel with shallow end slots. A spring overhead will keep the paper from unrolling too fast.

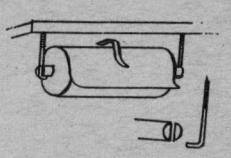

Utility Tray. Do some of the shelves in your workshop cabinet ever become crowded with nuts, bolts, and other odds and ends? A swinging utility tray, such as the one illustrated, will come in very handy to help sort out these items. All you do is bolt an ordinary cake pan to the underside of your bench or a shelf, so that it can be swung out when needed, and back underneath when not in use. You can also attach a wooden drawer pull to the outside of the pan for use as a handle.

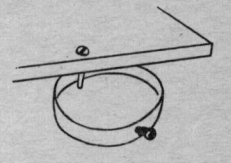

Wall Clamp. Here's a little different twist on making use of mousetraps. Nail an ordinary spring trap to the wall in your workshop or garage — or wherever you do lots of puttering. The spring will prove ideal for holding those easily-misplaced gloves, cloths, and so forth.

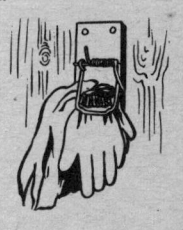

Workshop Lighting.

Bridge Lamp. An old, discarded bridge lamp makes a very efficient lamp for the workbench or shop. It

WROUGHT-IRON EFFECT

is easily moved about to pour its light down just where you want it — and for very close work you can use a reflector bulb in it.

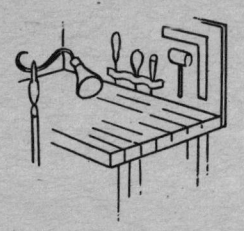

Mobile Light. A "traveling" bench light which can be slid back and forth to provide illumination to every area of your workbench can be very quickly made with a discarded, empty film spool. Just mount the spool on a taut wire stretched across and above your bench, and fasten the cord of your lamp to the spool, as illustrated, being sure to allow plenty of slack in the cord to permit the lamp to be slid from one end of the bench to the other.

Reflector. You can make an efficient lead light for your workshop by cutting off the small end of a medium-sized funnel and then soldering the remainder of the funnel to your light socket. This funnel serves as a spot reflector to provide you more light when you're searching about in dark corners for some illusive item, and at the same time it eliminates any direct glare of light in your face.

Wrench, see TOOLS, HAND.

Wrought Iron Furniture, see FURNITURE CARE.

Wrought Iron Effect. You can add a very attractive wrought iron effect to ordinary steel hardware by coating it with a mixture of water putty powder mixed with black asphalt varnish to the consistency of stiff paste. This will dry a dead black, but you can give it a gloss, if you wish, by varnishing.

XYZ

Yard Hydrant, see PLUMBING.

Yard Screen, see SCREEN, OUTDOOR.

Yarn. If you have some used yarn that is very kinky, wind it around a milk bottle, dip the bottle into water, and let stand a while. When the yarn has dried, the kinks will have disappeared.

Yarn that has been raveled from a knit or crocheted garment is difficult to handle until it has been smoothed out. To do this, wind the yarn around a board, dampen it with water, and let dry on the board. Then remove and wind into a ball.

Yarn Holder. When no helpful person is around to hold a hank of yarn for you while you wind it into a ball, drop the hank over a lampshade that revolves easily, and start winding.

Yarn Preserver. It's a good idea to wind your leftover yarn around a mothball, especially when you expect some time to elapse before you use the yarn again. This will discourage any moths from making a meal of your yarn.

Zinc. To clean zinc, rub carefully with kerosene, then polish with newspapers ... the combination of kerosene and printer's ink being an effective stain remover.

Zipper.

Handle. If you have lost or broken the pull handle on a zipper, a temporary repair or replacement for the handle can be provided with an ordinary paper clip. All you have to do is insert the clip through the hole at the top of the sliding portion of your zipper.

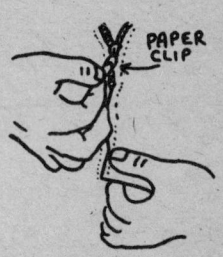

Lubricants. An excellent lubricant for a zipper is provided by an ordinary wax candle. Simply stroke the candle across the teeth on both sides and it will work like magic.

Run an ordinary lead pencil up and down a sticky zipper. The graphite will lubricate the parts and make the zipper run smoothly.

Protection. If you have ever damaged a nylon zipper with a hot iron, here is one way you can avoid this trouble. Place a double-thickness of medium-weight woolen material over the closed zipper placket. The heat of the iron will not affect the zipper and the area will be pressed nicely.

Repair. If the zipper refuses to budge on a wash-dress that has just come back from the laundry, rub over the zipper with some waxed paper, then watch it "run."

MORE HINTS AND HELPS

MORE HINTS AND HELPS

MORE HINTS AND HELPS

MORE HINTS AND HELPS

MORE HINTS AND HELPS

SPECIAL OFFER
REFERENCE LIBRARY

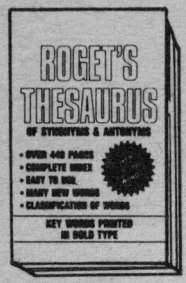

ROGET'S THESAURUS	 **LARGE PRINT WEBSTER'S DICTIONARY**	 **WEBSTER'S SPANISH-ENGLISH ENGLISH-SPANISH DICTIONARY**	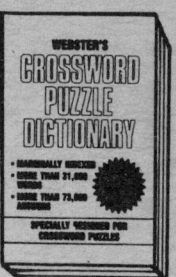 **WEBSTER'S CROSSWORD PUZZLE DICTIONARY**
$6.95	$5.95	$5.95	$5.95
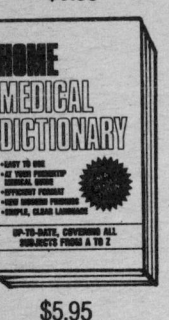 **HOME MEDICAL DICTIONARY**	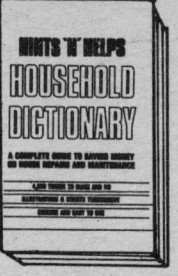 **HINTS 'N' HELPS HOUSEHOLD DICTIONARY**	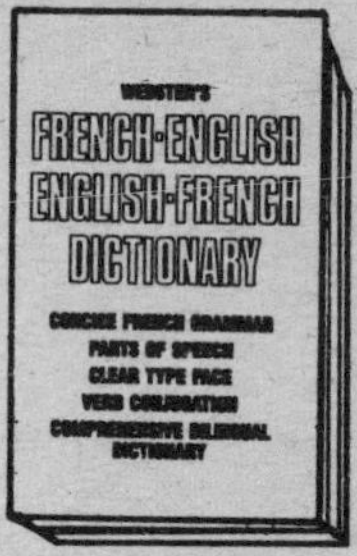 **WEBSTER'S FRENCH-ENGLISH ENGLISH-FRENCH DICTIONARY**	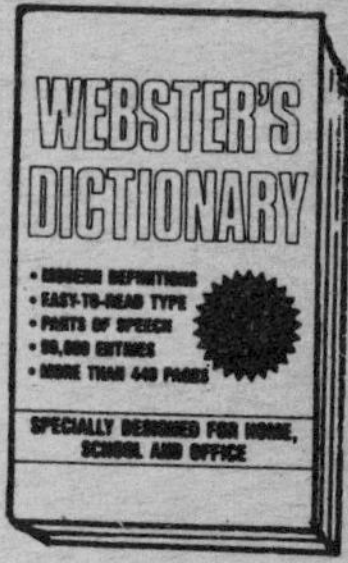 **WEBSTER'S DICTIONARY**
$5.95	$7.95	$5.95	$6.95

Please send me the following books:

_____ WEBSTER'S DICTIONARY   _____ CROSSWORD PUZZLE DICTIONARY
_____ LARGE PRINT DICTIONARY   _____ SPANISH/ENGLISH DICTIONARY
_____ ROGET'S THESAURUS   _____ WEBSTER'S FRENCH/ENGLISH DICTIONARY
_____ HOME MEDICAL DICTIONARY   _____ HINTS/HELPS/HOUSEHOLD DICTIONARY

Plus $1.50 for postage & handling for each book.

Name _____
Address _____
City _____ State _____ Zip _____

I have enclosed $ _____ for _____ books which includes all postage & handling costs. (No C.O.D.)

Send to: **P.S.I. & Associates, Inc.**
13322 S.W. 128th Street
Miami, Florida 33186